TIME AND MEMO

THE capacity to represent and think about time
mental and least understood aspects of human co.
This book throws new light on central issues in the study of the mind by unit-
ing, for the first time, psychological and philosophical approaches dealing
with the connection between temporal representation and memory. Fifteen
specially written essays by leading psychologists and philosophers investigate the way in which time is represented in memory, and the role memory
plays in our ability to reason about time. They offer insights into current
theories of memory processes and of the mechanisms and cognitive abilities
underlying temporal judgements, and draw out fundamental issues concerning the phenomenology and epistemology of memory and our understanding
of time. The chapters are arranged into four sections, each focused on one
area of current research: Keeping Track of Time, and Temporal
Representation; Memory, Awareness and the Past; Memory and Experience;
Knowledge and the Past: The Epistemology and Metaphysics of Time. A
general introduction gives an overview of the topics discussed and makes
explicit central themes which unify the different philosophical and psychological approaches.

CONSCIOUSNESS AND SELF-CONSCIOUSNESS

This series presents the fruits of a joint philosophy and psychology research project whose aim is to advance understanding of the nature of consciousness and self-consciousness by integrating philosophical work with experimental and theoretical work in developmental psychology, cognitive psychology, and neuropsychology.

Volumes are in preparation on agency and self-awareness and on joint attention.

Time and Memory

Issues in Philosophy and Psychology

edited by

Christoph Hoerl
and
Teresa McCormack

CLARENDON PRESS · OXFORD
2001

OXFORD

UNIVERSITY PRESS

Great Clarendon Street, Oxford OX2 6DP

Oxford University Press is a department of the University of Oxford.
It furthers the University's objective of excellence in research, scholarship,
and education by publishing worldwide in

Oxford New York

Athens Auckland Bangkok Bogotá Buenos Aires
Cape Town Chennai Dar es Salaam Delhi Florence Hong Kong Istanbul
Karachi Kolkata Kuala Lumpur Madrid Melbourne Mexico City Mumbai
Nairobi Paris São Paulo Shanghai Singapore Taipei Tokyo Toronto Warsaw
and associated companies in Berlin Ibadan

Oxford is a registered trade mark of Oxford University Press
in the UK and in certain other countries

Published in the United States
by Oxford University Press Inc., New York

British Library Cataloguing in Publication Data
Data available

Library of Congress Cataloging in Publication Data
Time and memory: issues in philosophy and psychology/edited by Christoph Hoerl and
Teresa McCormack.
p. cm.—(Consciousness and self-consciousness; no. 1)
Includes bibliographical references and index.
1. Time perception. 2. Time—Psychological aspects. 3. Time—Philosophy. 4. Memory.
5. Memory (Philosophy) I. Hoerl, Christoph. II. McCormack, Teresa. III. Series
BF468.T543 2001 153.1'2—dc21 2001016330

ISBN 0–19–825035–5
ISBN 0–19–825036–3 (pbk)

1 3 5 7 9 10 8 6 4 2

Typeset in Times by
Cambrian Typesetters, Frimley, Surrey
Printed in Great Britain
on acid-free paper by
Biddles Ltd,
Guildford & King's Lynn

The Consciousness and Self-Consciousness Project

The problem of explaining consciousness and self-consciousness is the central problem that any account of the relation between the brain and the mind must address. Despite the recent great proliferation of books and articles in this area, in a large number of academic disciplines, there are many stubborn problems that have so far resisted satisfactory explanation. Many of these turn on the difficult question of the relation between a priori, constitutive claims about the nature of consciousness and self-consciousness, on the one hand, and empirical findings about the workings of the mind, on the other, including findings about the brain.

The joint philosophy/psychology AHRB Project on Consciousness and Self Consciousness was set up in 1997 with the aim of addressing this specific problem. It is guided by two methodological tenets. The first is that psychology— because its methods are empirical while at the same time being guided by our everyday conceptions of consciousness and self-consciousness—is the place to look for the meeting-ground between the a priori (the concern of philosophy) and the empirical. Joint philosophical and psychological work therefore provides an essential bridge to any consideration of the relation between mind and brain. The second is that to make progress beyond generalities and metaphors here we need to focus on specific well-defined topics of research that are (i) central to understanding consciousness and self-consciousness, and (ii) already the subject of intensive work, empirical and theoretical, in distinct areas in psychology (such as developmental and cognitive psychology, the neurosciences and animal behaviour) and in various areas in philosophy (philosophy of mind, epistemology, theory of thought, metaphysics, and philosophy of psychology).

The choice of topics for the project to focus on is informed by the following two substantive theoretical ideas. The first is that the key bridging concept for relating philosophical and psychological work on consciousness and self-consciousness is the concept of a *point of view* or *perspective on the environment*. The second is that the key general question which will yield most dividends in relating philosophical and psychological work on the nature of consciousness and self-consciousness is: How do we distinguish what is involved in possessing a *merely conscious* point of view on the environment from what is required for possessing a *fully self-conscious* point of view?

More specifically, these questions are being approached by focusing on the following set of specific interdependent problems:

(a.) What are the *representational abilities* required for having a grip on *space, time, and minds*? In particular, what kinds of representation of space, time, and minds are required for a fully self-conscious perspective on the environment? And how are they distinguished from those required for a merely conscious perspective?

(**b**.) What are the *psychological mechanisms* underpinning such representational abilities? The three main areas the project has been focusing on are varieties of *attention* mechanisms, varieties of *monitoring* and *control* mechanisms, and the mechanisms involved in *motivation* and *affect*. Here the question is, then, how do we distinguish the mechanisms of attention, monitoring and control, and affect generation and regulation required for sustaining fully self-conscious perspectives, from the kind required for sustaining merely conscious perspectives?

The AHRB project is based at the University of Warwick, and is run in collaboration with philosophers and psychologists from University College London, Birmingham, Oxford, and the MRC Cognition and Brain Sciences Unit, Cambridge. Its method of work is to bring together for periods of intensive collaboration, in the course of several years, researchers from around the world working in adjacent but at present unconnected areas of both philosophy and psychology. This volume is the first of a series that is the product of this way of working. Others already in preparation include a volume on *Agency and Self-Awareness*, and one on *Joint Attention and Other Minds*. Also closely relevant to the kind of work represented in these volumes are *Spatial Representation: Problems in Philosophy and Psychology*, edited by Eilan, Brewer, and McCarthy (reissued by OUP in 1999), and *The Body and the Self*, edited by Bermudez, Marcel, and Eilan (MIT Press, 1995). Both of these books originated in the progenitor of the AHRB project, The Spatial Representation Project, which was based at the King's College Research Centre in Cambridge.

Naomi Eilan
Project Director

Acknowledgements

Most of the chapters in this volume had their origin in a series of seminars and discussion sessions held by the Joint Philosophy and Psychology Project on Consciousness and Self Consciousness, which is supported by a grant from the Arts and Humanities Research Board (AHRB). In addition to the chapters arising from this seminar series, two further chapters were commissioned for the volume. The relationship between time and memory has been one of the issues especially singled out for detailed study within the framework of the AHRB project. The guiding idea behind singling out this issue is that the ability to represent time is one of the most fundamental and least understood abilities constitutive of both consciousness and self consciousness. We are immensely indebted to Naomi Eilan, the director of the project, who has been instrumental in shaping our own thoughts in this area, and who has given us generous support, helpful advice, and stimulating input throughout the work on this volume. We have also benefited greatly from many discussions with Johannes Roessler.

The series of seminars and discussion sessions which gave rise to the idea for this book was an extraordinarily stimulating intellectual experience. We would like to thank all the participants at these meetings for their contributions and the constructive discussion. And we would like to thank the AHRB for providing financial support for holding these meetings as well as for other activities of the Project on Consciousness and Self Consciousness.

Work on this volume was further supported by funding for the two editors in the form of an AHRB Institutional Fellowship, and a grant from the Medical Research Council (G9608199), respectively.

C.H. and T.M.

Contents

IV. Knowledge and the Past: The Epistemology and Metaphysics of Time

Notes on Contributors

Richard A. Block is Professor of Psychology at Montana State University, Bozeman, Montana. His research is mainly on human memory and cognition, especially issues related to the psychology of time. Some of his recent work has entailed quantitative (meta-analytic) reviews, with Dan Zakay, of the literature on human duration judgements. He is editor of the book *Cognitive Models of Psychological Time* (Erlbaum, 1990).

Jill Boucher is Honorary Professor of Psychology at the University of Warwick. Her research interests are language-related developmental disorders, and she has published extensively in the field of autism.

Gordon D. A. Brown has been Professor in Psychology at the University of Warwick since 1994. He has research interests in models of timing, memory, and the relationship between them. He has edited three books and published some eighty research articles and chapters.

John Campbell is Fellow and Tutor in Philosophy at New College, Oxford. He has published on philosophy of psychology, metaphysics, and the philosophy of language. *Past, Space and Self* was published by MIT Press in 1994; *Reference and Consciousness* is forthcoming from Oxford University Press.

Nick Chater is Professor of Psychology at Warwick University. He works on cognitive science and its applications. With Mike Oaksford, he is the author of *Rationality in an Uncertain World* (Psychology Press, 1998) and editor of *Rational Models of Cognition* (Oxford University Press, 1998). He is co-editor, with Morten Christiansen, of *Connectionist Psycholinguistics*.

David Cockburn is Professor of Philosophy at University of Wales, Lampeter. He is the author of *Other Human Beings* (Macmillan, 1990) and *Other Times* (Cambridge University Press, 1997).

Martin A. Conway is Professor of Experimental Psychology at the University of Bristol. His research interests are in memory, consciousness, and the self. He has written and edited several books and academic journal papers on these topics. In his most recent work he has put forward a theory of autobiographical memory that brings all three topics together.

Jérôme Dokic is 'maître de conférences' at the University of Rouen, and member of CREA (Paris). He is the author of *La philosophie du son* (with Roberto Casati, Éditions Chambon, 1994), and *Penser en contexte* (with Eros Corazza, Éditions de l'Éclat). His forthcoming books include *L'esprit en mouvement. Essai sur la* *dynamique cognitive* (CSLI/Presses Universitaires de France), and *Ramsey: Vérité et succès* (with Pascal Engel, Presses Universitaires de France). He has also published several papers pertaining to epistemology and to the philosophy of language and mind.

William J. Friedman is Professor of Psychology at Oberlin College, Ohio. He is the author of *About Time: Inventing the Fourth Dimension* (MIT Press, 1990), editor of *The Developmental Psychology of Time* (Academic Press, 1982), and co-editor of *Time, Action and Cognition: Towards Bridging the Gap* (Kluwer, 1992).

Christoph Hoerl is Institutional Research Fellow in the AHRB Project on Consciousness and Self Consciousness at the Department of Philosophy, University of Warwick. He has published papers on memory and time perception.

Teresa McCormack is a lecturer at the Department of Psychology, University of Warwick. She has researched and published on the development of memory and temporal abilities in children. She is a member of the interdisciplinary Project on Consciousness and Self Consciousness based at Warwick.

M. G. F. Martin is Lecturer in philosophy at University College London. He has published a number of papers on the philosophy of perception and awareness of the body, and is currently working on a book on naïve realism in perception. He is the editor of *Mind*.

Andrew R. Mayes is Professor of Cognitive Neuroscience at the University of Liverpool. His recent book publications include *Human Organic Memory Disorders* (Cambridge University Press, 1988) and *Theories of Organic Amnesia* (co-edited with J. J. Downes; Psychology Press, 1997).

A. W. Moore is Tutorial Fellow in Philosophy at St Hugh's College, Oxford. His publications include *The Infinite* (Routledge, 1990) and *Points of View* (Oxford University Press, 1997). He has also edited two anthologies: *Infinity* (Dartmouth, 1993) and *Meaning and Reference* (Oxford University Press, 1993).

Christopher Peacocke is Professor of Philosophy at New York University. He is the author of books including *A Study of Concepts* (MIT Press, 1992), and *Being Known* (Oxford University Press, 1999), and of papers in the philosophy of psychology, the philosophy of language, and epistemology.

J. H. Wearden is Professor of Psychology at the University of Manchester. His current research interests range over most areas of animal and human timing. He has published extensively in these areas, particularly on the application of formal models of timing to humans.

Dan Zakay is Professor of Psychology at Tel Aviv University, Tel Aviv, Israel. His research is mainly on the psychology of time and on human judgement and decision-making. Some of his recent work has entailed quantitative (meta-analytic) reviews, with Richard A. Block, of the literature on human duration judgements. He is co-editor of the book *Time and Human Cognition: A Life-Span Perspective* (North-Holland, 1989).

Perspectives on Time and Memory
An Introduction

Christoph Hoerl and *Teresa McCormack*

What is the connection between the way we represent time and things in time, on the one hand, and our capacity to remember particular past events, on the other? This is the substantive question that has stood behind the project of putting together this volume. The methodological assumption that has informed this project is that any progress with the difficult and fascinating set of issues that are raised by this question must draw on the resources of various areas both in philosophy and in psychology.

Our aim in this introduction is to draw upon the various contributions to this volume in articulating the intuition that there is a deep connection between the capacity to remember particular past events and certain kinds of capacities for temporal representation or reasoning. In doing so, we cannot cover all the theoretical and empirical issues raised by the various authors. Instead, we hope to spell out some guiding ideas which are of common concern to their work.

One way of spelling out the intuition that there is a fundamental connection between our understanding of temporal reality and our capacity to remember past events can be found in Bertrand Russell's (1912: 66) remark that we should not be able to understand what it is for things to have happened in the past if it weren't for our ability, on occasion, to have 'immediately before the mind [something] which is recognized as past'. Yet, any such claim should lead us to ask just what kind of temporal understanding and what kind of memory ability is supposed to be in question here. Just what are the representational abilities involved in thinking about other times that are supposed to depend on our capacity to remember the past? And, equally, just what does it mean to say that the past can come before our minds when we remember—how does time enter into memory itself?

In short, the two terms that make up the title of this volume may be combined in two core questions:

(1) What role does memory play in our understanding of time?
(2) How is time represented in memory?

These two questions correspond to two directions from which the question about the relationship between memory and temporal understanding can be approached. One starting point would be a study of the ways we have of thinking about and representing things in time, leading us to ask which features of our understanding of temporal reality rely on our possession of memories. Conversely, we can start from the question as to the information about temporal reality which memory makes available to us, leading us to ask what it is about memory that gives it its role in temporal reasoning.

Within both philosophy and psychology, time and memory are each typically dealt with under quite different headings. In psychology, work on the mechanisms underlying timing abilities and temporal judgements has proceeded largely separate from work which has tried to distinguish different kinds of memory systems. In philosophy, debates on metaphysical questions regarding the reality of time have gone on in parallel to, and often independently of, work on the epistemology of memory and its role in accounts of the mind. There are indeed quite separate concerns for each of these various lines of research to address in their own right. However, an important challenge that faces any attempt to spell out in detail the connection between temporal understanding and memory is to clarify the relationships between those lines of research, both within each discipline and across them.

The force of that challenge is probably most obvious when it comes to the question as to what is involved in ascribing certain forms of temporal understanding or memory to a given individual. Constitutive philosophical claims about the different ingredients involved in having, say, a concept of the past or the idea of a chronological order of events often seem to postulate what, on the face of it, are quite sophisticated types of knowledge and reasoning abilities. As such, they seem to give us little to go on when it comes to deciding whether animals or children should be credited with similar temporal notions, or how to develop empirically plausible models of the representational mechanisms involved in mature temporal understanding. Conversely, cognitive and neuropsychological models describing different ways in which temporal information about events can be encoded, retained, and retrieved are cast in the technical vocabulary of the scientist. Further work is needed to show how such psychological models might illuminate our intuitive conception of what it is for someone to have a particular past event before her mind, and how such models might contribute to accounts of the phenomenology of memory, its role in our understanding of time, and our grasp of temporal concepts in general.

Clearly, an important task for any attempt to approach and clarify these issues is to distinguish different levels at which they can be addressed. There are many different senses in which someone can be said to remember something, just as there are many different ways in which someone can be said to be sensitive to, be aware of, or think about time. More to the point, both philosophy and psychology have their own reasons for talking about different types of memory and temporal understanding. In philosophy, such distinctions are motivated by epistemological, phenomenological, and thought-theoretic concerns; in psychology, they may ultimately involve the idea of different information-processing mechanisms which serve different functions, are located in different parts of the brain, emerge at different developmental stages, or can be selectively impaired. One task for this introduction is therefore to put some of the key issues discussed in the contributions to this volume into context by clarifying the grounds on which they draw such distinctions between different types of memory and temporal understanding. Another is to draw out in more detail in what sense different contributions may indeed be seen as addressing the same key issues.

TIME, REALITY, AND REPRESENTATION

Consider two commonplace perceptual situations: watching a ship sail down a river, and looking up and down the façade of a house. Immanuel Kant (1929: A189/B233 ff.) mentions these two examples to bring out how certain forms of temporal thought are basic to our thinking about the world around us. His point may be put like this. Fundamental to the way we represent the world is the ability to conceive of a temporal order of events which sometimes determines the course of our perceptions and sometimes does not. Without such an ability, we would be unable to distinguish between perceiving successive states of affairs (e.g. as the ship sails down the river) and successively perceiving coexistent states of affairs (e.g. as we glance at different parts of a house). Yet, without such a distinction, our perceptions would simply give way to one another without being integrated into a view of a mind-independent world 'out there' in which things are one way or another (see also Campbell, 1984). More generally, time provides us with a framework not just to order the events we know of, but also to wonder about what happens when we are not looking, what happened while we were asleep, or what will happen in the future. It is in this sense that temporal thought might be said to be a crucial part of thinking of the world as *objective*, as being the way it is independently of our interaction and engagement with it.

At the same time, temporal thought might also be said to be a crucial part of thinking about the world as something we have a certain *perspective* on, as the world we inhabit and in which our lives unfold. Just as we call things near or far from our point of view in space, we call things near or far from our point of view in time. And, from our point of view in time, certain things have already happened, others are currently taking place, and more are yet to come. More to the point, it would seem that we do not conceive of an event as real unless we conceive of the time of that event as having a particular bearing on our own point of view in this sense. Consider, for instance, the way we represent the events we read about in a piece of fiction (cf. McTaggart, 1927). Part of the force of saying that we do not represent them as real events is that we represent them in a way that is independent of our own point of view, as neither past, present, or future, near or far in time. By contrast, to think of events as real is, in part, to think of them as events in the world we inhabit—as events which have a specific bearing on us depending on whether they have already happened, are currently taking place or are yet to come (see also Cockburn, 1997).

Contemporary discussion on the role of temporal reasoning and concepts of time in our knowledge of the world owes much to a distinction first introduced by J. Ellis McTaggart (1927). He observes that there are two quite different ways we have of representing how events are positioned in time. First, we can think of the temporal position of an event purely in terms of its relations to other events. We do this, for instance, when we use notions such as 'before', 'after', or 'simultaneous with' to order two events, when we specify the length of the interval that separates them, or when we assign a date to an event. Thinking of the temporal position of an event in this way, however, still leaves open the question as to whether the event thus thought about lies in the past, the present, or the future, or how near or far in the past or future it lies. There is thus a second way of thinking of the temporal position of an event, and what is distinctive about it is that it brings in our own temporal perspective on the event in question. The answer to the question as to where in time an event lies, in this sense, depends crucially on when the question itself is asked, as an event which is now present, say, was once in the future, and will soon be past.

McTaggart's distinction has sparked an intense debate on the role these two ways of thinking of the temporal positions of events play in our reasoning about time as a feature of objective reality. In particular, a large amount of work in both epistemology and metaphysics has gone into attempts at spelling out the idea of a temporal perspective that manifests itself in our use of the past, present, and future tenses (see e.g. Chs. 14 and 13 by Moore and Peacocke in this volume). However, distinctions akin to that drawn by McTaggart are also made in the literature on psychological mechanisms underlying our ability to make temporal judgements. For instance, William Friedman (Ch. 5, this volume; see also Block and Zakay, Ch. 2) appeals to McTaggart in introducing a distinction between what he calls 'location-based' and 'distance-based' processes in memory for the time of past events. Starting with Friedman's distinction, we now wish to sketch three ways in which questions about the nature of memory may be connected with questions about temporal representation.

Memory for time

The question that Friedman addresses in his chapter is how we make 'when' judgements about remembered events. That is, how do we make judgements about the time at which past events occurred? He distinguishes between two processes on which judgements about the time of remembered events might be based. Location-based processes rely on information laid down at the time of encoding. That information either specifies or can be used to infer the location of an event in a conventional, natural, or personal time pattern. Distance-based processes, by contrast, rely on information which specifies or can be used to infer the recency of events (how long ago they happened) or the relative order of two remembered events with respect to the present.

The issue as to how 'when' judgements are made has typically been addressed quite separately from other work on memory. One potential reason for this may be that memories of events do not, on the face of it, appear to include 'when' information. In this sense, temporal information contrasts with other types of contextual information, which sometimes (although not always) seem to be given to one in the memory itself. For example, the way in which one remembers a word presented in a list-learning task may allow one to make judgements about the modality of presentation, or aspects of the surroundings in which the word was presented. However, one's memory does not in the same way seem to yield information about the temporal context in which one encountered the word. Given this, how do we make 'when' judgements? In answering this question, there is a second distinction that cuts across the distinction between distance- and location-based processes. We can distinguish between answers which appeal to specialized memory mechanisms that encode temporal information and answers which appeal to other, non-specialized, memory mechanisms which might be exploited in making 'when' judgements (see Block and Zakay, Ch. 2, this volume).

If there are specialized temporal encoding mechanisms in memory, it is necessary to characterize the content of the temporal information that such mechanisms specify. Friedman's distinction might provide us with two different ways in which this question can be addressed. A location-based account, on this view, would involve describing a 'time-tagging' process which specifies the temporal context in which the event occurred. A distance-based account would involve some mechanism by which temporal information about distance from the present was available in memory. Such information might somehow be available directly, but it might also result from computing the similarity between the temporal context in which the event occurred and the current temporal context (see Brown and Chater, Ch. 3, this volume).

The alternative is to assume that 'when' judgements involve inferences based on memory processes that are not specialized to encode temporal information. A location-based version of such an account would assume that information about 'when' an event occurred must be *reconstructed* by a chain of reasoning relating features of the remembered event to knowledge about time patterns (see Friedman's chapter, for example; note that on such an account it is necessary to give a separate explanation of how such time patterns are represented in memory). A distance-based version of such an account might claim that how long ago an event occurred is inferred from a memory property which happens to be correlated with the passage of time (such as the vividness of the memory).

The issue of how 'when' judgements are made, in this sense, involves considering a very particular way in which time and memory are related: Are there special memory mechanisms for remembering temporal information? Psychologists have tried to address this question in experimental studies, by modelling memory performance and by considering neuropsychological evidence. The different accounts that have emerged are debated in the chapters by Brown and Chater, Block and Zakay, and Friedman. Yet, the question may also be of philosophical relevance. A central claim in Peacocke's chapter is that our understanding of the past tense actually relies, in part, on the existence of mechanisms which are responsive to the passage of time.

Memory and chronology

A second issue regarding the way in which time and memory are related concerns descriptions of the organization of memory. As Friedman puts it, our intuitive conception of memory takes for granted that it is 'infused with chronology'.

However, there is considerable debate as to whether there are any substantive grounds for saying that memory itself is chronologically organized. Indeed, there also appear to be different descriptions of what it might mean to say that memory is chronologically organized.

On the one hand, Conway has argued that we possess abstracted personal histories, in which our lives are divided up into life-time periods (such as 'when I was at university'), which may themselves be nested within a hierarchy below extended periods or time eras (such as 'the twelve years in which I was married to Bob'). According to Conway, this knowledge about our past often serves to organize memory retrieval, in that we may often direct memory searches by accessing information from particular periods. Whether or not retrieval is conducted in this way is an empirical question (see Conway, 1993, for review). The point here is that Conway's claims constitute only one sense in which our memories could be described as infused with chronology. In particular, other authors imply that to claim that memory is chronologically organized is to make a stronger claim than this.

Friedman implies that it is only correct to describe memory as chronologically organized if there is a specialized memory mechanism that associates each memory with a temporal code. Thus, for him, to establish that memory is chronologically organized is a matter of establishing the existence of such a mechanism. He argues that there is no reason to believe that 'when' judgements depend upon such specialized temporal encoding mechanisms. Given that research on 'when' judgements seems to suggest that long-term memories are not consistently associated with a temporal code, he suggests that memory cannot be chronologically organized.

The general thrust of Brown and Chater's argument appears to work in the other direction: that there are reasons to believe that memory is chronologically organized, and therefore perhaps 'when' judgements are based on the output of specialized temporal encoding mechanisms. At the heart of Brown and Chater's argument is a mathematical model that assumes that the probability of remembering an event is related to its 'temporal distinctiveness' (see Ch. 3 below for more detail of their temporal distinctiveness model). In their model, the temporal distinctiveness of an event is calculated on the basis of how long ago it happened and how temporally close it was to other events. Very roughly speaking, the idea is that an event will be easy to retrieve if it occurred recently and if there were few temporally close neighbouring events.

The extent to which Brown and Chater's position conflicts with that of Friedman depends upon whether it is assumed that the principle of temporal distinctiveness is psychologically instantiated by means of a specialized temporal encoding mechanism. It is at least conceivable that this principle holds true because of emergent properties of memory storage and consolidation processes, rather than because memories are associated with temporal codes. If this were correct, then there may be a weak sense in which memory might be described as chronologically organized which does not hinge on establishing the existence of specialized temporal encoding mechanisms. In fact, however, Brown and Chater have in mind a stronger claim. They do describe the underlying psychological mechanisms governing memory retrievability as specialized temporal mechanisms (Brown, Preece, and Hulme, 2000; see also Boucher's Ch. 4 below). And part of their story is that it is precisely these mechanisms which are also sometimes used in making 'when' judgements.

Episodic memory

As we have outlined, several chapters in the volume discuss the psychological processes underlying 'when' judgements. The issue of how 'when' judgements are made would seem to arise only for certain kinds of memories. For example, when we recall facts such as titles of films, details of recipes, or what the capital of China is, what we recall is not something that we could make a 'when' judgement about. By contrast, when we recollect an event from our past lives, we can always raise the question as to when that event took place (even if we are actually unable to give an accurate answer to this question). For many years, the psychologist Endel Tulving has worked on the distinction between memory for facts and recollection of events, terming the latter type of memory *episodic memory*. Tulving describes episodic memory as a distinctive psychological system dealing with memories of events as particular past occurrences, which is distinct from the system that allows us to remember facts. Central to Tulving's way of setting up the distinction is the idea that remembered facts do not exist in time in the same way as remembered events do. He describes episodic memory as essentially memory for datable occurrences (Tulving, 1983). When we are episodically remembering, the question as to when the remembered event took place always at least makes sense to us, irrespective of how, or how well, we might go on to make 'when' judgements concerning that event.

Of course, some factual memories involve events for which one can raise 'when' questions. For example, one could remember the fact that there was a civil war in America, and then ask when that war actually happened. According to Tulving, the type of 'when' questions that one can raise about episodic memories are quite different in character to those that one raises about such factual memories. In characterizing this type of memory, Tulving quotes William James, and points out that an episodic memory 'requires more than the mere dating of a fact in the past. It must be dated in my past. In other words, I must think that I directly experienced its occurrence' (James, 1890: 650). Exactly what this requirement comes to is a question that is discussed by a number of contributors to this volume. The central claim which they share with Tulving, however, is that episodic memory is essentially memory for events that were 'personally experienced' (Tulving, 1972: 387) and thus occurred in one's personal past.

Tulving's description leads us on to a second sense in which episodic memory seems to lead to a special type of 'when' question. There is also a difference between judging 'when' an event normally happens, in the sense of remembering at what time of the day it usually occurs, and judging 'when' a past event happened. The latter type of 'when' judgement seems to involve thinking of an event as having a specific, unique temporal location in the past, whereas the former does not. Even when we are remembering a past event that may have repeated many times (for example, holidays to the same destination), we can still think of each individual occurrence of the past event as separate and distinct, and as having a unique temporal location. It is in this sense that episodically remembering seems to involve thought about particular past times (Campbell, 1994). Remembering what usually happens at a given time does involve some type of temporal competence, but episodic memory, as Tulving puts it, 'is the only form of memory that, at the time of retrieval, is oriented towards the past' (Tulving and Markowitsch, 1998). That is to say, episodic remembering essentially involves 'thinking back to' (ibid.) the time when the remembered event was experienced, in a way which is not the case for other forms of making use of previously acquired information and knowledge.

The distinction Tulving draws between episodic memory and memory for facts shares much with distinctions found in the philosophical literature, where what is sometimes called 'direct', 'personal', or 'experiential' memory is contrasted with 'factual memory' or 'remembering information' (cf. e.g. Ayer, 1956; Malcolm, 1963; Evans, 1982). Philosophers' starting point, in this context, has usually been the observation that we find it natural to distinguish between two sorts of memory ascription. In our use of the term 'remember' we typically distinguish between instances in which we would say that someone remembers that something is the case and instances in which we would say that she remembers a certain past event. One way of understanding Tulving's work is by saying that he wants to provide psychological grounds for this distinction, which philosophers have tried to analyse in terms of its epistemological and phenomenological significance. In what follows, we draw on material by psychologists and philosophers represented in this volume to discuss in more detail the specific ways in which temporal representation and temporal understanding might be involved in thinking back to particular events we have personally experienced.

TEMPORAL REPRESENTATION

At one point in his contribution to this volume (Ch. 13), Christopher Peacocke asks the following question. What is the difference between, on the one hand, being merely responsive to the temporal interval which has elapsed since a particular event occurred and, on the other hand, assigning to that event a position in one's history, and, correlatively, in the history of the world? When waiting in front of a familiar traffic light which had just turned red as we approached it, we may have a certain expectation as to when it will turn green again and ready ourselves to accelerate again just before it actually does so. Arguably, however, being thus sensitive to the typical length of the red phase of the traffic light is something quite different from recollecting the event of it turning red as a particular episode that just happened. What this example brings out is that episodically remembering a particular event seems to require the ability to think of this event as part of a sequence of events that make up, as Peacocke calls it, the history of the world. Several of the chapters in this volume attempt to spell out in detail some of the abilities that go into thinking about events in this way.

An echo of Peacocke's question can, for instance, be found in Teresa McCormack's contribution (Ch. 11) when she raises the empirical issue as to whether animals can be said to possess episodic memories. McCormack discusses at length an experiment in which it was shown that jays did not tend to search for worms they had cached if several days had elapsed since they had cached them, whereas they did search for the worms if the caching had taken place only a few hours before (see Clayton and Dickinson, 1998). According to McCormack's interpretation, this study shows that the birds were in some way sensitive to the length of the interval that had elapsed since the worms had been cached. This is important for the birds as the length of this interval affects whether the worms are still edible. Yet, for McCormack, demonstrating such a sensitivity to elapsed intervals falls short of demonstrating something equivalent to the human capacity to recall particular past events.

John Campbell has introduced a terminological distinction that might be used to capture the difference both Peacocke and McCormack are getting at. Drawing on Gibson's notion of an affordance, Campbell (forthcoming) describes a primitive level of engagement with the world that simply consists in the knowledge of affordances. Affordances, roughly, are behavioural options the environment offers us. Thus, for instance, a physical object may provide us with a variety of opportunities for moving around it, picking it up, putting something else on top, etc., in virtue of the shape and location it has. Yet, what Campbell argues is that it would be wrong to think of our ordinary perceptual experience of the object as providing us merely with knowledge of affordances in this sense. Instead, he says, we should think of perception as providing us with knowledge of the grounds of these affordances. Thus, for instance, in as far as the object's shape and location are themselves things we can be said to perceive when we look at the object, we can be said to be aware, in experience, of the reasons why various courses of action are open to us.

In the example we have just used to illustrate Campbell's distinction, the grounds of affordances are spatial. However, the examples we have mentioned in connection with the questions raised by Peacocke and McCormack seem to indicate that there are also affordances with what we might call temporal grounds. That is to say, behavioural options are sometimes also a matter of the amount of time that has elapsed since a certain event happened, given the amount of time certain kinds of processes normally take. Adopting Campbell's terminology, we might thus also speak of a knowledge of certain affordances when an individual shows a sensitivity to such temporal features. Yet, still following Campbell, we also have to distinguish knowledge of such affordances from knowledge of the grounds of such affordances.

Consider again the case of a driver who puts his foot on the accelerator just before the traffic light turns green again. The reasons why it is now the right time for him to put his foot back on the accelerator (i.e. the grounds of the affordance he responds to) are that the red phase of the traffic light normally lasts a certain amount of time, and that roughly this amount of time has now elapsed since the traffic light turned red. Those reasons would be apparent to him if he recalled previous occasions on which he has stood in front of that traffic light and also recalled the traffic light switching to red a certain amount of time ago. Yet, intuitively, something much less sophisticated is typically going on when we usually show this kind of behaviour. What is apparent to the driver might simply be that this is the suitable moment for putting the foot back on the accelerator (i.e. an affordance), and he may be quite oblivious to the question of why it is the right time to do so. If this is the right way of characterizing our own case, however, there is indeed a question as to whether the studies on animals discussed by McCormack should be seen as demonstrating the presence of episodic memory capacities in those animals. Here, perhaps the best way of describing the situation is that, after a certain time has elapsed, the opportunity to recover the buried worms no longer presents itself to the birds as an affordance. However, they might simply be sensitive to the interval that has elapsed since they buried the worms, and the interval of time it takes for worms to decay, in such a way that, after a certain point in time, it no longer occurs to them to look for those worms. We would only be justified in ascribing episodic memories to them if we could also say that they know the reasons why there is no longer any point in looking for those worms, since that would seem to require that they can remember the particular event of burying them.

There are a number of facets to this connection between episodic memory and the capacity to engage in certain forms of reasoning, which raise important questions about the requirements for possession of episodic memories. Some of the chapters in the volume can be seen as addressing such questions as they arise at various different levels of explanation. In what follows, we wish to discuss particularly questions relating to the temporal mechanisms, the types of temporal representation, and the temporal reasoning and understanding involved in episodic memory.

Episodes, phases, and intervals

The claim that there is a specific link between episodic memory and the representation of temporal information has entered the memory literature primarily through the idea that episodic remembering involves the retrieval of information about the context in which the remembered event was encountered (see McCormack Ch. 11, this volume, for a discussion of the notion of contextual information). Tulving's original definition of episodic memory, for instance, described it, among other things, as memory for events along with information about their temporal and spatial context. And the idea that episodic memory involves remembering specifically temporal contextual information can also be found in some contributions to this volume. One of the aims of Brown and Chater's chapter is to argue that the fundamental dimension of organization in episodic memory is a temporal one, and Boucher develops the claim that episodic memory deficits in autism can be explained in terms of impairments in temporal processing.

Very loosely speaking, something like the following seems to underpin some of the research in this area: episodic memories are memories for events which are associated with, linked to, or contain some kind of representation of the point in time at which the event occurred. There are various ways in which this claim could be assessed. For example, much hinges on the nature of the temporal information assumed to be involved, and the extent to which we want to say that episodic memory itself involves the encoding and storage of such temporal information. As we discussed above, several chapters address the issue of whether it is correct to describe event memories as routinely associated with temporal codes. For present purposes, the question is whether such an account of episodic memory could go some way towards describing what is interesting and distinctive about this type of memory.

A useful question to ask in this context is whether such an account might provide criteria for research on animal memory, which has been concerned with the thorny issue of attribution of episodic memory on the basis of non-verbal behaviour. In the animal literature, researchers have typically been concerned with explaining how animals seem to be able to anticipate the availability of food at certain times. The question is whether the theories developed in this context can also help us address questions regarding temporal representation in episodic memory.

A number of animals have been shown to be sensitive to the fact that some events recur at fixed times of the day (Church, 1984; Gallistel, 1990). For example, if food is provided in a location at a certain time each day, bees will tend to return to that location at the correct time (Kolterman, 1974). This sensitivity is known as *phase sense*. It is normally assumed that this sort of animal behaviour is based on the output of one or more oscillators—internal signals that repeat at regular intervals. The occurrence of food is thought to become associated with a particular state of the oscillator or oscillators, and when this state reoccurs it will trigger the appropriate behaviour. By using such mechanisms, animals can adjust to naturally occurring or experimentally contrived temporal regularities in the world.

Animals are sensitive not just to fixed times of the day at which some events recur, but also to the amount of time separating two events. This second type of timing is contrasted with phase sense, and is known as *interval sense*. In a typical experimental study, a signal such as a noise is used to indicate the start of an interval, and the animal must learn that food is available after a certain amount of time has elapsed (Gibbon, 1977; Killeen, 1975). Interval timing is discussed in detail in the chapters by Wearden and by Block and Zakay (Chs. 1 and 2). On the face of it, interval timing would appear to involve something like the ability to measure intervals of time and to store representations of such intervals in memory.

The chapter by Wearden in the present volume gives a detailed description of current psychological theorizing regarding such internal mechanisms. As applied to foraging behaviour of the type just described, the basic idea is this. Descriptions of the underlying mechanisms are typically in terms of oscillators which repeat their signals at regular intervals and pacemakers which produce a certain number of pulses per second. When the oscillator signal is in a certain state, or when a certain number of pulses have been accumulated, particular types of behaviour are triggered.

As sophisticated as behaviour based on such kinds of internal mechanism may possibly be, there are still powerful reasons to distinguish between the temporal representation involved in such behaviour and that involved in episodic memory. These are to do with the type of temporal information such timers may be said to provide (an issue developed in more detail in Campbell, 1994). Simply going on the description of the workings of such mechanisms we have just given, there seems to be nothing that would allow the animal to distinguish between events happening at different times, but corresponding to the same state of the internal timer. Indeed, the functioning of these mechanisms relies on the timer's being in the same state on what we would regard as quite different occasions, such as a certain time of day on different days, or each time a certain interval has elapsed since a certain type of event happened. On the face of it, therefore, explaining an animal's behaviour in terms of its possession of such timers is something quite different from explaining behaviour in terms of the possession of episodic memories, that is, memories of particular occasions on which a certain type of event happened (see also McCormack and Hoerl, 1999, where a similar type of point is made regarding children's early timing and sequencing abilities).

Episodic memory and temporal information

We now turn to considering whether the way time is represented in episodic memory can be explained in terms of the workings of particular kinds of temporal encoding mechanisms. Can the point made in the previous sub-section be met by introducing the idea of a temporal coding process which can, at least in principle, specify the temporal location of each event uniquely? (Brown and Chater, and Boucher, this volume, seem to assume that such a process potentially exists.) For example, there may be oscillator-based mechanisms which provide an output that is different for each point in time across the lifespan of the individual (see O'Keefe's, 1994, description of how this could be achieved without requiring oscillators with very long periods). There are several reasons, however, why one might cast doubt on the idea of such a mechanism, or at least argue that appeal to such a mechanism is not sufficient to explain what is interesting and distinctive about episodic memory.

One interesting issue raised by the suggestion that there might be mechanisms providing a unique signal for each point in time across one's lifespan is what type of use such information could be put to (see Friedman, 1993, and present volume). Recall that the contexts in which theorists typically appeal to the notion of an internal timer are contexts in which such timers serve to adjust the individual's behaviour to the regular recurrence of a certain type of event at a certain phase within a cycle, or a certain amount of time after another type of event has happened. In these contexts, the function of the timer is tied to the fact that it always provides the same signal on these different occurrences. Thus, the function of a mechanism that always provides different signals at different points in time, and never the same signal twice, would have to be explained in other terms (though see Brown and Chater's chapter for an attempt to provide such a function by drawing on work within the rational analysis framework).

Another question we can ask is why introducing the idea of mechanisms which assign each experienced event a unique temporal code should be the right move to make at this point. The idea of such a temporal coding process may only be one way of making good the intuitive idea that episodic memory involves thinking back to a particular event. An alternative possibility is that episodic memory, in as far as it involves keeping track of the time of events at all, exploits the same mechanisms as those involved in phase and interval timing, but that these mechanisms are put to work in a different way.

This possibility has been raised by Bill Brewer (1994), who points out a potential analogy between memory and perception. His argument is that the temporal information provided by internal mechanisms of the type we have been talking about might be compared with the egocentric spatial information provided by visual perception. We normally take it that visual perception allows us to pick out a particular object in virtue of its egocentric location, even though it is conceivable that we could be faced with an identical scene in another place in which a numerically different object occupied the same egocentric location. Thus, it would seem that our ability to represent the particular object we are faced with is simply a matter of our being in a context in which it is that object we are faced with, rather than a matter of assigning a unique spatial address to that object which would distinguish it from the qualitatively identical object we would be faced with in the counterfactual scenario. If this is true, however, it is difficult to see why our representing a particular event can't equally simply be a matter of being in a context where it is this particular event we have kept track of by means of an internal timing mechanism. The idea would be that, in as far as episodic memory relies on such mechanisms, we use exactly the same timing mechanisms in exactly the same way on different occasions to keep track of numerically different events.

If Brewer is right, we should not necessarily seek an explanation in terms of different timing mechanisms for the difference between an individual's merely being sensitive, say, to the time that has elapsed since a certain event happened, on the one hand, and his capacity to remember that event episodically, on the other. In fact, it is possible that the performance, in each case, relies on the same mechanisms, and that the difference lies in the way any information yielded by these mechanisms can be exploited by the individual. However, if this is true, we should be looking at other cognitive capacities necessary for episodic memory to explain the distinctive nature of episodic memory as a faculty for representing particular past events.

Temporal decentring

A number of contributions to this volume put centre stage questions as to the relation between a subject's past experience of an event and her present ability to think back to that particular event. For instance, an important set of questions in this context concerns the nature and significance of the causal link between the subject's past experience of an event and her present ability to make judgements about that event (cf. e.g. Chs. 8 and 7 below, by Dokic and Mayes). It may be argued, however, that purely causal notions do not suffice to explain the way in which our thinking is connected with the past in episodic remembering. To see what the problem here is, we can turn to an example used by John Campbell (Ch. 6, this volume). He considers the difference between a person remembering a past event and a person thinking, for instance, about the arrival of a cup of coffee as she orders it in a cafe. There may be very little difference between the kinds of information the person can give about that future event and the kinds of information we usually have about past events. Thus, she may know what the cup will look like and roughly when and where it will arrive. Furthermore, there is a causal connection between her ordering the coffee and its arrival, just as there is a causal connection between our memories of past events and our present recollection of them. Yet, intuitively, what this person knows about the arrival of the coffee falls short of the kind of knowledge we have when we remember a particular past event.

A central claim that can be found in Campbell's own contribution to this volume is that when we make judgements about past events on the basis of remembering them, our grasp of the meaning of these judgements possesses a diachronic aspect. That is to say, such memory judgements should be seen as being based on a kind of *temporally extended inference*, taking us from a judgement made at the time of witnessing the event to the judgement made at the time of recollecting the event, where the truth of the latter is implied by the truth of the former. (Though Campbell's model does allow for cases in which the memory judgement concerns aspects of our past experience which we did not think about at the time, as long as they would have provided grounds for making the relevant judgements then; see also Dokic, this volume (Ch. 8), and Martin, 1992.) If memory judgements do indeed involve something like a temporally extended inference in this sense, this might explain why they differ from judgements we can make about the future.

To bring out this point, Campbell focuses in particular on the kinds of demonstrative reference which might be involved in making judgements about the future and the past, respectively. He argues that in as far as we can use a demonstrative to refer to an object that will be encountered in the future (such as 'that cup'), it is only by fixing descriptive conditions that something must meet in order to be that object (e.g. 'the cup that will arrive at my table as a result of the order I have placed'). In this sense, grasp of the meaning of such demonstratives is underpinned by synchronic forms of reasoning, since it can only rely on the information we possess at the time of making the judgements in which they figure. By contrast, Campbell says, demonstrative reference based on an episodic memory of the circumstances in which a particular object was encountered does not rely on fixing a descriptive condition. Rather, it exploits a logical link between the present memory judgement and a past perceptual demonstrative judgement. And, as such, memory demonstratives can be said to be grounded in the same experience as that which provided grounds for perceptual demonstratives in the past.

The idea of a logical link between past and present is also a main theme of David Cockburn's contribution to this volume (Ch. 15). Cockburn's approach is to consider epistemological questions as to what is involved in our grasp of the past tense in the wider context of questions concerning the significance past events have in our lives. His strong claim is that a person's grasp of the past tense cannot be divorced from her grasp of the, broadly ethical, appropriateness of certain feelings and actions in the present. A person who consistently refused to see past events as providing her with reasons to be, say, ashamed, hurt, or proud could not be said to 'understand what happened' in the sense we normally assign to that phrase.

In this context, Cockburn also draws a distinction between thinking of one's current state as the present trace of a past event and thinking of it as the knowledge of a past event. For instance, to think of the shame with which one remembers a particular past deed merely as the present trace of a past event may involve thinking of it as an unpleasant condition which we would better be out of. Yet to think of it in this way, for Cockburn, falls short of a recognition of what has happened. Quite on the contrary, it may be seen as a method of refusing to acknowledge a certain understanding of what has happened. By contrast, to think of one's shame as an expression of one's grasp of what one has done requires seeing a logical, rather than a purely causal, connection between what is happening now and what has happened. It involves seeing the past as providing us with reasons to feel or do certain things now. In other words, what it is to think of one's memory in this sense, in as far as it involves a grasp of the appropriateness, now, of certain feelings and actions, cannot be spelled out without essential reference to the past.

If Campbell and Cockburn are right, then, it would seem that a theory of episodic memory must recognize the obtaining of a rational connection, through memory, between a subject's current mental state and her earlier experiences. Yet, as Cockburn himself draws out, we can also, at least sometimes, think of that connection in purely causal terms, conceiving of our memories as mere effects or traces of past events, in order to distance ourselves from any perceived demands the past may make on us (say, to avoid being prejudiced by our personal experience or to counter the forces of habit). It therefore seems appropriate to ask what constitutes the difference, for the subject, between thinking of a present mental state as the effect of a certain past event and seeing that past event as a reason for saying, doing, or feeling certain things.

Part of an answer to this question may be found in Campbell's contribution. For him, the ability to make what he calls 'temporally extended inferences', that is, to exploit a rational connection with the past in making memory judgements, is closely tied up with a capacity to engage in a certain form of imaginative exercise. He describes what he calls a certain form of 'decentring'. In decentring one adopts the pretence that it is now the time when the remembered event happened and, in doing so, simulates the making of certain perceptual judgements. To engage in such decentring requires some ability to keep track of the temporal or causal relation between the present time and the past time one reaches out to in one's imagination. Crucially, however, within the context of the imaginative project, judgements are made in the present tense. In other words, the judgements made within the context of the imaginative project exploit the same kind of understanding as goes into making perceptual judgements in the present. What Campbell argues, specifically, is that a subject's grasp of memory demonstratives referring to particulars encountered in the past rests on her ability to engage in this form of decentring. The subject's knowledge of the reference of such a demonstrative is provided by her ability to decentre to a past time and, in doing so, to conceive of it as the reference of a past perceptual demonstrative.

One way of understanding the point Campbell makes is by saying that our ability to make judgements about the past, on the basis of episodic memory, rests on the capacity to bring past events to mind by imaginatively adopting the temporal perspective of the time at which they happened. As such, ascribing an episodic memory to someone goes beyond ascribing to them a mere disposition to have certain beliefs, due to certain experiences they have had. Also, it is not the same as saying that they possess a theoretical understanding of the causal connections between their past experiences and their current mental state. Rather, as Campbell argues, the link between past and present is apparent to the subject through the capacity for decentring, in as far as it makes apparent a link between past perceptual judgements and present memory judgements.

The notion of a temporal point of view

There is an interesting question as to whether Campbell's theory, which puts a particular kind of imaginative ability at the core of our ability to make memory judgements, is compatible, for instance, with the kind of theory put forward by Martin (Ch. 10, this volume), which explicitly contrasts episodic memory and imagination. However, what Campbell says about memory also connects up with traditional concerns about temporal reasoning and the nature of time. The link between past perceptual judgements and present memory judgements which Campbell speaks of implies, at least on the face of it, a certain form of commensurability between judgements made at different times denied in some current accounts of the truth-conditions of tensed representations. Central to these accounts is the claim that tense is real, which is clarified and discussed in detail in A. W. Moore's contribution to this volume (Ch. 14). According to Moore, claiming that tense is real amounts to saying that there is something in reality that corresponds in a special way to the tense of any given representation. In other words, a tensed representation represents reality from a temporal point of view in such a way that the truth-conditions of that representation can only be given from that very same temporal point of view.

Moore traces back the motivation behind the claim that tense is real to a picture of reality as fractured into different worlds. On this picture, he says, each temporal point of view carries its own world with it. Consider, for instance, an utterance of 'It is raining today', made yesterday, and an utterance of 'It was raining yesterday', made today. Today, we might say of yesterday's utterance of 'It is raining today' that it was true if and only if it was raining yesterday. But, according to the view that tense is real, the fact we thereby express is not the fact that made this utterance true (if indeed it was true). In as far as the fact that made this utterance true belonged, so to speak, to the world of yesterday, it can only be expressed from the temporal point of view of yesterday. Conversely, we can express the fact that makes today's utterance of 'It was raining yesterday' true by saying that it was raining yesterday. Yet this fact is a fact that belongs to today's world and, as such, we could not have expressed it from the temporal point of view of yesterday.

The question Moore explores is whether we have any reasons to reject such a picture of reality as fragmented into different worlds, constituted by facts which can only be expressed from the corresponding temporal point of view. In particular, he looks at Kant's philosophy as a possible source for arguments which would show that temporal reality can't be thus fragmented but must be unified. What he says, following Kant (1929), is that, ultimately, there are no such arguments. Or rather, if we think that temporal reality can't be fragmented but must be unified, the source of this conviction cannot stem from any more basic principles that we can adduce to, but must stem from a self-conscious reflection on the way we think about the world and our place within it. Time, that is, is *given* to us as having the requisite unity, which is reflected in the nature of the judgements we in fact make.

A central element of Kant's philosophy which Moore appeals to in clarifying the idea that time, as it is given to us, is unified is the idea that time is given to us in a way that justifies our applying the same categories to what is present and what is not present. Interestingly, one example that Moore mentions in this context is our ability to apply the category of causation across different times. Recall that, in the previous section, we asked whether purely causal notions suffice to explain the way in which our thinking is connected with the past in episodic memory. What Moore argues, in effect, is that in order to judge, say, a present event to be the effect of a past event, we must already conceive of both events as belonging to the same categorical order, and we must think of the relation between them as obtaining independently of our particular point of view on one of them as past and the other as present (points also echoed in Peacocke's chapter). That is to say, we must represent them as occupying different positions within a single world on which we have different temporal points of view at different times. As such, making the required causal judgement, for instance, requires a certain understanding of what is involved in using the past tense. This understanding cannot be explained without an appeal to our ability to appreciate the links that obtain between judgements made from our current temporal point of view and judgements made from other points of view in time, in virtue of the fact that they are all points of view onto the same world.

Memory, temporal thought, and self consciousness

Some of the most intriguing questions with which the chapters in this volume leave us concern the connections between memory and temporal thought, on the one hand, and self-consciousness, on the other. Consider again, for instance, how Peacocke describes full-blown use of the past tense as a matter of assigning events positions in one's own history and, correlatively, in the history of the world. His words suggest that use of the past tense, in this sense, is underpinned by a combination of capacities for objective thought and capacities for first-person thought.

A crucial element in Peacocke's theory is the claim that a thinker's understanding of sentences in the past tense consists in part in her having information about a certain link that obtains between thoughts entertained or utterances made at different times. We have already seen a related idea at work in Moore's account when he says that our understanding of the past tense involves the ability to apply the same categories in our thinking about the past as we do in our thinking about the present. Peacocke's account tries to make sense of this idea by talking about a 'property–identity link' implicit knowledge of which informs our understanding of past-tense statements. For instance, he contends that a thinker's understanding of the utterance 'Yesterday it rained' consists in part in her having the information that that utterance is true just in case yesterday had the same property as today has to have for the utterance 'It is now raining' to be true when evaluated with respect to today.

Within Peacocke's theory, the claim that our understanding of the past tense is underpinned by implicit knowledge of such a property–identity link forms a centrepiece in an attempt at spelling out a particular brand of realism about the past. Realism about the past, in general, is the doctrine that there can be past-tense statements which are true, but unknowably so. What Peacocke argues, in effect, is that a subject who is in possession of the information given in the property–identity link can conceive of the truth-conditions of past-tense thoughts or utterances in a way that doesn't require her to know whether those thoughts or utterances are true or not. Furthermore, the property–identity link makes intelligible how there can be past-tense utterances or thoughts which are true even though there are no states of affairs obtaining now from which their truth could be inferred.

The particular task Peacocke sets himself is to show how we can square the idea that our understanding of the past tense can be realist, in the sense that it allows for the possibility of such unknowable truths about the past, with the idea that it also essentially rests upon a capacity for learning knowable truths about the past. Arguably, we can only credit a subject with an understanding of the past tense (including implicit knowledge of the property–identity link) if there are at least some instances in which that subject can recognize that the truth-conditions of past-tense utterances or thoughts obtain. More specifically, the question Peacocke tries to address is how memory can make available modes of thinking about past events in such a way that the events thus thought of could have happened without our knowing about them, then or now. And it is here that the idea of a connection between objective thought and first-person thought might be seen to have a crucial role to play.

The question, in short, is how the subject can make sense of the possibility that past-tense utterances or thoughts she knows to be true might be true without her knowledge. One possible suggestion (adapted from a similar suggestion made by Evans, 1982, about perceptual knowledge) runs as follows. The subject can make sense of the possibility of truths about the past she doesn't know about only if she can appreciate what makes certain truths about the past knowable. Put differently, the subject has to grasp that there are further conditions to be met, apart from things having been a certain way in the past, before she can know that they have been that way. Crucially, this gives us one way of understanding the connection Peacocke draws between the subject's ability to assign a remembered event a position in the history of the world and assigning it a place in one's own history (see also Hoerl, Ch. 12, this volume). Had the subject's own history been different, the very events she now remembers could have happened without her knowing that they did. Thus, the suggestions runs, it is only in as far as the subject can conceive of the contents of her memory as the joint upshot of her own history as well as the history of the world that she can make sense of how the truths she actually knows about could be beyond her ken.

Saying that, however, leaves wide open the question as to the specific kinds of reasoning about herself—the kind of self-conscious reasoning—a thinker needs to be capable of if she is to have the notion of her own history that is at issue here. And the views put forward in other chapters in this volume suggest that there are a number of possible answers to this question.

Perhaps the most central issue is whether possession of such a notion of one's own history requires what is typically called a 'theory of mind', that is, an understanding of the representational nature of mental states and of the causal relations in which they stand to the world and to each other. For instance, on a metarepresentational view, such as that proposed by Perner (1991) and further developed by Dokic (Ch. 8, this volume), it would seem that a subject's ability to make memory-judgements about particular past events depends on her capacity to think of her present mental state as the effect of an earlier experience of those events. If this is true, it suggests that an essential part of having the notion of one's own history, as it enters into such judgements, must be the ability to think of oneself as the bearer of certain representational states in the past. Therefore, on this account, the crucial issue would be to clarify what it takes to have access to one's own mind in this way.

Other contributors, however, suggest that it is not so much the thought of one's own mental states in the past that our memory-judgements are based upon, but our ability to evoke those mental states in the form of a memory image. In having the memory image we re-encounter, so to speak, the world from a point of view we once had. Admittedly, this leaves the question as to what it takes for the subject to be able to correlate her past point of view with her present one, as two different points of view on the same reality (this point is discussed below with reference to the chapters by Conway and Martin). But an explanation of this ability might not need to invoke a capacity to conceptualize one's own mental states as such. It could be more simply, for instance, that the subject must appreciate that what she knows about the past is determined by where she was at different time, that is, her own spatiotemporal location. In this sense, having a notion of one's history would be a matter of thinking of oneself as a physical object located in different places at different times, and the question would be what it takes for someone to think of herself as such an object in the world (cf. Povinelli, Landau, and Perilloux, 1996).

MEMORY AND EXPERIENCE

In one way or the other, the theories we have discussed all put special emphasis on the ability to remember particular past events that were personally experienced. According to these theories, our ability to represent and think about events in time in general is intimately connected with the ability to bring before the mind or think back to particular things which we have done or which happened to us. Yet what exactly is involved in this special kind of memory ability? In the remainder of this introduction, we wish to discuss the idea that considerations about the phenomenology of memory may hold the key to the question as to what it is to remember particular, personally experienced events. This idea can be found articulated in different ways in several of the contributions to this volume.

When Tulving first introduced the term 'episodic memory' to describe our ability to remember particular, personally experienced events, the idea of a difference between episodic memory and other types of memory had the status of a 'pretheoretical position' (Tulving, 1972: 384), based primarily on distinctions between different types of memory tasks. He writes: 'Nothing very much is lost at this stage of our deliberations if the reality of the separation . . . lies solely in the experimenter's and the theorist's, and not the subject's mind' (ibid.). However, the situation has changed significantly since then, and much current work on episodic memory can be seen as an attempt at finding more substantive grounds for talk about episodic memory as a distinct system.

A significant amount of work in this area has gone into pointing out ways in which episodic memory can fail. Dokic (Ch. 8, this volume), for instance, discusses at length a passage in which Goethe professes that there are certain events in his childhood which he probably only knows about because he was told by others. What Goethe's example brings home is that there is a sense in which we may forget events we have experienced even though we may still know that they happened from other sources, such as the word of others. Conversely, there are cases in which a person's knowledge goes back to the experience of a particular event, but in which information about the occurrence of that event has not been retained. Here we may think, for instance, about Claparède's famous experiment with an amnesic patient (Claparède, 1911, discussed in Kihlstrom, 1995; see also Campbell, Ch. 6, this volume). After a handshake during which he had pricked her with a pin that he had concealed in his own hand, she refused to shake hands with him again. Yet, asked why she was suddenly reluctant, she would only say things like 'Sometimes pins are hidden in people's hands' and seemed to have forgotten all about the actual incident.

The notion of episodic memory tries to capture a combination of two aspects, each of which is lacking in one of the examples just given. They correspond to two ways of understanding the idea that episodic memory is essentially memory for personally experienced events. Ascriptions of episodic memory signify that a person is able to make judgements about a particular sort of thing, that is, a specific event in his own life; at the same time, such ascriptions also indicate what puts the person into a position to make such judgements, namely his own experience of that event.

It can be argued, however, that there is also another respect in which episodic memory differs from the kinds of retention of information involved in the examples given above. A dominant theme in current research on episodic memory is that there is a specific kind of phenomenology to episodic recall as an aspect of the subject's conscious awareness. Thus, it has been argued that there really is a distinction 'in the subject's own mind' in as far as there is a difference between what it is like to recollect a particular, personally experienced event as opposed to retrieving other kinds of information or knowledge.

The conscious experience of recall (or 'recollective experience', as he puts it) has also become a major focus of Tulving's work. He writes that 'recollective experience should be the ultimate object of interest [in theories of episodic memory], the central aspect of remembering that is to be explained and explored' (Tulving, 1983: 184; see also Wheeler, Stuss, and Tulving, 1997). However, such claims are by no means uncontroversial (cf. Cockburn, Ch. 15, this volume). The idea that appeals to the phenomenology of recall can help to explain what is important and distinctive about our ability to remember particular, personally experienced events has come under attack from at least two, quite different, quarters—one within psychology and the other within philosophy.

One challenge to this idea has come from methodological considerations about the study of memory capacities in animals and infants. It has been argued that recent theories of episodic memory, which place special emphasis on the conscious experience of recall, make the question as to whether non- or pre-verbal populations possess episodic memories seemingly unanswerable. Some researchers have therefore preferred to say that all they are after is establishing whether animals or infants possess 'episodic-like' memories (cf. Griffiths, Dickinson, and Clayton, 1999; Meltzoff, 1990), implying that the behavioural measures they use cannot test whether there is an equivalent in animals or infants to the conscious experience of recall in adult humans. Often, however, such remarks also indicate a certain scepticism as to whether the concept of episodic memory can actually serve to single out a psychologically useful category, if claims about the representational abilities involved in episodic memory and its cognitive function cannot be considered separately from claims about the phenomenology of recall.

The idea that considerations about the phenomenology of episodic recall are central to giving an account of this kind of memory has also been challenged on epistemological grounds. Specifically, what theorists have been arguing against is a picture which assimilates our knowledge of events we have experienced ourselves to knowledge that is derived from the observation of certain features in our environment which we interpret as causal traces or effects of past events. Instead, it has been argued that memory delivers a peculiarly direct, non-inferential form of knowledge about the past. Indeed, without this form of knowledge, knowledge of the past by inference would never get off the ground, since we would have no conception of the kind of circumstance to infer to. It is in this context that theorists have also questioned the relevance of conscious experiences in giving an account of memory (Wittgenstein, 1958, 1980; Anscombe, 1976; Ayer, 1956). Specifically, they have argued that an appeal to such experiences cannot explain how there can be such direct, non-inferential knowledge of the past, since these experiences themselves stand in need of interpretation before they can tell us anything about the past. Rather, the argument goes, it is because we already know about the past that we can see such experiences as having anything to do with the fact that we remember.

Neither of the two lines of thought we have just described denies that we typically have certain conscious experiences when we remember particular past events. Instead, what they call into question is the significance we should assign to these experiences in ascribing episodic memory to others (including, perhaps, animals and children) and to ourselves. In short, they suggest that any conscious experiences we have when we remember past events are only contingently associated with our ability to make judgements about these events.

Several of the chapters in this volume can be seen as exploring an alternative conception of the relation between episodic memory and conscious experience, which is linked to the claim that episodic memory is essentially memory for personally experienced events. We have already said that this claim combines two aspects: that a person is able to make judgements about a specific event in his own life; and that he is in a position to make such judgements because he has experienced that event himself. However, this claim can also be understood to indicate that there is a specific connection between these two aspects, in the sense that there is a particular kind of judgement a subject can make about past events which he can only make if he has experienced these events himself. If this is true, it might give us a particular way of understanding the role of conscious experience in episodic memory. Basically, the idea would be that there is a certain experience which the subject would not have had he not experienced the event in question. And it is his having that experience which explains the sense in which he is able to make particular kinds of judgements about that event. Thus, an appeal to the phenomenology of episodic memory can serve to make clear how these two aspects of episodic memory are connected. In other words, talk about an 'experience of recall' can be seen as an attempt to capture the idea that someone who episodically remembers a certain event has available to him a particular way of thinking about that event, together with the idea that this way of thinking about that event would not be available to him had he not experienced it himself.

In what follows, we wish to discuss three concrete ways in which this general line of thought may be articulated. They correspond to three broad suggestions about the phenomenology of episodic remembering which can be extracted from contributions to this volume. Very simplified, the suggestions go as follows: (*a*) Episodic remembering involves an awareness that one's present mental state has been caused by one's own personal experience of the remembered event; (*b*) Episodic remembering involves having before the mind a memory image of the remembered event; (*c*) Episodic remembering involves having a temporal impression of the length of the interval that has elapsed since the remembered event occurred. We shall consider these three suggestions in turn.

Recollection and awareness of a causal link with the past

Both Jérôme Dokic and Andrew Mayes, in their contributions to this volume (Chs. 8 and 7), present theories in which the causal connection between the subject's past experience of an event and her present recollection of that event is assigned a particular role in explaining the phenomenology of recollection. Dokic's argument develops from considerations about the metarepresentational theory of episodic memory, first proposed by Perner (1991). According to Perner's original proposal, episodic memory makes available two kinds of information, namely information about the world and information about our own mental states. When we episodically remember an event, we not only possess information about the event, we also possess the information that this information was acquired perceptually. What Dokic aims to clarify is the role of this latter 'metarepresentational comment'. He notes that, as it stands, Perner's theory may make it look as though the metarepresentational comment is simply a further piece of factual information that was acquired in the original encounter with the event and is now being retrieved. Instead, what Dokic proposes is that the metarepresentational comment must be construed as a piece of information about the subject's current mental state. Thus, it cannot be said to be retrieved from memory in a similar way as a previously acquired piece of factual information. Retrieving factual information, for Dokic, means getting into much the same sort of mental state we were in when we first acquired that information. In episodic memory, by contrast, the way in which our present mental state has been caused by past experience makes a difference to what it is like to be in that mental state, in as far as we become aware of a new fact, namely that the conscious information available to us now derives from that past experience. In this sense, episodic remembering is thought to involve a special sort of conscious awareness which allows us to think of our past experience of a certain event as the cause of our present mental state, and thus to think about the event in a way in which this would not be possible had we not experienced it.

Mayes's theory shares much with that proposed by Dokic, in so far as one of Mayes's central claims is that recollection involves an awareness that the contents of one's present consciousness were encountered in specific ways in the past. Both authors also agree that this awareness cannot be explained by appeal to the retrieval of a particular kind of information that was encoded earlier. There is a difference between them, however, when it comes to the question as to what does explain this awareness. Dokic says little about this question apart from claiming that it needs to be addressed at the level of sub-personal mechanisms. Mayes, by contrast, thinks that it can be explained by appealing to a specific aspect of the subject's conscious awareness, namely in terms of the way the information comes into consciousness. The way in which information comes into consciousness is an aspect of our conscious awareness which cannot be reduced to features of the content of that information. Mayes identifies it instead as the fluency with which that information is activated. Thus, one way of understanding Mayes's proposal is that, for instance, the fact that we have acquired certain pieces of information through personal experience of an event might make a difference to the conscious experience of activating that information, since the information will be activated more fluently. If this is true, however, it implies that this conscious experience can serve as a basis for making a particular kind of judgement about the past, namely that a certain past experience is responsible for one's current mental state, and thus that one is remembering.

The theories put forward by Dokic and Mayes may give us a lead on a possible connection between our ability to recollect past events and our grasp of the kinds of temporal concepts that McTaggart talks about. One important observation made by McTaggart is that there is an intimate connection between thinking about an event as real and applying certain kinds of temporal concepts to that event. In particular, he suggests that in order to think of an event as real, we must be capable of thinking of it as having a determinate location with respect to our own temporal perspective (see McTaggart, 1927: 16). He asks us to consider, for instance, the sequence of adventures that are narrated by Cervantes in *Don Quixote*. The adventure of the galley slaves, say, is later than the adventure of the windmills, and, in this sense, they may be said to stand in a temporal relation to each other. Yet part of the force of saying that these are not real events, but only fictional ones, lies in the fact that they cannot be judged as either past, present, or future.

Now, it is at least possible to interpret what Dokic and Mayes say as implying that recollection, in as far as it involves seeing a remembered event as the cause of our present mental state, makes manifest to us our temporal perspective on that event in McTaggart's sense. That is to say, we can judge that this event has taken place in the past because it has left certain effects on us. We can locate it not just with respect to other events we know about, but also with respect to our own temporal point of view. Moreover, because it has left this effect on us, we can also judge that this event has really happened (see Peacocke, Ch. 13, this volume). Thus, the grounds we have for judging that the event has taken place in the past are at the same time grounds for thinking of it as a feature of reality.

However, it might also be thought that the accounts put forward by Dokic and Mayes still leave open some important questions regarding the way past events are represented in episodic memory. Arguably, thinking of one's current mental state as having been caused by one's experience of an event in the past can fall short of knowing which particular event one has actually experienced. It seems to imply only that there has been an event which fulfils a certain descriptive condition, namely that one's experience of it has caused one's current mental state. Indeed, Mayes's account makes this quite explicit in as far as he also allows that retrieval from factual memory can be accompanied by increased fluency. Thus, on his account, even when we retrieve facts from memory, such as the fact that the chemical formula of table salt is NaCl, we can be aware that we acquired that fact in the past.

Clearly, on the accounts of both Mayes and Dokic, part of an explanation of the distinctive nature of episodic memory (as contrasted with factual memory) also lies in the particular kind of information that was acquired when the remembered event was first encountered. But there are different ways in which this idea might be spelled out. One idea that has been very influential is that episodic memory depends on the retention of certain kinds of contextual information. Something like this may also be what Mayes and Dokic have in mind. An alternative idea, however, is that episodic memory inherits certain experiential characteristics from the original perception of the event (see McCormack, Ch. 11, this volume). In the next section, we will look at this latter idea in the context of the theories put forward by Conway and Martin. As we will see, however, they also differ from Dokic and Mayes on the role of the causal connection between past and present in episodic memory.

The idea of a memory image

The idea that episodic remembering involves a distinctive phenomenology is also a central theme of the theories presented by Martin Conway and M. G. F. Martin in this volume (Chs. 9 and 10). However, the key to understanding this distinctive phenomenology, for both of these authors, lies in the way imagery features in episodic recollection.

Conway's starting point is a finding which has by now been well established in empirical studies. Participants in memory tests can readily distinguish between two kinds of judgements they may be asked to make (see Tulving, 1985; Gardiner, 1988). A person who has witnessed a certain event may sometimes say that they know of this event but at the same time not be prepared to say that they remember it. It has also been shown that the likelihood of participants making one judgement rather than another can be selectively influenced by task variables at encoding or retrieval (see Gardiner and Java, 1993, for review). These studies also play a large part in Mayes's theory, but Conway's interest in them is somewhat different. Roughly speaking, for Mayes, the crucial question we must ask in the light of these studies concerns the awareness we have of our present mental state that allows us to judge that it is a state of remembering. Conway's interest, by contrast, is in the kind of awareness that goes into that mental state of remembering itself, and indeed he argues that being in that mental state involves a certain disengagement from the present.

The contrast between merely retrieving facts about the past and episodically recollecting a particular past event, for Conway, can be described by saying that the former involves no apparent change in one's consciousness of the external world, whereas the latter involves, as he puts it, an encounter with fragments of a past self. In a certain sense, episodic recollection takes us back to what it was like when we first experienced the event we now remember. Conway explains this feature of the phenomenology of episodic memory in terms of the retrieval of what he calls 'phenomenological records', sensory-perceptual details that were encoded when the subject experienced the event. The point of appealing to these phenomenological records, however, is not just to say that episodic remembering makes available more information than we would otherwise have. Rather, information becomes available in a specific, imagistic, form, and it is in this sense that episodic remembering of an event can be said to be phenomenologically similar to one's perceptual experience of that event.

We can turn to Martin's discussion for a further elucidation of the idea that there is a phenomenological similarity between episodic remembering and perceptual experience, and for an extended discussion of the notion of a memory image. Martin takes issue with an assumption that is shared by many traditional accounts of what it is to have a memory image (cf. e.g. James, 1890; Russell, 1912). The assumption, as he puts it, is that the imagistic forms a neutral, common core to perception, memory, and imagination. On this assumption, the difference between perceptual images, memory images, and images that are part of an imaginative exercise has nothing to do with the nature of those images themselves. Rather, it results from something like attaching different labels to these images. Martin, by contrast, argues that we should see the difference as one that obtains between the images as such. Specifically, both perceptual and memory images differ from images created in imagination in that the former are intrinsically particular or specific in their content, whereas the latter are not. That is to say, both perceptual images and memory images present or represent a particular object in virtue of the kinds of images they are, independently of the use to which they are put. In this, Martin argues, they differ from images created in imagination, where particularity can only arise if the subject intends to imagine a particular object he knows about.

An important question that might be raised is whether something like Conway's story about the role of phenomenological records in episodic memory can help us explain this difference. It would seem that the distinctive phenomenology of episodic memory, as Martin envisages it, has something to do with the difference between the way memory images are generated as opposed to, say, the way images might be generated on the basis of purely factual information (see also Hoerl, Ch. 12, this volume). In this context, it is interesting to note that Conway does not just say that imagery enters recall when phenomenological records are retrieved, but also that retrieval of these records can be an automatic process, given a suitable cue. This might be a way of explaining a sense in which the images generated in episodic remembering are not of our own making and, in this sense, have the particular content they have independently of our intentions or the use to which we put them.

Once we have distinguished memory images from images created in imagination on the basis of their intrinsic particularity, the question remains as to what distinguishes memory images from perceptual images, which share this feature of intrinsic particularity.

It is tempting to think that at least part of the difference between perception and memory, on the accounts put forward by Martin and Conway, must lie with the way time is represented in memory. Yet, at first blush, this is not how Martin and Conway see things. For instance, Martin's construal of the difference between episodic remembering and perceptual experience seems to have little to do with any temporal information which episodic memory might be said to make available to us. He describes the difference, instead, as that between having an experience, in perception, and representing an experience, in episodic remembering. He elucidates this difference by saying that, in this respect, episodic memory can be seen as sharing a feature with imagination, in as far as imagining is also a matter of representing an experience (only the experience represented in imagination lacks the intrinsic particularity of that represented in episodic memory). A similar idea can be seen at work in the way Conway spells out the difference between perceptual experience and episodic remembering. He argues that the contents of consciousness represented in the memory image are the result of the subject's past attention, guided by his goals at the time. As such, however, the memory image implicitly carries with it goals which the subject does not currently have. Thus, again, we have something which might be described as a contrast between having an experience, in perception, and representing an experience, in episodic memory.

How, then, does time get into the picture, if at all? There is still a close connection, on both Martin's and Conway's account, between episodic memory and temporal representation. But this connection is little to do with any temporal information that might be carried by episodic memory; rather, it is to do with the fact that the remembering subject needs to have a grasp of time as a structure in which events can be located. Martin draws this out by pointing to the relevance his theory may be thought to have for developmental psychology. What infants must come to understand, he says, is how there can be particular events of which they have conscious knowledge, which are nevertheless not part of the present scene. The key to such an understanding, according to Martin, lies in the idea of time as a causal structure which relates earlier causes to later effects, but also a causal structure in which the infants themselves are located. In other words, we can hold separate and relate remembered events and events that form part of the present scene only if we grasp that our own temporal perspective is changing over time. And what makes this change in perspective intelligible to us is the idea that our own mental states are part of the causal nexus, such that recalled experiences are causally prior to episodes of recall.

A developmental question of the kind posed by Martin could also be raised with respect to Conway's theory. Roughly, the form it would take is this: What does it take for an infant to grasp that a memory image presents it with a view of reality, even though this view of reality is not governed by the goals that direct its perceptual attention in the present? A possible answer to this question may be sought in Conway's notion of an autobiographical knowledge base. Being able to relate the reality presented in the memory image to present reality, according to Conway, depends on the possession of general knowledge about one's own activities or about different periods in one's own life to which that memory image can be linked. This knowledge provides us with a unitary framework in which the different goals we possess at different times can be integrated, such that experiences represented in memory, which correspond to one's goals at times in the past, can be separated from and related with perceptual experiences driven by one's current goals. What bestows unity on this framework is the autobiographical nature of the knowledge involved, that is, the fact that it is all knowledge about us as a thing that persists over time. In other words, for us to possess such a unified framework requires the ability to think of ourselves as possessing an internal causal connectedness (Campbell, 1997), as something whose condition at one time affects the condition it is in later. The crux of the developmental question, then, would lie in the issue as to when children can be said to be able to think about themselves in this way.

Just as with the theories put forward by Dokic and Mayes, Conway's and Martin's theories raise important questions about the connection between our grasp of causal notions and our grasp of temporal notions, specifically the notion of the past, involved in making memory-judgements. One issue here could be formulated as follows. There are two different reasons why one might think that an understanding of causality is linked to the ability to make memory-judgements. On the one hand, one might think that there is such a link because recollection itself is a matter of being conscious that one's present mental state was caused by a certain past experience. This, roughly, is the route taken by Dokic and Mayes. On the other hand, one might think, as Conway and Martin seem to do, that recollection is simply a matter of having before the mind an image of a particular past event. Thus, according to them, it would seem that the phenomenology of recollection can be spelled out without using causal notions. However, it is still the case, on their view, that the image can only be an image of a particular past event in as far as the subject has a general grasp of the causal conditions that make it possible for us to know about past events although they are not currently perceived.

Distance-based processes and temporal impressions

Traditionally, an important empirical impulse for theories of episodic memory has come from studies of different forms of memory-loss in patients with brain damage. In particular, studies have examined whether brain damage can lead to a selective impairment of episodic memory while leaving other types of memory intact (cf. Cermack, 1982; Hirst, 1982; Mayes, 1988; Parkin and Leng, 1993). Such studies have typically explored memory impairments in patients with damage to medial temporal lobe structures and diencephalic regions, but also frontal lobe damage (see Wheeler, Stuss, and Tulving, 1997).

Yet, as Jill Boucher points out in her contribution to this volume (Ch. 4), there is a case to be made that episodic memory impairments are also a feature that can be found in autism (see also Perner, 2000). More to the point, what her discussion makes vivid is that the study of autism might provide promising, and as yet largely unexplored, resources for studying and factoring out the different elements that are involved in thinking back to particular events we have experienced in the past.

One obvious reason why people with autism should be a very interesting population to look at in the context of the theories we have discussed is that they are often said to suffer from particular difficulties with what is typically called 'mentalizing', that is, intuitive recognition of and reasoning about their own and other people's mental states. Thus, we might expect them to have episodic memory impairments if, as several authors in this volume seem to suggest, episodic recollection of events depends on an appreciation of the causal link between one's present mental state and one's own past experiences.

Yet Boucher suggests that there is another possible reason why memory impairments might occur in autism. She observes that people with autism sometimes report feeling 'lost in time', and she presents other evidence that they appear to have what she calls 'an impaired sense of time on the intuitive level'. These findings seem to indicate impaired processing of temporal information, and Boucher explores the possibility that such an impairment might explain some of the difficulties people with autism have in recalling past events. She hypothesizes that they feel lost in time because the internal clock or oscillator mechanisms which normally underlie intuitive temporal judgements are disrupted.

A central issue that emerges from Boucher's chapter is whether our ability to think back to particular events we have experienced depends, at least in part, on a capacity to make certain kinds of intuitive judgements about the time of events. A similar concern is also raised by Peacocke. A central claim of Peacocke's chapter is that we must recognize certain externalist elements in our understanding of the past tense. Thus, for instance, the understanding that goes into making a memory-judgement of the kind 'Yesterday, it was the case that A' cannot be accounted for purely in terms of a response, on the part of the subject, to certain states of affairs that obtain in the present (see also Cockburn, Ch. 15, this volume). Rather, in as far as it is a judgement about the past, it must involve a sensitivity to temporal relations. That is to say, a complete account of the representational content of the subject's mental state must mention states of affairs at a time other than the present. And it is in this sense that the mental state must be individuated externally.

In this context, Peacocke makes a further claim that brings his account close to some of the ideas explored by Boucher. What he claims is that there is a connection between this sensitivity to temporal relations and the workings of certain subpersonal mechanisms which keep track of time. According to him, the particular temporal relations in which we stand to past events can, at least sometimes, explain certain temporal impressions we have when we remember those events. Thus, for instance, he says that a person's having left the room about ten minutes ago can causally explain a subject's impression that the person left the room a certain interval of time ago, where the length of that interval is in fact about ten minutes. What Peacocke contends, in short, is that our understanding of the past tense relies on our ability to be causally sensitive to temporal facts in this sense. But he also argues that an explanation of this ability must ultimately be sought on the level of computational mechanisms which are responsive to the passage of time.

Thus Peacocke's theory of our understanding of the past tense leads us right back to some of the issues we raised at the beginning of this introduction. A fundamental concern raised by Peacocke's chapter might be formulated as follows. If, as he claims, the idea of a temporal impression is to capture something essential about episodic memory and its role in our grasp of the concept of the past, there is something important left out by some of the other theories of episodic memory we have discussed. A complete account of episodic memory must look not just at the conditions that obtained when remembered events were first encountered, plus whatever factors have to be in place at the time of recall. It must also look at what happens in the interval between encoding and recall. In particular, Peacocke argues that we need to appeal to the idea of an internal clock to shed light on temporal impressions as a central aspect of the phenomenology of episodic remembering. If he is right, any account of our understanding of the past tense must remain incomplete unless we can give a plausible story of specific mechanisms for keeping track of the time of events we remember.

THE STRUCTURE OF THIS VOLUME

We have thought it helpful to group the contributions to this volume into four main sections. The chapters in the first section look in detail at different accounts of how temporal information might be processed and represented. They provide current views on the psychological foundations of timing and memory for time, discussing the notion of an internal clock and the idea that memory is temporally organized. A common theme of the chapters in the second section is the idea that certain forms of remembering involve a particular kind of awareness of time, or of causal relations between past and present. They also raise questions about particular kinds of temporal or causal reasoning abilities involved in making judgements about the past. The chapters in the third section focus specifically on the phenomenology of episodic memory and the way particular past events can be said to come before the mind in episodic remembering. They explore connections between episodic memory and perceptual experience, and discuss the idea of a memory image. The chapters in the fourth section discuss different accounts of memory in the context of traditional concerns in epistemology and metaphysics. They highlight in particular connections between questions concerning the nature of memory and philosophical questions regarding the reality of time and our understanding of the past tense.

In these introductory comments, we have tried to sketch some of the issues raised in these chapters, which represent a variety of philosophical and psychological approaches to memory and temporal representation. However, we also hope to have given a sense of the interest in bringing together these various approaches, both within each discipline and across them, to address questions as to the relation between our understanding of time and our ability to represent particular past events.

REFERENCES

ANSCOMBE, G. E. M. (1976), 'Memory, "experience" and causation', in H. D. Lewis (ed.), *Contemporary British Philosophy,* 4th series. London: Allen and Unwin.

AYER, A. J. (1956), *The Problem of Knowledge*. Harmondsworth: Penguin.

BREWER, B. (1994), 'Thoughts about objects, places and times', in C. Peacocke (ed.), *Objectivity, Simulation, and the Unity of Consciousness: Proceedings of the British Academy 83.* Oxford: Oxford University Press.

BROWN, G. D. A., PREECE, T., and HULME, C. (2000), 'Oscillator-based memory for serial order', *Psychological Review*, 107: 127–81.

CAMPBELL, J. (1984), 'Possession of Concepts', *Proceedings of the Aristotelian Society*, 85: 149–70.

—— (1994), *Past, Space, and Self*. Cambridge, Mass.: MIT Press.

—— (1997), 'The structure of time in autobiographical memory', *European Journal of Philosophy*, 5: 105–18.

—— (forthcoming), *Reference and Consciousness*. Oxford: Oxford University Press.

CERMACK, L. S. (1982) (ed.), *Human Memory and Amnesia*. Hillsdale, NJ: Erlbaum.

CHURCH, R. M. (1984), 'Properties of the internal clock', in J. Gibbon and L. G. Allan (eds.), *Timing and Time Perception*. New York: New York Academy of Sciences, 566–82.

CLAPARÈDE, E. (1911), 'Recognition and "me-ness",' trans. D. Rapaport, in D. Rapaport (ed.), *Organization and Pathology of Thought: Selected Sources*. New York: Columbia University Press, 1951.

CLAYTON, N. S., and DICKINSON, A. (1998), 'Episodic-like memory during cache recovery by scrub jays', *Nature*, 395: 272–4.

COCKBURN, D. (1997), *Other Times: Philosophical Perspectives on Past, Present and Future*. Cambridge: Cambridge University Press.

CONWAY, M. A. (1993), *Autobiographical Memory: An Introduction*. Milton Keynes: Open University Press.

EVANS, G. (1982), *The Varieties of Reference*, ed. John McDowell. Oxford: Oxford University Press.

FRIEDMAN, W. J. (1990), *About Time: Inventing the Fourth Dimension*. Cambridge, Mass.: MIT Press.

—— (1993), 'Memory for the time of past events', *Psychological Bulletin*, 113: 44–66.

GALLISTEL, C. R. (1990), *The Organization of Learning*. Cambridge, Mass.: MIT Press.

GARDINER, J. M. (1988), 'Functional aspects of recollective experience', *Memory and Cognition*, 16: 309–13.

—— and JAVA, R. I. (1993), 'Recognizing and remembering', in A. E. Collins, S. E. Gathercole, M. A. Conway, and P. E. M. Morris (eds.), *Theories of Memory*. Hove: Erlbaum.

GIBBON, J. (1977), 'Scalar expectancy theory and Weber's law in animal timing', *Psychological Review*, 84: 278–325.

GRIFFITHS, D., DICKINSON, A., and CLAYTON, N. (1999), 'Episodic memory: what can animals remember about their past?', *Trends in Cognitive Sciences*, 3: 74–80.

HIRST, W. (1982), 'The amnesic syndrome: descriptions and explanations', *Psychological Bulletin*, 91: 435–60.

JAMES, W. (1890), *Principles of Psychology*, i. London: Macmillan.

KANT, I. (1929), *Critique of Pure Reason*, trans. Norman Kemp Smith. London: Macmillan.

KIHLSTROM, J. F. (1995), 'Memory and consciousness: an appreciation of Claparède and *Recognition et Moïté*', *Consciousness and Cognition*, 4: 379–86.

KILLEEN, P. (1975), 'On the temporal control of behavior', *Psychological Review*, 82: 89–115.

KOLTERMAN, R. (1974), 'Periodicity in the activity and learning performance of the honey bee', in L. B. Browne (ed.), *The Experimental Analysis of Insect Behavior*. Berlin: Springer-Verlag, 218–26.

MCCORMACK, T., and HOERL, C. (1999), 'Memory and temporal perspective: the role of temporal frameworks in memory development', *Developmental Review*, 19: 154–82.

McTAGGART, J. E. (1927), *The Nature of Existence*, ii, ed. C. D. Broad. Cambridge: Cambridge University Press.

MALCOLM, N. (1963), *Knowledge and Certainty*. Englewood Cliffs, NJ: Prentice-Hall.

MARTIN, M. G. F. (1992), 'Perception, concepts, and memory', *The Philosophical Review*, 101: 745–63.

MAYES, A. R. (1988), *Human Organic Memory Disorders*. New York: Cambridge University Press.

MELTZOFF, A. N. (1990), 'Towards a developmental cognitive science: the implications of cross-modal matching and imitation for the development of representation and memory in infancy', in A. Diamond (ed.), *Annals of the New York Academy of Science,* 608: *The Development and Neural Bases of Higher Cognitive Functions*. New York: New York Academy of Science.

O'KEEFE, J. (1994), 'Cognitive maps, time, and causality', in C. Peacocke (ed.), *Objectivity, Simulation, and the Unity of Consciousness: Current Issues in the Philosophy of Mind*. Oxford: Oxford University Press.

PARKIN, A. J., and LENG, N. R. C. (1993), *Neuropsychology of the Amnesic Syndrome*. Hillsdale, NJ: Erlbaum.

PERNER, J. (1991), *Understanding the Representational Mind*. Cambridge, Mass.: MIT Press.

—— (2000), 'Memory and theory of mind', in E. Tulving and F. I. M. Craik (eds.), *The Oxford Handbook of Memory*. New York: Oxford University Press.

POVINELLI, D. J., LANDAU, K. R., and PERILLOUX, H. K. (1996), 'Self-recognition in infancy using delayed versus live feedback: evidence of a development asynchrony', *Child Development*, 67: 1540–54.

RUSSELL, B. (1912), *The Problems of Philosophy*. London: Oxford University Press.

TULVING, E. (1972), 'Episodic and semantic memory', in E. Tulving and W. Donaldson (eds.), *Organization of Memory*. New York: Academic Press.

—— (1983), *Elements of Episodic Memory*. Oxford: Oxford University Press.

—— (1985), 'Memory and consciousness', *Canadian Psychology*, 26: 1–12.

—— and MARKOWITSCH, H. J. (1998), 'Episodic and declarative memory: role of the hippocampus', *Hippocampus*, 8: 198–204.

WHEELER, M. A., STUSS, D. T., and TULVING, E. (1997), 'Toward a theory of episodic memory: the frontal lobes and autonoetic consciousness', *Psychological Bulletin*, 121: 331–54.

WITTGENSTEIN, L. (1958), *Philosophical Investigations*, ed. G. E. M. Anscombe and R. Rhees, trans. G. E. M. Anscombe. Oxford: Basil Blackwell.

—— (1980), *Remarks on the Philosophy of Psychology*, ed. G. H. von Wright and G. E. M. Anscombe, trans. G. E. M. Anscombe. Oxford: Basil Blackwell.

I

*Keeping Track of Time, and
Temporal Representation*

1

Internal Clocks and the Representation of Time

J. H. Wearden

Time is represented in many ways. Our language, with its structure of tenses, and prepositions such as 'before' and 'after', embodies some temporal codes into its very structure (and different languages do this differently, see Brée, 1992). Language also employs temporal metaphors ('time flies' etc.) to give flavour to written and spoken discourse (see Jackson and Michon, 1992, for many examples). Physics employs several concepts of time, often in a subtle and occasionally counter-intuitive way (see Davies, 1995), but then so does film-making, where the actual duration of events is telescoped for dramatic effect (DeWied, Tan, and Frijda, 1992), and stories in various media can be narrated in total or partial 'flashback' (Proust's *A la recherche du temps perdu*, which has not escaped the attention of psychologists, see Fraisse, 1992, being probably the best-known example, certainly the longest one).

Time is the 'primordial context' in which all the events in our lives take place, but, unfortunately, pointing out this obvious fact, and expanding the paragraph above to fill this whole chapter, giving example after example of the way time is measured and represented (time in different cultures, time among the ancient Greeks, the development of time-measuring devices such as clocks, to name but a few) may weary the reader after a page or two. Perhaps, to be studied profitably, time needs to be cut down to manageable size, and small domains defined in which real progress can be made.

The present chapter seeks to introduce the reader to the way that time is represented in psychological models based on the idea of an 'internal clock', a notion which has been central to recent conceptions of psychological time.

The idea that organisms perform timing tasks using some sort of internal clock is by no means new, and has even been present in experimental studies in psychology since the 1920s (e.g. François, 1927). Of early researchers, Hoagland's name is perhaps the best known, and he proposed that humans possess a 'chemical clock', the rate of operation of which is governed by, among other things, body temperature (Hoagland, 1933). This idea, stemming from observation of his own wife when suffering from influenza, spawned some of serious psychology's most bizarre experimental manipulations, involving heated rooms and helmets, and even subjects pedalling exercise bicycles in a tank of water (Bell, 1975). As a recent review (Wearden and Penton-Voak, 1995) has shown, when body temperature rose, people usually behaved as if some internal pacemaker they possessed ran faster, thus supporting Hoagland's general idea.

The notion of an internal clock has been employed extensively in recent years as an explanation of the performance of animals and humans on a range of timing tasks. But not all the timed behaviours of humans are explainable by internal clocks. Humans may accurately perform time judgements on the basis of real world knowledge, such as how long events habitually last, by translating a non-temporal dimension into a temporal one (as where judgements of the length of time required for some action are derived from the number of events the action contains, or distance traversed) or, in what are called *retrospective timing* tasks, by using the amount of information processing during a period, or the number of contextual changes occurring, as an indicator of its duration (see Ch. 2 by Block and Zakay in this volume). The situations in which internal clock models are used are those involving, first, *prospective timing*, where subjects are alerted in advance that time judgements will be required and, secondly, those which I called elsewhere (Wearden, 1994) *biopsychological* time. Biopsychological time concerns time judgements based directly on real or hypothetical biological processes such as internal clocks or oscillators which, by implication, there is some chance that animals and humans might share.

The discussion of the use of internal clock-based mechanisms to represent time given in this chapter focuses on several issues. First, I discuss the most popular form of internal clock used in contemporary theory, the pacemaker-accu-mulator clock. I then discuss some of the uses to which this idea has been put in recent work, before introducing a more elaborate timing model, that of scalar timing theory, of which the clock is only a part. I then discuss two alternatives to pacemaker-accumulator clocks, an oscillator-based system and one that uses behavioural states to mediate the passage of time. I next discuss some conditions in which differences in 'internal clock speed' between conditions can be measured, as well as others in which it cannot, even though differences may exist. Before some concluding remarks, I briefly outline some, mostly very recent, work on the physiological basis of timing in animals and humans.

PACEMAKER-ACCUMULATOR CLOCKS

In the 1960s the idea that humans and animals might possess an internal clock was boosted by the development of quantitative models of how plausible internal clocks might work by Creelman (1962), and in particular in the pioneering model of Treisman (1963). One common idea was that of a *pacemaker-accumulator* clock, a device in which the clock consists of a pacemaker, an accumulator, and a switch which connects the two.

To illustrate the operation of such a clock, consider the problem of timing the duration of a stimulus. Onset of the stimulus causes the switch connecting the pacemaker and accumulator to close, allowing pulses (the 'clock ticks' of the internal clock system) to flow, then later stimulus offset causes the switch to open again, cutting the connection. Closing and opening of the switch may take some time, which need not be the same for stimulus onset and offset, nor constant from one trial to the next; that is, switch operations can contribute to the mean and variability of the number of 'ticks' accumulated when a stimulus, or other event, is timed.

To provide quantitative models of timed behaviour, some assumptions have to be made about how the pacemaker itself operates. Treisman (1963) proposed that it 'ticked' regularly, but more recent models have generally assumed a 'Poisson pacemaker' (Gibbon, 1977). This is a mechanism which produces pulses at random, but with some averagely constant rate, so the time between any two ticks may be unpredictable but the *average* rate of ticks per second over a longer period is fixed. The Poisson pacemaker idea has perhaps been popular because it represents a 'worst' case of completely random pulsations, and needs few additional assumptions. If the 'ticking' of the pacemaker was proposed not to be completely random, some assumptions as to exactly how it deviated from randomness would be needed to develop the proposal, and these would not only raise further questions, but have implications for properties of the pacemaker itself.

A Poisson pacemaker produces raw time representations with a number of interesting properties, but I want to concentrate on only one of these at present. This is the property of *linearity*. For example, if the pacemaker 'ticks' at some averagely constant rate, then pulses will accumulate in the pacemaker as a linear function of real time. For example, if n ticks accumulate in some real time, t, then, on average, $2n$ ticks will accumulate in $2t$, $3n$ in $3t$, and so on. In other words, accumulator contents will grow linearly with real duration. Although the result that short durations tend to be overestimated and long durations underestimated (Vierordt's law, see Fraisse, 1964) is frequently quoted, most modern studies support the prediction of linearity by finding linear relations between measures of timed behaviour and imposed temporal constraints (Gibbon, 1977; see also Lejeune and Wearden, 1991, for data from a wide range of animal species, and Wearden and McShane, 1988, and Wearden *et al.*, 1998, for data from humans).

WHAT PACEMAKER-ACCUMULATOR INTERNAL CLOCKS CAN DO

The sketch given above of how pacemaker-accumulator clocks might work is sufficient to understand some of the uses to which the idea has been put. One problem that can be treated is that in which it is known that judgements of the duration of one sort of event are reliably longer than those of another, when the two in fact have the same length. For example, it has been known since the nineteenth century that 'tones are judged longer than lights' (Goldstone and Lhamon, 1974; Wearden *et al.*, 1998). In other words, for the same real-time duration, auditory stimuli appear longer than visual ones. Wearden *et al.* (1998) showed that the visual/auditory difference in duration judgements could be modelled in terms of a difference in pacemaker speed for the two modalities. That is, if we assume that, for some reason, the pacemaker 'ticks' about 20 per cent faster for the auditory stimulus than the visual one, we can simulate the results obtained with a high degree of quantitative precision.

In fact, the mathematics of pacemaker-accumulator clocks (discussed in detail in Wearden *et al.*, 1998: 103–4) make stronger predictions about behaviour in situations where pacemaker speed is supposed to vary. In general, if the pacemaker runs faster for stimulus type A than for type B, the difference in subjective time representations between the two types of stimuli should get larger as the stimuli timed get longer. If judgements are plotted against real-time duration over a range, a hypothesized pacemaker-speed difference predicts that the two estimate functions will differ mostly in slope. Exactly this effect was found in the tone/light comparison in Wearden *et al.* (1998).

Another case might be one where judgements of one stimulus type are significantly more variable than those of another, even when they do not differ in mean duration estimate. The latency of the switch processes which start and stop accumulation can be invoked here: stimuli which engender more variable start and stop latencies will, on average, result in more variable numbers of pacemaker ticks accumulating from one trial to another. The tone/light case is again illustrative, as Wearden *et al.* (1998) showed that the tones were not only subjectively longer than the visual stimuli, but significantly less variable too. An explanation in terms of differential switch variability was proposed for this case and, although this is not the only possible explanation, the overall body of data reported by Wearden *et al.* (1998) tended to support it.

Another situation in which internal clock processes might account for differences in subjective time is where some manipulation is used which affects the subjective duration of the same stimulus. For example, Penton-Voak, Edwards, Percival, and Wearden (1996) used a technique introduced by Treisman, Faulkner, Naish, and Brogan (1990) to apparently change pacemaker speed in humans. Treisman *et al.* (1990) reported that trains of repetitive stimulation (clicks or flashes) produced, among other effects, an increase in 'arousal' which increased pacemaker speed. Penton-Voak *et al.* (1996) showed that brief trains of clicks (from 1 to 5 seconds long) changed the subjective duration of auditory and visual stimuli, as well as intervals produced by the subjects themselves, in a manner consistent with the idea that pacemaker speed had been increased by the clicks (see also Wearden *et al.*, 1998, and Wearden, Philpott, and Win, 1999, for replications of this effect). The difference in duration estimates occasioned by the click manipulation was a slope effect, consistent with an increase in pacemaker speed, as discussed above.

One cautionary note to be sounded here is that the issue of what effects changes in pacemaker speed will have on duration judgements can in some cases be more complicated than in the examples quoted above. This will be discussed in a later section.

Although a number of experimental results make sense when discussed just in terms of the operation of a pacemaker-accumulator clock itself, in fact all developed quantitative models of timing involve more than just the clock. This was true of the model devised by Treisman (1963), but can probably be best illustrated with reference to the current leading theory of animal timing, the scalar timing theory (or scalar expectancy theory: SET) of Gibbon, Church, and Meck (1984).

SCALAR TIMING THEORY

There is little doubt that SET is the most influential model of animal timing, and it has been recently applied with increasing frequency to data from humans (Allan, 1998; Wearden, 1991*a*, *b*; Wearden and McShane, 1988). An important feature of SET, and something that was true also of Treisman's earlier, and very similar, model is that the timing model contains much more than just an internal clock. Figure 1.1 provides a diagram of the SET system.

The first part is the pacemaker-accumulator internal clock itself, assumed to be a Poisson mechanism of the type described above. The second part comprises mechanisms for the storage of duration representations (for example, some mechanism for storing the number of ticks produced by an internal clock at time t). Such storage may be either short-term or long-term. A moment's thought suggests that storage mechanisms are essential for time judgements. For example, humans and animals can perform judgements where each trial presents them with two stimuli of possibly different durations, t_1 and t_2, and the task is to indicate something about the temporal relation of t_1 and t_2 (e.g. whether they were equal in length, whether the second was longer than the first). This task could not be performed if the duration of the first stimulus could not be stored until after the second one had been presented. In other studies, people and animals may be asked to compare a number of current stimulus durations with a 'standard' duration they learned minutes, hours, or days ago. Here, obviously, some long-term memory (sometimes called 'reference memory') is implicated.

The third and final part of the SET model is a comparison or decision process. Why is this needed? Consider again the problem posed in the task where people are given two successive stimuli and asked whether or not their duration was the same. How is the response generated on this task? One possibility is that the difference in duration between the two stimuli is calculated and if this is greater than zero the response is 'Different', but this simple model implies an infinite precision of both representation and discrimination. In practice, the representation of the duration even of some fixed time may vary slightly from one trial to another (e.g. because of slight differences in pacemaker speed between trials, or because of variance from other sources), so a zero difference between the subjective durations of events may never actually occur even though the events have the same real-time duration. A modification is to have some decision threshold, b, so that if the difference is less than b, the response 'Same' occurs (i.e. the two durations are 'close enough') but introducing this threshold clearly demonstrates the need for a decision process

In practice, on many timing tasks the three levels of the SET system (clock,

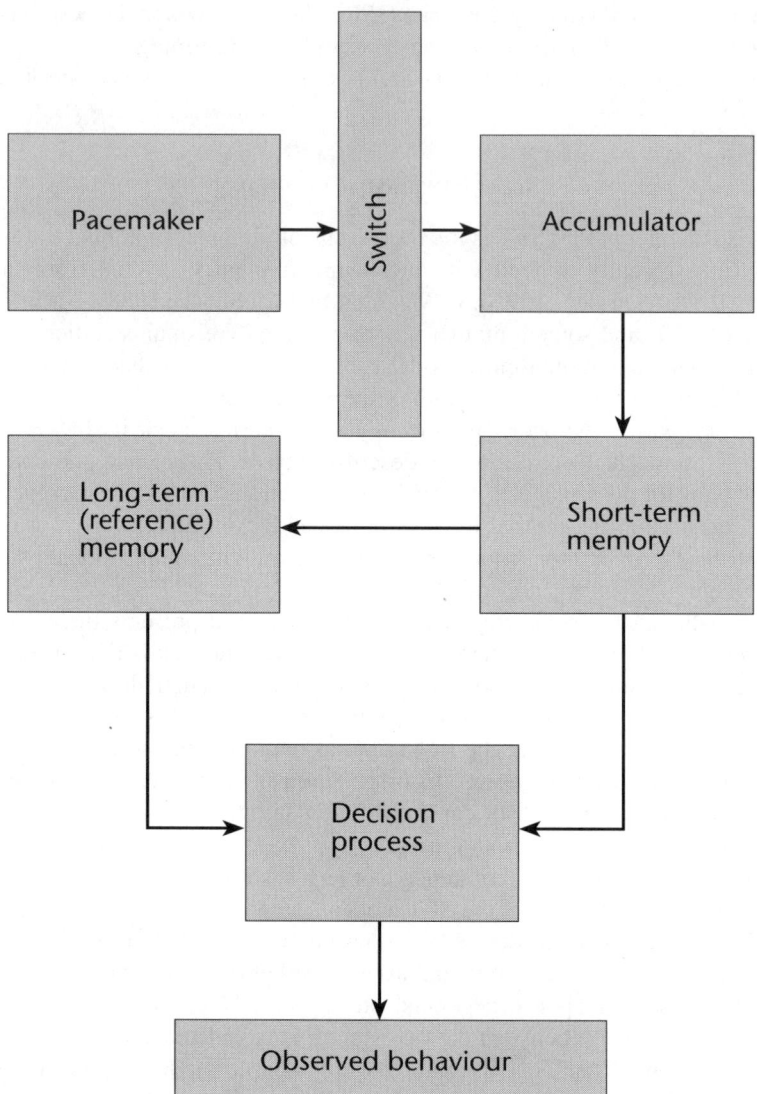

FIGURE 1.1. Outline of the temporal information processing system proposed by scalar timing theory. The upper part shows the pacemaker-switch-accumulator system. Accumulator contents are transferred to a short-term memory and some values in short-term memory (e.g. those associated with reinforcement in animal studies or identified as standards in studies with humans) can be transferred to a longer-term reference memory. Observed behaviour results from comparison of a current duration value with a sample or samples derived from reference memory.

memory, and decision) operate together to determine performance. A simple illustration of this is the task of *temporal generalization*. Both the initial version used with rats (Church and Gibbon, 1982) and the variant developed by Wearden (1992) for use with humans, involve comparisons between a just-presented duration, *t*, and a previously learned standard, *s*. For example, consider a task where a person receives a number of presentations of a 400 msec tone, identified as a 'standard' duration. Following this, tones of different durations (e.g. from 100 to 700 msec in 100-msec steps) are presented in random order, and the subject's task is to decide whether or not the just-presented tone is the standard. Feedback as to performance accuracy may (Wearden, 1992; Wearden, Wearden, and Rabbitt, 1997) or may not (Wearden, Pilkington, and Carter, 1999) be given.

The usual theoretical treatment of performance on this task assumes that behavioural responses (e.g. Yes [i.e. it's the standard] or No) are generated by a three-stage process. First, the pacemaker-accumulator internal clock times the presented stimulus, *t*, and the representation of *t* is stored in short-term memory. Next, the long-term, reference, memory which contains representations of the standard duration, *s*, is sampled and a sample value, s^*, is extracted. Finally, s^* and *t* are compared, and if they are 'close enough' according to some decision rule, the response *Yes* occurs, otherwise *No* occurs.

Note here that the behaviour observed reflects internal clock properties only indirectly; the response which occurs is a function of clock, memory, and decision processes, and may be influenced by changes in any of these three stages. For example, behaviour will vary with pacemaker speed or switch latency variance differing between conditions (and everything else equal), or by short- or long-term memory processes differing (and everything else being equal), or by the decision process being different (with clock and memory processes being the same). In fact, the difference in temporal generalization performance between rats and humans (discussed in Wearden, 1992) can be modelled by assuming that the decision processes used by the two species are different, while clock and memory processes are similar.

Time judgements are variable from one occasion to another. If a person verbally estimates the duration of some stimulus of real duration *t*, his or her estimates vary from one trial to the next; if on temporal generalization a just-presented duration *t* has to be compared with a standard *s*, the response is not always the same (except perhaps when *s* and *t* are very different); when two similar durations t_1 and t_2 are presented on the same trial and the judgements *Same* or *Different* are required, the response is not always the same, even when the two stimuli are. In other words, timing behaviour contains variance. Furthermore, a large number of studies agree about the properties of such variance. It is *scalar*, and it is this property which gives SET its name.

Scalar variance occurs when the standard deviation of judgements is a constant fraction of the mean, so that a coefficient of variation statistic (standard deviation/mean) is constant as the duration to be timed varies. This coefficient of variation is akin to a Weber fraction, so such scalar timing is consistent with

Weber's law, and implies a mechanism with constant sensitivity as the interval timed varies. Gibbon (1977) gives numerous examples of scalar timing from the earlier animal literature, and Wearden and McShane (1988) an example in data obtained from humans. In this latter study, humans produced intervals ranging from 0.5 to 1.3 sec, and were given feedback as to the accuracy of the time they had just produced. The relative frequency of the times produced, plotted against duration, showed near perfect scalar timing. The standard deviation was an almost exactly constant fraction of the mean, resulting in a nearly constant coefficient of variation.

The scalar property of timing can be tested by calculating the coefficient of variation of timed behaviours and observing that they remain constant, or by *superimposition* (called *superposition* in the American literature). Here measures of timed behaviour from different time intervals are plotted on the same relative scale. For example, the proportion of *Yes* responses (identifications of a stimulus duration as being the same as the standard) from temporal generalization with different standard values are plotted against duration, where the latter is expressed on a relative scale, for example as a proportion of the standard in force. If scalar timing holds, the different temporal generalization functions should superimpose perfectly, and this is exactly the result found in both animals (Church and Gibbon, 1982) and humans (Wearden, 1992; Wearden and Towse, 1994; Wearden *et al.*, 1997). Violations of scalar timing can occur in animals when exceptionally long intervals are timed (e.g. up to 15 minutes, see Lejeune and Wearden, 1991), but such deviations from scalar timing can be modelled by additional processes over and above timing itself (see Lejeune and Wearden, 1991: 98–104 for discussion), and some time judgements produced by humans, such as verbal estimates of duration (Wearden, 1999) can violate scalar timing on occasion, for reasons which are at present unclear. However, there is little doubt that the scalar property of variance holds across a wide range of timing tasks, durations timed, and species tested.

The problem of interest here is where the scalar property of variance comes from, a problem which some authors (e.g. Wearden, 1999) regard as being far from solved. One possibility is that the scalar property of variance comes from the pacemaker-accumulator clock itself; in other words, the scalar property is generated by the earliest stage of the timing system, and the representations which possess this variance property are passed through the memory and decision processes intact. However, the commonest proposal for the operation of the pacemaker is that it is a Poisson timer (as discussed earlier). Poisson pacemakers produce accumulator contents which grow linearly with real time, but another property is of interest here. With Poisson timing, it is the *variance* that grows in proportion to the mean rather than the *standard deviation*, so the coefficient of variation (sd/mean) will *decrease* as the interval timed lengthens. In other words, with Poisson timers, longer intervals have *relatively* less variability than shorter ones. This violates scalar timing which, as mentioned above, is nearly ubiquitous in data from timing experiments.

How can this problem be resolved? One possibility is to modify the property of the pacemaker so that it generates scalar, rather than Poisson, output (e.g. Gibbon, Church, and Meck, 1984), but another is to assume that the principal source of scalar variance is in the *reference memory* (see Wearden, 1999, for discussion). Models with scalar variance built into the reference memory of 'standard' durations (such as those associated with reinforcement on animal timing tasks, or identified by instructions as being in some way special in tasks with humans) fit data well. However, as Wearden (1992) showed, models with scalar variance elsewhere in the system (e.g. in the clock itself) fit equally well. The problem of where variance comes from in the scalar system can be potentially resolved, at least in large measure, by the use of tasks in which reference memory is excluded (Wearden, 1999). If such tasks still produce behaviour with scalar variance, reference memory cannot, obviously, be implicated. However, such tasks are extremely difficult to design for animals (who in most timing tasks have some standard duration associated with reinforcement), and difficult to arrange even for humans, but some suggestions are given in Wearden (1999), and work is under way to test these ideas.

SOME ALTERNATIVE CLOCK MODELS

Although SET is the dominant theory of animal timing, and the theory in which the old idea of the pacemaker-accumulator clock finds its fullest expression, some alternative approaches that use clock-like mechanisms do exist, and these will be briefly discussed here.

A popular alternative to pacemaker-accumulator internal clocks has been the measurement of elapsing time by some kind of oscillator-based system. The idea that oscillators might be used to represent psychological time is not new (e.g. Pöppel, 1972), but a persistent problem has been to go beyond the simple idea that oscillators might be used to represent time to develop an oscillator-based model that could actually model existing timing data. Church and Broadbent (1990; see also Wearden and Doherty, 1995, for discussion of their theory) is perhaps the best-developed oscillator-based model of timing in the current literature. Not only can the Church/Broadbent model address a range of timing data, but its unusual way of representing time would make it worthy of discussion even without the number of empirical successes it has enjoyed.

The Church/Broadbent model departs from conventional wisdom about how oscillators might represent elapsing time. The obvious idea is that if an oscillator cycles through its positive and negative phases every p seconds, then counting the number of times the phase change occurs in some time to be judged, t, will enable t to be measured. Essentially, some accumulation variable n represents the number of phase changes during t, so that $n = t/p$, with phase changes taking the place of clock ticks in pacemaker-accumulator clocks, and n representing accumulator contents. Such a formulation might well provide an oscillator-compatible model of a pacemaker-accumulator internal clock, but the Church/Broadbent model in fact represents time in a radically different way.

Instead of a single oscillator changing state every p seconds, the Church/Broadbent model measures time by using a *set* of oscillators. Their model incorporates eleven oscillators, but the oscillator set size, and oscillator values, are both arbitrary, although the actual oscillator values selected have some consequences for time representation (Wearden and Doherty, 1995), as discussed further below. In the original formulation of Church and Broadbent's model, the eleven oscillators chosen all had progressively doubling periods, beginning with 0.2 sec, and increasing progressively to 204.8 seconds. So, for example, the first oscillator in the set would cycle every 0.2 sec, the second every 0.4 sec, the third every 0.8 sec, and so on. Such a set enables the representation of durations over a more than 100-fold range of values with the same oscillator set, so is a highly economical form of representation.

Church and Broadbent departed from the obvious idea described above, that of counting the number of oscillations occurring during an elapsed time period, in favour of a representation in terms of a vector of oscillator *phases* at the critical time. That is, the model merely notes the *phase* of the eleven oscillators at time t, with a value of +1 representing the positive phase and −1 the negative one. A particular time value, t, is thus represented as a vector of +1 and −1 values, and the number of times that any particular oscillator has changed state in t is ignored.

For example, using the oscillator set starting at 0.2 sec and progressively doubling, the vectors at 15 and 40 seconds will be:

15 seconds: +1 +1 −1 +1 −1 −1 +1 −1 −1 −1 −1
40 seconds: −1 −1 −1 +1 −1 −1 +1 +1 −1 −1 −1

Note here that the two different time values differ in only three of the eleven vector elements, so can be considered 'similar', a point discussed later.

The vector form of representation is an example of what Wearden (1994) called *qualitative* encoding of time; that is, different times are represented by *different* states of the same number of elements, in contrast to the *quantitative* encoding of time resulting from internal clock models where longer times are represented by *more* of something (clock ticks, for example).

Variability was introduced into the Church/Broadbent model by making the oscillator periods variable from one trial to another. The method used was to multiply each period, p, by a random value taken from a Gaussian distribution with mean 1.0 and coefficient of variation, c. This produced oscillator periods where the standard deviation of the period was a constant fraction, c, of the mean, effectively introducing scalar variance into the oscillator periods themselves. That is, the scalar property of variance so characteristic of data from experiments on timing in humans and animals was built into the model from the outset, so it is perhaps no surprise that the model simulated data with scalar properties well. There is, however, a more subtle consequence of introducing variance into oscillator periods, as pointed out by Wearden and Doherty (1995). Consider some time value, t, which is to be represented by the model. If t is considerably longer than the period of some particular oscillator (e.g. $t = 20$ sec, and $p = 0.2$ sec), then the introduction of variance into the oscillator period means that the state of this particular oscillator (i.e. $+1$ or -1) at t will be, from trial to trial, effectively random. In other words, little of the burden of representing t will be borne by oscillators which are effectively random in phase from trial to trial at t. Oscillator periods which are much longer than t (e.g. $p = 256$ sec at $t = 20$ sec) will likewise play little role in representing t, as these oscillators will be in their initial state (arbitrarily chosen to be -1, that is, negative) at t on all trials; that is, they will hardly ever have changed state at the time t. Wearden and Doherty (1995) showed that oscillators which were 'remote' from t (having periods much shorter or longer than t) actually made no contribution to the representation of t within the Church/Broadbent model.

In the Church/Broadbent model, long-term storage of time intervals ('reference memory') is accomplished in terms of a matrix of correlations representing the degree of similarity of phase of any pair of oscillators at the time reinforcement was delivered. So, for example, if oscillators a and b were always in the same phase (either positive or negative) at the time of reinforcement, their correlation would be 1.0; if they were always in different phases, their correlations would be -1.0; if they were in random phases relative to one another, the correlation would be 0. To generate behaviour, the Church/Broadbent model compares the oscillator representation of elapsing time continuously with a value retrieved from the matrix contents, and when the two values are 'close enough' (i.e. the current time is sufficiently close to the time of reinforcement) the model responds. The details of operation of this model are discussed fully in Wearden and Doherty (1995).

A peculiarity of the oscillator-based representation of duration employed by Church and Broadbent (1990) is that it is fundamentally non-linear. Recall that the hypothesized Poisson clock of SET generates fundamentally linear representations of duration by accumulating ticks from the pacemaker. In the Church/Broadbent model, however, how 'similar' two durations are depends on how similar their oscillator-based representations are, and this depends on both the actual time values and the oscillators used to represent them. As shown above, using the oscillators from the original Church/Broadbent model (with periods of 0.2, 0.4, 0.8 ... 204.8 seconds), an elapsed time of 15 seconds is 'similar' to 40 seconds, in fact more similar than 30 seconds is, and with appropriate response-generating rules these 'similarity coincidences' can cause the model to respond at 'inappropriate' times.

Whatever oscillator set is chosen to represent duration, similarity coincidences will occur somewhere, so the oscillator-based model has to be finely tuned in order to simulate observed behaviour. Nevertheless, it can be so tuned, and when this is done it will produce output bearing a striking resemblance to data obtained in a range of circumstances (e.g. Wearden and Doherty, 1995, figures 10 and 11). The Church/Broadbent oscillator-based model is sometimes referred to as a connectionist version of SET, with the oscillator vector taking the place of the clock and short-term memory, and the matrix of phase intercorrelations representing long-term storage of time. An oscillator-based model might also have advantages over the pacemaker-accumulator version of SET in terms of potential physiological probability, although, as discussed later, we are at present very far from physiologically plausible models of how timing is performed in the brain.

An unusual variant of internal clock theories is the *Behavioral Theory of Timing* (BeT) of Killeen and Fetterman (1988). I classify this approach, perhaps rather controversially, as an internal clock theory, since the basis of timed behaviour is a pacemaker, somewhat like that proposed by SET. In other respects, however, the theory departs radically from the framework of a conventional clock-based model like SET, or at least it seems to. BeT, as its name suggests, is a *behavioural* theory, with two core ideas. The first is that measured timed behaviour (e.g. lever-presses or key-pecks) is mediated by a sequence of *adjunctive* behaviours. These are a sequence of actions, sometimes highly stereotyped, which occur between measured behaviours, and themselves are usually unmeasured. It has been known since Skinner (1948) that presenting food periodically to animals will induce stereotyped sequences of actions, that is, the animal emits some behaviour sequence B_1, B_2, ... B_N, in the time between reinforcer deliveries. BeT assumes that these adjunctive behaviours act as cues for the emission of measured activities, so, for example, an animal may start lever pressing just after it has completed activity B_X. According to BeT lever-pressing is just another part of the sequence, distinguished from other behaviours merely by its special significance to the experimenter and the fact that it usually precedes reinforcement.

The transition from one adjunctive behaviour, B_N, to the next, B_{N+1} is governed by pulses from an internal pacemaker. This pacemaker is of the Poisson type but, as noted above, by itself the Poisson pacemaker will produce behaviours which are incompatible with the scalar property usually found. To 'correct' the Poisson pacemaker so that the scalar property can be derived, BeT assumes that the rate of the pacemaker is a linear function of the rate of reinforcement in the experimental situation, which usually itself varies according to the interval timed. So, for example, when animals were subjected to an inter-reinforcement time of 20 seconds, the pacemaker would run about twice as fast as when the inter-reinforcement time was 40 seconds, thus the adjunctive behaviours serving as cues for measured behaviours like lever-pressing also vary in their rate of emission with pacemaker rate and hence with rate of reinforcement. This variation of pacemaker rate with reinforcement rate is the second core idea of BeT.

Although it is a pacemaker-based theory, BeT seems to dispense with most of the apparatus needed by other internal clock models, particularly SET. At first sight there are no memory or decision processes, but a deeper consideration suggests that the theories may not be as different as supposed at first. Although BeT has no memories for duration, long-term representation of duration is embodied in a particular adjunctive sequence, and the rate of transition from one behaviour to another. Thus the adjunctive sequences proposed by BeT form a kind of 'behavioural' long-term memory representation of critical durations.

In spite of its apparent simplicity, BeT is a subtle theory, whose exact predictions are at times somewhat surprising, and which is much more difficult to confirm or falsify by observation than might be thought at first. For example, the question of whether the proposed adjunctive sequences are actually observed might seem fundamental, and indeed it is, but in practice it can be hard to judge whether any particular observation of adjunctive behaviour is or is not compatible with BeT. Lejeune, Cornet, Ferreira, and Wearden (1998) conducted what is probably the most extensive study of relations between measured timed behaviours and adjunctive sequences. In their work, gerbils were reinforced for staying on a small platform for more than t sec, where t was varied across conditions. The activities emitted by the animal during this automatically measured response were observed directly, a remarkably time-consuming process which by itself accounts for the paucity of studies of this type.

One of the results of Lejeune and colleagues strikingly supported BeT's predictions: the observed rate of adjunctive behaviour did vary linearly with reinforcement rate, thus allowing the Poisson mechanism supposedly underlying the adjunctive transitions to generate the scalar properties noted in measured behaviours. However, more problematically for BeT, Lejeune and colleagues found that the behaviour sequences emitted were more variable than some expositions of the theory suggest they would be, although nothing in BeT *logically* requires the adjunctive sequence to be exactly stereotyped from one trial to the next. In fact, a number of different adjunctive sequences could all act to mediate measured operant behaviour.

Lejeune *et al.* (1998) also found many instances of what appeared to be repeats of the same behaviour in different parts of single adjunctive sequences. This is potentially damaging to BeT, as the distinct adjunctive behaviours are supposed to act as cues for measured operants, so repeating actions causes problems of discrimination. Of course, as Lejeune and colleagues point out, behaviours which seem sufficiently similar to the experimenter to be classified as the same may from the animal's point of view have distinguishing features.

BeT is of particular interest here in that it offers a unique type of 'representation' of durations and, in spite of the fact that BeT dispenses with much of the apparatus of SET and its connectionist variant, it provides an excellent account of animal performance on a range of timing tasks. The limited space available cannot, however, do justice to this interesting approach to timed behaviour, and the reader is referred to Lejeune *et al.* (1998) for discussion and for a list of relevant references. BeT's most serious drawback is probably the fact that it cannot easily be applied to timing in humans, except perhaps by regarding the 'adjunctive' behaviours as internal—for example, silent counts or microscopic movements which are not usually observable. Whether a development along these lines can be provided without robbing the theory of its behavioural character and turning it effectively into a version of SET (with 'clock ticks' as the internal behaviours) remains to be seen.

CLOCK SPEED REVISITED

A previous section discussed the use of a pacemaker-accumulator clock model to deal with situations where either it was believed a priori that the speed of the pacemaker of the clock (which from now on I just call 'clock speed') varied between conditions or, conversely, behavioural differences between conditions were explained with reference to different clock speeds. Although the treatment given in the section above was not incorrect, it was incomplete, and glossed over some logical and methodological problems in using clock speed as an explanation of behavioural differences. To be strictly accurate, clock speed differences can account for behavioural effects most easily (or perhaps even only) in conditions involving *state change without recalibration.* State change here means that the *same* subjects are tested under conditions where clock speed is manipulated (i.e. the clock speed varies between two states), and their behaviour in the two different conditions is directly compared.

The classic studies of the psychopharmacology of animal timing published in the early 1980s (Maricq, Roberts, and Church, 1981; Meck, 1983; see Meck, 1996, for a review) exemplify the state change idea most clearly. Consider the work of Maricq, Roberts, and Church (1981) examining the effect of amphetamine, a drug proposed to increase clock speed, on animal timing. The techniques they used were considerably more complicated than my exposition will be, but essentially the logic was as follows. Suppose that a rat is trained, after saline injections (a control condition, where the clock speed is putatively 'normal': state 1), to respond for reinforcement at time *t*. The animal will learn to associate the *n* ticks of the internal clock which accumulate in *t* with reinforcement. Next, the animal is injected with amphetamine (state 2), and its behaviour tested *without responding being reinforced*. If amphetamine speeds up the clock, the *n* ticks will accumulate in some time less than *t*, so the animal will respond *early*. Consider next the converse case. The animal is trained under amphetamine with a putatively 'fast' clock, and associates *m* ticks with *t* (where *m* > *n*). Subsequent to this training, the animal is tested, without reinforcement, after a saline injection. Now, the clock runs more slowly than during training, so a time period longer than *t* is needed to accumulate the *m* ticks, and the animal responds *late*.

The two control conditions (saline/saline and amphetamine/amphetamine) do not involve any state change, and the behaviour should be the same during the test as during original training. Furthermore, consider a rat shifted from saline to amphetamine, who continues, under amphetamine, to be reinforced at time *t*. Initially, the rat will respond before *t,* but over a number of sessions the rat will learn that in fact *m* ticks should now be associated with reinforcement rather than the *n* used before, so its behaviour will adjust appropriately, with responding shifting towards *t*. The same is true for rats receiving the other transition (amphetamine/saline) with continued training under saline. The conditions where the state is changed but reinforcement continues allow the animal to 'recalibrate', that is, compensate for the change in the number of ticks associated some reinforced time *t*, by responding after the 'new' number of ticks rather than the 'old' one. Even when responding in the new state is reinforced, adjustment in animals may take a number of sessions; in humans, however, recalibration may be very rapid, and at a limit may occur after a single trial in the new state.

Maricq, Roberts, and Church (1981) obtained all the different elements of the pattern of results discussed above, when all four combinations of saline and amphetamine were used. Animals responded early when trained under saline and tested under amphetamine, late when the training and testing states were reversed, and showed no change when trained and tested in the same state, whatever it was.

Wearden, Philpott, and Win (1999) performed an experiment with humans similar in principle to that of Maricq, Roberts, and Church. People learned standard durations, which were either timed normally, or with a 'speeded-up' clock, the latter effect achieved by preceding the standards with click-trains then comparison durations were presented, again sometimes preceded by clicks. People responded 'early' if the standards had been timed by a 'normal' clock and the comparisons were 'speeded up', and 'late' if the conditions were reversed.

The assertion that state-change without recalibration is the best situation for demonstrating changes in 'clock speed' probably commands wide assent, and all the best examples from animal and human subjects use this method. What is more controversial is whether clock-speed effects can be detected in other conditions, for example, those in which state-change is impossible.

Situations of the latter sort are extremely common, and involve some questions that it would be important to be able to answer. For example, do different animal species have internal clocks which run at different speeds? As people get older, does their internal clock slow down or speed up? Do various sorts of brain damage or cerebral degeneration affect internal clock speed?

All these questions obviously involve situations where state-change is impossible. We cannot train an organism as a pigeon and test it as a rat, train persons as old and test them as young, train brain-damaged persons then test them intact. Having acknowledged these problems, however, the questions raised in these sorts of comparison seem among the most interesting that timing research could address and, furthermore, some of them have given rise to plausible speculation. For example, as Wearden, Wearden, and Rabbitt (1997) note, 'clock-speed' differences between old and young people have long been conjectured, with the general, but not unanimous, consensus being that the internal clock slows down with age. Similarly, given the physiological and behavioural differences between animal species, it would be hard to imagine that clock-speed differences did not exist between at least some of them, for example, between a sloth and a humming-bird, to give one experimentally somewhat impractical, but convincing, example.

Can anything be done in these situations? One thing that obviously can be done is some kind of empirical comparison of timing behaviour. Lejeune and Wearden (1991), for example, examined the behaviour of a range of animal species (cats, rats, mice, pigeons, doves, fish, and turtles) on a standard experimental procedure, a fixed-interval (FI) schedule of reinforcement. In this procedure, the first response that occurs t seconds after the previous reinforcement is itself reinforced, and resets the interval, thus separating the opportunity to obtain reinforcement by a minimum of t sec. In practice, reinforcers are delivered with a periodicity very close to t. The pattern of behaviour averaged from a number of sessions of FI, after animals have been well trained, is as follows. The reinforcer delivery is followed by a period of little or no responding, then response rates accelerate throughout the interval, peaking at t. The rapidity of the acceleration within the interval can be taken as a measure of the precision of temporal control: if animals time very precisely, their responses will tend to be concentrated in the latter parts of the interval; if their timing is poorer, responses will be more uniformly distributed between reinforcer deliveries. All the species tested (with the exception of turtles who exhibited a minor deviation) showed the averagely accelerating response pattern, peaking at t.

Lejeune and Wearden (1991) derived a coefficient of variation statistic from quantitative analyses of performance of the different species on FI, and found that temporal control varied systematically across species. Cats were best, followed by rats and mice, then pigeons, then fish, then finally turtles. Does this mean that the different species differed in clock speed?

Unfortunately, this conclusion cannot be unequivocally supported. Suppose that we return to the Poisson properties usually ascribed to the pacemaker of the internal clock. The mathematics of Poisson pacemakers (Gibbon, 1977) shows that *slower* pacemakers generate *more variable* time representations, so perhaps variability (rather than responding shifts as in the state-change studies) can be taken as an index of clock speed. This idea would suggest, of course, that animals showing greater temporal precision had faster internal clocks. However, as mentioned above, most instantiations of SET assume that the main source of variability in responding is reference memory, not the internal clock itself, so Lejeune and Wearden's results might be interpreted in these terms. Fish, for example, might encode the time of reinforcement less precisely than cats (although both are on average accurate), but this is usually taken as a memory, rather than clock-speed, effect. The fact that the FI performance of the different species showed scalar properties, at least over a wide part of its range, also implicates some source of variance other than that of the internal clock itself (Gibbon, 1992) which by using its hypothesized Poisson pacemaker would generate Poisson variance in the data, contrary to what was found. Thus, unfortunately, even finding systematic timing differences between species does not permit us to draw conclusions about relative clock speed, however intuitively plausible these conclusions might be.

A recent comparison of old and younger humans (e.g. Wearden, Wearden, and Rabbitt, 1997) produced much less dramatic results than Lejeune and Wearden's cross-species comparisons, with timing behaviour of elderly people usually showing no overall age effect within the elderly group, and often being strikingly similar to that of students more than fifty years younger. However, what differences were found tended to suggest that timing variability increased with age, a result consistent with the slowing down of a Poisson pacemaker, but also, of course, consistent with increased variability of temporal memory.

Overall, therefore, although the idea of a pacemaker-accumulator internal clock can deal convincingly with some instances of behavioural differences by appealing to clock-speed differences, many comparisons that we might like to be able to make seem logically inaccessible, even when marked behavioural differences between groups or species compared do exist.

TIME AND THE BRAIN: FROM METAPHOR TO MECHANISM

The idea of an internal clock has progressed from just a verbally expressed idea, a kind of metaphor for how internal timing processes might work, to the development of quantitative models like SET, which are among the most precisely specified and successful theoretical models in any area of psychology. But is the internal clock more than a metaphor? Is there some mechanism in the brain which corresponds, more or less exactly, to the different parts of a model like SET?

For the last twenty or so years, there have been extensive efforts to uncover the brain processes underlying timing, largely by proponents of SET such as Gibbon, Church, and Meck, who began in the early 1980s with a number of studies on the pharmacology and physiology of timing in rats. For example, the study of Maricq, Roberts, and Church (1981), discussed above, showed that amphetamine apparently increased clock speed, thus suggesting a dopaminergic basis for the internal clock. This idea was supported by the general finding that drugs which stimulate dopaminergic neurons (such as amphetamine) make animals behave as if the clock runs faster, whereas drugs inhibiting dopamine (such as haloperiodol) appeared to decrease clock speed (see Meck, 1996, for a review and a discussion of the general logic of these experiments, particularly his pages 235–9). Other drugs, rather than changing clock speed, made animals behave as if the time associated with reinforcement was being systematically misremembered, so no amount of reinforced training under the drug produced a 'recalibration' towards accurate responding. These drugs generally affected acetylcholine-based neurons, rather than dopamine systems. It appeared, therefore, as if the distinction made by models like SET between the internal clock itself and mechanism for short- and longer-term storage of temporal representations had some basis in pharmacological reality, in the sense that clock and memory systems appeared to depend on different neurotransmitters.

Timing is not, however, radically affected by all pharmacological manipulations which have psychoactive effects. Bradshaw, Szabadi, and colleagues have worked extensively on manipulations of the 5-HT system, generally finding that very marked changes in 5-HT levels in rats had no effect on timing behaviour, or at best minimal effects (see Al-Ruwaitea *et al.*, 1997, for a review).

Attempts to uncover the underlying physiology of timing in humans have tended to rely on neuropsychological investigations of patients with brain damage rather than pharmacological studies, although these do exist (e.g. Rammsayer, 1997). Interest has focused on effects on human timing of damage to two brain areas, the cerebellum and the basal ganglia.

It has long been known that damage to the cerebellum will perturb timing of motor activities, particularly movements involving fine motor control (Ivry and Keele, 1989), but Nichelli, Alway, and Grafman (1996) showed that timing of short durations (< 1 sec) was impaired by cerebellar damage even when the task involved stimulus, rather than motor, timing. Furthermore, Malapani, Dubois, Rancurel, and Gibbon (1998) have recently shown that timing of longer intervals (up to 21 seconds) was affected by cerebellar damage, although the task used involved the motor reproduction of durations.

Patients with disturbances of basal ganglia functions (mainly those with Parkinson's disease and related disorders) have also been found to have timing deficits on motor tasks such as repetitive tapping (O'Boyle, Freeman, and Cody, 1996), and also on tasks where previously presented intervals were reproduced (Malapani, Rakitin, Meck, Deweer, Dubois, and Gibbon, 1998). Deficits may also occur on timing tasks without a large motor component, as in Harrington, Haaland, and Hermanowicz's (1998) finding that Parkinson's patients had higher thresholds for duration discrimination than controls.

Although interest has mainly focused on the cerebellum and basal ganglia, some other areas of the brain, such as the suprachiasmatic nucleus of the hypothalamus (Cohen, Barnes, Jenkins, and Albers, 1997) and parts of the cortex (Rao *et al.*, 1997), have also been implicated in the control of various forms of timing.

Overall, therefore, it appears that many brain regions may be involved in timing in both animals and humans, and that uncovering simple circuits subserving timed behaviour may be very difficult. Gibbon, Malapani, Dale, and Gallistel (1997) review the complex and confusing literature and point to important roles for the basal ganglia, cerebellum, and thalamic and cortical areas.

It should be noted that none of the neuropsychological studies with humans have used methods which permit behavioural differences to be unequivocally attributed to differences in internal clock processes alone. None so far have used the idea of state-change without calibration method, even when this might be possible. For example, Parkinson's disease patients can be tested after their usually dopamine-stimulating medication and without it, so opening up the possibility of a state-change study, similar to that of Maricq, Roberts, and Church (1981) or Meck (1983). However, even when Parkinson's patients have been tested both on and off their medication (as in O'Boyle, Freeman, and Cody 1996, and Malapani *et al.*, 1998) patients received both training and testing in both conditions, so 'recalibration' of the timing system was possible.

Another general problem is that although the neuropsychological studies have identified some brain regions as being important for timing, they do little to suggest a mechanism for processes like the internal clock. For example, finding out that the pacemaker of the internal clock is affected by dopaminergic manipulations tells us little about how the units of which the brain is composed might actually subserve timing. Although neurons with oscillatory or repetitive activity might be able to produce the 'ticks' of the hypothesized pacemaker, how can these ticks be accumulated neurally? Even if some mechanism for very temporary storage of time representations can be devised, problems remain when attempting to model longer-term memory for duration, the 'reference memory' of SET. Such a reference memory may persist for long periods, so appears highly stable, yet, paradoxically, reinforcement experiences with 'new' reinforcement times can shift behaviour very rapidly (Lejeune *et al.*, 1997), suggesting that the reference memory can be highly flexible. Even simulating the scalar property of time representations with a neurally plausible model remains an unmet challenge.

At present, we have few computational models of how any part of the brain might perform tasks explainable by internal-clock models, and this lack renders neuropsychological studies somewhat incomplete so far as finding the mechanism of internal clocks is concerned.

Even though we may be far from understanding how even simple timing tasks are performed by the brain, so the notion of an internal clock remains for the moment a hypothesis, the material presented in this chapter testifies, I hope, to the vitality of the idea and its usefulness in both integrating a range of data and stimulating new research. It may be that in years to come the clock metaphor is replaced by something else: oscillators, neural nets, shifting potentials, or physiological processes of some type yet unimagined. Even if this is true, the idea of the internal clock will have played a central role in our attempts to understand how organisms can be sensitive to the passage of time, and how they adjust their behaviour to mesh with the temporal imperatives of the environment that surrounds them.

REFERENCES

AL-RUWAITEA, A. S. A., AL-ZAHRANI, S. S. A., HO, M.-Y., BRADSHAW, C. M., and SZABADI, E. (1997), '5-Hydroxytryptamine and interval timing', in C. M. Bradshaw and E. Szabadi (eds.), *Time and Behaviour: Psychological and Neurobehavioural Analyses*. Amsterdam: Elsevier.

ALLAN, L. G. (1998), 'The influence of the scalar timing model on human timing research', *Behavioural Processes*, 44: 101–17.

BELL, C. R. (1975), 'Effects of lowered temperature on time estimation', *Quarterly Journal of Experimental Psychology*, 27: 531–8.

BRÉE, D. S. (1992), 'Words for time', in F. Macar, V. Pouthas, and W. J. Friedman (eds.), *Time, Action, and Cognition*. Dordrecht: Kluwer.

CHURCH, R. M., and BROADBENT, H. (1990), 'Alternative representations of time, number, and rate', *Cognition*, 37: 55–81.

—— and GIBBON, J. (1982), 'Temporal generalization', *Journal of Experimental Psychology: Animal Behavior Processes*, 8: 165–86.

COHEN, R. A., BARNES, H. J., JENKINS, M., and ALBERS, H. E. (1997), 'Disruption of short-duration timing associated with damage to the suprachiasmatic region of the hypothalamus', *Neurology*, 48: 1533–9.

CREELMAN, C. D. (1962), 'Human discrimination of auditory duration', *Journal of the Acoustical Society of America*, 34: 582–93.

DAVIES, P. (1995), *About Time*. Harmondsworth: Penguin.

DEWIED, M., TAN, E. S. H., and FRIJDA, N. H. (1992), 'Duration experience under conditions of suspense in films', in F. Macar, V. Pouthas, and W. J. Friedman (eds.), *Time, Action, and Cognition*. Dordrecht: Kluwer.

FRAISSE, P. (1964), *The Psychology of Time*. London: Eyre and Spottiswode.

—— (1992) 'From time lost to time regained', in F. Macar, V. Pouthas, and W. J. Friedman (eds.), *Time, Action, and Cognition*. Dordrecht: Kluwer.

FRANÇOIS, M. (1927), 'Contributions à l'étude du sens du temps: La température interne comme facteur de variation de l'appréciation subjective des durées', *L'Année Psychologique*, 27: 186–204.

GIBBON, J. (1977), 'Scalar expectancy theory and Weber's law in animal timing', *Psychological Review*, 84: 279–325.

—— (1992) 'Ubiquity of scalar timing with a Poisson clock', *Journal of Mathematical Psychology*, 36: 283–93.

—— CHURCH, R. M., and MECK, W. (1984), 'Scalar timing in memory', in J. Gibbon and L. Allan (eds.), *Annals of the New York Academy of Sciences*, 423: *Timing and Time Perception*. New York: New York Academy of Sciences.

—— MALAPANI, C., DALE, C. L., and GALLISTEL, C. R. (1997), 'Toward a neurobiology of temporal cognition: advances and challenges', *Current Opinion in Neurobiology*, 7: 170–84.

GOLDSTONE, S., and LHAMON, W. T. (1974), 'Studies of auditory-visual differences in human time judgment, 1: Sounds are judged longer than lights', *Perceptual and Motor Skills*, 39: 63–82.

HARRINGTON, D. L., HAALAND, K. Y., and HERMANOWICZ, N. (1998), 'Temporal processing in the basal ganglia', *Neuropsychology*, 12: 3–12.

HOAGLAND, H. (1933), 'The physiological control of judgments of duration: evidence for a chemical clock', *Journal of General Psychology*, 9: 267–87.

IVRY, R. L., and KEELE, S. W. (1989), 'Timing functions of the cerebellum', *Journal of Cognitive Neuroscience*, 1: 136–52.

JACKSON, J. L., and MICHON, J. A. (1992), 'Verisimilar and metaphorical representations of time', in F. Macar, V. Pouthas, and W. J. Friedman (eds.), *Time, Action, and Cognition*. Dordrecht: Kluwer.

KILLEEN, P. R., and FETTERMAN, J. G. (1988), 'A behavioral theory of timing', *Psychological Review*, 95: 274–95

LEJEUNE, H., and WEARDEN, J. H. (1991), 'The comparative psychology of fixed-interval responding: some quantitative analyses', *Learning and Motivation*, 22: 84–111.

—— CORNET, S., FERREIRA, J., and WEARDEN, J. H. (1998), 'How do Mongolian gerbils (*Meriones unguiculatus*) pass the time? Adjunctive behavior during temporal differentiation in gerbils', *Journal of Experimental Psychology: Animal Behavior Processes*, 24: 325–34.

—— FERRARA, A., SIMONS, F., and WEARDEN, J. H. (1997), 'Adjusting to changes in the time of reinforcement: peak interval transitions in rats', *Journal of Experimental Psychology: Animal Behavior Processes*, 23: 311–31.

MALAPANI, C., DUBOIS, B., RANCUREL, G., and GIBBON, J. (1998), 'Cerebellar dysfunctions of temporal processing in the seconds range in humans', *Neuroreport*, 9: 3907–12.

—— RAKITIN, B., MECK, W. H., DEWEER, B., DUBOIS, B., and GIBBON, J. (1998), 'Coupled temporal memories in Parkinson's disease: a dopamine-related dysfunction', *Journal of Cognitive Neuroscience,* 10: 316–33.

MARICQ, A. V., ROBERTS, S., and CHURCH, R. M. (1981), 'Metamphetamine and time estimation', *Journal of Experimental Psychology: Animal Behavior Processes,* 7: 18–30.

MECK, W. H. (1983), 'Selective adjustment of the speed of internal clock and memory processes', *Journal of Experimental Psychology: Animal Behavior Processes,* 9: 171–201.

——— (1996) 'Neuropharmacology of timing and time perception', *Cognitive Brain Research,* 3: 227–42.

NICHELLI, P., ALWAY, D., and GRAFMAN, J. (1996), 'Perceptual timing in cerebellar degeneration', *Neuropsychologia,* 34: 863–71.

O'BOYLE, D. J., FREEMAN, J. S., and CODY, F. W. J. (1996), 'The accuracy and precision of timing of self-paced repetitive movements in subjects with Parkinson's disease', *Brain,* 119: 51–70.

PENTON-VOAK, I. S., EDWARDS, H., PERCIVAL, A., and WEARDEN, J. H. (1996), 'Speeding up an internal clock in humans? Effects of click trains on subjective duration', *Journal of Experimental Psychology: Animal Behavior Processes,* 22: 307–20.

PÖPPEL, E. (1972), 'Oscillations as the possible basis for time perception', in J. T. Fraser, F. C. Haber, and G. H. Muller (eds.), *The Study of Time.* New York: Springer-Verlag.

RAMMSAYER, T. H. (1997), 'Are there dissociable roles of the meostriatal and mesolimbocortical dopamine systems on temporal information processing in humans?', *Neuropsychobiology,* 35: 36–45.

RAO, S. M., HARRINGTON, D. L., HAALAND, K. Y., BOBHOLZ, J. A., COX, R. W., and BINDER, J. R. (1997), 'Distributed neural systems underlying the timing of movements', *Journal of Neuroscience,* 17: 5528–35.

SKINNER, B. F. (1948), 'Superstition in the pigeon', *Journal of Experimental Psychology,* 38: 168–72.

TREISMAN, M. (1963), 'Temporal discrimination and the indifference interval: implications for a model of the "internal clock" ', *Psychological Monographs,* 77: whole number 576.

——— FAULKNER, A., NAISH, P. L. N., and BROGAN, D. (1990), 'The internal clock: evidence for a temporal oscillator underlying time perception with some estimates of its characteristic frequency', *Perception,* 19: 705–48.

WEARDEN, J. H. (1991*a*), 'Do humans possess an internal clock with scalar timing properties?', *Learning and Motivation,* 22: 59–83.

——— (1991*b*), 'Human performance on an analogue of an interval bisection task', *Quarterly Journal of Experimental Psychology,* 43B: 59–81.

——— (1992), 'Temporal generalization in humans', *Journal of Experimental Psychology: Animal Behavior Processes,* 18: 134–44.

——— (1994), 'Prescriptions for models of biopsychological time', in M. Oaksford and G. Brown (eds.), *Neurodynamics and Psychology.* London: Academic Press.

——— (1999), ' "Beyond the fields we know . . .": exploring and developing scalar timing theory', *Behavioural Processes,* 45: 3–21.

——— and DOHERTY, M. F. (1995), 'Exploring and developing a connectionist model of animal timing: peak procedure and fixed-interval simulations', *Journal of Experimental Psychology: Animal Behavior Processes,* 21: 99–115.

——— and McSHANE, B. (1988), 'Interval production as an analogue of the peak procedure: evidence for similarity of human and animal timing processes', *Quarterly Journal of Experimental Psychology,* 40B: 363–75.

WEARDEN, J. H., and PENTON-VOAK, I. S. (1995), 'Feeling the heat: body temperature and the rate of subjective time, revisited', *Quarterly Journal of Experimental Psychology*, 48B: 129–41.

—— and TOWSE, J. (1994), 'Temporal generalization in humans: three further studies', *Behavioural Processes*, 32: 247–64.

—— PHILPOTT, K., and WIN, T. (1999), 'Speeding up and (. . . relatively . . .) slowing down an internal clock in humans', *Behavioural Processes*, 46: 63–73.

—— PILKINGTON, R., and CARTER, E. (1999), ' "Subjective lengthening" during repeated testing of a simple temporal discrimination', *Behavioural Processes*, 46: 25–38.

—— WEARDEN, A. J., and RABBITT, P. (1997), 'Age and IQ effects on stimulus and response timing', *Journal of Experimental Psychology: Human Perception and Performance,* 23: 962–79.

—— DENOVAN. L., FAKHRI, M., and HAWORTH, R. (1997), 'Scalar timing in temporal generalization in humans with longer stimulus durations', *Journal of Experimental Psychology: Animal Behavior Processes*, 23: 502–11.

—— EDWARDS, H., FAKHRI, M., and PERCIVAL, A. (1998), 'Why "sounds are judged longer than lights": application of a model of the internal clock in humans', *Quarterly Journal of Experimental Psychology*, 51B: 97–120.

2

Retrospective and Prospective Timing: Memory, Attention, and Consciousness

Richard A. Block and *Dan Zakay*

For millions of years, organisms have been products of evolution, gradually becoming increasingly adapted to their changing environments. Plants regulate their metabolism according to seasons, daily rhythms, and weather. Animals regulate their behaviour according to temporal constraints as well. Their nervous systems, down to at least planarians if not more simple organisms, have evolved to time events. However, only in the last several hundred years have humans consciously developed various external timing mechanisms, including four different kinds of chronometers (Roberts, 1998). This reflects the needs of humans for accurate timing that is not provided by natural mechanisms.

Relatively accurate timing of events and durations is essential to ensure the optimal functioning of organisms, who must have some way to remember the timing of past events and to anticipate the timing of future events. Organisms must encode temporal properties of important events, store representations of those properties, and use those representations for actions. For example, people must learn the temporal order of components of actions, such as getting dressed, making coffee, and driving a car. Such actions require that a person time durations to perform appropriate actions in the correct order and with the correct durations of components.

There are several qualitatively different kinds of temporal experiences: simultaneity, successiveness, temporal order, duration, and temporal perspective (Block, 1979, 1990). We mainly focus here on temporal order and duration judgements, especially in the range of seconds and minutes. Timing in this range is essential for representing present and past episodes. Duration timing is the most researched aspect of psychological time, probably because it is a complex and important aspect in terms of environmental adaptation. No single sensory organ or perceptual system subserves psychological time. Consequently, most theorists explain duration timing in terms of cognitive processes or interactions between cognitive and biological processes (such as involving biological clocks). Duration timing requires attention and memory, and the study of duration judgements reveals and clarifies the underlying cognitive processes (Block and Zakay, 1996; Zakay and Block, 1997).

TEMPORAL DATING: SERIAL POSITION AND RECENCY JUDGEMENTS

Cognitive evidence

Research investigating temporal dating judgements reveals some interesting and relevant conclusions. In one experiment (Hintzman and Block, 1971), participants were told to pay attention to a series of words for a later memory test. They were not forewarned that temporal dating would be required. After all words had been presented, participants were unexpectedly asked to judge the approximate serial (temporal) position of each word in the series. They were able to do so with considerable accuracy. Temporal information seems to be encoded in memory even under incidental conditions, and this process does not require the conscious intent to encode temporal information.

Several subsequent experiments clarified this finding. In one of them (Hintzman, Block, and Summers, 1973), participants viewed two separate series of words, again under incidental conditions. Afterwards, they were unexpectedly asked to judge whether each word had occurred in the first list or the second list, then to judge whether it had occurred near the beginning, middle, or end of the list. Again, participants were able to make these judgements with considerable accuracy. However, the errors that they made were particularly revealing. If a person incorrectly judged that a word had occurred in a particular list, the person nevertheless tended to judge that it had occurred in the correct part of the list. Thus, incorrect position judgements did not simply migrate to temporally adjacent locations. This finding suggests that participants based their position judgements on incidentally encoded contextual information instead of on hypothetical time tags that locate events on a continuous scale of absolute time. Alternative explanations are possible. For example, oscillators with different characteristic frequencies may separately encode within-list and between-list information (cf. G. D. A. Brown and Vousden, 1998). This kind of explanation is weakened by the findings of other studies, which show that people can remember contextual information that has no temporal basis even if they are not forewarned that they will be required to do so. In one such experiment, each word in a long series was presented either auditorily or visually, and people were subsequently able to remember the presentation modality of tested words with above-chance accuracy (Hintzman, Block, and Inskeep, 1972).

Additional supporting evidence comes from studies of autobiographical memory in which participants are asked to date personal memories of events that occurred during relatively long time periods, such as months and years. People can make such judgements with some accuracy. However, their judgements also reveal systematically biased inaccuracy, called *scale effects*: a person may show relatively good accuracy in dating an event as having occurred during a particular time of day but show considerable inaccuracy in remembering the day, month, or year during which the event occurred (Friedman and Wilkins, 1985). Friedman (1993; see also this volume, Ch. 5) interpreted this kind of evidence as supporting what he called *location-based* rather than *distance-based* processes. Location-based processes are those that involve judging the recency of an event in a way that is influenced by important contextual landmarks (Shum, 1998), whereas distance-based processes are those that involve judging recency in a more absolute way, such as in terms of the strength of a memory trace. Evidence for location-based processes suggests that relative contextual information, rather than absolute time tags or memory strength, subserves temporal memory judgements.

Evidence that contextual information is automatically encoded comes from two main sources. First, participants can make reasonably accurate temporal dating judgements without being forewarned that they will have to do so (Hintzman and Block, 1971). Second, some experimenters have compared incidental and intentional memory conditions, in which the latter involves informing participants in advance that they will be asked to remember the temporal location of events. These studies reveal that there is little or no greater accuracy in the intentional condition (Auday, Sullivan, and Cross, 1988; but see Jackson, 1990). In short, people automatically encode contextual information concerning experienced events, a process that does not require conscious intention. When they later need to make a temporal order or recency judgement, they rely on whatever information is available in memory to reflect the temporal dimension, and they use contextual information and logical inferences based on it.

Memory for the recency of an event is apparently not limited to humans. Scrub jays are able to remember how long ago they cached (stored for later use) certain food items, either wax-moth larvae or peanuts (Clayton and Dickinson, 1998, 1999). When the scrub jays were allowed to recover wax-moth larvae, which are their preferred food items, with only a short delay, they chose to recover them instead of peanuts. However, when they were not allowed to recover wax-moth larvae until after the larvae would have perished, the scrub jays instead chose to recover the non-perishable peanuts. Clayton and Dickinson argued that this evidence meets the criteria for episodic-like memory in nonhuman animals—that is, memory for spatial and other contextual associations to personally experienced events, which in this case was the act of caching the food items. As such, non-human animals may automatically encode contextual information along with other information about their own actions. When a subsequent temporal judgement becomes important and relevant, they may rely on this contextual information. The extent to which non-human animals use encoded contextual information is probably limited compared to the extent to which humans use encoded contextual information. Non-human animals probably cannot make logical inferences about temporal order, position, and duration.

Neuropsychological evidence

People with brain damage in the prefrontal cortex usually show relatively little impairment in remembering events. However, they have difficulty performing memory tasks that require temporal judgements. For example, they are seriously impaired in judging which of two remembered events occurred more recently (e.g. Milner, 1982; Milner, McAndrews, and Leonard, 1990; Petrides and Milner, 1982). This impairment of temporal memory occurs mainly if there is damage to the dorsolateral prefrontal cortex, specifically in and around Brodmann's area 46. In addition, encoding the temporal order of external events more heavily involves the right prefrontal cortex, whereas encoding the temporal order of internal events more heavily involves the left prefrontal cortex (see Milner, 1982).

Milner, McAndrews, and Leonard (1990) proposed two hypotheses concerning the role of the frontal lobes in temporal-order encoding: (1) 'If the frontal lobes parse and organize the temporal contexts of events, one outcome of such operations could be thought of as a direct encoding of temporal tags for events in memory' (1990: 991), and (2) the frontal lobes 'develop appropriate encoding and retrieval strategies for the reconstruction of temporal order' (1990: 992). Although they favoured the second hypothesis, the first hypothesis is also tenable, and the two functions are not mutually exclusive. Thus the dorsolateral prefrontal cortex may encode contextual information, thereby enabling a person subsequently to remember the order of recent events (Fuster, 1995, 1997). Because the prefrontal cortex is critically involved in control of behaviour across time, Moscovitch (1992) proposed calling the corresponding memory system *working with memory* rather than simply *working memory*. Some controversy remains concerning whether the prefrontal cortex subserves the encoding of both temporal and spatial context. Schacter (1987) proposed that the prefrontal cortex is implicated in both, whereas Lewis (1989) argued that the prefrontal cortex subserves the encoding of only temporal context. According to Lewis, the hippocampus plays a more important role in processing information about spatial context.

The role of the dorsolateral prefrontal cortex may also include timing short durations (experiencing duration in passing). In other words, it may contain specialized neural circuits that are part of an internal-clock mechanism which is necessary for judgement of durations in the range of seconds to minutes (for relevant discussion, see Block, 1996; Block and Zakay, 1996; Church, 1989; Rubia *et al.*, 1998). Nichelli *et al.* (1995) interpreted the decreased accuracy shown by patients with frontal lobe damage in terms of an impaired reference memory system for time intervals. Although the dorsolateral prefrontal cortex seems to be crucially involved in various temporal tasks, its exact role in these phenomena remains unclear (Nichelli, 1993).

The neurotransmitter dopamine is found throughout the prefrontal cortex. Some evidence suggests that the dopamine D1 receptor site plays an important role in working memory (Goldman-Rakic, 1992; Sawaguchi and Goldman-Rakic, 1991). Some drugs that influence prospective temporal judgements may influence D1 dopamine receptor sites in the dorsolateral prefrontal cortex. Dopamine agonists lengthen prospectively experienced duration (i.e. they increase the subjective time rate), whereas dopamine antagonists shorten prospectively experienced duration (Hicks, 1992).

McAndrews and Milner (1991) studied patients with damage to the medial temporal lobes (i.e. the hippocampus and adjacent structures). They presented a series of stimuli and then tested the patients' memory by presenting test stimuli in pairs and asking them to judge which of the two had occurred more recently. When the patients were able to remember both stimuli, they performed normally on the recency judgement task. Thus, although patients with medial temporal-lobe damage show deficits in encoding permanent episodic memories, when they are able to acquire and explicitly retrieve an episodic memory, they often can remember associated contextual information, which they may use to make temporal judgements about the events. As we noted earlier, frontal-lobe patients show roughly the opposite: impaired memory for temporal information but normal memory for event information. These findings suggest that the hippocampus and the dorsolateral prefrontal cortex may perform somewhat separate (but interrelated) functions. Schacter proposed 'that remembering of temporal order constitutes one component of episodic memory, subserved by the frontal regions, and that remembering of recently presented items constitutes another component of episodic memory, likely subserved by the medial temporal regions' (1989: 704). The dorsolateral prefrontal cortex may supply the hippocampus with information about the cognitive context of events, and the hippocampus may encode this information in association with information about the content of events. In a subsequent section, we discuss the role of medial temporal lobe structures in retrospective duration judgements.

DURATION JUDGEMENTS

We need to distinguish between two kinds of duration judgements: (1) judging the duration of a single event (i.e. a stimulus), and (2) judging the duration of a series of events (i.e. a time period). These two kinds of duration judgement almost certainly involve different processes, and failing to distinguish between them may lead to conclusions that seem to be, but are not actually, contradictory.

Research reveals that non-human animals can learn to make one response to a relatively short stimulus, such as a 2-second light flash, and another response to a relatively long stimulus, such as a 10-second light flash (e.g. Fetterman, 1995). People can remember the duration of each event (e.g. word) in a long series of events with some accuracy even if they are not forewarned that they will be asked to do so (Hintzman, 1970). Duration information is apparently encoded relatively automatically as an integral part of the experience of an event.

A substantially larger body of research has focused on processes involved in judging the duration of a series of events. In this case, duration is not an integral property of a single stimulus, and the processes involved in experiencing and remembering the duration of a series of events are probably relatively complex. In his famous chapter in *The Principles of Psychology*, James (1890) made an important distinction. He claimed that different variables influence the 'retrospective and prospective sense of time' (p. 624): the apparent magnitude of a past duration lengthens as a function of 'the multitudinousness of the memories which the time affords' (p. 624), whereas the apparent magnitude of a duration in passing lengthens when 'we grow attentive to the passage of time itself' (p. 626). Researchers have investigated James's claims by using two kinds of methodology. In one kind, participants prospectively expose stimuli at a rate of one per subjective second until stopped by the experimenter, and then they retrospectively estimate the total duration (e.g. Frankenhaeuser, 1959; Hicks, 1992). The typical finding is that the retrospective verbal (numerical) estimate is less than the total duration produced prospectively. However, this kind of experiment does not afford a valid comparison of prospective and retrospective timing, because the duration is judged with two different methods.

A better way to test James's claim is by comparing duration estimates in what researchers now call the *prospective paradigm* and the *retrospective paradigm*. In the prospective paradigm, participants know in advance that they will later be asked to judge the duration of a time period. In the retrospective paradigm, participants do not have this knowledge. In both cases, participants experience a time period containing the same external information and nominal processing task, if any. However, the way in which they experience the duration and the various cognitive processes involved may differ. In the prospective paradigm, a person may intentionally (effortfully) encode temporal information as an integral part of the experience of the time period. This is partly why Block (1990) and others have used the term *experienced duration* to refer to the prospective paradigm. In the retrospective paradigm, a person may automatically and incidentally encode contextual information and may later need to effortfully retrieve from memory whatever information is relevant. Hence, the term *remembered duration* refers to the retrospective paradigm.

Many researchers have used the prospective paradigm, but few have used the retrospective paradigm. The main reason is that after a person is asked to provide a retrospective judgement, the person becomes aware that he or she may be asked to judge a subsequent duration. This is the defining characteristic of prospective judgement. Gilliland, Hofeld, and Eckstrand (1946) questioned whether the duration judgement paradigm would influence a person's duration judgements, but they did not report any evidence. Bakan (1955) conducted the first experiment, but he found no significant difference in duration judgements. The issue lay dormant for twenty years. Investigations of the duration judgement paradigm did not become common until after Hicks, Miller, and Kinsbourne's (1976) seminal study. In this study, participants sorted playing cards according to a rule requiring the processing of either zero, one, or two bits of information per card. In the prospective paradigm, verbal estimates of the duration were an inverse linear function of the amount of information processed. In the retrospective paradigm, the amount of information processed did not influence duration judgements.

More convincing evidence that prospective and retrospective duration judgements involve somewhat different processes or systems comes from findings that several variables differentially influence judgements in the two paradigms. For example, Block (1992) replicated Hicks and colleagues' finding. In the first experiment, experienced duration decreased when a person performed a more difficult processing task, but remembered duration was not affected. In the second experiment, remembered duration increased when participants performed several different kinds of tasks during the duration, but experienced duration was not affected. These findings reveal a double dissociation, thereby providing strong evidence that different processes or systems subserve the duration judgements in the two paradigms.

Most theorists have interpreted this kind of evidence as supporting a distinction between processes subserving prospective and retrospective judgements (e.g. Block, 1992; Hicks, Miller, and Kinsbourne, 1976). However, some theorists have emphasized the essential similarity of the timing processes involved. For example, S. W. Brown concluded that 'the most important feature of [his] results is the similarity of prospective and retrospective judgments' (1985: 119). This statement is striking, especially because he found that prospective judgements were greater in magnitude and more accurate than retrospective judgements.

Cognitive variables, such as task difficulty, greatly influence judgements of short durations. In attempts to explain this pervasive kind of finding, theorists have proposed various cognitive models of psychological time. Psychological time depends on complex interactions among the various conditions under which a duration is experienced and the context at the time the person makes a duration judgement (Block, 1989). Perhaps the most important factor is the time estimation paradigm; differences between prospective and retrospective timing are becoming clear (Block and Zakay, 1997). Under retrospective conditions, participants must construct a duration judgement from the contextual changes that were automatically encoded in memory during a time period. Under prospective conditions, this automatic encoding of context also occurs, but it plays a relatively minor role. The reason is that under prospective timing conditions participants effortfully attend to time during a duration and thereby accumulate relevant temporal information. This information is the most salient information at the time the person judges the duration. In short, different cognitive processes underlie prospective and retrospective judgements of duration.

Outside the laboratory, it may sometimes be difficult to tell whether any particular time estimate is being made primarily prospectively or retrospectively, and it may also be difficult to tell whether some behaviours involve time at all. In some cases, however, it is clear that a temporal judgement must be made retrospectively. Consider research in which a person is asked to temporally date (i.e. judge the recency of) many past events that he or she experienced. A person can usually do so with at least some accuracy. These judgements are similar to retrospective duration judgements if one considers each time period to have begun when a person experienced an event and to have ended at the time the recency judgement was made. It would be nearly impossible for a person to have been prospectively attending to the duration of each of these time periods, because the ending point of each time period is arbitrary. Further, when a person is asked (under prospective conditions) to track the duration of several concurrent events, accuracy of timing decreases if the person has more events to track (S. W. Brown, 1997).

RETROSPECTIVE DURATION JUDGEMENTS

Cognitive evidence

Theorists typically propose memory-based models of remembered duration. Specific theories focus on stored and retrieved information, or 'storage size' (Ornstein, 1969); remembered changes (Fraisse, 1963); encoded and retrieved contextual changes (Block and Reed, 1978); or interval segmentation (Poynter, 1983). Most theorists ignore the role of a person's attention to time unless there is little information to process, there are frequent feelings of boredom, or there are other conditions that arouse a temporal motive (Doob, 1971). Memory-based explanations, which do not involve attention to time *per se*, are more typically needed. To the extent that a person can retrieve a greater number of events, he or she remembers the duration of a time period as being longer (Ornstein, 1969). However, retrospective duration judgements are not simply based on the degree of recallability of individual events (Block, 1974; Block and Reed, 1978); other factors are involved. Even if people use this strategy, they do not attempt to retrieve all available memories of events from the time period. Instead, they may rely on an availability heuristic in which they remember a duration as being longer to the extent that they can easily retrieve some of the events that occurred during the time period.

Changes in cognitive context have a more important influence on remembered duration than does the number of stimulus events encoded and retrieved. Contextual changes may occur as a result of variation in environment stimuli, interoceptive stimuli, and the processing context. Block and Reed (1978) found that people remembered a time period as being longer in duration to the extent that there were greater process context changes. These are changes that occur when a person employs different kinds of cognitive processes to encode information. For example, a time period containing some words that required structural processing and other words that required semantic processing was remembered as being longer in duration than an equal time period containing words that only required structural processing or only required semantic processing. Memory for individual words was best in the semantic-only condition, intermediate in the mixed-processing condition, and worst in the structural-only condition. Taken together, these findings lead to the rejection of simple event-memory explanations of remembered duration, such as Ornstein's (1969) storage-size model. Block (1982) investigated environmental context as another salient source of contextual changes. A person's previous experience in a particular environment shortened the remembered duration of a subsequent time period spent in it. Poynter (1989; see also Zakay *et al.*, 1994) found that remembered duration is longer to the extent that a to-be-estimated interval is segmented by high-priority events which attract attention (like politicians' names inserted among names of furniture). Segmentation, however, may be interpreted to be a particular case of contextual changes created as a result of the appearance of the high-priority events.

A contextual-change model predicts a positive time-order effect in remembered duration, especially if relatively long time periods and a comparative duration-judgement task are used. A positive time-order effect is the finding that a person will usually remember the first of two equivalent time periods as being longer than the second (Block, 1982, 1985). More generally, a positive time-order effect is revealed when a person makes longer judgements of durations presented earlier in a series of several durations (see, for example, S. W. Brown and Stubbs, 1988). According to a contextual-change model, a person encodes a greater number of changes in contextual elements during a more novel experience, such as during the first of several durations. Two additional findings support the notion that contextual changes underlie the positive time-order effect. The effect is eliminated if the environmental context prevailing during the second of two durations is different from that prevailing during the first (Block, 1982). It is also eliminated if changes in emotional context that would ordinarily occur during the first duration occur instead during a preceding time period (Block, 1986). Note that the positive time-order effect is somewhat counter-intuitive. Ornstein's storage-size model predicts the opposite, a negative time-order effect attributable to 'items dropping out of storage' (1969: 107). In fact, some of Ornstein's data reveal a positive time-order effect rather than a negative time-order effect.

To the extent that the first of two time periods becomes relatively less recent and the second becomes relatively more recent (i.e. the interval between the two increases), a person may have relatively more difficulty remembering the contextual changes that occurred during the first time period. In such a case, the typical positive time-order effect may reverse, becoming a negative time-order effect. Wearden and Ferrara (1993), who used two brief stimuli and asked people to judge the relative duration of the two, obtained such evidence. They called it a *subjective shortening* effect.

It is nearly impossible to find evidence revealing that non-human animals can make retrospective duration judgements. There are at least two possible explanations for why this is the case. One possibility is that researchers have not attempted to devise conditions testing animals' abilities to make retrospective duration judgements. Although such testing is difficult, it is possible. It requires subsequently using differential reinforcement of at least two responses, one indicating one kind of duration judgement regarding a previously presented time period (e.g. 'shorter in duration') and another indicating a second kind of temporal judgement (e.g. 'longer in duration'). The main problem may be devising a way to present test stimuli, because each stimulus would have to symbolize a previously experienced time period. Another possibility is that animals do not encode temporal information unless they experience a stimulus or a time period under prospective conditions. Compared to prospective timing, retrospective timing may involve evolutionarily more complex processes, perhaps because it has not been essential to the survival and subsequent reproduction of organisms.

Neuropsychological evidence

The long-term encoding of episodic memories requires the intact functioning of medial temporal lobe structures, especially the hippocampus, apparently working in conjunction with information supplied by the prefrontal cortex. Medial temporal lobe structures are also involved in judgements of the duration of past time periods. Patients with damage to the medial temporal lobes, especially the hippocampus, show abnormally short reproductions of durations greater than about 5–15 seconds (Richards, 1973; Williams, Medwedeff, and Haban, 1989). The prefrontal cortex and the hippocampus are intimately connected and apparently play a conjoint role in the processing of working memory and episodic-memory information (Goldman-Rakic, Selemon, and Schwartz, 1984; Olton, 1989). The working memory system of the prefrontal cortex apparently generates encodings of contextual information, which a person may use to make various temporal memory judgements. Temporal memory judgements concerning past events and episodes depend on retrieving encoded contextual changes, including changes in process context, environmental context, emotional context, and other contextual associations (Block, 1982, 1986, 1992; Block and Reed, 1978). To the extent that retrospective order, recency, duration, and other similar temporal judgements rely on event information no longer represented in the working memory system, these kinds of judgements also require the hippocampus for the permanent encoding of events and associated contextual information.

The frontal lobes may also subserve a person's ability to organize various strategic processes required for retrieval of information from memory (Mangels *et al.*, 1996; Moscovitch and Melo, 1997; see also Friedman, Ch. 5, this volume). This function may be somewhat different from that involved in generating contextual information, although evidence on that issue is unclear.

PROSPECTIVE DURATION JUDGEMENTS

Cognitive evidence

Attention-demanding processes that occur concurrently with the processing of non-temporal (task) information influence prospective duration timing. Diverse research has revealed that experienced duration typically increases if the number of stimuli requiring processing is small, if a processing task is easy, or if participants do not need to respond actively to stimulus information (Hicks, Miller, and Kinsbourne, 1976; Zakay, 1993; Zakay and Block, 1997). Thus prospective timing is a dual-task condition in which attention must be shared between temporal and non-temporal information processing. Attending to time requires access to some of the same resources that non-temporal tasks do. For this reason, most theorists propose attention-based models of experienced duration (Block and Zakay, 1996; S. W. Brown, 1998; Macar, Grondin, and Casini, 1994; Thomas and

Weaver, 1975; Zakay and Block, 1996). In these models, experienced duration increases to the extent that a person allocates more attentional resources to processing temporal information.

Evidence supporting attentional models comes from studies that have used a dual-task paradigm (S. W. Brown, 1997; Macar, Grondin, and Casini, 1994). If a person receives instructions on how much attention to allocate for stimulus information processing and how much to allocate for temporal information processing, prospective duration judgements are a function of the latter. For example, Zakay (1998) used a primary–secondary task paradigm. The magnitude of prospective duration judgements increased when participants were told that a temporal task was the primary task and that a simultaneous non-temporal task was the secondary task. The magnitude of the duration judgements decreased when the instructions were reversed. Zakay (1992) used another kind of experimental manipulation, in which a stimulus that attracted attention was presented during some intervals that required an ongoing temporal judgement. On those trials, the magnitude of the prospective duration judgement decreased.

In making a prospective duration judgement, a person compares the accumulated temporal units with the typical number of such units stored during reference durations. In the attentional-gate model (Zakay and Block, 1996, 1997), for example, the pulse count accumulated during the duration is compared to those stored in reference memory. This is a long-term memory store containing learned pulse counts, as well as (in the case of humans) translations of these total pulse counts into verbal (numerical) units. Some of these total pulse counts may originally have been stored in a retrospective way. For example, a person who encounters a certain traffic (stop) light repeatedly may initially encode the duration retrospectively. Later, the person may attend to time in a prospective way, storing additional pulse totals for this particular duration. As the person acquires expertise with a particular duration, his or her duration estimates presumably become more accurate and less variable (Zakay and Block, 1999).

Animals such as rats may be trained on a fixed-interval schedule, in which the animal is reinforced for the first response made after a fixed duration since the previously reinforced response (see Church, 1989, for a review). Research on animal timing more often uses a variant of this called the *peak procedure*, in which randomly interspersed discrete trials contain either fixed-interval reinforcement or no reinforcement at the usual time. A fixed-interval schedule essentially entails what is called the *method of production* in human research, in which a person is told to respond at the end of some previously defined duration (e.g. 'Say stop when you think that 30 seconds has elapsed'). As such, this schedule is by definition an example of the prospective paradigm. Animal researchers have typically had no need to propose an attentional mechanism, and they have not done much relevant research that might have revealed it. Do animals' prospective duration judgements show the same sort of attentional effects as those of humans? Research to date has left that important question unanswered.

Neuropsychological evidence

As we noted earlier, a working-memory system that is apparently subserved by the dorsolateral prefrontal cortex appears to play a role in the experience of time in passing. Short-duration judgements as well as subsequent recency and temporal-order judgements presumably require the functioning of this system. Prospective timing may also require a biological-clock mechanism. Scalar timing theory proposes that this mechanism consists of a pacemaker (which produces pulses), a switch, and an accumulator, with a comparison made between pulse totals in working memory and in reference memory (Church, 1984, 1989). Although scalar timing theory proposes a single mechanism, several partially dissociable brain systems may be involved in prospective duration judgements (Block, 1996).

Payk (1977) reviewed various case studies of what has come to be called the *Zeitrafferphänomen*, or *accelerated time phenomenon*. (A Zeitraffer is a mechanical apparatus to accelerate the apparent motion in a film, as in time-lapse cinematography, so common translations of *Zeitrafferphänomen* usually focus on accelerated motion of events or accelerated experience of time.) Binkofski and Block (1996) described a Zeitraffer patient (B.W.) with damage in his left-hemisphere prefrontal cortex resulting from a glioblastoma. The onset of his symptoms was surprisingly sudden: As B.W. was driving his automobile, he noticed that external objects seemed to be rushing towards him at an unusually fast rate. He stopped his car, unable to drive. He later described his experience as that of an 'accelerated motion' of events, and he complained that he could not even watch television because the progression of events was too quick for him to follow. When B.W. was asked to produce 60-second durations, his productions were greatly lengthened, averaging 286 seconds. (He made these productions under conditions of minimal environmental stimulation.) This evidence converges with B.W.'s description of his condition. He experienced events in much the way a normal person would experience events on a video-cassette recording being played on 'fast forward' (i.e. occurring at approximately six times their normal rate). Binkofski and Block concluded that the most likely explanation for these data was that the pacemaker component of B.W.'s internal clock was now producing pulses at a considerably decreased rate (see also Nichelli, 1993).

Researchers who have administered drugs to animals trained on fixed-interval schedules suggest that the internal clock may be subserved by dopaminergic neurons, which the prefrontal cortex is known to contain. The internal clock may also involve older brain areas such as the basal ganglia (Meck, 1996).

Brain areas that subserve the internal-clock mechanism may be separate from, but interconnected with, other areas that subserve the proposed role of attentional processes in prospective duration judgement. It is unclear which areas of the brain may subserve attention to time, a process that is implicated in research using the prospective paradigm. Studies using positron emission tomography suggest that several anatomically separate brain areas, including the thalamus, the parietal lobes, and the anterior cingulate gyrus, are involved in various aspects of attentionally guided task performance (for a review, see Posner and Raichle, 1994). These areas may also play somewhat different roles. The likely candidate for an area that subserves the allocation of attention to external events or to time is the anterior cingulate cortex. This area, located in an evolutionarily new part of the brain, may be the essential component of an executive attention network that directly influences the working-memory functions of the dorsolateral prefrontal cortex. As such, it may subserve the role of attention in the prospective timing of stimuli and durations.

Our conclusions about the likely roles of various brain areas in subserving prospective duration judgements differ from those of Kesner (1998). Kesner concluded that people with damage to the prefrontal cortex are not impaired on a task requiring short-term memory for the duration of a stimulus, but people with damage to the hippocampus are impaired on such a task. Perhaps the contradiction is more apparent than real: as we noted earlier, memory for the duration of an event and memory for the duration of a series of events may entail different processes. Additional research is needed, however, to clarify the roles of the anterior cingulate cortex, the dorsolateral prefrontal cortex, and the hippocampus in various kinds of tasks requiring temporal judgements.

DIRECTIONS FOR FUTURE RESEARCH

Research on various kinds of prospective and retrospective temporal judgements is needed to identify all the variables that influence them. Nevertheless, three issues call for special attention by time researchers:

1. In what ways do various kinds of temporal judgements involve similar processes and in what ways do they involve different processes? In particular, how are temporal dating judgements (e.g. recency, temporal location, and temporal order judgements) related to duration judgements? How are judgements of the duration of an event related to judgements of the duration of a series of events? Answering these questions requires an integration of cognitive and neuropsychological research.

2. Is it possible to create a unified model of prospective and retrospective duration judgements? Evidence strongly suggests that these two kinds of duration judgements rely on somewhat different processes (Block and 'Zakay, 1997). Nevertheless, it may be possible to combine the two kinds of judgement in a unified model.

3. Is human temporal cognition simply an elaborated version of temporal mechanisms that evolved during the course of evolution, or is it based on principles different from those that characterize non-human animals' temporal processes? This issue is related to the need to identify brain areas and mechanisms that subserve temporal processes in general and duration judgements in particular.

SUMMARY AND CONCLUSIONS

Relatively accurate timing of events and durations is essential to ensure the optimal functioning of organisms. Several kinds of temporal judgements, such as order, recency, and even recognition memory judgements, can be made retrospectively, based mainly on contextual information. The relevant information is encoded relatively automatically, as revealed by studies in which participants do not know that temporal information will be needed later (incidental memory). Evolutionarily newer cortical areas (e.g. dorsolateral prefrontal cortex, parahippocampal cortex, and hippocampus) apparently subserve this relatively automatic encoding of contextual information. Evidence indicates that duration judgements depend on several variables, most importantly the duration-judgement paradigm—that is, whether the judgement is made retrospectively or prospectively. Although it may sometimes be difficult to tell whether any naturally occurring duration judgement is retrospective or prospective, prospective judgements may ordinarily be more common. Retrospective duration judgements depend on the relatively automatic encoding of event and associated contextual information, which is retrieved in a controlled (non-automatic) way. In contrast, some temporal judgements are made prospectively—that is, in situations in which a person is aware that temporal information is needed, either immediately or later. Although the same contextual information may be encoded as in a retrospective paradigm, other information is also encoded. This information is encoded only in a deliberate (controlled) way, involving attention and hence more complete involvement of mechanisms of consciousness. Attending to temporal information apparently competes for the same pool of attentional resources as does attending to non-temporal information. Evidence suggests the additional involvement of evolutionarily older subcortical (and some newer cortical structures) in prospective situations.

We thank William Friedman, Françoise Macar, and Teresa McCormack for comments on a draft of this chapter.

R.A.B. and D.Z.

REFERENCES

AUDAY, B. C., SULLIVAN, C., and CROSS, H. A. (1988), 'The effects of constrained rehearsal on judgments of temporal order', *Bulletin of the Psychonomic Society*, 26: 548–51.

BAKAN, P. (1955), 'Effect of set and work speed on time estimation', *Perceptual and Motor Skills*, 5: 147–8.

BINKOFSKI, F., and BLOCK, R. A. (1996), 'Accelerated time after left frontal cortex lesion', *Neurocase*, 2: 485–93.

BLOCK, R. A. (1974), 'Memory and the experience of duration in retrospect', *Memory & Cognition*, 2: 153–60.

—— (1979), 'Time and consciousness', in G. Underwood and R. Stevens (eds.), *Aspects of Consciousness, Volume 1: Psychological Issues*. London: Academic Press, 179–217.

—— (1982), 'Temporal judgments and contextual change', *Journal of Experimental Psychology: Learning, Memory, and Cognition*, 8: 530–44.

—— (1985), 'Contextual coding in memory: studies of remembered duration', in J. A. Michon and J. L. Jackson (eds.), *Time, Mind, and Behavior*. Berlin: Springer-Verlag, 169–78.

—— (1986), 'Remembered duration: imagery processes and contextual encoding', *Acta Psychologica*, 62: 103–22.

—— (1989), 'Experiencing and remembering time: affordances, context, and cognition', in I. Levin and D. Zakay (eds.), *Time and Human Cognition: A Life-Span Perspective*. Amsterdam: North-Holland, 333–63.

—— (1990), 'Models of psychological time', in R. A. Block (ed.), *Cognitive Models of Psychological Time*. Hillsdale, NJ: Erlbaum, 1–35.

—— (1992), 'Prospective and retrospective duration judgment: the role of information processing and memory', in F. Macar, V. Pouthas, and W. J. Friedman (eds.), *Time, Action and Cognition: Towards Bridging the Gap*. Dordrecht: Kluwer Academic, 141–52.

—— (1996), 'Psychological time and memory systems of the brain', in J. T. Fraser and M. P. Soulsby (eds.), *Dimensions of Time and Life*. Madison, Conn.: International Universities Press, 61–76.

—— and REED, M. A. (1978), 'Remembered duration: evidence for a contextual-change hypothesis', *Journal of Experimental Psychology: Human Learning and Memory*, 4: 656–65.

—— and ZAKAY, D. (1996), 'Models of psychological time revisited', in H. Helfrich (ed.), *Time and Mind*. Kirkland, Wash.: Hogrefe and Huber, 171–95.

—— and ZAKAY, D. (1997), 'Prospective and retrospective duration judgments: a meta-analytic review', *Psychonomic Bulletin & Review*, 4: 184–97.

BROWN, G. D. A., and VOUSDEN, J. I. (1998), 'Adaptive sequential behavior: oscillators as rational mechanisms', in M. Oaksford and N. Chater (eds.), *Rational Models of Cognition*. Oxford: Oxford University Press, 165–93.

BROWN, S. W. (1985). 'Time perception and attention: the effects of prospective versus retrospective paradigms and task demands on perceived duration', *Perception & Psychophysics*, 38: 115–24.

—— (1997), 'Attentional resources in timing: interference effects in concurrent temporal and nontemporal working memory tasks', *Perception & Psychophysics*, 59: 1118–40.

—— (1998), 'Automaticity versus timesharing in timing and tracking dual-task perfor-mance', *Psychological Research/Psychologische Forschung*, 61: 71–81.

—— and STUBBS, D. A. (1988), 'The psychophysics of retrospective and prospective timing', *Perception*, 17: 297–310.

CHURCH, R. M. (1984). 'Properties of the internal clock', *Annals of the New York Academy of Sciences*, 423: 566–82.

—— (1989), 'Theories of timing behavior', in S. B. Klein and R. R. Mowrer (eds.), *Contemporary Learning Theories: Instrumental Conditioning Theory and the Impact of Biological Constraints on Learning*. Hillsdale, NJ: Erlbaum, 41–71.

CLAYTON, N. S., and DICKINSON, A. (1998), 'Episodic-like memory during cache recovery by scrub jays', *Nature*, 395: 272–4.

—— (1999), 'Memory for the content of caches by scrub jays (*Aphelocoma coerulescens*)', *Journal of Experimental Psychology: Animal Behavior Processes*, 25: 82–91.

DOOB, L. W. (1971), *Patterning of Time*. New Haven: Yale University Press.

FETTERMAN, J. G. (1995), 'The psychophysics of remembered duration', *Animal Learning & Behavior*, 23: 49–62.

FRAISSE, P. (1963), *The Psychology of Time*, trans. J. Leith. New York: Harper and Row. (Original work published 1957.)

FRANKENHAEUSER, M. (1959), *Estimation of Time: An Experimental Study*. Stockholm: Almqvist and Wiksell.

FRIEDMAN, W. J. (1993), 'Memory for the time of past events', *Psychological Bulletin*, 113: 44–66.

—— and WILKINS, A. J. (1985), 'Scale effects in memory for the time of events', *Memory & Cognition*, 13: 168–75.

FUSTER, J. M. (1995), 'Temporal processing', *Annals of the New York Academy of Sciences*, 769: 173–81.

—— (1997), *The Prefrontal Cortex: Anatomy, Physiology, and Neuropsychology of the Frontal Lobe*, 3rd edn. Philadelphia: Lippincott-Raven.

GILLILAND, A. R., HOFELD, J. B., and ECKSTRAND, G. (1946), 'Studies in time perception', *Psychological Bulletin*, 43: 162–76.

GOLDMAN-RAKIC, P. S. (1992), 'Working memory and the mind', *Scientific American*, 267: 111–17.

—— SELEMON, L. D., and SCHWARTZ, M. L. (1984), 'Dual pathways connecting the dorsolateral prefrontal cortex with the hippocampal formation and parahippocampal cortex in the rhesus monkey', *Neuroscience*, 12: 719–43.

HICKS, R. E. (1992), 'Prospective and retrospective judgments of time: a neurobehavioral analysis', in F. Macar, V. Pouthas, and W. J. Friedman (eds.), *Time, Action and Cognition: Towards Bridging the Gap*. Dordrecht: Kluwer Academic, 97–108.

—— MILLER, G. W., and KINSBOURNE, M. (1976), 'Prospective and retrospective judgments of time as a function of amount of information processed', *American Journal of Psychology*, 89: 719–30.

HINTZMAN, D. L. (1970), 'Effects of repetition and exposure duration on memory', *Journal of Experimental Psychology*, 83: 435–44.

—— and BLOCK, R. A. (1971), 'Repetition and memory: evidence for a multiple-trace hypothesis', *Journal of Experimental Psychology*, 88: 297–306.

—— —— and INSKEEP, N. R. (1972), 'Memory for mode of input', *Journal of Verbal Learning and Verbal Behavior*, 11: 741–9.

—— —— and SUMMERS, J. J. (1973), 'Contextual associations and memory for serial position', *Journal of Experimental Psychology*, 97: 220–9.

JACKSON, J. L. (1990), 'A cognitive approach to temporal information processing', in R. A. Block (ed.), *Cognitive Models of Psychological Time*. Hillsdale, NJ: Erlbaum, 153–80.

JAMES, W. (1890), *The Principles of Psychology*. New York: Holt.

KESNER, R. P. (1998), 'Neural mediation of memory for time: role of the hippocampus and medial prefrontal cortex', *Psychonomic Bulletin & Review*, 5: 585–96.

LEWIS, R. S. (1989), 'Remembering and the prefrontal cortex', *Psychobiology*, 17: 102–7.

MACAR, F., GRONDIN, S., and CASINI, L. (1994), 'Controlled attention sharing influences time estimation', *Memory & Cognition*, 22: 673–86.

MCANDREWS, M. P., and MILNER, B. (1991), 'The frontal cortex and memory for temporal order', *Neuropsychologia*, 29: 849–59.

MANGELS, J. A., GERSHBERG, F. B., SHIMAMURA, A. P., and KNIGHT, R. T. (1996), 'Impaired retrieval from remote memory in patients with frontal lobe damage', *Neuropsychology,* 10: 32–41.

MECK, W. H. (1996), 'Neuropharmacology of timing and time perception', *Cognitive Brain Research,* 3: 227–42.

MILNER, B. (1982), 'Some cognitive effects of frontal-lobe lesions in man', in D. E. Broadbent and L. Weiskrantz (eds.), *The Neuropsychology of Cognitive Function.* London: Royal Society, 211–26.

—— MCANDREWS, M. P., and LEONARD, G. (1990), 'Frontal lobes and memory for the temporal order of recent events', *Cold Spring Harbor Symposia on Quantitative Biology,* 55: 987–94.

MOSCOVITCH, M. (1992), 'Memory and working-with-memory: a component process model based on modules and central systems', *Journal of Cognitive Neuroscience,* 4: 257–67.

—— and MELO, B. (1997), 'Strategic retrieval and the frontal lobes: evidence from confabulation and amnesia', *Neuropsychologia,* 35: 1017–34.

NICHELLI, P. (1993), 'The neuropsychology of human temporal information processing', in F. Boller and J. Grafman (eds.), *Handbook of Neuropsychology.* Amsterdam: Elsevier Science, 339–71.

—— CLARK, K., HOLLNAGEL, C., and GRAFMAN, J. (1995), 'Duration processing after frontal lobe lesions', *Annals of the New York Academy of Sciences,* 769: 183–90.

OLTON, D. S. (1989), 'Frontal cortex, timing and memory', *Neuropsychologia,* 27: 121–30.

ORNSTEIN, R. E. (1969), *On the Experience of Time.* Harmondsworth: Penguin.

PAYK, T. R. (1977), 'Störungen des Zeiterlebens bei den endogenen Psychosen [Disturbances of time experience in endogenous psychoses]', *Schweizer Archiv für Neurologie, Neurochirurgie und Psychiatrie,* 121: 277–85.

PETRIDES, M., and MILNER, B. (1982), 'Deficits on subject-ordered tasks after frontal- and temporal-lobe lesions in man', *Neuropsychologia,* 20: 249–62.

POSNER, M. I., and RAICHLE, M. E. (1994), *Images of Mind.* San Francisco: Freeman.

POYNTER, W. D. (1983), 'Duration judgment and the segmentation of experience', *Memory & Cognition,* 11: 77–82.

—— (1989), 'Judging the duration of time intervals: a process of remembering segments of experience', in I. Levin and D. Zakay (eds.), *Time and Human Cognition: A Life-Span Perspective.* Amsterdam: North-Holland, 305–31.

RICHARDS, W. (1973), 'Time Reproductions by H.M.', *Acta Psychologica,* 37: 279–82.

ROBERTS, S. (1998), 'The mental representation of time: uncovering a biological clock', in D. Scarborough and S. Sternberg (eds.), *Methods, Models, and Conceptual Issues: An Invitation to Cognitive Science,* iv. Cambridge, Mass.: MIT Press, 53–106.

RUBIA, K., OVERMEYER, S., TAYLOR, E., BRAMMER, M., WILLIAMS, S., SIMMONS, A., ANDREW, C., and BULLMORE, E. (1998), 'Prefrontal involvement in "temporal bridging" and timing movement', *Neuropsychologia,* 36: 1283–93.

SAWAGUCHI, T., and GOLDMAN-RAKIC, P. S. (1991), 'D1 dopamine receptors in prefrontal cortex: involvement in working memory', *Science,* 251: 947–50.

SCHACTER, D. L. (1987), 'Memory, amnesia, and frontal lobe dysfunction', *Psychobiology,* 15: 21–36.

—— (1989), 'Memory', in M. I. Posner (ed.), *Foundations of Cognitive Science.* Cambridge, Mass.: MIT Press, 683–725.

SHUM, M. S. (1998), 'The role of temporal landmarks in autobiographical memory processes', *Psychological Bulletin,* 124: 423–42.

THOMAS, E. A., and WEAVER, W. B. (1975), 'Cognitive processing and time perception', *Perception & Psychophysics*, 17: 363–7.

WEARDEN, J. H., and FERRARA, A. (1993), 'Subjective shortening in humans' memory for stimulus duration', *Quarterly Journal of Experimental Psychology*, 46B: 163–86.

WILLIAMS, J. M., MEDWEDEFF, C. H., and HABAN, G. (1989), 'Memory disorder and subjective time estimation', *Journal of Clinical and Experimental Neuropsychology*, 11: 713–23.

ZAKAY, D. (1992), 'The role of attention in children's time perception', *Journal of Experimental Child Psychology*, 54: 355–71.

—— (1993), 'The roles of non-temporal information processing load and temporal expectations in children's prospective time estimation', *Acta Psychologica*, 84: 271–80.

—— (1998), 'Attention allocation policy influences prospective timing', *Psychonomic Bulletin & Review*, 5: 114–18.

—— and BLOCK, R. A. (1996), 'The role of attention in time estimation processes', in M. A. Pastor and J. Artieda (eds.), *Time, Internal Clocks and Movement*. Amsterdam: North-Holland/Elsevier Science, 143–64.

—— —— (1997), 'Temporal cognition', *Current Directions in Psychological Science*, 6: 12–16.

—— —— (1999), 'The negative asynchrony phenomenon: a prospective timing perspective', in G. Aschersleben, T. Bachmann, and J. Müsseler, (eds.), *Cognitive Contributions to the Perception of Spatial and Temporal Events*. Amsterdam: Elsevier Science, 251–7.

—— TSAL, Y., MOSES, M., and SHAHAR, I. (1994), 'The role of segmentation in prospective and retrospective time estimation processes', *Memory & Cognition*, 22: 344–51.

3

The Chronological Organization of Memory: Common Psychological Foundations for Remembering and Timing

Gordon D. A. Brown and *Nick Chater*

Time and memory are related at several different levels, many of which are explored in the present volume. In this chapter we focus on recent psychological models of human timing and human memory, show that there has recently been a clear convergence between models in these two different areas, and explore reasons for this convergence. Thus, according to many current models, memories are chronologically organized, and similar cognitive mechanisms may underpin human memory and timing behaviour. Why should memory be chronologically organized, and why should there be such a strong similarity between models of memory and models of timing?

Our discussion of why models of memory and models of timing have come to look so similar will have several strands. We review evidence that memories are temporally organized, show how this is reflected in current models of memory, and draw on ecological analyses and the 'rational analysis' approach within cognitive psychology to show why possession of a chronologically organized memory may confer adaptive utility. We argue that there is a deep relationship between human memory and timing ability, although it is only recently that detailed models of memory and timing have reached a level of sophistication at which this relationship becomes explicit.

Psychologists have distinguished many different types of memory, and such distinctions have themselves been controversial. What particular variety of memory are we concerned with here? Within the psychological literature, much of the discussion on the relationship between time and memory has arisen from the study of *episodic* memory. Conceptions of the nature of episodic memories typically depend in various ways upon the temporal datability of such memories by the rememberer. Thus Tulving (1972) viewed episodic memory as a sub-system of memory designed specifically for storing temporally dated episodes or events and relations between such events. More recent accounts have emphasized the kind of experience involved in episodic remembering, with the characteristic ability to reinstate one's past mentally and to recognize retrieved memories as belonging to that past (Wheeler, Stuss, and Tulving, 1997). As McCormack and Hoerl (1999) emphasize, episodic remembering seems to require the ability to represent an event as having happened at a particular time in the past, and this ability requires a certain kind of temporal decentring on the part of the rememberer. McCormack and Hoerl also argue that because of the close linkage between conceptions of time and episodic remembering, adult-like episodic memory cannot emerge in children until they possess the requisite concept of time. In both developmental and conceptual terms, therefore, there is a close connection between episodic memory and temporal representation.

In the present chapter we maintain a focus on memory and temporal representation. However, our concern is not with the conceptual relationships between memory and timing or temporal perspective-taking, but with relationships at the level of empirical data, psychological mechanism, and adaptive functionality. We examine memory over a wide range of time-scales, including shorter times than those traditionally considered under the heading of 'episodic memory'.

This chapter has four parts. In the first section we review evidence that much of human memory is indeed temporally organized, particularly over relatively short time-scales. The second part of the chapter briefly reviews the classes of model that have been developed to account for short-term episodic memory and timing behaviour, and points to striking convergences in the mechanisms assumed by models of memory and of timing. The third section is concerned with possible *reasons* for the close connection between memory and time that is evident at the level of empirical data and models. We show how the 'rational analysis' approach to memory adopted by Anderson and his colleagues enables an understanding of why memories might be organized in terms of their temporal distance from the present. It is claimed that an efficient memory system, that is, one that adaptively reflects the statistical structure of the world it remembers, must have time as a fundamental organizing dimension. Finally, we summarize and address arguments that have been put forward by other researchers to support that idea that memories are *not* chronologically organized.

EMPIRICAL DATA: EVIDENCE THAT TIME IS USED TO INDEX MEMORY

What kind of psychological evidence could underpin the claim that memories are temporally organized? We consider three kinds of empirical evidence that might support the case: the observation of time-based forgetting from memory; the ability to make judgements about the relative temporal recency of episodic memories; and the tendency to confuse the relative positions of temporally close items in recall of order information. We argue that data from the last two cases provide clear evidence that time is an important dimension underpinning the structure of memory.

As a preliminary, we state our specific claim. The claim is simply that an important dimension underlying the organization of memories is one that represents the temporal relationship between the time an event occurred and the time of remembering. More specifically, we argue that memories are organized in terms of time relative to the present rather than time relative to some other (e.g.

arbitrary calendar) date. This claim is separate from (although related to) the claim that all memories are 'date-stamped' in some way with the absolute time that they occurred. Indeed there is plenty of evidence against the idea of calendar dating of events (e.g. Burt, 1992; Friedman, 1987; Wagenaar, 1986; see Friedman, Ch. 5, this volume, for a review). In Friedman's terms, our concern is with 'distance' rather than 'location' models. We note that the claim that memory is chronologically organized does not imply that memory is searched serially in reverse chronological order so that older memories invariably take longer to retrieve. (If I need to remember the name of someone from an appointment about six weeks ago, I can locate the appropriate region of my diary without scanning backwards through every page.)

Much of the data we cite in favour of the idea of a temporally organized memory comes from experimental paradigms such as 'free recall' and 'serial recall' tasks, in which subjects must recall relatively meaningless information over short periods (typically minutes; sometimes days or weeks). We will suggest that this is because temporal information is a particularly useful memory retrieval cue over short time-scales and when no other useful cues are available. After longer periods, as memories recede into the past, it becomes gradually harder to distinguish and identify memories in terms of their position along the temporal dimension, and other dimensions of memory organization play a relatively greater role. However, as we shall see, there is ample evidence for the temporal dimension of organization even at much longer time-scales (e.g. Glenberg *et al.*, 1983; see Brown, Neath, and Chater, 2000).

We now turn to the empirical evidence.

Forgetting

Evidence that elapsed time is an important dimension underlying the organization of memory might seem to come from the simple fact that memory declines over time. Other things being equal, an event from a minute ago will be more memorable than an event from an hour ago; an event from a week ago will be more memorable than a memory from a month ago, and a memory from a month ago will be more retrievable than a memory from a year ago. Forgetting is also seen after very short time-scales: In a typical immediate free recall task, where experimental subjects listen to and then recall a list of fifteen or twenty unrelated words, the more recently encountered words will be better remembered.[1] Indeed it seems that forgetting over time is describable by similar laws over many different time-scales (see J. R. Anderson and Schooler, 1991; Baddeley, 1976; Bjork and Whitten, 1974; Brown, Neath, and Chater, 2000; Glenberg *et al.*, 1983; Rubin and Wenzel, 1996; Wixted and Ebbesen, 1991, 1997).

---

[1] Primacy effects represent an exception to this general rule. However, it is widely assumed that primacy effects reflect the operation of separate processes (see e.g. Crowder, 1976) and we do not discuss them further here.

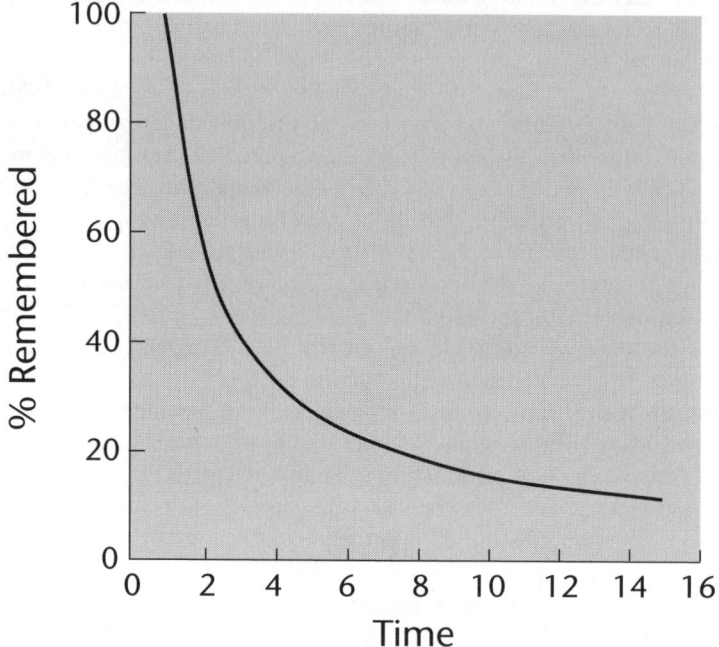

FIGURE 3.1. A typical power-law forgetting curve. Units of time are arbitrary because the curve has the same shape over all time-scales.

Of course, other things are often not equal. Events that are less salient, less meaningful, or of less personal significance are less likely to be remembered. Furthermore, there is a well established 'reminiscence bump' such that memories from subjects' late adolescent years tend to be better remembered than events from earlier or later periods of life (e.g. Rubin and Schulkind, 1997). In general, however, it is clear that forgetting occurs over time, and that time elapsed can be used as a good, although far from perfect, predictor of memory availability. When memory for arbitrary and unrelated information is studied, under conditions that exclude the opportunity for 'special factors' to intervene, highly orderly forgetting functions are obtained (see Figure 3.1).

To what extent does forgetting over time provide evidence for a temporal dimension underlying memory? Forgetting over time, however caused, will result in a memory system in which more recent events are more retrievable than less recent events. In terms of their retrievability, therefore, memories could be said to be temporally organized. However, it is more natural to think of this limited temporal organization as a side-effect of forgetting, rather than as a design principle of any particular functional or adaptive significance. This impression is strengthened by two further considerations. First, as a number of authors have made clear, at a mechanistic level it makes little sense to think of time as a causal factor in itself; instead some process correlated with the passage of time (analogous to rusting or immersion in a bath of acid) must provide the causal mechanism of time-based forgetting (see McGeogh, 1942; Posner and Konick, 1966). An analogy can be made of a car scrapyard. The cars that have been exposed in the yard for longest will have rusted most, and in that sense degree of rusting is correlated with yard residence time. Here we would not wish to say that the cars in the scrapyard were 'temporally organized'. However, it is possible to imagine an alternative scenario in which the scrapyard owner has deliberately organized the spatial layout of her yard in terms of the arrival dates of the cars (perhaps because she wishes to destroy all cars after they have been in the yard for a certain number of years). In such a case we would perhaps be less reluctant to describe the scrapyard as 'temporally organized'. This example activates the intuition that if we are to describe memory as temporally organized in more than an accidental way, or to say that time is an important dimension underpinning memorial representations, we would like to identify some functional or adaptive reason for such an organization. The later part of this chapter will provide just such reasons. But the simple fact of time-based forgetting is not in itself evidence for the temporal organization of memory in any interesting sense.

A second reason for being unwilling to infer 'temporal organization' from 'forgetting over time' is that fact that interference, rather than time-based decay, appears to be the causal factor that underpins forgetting. Psychologists have devoted much attention to delineating the factors that cause forgetting (see Crowder, 1976; McGeoch and Irion, 1952, for reviews), and the debate has often been cast as one between 'interference' and 'trace decay' as causal factors in forgetting. Interference accounts assume that memories becomes impossible to retrieve because they are overwritten by other memories, or because available retrieval cues do not uniquely identify the target memory. Decay accounts, in contrast, typically assume that there is some spontaneous degradation of memories over time, independently of any other causal factor. As only trace decay is explicitly a time-based factor, the fact that most evidence seems to favour interference-based rather than decay-based explanations of forgetting[2] further undermines the inference from 'forgetting over time' to 'temporally organized memories', and is instead consistent with the suggestion that the tendency for remote memories to be less memorable might simply be a consequence of some non-temporal causal factor.

Judgements of temporal recency

More direct evidence for the importance of elapsed time as an underlying organizational dimension of memory comes from the fact that subjects in psychological experiments can reliably make judgements about the relative temporal recency even of arbitrary and unrelated events. For example, if subjects are

---

[2] Although this is not universally accepted.

presented with all the letters of the alphabet in random order and are then presented with two letters from random positions in the list, they are able, with a reasonably high degree of accuracy, to judge which letter they viewed more recently (e.g. Hacker, 1980). Similar abilities have been demonstrated over much longer time-scales in both adults and children (e.g. Friedman, 1991; Friedman, Gardner, and Zubin, 1995; Friedman and Huttenlocher, 1997; Friedman and Kemp, 1998). This ability in itself does not provide strong evidence that memories are organized in terms of the amount of time elapsed between learning and retrieval, however, because accounts are possible that do not assume explicit availability of memories' position along a temporal dimension. Four general mechanisms that could underpin the ability to perform recency judgements can be distinguished, only one of which requires direct availability of time elapsed.

First, according to *familiarity* or *trace-strength* accounts, subjects may simply use the strength or availability of a memory trace as a proxy for the temporal recency of the episode (Morton, 1968). For example, if memories simply become weaker or less available over time (Hinrichs, 1970), and if temporal information is neither represented in memory nor causally responsible for the decline in retrievability over time, subjects could none the less perform the recency judgement task described above simply by comparing the strengths or availabilities of different memory traces. In terms of the car scrapyard analogy, this would be like equating 'rustier' with 'older'. How can this alternative account of our ability to make recency judgements be excluded? If the strength/familiarity were correct, subjects should have trouble distinguishing between familiar events and recent events (because if familiarity or memory availability is used as a proxy for recency, the two types of event should be psychologically indistinguishable). For example, imagine that on Monday and Tuesday you have red wine with your evening meal, while on Wednesday you have white wine. On Thursday you are asked whether you have drunk red wine or white wine more recently. You have no trouble in distinguishing the recent episode (white wine drinking) from the more frequent but less recent episode (red wine drinking). Psychologists have examined this question directly in recency judgement experiments by boosting the familiarity of some items by repeating them, and then examining whether subjects erroneously judge that they have encountered these familiar items more recently (see e.g. Morton, 1968). This is illustrated in Figure 3.2, which illustrates the case where a sequence of letters is presented, with one letter occurring twice, and then subjects are presented with two letters from the list (one of which occurred twice). Even if older memories have weaker strengths, Y may nevertheless have a higher strength than the more recent X, because Y is repeated. (In the diagram, at the time of testing when X and Y are presented together for recency judgement X has a 'strength' or 'familiarity' of 26.5, while Y has a total strength of $13.3 + 18.4 = 31.7$.)

Therefore, if strength is used as a proxy for recency, subjects may erroneously judge the more frequently presented item to be the more recent. Crucially, however, normal adults can generally distinguish between familiarity and

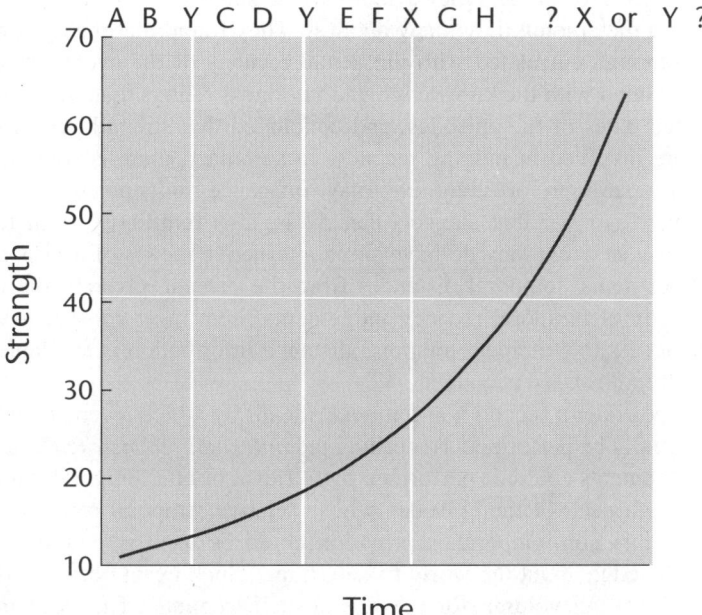

FIGURE 3.2. The summation of strengths due to repeated presentations of an item (see text for details).

recency, suggesting that they are not using strength/familiarity as a proxy for temporal recency (see also Flexser and Bower, 1974; Friedman and Kemp, 1998; Guttentag and Carroll, 1997; McCormack and Russell, 1997).[3] Hintzman and Block (1971) found that subjects can remember the two distinct temporal locations of a repeated item in a list—a result difficult to accommodate on a strength-based theory (see Crowder, 1976, for a review of relevant evidence).

The evidence is somewhat mixed, however: recency and familiarity are more likely to be confused by individuals with memory impairments (e.g. Mayes *et al.*, 1989), and accuracy in performing recency judgements may be reduced when familiarity and recency are set in opposition, as in the experiment described above (but see Flexser and Bower, 1974, for arguments that such effects do not in any case force the adoption of strength-based models). Furthermore, the vividness of memories can be related to recency judgements. Kemp and Burt (1998) asked subjects to squeeze a dynamometer with a strength proportional to the

---

[3] Whether or not a repeated old item will have a stronger memory representation than a non-repeated recent item will, of course, depend on rather detailed assumptions about the form and slope of the function relating elapsed time to memory strength. In implementing models of this process we have found that plausible strength-based models can for just this reason often distinguish recency from familiarity. Therefore the fact that humans can make the distinction does not exclude all familiarity-based accounts.

recency of a given event, and they also asked the subjects to rate the vividness of the event and the amount they knew about it. They found that the dynamometer readings, although correlated with the actual recency of the events, were more closely associated with the knowledge and vividness ratings than they were with the estimated dates of the episodes, and concluded that strength/distance-based metrics were involved in judging recency. In summary, there is some evidence that memory strength or vividness may influence judgements of temporal recency, but it is clear that subjects can distinguish familiarity from temporal recency, and hence that they do have some alternative means of access to information about items' temporal distances from the present. Overall, the findings from the study of temporal recency judgements seem most consistent with the claim that access to genuinely temporal distance information is available, rather than with strength-based accounts.

We now consider a second non-temporal means by which recency judgements could potentially be performed. According to *contextual reconstruction* accounts, recency judgements could be performed by retrieval of non-temporal information associated with each of the episodes whose relative temporal recency must be judged, and this non-temporal information could be used in conjunction with general knowledge about the world to determine which event occurred first (see Friedman, Ch. 5, this volume, for a review of such accounts). The idea here is that general, rather than specific and episodic, information about temporal relations is used.[4] For example, in deciding whether I wrote paper X before paper Y, I might remember that I wrote paper X on a more modern computer than the one I used to write paper Y. It is undoubtedly true that reconstructive processes of this type are often invoked in performing relative recency judgements. However, when subjects are required to make decisions about the relative recency of a pair of arbitrary and unrelated items, such as letters in a randomly ordered list, and there are no non-temporal contextual changes in the experimental environment, subjects can still decide which of a pair of items occurred first in the list (e.g. Hacker, 1980). Given that there has been no external contextual change that can be associated with the items, the most plausible basis for performing recency judgements is temporal position. Although it would always be possible to argue that there is some internal contextual change associated with the time course of an experiment (such as feelings of fatigue or boredom) such explanations would either risk unfalsifiability or simply reduce to the assumption of the existence of an internal clock of some kind. (We note, however, that some contextual models, such as that of Block (see Ch. 2, present volume) offer the prospect of a richer and more elaborated notion of 'context' than the purely time-based notion discussed here.) It therefore seems that, at least under circumstances where non-temporal cues are unavailable, a chronological dimension that underpins memory organization is both available and accessible.

----

[4] Although it is difficult to see how the general knowledge could be acquired except via the ability to represent such temporal relations episodically in the first place.

A third possibility is that every possible pairwise ordinal relation between every list item is explicitly stored and represented. Such an account seems implausible on computational grounds because of the combinatorial explosion that would ensue if all pairwise ordinal relations from a realistically long list were retained in memory, and there is independent evidence against the idea that chaining representations are used (see e.g. Burgess and Hitch, 1992; Henson *et al.*, 1996; although see Serra and Nairne, forthcoming; Stuart and Hulme, 2000). Although some accounts (e.g. Tzeng and Cotton, 1980) assume that explicit ordinal codes are formed at encoding between semantically related items ('study-phase retrieval'), it is difficult to see how such accounts can be extended to account for recency judgements on unrelated items.

The fourth and final account of relative recency judgement performance assumes that subjects do have information about the temporal recency of events available to them. It does appear from the study of judgements of temporal recency that some temporal information is associated with episodic memories. Such information seems more likely to be used in the short term than in the long term. When subjects are required to judge the relative temporal recency of events from the more distant past, factors such as reconstruction and the recruitment of general knowledge about the world are more often relevant. For example, if I have to judge the relative recency of my first house purchase and my first car purchase, I do this primarily by methods other than the simple reading-off of information about purely temporal recency. In the much shorter term, when no evidence other than the passage of time alone is available to determine the relative order of semantically unrelated events, it is more plausible that information about temporal recency is utilized. Thus the suggestion here is not that *only* information about time elapsed is used in making a temporal recency judgement. Rather, the suggestion is that such information is under some circumstances both the more available and most useful information for performing the task.

Given that temporal information seems to be retrieved and used to make temporal recency judgements under some conditions, while reconstructed information is used in others, two types of account are possible. A 'separate systems' account might suggest that temporal information is used in the short term, while non-temporal information is used in the long term. According to such a model, the evidence we have outlined above would provide little evidence for the chronological organization of long-term episodic memories. An alternative model is that there is no sharp distinction between the different conditions, and that a temporal dimension always underpins memory organization but there is a graded tendency for temporal information to become relatively less useful with the passage of time. We describe such a model below, as we believe there is considerable evidence to prefer it (Brown, Neath, and Chater, 2000). In any case, reconstructive accounts of temporal recency judgements for arbitrary events must themselves assume some form of chronological organization of memory, for without such organization there would be no way for chronologically proximal items to activate one another as is necessary if general world knowledge is subsequently to be brought to bear on the judgement. Thus one recent model of date estimation (Kemp, 1999) explicitly assumes that memories can be accessed in order of their temporal proximity to a target item.

Temporally adjacent items are confusable in memory

A third source of evidence in favour of the idea that memories are chronologically organized is the observation that in many domains of human memory items the relative temporal position of items is more likely to be confused when those items occur close together in time. In human speech production, for example, errors in which phonemes are inadvertently exchanged often occur (e.g. '**p**ick as a **s**arrot' for '**s**ick as a **p**arrot'). A striking characteristic of such errors is that they are much more likely to occur between nearby phonemes than between distant phonemes (subject to syllabic position constraints: MacKay, 1970; Vousden and Brown, 1998; Vousden, Brown, and Harley, 2000). Similar constraints occur in everyday tasks such as remembering telephone numbers or arbitrary lists of letters (e.g. Healy, 1974). For example, if subjects are required to recall the sequence K B R D F X in order, they may erroneously recall it as K B R **F D** X, that is, with the fourth and fifth items recalled in the wrong relative order. However, a recall such as K **F** R D **B** X, in which items further apart have exchanged, is much less likely. Similar effects are observed in other domains of human sequential behaviour such as typing and playing the piano. It seems, therefore, that there is a tendency to confuse temporally proximal items. If so, this would further suggest that memory is temporally organized.

As in the case of temporal recency judgements, however, it is necessary to exclude alternative, non-temporal, interpretations of human performance. At least three types of account could explain the predominance of nearby exchanges of this type. First, it may be that temporally nearby items are indeed confusable because they have similar representations in memory due to temporal information being a part of those representations. A second, non-temporal, possibility is that the memory representations are similar (and hence confusable) for items that occupy similar *positions* in a list. Thus the second and third items in a list are positionally closer to one another than are the second and fourth items, irrespective of the temporal relationships between those items. Although memories that incorporate positional information do not directly represent the relative order of items, temporal order information can easily be inferred. Finally, it may be that the memory representation of a given item incorporates that item's ordinal (i.e. not positional or temporal) relations to other items. Ordinal information for a pair of items would specify which item of the pair came first in the list, without explicitly representing information about the absolute list position of either of the items. If such ordinal relations are more likely to be represented accurately for ordinally close items, the observed data could be explained.

It is therefore necessary to consider cases in which temporal, positional, and ordinal position are unconfounded. Such experiments have been conducted by

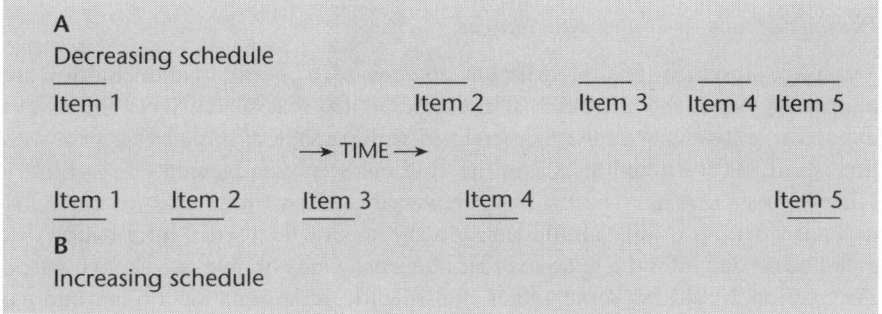

FIGURE 3.3. Illustration of increasing and decreasing presentation schedules for a list of items in a memory task.

Ian Neath and his colleagues (e.g. Crowder and Neath, 1991; Neath and Crowder, 1990, 1996). These experiments separate temporal and ordinal position by increasing or decreasing the rate of presentation of items in a list in the manner depicted in Figure 3.3. In Condition B the first, second, and third items in the list occur relatively close to each other in time, while the fourth and fifth items are more widely separated in time. In Condition A, the reverse is the case. Subjects are required to recall as many items as possible from sequences of words presented in these different ways. If items that are temporally close in the list are represented as such in memory, then performance should be relatively worse on the early list items from Condition A, but the late list items from Condition B. If, in contrast, it is purely positional or ordinal information that is represented in memory, there is no reason to expect these conditions to differ. Typical results from such experiments reveal that items that occurred relatively close to one another in time are less well remembered (Neath and Crowder, 1996), consistent with the suggestion that some form of temporal (not merely positional or ordinal) information is stored with items in memory. Such data have motivated many psychological theorists to develop models in which temporally proximal items are assigned memory representation that are more similar to one another than are memory representations of items more widely separated in time (e.g. Burgess, 1995; Burgess and Hitch, 1996; Henson, 1998; Houghton, 1990; Brown, Preece, and Hulme, 2000; but see Henson, 1999).

The experiments reviewed in the above paragraphs explicitly require subjects to reconstruct the serial order of items, and it may be that this emphasis causes memories to be temporally organized at encoding in a task-specific manner. However, even when unordered recall is required, subjects show a strong unprompted tendency to recall temporally adjacent items together (e.g. Laming, 1999), providing further evidence of an underlying temporal organization. Furthermore, temporally adjacent items tend to have their positions recalled in the wrong relative order even after quite long periods, such as twenty-four hours (Nairne, 1992) or weeks or more (Huttenlocher, Hedges, and Prohaska, 1988, 1992).

Passage of time or contextual change?

We have presented several different sources of evidence that memories are temporally organized. However it could be argued that such effects are always due to contextual change that is correlated with passage of time, rather than with time itself. As we noted above, in the case of recency judgements for arbitrary related events that have occurred in the very recent past (e.g. a list of randomly ordered letters) it is difficult to identify non-temporal contextual information that could be used to infer the relative order of events. One possible candidate for such information would be some rather non-specific representation of the internal cognitive state that obtained at the time of episode learning. If the rate of change of such contextual information was correlated with the passage of time, retrieval of this contextual information assumed to be associated with each item could be used to infer relative recency. A contextual account of this type could only account for such results on the assumption that changes in the context associated with each item are very highly correlated with the amount of time passing between each item's occurrence. If the correlation were perfect, such a contextual mechanism would effectively be operating as a clock. Indeed, as we show below, a good quantitative fit to such data can be given by formal models that assume items are represented in terms of their position along a temporal dimension using clock-like oscillatory mechanisms (see Brown, Preece, and Hulme, 2000; Brown and Vousden, 1998; Burgess and Hitch, 1992; 1996).

It is clearly difficult to distinguish between mechanism-level accounts in which some kind of simple internal cognitive contextual representation changes gradu-ally in a way that is correlated with the passage of time, and accounts in which there are internal 'clocks' of some kind. The fact that both animals and humans are able accurately to reproduce short time intervals without external time-providing cues strongly suggests that they possess some internal analogue of clocks. But what 'clock' normally refers to in such a context is some physical mechanism which has a rate of change that correlates with the passage of actual time. Therefore, at least over short intervals, it is possible in principle to give an account of simple animal timing behaviours in terms of a dynamically changing internal contextual milieu, but only at the cost of assuming that rate of contextual change is perfectly correlated with the passage of time. In such a case the mechanisms that instantiate the putative contextual change incorporate the relevant functions of clocks. If on the other hand non-temporal factors can give rise to contextual change, then a separate role for chronological organization needs to be preserved.

PSYCHOLOGICAL MODELS: RELATIONS BETWEEN TIME AND MEMORY

In the previous section, we adduced evidence consistent with the claim that an important part of memory representations is information about the time elapsed since the remembered event occurred. Before going on to consider possible reasons for this (in terms of the adaptive utility of such a system), we summarize some recent trends in models that have been developed to account for human and animal timing behaviour and episodic memory. We seek to establish two points. The first is that researchers working in independent traditions (episodic memory and timing behavior) have developed models of memory and timing that are in important respects remarkably similar. The second is that several current models of human memory accord an essential role to temporal representation in memory formation and retrieval. Such models also enable us to give a more precise meaning to the idea of temporal organization in the context of memory over different time-scales.

Models of timing

Models of animal timing have been developed to account for animals' ability to represent, remember, and respond on the basis of learned temporal durations. For example, animals can learn that they will be rewarded for the first response they make after a fixed amount of time has elapsed (the 'peak procedure', e.g. Roberts, 1981). After such an interval has been learned, animals' responding can be seen to reach a peak level at or about the time at which a reward has been experienced in the past, indicating that some representation of the remembered temporal interval is available to guide behaviour. Using different experimental procedures ('temporal bisection'), animals can learn to respond selectively to stimuli of a specific duration (e.g. Church and Deluty, 1977). Furthermore, the precision of animals' temporal representations is evident in more naturalistic foraging situations (e.g. Bateson and Kacelnik, 1996; Brunner, Kacelnik, and Gibbon, 1996; see Gallistel, 1990, for a review). Several different specific models have been developed to account for the wealth of empirical data obtained from such tasks (see Wearden, Ch. 1, this volume, for a review), but for present purposes we can divide these into two categories.

The scalar timing model of Gibbon and colleagues assumes the existence of a clock-like central pulse generator. While a to-be-learned duration is unfolding, pulses from this generator accumulate in a working memory, which provides a basis for the comparison of stored and experienced durations (see Wearden, 1994, and Ch. 1 above, for a review). Many detailed features of the model are responsible for its success in accounting for data from a wide range of experimental paradigms. Here, however, the crucial element is the clock-like aspect of the pulse generator plus working memory. The effect of these mechanisms is that temporal durations are effectively represented in memory as a number (of pulses), with larger numbers representing longer intervals. Recent work (e.g. Harrington, Haaland, and Hermanowicz, 1998) has discussed how such mechanisms may be implemented neurobiologically. An alternative, but related, account was developed by Church and Broadbent (1990). The Church and Broadbent model assumes the existence of an array of thresholded oscillators, with some oscillators

(a)

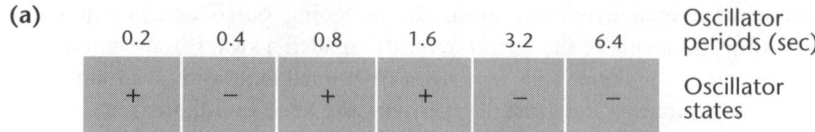

(b)

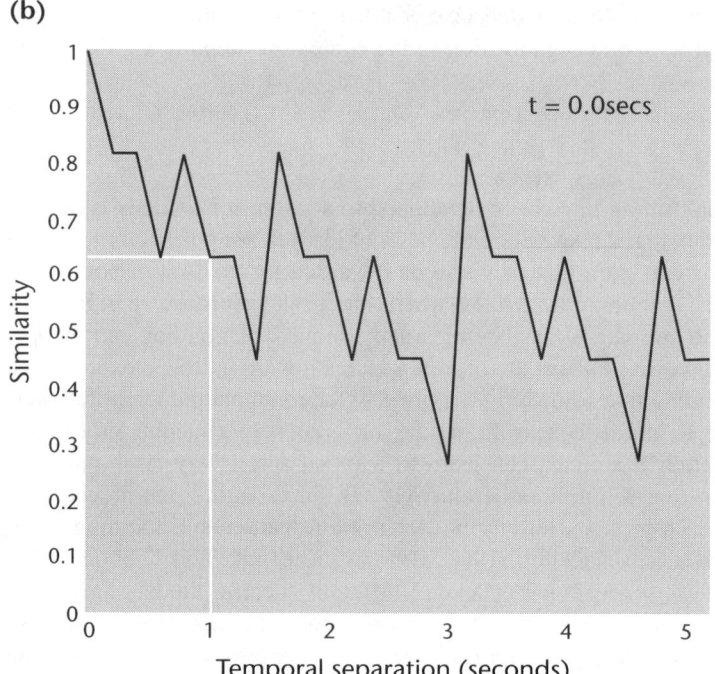

FIGURE 3.4. (*a*) The oscillator-based contextual-clock signal used by Church and Broadbent (1980). (*b*) The similarity function of the contextual-clock signal used by Church and Broadbent (1980).

changing their state much more often than others (Figure 3.4*a*). For example, one oscillator might change its state between −1 and +1 every 200 ms, while the next oscillator changes its state every 400 ms, the next every 800 ms, and so on. The net result of this system is that the array of oscillators acts a bit like a clock-face with many different hands—some fast and some slow. The thresholded nature of the oscillators simply means that each hand moves round the clock in discrete steps rather than a smooth continuous motion. Generally similar behaviour can be obtained from a number of different mechanisms; it is not necessary, for example, that successively slower oscillators are exactly twice as slow as their faster neighbours. Such a mechanism allows relatively distinct representations to be assigned to points nearby in time (because the fast changing oscillators will have switched state after relatively short intervals). However, different representations can also be assigned to points in time that lie arbitrarily far away from each other in real time, because the slowest oscillator can be made as slow as is required for this to be the case (or because, more plausibly in the context of long temporal intervals, other non-repeating factors influence the composition of the signal). In summary, the state of the array of oscillators as a whole is used to represent temporal states. Church and Broadbent show that this model can account for a range of empirical data concerning animal timing. Wearden and Doherty (1995) identify some difficulties for the model (see also Wearden, Ch. 1, this volume), but the central point for present purposes is the nature of the temporal representations employed in this oscillator-based clock signal. The state of the signal gradually changes over time, as illustrated in Figure 3.4*b*. Thus states of the signal that are close to one another in time are more similar than are states more distant in time, rather like an analogue clock-face (the representations of 3.05 and 3.10 are generally more similar to one another than are the representations of 3.05 and 3.20). Like a clock-face, the states of an oscillator-based control signal will eventually repeat themselves, although this can be prevented by the inclusion of arbitrarily slow-moving oscillators. Also, as illustrated in Figure 3.4*b*, the decline in similarity between states of the signal as a function of their temporal separation may not be monotonic, although it can be made arbitrarily close to monotonic (as in our own model described below). However, the general tendency for temporally adjacent states of the signal to be similar to one another allows temporal generalization to occur.[5] In terms of the Church and Broadbent (1990) model, for example, imagine that an animal has been trained to produce a reward after a fixed period of time (say 20 seconds). The reward-producing action is associated with the state of the clock-like signal after 20 seconds. On future occasions, the 20-second state of the signal will lead to the highest probability of responding, but similar temporal periods (18 seconds, or 20 seconds) will also be associated with a high probability of responding just to the extent that the representations of 18 or 22 seconds are similar to the representation of 20 seconds. This is just the behaviour that is observed experimentally in the 'peak procedure' task.

In summary, the array of available models have all proved highly successful in accounting for empirical data in both animals and humans, and the success of such models can be seen as strong evidence for the existence of clock-like mechanisms (e.g. neurobiological oscillators) that can be recruited to underpin performance on tasks where representations of temporal durations are essential.

[5] To the extent that the similarity function is non-monotonic, temporally distant memories may become confused. As illustrated in Figure 3.4, for example, states of the signal that are 0.6 s and 1 s away are equally similar to the reference time, and so their temporal distances cannot be distinguished by similarity. Such problems can be overcome be averaging noisy versions of the signal.

Models of memory

Researchers in the field of human memory have independently developed models to account for human memory performance on memory tasks involving recall of the temporal or serial order of events. What is striking is that many of the most recent successful models make use of oscillator-based clock-like representations very similar to that discussed in the context of animal timing by Church and Broadbent (1990). Items are stored in memory by associating them with states of the clock-like signal. Although such models have typically been applied to memory over relatively short periods, they are now being extended to account for similar phenomena over much longer time-scales. We now briefly describe these models.

Oscillator-based models of memory.   Several recent models of memory for serial order are based around the assumption successive items in a sequence become associated to successive states of a time-varying control or learning-context signal (Brown, Preece, and Hulme, 2000; Brown and Vousden, 1998; Burgess, 1995; Burgess and Hitch, 1992, 1996; Glasspool, 1995; Gupta, 1996; Hartley and Houghton, 1996; Henson, 1998; Henson and Burgess, 1998; Hitch *et al.*, 1996; Houghton, 1990, 1994). In other words, a series of item-to-context associations is learned. Our own model of memory for order, OSCAR (for OSCillator-based Associative Recall) uses an array of oscillators, of different frequencies, to provide the dynamic learning-context signal to which successive items in a sequence become associated. The resulting learning-context signal is similar in many respects to that of Church and Broadbent (1990) described above, although the function that related the similarity of successive states of the signal to their temporal separation is smoother (see Figure 3.5); this is important to the successful functioning of the model.

The full model, which is implemented in the form of a computer program, is described in Brown, Preece, and Hulme (2000). Here we just describe the general principles of operation. Successive states of the dynamic learning-context signal can be seen as analogous to successive states of a clock-face. The memory of a sequence of items (e.g. a list of letters to be recalled in order) is analogous to a set of associations between successively presented list items and successive states of the clock-face. For example, suppose that the sequence of items A B C D must be learned, starting at 2.00. Item A might be associated to the representation of 2.00; item B to 2.05; C to 2.10, and D to 2.15. This set of four learned item-to-context associations is the stored memory representation of the sequence.

Recall of the sequence is enabled by a process analogous to rewinding the clock to its state at the start of list-learning. After this initial state (2.00) has been specified, successive states (2.05, 2.10, etc.) are obtained 'for free' as the clock runs forward under its own intrinsic dynamics. Each state of the learning-context signal can be used as a probe to recall each successive list item.

The implementation of these models is complex, but they can account for a

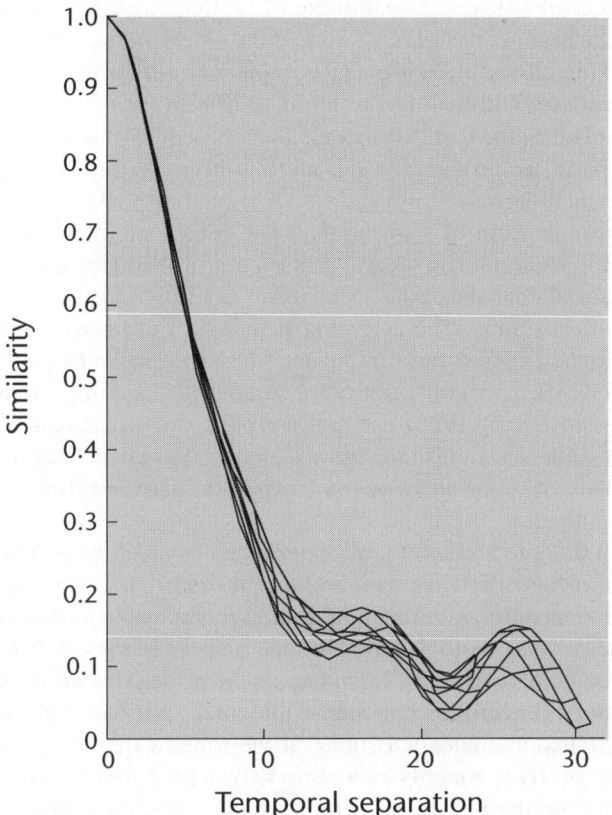

FIGURE 3.5. The similarity function of the contextual-clock signal used in Brown, Preece, and Hulme (2000).

wide range of memory data (e.g. Brown, Preece, and Hulme, 2000). In particular, they can account for the experimental evidence we brought forward in the first section of this chapter to support the claim that memory is chronologically organized. For example, temporally (rather than positionally or ordinally) adjacent items in a sequence are likely to become confused in memory, because they are associated with similar retrieval cues (i.e. similar states of the oscillator-based learning-context signal). Furthermore, with the addition of oscillators of particular frequencies, such models can account for hierarchical effects in memory (such as effects of temporal grouping) and memory over both short and long timescales (see Brown, Preece, and Hulme, 2000).

Relation to timing models. It can be seen that this kind of model of memory is essentially identical to the model of animal timing behaviour developed by Church and Broadbent (1990). In both models, actions are associated to states of a time-varying clock-line contextual or control signal, in such a way that actions will be elicited whenever the relevant state of the clock/contextual signal is reproduced. In the Church and Broadbent model, just one action (e.g. a pigeon pecking a key to produce food) will be produced, at or near the temporal interval that has been rewarded. In the OSCAR model, a whole sequence of actions (recalling items from a list) are produced, each after a different time. Thus short-term memory for serial order, as in tasks such as remembering a telephone number, can be seen as a simple kind of sequential motor behaviour (see also Brown and Vousden, 1998). We note that several motor control theorists (e.g. Rosenbaum, 1985) have argued that the same mechanism controls movement ordering as controls movement timing. The correct sequencing of events is sometimes seen as secondary to their correct timing (but see MacKay, 1987*a*, *b*).

Thus the OSCAR model of memory for serial order, and other similar models (e.g. Burgess and Hitch, 1996) can be interpreted as time-stamping memory models, in the sense that episodic memories are associated with their time of occurrence relative to some anchor point (such as the start of a to-be-remembered list).

However, in order to account for all the relevant psychological data (including data from judgements of relative temporal recency) such models of memory need to be extended to incorporate a temporal distance component. Fortunately, temporal distance metrics can come 'for free' in such models. In the OSCAR model, for example, the temporal distance of any memory can be determined simply in terms of the similarity between the temporal-contextual signal associated with that item, and the temporal-contextual signal at the time of determination. Because such similarity declines roughly monotonically with temporal separation (see Figure 3.5) the similarity between the current context and the remembered context can be used as a proxy for temporal distance of the memory. In terms of the clock-face analogy, this is like assessing the recency of a 3.05 item and a 3.10 item at 3.15. Because 3.10 is more similar to 3.15 than is 3.05, it can be concluded that the 3.10 item is more temporally recent (Brown, Preece, and Hulme, 2000). Such similarity need not be the outcome of a process of explicit comparison, but can be viewed instead as an implicit property of the system at any given point in time. Provided that item-to-context associations are separate and do not sum together (Brown *et al.*, 1999), such a model can readily distinguish between recency and familiarity.

Note from Figure 3.5 that the similarity between two states of the temporal-contextual signal declines quickly over short temporal separations (because of high frequency oscillators) but only more slowly at longer temporal intervals. This means that two memories separated by unit time in the recent past will possess more temporally distinctive locations in memory than will two memories separated by unit time when the two memories are further in the past. Thus, given the similarity function in Figure 3.5, signals 5, 10, and 15 time units back in the past will have similarities to the present signal of approximately 0.65, 0.3, and 0.15 respectively. The values associated with the two more temporally distant memories (0.3 and 0.15) are much more similar than are the values for the two more recent memories (0.65 and 0.3), and therefore more recent memories will be more easily distinguishable along the temporal distance dimension.

This general picture is consistent with the observation we made earlier to the effect that evidence for the chronological organization of memory comes mainly from memory tasks carried out over relatively short periods of time. Over longer periods, the relative lack of temporal distinctiveness means that other (e.g. reconstructive) processes will assume relatively greater importance in temporal dating whenever additional information is available.

The OSCAR model has not been applied in detail to general unordered recall from long-term memory, but instead focuses on memory for order over both long and (especially) short periods. We have therefore more recently attempted to capture the temporal distance features of the model in a simpler (and more tractable) mathematical framework, and this model has been applied to serial recall, unordered ('free') recall, and human timing data directly. Furthermore, the model is intended to apply to memory over all time-scales, not just the short-term.

A temporal distance model of memory: SIMPLE

SIMPLE (for Scale Invariant Memory, Perception, and LEarning) is a model of memory that we developed (Brown, Neath, and Chater, 2000) to capture directly the notion that a central dimension underpinning the representation of all episodic memories (over both short and long time-scales) is the amount of time that has elapsed since that memory was laid down—the temporal distance of the memory. The model is intended to apply to both episodic memory as traditionally conceived, and also memory over much shorter time-scales normally associated with concepts such as 'short-term memory' and 'free recall'. Brown, Neath, and Chater (2000) summarize evidence consistent with the idea that similar principles govern memory performance over all time-scales (see e.g. Anderson and Schooler, 1991; Rubin and Wenzel, 1996; Nairne, 1991, 1992); this temporal 'Scale Invariance' in memory is central to the SIMPLE model. According to the model the retrieval of a memory involves locating a region in psychological space (memory) that is sufficiently well specified that it contains only the target memory and no others. To the extent that a region of psychological memory space is psychologically crowded (e.g. for memories far in the past), a given retrieval cue will be less likely to activate the target memory uniquely. Indeed, often an important part of this retrieval cue will simply be the temporal distance of the memory (especially when relatively short retention intervals are involved). Whether or not position along a remembered temporal dimension forms the primary retrieval cue, all items in memory are located in terms of their position along a temporal dimension even though positional information along this dimension may be increasingly less accurate and available as items recede into the past.

Thus, according to the model, memories can be discriminated from one another in terms of their distance along the dimension of 'time elapsed' in exactly the same way as a set of tones may be discriminated from one another in terms of their position along a frequency dimension, or objects may be discriminated from one another in terms of their position along a weight dimension, etc. (Murdock, 1960).

Crowder (1976) famously introduced a related temporal-spatial analogy to account for the fact that temporally distant items will become harder to identify (i.e. forgetting will occur):

The items in a memory list, being presented at a constant rate, pass by with the same regularity as do telephone poles when one is on a moving train. The crucial assumption is that just as each telephone pole in the receding distance becomes less and less distinctive from its neighbours, likewise each item in the memory list becomes less distinctive from the other list items as the presentation episode recedes into the past. Therefore, retrieval probability is assumed to depend on discriminability of traces from each other. (Crowder, 1976: 462)

This basic idea captures the idea that the retrievability of items from memory will have ratio-like qualities—that is, the relative discriminability (and hence retrievability) of two items will depend on the ratio of their temporal distances. Thus memories learned one hour and two hours ago will, in the absence of other factors, be as discriminable from one another as will memories learned ten minutes and twenty minutes ago. This kind of ratio-like scale invariant quality of temporal memory has been identified and characterized by many researchers (Bjork and Whitten, 1974; Glenberg *et al.*, 1983).

The SIMPLE model is not quite an instantiation of the telephone pole analogy, for SIMPLE assumes that the retrievability of a memory will be determined not just by the nearest temporal neighbour of a word, but by all the temporally close neighbours (with the interference from a neighbour reducing as that neighbour is more temporally distant, so that items are harder to retrieve from crowded regions of temporal space). Furthermore, as we show below, unlike the telegraph pole model SIMPLE does not assume that only a single temporal dimension can be represented—hierarchical temporal representations are possible. The model operates along generally similar principles to those assumed to take place in simple categorization tasks (e.g. Nosofsky, 1986). More specifically, the SIMPLE model assumes that items in memory are represented in terms of their position along a logarithmically transformed dimension of 'time elapsed since memory formation' (see Figure 3.6). Part of the retrieval cue for a given item is assumed often to be an imprecise representation of the position of an item along this 'time-elapsed' dimension. The similarity of the value of the retrieval cue to the value of the retrieval cues for every item in memory is calculated, with similarity being an exponential function of distance along the logarithmically transformed temporal distance measure. The probability of retrieving a given item is then proportional to the similarity of the retrieval cue to that item's temporal dimension value relative to the similarity of the retrieval cue to all items' temporal dimension values. Memories will, of course, be represented in terms of their positions along other

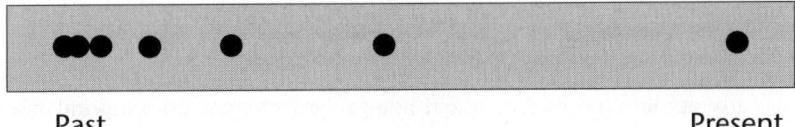

Past   Present

FIGURE 3.6. Items arrayed along a logarithmically transformed temporal dimension. Items become closer to one another on the temporal dimension as they recede into the past.

dimensions, and these values may also form retrieval cues (see Brown, Neath, and Chater, 2000, for full details).

The result of this simple mechanism is that items are more easily retrievable when they are in less crowded regions along the time-elapsed dimension. Thus, for example, more recent items will be more easily recalled, because the memory representations of recent episodes are more widely spaced. The SIMPLE model can also account for retrieval of memories from more complex (multidimensional) psychological spaces along the same principles. Brown, Neath, and Chater (2000) show that this kind of model can account for several dozen empirical results from the study of free recall; serial recall, and perceptual identification experiments, using the same kind of psychological principles as are used in exemplar-based models of categorization (e.g. Nosofksy, 1986); and perhaps perceptual grouping (Kubovy, Holcombe, and Wagemans, 1998), and attention (Wolfe, 1994). To the extent that the model is successful in accounting for memory data, it is consistent with the claim of the present chapter that time is an important underlying dimension of memory, in that temporal distance may be used as a retrieval cue.

A major advantage of this kind of account is that the same framework can be used to characterize many different aspects of human perceptual identification, categorization, and episodic memory. Thus temporal location can be used as an identifying cue using exactly the same psychological mechanisms as spatial location, or indeed location along any psychological dimension (cf. Shum, 1998). More specifically, the same psychological machinery assumed to be used to identify, for example, a tone from other tones of different frequencies, or a weight from other different weights, can be used to identify a memory of a given temporal distance from other memories with different temporal distances. This is advantageous because the relevant psychological mechanisms have been widely investigated and are relatively well understood.

Due to the logarithmic compression of the temporal scale, the SIMPLE model also assumes that the same principles govern memory over all time-scales (see Brown, Neath and Chater, 2000, for extensive discussion) consistent with a range of psychological evidence (Nairne, 1992; Wixted and Ebbesen, 1991, 1997) and with the suggestion that scale invariance in the mind is reflected in scale invariance in cognitive and perceptual processes (Chater and Brown, 1999).

Thus the SIMPLE model as applied to memory instantiates the assumption that 'time elapsed' is an important organizational dimension of memory and, by making such an assumption, is able to account for a very wide range of data obtained from the study of human memory. Exactly the same model has been successfully applied to children's and adults' performance on temporal interval estimation tasks (McCormack *et al.*, 1999). The wide-ranging success of this and other models can be seen as evidence consistent with the basic mechanism of temporal organization that they assume to underpin memory over many different time-scales.

How does this kind of model relate to the oscillator-based timing and memory representations described earlier? The SIMPLE model provides a higher-level, more abstract characterization of the idea that is expressed at an implementational level by the OSCAR memory model. The OSCAR model provides a mechanism by which representations of episodes can become associated to representations of an internal time-varying clock-like signal; OSCAR also instantiates the assumption that episodes that have occurred in close temporal proximity will, other things being equal, have more confusable memory representations from the temporal perspective of retrieval. Oscillator-based models also specify the mechanism by which a sequence of temporal retrieval cues can be generated, and also can be used to specify the implementation-level mechanism by which temporally distal episodes have representations that are more confusable along the temporal distance dimension. Hierarchical temporal representations can be represented in both models—as an additional dimension of memory organization in the SIMPLE model, or in terms of repeating oscillators within the OSCAR model.

Summary

The claim being made here is essentially a psychological one. The claim is that the most successful current models of human memory for serial order, and perhaps of human memory more generally, are showing encouraging signs of convergence. Specifically, they are converging on the idea that models must accord a central role to temporal representation in memory retrieval if we are to arrive at a psychological understanding of human memory, its successes, and its limitations.

WHY TIME AND MEMORY ARE RELATED: ADAPTIVE ANALYSES

The previous sections of this chapter have reviewed evidence that time is an important underlying dimension of memory, and have shown how timing mechanisms are central to many current models of memory. However, we have as yet given no attention to the question of *why* this should be so. We attempt to remedy this here.

Three types of consideration are relevant to such an understanding. First, at a design level timing and memory mechanisms need to be closely related because there are links between the time elapsed since a memory was laid down and the probability of retrieval of that memory being necessary. This has been made clear by the analyses of J. R. Anderson and his colleagues (e.g. Anderson and Milson, 1989; Anderson and Schooler, 1991; Schooler and Anderson, 1997); we outline the relevant work below. Secondly, animal timing, memory, and sequential behaviour can be seen to have common roots in simple animal navigation and foraging behaviours (e.g. Bateson and Kacelnik, 1997; Brown and Vousden, 1998; Gallistel, 1990). Thus memory and timing may have common developmental or evolutionary origins. Thirdly, human memory and timing capacities may have common origins in terms of the common ontogenetic or phylogenetic mechanisms used to underpin them. We deal with these three arguments in turn.

Adaptive approaches

Of particular interest in the present context is the rational modelling approach (e.g. J. R. Anderson, 1990; Shepard, 1987). This research tradition aims to understand human cognitive behaviour as an adaptive reflection of the statistical structure of the environment. J. R. Anderson and Milson (1989) and Anderson and Schooler (1991) have applied the rational modelling methodology to the case of forgetting from memory. In particular they focus on why we forget, and on why the forgetting curve (i.e. the curve that characterizes loss of memory retrievability over time) has the particular form that it does. A central plank of the rational modelling approach involves an initial analysis of the statistical structure of the relevant aspects of the world, as only after this analysis is it possible to determine whether human psychological processing mechanisms, such as memory, are adapted to a world with that structure. In the case of memory, Anderson and his colleagues identified the relevant characteristic of the world as being concerned with the changing probability, over time, that some piece of information would need to be retrieved from memory. Assuming that there is some cost to retrieving memories, memories that are more likely to have to be recalled (that have a high 'need probability', in Anderson's terms) should be more memorable. In other words, the retrievability of a memory in the human cognitive system should be related at any given time to the probability that the memory will need to be accessed.

By examining a variety of domains (e.g. the times of arrival of e-mail messages from different senders), Anderson and his colleagues demonstrated that the probability of access to some piece of information (e.g. information about the sender of an e-mail message) being needed declines monotonically as a function of the time since the same information was last required, in exactly the same way as memory retrievability declines over time. More specifically, it was argued that the mathematical form of the forgetting curve of human memory is exactly the same as the form of the curve that describes the decline over time in the probability that some piece of information will be retrievable (J. R. Anderson and Schooler, 1991; see also R. B. Anderson, 1998). Thus the suggestion is that memory is organized to reflect the probabilities that memories will need to be retrieved, and that these probabilities are themselves a function of the temporal distance of the events to be remembered.

Of course contextual factors are also relevant—the 'need probability' of a memory will be determined not only by the amount of time that has elapsed, but also by the similarity between the context of initial learning and the context with respect to which need probability is calculated (Schooler and Anderson, 1997). Such factors are also taken into account in the approach of Anderson and his colleagues; here we have presented a simplified approach. However, the suggestion is clear: it may be that possession of a chronologically organized memory enables adaptive retrieval probabilities.

Foraging

Timing ability, memory for temporal durations, and episodic memory are all central to simple animal foraging and navigation behaviours, which provide one possible ecological basis for human episodic memory. Time of day information, and the ability to remember the day-time at which particular sources of food are available, are made use of by many animals in both navigation and foraging (see Gallistel, 1990, for a review). In addition to the role of timing mechanisms in navigation to food locations, birds make near-optimal decisions on when to leave a patch of food and travel to another, taking into account the time spent on the current patch, the yield of the current patch, and the energy expenditure required to travel to a different patch (e.g. Brunner, Kacelnik, and Gibbon, 1996). Such decision requires accurate timing ability.

Clayton and Dickinson (1998) have shown that animals can make use of remembered duration information to make choices between different sources of food, and show preference reversals that take account of the perishability over time of certain food types. They argued that this constitutes evidence for episodic-like memory in these animals (see Griffiths, Dickinson, and Clayton, 1999). Elsewhere, we have argued that simple oscillator-based timing mechanisms, of the type that may have evolved to subserve the control of internally generated foraging-related sequential behaviour, can be viewed as having provided the evolutionary foundation for human memory for serial order (Brown and Vousden, 1998). Finally, it is important to remember both the temporal and spatial locations of food sources—important events need to be linked to both the spatial and temporal content of their occurrence (Gallistel, 1990); it would therefore not be surprising if similar mechanisms, perhaps hippocampal, may have evolved to do both.

In summary, there is ample evidence that time and memory are involved in basic foraging behaviour. Many current models of memory can be seen as evolutionary extensions of these same basic mechanisms. More particularly, foraging considerations can help to understand the particular links between psychological representations of space, memory, and time. The evidence for these links takes two specific forms. First of all, regarding the energy expenditure required to reach a nutrition source, time and distance can be seen as equivalent in that longer distances equate to longer times. Secondly, both spatial and temporal discounting occur, in that rewards are less valuable to the extent that they are temporally or spatially distant. Furthermore, both temporal and spatial discounting seem to be describable by similar (hyperbolic, or power law) functions (Kacelnik, 1998; Wixted and Ebbesen, 1991). Shum (1998) has described the way in which the use of 'temporal landmarks' may be used in memory retrieval; such use of landmarks to navigate one's way around a chronologically organized memory is strikingly similar to the way in which spatial landmarks are used by animals to locate themselves with respect to the physical world.

It is therefore not surprising that spatial metaphors for episodic memory are so compelling (cf. Crowder's telephone pole analogy described earlier). But despite the similarities between space and time, there is an important difference between them with regard to episodic memory. The association of memories to temporal-contextual cues allows a unique address in memory (i.e. an unambiguous retrieval cue) to be given to each episodic memory. The association of memories solely to spatial-contextual cues, in contrast, would not provide a unique address for each memory, because spatial locations can be visited on more than one occasion and so more than one memory could be attached to a given location cue. Note that this only applies to episodic memory: multiple events that occurred at the same time but at different locations can, of course, be represented in general memory without difficulty.

Dynamical systems

Our final argument for a close relationship between time and memory comes from a consideration of the kinds of implementation-level mechanisms that may have evolved to subserve them. There has been much recent interest in the kinds of dynamic, orderly behaviour that can emerge in complex interconnected dynamical systems (e.g. Kauffman, 1993). As Kauffman and others have shown in studies of self-organizing networks, 'order for free' can emerge spontaneously in complex interconnected systems. Because oscillatory dynamics emerge spontaneously in such networks (of which the brain is an example), they provide a natural building-block for dynamic cognitive theories (Brown and Vousden, 1998). As we noted above, we (Brown, Neath, and Chater, 2000; Brown, Preece, and Hulme, 2000; Vousden and Brown, 1998) and others (Burgess and Hitch, 1996; Henson and Burgess, 1998) have shown that oscillatory dynamics can provide a good account of the detailed pattern of data in speech production and short-term memory for serial order. As we also noted above, similar oscillatory systems are involved in some models of timing (Church and Broadbent, 1990; Gallistel, 1990). Thus memory and timing may be related in an important further sense, in that they can both be seen as behaviours that make use of the same kinds of underlying oscillatory mechanisms—mechanisms of the type that we may expect to be available 'for free' in complex interconnected dynamical systems such as the brain.

SUMMARY

We have provided some evidence that time is an important dimension along which memory is organized, and we have also reviewed evidence for the adaptive significance of such a system. In this final section we briefly address a variety of arguments that have been used against the idea that memories are not temporally organized. For example, Friedman (Ch. 5, present volume) argues that 'events are not chronologically organized in memory' and that there is no 'special system for assigning temporal codes to individual memories'.

First of all, we emphasize that the claim here is not that time is the only dimension underpinning memory organization. Rather, our claim is that time is always a factor, although it will be of relatively little importance under conditions where other retrieval and organizational cues are available or of greater utility (e.g. when general knowledge about the world can be brought to bear, or when more temporally distant memories are concerned), and of relatively greater importance after short time intervals and under conditions where other, non-temporal, cues are unavailable. It is no accident that most of the evidence we have cited in favour of the chronological dimension comes from experiments where memory is examined over relatively short time-frames (minutes rather than years) and where there are few non-temporal cues available to date or retrieve memories (because memory for arbitrary and unrelated materials is examined in relatively constant experimental contexts).

Argument 1. Recency judgements are made by non-temporal means.   The fact that temporal recency (as indexed by grip force) is more strongly related to rated memory vividness than is dating (Kemp and Burt, 1998), after actual date has been controlled for, does suggest that some kind of strength measure can be used in recency judgement, and that separate reconstructive processes are involved to a greater extent in date estimation than in the grip force task. As we noted above, the apparent occasional tendency to confuse recency with frequency (Morton, 1968), even when item memory is controlled for (Flexser and Bower, 1974), is also consistent with a role for some kind of familiarity dimension in the judgement of absolute recency (although Flexser and Bower themselves report evidence they take to be consistent with a multiple-trace model). However, all that these examples show is that non-temporal factors can enter into temporal dating and/or recency judgements. They do not show that temporal factors are not involved in the process. And, as we demonstrated above, there is ample evidence that a purely temporal factor can be drawn upon, for humans can reliably distinguish familiarity and frequency from recency over a variety of time-scales (see e.g. Burt, 1992; Friedman and Kemp, 1998; Kemp, 1988; McCormack and Russell, 1997; Wright, Gaskell, and O'Muircheartaigh, 1997). The most plausible conclusion seems to be that information about items' locations along a purely temporal dimension is available and can be used to inform recency judgement, although other factors are also relevant.

Argument 2. Retrieval of a memory does not lead to retrieval of temporally prox-imate memories.   The retrieval of a memory from a particular time in the past does not lead to the easy retrievability of other memories from nearby points in the past (Friedman and Huttenlocher, 1997), and this has been taken as evidence against the existence of a temporally organized memory (e.g. Friedman, Ch. 5, this volume). However, when memories must be retrieved in order after fairly short time periods, there is in fact a strong tendency to confuse items from tempo-rally close positions, as we demonstrated earlier—the attempt to retrieve an item from one temporal location often leads to the recall of items from neighbouring temporal positions (leading to order errors in serial recall). This seems strong evidence for a chronologically organized memory. Furthermore, similar effects occur after much longer periods, from twenty-four hours (Nairne, 1992) to weeks (Huttenlocher, Hedges, and Prohaska, 1988, 1992). Furthermore, in free recall there is a strong tendency for groups of temporally close items to be recalled together, usually in forward order (Kahana, 1996; Laming, 1999; Murdock and Okada, 1970). Thus it seems that temporally proximate items are indeed stored near to one another, although the effects of this may only be apparent when few other cues are available for retrieval.

When other, non-temporal, retrieval cues are of greater relative importance, on the other hand, there seems in any case no reason to believe that memories of temporally proximate memories should act as cues for one another. Suppose that a memory, M1, is associated with a time of event occurrence T1 and a context C1. A second memory, M2, is separately associated with T2 and C2. Even if T1 and T2 are similar, there seems little a priori reason to believe that retrieval of M1 should aid retrieval of M2. T1 and T2 may not activate each other. Even if they do activate each other, M2 may not be strongly associated to T2, and may not be retrievable via activation of T2 via T1.

Argument 3. Hierarchical effects.   A further argument against the idea that memory is temporally organized along a linear time dimension is the observation of hierarchical temporal effects (see e.g. Friedman and Wilkins, 1985; Hintzman, Block, and Summers, 1973; Huttenlocher, Hedges, and Bradburn, 1990; Ryan, 1969). For example, consider an experiment where several separate lists of items are presented, and subjects are asked to reconstruct the temporal order of items. Subjects will tend to confuse the times of end-list items with one another, and start-list items with one another, rather than confusing items at the end of one list with items at the start of the next list. Many experiments and paradigms have produced related results, showing that it is not always items temporally closest to one another that become confused—instead, more temporally distant items may be more likely to become confused if they are close together at a higher level in a temporal hierarchy (this can be seen as analogous to confusing a 3.30 meeting with a 4.30 meeting, rather than confusing the 3.30 meeting with the temporally closer 3.15 meeting). Such evidence does show that memories are not simply arranged along a linear temporal dimension, but does not go against the idea that

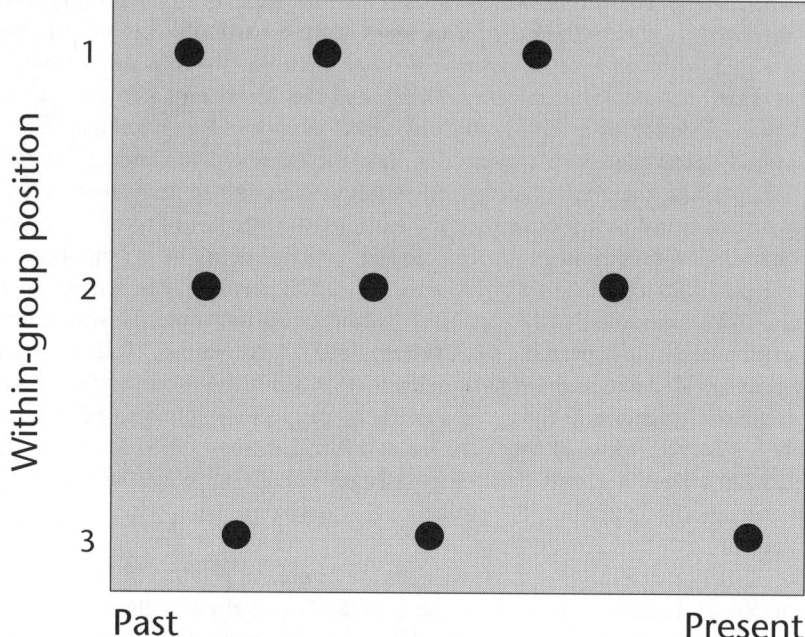

FIGURE 3.7. The position of items from three separate lists of three items in a two-dimensional space, where one dimension represents distance from the present and the other represents position within a list. Items that occupy identical positions within a list have more similar representations than do items that are closer to one another on the dimension representing temporal distance in the past.

memories are chronologically organized. Rather, the implication is simply that some kind of hierarchical representation of temporal position must be appealed to; such representations have been shown to account for the relevant data (e.g. Brown, Neath, and Chater, 2000; Brown, Preece, and Hulme, 2000) while preserving the centrality of time as an organizing dimension of episodic memory. An example is shown in Figure 3.7, in which the positions of items in memory are represented along two temporal dimensions—a non-repeating dimension, as discussed previously, and a repeating dimension.

Argument 4. Dating accuracy is correlated with amount remembered. The fact that the accuracy with which a memory can be temporally dated is correlated with measures of the richness of that memory (e.g. Wright, Gaskell, and O'Muircheartaigh, 1997) has been taken as evidence against the idea that position along a purely temporal dimension is used in dating. Although we have acknowledged above that strength/familiarity processes, or reconstruction, may additionally contribute to temporal judgements, the greater dating accuracy of richer memories can be explained (and modelled) simply by assuming stronger associative links between memories and their associated temporal contexts when the memories are more thoroughly encoded.

In summary, while a range of arguments have been advanced against the suggestion that time is a central organizing dimension of memory, such data can only suggest that other information (i.e. in addition to location along a temporal dimension) is involved. In combination with the data described earlier, which seem to demand reference to temporal organization of memory, the most tenable conclusion seems to be that memories are indeed temporally organized, but that other, non-temporal, information may also be used where it is available in a number of temporal tasks.

This research was supported by grants from the Medical Research Council, UK (G9608199) and the Leverhulme Trust (F/215/AY). We thank William Friedman, Richard Block, and the editors for many helpful comments.

G.D.A.B. and N.C.

REFERENCES

ANDERSON, J. R. (1990), *The Adaptive Character of Thought*. Hillsdale, NJ: Erlbaum.

—— and MILSON, R. (1989), 'Human memory: an adaptive perspective', *Psychological Review*, 96: 703–19.

—— and SCHOOLER, L. J. (1991), 'Reflections of the environment in memory', *Psychological Science,* 2: 396–408.

ANDERSON, R. B. (1998), 'Rational and non-rational aspects of forgetting', in M. Oaksford and N. Chater (eds.), *Rational Models of Cognition*. Oxford: Oxford University Press, 155–64.

BADDELEY, A. D. (1976), *The Psychology of Memory*. London: Harper and Row.

BATESON, M., and KACELNIK, A. (1997), 'Starlings' preference for predictable and unpredictable delays to food', *Animal Behaviour*, 53: 1129–42.

BJORK, R. A., and WHITTEN, W. B. (1974), 'Recency-sensitive retrieval processes in long-term free recall', *Cognitive Psychology*, 6: 173–89.

BROWN, G. D. A., and VOUSDEN, J. I. (1998), 'Adaptive analysis of sequential behavior: oscillators as rational mechanisms', in M. Oaksford and N. Chater (eds.), *Rational Models of Cognition*. Oxford: Oxford University Press, 165–93.

—— NEATH, I., and CHATER, N. (2000), 'SIMPLE: a local distinctiveness model of scale-invariant memory and perceptual identification', MS submitted for publication.

—— PREECE, T., and HULME, C. (2000), 'Oscillator-based memory for serial order', *Psychological Review*, 107: 127–81.

—— VOUSDEN, J. I., McCORMACK, T., and HULME, C. (1999), 'The development of memory for serial order: a temporal—contextual distinctiveness model. *International Journal of Psychology*, 34: 389–402.

BRUNNER, D., KACELNIK, A., and GIBBON, J. (1996), 'Memory for inter-reinforcement interval variability and patch departure decisions in the Starling, *Sturnus vulgaris*', *Animal Behaviour*, 51: 1025–45.

BURGESS, N. (1995), 'A solvable connectionist model of immediate recall of ordered lists', in G. Tesauro, D. Touretzky, and T. K. Leen (eds.), *Neural Information Processing Systems*, 7. Cambridge, Mass.: MIT Press.

—— and HITCH, G. J. (1992), 'Towards a network model of the articulatory loop', *Journal of Memory and Language,* 31: 429–60.

—— —— (1996), 'A connectionist model of STM for serial order', in S. E. Gathercole (ed.), *Models of Short-Term Memory.* Hove: Psychology Press, 51–72.

BURT, C. D. B. (1992), 'Retrieval characteristics of autobiographical memories: event and date information', *Applied Cognitive Psychology*, 6: 389–404.

CHATER, N., and BROWN, G. D. A. (1999), 'Scale invariance as a unifying psychological principle', *Cognition*, 69: B17–B24.

CHURCH, R. M., and BROADBENT, H. (1990), 'Alternative representations of time, number, and rate', *Cognition*, 37: 55–81.

—— and DELUTY, M. Z. (1977), 'Bisection of temporal intervals', *Journal of Experimental Psychology: Animal Behavior Processes*, 3: 216–28.

CLAYTON, N. S., and DICKINSON, A. (1998), 'Episodic-like memory during cache recovery by scrub jays', *Nature*, 395: 272–4.

CROWDER, R. G. (1976), *Principles of Learning and Memory*. Hillsdale, NJ: Erlbaum.

—— and NEATH, I. (1991), 'The microscope metaphor in human memory', in W. E. Hockley and S. Lewandowsky (eds.), *Relating Theory and Data: Essays on Human Memory in Honor of Bennet B. Murdock*. Hillsdale, NJ: Erlbaum, 111–25.

FLEXSER, A. J., and BOWER, G. H. (1974), 'How frequency affects recency judgments: a model for recency discrimination', *Journal of Experimental Psychology*, 103: 706–16.

FRIEDMAN, W. J. (1987), 'A follow-up to "Scale effects in memory for time of events": the earthquake study', *Memory & Cognition*, 15: 518–20.

—— (1991), 'The development of children's memory for the time of past events', *Child Development*, 62: 139–55.

—— and HUTTENLOCHER, J. (1997), 'Memory for the times of "60 Minutes" stories and news events', *Journal of Experimental Psychology: Learning, Memory, and Cognition*, 23: 560–9.

—— and KEMP, S. (1998), 'The effects of elapsed time and retrieval on young children's judgments of the temporal distances of past events', *Cognitive Development*, 13: 335–67.

—— and WILKINS, A. J. (1985), 'Scale effects in memory for the time of past events', *Memory & Cognition*, 13: 168–75.

—— GARDNER, A. G., and ZUBIN, N. R. E. (1995), 'Children's comparisons of the recency of 2 events from the past year', *Child Development*, 66: 970–83.

GALLISTEL, C. R. (1990), *The Organization of Learning*. Cambridge, Mass.: MIT Press.

GLASSPOOL, D. (1995), 'Competitive queueing and the articulatory loop', in J. P. Levy, D. Bairaktaris, J. A. Bullinaria, and P. Cairns (eds.), *Connectionist Models of Memory and Language*. London: UCL Press, 5–10.

GLENBERG, A. M., BRADLEY, M. M., KRAUS, T. A., and RENZAGLIA, G. J. (1983), 'Studies of the long-term recency effect: support for a contextually guided retrieval hypothesis', *Journal of Experimental Psychology: Learning, Memory, and Cognition*, 9: 231–55.

GRIFFITHS, D., DICKINSON, A., and CLAYTON, N. (1999), 'Episodic memory: what can animals remember about their past?', *Trends in Cognitive Sciences*, 3: 74–80.

GUPTA, P. (1996), 'Verbal short-term-memory and language processing—a computational model', *Brain and Language,* 55: 194–7.

GUTTENTAG, R., and CARROLL, D. (1997), 'Memorability judgments for high- and low-frequency words', *Memory & Cognition*, 26: 951–8.

HACKER, M. J. (1980), 'Speed and accuracy of recency judgments for events in short-term memory', *Journal of Experimental Psychology: Human Learning and Memory*, 6: 651–75.

HARRINGTON, D. L., HAALAND, K. Y., and HERMANOWICZ, N. (1998), 'Temporal processing in the basal ganglia', *Neuropsychology*, 12: 3–12.

HARTLEY, T., and HOUGHTON, G. (1996), 'A linguistically constrained model of short-term memory for nonwords', *Journal of Memory and Language*, 35: 1–31.

HEALY, A. F. (1974), 'Separating item from order information in short-term memory', *Journal of Verbal Learning and Verbal Behavior*, 13: 644–55.

HENSON, R. N. A. (1998), 'Short-term memory for serial order: The start–end model', *Cognitive Psychology*, 36: 73–137.

—— (1999), 'Positional information in short-term memory: relative or absolute?', *Memory & Cognition*, 27: 915–27.

—— and BURGESS, N. (1998), 'Representations of serial order', in J. A. Bullinaria, D. W. Glasspool, and G. Houghton (eds.), *Proceedings of the Fourth Neural Computation and Psychology Workshop: Connectionist Representations*. London: Springer-Verlag, 283–300.

—— NORRIS, D. G., PAGE, M. P. A., and BADDELEY, A. D. (1996), 'Unchained memory: error patterns rule out chaining models of immediate serial recall', *Quarterly Journal of Experimental Psychology*, 49A: 80–115.

HINRICHS, J. V. (1970), 'A two-process memory-strength theory for judgment of recency', *Psychological Review*, 77: 223–33.

HINTZMAN, D. L., and BLOCK, R. A. (1971), 'Repetition and memory: evidence for a multiple-trace hypothesis', *Journal of Experimental Psychology*, 88: 297–306.

—— —— and SUMMERS, J. J. (1973), 'Contextual associations and memory for serial position', *Journal of Experimental Psychology*, 97: 220–9.

HITCH, G. J., BURGESS, N., TOWSE, J. N., and CULPIN, V. (1996), 'Temporal grouping effects in immediate recall: a working memory analysis', *Quarterly Journal of Experimental Psychology*, 49A: 116–39.

HOUGHTON, G. (1990), 'The problem of serial order: a neural network model of sequence learning and recall, in R. Dale, C. Mellish, and M. Zock (eds.), *Current Research in Natural Language Generation*. London: Academic Press, 287–319.

—— (1994), 'Inhibitory control of neurodynamics: opponent mechanisms in sequencing and selective attention, in M. Oaksford and G. D. A. Brown (eds.), *Neurodynamics and Psychology*. London: Academic Press, 107–55.

HUTTENLOCHER, J., HEDGES, L. V., and BRADBURN, N. M. (1990), 'Reports of elapsed time: Bounding and rounding processes in estimation', *Journal of Experimental Psychology: Learning, Memory, and Cognition*, 16: 196–213.

—— —— and PROHASKA, V. (1988), 'Hierarchical organization in ordered domains: estimating the dates of events', *Psychological Review*, 95: 471–84.

—— —— —— (1992), 'Memory for day of the week: a 5 + 2 day cycle', *Journal of Experimental Psychology: General*, 121: 313–26.

KACELNIK, A. (1998), 'Normative and descriptive models of decision making: time discounting and risk sensitivity', in M. Oaksford and N. Chater (eds.), *Rational Models of Cognition*. Oxford: Oxford University Press, 54–70.

KAHANA, M. J. (1996), 'Associative processes in free-recall', *Memory & Cognition*, 24: 103–9.

KAUFFMAN, S. A. (1993), *The Origins of Order*. Oxford: Oxford University Press.

KEMP, S. (1988), 'Dating recent and historical events', *Applied Cognitive Psychology*, 2: 181–8.

—— (1999), 'An associative theory of estimating past dates and past prices', *Psychonomic Bulletin and Review*, 6: 41–56.

—— and BURT, C. D. B. (1998), 'The force of events: cross-modality matching the recency of news events', *Memory*, 6: 297–306.

KUBOVY, M., HOLCOMBE, A. O., and WAGEMANS, J. (1998), 'On the lawfulness of grouping by proximity', *Cognitive Psychology*, 35: 71–98.

LAMING, D. R. J. (1999), 'Testing the idea of distinct storage mechanisms in memory', *International Journal of Psychology*, 34: 419–26.

MCCORMACK, T., and HOERL, C. (1999), 'Memory and temporal perspective: the role of temporal frameworks in memory development', *Developmental Review*, 19: 154–82.

—— and RUSSELL, J. (1997), 'The development of recency and frequency memory: is there a developmental shift from reliance on trace-strength to episodic recall?', *Journal of Experimental Child Psychology*, 66: 376–92.

—— BROWN, G. D. A., MAYLOR, E. A., DARBY, R. J., and GREEN, D. (1999), 'Developmental changes in time estimation: comparing childhood and old age', *Developmental Psychology*, 35: 1143–55.

MCGEOCH, J. A. (1942), *The Psychology of Human Learning*. New York: Longmans.

—— and IRION, A. L. (1952), *The Psychology of Human Learning*. New York: Longmans.

MACKAY, D. (1970), 'Spoonerisms: the structure of errors in the serial order of speech', *Neuropsychologia*, 8: 323–50.

—— (1987a), *The Organization of Perception and Action*. New York: Springer-Verlag.

—— (1987b), 'Constraints on theories of sequencing and timing in language production', in A. Allport, D. MacKay, W. Prinz, and E. Scheerer (eds.), *Language Perception and Production: Relationships between Listening, Speaking, Reading and Writing*. London: Academic Press, 407–29.

MAYES, A. R., BADDELEY, A. D., COCKBURN, J., MEUDELL, P. R., PICKERING, A., and WILSON, B. (1989), 'Why are amnesic judgements of recency and frequency made in a qualitatively different way from those of normal people?', *Cortex*, 25: 479–88.

MECK, W. H., CHURCH, R. M., and OLTON, D. S. (1984), 'Hippocampus, time and memory', *Behavioral Neuroscience*, 102: 54–60.

MILNER, B., CORSI, P., and LEONARD, G. (1991), 'Frontal lobe contribution to recency judgements', *Neuropsychologia*, 29: 601–18.

MORTON, J. (1968), 'Repeated items and decay in memory', *Psychonomic Science*, 10: 219–20.

MURDOCK, B. B. (1960), 'The distinctiveness of stimuli', *Psychological Review*, 67: 16–31.

—— and OKADA, R. (1970), 'Interresponse times in single-trial free recall', *Journal of Experimental Psychology*, 86, 263–7.

NAIRNE, J. S. (1991), 'Positional uncertainty in long-term memory', *Memory & Cognition*, 19: 332–40.

—— (1992), 'The loss of positional certainty in long-term memory', *Psychological Science,* 3: 199–202.

NEATH, I., and CROWDER, R. G. (1990), 'Schedules of presentation and distinctiveness in human memory', *Journal of Experimental Psychology: Learning, Memory, and Cognition*, 16: 316–27.

—— —— (1996), 'Distinctiveness and very short-term serial position effects', *Memory*, 4: 225–42.

NOSOFSKY, R. M. (1986), 'Attention, similarity, and the identification–categorization relationship', *Journal of Experimental Psychology: General*, 115: 39–57.

POSNER, M. I., and KONICK, A. F. (1966), 'On the role of interference in short-term retention', *Journal of Experimental Psychology*, 72: 221–31.

ROBERTS, S. (1981), 'Isolation of an internal clock', *Journal of Experimental Psychology: Animal Behavior Processes*, 7: 242–68.

ROSENBAUM, D. A. (1985), 'Motor programming: a review and scheduling theory', in H. Heuer, U. Kleinbeck, and K.-M. Schmidt (eds.), *Motor Behavior: Programming, Control, and Acquisition*. Berlin: Springer-Verlag, 1–33.

RUBIN, D. C., and SCHULKIND, M. C. (1997), 'The distribution of autobiographical memories across the lifespan', *Memory & Cognition*, 25: 859–66.

—— and WENZEL, A. E. (1996), 'One hundred years of forgetting: a quantitative description of retention', *Psychological Review*, 103: 734–60.

RYAN, J. (1969), 'Grouping and short-term memory: different means and patterns of grouping', *Quarterly Journal of Experimental Psychology*, 21: 137–47.

SCHOOLER, L. J., and ANDERSON, J. R. (1997), 'The role of process in the rational analysis of memory', *Cognitive Psychology*, 32: 219–50.

SERRA, M., and NAIRNE, J. S. (forthcoming), 'Part-set cuing of order information: implications for associative theories of serial order memory', *Memory & Cognition*.

SHEPARD, R. N. (1987), 'Evolution of a mesh between principles of the mind and regularities of the world', in J. Dupré (ed.), *The Latest on the Best: Essays on Evolution and Optimality*. Cambridge, Mass.: MIT Press.

SHUM, M. S. (1998), 'The role of temporal landmarks in autobiographical memory processes', *Psychological Bulletin*, 124: 423–42.

STUART, G., and HULME, C. (2000), 'The effects of word co-occurrence on short-term memory: associative links in long-term memory affect short-term memory performance', *Journal of Experimental Psychology: Learning, Memory, and Cognition*, 26: 796–802.

TULVING, E. (1972), 'Episodic and semantic memory', in E. Tulving and W. Donaldson (eds.), *Organization of Memory*. New York: Academic Press, 381–403.

TZENG, O. J. L., and COTTON, B. (1980), 'A study-phase retrieval model of temporal coding', *Journal of Experimental Psychology: Human Learning and Memory*, 6: 705–16.

VOUSDEN, J., and BROWN, G. D. A. (1998), 'To repeat or not to repeat: the time course of response suppression in sequential behaviour', in J. A. Bullinaria, D. W. Glasspool, and G. Houghton (eds.), *Proceedings of the Fourth Neural Computation and Psychology Workshop: Connectionist Representations*. London: Springer-Verlag.

—— —— and HARLEY, T. A. (2000), 'Serial control of phonology in speech production: a hierarchical model', *Cognitive Psychology* 41: 101–75.

WAGENAAR, W. A. (1986). 'My memory: a study of autobiographical memory over six years', *Cognitive Psychology*, 18: 225–52.

WEARDEN, J. H. (1994), 'Prescriptions for models of biopsychological time', in M. Oaksford and G. D. A. Brown (eds.), *Neurodynamics and Psychology*. London: Academic Press, 215–36.

—— and DOHERTY, M. F. (1995), 'Exploring and developing a connectionist model of animal timing—peak procedure and fixed-interval simulations', *Journal of Experimental Psychology: Animal Behavior Processes*, 21: 99–115.

WHEELER, M. A., STUSS, D. T., and TULVING, E. (1997), 'Toward a theory of episodic memory: the frontal lobes and autonoetic consciousness', *Psychological Bulletin*, 121: 331–54.

WIXTED, J. T., and EBBESEN, E. B. (1991), 'On the form of forgetting functions', *Psychological Science,* 2: 409–15.

—— —— (1997), 'Genuine power curves in forgetting: a quantitative analysis of individual subject forgetting functions', *Memory & Cognition*, 5: 731–9.

WOLFE, J. M. (1994), 'Guided search 2.0—a revised model of visual-search', *Psychonomic Bulletin & Review*, 1: 202–38.

WRIGHT, D. B., GASKELL, G. D., and O'MUIRCHEARTAIGH, C. A. (1997), 'Temporal estimation of major news events: re-examining the accessibility principle', *Applied Cognitive Psychology*, 11: 35–46.

4

'Lost in a Sea of Time': Time-Parsing and Autism

Jill Boucher

ABNORMAL TIME PROCESSING IN AUTISM

A problem in sensing time

It is well known that autism is defined in terms of a triad of impairments affecting social interaction, communication, and creativity. It is also widely known that other impairments, such as general learning difficulties (mental handicap) and motor incoordination often co-occur with autism, but that people with autism may also show peaks of relatively high ability typically in rote learning and memory, and sometimes on visuo-spatial tasks. What is much less widely recognized, except by those regularly in contact with people with autism, is that they have—probably universally—a very poor intuitive sense of time.

Donna Williams, a highly able individual with Asperger syndrome, writes:

For me, a problem with sequencing is also about sense of time and the continuity (or lack of it) in my sense of personal history. . . . Labelling clocks with symbols for the sort of things that happen when the hands get to different points can be one way of keeping track of time and how it relates to things that get done at different times. . . . Albums with the day's events, keywords, objects collected through that day to do with smells and tastes and textures experienced and pictures or photos that capture things that happened that day, can all be put together in a way that can make up month by month accessible libraries. These can be kept year after year so that a person can look through them at any time and get some sort of composite sense of who they are. (Williams, 1996: 165)

Firsthand accounts by autistic people are often considered suspect on the grounds that they have been 'ghosted', or otherwise 'fed in' by other people. However, problems with intuitive time processing are also well recognized by clinicians and educationists who work with people with autism. So, for example, one of the most authoritative clinicians and researchers into autism in the UK, Lorna Wing, writes of autistic people's 'basic inability to make sense of past and present experiences' and continues:

The problems of time are not related to telling the time by the clock, which some people with autistic disorders are able to do well. The difficulties lie in comprehending the passage of time and linking it with ongoing activities. . . . One of the most obvious examples of confusion with time is the way in which those with enough speech continually ask for reassurance about future events and when they will happen. . . . Another aspect of this problem is the lack of awareness that an event, once started, will come to an end. . . . The fear generated by being lost in time also explains why there is often such a strong adverse reaction to any unpredicted change in the expected timetable. Some more able children who can tell time by the clock become obsessed with time and demand that everything happens at the precise pre-ordained moment. (Wing, 1996: 88)

Wing concludes (p. 89): 'Most people are born with the ability to understand [time] in everyday terms. People with autistic disorders seem to lack this understanding to a degree that is markedly discrepant with their level of intelligence.'

Peeters and Gillberg, who are also primarily practitioners, echo Wing's words. They write:

Most people with autism feel lost in a sea of time. If they cannot 'see' the time, they will often try to develop routines and rituals by way of compensation. They want all activities to be undertaken in the same sequence every day . . . and if the sequence of activities changes on a certain day, then they have behavioural problems. (Peeters and Gillberg, 1999: 87)

Parents, teachers, and others caring for people with autism have many strategies for reducing the autistic person's disorientation in time. Peeters (1997) describes how duration can be concretized for the less able autistic child by using a kitchen timer with a dial and pointer which the child can watch, or by using an egg-timer, or by playing a set number of familiar songs on a cassette: 'After the music stops, it is time to go out.' Use of pictorial timetables is universal in schools and units catering for less able children with autism, and more able people, as Lorna Wing points out, rely greatly on clocks and calendars.

An excessive, and sometimes obsessional, reliance on clocks, calendars, and other timing devices can be illustrated anecdotally. I once asked a boy when he last went swimming, and he replied by giving me a date, rather than responding 'yesterday', 'last week', 'a few days ago', as might have been expected. Another boy I know of can tell you what he did on any date of the recent year or more (I have not asked how far back in time his abilities go). I am currently working with a group of able young adults with autism. One—a university student—had been having some trouble with his university coursework. When I asked him how the coursework was going, he went to a calendar on the wall, turned back a month or two, and proceeded to give me a date by date account of when he had handed a particular piece of work in, when he had had it returned, when he had been to see his tutor about it, when his father had written to his tutor about it, and so on up to the present. Another highly intelligent person I know who has Asperger syndrome uses an electric timer to ensure that the tea bags remain in his tea for a precise length of time. This person likes to travel, and he can tell me the exact dates on which he went to numerous places. He is also a calendrical calculator—that is to say, he can calculate what day of the week past dates fell on and future dates will fall on.

Impaired processing of information with a temporal dimension: evidence from research

If people with autism have an impaired sense of time at the intuitive level, then it would be expected that they would perform particularly poorly on tests of intelligence involving time-based systems or knowledge, as opposed to those predominantly involving the ability to process static visuo-spatial stimuli. This is in general the case. In children with classic autism as originally described by Kanner (1943), verbal IQ is lower than performance IQ. Moreover, within the sets of subtests which may be used in assessing performance IQ, children with classic autism generally perform better on tasks which involve processing static visuo-spatial information as opposed to tasks which involve verbal mediation (Lincoln, Allen, and Kilman, 1995). So, for example, they perform consistently better on a subtest which involves assembling coloured blocks to make given patterns than they do on a subtest which involves placing a sequence of pictures in order so as to tell a coherent story. On the Kaufman Assessment Battery (Kaufman and Kaufman, 1983), which is specifically designed to compare performance on tasks requiring temporal processing as opposed to the processing of static visuo-spatial material, children with autism perform particularly poorly on the former type of task (Freeman *et al.*, 1985; Allen, Lincoln, and Kaufman, 1991). There is also evidence to suggest that where a particular task can be solved using either a temporal or a spatial strategy, children with autism utilize a spatial rather than a temporal strategy (Hermelin and O'Connor, 1975). In this they resemble deaf children, and not typically developing children. There is also evidence to suggest that adults with high-level autism think visually, rather than verbally, again suggesting an unusual avoidance of a time-based system (Hurlbert, Happé, and Frith, 1994).

In individuals with high-level autism, sometimes referred to as Asperger syndrome, the discrepancy between verbal and non-verbal IQ scores which is seen in classic autism does not occur. This is not surprising, because people with Asperger syndrome have, by definition, a normal language system in terms of vocabulary and knowledge of grammar. However, although people with Asperger syndrome have normal vocabularies and knowledge of grammar, their performance on tests of verbal reasoning and reading comprehension are relatively poor (Minshew, Goldstein, and Siegel, 1997). They also have problems in understanding figurative or non-literal language (Happé, 1994). Possible differences between the time-processing impairment as it occurs in classic autism, in Asperger syndrome, and also in those children whose autism is accompanied by general learning difficulties are considered below.

The problems which people with autism have in processing time-based information are not associated with the strictly linear sequencing of successive items of information through time. Indeed, people with autism perform well on a variety of tasks involving linear sequencing of the kind in which A is reliably followed by B is followed by C. Rather, the problem is likely to relate to the hierarchical analysis and organization of complex time-based inputs and outputs. So, for example, children with classic autism consistently perform worse on a test of verbal comprehension than they do on tests of the ability to remember short strings of unrelated words or digits (Allen, Lincoln, and Kaufman, 1991). Similarly, adults with Asperger syndrome are slow in carrying out a peg-moving task, but not on a repetitive finger-tapping task (Minshew, Goldstein, and Siegel, 1997).

It will be suggested below that the discrepancy between relatively spared linear temporal sequencing and impaired hierarchical temporal sequencing reflects the fact that whereas at least some individual biological clocks or timers operate normally in people with autism, the integration of individual timers into a co-ordinated hierarchy is defective. This is analogous to an individual's having one clock showing hours, another showing minutes, and another showing seconds, rather than having a single clock representing hours, minutes, and seconds simultaneously. With three separate clocks an individual would be able to locate extended events temporally within the hours in which they occurred, and to record their temporal succession. They would also be able to locate shorter, more rapidly successive events within the minutes in which they occurred, and to record their temporal succession; and also to locate very rapidly successive events within the seconds in which they occurred, and to record their temporal succession. However, they would not be able to encode the temporal relations *between* these three sets of events, resulting in difficulty in encoding the briefer events as parts of more extended wholes, and a corresponding difficulty in breaking down more extended events in terms of constituent parts. Alternatively, if certain biological timers were simply missing, the hierarchical parsing of time-based events would be just as much impaired as if timers were present, but not integrated. More is said below about possible mechanisms underlying impaired time-parsing in autism.

Evidence of selective, time-related, memory impairments

If people with autism have an impaired sense of time of the kind indicated, they would also be expected to have selective memory problems. In particular, they might be expected to have impaired declarative memory for when events occurred. This problem would arise because remembering 'when' (without resorting to dates and times) involves several biological timers recording, for example (and again using the ordinary clock analogy), the positions of the hour, minute, and second hands *simultaneously and in combination.* On the other hand, the individual might be able to remember what occurred and thereby acquire semantic memories of facts. Memories and learning based on the linear temporal succession of certain events or items of information would also be intact. Thus associations between temporally successive pairs of events or items of information and rote memory for strings of temporally successive items would be intact, subserving the acquisition of habits and procedures. I will consider evidence relating to each of these predictions, in reverse order.

Regarding the prediction that people with autism will have spared habit and procedural memory, this prediction is consistent with the set of peak abilities in associative and rote memory noted by Kanner (1943) and confirmed by both clinical observation and research. At the clinical and observational level the common occurrence of echolalia, the excessive use of formulaic language, and autistic people's renowned memory for television jingles or the words of songs, are all evidence of good rote memory for speech. Equally, clinical observation of the tendency to do things in the same way, in the same order time after time, indicates intact habit and procedural memory and an unusual degree of reliance on these intact abilities. There are intriguing suggestions in the firsthand accounts of autism to the effect that people with autism, even the most able, think in strings of tightly interlinked images. For example, Temple Grandin is quoted as saying: 'My mind is like a CD-ROM in a computer—like a quick-access videotape. But once I get there I have to play the whole part [i.e. she has to play a whole memory-episode through]—no fast forward . . . I actually have the machine in my head. I run it in my mind. I play the tape' (Sacks, 1995: 269).

Research data on memorizing temporally successive events or items of information is quite sparse. However, it has been shown that people with autism perform well on tests of paired associate learning (Boucher and Warrington, 1976; Minshew, Goldstein, and Siegel, 1997). They also perform relatively normally on tests of the ability to learn supra-span strings of digits or words over repeated trials (Boucher, 1975; Rumsey and Hamburger, 1988), and on a test of the ability to learn to track the route of a maze (Minshew, Goldstein, and Siegel, 1997).

With regard to the prediction that semantic memory will be relatively unimpaired by temporal processing problems, such research evidence as there is supports the prediction. So, for example, people with Asperger syndrome may have excellent vocabulary knowledge (although performing poorly on tests of verbal reasoning and tests of reading comprehension). The overwhelming evidence of a capacity to acquire factual knowledge comes, however, from clinical and anecdotal observation of individuals with encyclopaedic knowledge concerning topics of obsessional interest. These topics quite often involve transport systems and timetables, which is of interest in itself. However, I have known individuals with an encyclopaedic knowledge of pop music, cooling towers and electricity generating stations, geographical information, spiders, and military hardware.

Although the ability of the more able person with autism to amass facts is not in question, nor does there appear to be any problem in accessing these memories, it is questionable whether the *kinds* of memories which people with autism have in their semantic and general knowledge bases are fully normal. In the first place, the range of subjects which any one individual with autism knows about is narrow (they perform poorly on the general knowledge subtest of a standard intelligence test). More importantly than this, however, is the fact that if, as I suggest below, memory for events is impaired, and if in particular there is an impairment of the ability to analyse and encode the temporal structure of complex events, then the contents of semantic memory will also lack information about temporal relationships between items. Such research as there is concerning the semantic-lexical knowledge base in autism suggests a normal categorical structure (Klinger and Dawson, 1995). However, there has been very little research in this area and none that touches on the issue in question.

With regard to the prediction that declarative memory for the 'when' of events would be impaired by problems in sensing time, such research evidence as there is again supports the prediction. Free recall tasks are the most commonly used tests of event memory. In two experiments in which children with autism were asked to recall everything they had done with a particular tester over the last term (in one case) and over the last year (in another case), the children with autism performed poorly, relative to the controls (Boucher, 1981a; Boucher and Lewis, 1989). This was not because they had forgotten the activities they had taken part in: they were able to recall most of the activities when cued. However, they were poor at remembering them unaided, and this could have been caused by a lack of information in the memory store concerning when these particular activities had been carried out: in other words, a crucial retrieval cue may have been missing. The plausibility of this explanation is increased by the common complaint of parents and teachers that children with autism seem unable to answer accurately questions like 'What did you do on the weekend', 'What did you do last night', 'What did you do at school today?', although when prompted with some or other more salient and discriminating piece of information, such as 'What did you do at Grandma's on the weekend?' or 'Where did you go on the coach last night?' they are able to respond appropriately. Anyone who has tried to have a conversation with someone with autism will know that any non-standard (i.e. non-routine, or stereotypical) information has to be elicited by such highly structured, information-giving questions (Dobbinson, Perkins, and Boucher, 1998).

Free recall in other tasks is fragile. By that I mean that if the material or 'event' to be recalled is simple (such as a list of digits, or unrelated words) and recall is immediate, then children with autism are not impaired, relative to controls: their immediate memory spans are commensurate with their overall abilities (Hermelin and O'Connor, 1970; Lincoln *et al.*, 1992). However, if the material to be remembered is more structured (for example, sentences or a whole story, rather than word lists), then recall deteriorates relative to controls (Hermelin and O'Connor, 1970; Tager-Flusberg, 1991; Minshew, Goldstein, and Siegel, 1997). Similarly, if the number of words or digits to be remembered is increased to be supra-span, or if a delay is inserted prior to recall, the performance of children with autism deteriorates relative to that of controls (Boucher and Warrington, 1976; Boucher, 1981b; Boucher and Lewis, 1989). The performance of younger and less able children with autism is, not surprisingly, more vulnerable than that of older, or more able individuals. Nevertheless, even the performance of able adults with Asperger syndrome breaks down relative to that of controls when the event to be recalled is of a certain level of time-related difficulty (Minshew, Goldstein, and Siegel, 1997).

It is perhaps surprising that the immediate memory span is unimpaired in able people with autism, because it is likely that memory for serially ordered lists involves complex temporal processing mechanisms (Church and Broadbent,

1990; Burgess and Hitch, 1996; Brown, Preece, and Hulme, 2000). However, it seems possible that people with autism, unlike others, use an associative, chaining strategy for word list recall, and that this works up to a certain list length but not beyond. There is evidence to suggest that people with autism do use unusual methods of memorising within span word lists (Boucher, 1976; Renner, Klinger, and Klinger, 2000). Dependence on a chaining strategy could also help to explain why introducing meaning and structure into word strings is less helpful to people with autism than to non-autistic controls (Hermelin and O'Connor, 1970; Tager-Flusberg, 1991).

The impairments of free recall which occur in people with autism probably do not reflect problems of consolidation or storage. In all cases where memory for the events presented in laboratory tasks has been probed using retrieval cues, or by asking children if they recognize a word or picture, children with autism perform well, indicating that the event itself is stored and available, although the child has not been able to access the information in free recall (Boucher and Warrington, 1976; Boucher, 1981a; Tager-Flusberg, 1991: Ameli et al., 1988). There are various possible reasons for this. However, a lack of temporal contextual information, and/or a lack of temporal binding of target information and contextual information in general, are possible explanations.

Event memory of the kinds described above is impersonal. That is to say, when remembering a list of words, or a story, or a set of activities which one has experienced in a laboratory setting, there is not necessarily any recall or re-experience of what it felt like to be listening to the words, or looking at the set of pictures. Episodic memory, by contrast, can be defined as memory for events combined with memory for one's personal involvement in the event (Wheeler, Stuss, and Tulving, 1997). Certain evidence suggests that people with autism have impaired episodic memory, using the term in this narrowed sense.

First, the two experiments testing autistic children's free recall of activities reported in Boucher (1981a) and in Boucher and Lewis (1989) were carried out in naturalistic settings and involved activities such as drawing pictures, or playing with an old camera, designed to be of some interest to the children with autism. It seems reasonable to suggest that some at least of these activities were sufficiently distinctive and enjoyable to have been candidates for registration in episodic memory. As noted above, the autistic children performed poorly relative to controls in both of these experiments.

Secondly, in a test of source memory, Russell and Jarrold (1999) showed that non-autistic children had significantly better recall of actions which they themselves had carried out in the course of a game than they had of actions which they had observed others carrying out. For children with autism, the reverse was true. A similar finding has been reported by Millward et al., (2000) utilizing an even more naturalistic and child-friendly setting. In this experiment, children with autism were taken on a walk in which particular objects were found, or played with, or purchased in distinctive settings encountered on the walk. A 'non-autistic companion' child was also taken on the walk, but they did slightly different things in the different settings. On their return from the walk, the non-autistic children had better recall of the things they had done themselves than they had of things which they had observed the child with autism doing, whereas the reverse was true for the children with autism. In another test of children's memory for their own or others' actions, a different result was obtained, in that there was no difference between the non-autistic controls and the children with autism (Farrant, Blades, and Boucher, 1998). However, methodological differences probably explain the discrepancy between the finding on this experiment and on the two other experiments assessing source memory.

An experiment reported by Benneto, Pennington, and Rogers (1996) purports to investigate source memory, but actually assesses what is more usually referred to as memory for recency. However, the experiment is relevant to the issue of whether or not people with autism encode information concerning the intuitively experienced 'when' of events. These authors gave their participants two lists of words to remember, and then tested recognition memory for the words and also memory for the list in which any word occurred. The autistic participants performed significantly worse than controls on the test of list membership.

A third type of evidence concerning an impairment of episodic memory comes from an experiment reported by Bowler, Gardiner, and Grice (2000) using a remembering v. knowing recognition test. In this paradigm, participants are given a list of words to try to remember, and are subsequently tested on their ability to recognize the words. When they make a correct recognition response, they are asked if they *know* that they saw the word before but cannot remember any details about seeing it in the original list; or whether they also *remember* something about what they experienced when they saw the word in the original list. The participants with Asperger syndrome were significantly more likely than controls to give 'knowing' rather than 'remembering' responses, and this finding provides direct evidence of impaired episodic memory in people with autism. Impaired recall of self-related information by people with autism could, of course, be explained in terms of a defective sense of self. However, able people with autism have a well-developed sense of themselves (Wolff, 1995), and the problem can be more plausibly explained by a lack of temporal binding of target and contextual memories.

If, as the evidence suggests, event and episodic memory are both impaired in autism, then it follows that autobiographical memory will be partially impaired. In particular, that part of the contents of autobiographical memory which consists of episodic and event memories will be impaired, although factual autobiographical knowledge may be relatively normal. There is no evidence, to the best of my knowledge, relating to this prediction. However, it could be quite easily tested.

Evidence of time-related output abnormalities

The amount of time we spend thinking about the past is dwarfed by the amount of time we spend thinking about the future ('I'll have to stop typing soon and feed the cat'; 'Time for another cup of coffee'; 'What am I doing this evening?'). Even more of our time is spent doing things, and we do things forwards in time, usually without conscious planning of our immediate actions but still with some kind of advance programming. This could not be done without an intuitive temporal framework by means of which to construct the future.

People with acquired global amnesia are not able to think forwards in time any more than they are able to think backwards (Tulving, 1985; Friedman, 1990). When he tried to imagine his future, Tulving's patient described his mind as a blank. People with the lesser form of amnesia associated with frontal lobe lesions also have both memory and planning impairments (Schacter, 1987). However, in their case there is no loss of explicit memories *per se* (as there is in global amnesia), since recognition memory is unimpaired. Rather, event and episodic memory are impaired by a loss of the ability to recall when an event occurred (Fuster, 1989). Similarly, the performance of people with frontal lobe lesions is impaired on tasks involving the capacity to 'visualize' time (and movement through space) such as the Tower of London task (Owen *et al.*, 1990).

The evidence from acquired amnesia suggests that whatever intuitive time sense is used in determining the non-calendrical 'when' of past events is also used in establishing a non-calendrical temporal framework for imagining and planning. Similarly, it can be argued that the biological mechanisms involved in the temporal analysis of speech, seen or felt motion, and other sensory information which changes through time are also likely to be used in establishing temporal frameworks for motor action (Treisman, Faulkner, and Naish, 1992). If these suppositions are correct, and if people with autism have an impaired biological time sense, they will not only have impairments of perception, input encoding, and memory, but they will also have impairments of the organization of motor outputs, and of generativity, imagining, and planning. Moreover, the problems with time future will reflect the problems with time past.

Specifically, planning which involves the recycling of learned associations, habits, or procedures, and the actual production of associative responses and linear sequences of behaviour will be spared (corresponding to the sparing of associative, rote, and procedural memory). Some facts and knowledge such as can be utilized in forward planning will be available (corresponding to the relative sparing of semantic memory). However, it is important to reiterate that impaired event-processing will cause abnormalities in the knowledge base: not least, impaired event-processing will interfere with the abstraction of event scripts and certain types of conceptual knowledge. Finally, planning or imagining which involves the temporal organization of thoughts and ideas in novel combinations through future time will be impaired, especially where a superordinate plan breaks down into a hierarchy of temporally related constituents. Equally, the enactment of plans whether at the level of motor programmes or at the level of a game of chess or a varied day's work will be impaired if temporal processors with relevant periodicities are either not available or not hierarchically integrated. (These impairments correspond to the input impairments of event analysis, encoding, and memory.)

The predicted sparing of the production of associative, rote learned, or habitual behaviours is supported by the fact that all definitions and clinical descriptions of autism refer to the repetitiveness of autistic behaviour and to the tendency to adhere to inflexible routines or rituals (APA, 1994). A lack of spontaneous pretend play is also seen as diagnostic of autism, such spontaneous pretence as is produced consisting of learned routines (Wing and Gould, 1979). A nice indication that even highly able adults with autism are most comfortable when generating a linear temporal succession of output units is provided by a remark made by Donna Williams about her preferred mode of communication: 'I personally prefer mime to using spoken language alone. . . . Mime as signing can be used as one simple single action per word and those single actions can be used to make linear sentences' (Williams, 1996: 157).

The tendency to produce abnormally invariant sequences of behaviour has been noted in the research literature since the 1970s. Frith, for example, demonstrated excessively rule-bound spontaneous sequence production in early experiments (Frith, 1970), something which I also observed in an early study (Boucher, 1977). In one of Frith's studies, children were given blue and red counters and a row of slots into which the counters could be placed to make a pattern. Whereas typically developing children made quite variable patterns, the children with autism showed a strong tendency to produce lines of entirely red or entirely blue counters, or simply alternated the two colours, as if reproducing over and over again a simple red–blue (or blue–red) unit. This kind of observation led several theorists of the time to suggest that 'sequencing' abnormalities were at the heart of autism (Tanguay, 1984; Ricks and Wing, 1975; Rutter, 1983), a suggestion which has been explored again by Lincoln and his colleagues in work referred to above. This suggestion is, however, misleading, since, as pointed out above, linear sequencing is in fact a peak ability in people with autism. What people with autism cannot do, it seems, is break out of the linear chains to produce more complex, varied, and original outputs.

The predicted abnormalities in the facts and knowledge available for use in productive behaviour emerge from an examination of the units of repetition which occur in the stereotypic, routinized, or rule-bound outputs of people with autism. I have suggested that the children in Frith's experiment either repeated a unit consisting of a single colour, or they repeated a unit consisting of the two colours. The children tested by Frith were quite young and not highly able, and it may be speculated that their repetitive habits and preferred routines were also made up of quite simple bits of behaviour of brief duration. The routines of an able adult with autism or Asperger syndrome may, by contrast, be made up of complex higher-order units of relatively extended temporal duration. So, for example, an able person living independently may have a daily routine consisting of going to the local library to read the paper, calling in at a café for a cup of coffee, shopping at the local corner shop, and returning home in time to make a cheese and pickle sandwich and watch 'Neighbours'. The able adult with autism is thus just as rigid and repetitive as the younger or less able individual, but the units of perseveration are different.

It may be, therefore, that one of the things which distinguishes the older and more able autistic person from younger or less able individuals is the temporal span (and related complexity) of their repeating units of behaviour. By contrast, one of the things which all individuals with autism have in common is that their units of repetition, whether short and simple or long and complex, are not treated as components of behaviour which are free and available for creative and original combination and recombination. Instead, they tend to be produced in predictable order, over and over again. From the differences in the temporal duration (and complexity) of the units of repetition in younger/less able and older/more able individuals, it may be inferred that younger or less able individuals lack the biological mechanisms needed to process events of even short durations. Similarly, it may be inferred that older or more able individuals can process events of relatively short durations, but lack the means of intuitively processing temporally extended events.

To appreciate the effects which such timing deficits would have on thinking forward through time, try to imagine periods of time longer than the lifetime of the universe, and invent a science fiction plot describing the course of cosmological events during that period. In fact, one cannot imagine a period of time longer than the lifetime of the universe except by thinking of a temporal succession of universes with cumulative lifetimes: there are no superordinate temporal spans within which events can be imagined, only a string of slots to be filled in a set order (lifetime of universe 1, lifetime of universe 2, and so on). Just so, if able people with autism lack the capacity to imagine extended time frames, then the only way they can plan the events of a day (other than by resorting to external clocks) is by stringing together a succession of short temporal slots. So, for example, flexible planning and imagining within hours might be possible, but flexibility across hours might not be possible. Similarly, the less able or younger individual might be able to plan, imagine, and generate novel combinations of behaviour only within very limited time periods, forcing them into repetition, random behaviour, or inertia for much of their waking hours, which is precisely what is seen in less able individuals.

I have recently had the chance to study the humorous productions of a woman with borderline Asperger syndrome, who nicely illustrates both the scope for, and the limitations of, creativity in more able autistic people (Werth, Perkins, and Boucher, 2000). This woman produces truly comical neologisms and puns. For example, when showing a visitor round her Camphill village and approaching the weaving centre she said: ' Here's the weavery looming up'. And describing a day out: 'Well, I got a bit grizzly-grizzly, but I wisted over it, then I had tea . . . Later on I felt happier, I listened to scruples and scruples of Grandpa's tape decca-ised music. Then I keshed out the kettle'. She also draws cartoons and Heath Robinson creations which people an ongoing fantasy world. This woman's humour might seem to contradict the generalization that people with autism do not have combinatorial, generative behaviour. However, the drawings combine components in space, rather than in time, and the successful word play operates over the acoustics and semantics of individual words and phrases. When she tries to tell jokes with formal structures which are more extended through time, such as riddles, or question and answer jokes, this exceptional woman is much less successful.

It seems unlikely that generative use of language would have been within the capacities of the children Frith tested in her pattern-making experiment, and the contrast between the limited generative capacities of young or less able individuals with autism, and the less limited but nevertheless restricted capacities of more able individuals such as the woman described above suggests how differences in time-processing capacities would affect language acquisition and use. Specifically, younger or less able individuals may be able to analyse sensory inputs over only very short time-spans, perhaps sufficient to enable them to, for example, correctly echo single words or two-word phrases. Somewhat more able individuals can both memorize longer phrases of language and analyse some of the rapid rate components, sufficient to acquire knowledge of the phonology of their language and to subserve mechanical reading (hyperlexia). Further increases in the span of items which can be both held in memory and temporally analysed would contribute to the capacity to acquire grammar and meaning. Yet further increases would be required for coherent conversational turn-taking, and further increases for the capacity to comprehend narrative and to participate in extended conversation. Individuals with these time-processing capacities would, of course, no longer have the problems of generativity, planning, imagination, and motor programming which are typical of autism.

A BIOPSYCHOLOGICAL TIME-PARSING SYSTEM

In this section, I tentatively propose an informal model of a biopsychological time-parsing system. The model is provisional and crude. However, it is based on research from a number of independent sources; it fills a hole in our understanding of human psychology (building on, as I have said, the work of others); and it has potentially powerful explanatory value, not just for autism, but for a fuller understanding of intelligence, language, and other cognitive capacities which are unique to humans. The model therefore has relevance for evolutionary psychology, and this application of the model will be explored elsewhere. In the present chapter, I briefly outline the structure of the model and its functions, and speculate concerning the physical and psychological time-processing deficits which may be involved in autism.

Structure

How might the notion of 'having a sense of time' be cashed out in terms of underlying processes and mechanisms? The first thing to say is that if we try to cash out this notion in terms of such things as 'experiencing change' or 'noticing the succession of events' we are putting the cart before the horse, since these descriptions of behaviour assume that we start with a sense of time—at least with a distinction between what is happening now and what happened in the past. Equally, as Friedman points out, 'there is no environmental time that can excite a time sense, only the physical events that we consider as contained in time' (1990: 10). This suggests that preconceptual infants, and also animals which, like people, live in a temporal world, must have biologically based mechanisms for analysing those temporal aspects of experience which are important for their survival, much as they have biologically based mechanisms for analysing the spatial aspects of experience. It is these primitive biopsychological mechanisms which may be lacking or dysfunctional in some way or other in people with autism, and which have to be effortfully compensated for by those caring for people with autism, and by able autistic people themselves.

I envisage a preconceptual, biopsychological 'time-parsing' system based on 'biological clocks' or cyclic 'timers', with periodicities ranging from milliseconds to a year, and computations over the outputs of such timers. Some of these cyclic timers are instantiated in the form of cycles of physiological changes within the brain, and some are instantiated in the form of oscillatory neural activity. Additional representations of cyclic time are likely to be provided by computing multiples or factors of physically instantiated cycles. The proposed system is based largely on the work of Gallistel (1990). However, the notion of a system based on biological clocks also gains plausibility from work utilizing explicit timing signals in connectionist modelling of memory (Church and Broadbent, 1990; Burgess and Hitch, 1996; Brown, Preece, and Hulme, 2000) and speech production (Vousden, Brown, and Harley, forthcoming). The proposed system is also consistent with findings from neurobiological and neuropsychological research into explicit timing mechanisms in the human brain (see e.g. Mangels, Ivry, and Shimuzu, 1998; Harrington and Haaland, 1998).

The essential components of the proposed time-parsing system are illustrated schematically in Figure 4.1.

Functions

Registering the temporal characteristics of experience.   Each cycle, or 'clock', in the system sets up a linear series of intervals or time windows with fuzzy boundaries. The smallest-sized time windows are provided by the highest-frequency cycles within any system, and the largest-sized windows are provided by the lowest-frequency cycles, with windows of intermediate and proportional sizes in between. Each window contains a phasic temporal context signal provided by the continuous changes in bodily state within any physiologically instantiated cycle, or the continuous changes in the wave form within any neurally instantiated cycle.

The temporal characteristics of experience can be registered in three distinct ways. First, particulate items of information, or events, can be registered as

Jill Boucher

Cyclic frequencies

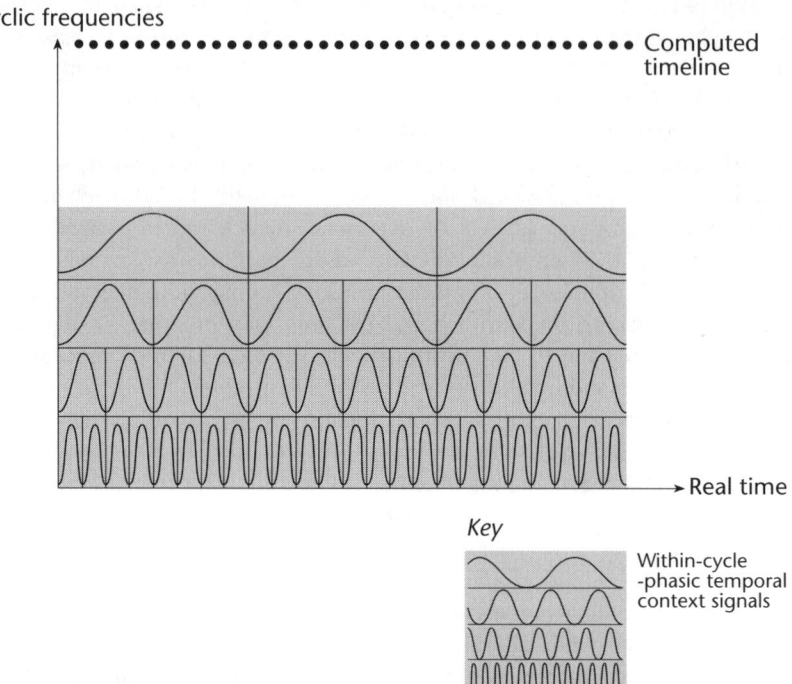

FIGURE 4.1. Schematic diagram of the proposed time-parsing system showing a sample of biological cycles with harmonically related frequencies, and the computed temporal context signal, or time-line. The key shows a sample of within-cycle phasic temporal context signals, or phase signals. The vertical lines illustrate the time intervals, or 'time windows' within which individuated items may be registered, and the combination of vertical and horizontal lines illustrates the hierarchical grid referred to in the text as the time map.

falling within a particular time window at a particular level of analysis, and as falling across a range of subordinate time windows at lower levels of analysis. This is analogous to registering that a particular earthquake occurred within a certain hour, and across certain minutes, seconds, and milliseconds. Secondly, the temporal course of continuous (non-particulate) items or events can be registered in terms of the phasic temporal context signal within a particular time window, or across a number of successive time windows. This is analogous to registering that the first shock of the earthquake showed a fluctuating pattern of severity over the period in which the second hand of a clock travelled around an unmarked clock-face, the fluctuations in the shock waves being registered against the continuously changing position of the second hand. Thirdly, the time of occurrence of a particulate item or event can be registered in terms of a 'time-line' derived from computations across the combined outputs of all the timers in a system. This is analagous to using the hour, minute, and second hands of a clock in order to determine that the earthquake began at 4 hours, 32 minutes and 7 seconds in the morning and ended at 4 hours, 32 minutes, and 40 seconds. There are two important points to make about the time-line. First, it recycles within the periodicity of the slowest-rate cycle in a system, and in a system with only rapid-rate cycles, time-of-occurrence information will lack distinctiveness. Secondly, because the time-line is composed of the combined outputs of all the timers in a system, it can be decomposed into information concerning the position of a particulate item or event within a hierarchy of time windows. The time-line and what may be described as a hierarchical time map therefore contain the same information. However, the information is in summary form in the former case, and in more detailed form in the latter case.

Segmenting and individuating time-based items and events: determining the processing capacity of a system in terms of particulate items.   Time windows contribute to the segmenting and individuation of time-based items and events. They therefore have a role in determining the processing capacity of an organism in so far as the number of particulate items in the knowledge base contributes to processing capacity.

The analysis and encoding of experience in terms of inter-item temporal relationships.   Particulate items and events can be encoded within the temporal framework provided by the hierarchical array of time windows, in terms of (1) their linear temporal relations to preceding and successive items at the same level of temporal analysis, (2) their relations to items at superordinate levels, and (3) their relations to items at subordinate levels. So, for example, a word can be encoded in relation to other words immediately preceding or following it, and in terms of the phrase or sentence of which it forms a part, and also in terms of its constituent syllables and phonemes. It is important to notice, however, that items which fall within the time windows determined by the slowest-rate cycle in any system cannot be encoded in terms of their relations with superordinate items, since there are no superordinate items. Equally, items which fall within the time windows determined by the fastest-rate cycles within a system cannot be encoded in terms of their relations with particulate subordinate items, because there are no particulate subordinate items. (However, the temporal characteristics of items falling within the smallest time windows can be registered against the phasic temporal context signal—see above.)

Rote learning, and procedural or habit memory.   Within the terms of the model, rote and procedural memory are subserved by the linear sequences of time windows yielded by individual cycles in any system. As pointed out above, items individuated by the slowest-rate cycle in a system cannot be encoded in terms of their relations with superordinate items, since there are no superordinate items.

The only way in which these items can be utilized in productive behaviour, therefore, is in isolation, or in associative pairs or linear strings.

Event memory and episodic memory: temporal addressing and temporal binding. Within the terms of the model, the computed time line provides a time-of-occurrence 'temporal address' by means of which events may be retrieved. When memory for an event shares a temporal address with memory of having personally experienced that event the two parts of the total memorial event are bound together in time, and episodic memory results. In just the same way, memory for an event is temporally bound to other concurrent contextual information, which may therefore be used to cue recall of the event.

Semantic memory and the knowledge base. The time-of-occurrence information attached to any item in event memory becomes decreasingly discriminable over repeated occurrences of the same event at different times. Such events then form part of the knowledge base in semantic memory, and the event memories from which they derived can no longer be retrieved. So, for example, I may learn the meaning of the word 'chauvesouris' in my French lesson this week, and be able to remember the occasion of learning the word. However, after repeated occurrences of 'chauvesouris' in subsequent lessons, I will not be able to recall these events individually (except, possibly, the most recent) although the meaning of the word will—hopefully—be lodged in my semantic memory.

Planning and programming motor action: off-line representations of biopsychological time. It is proposed that the temporal framework, or time map, illustrated in Figure 4.1 is utilized in temporally structuring future action. This entails that representations of the time map can be run off line as well as being utilized on line.

Generativity. The contribution of the time-parsing system to the segmentation and individuation of particulate items of knowledge contributes to generativity (Abler, 1989; Studdert-Kennedy, 1998; Bloom, 1994). Rules for combining particulate items in combinatorial systems such as language include constraints on the temporal relations which an item can have with other items at the same level of analysis and at superordinate levels. These rules are derived in part by abstracting from past experiences of an item's temporal relations with other items as registered on the time map and stored in semantic memory.

Language acquisition. It is suggested that time-parsing contributes to the acquisition of language by (1) contributing to the segmentation of linguistic units at various levels in parallel; (2) analysing and encoding linguistic data within a temporal framework, and simultaneously analysing and encoding non-linguistic data within the same framework; thereby (3) providing information on the basis of which structural and semantic dependencies between linguistic units at all levels can be computed (cf. Cromer, 1983; Bishop, 1997).

Defective functioning of the time-parsing system at the physical level in autism: hypotheses, and evidence

In connection with the hypothesis that defective time-processing is implicated in developmental dyslexia, Llinas (1996) makes several suggestions concerning the kinds of abnormality which might occur within neural oscillatory timing systems. For example, oscillatory activity at some frequencies might be absent, or fluctuating; activity at different frequencies could be poorly co-ordinated, or unresponsive to calibratory control; computations across outputs might be impaired; or output connections from particular oscillatory mechanisms and their target effectors might be dysfunctional. In other words, if biological time-processing mechanisms are importantly dependent on a complex system of interactive brain waves and biorhythms, it seems likely that these could break down in many ways and at many points in the system.

Given the uncertainties concerning the precise physical mechanisms underlying the kind of time-parsing system I have described, I do not want to make any strong claims concerning the precise mechanisms underlying hypothetical time-parsing deficits in autism. In general terms, however, I hypothesize the following:

1. Individuals with low functioning autism have pervasive deficits across the whole timing system (short of having a complete absence of timing mechanisms, which is not consistent with life).

2. Individuals with classic autism/Kanner's syndrome have less pervasive deficits, leaving intact at least some of the rapid-rate timers which subserve the acquisition of a language system, but affecting those timers which are necessary for encoding and extracting meaning from events lasting longer than a few seconds.

3. Individuals with Asperger syndrome have only patchy deficits among relatively rapid-rate timers (affecting, for example, the interpretation and use of facial expression, body language, and prosody); and similarly patchy deficits among slower-rate timers such as are involved in analysing, encoding, and learning from events such as conversations, and those events from which an understanding of mental states can be derived. It seems likely that 'counter' mechanisms (Wearden, 1994) are impaired, since people with Asperger syndrome (and no doubt people with more severe forms of autism) appear to have little sense of their own life-span, except in terms of dated years.

There is some physical evidence in support of these linked hypotheses. In the first place there is evidence which suggests that the circadian 24-hour cycle is abnormal in autism. Numerous studies have demonstrated abnormalities in autistic children's circadian rhythms using a number of different measures: for example, salivary cortisol (Takahagi *et al.*, 1986), blood cortisol and body temperature (Hill *et al.*, 1977), and melatonin (Ritvo *et al.*, 1993; Nir, 1995). A majority of autistic children experience sleep problems especially in their early years, and these problems are likely to be severe (Richdale and Prior, 1995). Richdale and Prior suggest that sleep problems may have some specificity for autism, as they are not common in normally developing children or in children with mental retardation. Disturbances in circadian rhythms are more common in young children with autism and in older low-functioning individuals with autism, than in older high-functioning individuals. It does not appear, therefore, that abnormal circadian rhythm is a necessary feature of autism. However, there is evidence to suggest that circadian rhythms are established very soon after birth in normally developing infants (Attansio, Rager, and Gupta, 1986), and it has been suggested that an absence or irregularity of the normal 24-hour neuroendocrinological cycle could have a cascade of effects on the developing brain in infants with autism (Segawa *et al.*, 1992). The effects of delayed establishment of circadian rhythms in autism could therefore persist after relatively normal circadian rhythms became established.

In the second place, there is ample evidence of abnormalities in the EEGs of people with autism such as might be associated with abnormal oscillatory activity. Abnormal EEGs in people with autism may be related to the mental retardation and seizures which frequently co-occur with autism, rather than with the autism *per se*. Recently, however, it has been claimed by one authoritative group of researchers that different patterns of EEG abnormalities can be used not only to differentiate between children with autism and normally developing children, but also to differentiate between children with different patterns of autism-related social abnormalities (Dawson *et al.*, 1995). Moreover, a higher rate of EEG abnormalities and a raised vulnerability to seizures in those less able individuals who do not acquire speech and language is consistent with the suggestion that rapid-rate timing mechanisms (in addition to slow-rate timers) are more affected in low-functioning individuals with autism than in those more able individuals who acquire at least some language.

In addition to the physical evidence which supports, or is consistent with, the proposed hypotheses, there is other evidence from the broader field of normal and abnormal development which can be interpreted as suggesting that fully adult timing systems develop gradually during early childhood, and that delayed maturation of these systems can cause developmental disorders. In particular, early changes in the immediate memory span, the emergence from infantile amnesia, and certain aspects of representational change are easy to explain in terms of an initially skeletal, but gradually expanding, timing system. Moreover, when the immediate memory span does not expand normally, language acquisition is always impaired (Boucher, 1998), supporting the claim that pervasive deficits affecting rapid-rate timers cause the failure of language acquisition in children with low-functioning autism. One of the most persistent theories concerning the cause of specific language impairments (SLI) in children is that temporal processing is defective (Leonard, 1998), and the hypotheses proposed here help to explain the higher than expected rate of language impairments in the relatives of individuals with autism (Bolton *et al.*, 1994).

If it is correct to surmise that normal infants are born with a skeletal timing system (consisting, perhaps, of a circadian cycle and associated intradian biorhythms, and sufficient rapid rate neural timers to co-ordinate the perceptions and actions necessary for sucking, crying, and so forth), the question arises as to the processes involved in expanding the system to adult levels. If the theory that SLI is caused by defective rapid-rate temporal processing is correct, maturation under genetic control would appear to be involved, since there is no evidence to suggest that SLI is strongly associated with deprivation. If autism and SLI are genetically related, as is also likely, then it seems probable that timing deficits in autism are at least partly caused by genetic abnormalities. However, there is also evidence from the study of SLI and people with phonological dyslexia which suggests that intensive training may ameliorate whatever temporal processing deficits were originally operative (Merzenich *et al.*, 1996). This supports other evidence which suggests that many bodily cycles develop as a result of entrainment with rhythmic cycles within the environment, whether these are naturally occurring, or whether they occur by social convention (Levine, 1998). This raises the possibility that timing is defective in people with autism as a result of a failure of entrainment, as has in fact been suggested by Richdale and Prior (1995). There is a chicken–egg problem here, because a failure of entrainment of interpersonal and social rhythms could result from primary intersubjectivity deficits (Hobson, 1993). On the other hand, intersubjectivity impairments could result from primary deficits in timing mechanisms, causing the infant's behaviour to be 'out of synch.' with the daily rhythms of life and with the rhythmicities of other people's behaviour. Finally, if, as suggested above, people with autism lack the usual 'counter' mechanisms, this quite strongly suggests that the timing system in people with autism could be impoverished as a result of computational abnormalities. Such abnormalities could affect the range of timers within a system (see above), and also integration across the outputs of functional timers.

At present there is no way of deciding between these various possible causes of defective timing in autism. However, it seems most probable that initial deficits within the skeletal timing system result from genetic abnormalities and lead to a cascade of secondary timing deficits, as suggested by Segawa *et al.* (1992). These secondary deficits could include impairments of computational mechanisms. The child with a reduced or abnormal set of internal cyclic mechanisms has reduced possibilities for entraining internal rhythms with rhythmicities in the physical and social environment. This would disrupt reciprocal social interaction from the earliest age, reducing the opportunities for socially stimulated entrainment.

Defective functioning of the time-parsing system at the psychological level in autism

In earlier sections I have suggested that the biopsychological time-parsing system in normal people has the following functions:

- contributing to the segmentation and individuation of time-based items and events at multiple levels of analysis, thereby helping to determine the processing capacity of a system in terms of individuated items;

- registering the temporal characteristics of experience, including registering the temporal course of continuous experience, registering the time of occurrence of individuated events, and registering the temporal relations between items at different levels of analysis;
- providing a mechanism for registering temporal succession and thereby enabling associate, rote, habit, and procedural memories to be acquired;
- binding together, via shared time-of-occurrence information, memories of individuated events and contextual memories including those representing one's personal involvement in an event, thereby contributing to both event memory and episodic memory;
- providing the material in memory from which events scripts, certain concepts, and knowledge of regularities and rules can be extracted, thereby helping to make representational material available *to* the system in addition to being available *within* the system (Karmiloff-Smith, 1992),[1] thereby contributing to semantic memory and the knowledge base;
- providing representations of time which can be utilized off line in all forms of future-based programming, planning, problem solving, and imagining;
- providing the particulate items, knowledge of rules, and representations of future time which are required for generating all forms of time-based novel behaviour; thereby contributing to language acquisition and use, *inter alia*.

The suggestion here is that some or all of these functions are impaired in people with various forms of autism ranging from very low-functioning autism to the mildest forms of Asperger syndrome.

However, it is difficult to summarize precisely how these impairments are manifested in different individuals across the spectrum, because the effects of defective time-parsing will vary according to the pervasiveness of the timing deficits and according to their distribution across the whole range of timers, from those with periodicities of milliseconds to those with periodicities of days, lunar months, and possibly years. It is certain, moreover, that time-parsing has other functions, not mentioned above. For example, there is an expanding literature on the role of temporal binding in perception, and it is possible that abnormalities in this area can help to explain some of the perceptual abnormalities which occur in autism, including some of the evidence relating to the theory of weak central coherence (Brock *et al.*, forthcoming).[2] However, probably enough has been said in previous sections to illustrate both the differences in the impairments which would result from different patterns of timing deficits, as well as the commonalities which can be identified.

---

[1] This suggestion was not introduced above, except obliquely, and cannot be developed here for lack of space. However, fuller arguments for the role of time-parsing in representational change will be presented in a future paper.
[2] Again, lack of space precludes discussion of this interesting possibility.

CONCLUSION

A case has been made for the importance of problems of biopsychological timing for our understanding of autism, and a time-parsing system has been outlined which, it is hypothesized, may be defective in autism. The probable effects of defective time-parsing on memory and generativity have been stressed, with some mention of the likely effects on peripheral input and output processing. More could be said about the possible effects of defective time-parsing on perception, on representational abilities, on the acquisition and function of speech, language, and communication, on the development of a concept of self, and on reciprocal social interaction. However, consideration of these topics could not be included in a single chapter. It will be important in future work to explore the relationship between any time-parsing problems and the social problems of autism: the theory as it stands appears to be capable of explaining—or contribut-ing to an explanation of—the linguistic and creativity impairments which define autism, but has less power to explain the social impairments. If the theory is supported by planned empirical work, then it will also be important to consider how it relates to other influential and well supported theories concerning the psychological origins of autism.

It will also be of interest to consider how the theory meshes with existing theo-ries concerned with the development of temporal concepts in normal children (Friedman, 1990; McCormack and Hoerl, 1999). To date very little if anything has been written about the biological mechanisms which supply the raw material for concepts of time, and the time-parsing mechanism outlined here could provide a starting point for work in this area.

I am grateful to Teresa McCormack and Christoph Hoerl for their perceptive, patient, and always constructive comments on earlier drafts of this chapter, and for their ongoing contributions to my still very incomplete learning curve about the psychology of time. I am particularly indebted to Gordon Brown for the same reason.

J.B.

REFERENCES

ABLER, W. (1989), 'On the particulate principle of self-diversifying systems', *Journal of Social and Biological Structures*, 12: 1–13.

ALLEN, M., LINCOLN, A. J., and KAUFMAN, A. S. (1991), 'Sequential and simultaneous processing abilities of high functioning autistic and language impaired children', *Journal of Autism and Developmental Disorders*, 21: 483–502.

AMELI, R., COURSCHESNE, E., LINCOLN, A., KAUFMAN, A. S., AND GRILLON, C. (1988), 'Visual memory processes in high-functioning individuals with autism', *Journal of Autism and Developmental Disorders*, 18: 601–16.

American Psychiatric Association [APA] (1994), *Diagnostic and Statistical Manual of Mental Disorders,* 4th edn. (DSM-IV). Washington, DC: APA.

ATTANASIO, A., RAGER, K., and GUPTA, D. (1986), 'Ontogeny of circadian rhythmicity for melatonin, serotonin and N acetylserotonin in humans', *Pineal Research,* 3: 251–6.

BENNETTO, L., PENNINGTON, B. F., and ROGERS, S. J. (1996), 'Intact and impaired memory functions in autism', *Child Development,* 67: 1816–35.

BISHOP, D. V. M. (1997), *Uncommon Understanding.* Hove: Psychology Press.

BLOOM, P. (1994), 'Generativity within language and other cognitive domains', *Cognition,* 54: 177–89.

BOLTON, P., MACDONALD, H., PICKLES, A., RIOS, P., GOODE, S., CROWSON, M., BAILEY, A., and RUTTER M. (1994), 'A case-control family history study of autism', *Journal of Child Psychology and Psychiatry,* 35: 877–900.

BOUCHER, J. (1975), 'Two neuropsychological theories of autism', Ph.D. thesis (ch. 8), University of Birmingham.

—— (1976), 'Echoic memory capacity in autistic children', *Journal of Child Psychology and Psychiatry,* 19: 161–6.

—— (1977), 'Alternation and sequencing behaviour, and response to novelty in autistic children', *Journal of Child Psychology and Psychiatry,* 18, 67–72.

—— (1981*a*), 'Memory for recent events in autistic children', *Journal of Autism and Developmental Disorders,* 11: 293–301.

—— (1981*b*), 'Immediate free recall in early childhood autism: another point of behavioural similarity with the amnesic syndrome', *British Journal of Psychology,* 72: 211–15.

—— (1998), 'The prerequisites for language acquisition: evidence from cases of anomalous language development', in P. Carruthers and J. Boucher (eds.), *Language and Thought: Interdisciplinary Themes.* Cambridge: Cambridge University Press, 55–75.

—— and LEWIS, V. (1989), 'Memory impairment and communication in relatively able autistic children', *Journal of Child Psychology and Psychiatry,* 30: 99–122.

—— and WARRINGTON, E. K. (1976), 'Memory deficits in early infantile autism: some similarities to the amnesic syndrome', *British Journal of Psychology,* 67: 73–87.

BOWLER, D., GARDINER, J., and GRICE, S. (2000), 'Episodic memory and remembering in high-functioning adults with autism', *Journal of Autism and Developmental Disorders,* 30: 295–304.

BROCK, J., BROWN, C., BOUCHER, J., and PLEYDELL-SMITH, K. (forthcoming), 'Local and global neural networks and weak central coherence in autism'.

BROWN, G. D. A., and VOUSDEN, J. (1998), 'Adaptive analysis of sequential behaviour: oscillators as rational mechanisms', in M. Oaksford and N. Chater (eds.), *Rational Models of Cognition.* Oxford: Oxford University Press, 165–93.

—— PREECE, T., and HULME, C. (2000), 'Oscillator-based memory for serial order', *Psychological Review,* 107: 127–81.

BURGESS, N., and HITCH, G. J. (1996), 'A connectionist model of STM for serial order', in S. E. Gathercole (ed.), *Models of Short-Term Memory.* Hove: Psychology Press, 51–72.

CHURCH, R. M., and BROADBENT, H. (1990), 'Alternative representations of time, number and rate', *Cognition,* 5: 105–18.

CROMER, R. (1983), 'Hierarchical planning disability in the drawings and constructions of a special group of severely aphasic children', *Brain and Cognition,* 2: 144–64.

DAWSON, G., KLINGER, L., PANAGIOTIDES, H., LEWY, A., and CASTELLOE, P. (1995), 'Subgroups of autistic children based on social behaviour display distinct patterns of brain activity', *Journal of Abnormal Child Psychology,* 23: 569–83.

DOBBINSON, S., PERKINS, M., and BOUCHER, J. (1998), 'Structural patterns in conversations with a woman who has autism', *Journal of Communication Disorders*, 31: 113–34.

FARRANT, A., BLADES, M., and BOUCHER, J. (1998), 'Source memory in high functioning children with autism', *Journal of Autism and Developmental Disorders*, 28: 43–50.

—— BOUCHER, J., and BLADES, M. (1999), 'Metamemory in relatively able children with autism', *Child Development*, 70: 107–31.

FREEMAN, B. J., LUCAS, J. C., FORNESS, S. R., and RITVO, E. (1985), 'Cognitive processing of high-functioning autistic children: comparing the K-ABC and the WISC-R', *Journal of Psychoeducational Assessment*, 4: 357–62.

FRIEDMAN, W. J. (1990), *About Time: Inventing the Fourth Dimension*. Cambridge, Mass.: MIT Press.

FRITH, U. (1970), 'Cognitive mechanisms in autism: experiments with color and tone sequence production', *Journal of Autism and Childhood Schizophrenia*, 2: 160–73.

FUSTER, J. M. (1989), *The Prefrontal Cortex: Anatomy, Physiology, and Neuropsychology of the Frontal Lobe*, 2nd edn. New York: Raven.

GALLISTEL, C. R. (1990), *The Organization of Learning*. Cambridge, Mass.: MIT Press.

HAPPE, F. (1994), *Autism: An Introduction to Psychological Theory*. London: UCL Press.

HARRINGTON, D. L., and HAALAND, K. Y. (1998), 'Sequencing and timing operations of the basal ganglia', in D. A. Rosenbaum and C. E. Collyer (eds.), *Timing of Behavior: Neural, Psychological, and Computational Perspectives*. Cambridge Mass.: MIT Press, 35–61.

HERMELIN, B., and O'CONNOR, N. (1970), *Psychological Experiments with Autistic Children*. Oxford: Pergamon Press.

—— —— (1975), 'The recall of digits by normal, deaf, and autistic children', *British Journal of Psychology*, 66: 203–9.

HILL, S., WAGNER, E., SHEDLARSKI, J., and SEARS, S. (1977), 'Diurnal cortisol and temperature variation of normal and autistic children', *Developmental Psychology*, 10: 579–83.

HOBSON, P. (1993), *Autism and the Development of Mind*. Hove: Erlbaum.

HURLBERT, R., HAPPÉ, F., and FRITH, U. (1994), 'Sampling the inner experience of autism: a preliminary report', *Psychological Medicine*, 24: 385–95.

KANNER, L. (1943), 'Autistic disturbance of affective contact', *Nervous Child*, 2: 217–50.

KARMILOFF-SMITH, A. (1992), *Beyond modularity*. Cambridge, Mass.: MIT Press.

KAUFMAN, A. S., and KAUFMAN, N. L. (1983), *Kaufman Assessment Battery for Children*. Circle Pines, Minn: American Guidance Service.

KLINGER, L. C., and DAWSON, G. (1995), 'A fresh look at categorization abilities in persons with autism', in E. Schopler and G. Mesibov (eds.), *Learning and Cognition in Autism*. New York: Plenum Press, 119–36.

LEONARD, L. (1998), *Children with Specific Language Impairment*. Cambridge, Mass.: MIT Press.

LEVINE, ROBERT N. (1998), *A Geography of Time: On Tempo, Culture, and the Pace of Life*. New York: Perseus Books.

LINCOLN, A. J., DICKSTEIN, P., COURSCHESNE, E., ELMASIAN, R., and TALLAL, P. (1992), 'Auditory processing abilities in non-retarded adolescents and young adults with developmental language disorder and autism', *Brain and Language*, 43: 613–22.

—— ALLEN, M. H., and KILMAN, A. (1995), 'The assessment and interpretation of intellectual abilities in people with autism', in E. Schopler and G. Mesibov (eds.), *Learning and Cognition in Autism*. New York: Plenum Press, 89–118.

LLINAS, R. (1996), 'Is dyslexia a dyschronia?', *Annals of the New York Academy of Science*, 682: 48–56.

MCCORMACK, T., and HOERL, C. (1999), 'Memory and temporal perspective: the role of temporal frameworks in memory development', *Developmental Review*, 19: 154–82.

MANGELS, J., IVRY, R. B., and SHIMIZU, N. (1998), 'Dissociable contributions of the prefrontal and neocerebeller cortex to time perception', *Cognitive Brain Research*, 7: 15–39.

MERZENICH, M., JENKINS, W., JOHNSTON, P., SCHREIMER, C., MILLER, S., and TALLAL, P. (1996), 'Temporal processing deficits of language-learning impaired children amelio-rated by training', *Science*, 271: 77–81.

MILLWARD, C., POWELL, S., MESSER, D., and JORDAN, R. (2000), 'Recall for self and other in autism: children's memory for events experienced by themselves and their peers', *Journal of Autism and Developmental Disorders*, 30: 15–28.

MINSHEW, N. J., GOLDSTEIN, G., and SIEGEL, D. J. (1997), 'Neuropsychologic functioning in autism: profile of a complex information processing disorder', *Journal of the International Neuropsychological Society*, 3: 303–16.

NIR, I. (1995), 'Circadian melatonin, thyroid stimulating hormone, prolactin and cortisol levels in serum of young adults with autism', *Journal of Autism and Developmental Disorders*, 25: 641–54.

OWEN, A. M., ROBERTS, A. C., POLKEY, C. E., SAHAKIAN, B. J., and ROBBINS, T. W. (1990), 'Planning and spatial working memory following frontal lobe lesions in man', *Neuropsychologia*, 29: 993–1006.

PEETERS, T. (1997), *Autism: From Theoretical Understanding to Educational Intervention.* London: Whurr Press.

—— and GILLBERG, C. (1999), *Autism: Medical and Educational Aspects.* London: Whurr Publishers.

RENNER, P., KLINGER, L. G., and KLINGER, M. (2000), 'Implicit and explicit memory in autism: is autism an amnesic disorder?' *Journal of Autism and Developmental Disorders*, 30: 3–14.

RICHDALE, A., and PRIOR, M. R. (1995), 'The sleep/wake rhythm in children with autism', *European Child and Adolescent Psychiatry*, 4: 175–86.

RICKS, D., and WING, L. (1975), 'Language, communication and the use of symbols in normal and autistic children', *Journal of Autism and Childhood Schizophrenia*, 5: 191–221.

RITVO, E., RITVO, R., YUWILER, A., and BROTHER, A. (1993), 'Elevated daytime melatonin concentrations in autism: a pilot study', *European Child and Adolescent Psychiatry*, 2: 75–8.

RUMSEY J., and HAMBURGER, S. D. (1988), Neuropsychological findings in high-function-ing men with infantile autism, residual state', *Journal of Clinical and Experimental Neuropsychology*, 10: 201–21.

RUSSELL, J. (1996), *Agency: Its Role in Mental Development.* Hove: Erlbaum (UK) Taylor and Francis.

—— and JARROLD, C. (1999), 'Memory for actions in children with autism: self versus other', *Cognitive Neuropsychiatry*, 4: 303–31.

RUTTER, M. (1983), 'Cognitive deficits in the pathogenesis of autism', *Journal of Child Psychology and Psychiatry*, 24: 513–31.

SACKS, O. (1995), *An Anthropologist on Mars: Seven Paradoxical Tales.* London: Picador, ch. 7.

SCHACTER, D. L. (1987), 'Memory, amnesia, and frontal lobe dysfunction', *Psychobiology*, 15: 21–36.

SEGAWA, M., KATOH, M., KATOH, J., and NOMURA, Y. (1992), 'Early modulation of sleep parameters and its importance in later behaviour', *Brain Dysfunction*, 5: 211–23.

STUDDERT-KENNEDY, M. (1998), 'The particulate origins of language productivity: from syllable to gesture', in J. Hurford, M. Studdert-Kennedy, and G. Knight (eds.). *Approaches to the Evolution of Language: Social and Cognitive Bases*. Cambridge: Cambridge University Press, 202–21.

TAGER-FLUSBERG, H. (1991), 'Semantic processing in the free recall of autistic children: further evidence for a cognitive deficit', *British Journal of Developmental Psychology*, 9: 417–30.

TAKAHAGI, K., YOKOYAMA, F., MURATA, S., WATANABE, M., HOSHINO, Y., KANEKO, M., and KUMASHIRO, H. (1986), 'Diurnal rhythm in the salivary cortisol concentrations of children with psychiatric disorders', *Neurosciences (Kobe)*, 12: 94–5.

TANGUAY, P. E. (1984), 'Toward a new classification of serious psychopathology in children', *Journal of American Academy of Child Psychiatry*, 23: 373–84.

TREISMAN, M., FAULKNER, A., and NAISH, P. (1992). 'On the relation between time perception and the timing of motor action: evidence for a temporal oscillator controlling the timing of movement', *Quarterly Journal of Experimental Psychology*, 45A: 235–63.

TULVING, E. (1985), 'Memory and consciousness', *Canadian Psychology*, 25: 1–12.

TURNER, M. (1997), 'Towards an executive dysfunction account of repetitive behaviour in autism', in J. Russell (ed.), *Autism as an Executive Disorder*. Oxford: Oxford University Press, 57–100.

VOUSDEN, J., BROWN, G. D. A., and HARLEY, T. (forthcoming), 'Serial control of phonology in speech production', *Cognitive Psychology*.

WEARDEN, J. H. (1994), 'Prescriptions for models of biopsychological time', in M. Oaksford and G. D. A. Brown (eds.), *Neurodynamics and Psychology*. San Diego: Academic Press, 215–36.

WERTH, A., PERKINS, M., and BOUCHER, J. (1999), ' "Here's the weavery looming up": the creative word-play of a woman with high-level autism', paper presented at the Conference of the International Clinical Phonetics and Linguistics Association, Montreal, May.

WHEELER, M. A., STUSS, D. T., and TULVING, E. (1997), 'Toward a theory of episodic memory: the frontal lobes and autonoetic consciousness', *Psychological Bulletin,* 121: 331–54.

WILLIAMS, D. (1996), *Autism: An Inside-out Approach*. London: Jessica Kingsley Publishers.

WING, L. (1996), *The Autistic Spectrum*. London: Constable.

—— and GOULD, J. (1979), 'Severe impairment of social interaction and associated abnormalities in children: epidemiology and classification', *Journal of Autism and Childhood Schizophrenia*, 9: 11–29.

WOLFF, S. (1995), *Loners: The Life Path of Unusual Children*. London: Routledge.

II

Memory, Awareness, and the Past

5

Memory Processes Underlying Humans' Chronological Sense of the Past

William J. Friedman

How do we remember the times of past events? What information in memory allows us to know *when* an event occurred? Usually, we take for granted that memory is infused with chronology. The term 'autobiographical memory', used by some cognitive psychologists to describe memory for personal events, seems to imply a particular metaphor: that memory is like a narrative of one's life, organized by chronology, much as the sequence of chapters and pages of a book might reflect the order in which the events of a life unfold. In this chapter I will try to show that events are not chronologically organized in memory nor is there even a special system for assigning temporal codes to individual memories. Personal memories, instead, are individual episodes—islands in time. Only by reconstructing when an event must have occurred or by assessing the vividness of a memory can we place it in time. And even this latter, intuitive sense of how long ago an event took place is distorted, with considerable compression of the subjective ages of events beyond the recent past.

To understand psychological research on memory for the times of past events, it is useful to introduce a distinction between two ways of knowing when an event occurred, which I will call 'distances' and 'locations'. A temporal distance is the amount of time that has elapsed between some event and the present. A particular event might have occurred two week ago, one year ago, and so forth. Temporal locations, by contrast, are parts of conventional, natural, or personal time patterns. For example, the spring, Wednesday, and my last year of college are all locations in time patterns in which a particular event may have occurred, but which we also understand apart from their contents. This distance-location distinction bears similarities to the contrasts sometimes drawn between egocentric and exocentric reference and between McTaggart's (1927) A series and B series.

The distinction between temporal distances and locations may seem artificial, because adults can easily translate distances to locations and vice versa. For example, if I know that an event happened last June, I can determine how long ago the event occurred; or if I know it was a month ago, I can tell the month and season in which it occurred. But these sorts of inference are the end products of human temporal cognition, not the fundamental information on which our memory for time is based. I will try to demonstrate the psychological relevance of the distance-location distinction by presenting evidence for the existence of the two kinds of processes, describing their properties, and discussing the roles they play in human thought.

THEORIES OF MEMORY FOR THE TIMES OF PAST EVENTS

Location-based theories

A number of theorists have proposed that humans' ability to remember the times of past events depends on information about unchanging locations in time patterns (as opposed to ever-changing *distances* from the present). (See Friedman, 1993, for a more complete description and evaluation of theories of memory for time.) In one such theory, specific temporal information, or 'time tags', are uniformly and automatically stored with representations of an event at the time when the event occurs (e.g. Hasher and Zacks, 1979; Yntema and Trask, 1963). If we later need to determine the time of the event, we access the time tag associated with it in memory. Although this idea is appealing, the theory has been criticized for its vagueness (Friedman, 1993). Without specifying the nature of the temporal information that is assigned to each memory, the theory's predictions are difficult to distinguish from any of the other explanations of our ability to remember when an event occurred. Worse for the theory, the few empirical implications that can be pinned down appear to be inconsistent with research findings. One such finding is that memory for time is generally more accurate in laboratory tasks in which participants know in advance that they must remember the material than in tasks where the time-memory test comes as a surprise (e.g. Naveh-Benjamin, 1990). If time-tagging were automatic, no such differences would be expected.

The most successful location theories are reconstructive theories (e.g. Brown, Rips, and Shevell, 1985; Friedman and Wilkins, 1985; Hintzman, Block, and Summers, 1973). According to these theories, we judge the times of past events by retrieving whatever information is associated with them in memory and, where possible, relating this information to our rich store of knowledge about personal, natural, or social time patterns. For example, I might remember that a particular visit to London occurred at the end of the summer by recalling that the weather was hot and the grass was parched in Kensington Gardens or that my visit to the National Gallery must have occurred in the middle of the day, because I remember having lunch at the museum restaurant. No special time tags are assumed in these theories. Instead, ordinary contextual information (such as percepts, activities, or other events that happened at about the same time) are related to our general knowledge about time patterns (e.g. that summer is hot, and lunch is eaten in the middle of the day).

Distance-based theories

Some psychologists have proposed that memory is itself organized according to the times at which events occur. For example, Murdock reasoned that: 'Somehow the brain must encode or represent temporal information in a spatial format' (1974: 266), 'The older the trace, the farther removed it is from the psychological present . . . in whatever way the brain preserves a record of human experience' (p. 270). In such chronological-organization theories, the time of an event is determined by its distance from the present in the memory store. There is, to my knowledge, no neurological evidence to support chronological-organization theories, and most such theories have proved difficult to evaluate in psychological experiments because most of their predictions are readily explained by other theories (Friedman, 1993). Furthermore, one unique prediction that would seem to follow from the notion of chronological organization appears to be incorrect. If the memory store is chronologically organized, one would expect that, when provided with a description of some event, we should easily remember the nearness in time of some other unrelated but temporally contiguous event. Several studies show that we cannot do this with any consistency. For example, Friedman and Huttenlocher (1997) asked viewers of the television show '60 Minutes' to judge whether pairs of stories from the past year (both of which respondents reported recognizing) had been presented the during the same weekly episode or whether story A was presented in an earlier or later week than story B. The results showed that same-week pairs were no more likely to be judged to be contiguous in time than different-week pairs. Finally, Brewer (1996) notes that these theories are implausible, because of the large amount of time that would be required to retrieve an event if memory were organized by time of occurrence.

A more influential type of distance theory is that changes in the characteristics of memories with the passage of time provide cues to their ages. According to these strength theories, the strength, accessibility, or elaborateness of memory traces allows us to determine the ages of memories (e.g. Brown, Rips, and Shevell *et al.*, 1985; Hinrichs, 1970; Morton, 1968). For example, I may judge a news story that I heard last night to be quite recent because the memory is vivid, whereas one from several years ago might seem rather old because my memory of it is dim or sketchy. These sorts of theories are discussed in greater detail in a separate section later in this chapter.

In the present book, Gordon Brown and Nick Chater present another theory that they describe as distance-based but which seems to the present author to incorporate aspects of both distance and location theories. Brown and Chater propose that all memory representations contain information about the time elapsed since the event occurred, that is, they contain information about distances from the present. They also suggest that the source of temporal information is the attachment of readings from a set of clocks, each with a different periodicity, at the time when an event occurs. This seems to imply that the temporal information associated with memories is locations—the clock readings when the events occurred.

Brown and Chater believe that the theory is consistent with available evidence, as long as one assumes that other processes, such as reconstruction, sometimes play a role in memory for time. My own view is that the theory has difficulty accounting for a number of phenomena. For example, one of the most robust phenomena in laboratory studies is sometimes called 'primacy' (see Friedman, 1993). (This phenomenon is also discussed in the later section on location theories.) Participants are especially accurate in judging the within-list position of items that were presented near the beginning of the list. This finding presents problems for theories that assume that the basic temporal information in memory is distances from the present, because the beginning of a list is an arbitrary distance in the past; it is only special as a location in a time pattern—the list itself. Brown and Chater would probably explain primacy by the time-stamping of memories relative to the start of the list, a mechanism assumed in their OSCAR model. But if this is the case, then it would seem incorrect to maintain that memory is organized in terms of time relative to the present. Of course it is theoretically possible to compute distances and locations from one another if all events, including the present, have time codes relative to some arbitrary starting point assigned to them. But if the times of past events are known by the subtraction of time codes, why is the accuracy of items near the start of the list so much greater than that for items in the middle of the list? Another problem is the theory's explanation of what Brown and Chater call hierarchical effects. This problem is discussed later, in the section 'Scale effects'.

Other theories

In this chapter I will focus on the two main explanations of humans' memory for time, reconstructive, and strength theories. However, it is important to note that there is a third way in which one can know the times of past events. We sometimes remember the *order* of a pair of events, even when neither can be located in a time pattern and their relative distances from the present cannot be judged. This may be true for pairs of news stories when a particular story causes us to recall an earlier, related event. People who remember that Robert Kennedy was assassinated after his brother John may do so in part because they retrieved the earlier event when the later one occurred and stored this relation in memory. When asked which of the two events was more recent, we might access a kind of temporal pointer linking the later event to the earlier one. It is inconceivable that the order of all possible pairs of events is stored. Instead, advocates of this order-code theory (e.g. Tzeng and Cotton, 1980) predict that the order of a pair of events will be stored only when a later event reminds us of an earlier event. The order-code theory successfully predicts that the order of pairs of words presented in a laboratory task will be better remembered if the two words have related meanings than if the two are unrelated (e.g. Tzeng and Cotton, 1980; Winograd and Soloway, 1985). It seems that order codes *do* play a role in our memory for the times of events, but that their utility is restricted to cases where it is order information that is sought and the events happen to be related. These occasions are probably uncommon, though order information is likely to be one of several kinds of information that help us reconstruct the locations of past events.

RESEARCH ON MEMORY FOR TIME

Research methods

Most psychological research on memory for time has been conducted in the laboratory using the brief time-scales that a single laboratory session allows, typically less than one hour. Participants are presented with a series of events, usually a list of words, and then asked to judge the times that particular events occurred. For example, a researcher might present four lists of twenty words each and later ask a participant to judge in which list a particular word had been presented, or the researcher might present a single list of twenty words and ask the participant to indicate in which position, from one to twenty, the word had been presented. Laboratory studies allow experimenters to control the nature and timing of the stimuli and to minimize the influence that simple strategies, such as looking at a clock, might have on performance. But these studies cannot tell us directly how we remember times on much longer scales nor how we remember the times of events that are more meaningful. For this reason, a number of students of memory for time have used tasks in which participants judge the times of news events or personal events. For example, participants might be asked to give the date of an event they had earlier recorded in a diary or the month and year in which Nelson Mandela was elected president of South Africa. Each of these approaches contributes information that is useful in evaluating the theories of memory for time.

Location-based theories

Scale effects. One of the most persuasive lines of evidence for reconstructive theories, and against distance theories, is a phenomenon called scale effects. Scale effects occur when we are able to recall accurately the time of an event on a fine time-scale, such as the time of day that the event happened, while being inaccurate on a grosser scale, such as the month. Scale effects cannot be explained by distance theories which require that the information underlying memory for time be unitary, such as the strength of the memory trace or its location in the memory store. If information about strength or location in memory is too imprecise for us to judge the month of an event, how could the information be accurate for time of day? This would be like estimating the distance of some object we see from our window and getting the number of centimetres within the last metre correct but being inaccurate by several metres.

In this volume, Brown and Chater offer another explanation of scale effects (which they call 'hierarchical effects'). They believe such effects can be explained by the coding of times by multiple, endogenous oscillators, each with a different frequency. However, this seems to require the implausible assumption that some of the oscillators happen to be tuned to arbitrary intervals, such as the length of lists in laboratory experiments. Without such an assumption, it is difficult to see how within-list position can sometimes be better remembered than the list in which an item appeared.

In reconstruction theories the information used to judge the times of past events is not assumed to be some integral quantity or time-stamps from multiple oscillators but rather the ordinary contents of memory. If the information we happen to recall is sufficient to constrain the time within some pattern, we can infer the location within that pattern. But we might well lack information that can constrain the time on another scale, even if that other scale is a grosser one.

Scale effects have been demonstrated both in the laboratory (Hintzman, Block, and Summers, 1973) and in studies of memory for personal or news events (Bruce and Van Pelt, 1989; Friedman, 1987; Friedman and Wilkins, 1985; White 1982, 1989). For example, Friedman and Wilkins (1985) asked a group of British women to recall the times of ten news events from the preceding twenty years. Table 5.1 lists the events and gives the times at which they occurred. (Testing took place in May 1983.) The participants were asked to make separate judgements on the following time scales: year, month, day of the month, day of the week, and hour of the day. We calculated the average error in years for the year estimates, and, for the remaining, cyclic scales, errors were calculated as a proportion of the amount of error that would be expected by chance alone. For example, if you simply guess the month of some event, you will be off by three months on average—half the maximum distance that you could be wrong in a twelve-month cycle. If your actual estimate was one month away from the true

TABLE 5.1 *Stimulus events and times of occurrence*

Event description	Day of week	Date	Approximate GMT
1. John F. Kennedy is assassinated	Friday	22 November 1963	19:00
2. Donald Campbell is killed in a speedboat accident on Lake Windermere.	Wednesday	4 January 1967	9:00
3. The first spaceman sets foot on the moon.	Monday	21 July 1969	3:00
4. Lord Mountbatten is killed by an explosion aboard his boat.	Monday	27 August 1979	12:00
5. Former Beatle John Lennon is shot.	Tuesday	8 December 1980	4:00
6. Pope John Paul II is shot.	Wednesday	13 May 1981	16:00
7. Prince Charles and Lady Diana exchange rings.	Tuesday	29 July 1981	12:00
8. Egyptian president Anwar Sadat is assassinated.	Thursday	6 October 1981	13:00
9. Prince William is born.	Tuesday	22 June 1982	21:00
10. The ship *Mary Rose* rises above the surface.	Monday	11 October 1982	9:00

Source: W. J. Friedman and A. J. Wilkins (1985), by permission of the Psychomonic Society.

TABLE 5.2 *Mean error of time estimates for each scale for each event*

Event	Actual year	Absolute deviation Year	Proportion of chance deviation				
			Month	Day of month	Day of week	Hour	Mean of the four
1. Kennedy	1963	1.75	.98	.79	.62**	.64**	.76
2. Campbell	1967	3.78	1.51	1.08	.86	.57**	1.00
3. Moon	1969	2.67	.55***	.93	1.06	1.14	.92
4. Mountbatten	1979	.71	.10***	.93	1.10	.41***	.64
5. Lennon	1980	1.35	.76*	1.18	.86	1.34	1.04
6. John Paul II	1981	.76	.65**	.82	1.10	.45***	.76
7. Wedding	1981	.06	.04***	.77	.99	.14***	.48
8. Sadat	1981	.94	.92	1.32	.93	.31***	.87
9. Prince	1982	.06	.23***	.76	.65**	.85	.62
10. *Mary Rose*	1982	.29	.73*	.73*	.75	.55***	.69
Mean		1.24	.65	.93	.89	.64	

Note: Significance levels are for one-tailed t tests with the null hypothesis that entries are equal to or greater than chance deviations. Italicized entries are also significantly lower than the corresponding deviation scores in Experiment 2.
*p < .05.   **p < .01.   ***p < .001.

Source: Friedman and Wilkins (1985), by permission of the Psychonomic Society.

month of the event, your error would be .33 by this metric. This way of computing average error allowed us to compare participants' accuracy on different time-scales.

Table 5.2 presents the average error values for each event. For the cyclic scales (from month through hour), values of less than 1.0 mean that participants were more accurate than would be expected by pure guessing, and the asterisks indicate values significantly less than 1.0 by *t*-tests. Comparison of the year and month columns show a number of instances where participants were inaccurate by more than a year but judged the month with greater accuracy than would be expected by chance. Even more striking are the many instances where hour estimates are significantly accurate. The bottom row shows that while the average error on the year scale was more than one year, the average error in months was only .65 of what would be expected by chance. This row also reveals that accuracy, expressed as proportion of chance error, was as great for hour as for months, a finding that would be very difficult to explain by a unitary distance-based process. On the other hand, the results are easy to explain if we assume that participants sometimes remember aspects of the events that allow them to reconstruct the likely times on fine time-scales.

The findings in Table 5.2 do not allow us to distinguish between reconstruction based on memory for the events and inference based on the event descriptions. For example, even someone who had no recollection of the royal wedding might guess it took place in the middle of the day, and would have been very accurate on the hour scale. One example of *inaccuracy* suggests that non-memory-based inference did contribute to participants' judgements. The month estimate for event 2 was 1.51 times as many months away from the true month as would be expected by chance. Apparently, few participants believed it likely that a water-speed record would be attempted in midwinter. Friedman and Wilkins also found that participants in a follow-up study (1985, experiment 2) were able to guess the times of fictitious events with descriptions similar to those in Table 5.1 in a way that often matched significantly the times when the real events occurred. Again, these findings suggest that logical inference alone can contribute to scale effects.

However, two lines of evidence show that memory-based reconstruction also contributes to the unexpected accuracy of month and hour estimates. First, a comparison of the accuracy in Friedman and Wilkins's (1985) follow-up study and the main study showed that many of the month and hour estimates of the real events were significantly more accurate than the corresponding fictitious events (see the italicized entries in Table 5.2). Secondly, a later study (Friedman, 1987) demonstrated scale effects with an event whose time could not be reconstructed by general knowledge, an earthquake.

In January 1986 a mild but noticeable earthquake struck north-eastern Ohio. Earthquakes are rare in this region, so the event was distinctive and memorable. Earthquakes also have a property that is valuable for distinguishing reconstruction based on memory from reconstruction based on general knowledge alone: They can happen at any time. About eight months after the earthquake, employees of a college in the region were mailed a survey in which they were asked to recall, without consulting a diary or talking to anyone else, the time of the earthquake on each of the time-scales used in Friedman and Wilkins's (1985) study. The average absolute errors were .11 for year, 1.94 for month, 9.45 for day of the month, 1.57 for day of the week, and 1.04 for hour. Month estimates are close to what one would expect given the participants' accuracy for year, but hour estimates are far more accurate than would be expected for this level of accuracy for month and year. Whereas the year and month errors, expressed in years, were .11 and .16 respectively, the hour error was .0001 years. As in Friedman and Wilkins's study, the extreme accuracy for hour cannot be explained by unitary distance-based processes; participants must be reconstructing the time of day when the earthquake occurred. However, because earthquakes can happen at any time of the day or night, the accuracy must be based on information remembered about the event.

Method reports. Another kind of support for reconstructive theories comes from these same two studies and others of memory for personal or news events (Baddeley, Lewis, and Nimmo-Smith, 1978; Brown, Shevell, and Rips, 1986; Friedman, 1987; Friedman and Wilkins, 1985; Lieury *et al.*, 1979; Linton, 1975). When participants in these studies were asked to explain how they arrived at their estimates, they often reported using the sorts of processes predicted by reconstructive theories: linking information remembered about the events with general knowledge of time patterns. For example, many of the participants in Friedman and Wilkins's (1985) study explained their estimates of the month at which Prince William was born by pointing out that they recalled that it was about one year after the July wedding of his parents. In the earthquake study, eighty-four of the ninety-nine participants related the earthquake to a daily routine, such as lunch, or some other event whose time of day was recalled (Friedman, 1987). These examples illustrate a very common method of reconstructing the times of events, relating the event to be judged to some other event whose time is known. Another common method is to use some remembered aspect of the event itself, such as the weather, to infer the time.

Temporal landmarks.   Even laboratory experiments, which deprive participants of most conventional cues to time, provide ways of linking stimulus events to temporal landmarks. The start and end of a list of words are unavoidable landmarks in most studies, and participants are more accurate in their judgements of the times of words presented near these landmarks than for words in the middle of lists (e.g. Block, 1982; Hintzman and Block, 1971; Toglia and Kimble, 1976; Zimmerman and Underwood, 1968). The end-of-list finding might be explained by distance theories as the result of the strength of memory traces declining most rapidly in the time shortly after a word is presented. According to these theories, the recent past is a distinctive distance in the past, one easily discriminated from greater distances. But the finding for words near the start of a list is particularly important for location theories, because the start of a list is a notable location but, across experiments, an arbitrary distance in the past. In some experiments it might be about one minute ago, in others two minutes ago, and so forth. The fact that participants none the less show particular accuracy for the earliest words of a list must be due their linking the words with the location: start of the list.

   In addition, some researchers have deliberately provided artificial time patterns by choosing the words for each of a series of lists from particular categories (e.g. all in a given list are fruits or all are tools). When word lists are 'blocked' by category, temporal judgements are more accurate than when the members of each list come from varied categories (e.g. Tzeng and Cotton, 1980; Underwood and Malmi, 1978). Another way of increasing temporal information is to play a tape recording of a story at the same time as a sequence of stimuli is presented (Guenther and Linton, 1975). Participants who were tested in this condition made more accurate judgements of the times when particular pictures had been presented than those who did not hear a story. This technique, too, suggests that participants form associations between stimulus items and locations, in this case parts of the story. All of these findings show that people are more accurate when they can use temporal locations to judge the times of past events.

Amount remembered about events.   One of the clearest findings in research on memory for time is that when participants remember an event especially well, they are also particularly accurate in judging the time when it occurred (e.g. Bartlett and Snelus, 1980; Fozard and Weinert, 1972; Wells, 1974; Wright, Gaskell, and O'Muircheartaigh, 1997). This finding is important for reconstruction theories because it suggests that the greater the amount of information available about an event, the better we can infer the time when it occurred. But the finding is difficult for strength-based distance theories to explain. Judgements of very well remembered events should be displaced towards the present, not placed more accurately in time, if we rely on strength or vividness to judge when they occurred. However, most studies have failed to support the prediction that well-remembered events are displaced towards the present (Burt, 1992; Kemp, 1988; Thompson, Skowronski, and Lee, 1988; Wright, Gaskell, and O'Muircheartaigh, 1997; but see Brown, Rips, and Shevell, 1985).

Neurological evidence. A number of studies of patients with brain damage provide indirect support for reconstructive theories of memory for the times of events. (See also Ch. 2 by Block and Zakay in this volume for discussions of brain mechanisms involved in time perception and memory.) Patients with lesions in specific frontal regions of the cerebral cortex are poor at performing laboratory tasks of temporal memory and tasks measuring memory for the times of public events (McAndrews and Milner, 1991; Milner, Corsi, and Leonard, 1991; Shimamura, Janowsky, and Squire, 1990). This finding of impaired temporal judgements in frontal patients has led to the question of whether the frontal lobes play a special role in the initial coding of temporal information, as one theorist suggested (Schacter, 1987), or whether the deficits are in more general processes that allow the reconstruction of times (Moscovitch, 1995; Shimamura, Janowsky, and Squire, 1990; Wheeler, Stuss, and Tulving, 1997).

Evidence supports the latter position. Although frontal patients do not show across-the-board impairment of cognitive ability, and many perform normally on intelligence tests, they are impaired on a variety of tasks that require the reconstruction of both temporal and non-temporal information (Mangels *et al.*, 1996; Moscovitch and Melo, 1997). For example, Moscovitch and Melo (1997) found that frontal patients not only gave inaccurate dates for personal and historical events but made up a variety of details about them. Other studies show that whereas frontal patients may be only slightly impaired in recognizing an old event that is presented to them, they are disproportionately impaired at independently retrieving past events on their own or at recalling their times (Mangels *et al.*, 1996; Milner, Corsi, and Leonard, 1991; Shimamura, Janowski, and Squire, 1990; Wheeler, Stuss, and Tulving, 1997). These findings suggest that the problem is not the storage of information but rather the ability to use strategic processes to get at the information. Moscovitch believes that the frontal lobes perform strategic tests of information that is stored in more posterior parts of the cortex: '[T]he frontal lobes are necessary for converting remembering from a stupid, reflexive act triggered by a cue to an intelligent, reflective, goal directed activity that is under conscious, voluntary control' (1995: 1353). This sort of intelligent, goal-directed activity is necessary to reconstruct the times of events, so it seems likely that its impairment is the source of the deficits of memory for time found in frontal patients.

Distance-based theories

As explained in the section on theories, distance-based models are built on the assumption that natural memory processes, such as declines in the vividness, elaborateness, or accessibility of memories, create clues to the ages of memories. If a memory is clear, the event is assigned to the recent past; if it is dim, the event is judged to be old. Despite the intuitive appeal of these explanations, the large literature on memory for time has usually failed to support them (Friedman, 1993). In the previous section, we considered a number of findings from this literature that are difficult for distance-based theories to explain, including scale effects and the particular accuracy of the first items on a list. Indeed, some thirty years ago, when research on memory for time was just beginning, Tulving and Madigan (1970) offered an interesting criticism of the theories using a hypothetical experiment:

We suggest the following simple experiment to those who believe in the strength hypothesis. Present to the subject a series of items, one of which is the subject's own name or some other very conspicuous item . . .Then ask the subject to estimate the recency of various items, including the name. If the subjects say that the name was the last item in the series, please write to us, and to *Science* or *Nature*. If subjects are reasonably accurate in their judgments about the name, do some more thinking about the strength hypothesis. (1970: 463–4)

As we saw earlier, their expectation was borne out. In most studies well-remembered events are not displaced towards the present. Rather, their times are judged with particular accuracy.

Clearly distance-based theories are inconsistent with much of the research literature, but do distance processes play a role in our chronological sense of the past? I think the research literature has been biased against distance processes, because in formal studies participants are implicitly asked to be accurate. Most of us have probably learned that reconstruction is the most accurate method for estimating the times of past events. (Few of us would rely on impressions of distance in the past if we were questioned in a criminal investigation.) But this does not mean that distance-based information is unavailable to us. We might limit our use of direct impressions of the ages of events to relatively unimportant matters, where reconstruction seems to be too much trouble. I might use impressions of recency in deciding which of two shirts I wore less recently or whether I have eaten in a Chinese or Italian restaurant more recently.

If most studies of memory for time lead participants to attempt to reconstruct the times, special measures may be needed to study direct impressions of distances in the past. In this section I describe a series of studies that use situations in which reconstruction is difficult. These studies were designed to determine whether distance processes are used by humans to judge the times of past events and, if so, to learn about the properties of these processes.

Studies of young children.   Although children as young as 4 to 6 years are aware of the order of the main events within the day (Friedman, 1990), and can even use this knowledge to reconstruct the time of a past event within the day (Friedman, 1991), it is not until after 6 years that most children learn about longer time patterns, such as days of the week, seasons, and months of the year (Friedman, 1978, 1982). Even 8- and 9-year-olds often have difficulty using their knowledge of the year to determine which of two holidays occurred more recently (Friedman, 1992). The late development of representations of long-scale time patterns means that children younger than 9 or 10 years may need to rely on order codes or direct impressions of the ages of events if they are to compare accurately the recency of events from the past weeks and months. If the two events are unrelated, then order codes are unlikely to be available, so studies of young children may be one of the best methods for learning about distance-based processes in memory for time.

A first series of studies (Friedman, 1991) demonstrated that children as young as 4 to 5 years of age can discriminate the recency of an event presented one week before testing from that of another event that happened seven weeks before the test. In these experiments 4-, 6-, and 8-year-old children were presented with special events, such as a visitor making a videotape of the class or leading children in a novel game, seven weeks before the test session. Six weeks later teachers presented a distinctive lesson to their classes, such as demonstrating proper tooth-brushing technique with a large toothbrush and tooth. To decrease the likelihood that children would be reminded of the earlier event when the later one occurred, the pairs of events were selected to be unrelated by the content or the adults who were present. One week after the second event, children were shown cards representing the two events and asked which of the two was a long time ago and which a short time ago. The results showed that even the 4-year-olds were able to make this discrimination with greater-than-chance levels of accuracy.

To rule out the possibility that this youngest group solved the problems by reconstructing the times, children were also asked to judge the *location* of the older event: its time of day, month, and season. The 4-year-olds were at chance levels in judging the month and season of this event. The only time-scale on which they could accurately judge the time of this event was its time of day. Because only locations on the longer time-scales could logically constrain the order of the events, it seems that the children must have been relying on impressions of the ages of the events to make the discrimination. Thus these studies demonstrate that humans can use distance information to discriminate times on long time-scales.

Although these first studies show the ability to use distance information to discriminate the ages of 1- and 7-week-old events, they do not tell us whether the ability is present for even longer time-scales. To learn more about the temporal properties of distance-based processes, my colleagues and I conducted four additional studies, with more than 2,000 children, in which children were asked to discriminate the ages of two events (Friedman, Gardner, and Zubin, 1995; Friedman and Kemp, 1998, experiment 1). Here we used naturally occurring events: the child's birthday and the holidays Christmas or (in a study with New

Zealand children) Guy Fawkes Day. Birthdays, of course, are distributed throughout the year. We also conducted testing at several times of the year, so the comparison holidays were at distances ranging from the past few weeks to more than nine months ago. Collectively these studies allow us to examine children's accuracy as a function of the distances of the two events over a broad range of elapsed times.

It is important to recognize that these tasks would be easy for adults and would produce no effects of the distances of the events on accuracy. Because of their knowledge of locations within the calendar year, adults can determine whether their birthday or Christmas was more recent with equal accuracy at any time of the year. In contrast, children as old as 9 years made many errors on these tasks, suggesting that well into middle childhood children are unable to exploit knowledge about locations to determine which of two events is a longer time ago. But children younger than 9 years *are* accurate in some conditions, leading to the conclusion that they are able to compare intuitive impressions of the ages of the two events. For what distances in the past can accurate judgements be made?

First, it is evident that children are not limited to discriminating events that fall in the past seven weeks. Birthdays from the past two or three months are accurately discriminated from Christmas when the latter is about ten months in the past. On the other hand, the discrimination is quite difficult when both events are of similar ages, even when both occurred in the relatively recent past. When their birthday and Christmas were both within the past month, children were much less accurate than when one event was within the past month and the other many months ago. These findings suggest that children are comparing two quantities, and it is the relative values of these quantities that determine accuracy. Across studies, the best way to predict accuracy is not the absolute distance of either event alone but the ratio of the two distances. Mathematical analysis shows that ratio is a good predictor of accuracy when we are comparing two quantities that decrease at a decelerating rate with the passage of time. This is the time function predicted by some strength theorists. We will encounter further evidence that the quantity underlying distance-based judgements follows such a function in many of the remaining studies, including the developmental studies that follow.

To learn more about the temporal properties of distance-based processes, Friedman and Kemp (1998) conducted two studies in which children of about 3 to 6 years (mean age about 4 years, 9 months) were asked to judge the ages of individual events using a direct scaling method: placing events on a spatial continuum representing the ages of the events. Of course, children this young cannot use a scale that is based on conventional units, such as months. But the studies showed that they were able to use the spatial continuum, a kind of ruler, to make differentiated judgements of the times of past events.

The children were taught that the near end of the ruler represents times from the recent past, using the example of getting to school today. The far end was labelled 'a very long time ago', and the example of when the child learned to walk was given. After the training portion of the experiment, children were asked to point to locations representing their last birthday and last Valentine's Day, summer, Halloween, Thanksgiving, and Christmas.

In the first experiment, children were tested between 2 March and 2 May. The average distances along the ruler for their birthday are shown in Figure 5.1 and for the holidays and summer in Figure 5.2. In both figures the average number of days in the past is plotted on the horizontal axis, and the number of centimetres from the front of the ruler is plotted on the vertical axis. In Figure 5.1 children's responses are grouped in twelve 30-day categories of distances in the past. For example, the left-most point represents the children whose birthdays were within the 30 days prior to testing. In Figure 5.2 the points represent, from left to right, Valentine's Day, Christmas, Thanksgiving, Halloween, and summer (assumed to be 15 July).

The birthday results in Figure 5.1 seem to show the effects of two processes: an increase in subjective distances as true distances increase, up to about seven to nine months, and relatively low values for birthdays of nine to twelve months ago. The overall pattern is well described by the quadratic function plotted in this figure. There is no theory of memory for time that predicts that events will be judged as particularly recent as they approach one year in the past. Instead, the values of the three right-most points in Figure 5.1 are almost certainly the result

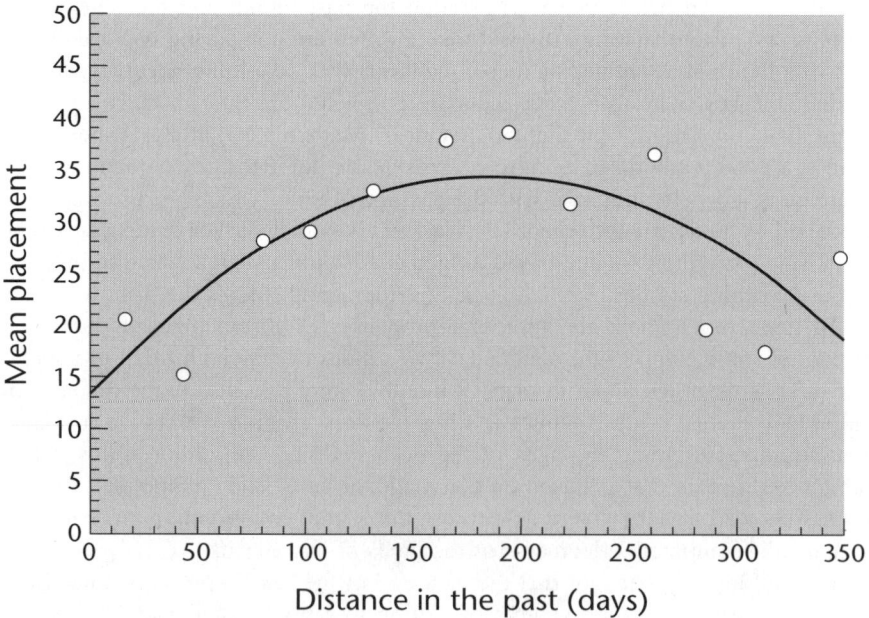

FIGURE 5.1. Mean placements for birthdays as a function of their distances in the past in days in Friedman and Kemp (1998), study 2. Reprinted by permission of Ablex

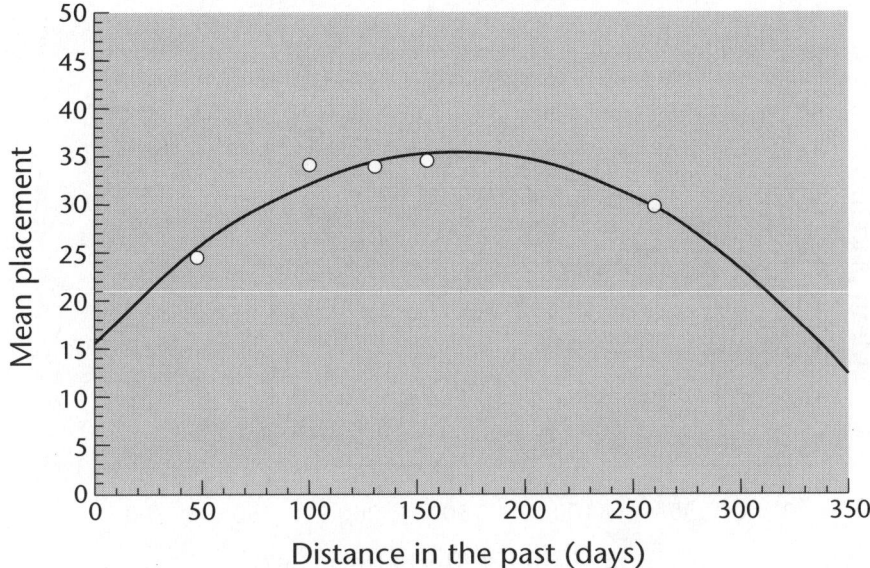

FIGURE 5.2. Mean placements for holidays and summer as a function of their distances in the past in days in Friedman and Kemp (1998), study 2. Reprinted by permission of Ablex Publishing.

of children anticipating the approach of their birthdays and confusing their future proximity with the category 'short time ago' used in the instructions. A similar effect was found in Friedman, Gardner, and Zubin's (1995) study of comparisons of the ages of birthdays and Christmas. In that study children less than 9 years of age were especially inaccurate when their birthday fell within the month after testing.

Although it is notable that young children sometimes confuse the near future with the recent past, our main interest was in the effects of memory on impressions of distances in the past. The points representing birthdays 0 to 9 months in the past show an impressive degree of differentiation for such a young group. It appears from these points that subjective distance increases rapidly in the first 3 to 5 months and shows little change thereafter. These nine points are well described by a function which shows decelerating change with the passage of time. As we saw earlier, decelerating change is predicted by some strength theories and is consistent with the effects of the ratios of distances in predicting the results of the birthday-holiday-comparison studies. Figure 5.2 shows a pattern similar to that found in Figure 5.1. Subjective ages of the holidays appear to increase up to about three months in the past, with little change thereafter.

We conducted a second study in which children were tested in January and February so that we would have a denser sampling of holidays in the past four

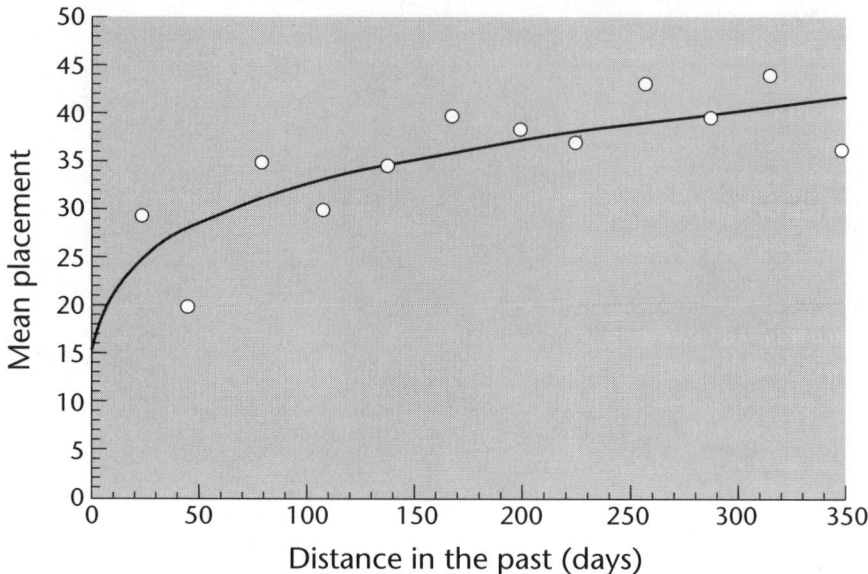

FIGURE 5.3. Mean placements for birthdays as a function of their distances in the past in days in Friedman and Kemp (1998), study 3. Reprinted by permission of Ablex

months. The results for birthdays are shown in Figure 5.3. Again we see an increase in subjective distance up to about three months, with little change in the perceived ages of older events. There was no evidence of an anticipation effect in this study. Perhaps parents discuss upcoming birthdays with children less frequently in the weeks following Christmas, so fewer children were aware that their birthdays were coming soon.

Figure 5.4 shows the judgements for the holidays and summer. From left to right, these points correspond to Christmas, Thanksgiving, Halloween, summer, and Valentine's Day. Again, we find rapid change in the subjective ages of events from the previous three months and slower change thereafter. There is no anticipation effect evident in Figure 5.4, but if we plot separately the data of children tested in the two weeks before Valentine's Day, we find placements for this holiday that are significantly closer to the near end of the ruler than for the children tested in January.

The results of these direct-scaling studies reinforce the earlier developmental studies that showed that children can discriminate the distances of events from the past months well before they are able to use information about their locations within the year. The scaling studies are also consistent with the position that the quantity underlying distance-based judgements changes at a decelerating rate with the passage of time. Finally, the scaling studies provide information about the time course of subjective recency. When children must

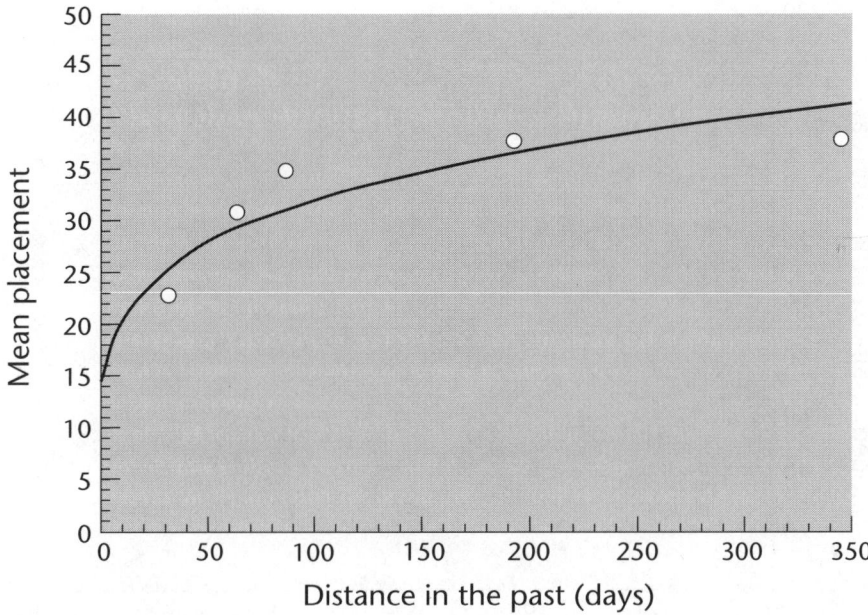

FIGURE 5.4. Mean placements for holidays and summer as a function of their distances in the past in days in Friedman and Kemp (1998), study 3. Reprinted by permission of Ablex Publishing.

rely on direct impressions of the ages of events, subjective distance increases continuously over about three to five months, with no clear increase thereafter.

Studies of adults. If we are to obtain convergent evidence for adults, we must arrange situations in which reconstruction of past times is difficult. In one such approach, a colleague and I selected for our study segments of a television news magazine show, '60 Minutes', that were difficult to relate to contemporaneous events in the news and that were probably watched in relatively unchanging contexts: viewers' Sunday evening routines (Friedman and Huttenlocher, 1997). The segments focused on a variety of topics, such as exposés of fraud or interviews with celebrities, but each was required to be difficult to localize in time. In a comparison condition, we presented news events, which should be subject to the usual reconstructive approaches that predominate in past studies. Participants were contacted by telephone and asked if they were regular viewers of '60 Minutes'. Regular viewers who agreed to participate in the brief interview were read descriptions of '60 Minutes' segments from about the past year and of major news events from a similar interval. Participants were first asked if they recognized a '60 Minutes' segment or news event and then asked when it had occurred.

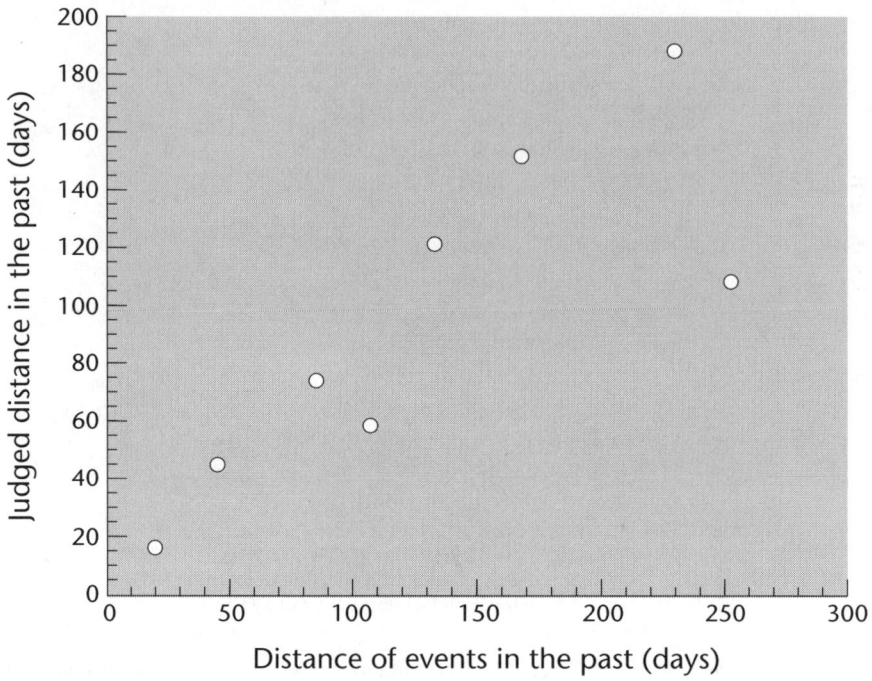

FIGURE 5.5. Antilog of the mean log time estimate for each distance category for the news events in Friedman and Huttenlocher (1997), study 1.

Figure 5.5 shows the results for the news events. With the exception of the right-most point, the data show the sort of linear function usually found in studies where events are well remembered and reconstruction is possible. The single point that falls far from an upward-sloping line apparently was caused by a confusion of two news events, one of which occurred shortly before testing (the 4 May 1994 meeting between Israeli Prime Minister Rabin and the PLO Chairman Arafat in Cairo) and the other about eight months earlier (the 13 September 1993 meeting between the same leaders in Washington).

A very different pattern is found for the '60-Minutes' segments (Figure 5.6). Here there is a roughly linear increase of judged distance with true distance through about sixty days, and a very gradual change thereafter. Events of about one year ago were judged to be farther in the past than those two to nine months old, but the difference is small.

The news and '60 Minutes' conditions show very different effects of the age of events. In the news condition, with the exception noted, participants were quite accurate throughout the range of times studied. In the '60-Minutes' condition, events were clearly differentiated if they fell within about the past two months. Beyond two months there is little change in the subjective distances of events

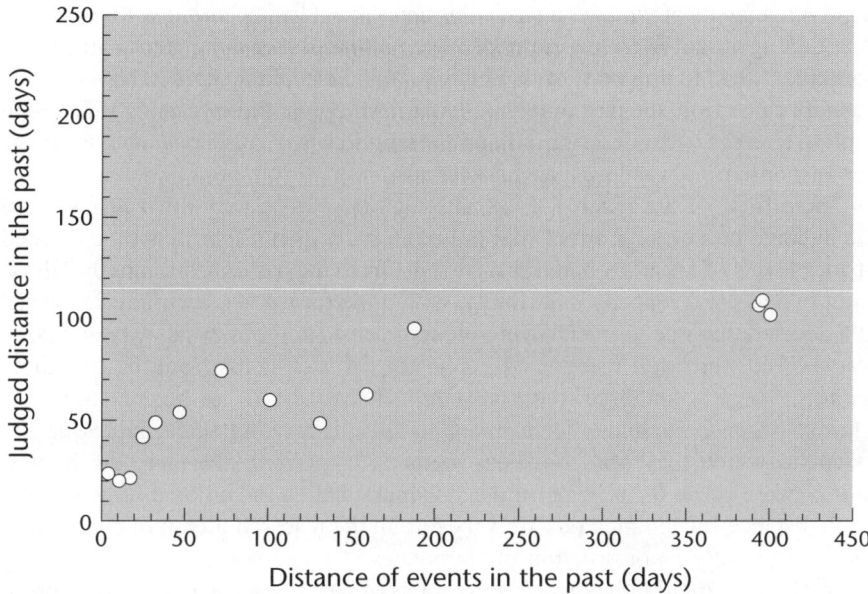

FIGURE 5.6. Antilog of the mean log time estimate for each distance category for the '60 Minutes' stories in Friedman and Huttenlocher (1997), study 2.

with true age, and the ages of events about one year old are grossly underestimated. One might suppose that the difference between these two conditions is due to the fact that the news events are more memorable. But the same difference in functions emerges if the data are reanalysed using only news stories and '60 Minutes' segments that were well recognized. It seems instead that the different functions result from different processes, reconstruction for the news events and impressions of distances for the '60-Minutes' segments.

The particular function found for the '60-Minutes' segments flattened at a shorter distance in the past than the ones found in the scaling studies with children. This may be because the '60 Minutes' segments were less memorable than birthdays and holidays, and the subjective distances of less memorable events might approach an asymptote more rapidly than more memorable ones. In any case it is notable that studies using such different methods and ages of participants produced similar functions, ones which show little change once events are more than about two to three months old.

Another approach to studying distance-based processes in adults is to require them to make very rapid judgements. Impressions of distance may be directly available, whereas reconstruction, by its nature, must be a slow process (Friedman, 1993). In the literature on memory for time, participants are usually given plenty of time to make judgements, so reconstruction is possible. In a series of unpublished studies (described in Friedman, 1996), I asked adults to make very rapid judgements of whether a particular news event had occurred within the past year or longer ago. Event descriptions were presented on a computer monitor, and participants had to press one of two buttons to indicate their choices. News events actually came from the past nine months or from two to three years ago. The time limit to read the event descriptions and to respond was 1.75 seconds, but the average response time was less than 1.3 seconds.

Three findings are notable. First, although this was a very difficult task, and the average proportion correct was only .63, participants significantly exceeded chance levels of accuracy both for the events from the past nine months and those from two to three years ago. Secondly, within the former set, accuracy decreased at a decelerating rate as events were older, at least for those events which a post-test showed were well recognized. Accuracy for such items from the past three months was .85, for three to six months .74, and for six to nine months .76. Thirdly, when participants were asked to fill out a rating scale indicating the extent to which they used different methods to perform the task, the highest ratings were given for relying on the vividness and on the amount remembered. Such distance-related methods are very rare in the research literature on memory for time; usually reconstruction predominates. These findings show that adults can make very rapid judgements of the times of past events, and when they do so their accuracy varies with the age of events in a similar manner to the accuracy pattern in the developmental-scaling and '60-Minutes' studies. Finally, participants' method reports suggest that they were using some strength-like quality to arrive at their judgements.

Another line of evidence supports the distinctness of distance-based processes. Kemp and Burt (1998) measured adults' impressions of the recency of a set of news events by asking them to squeeze a grip meter with a force proportional to how recent the event seemed to be. Similar methods are sometimes employed to directly scale the perception of sensory dimensions, such as loudness. The authors assumed that this approach would more directly tap distance-based processes than the date estimates used in most experiments. In other parts of their experiment, Kemp and Burt asked participants to date events in the traditional way and also to rate how vividly they remembered the experience of first hearing of the event. If distance-based processes are distinct from reconstruction, one would expect that vividness ratings would be more closely related to grip force than to date estimates (after statistically controlling for actual dates). This is what the authors found. As Kemp and Burt point out, this and previous studies show that impressions of vividness make only a modest contribution to how adults normally estimate the dates of news event, but their study does suggest that adults have direct impressions of the strengths of memories, impressions that are separable from location-based processes.

Surprisingly, little is known about how these impressions of the strengths of memories change with the passage of time. Distance-based theories of memory for time are based on the assumption that strength-like qualities of memories

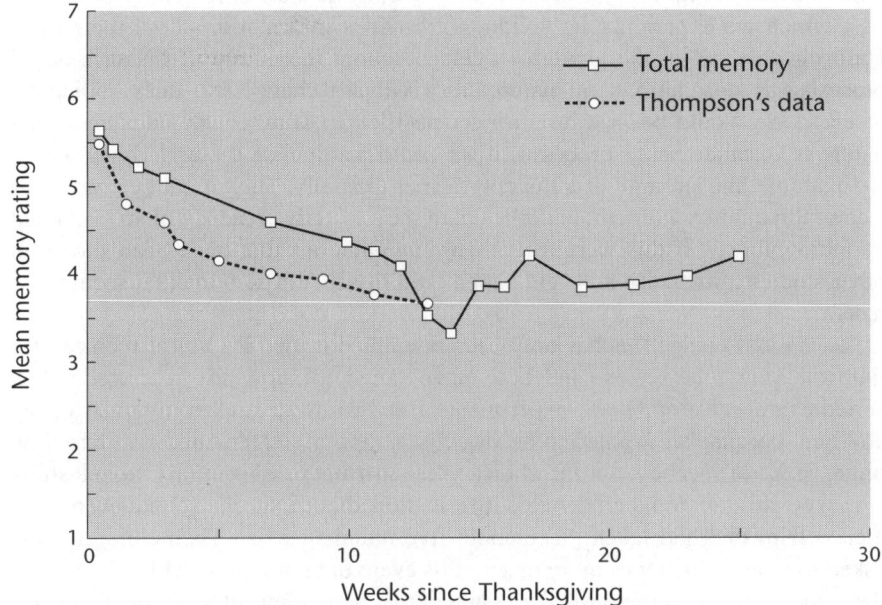

FIGURE 5.7. Mean ratings as a function of weeks since the event in Friedman and deWinstanley (1998), Thanksgiving survey, and Thompson (1982), study of memory for personal events. Reprinted by permission of Psychology Press Ltd.

decline in a regular way as the memories grow older, thus providing the information that leads to impressions of recency. But there is little evidence that examines this phenomenon directly, particularly on long time-scales, such as weeks and months. Figure 5.7 shows the results of two such studies. Thompson (1982) asked college students to record personal events over a fourteen-week period and subsequently to rate how well they remembered the events (1 = barely at all; 7 = perfectly). In the second study, a colleague and I (Friedman and deWinstanley, 1998) asked students to rate their memory for the Thanksgiving holiday at various times in the six months after the event occurred. The values of nine different 1-to-7 scales reflecting the completeness of their memories were averaged and plotted as a function of time. Thompson's data are shown by the dotted line in Figure 5.7, and Friedman and deWinstanley's findings are represented by the solid line. Together these curves reveal that the greatest change in the clarity of memories occurs over the first twelve weeks, with no systematic change thereafter. Although these measures do not directly tap memory for time, the results do show that changes in vividness *could* provide a mechanism that allows people to judge the distances of events in the past. Not only does vividness change in a regular way with the passage of time, but its time course resembles the function seen in several of the studies of subjective recency described above.

Experimental manipulations of strength. It appears that some quality of memories, which we experience as vividness, provides information about their ages. Unfortunately, all of the available evidence about the nature of distance-based processes is correlational in nature: as vividness changes so does subjective recency. We would be in a far stronger position to draw conclusions about the nature of distance-based processes if we could manipulate the underlying entity, for example, the strength of a memory, experimentally. This might be possible if a common quality, strength, underlies both the subjective recency of an event and its memorability. If this were true, then manipulations that have been shown in other studies to increase an event's memorability should also make it seem more recent.

To my knowledge this has only been attempted in two studies of memory for time on long time-scales, and both have failed to show the predicted effect (Friedman and Kemp, 1998, experiments 1 and 3). Both studies involved young children, because we wanted to be sure that temporal judgements were based on impressions of recency, not the ability to reconstruct past locations. In one study we asked children to recall detailed information about a special school event (e.g. a class trip) that had taken place about five months earlier. Then children were asked to judge which was more recent, this event or another one which was about the same distance in the past. We assumed that activating information about one of two events that were close in time would make that event seem more recent than the one that was simply mentioned. Despite the very large sample size, 537 children, there was no reliable effect of retrieving information about an event on which event was judged to be more recent. In a follow-up study, children either retrieved information about a holiday (e.g. 'What do you remember about last Halloween?'), memorized a list of words related to a holiday (e.g. costume, candy, pumpkin), or did not engage in either memory task. Impressions of the distance of the holiday were measured by the ruler task described earlier. Both kinds of memory tasks are known to increase the memorability of items, but neither affected judgements of how long ago the holidays took place. These experiments suggest that strength is not a unitary quality of memories: separate qualities appear to be responsible for impressions of the age of a memory and the likelihood that the event can be remembered.

These findings leave us with the question, what sort of information is used to make judgements of distances in the past? The failure of manipulations known to improve the likelihood of recall suggests that ease of retrieval is not the critical information. Another possibility is that the amount remembered about an event once it is retrieved is the cue (Brown, Rips, and Shevell, 1985). The evidence for this possibility is mixed. Brown and his colleagues found that when participants remembered more about a news event, it tended to be judged as somewhat more recent than when they remembered little about it. But Burt (1992), Kemp (1988), Thompson, Skowronski, and Lee, (1988), and Wright, Gaskell, and O'Muircheartaigh (1997) all failed to replicate these findings. Of course, it may be that the effect is obscured by the predominance of reconstruction in these studies.

For now, our best evidence about the information underlying distance-based judgements of the times of past events may come from participants' reports and the similar time course of reported vividness and subjective distance. Some quality experienced as vividness seems to be involved.

Neurological evidence.   Another important unresolved question is what brain structures and processes underlie distance-based judgements of time. In contrast to the evidence suggesting the involvement of the frontal cortex in the reconstruction of temporal locations, there have been no studies demonstrating that particular regions of the brain are responsible for direct impressions of recency. However, it is possible that information about the ages of memories can be derived from the degree to which a memory is 'consolidated'. Consolidation is a hypothetical process that has been used to explain the fact that a kind of memory loss, called 'temporally graded retrograde amnesia', is selective to the time period before the injury (e.g. Squire, 1992; Squire, Haist, and Shimamura, 1989; but see Nadel and Moscovitch, 1997). Events occurring shortly before the damage to the brain cannot be remembered, whereas events that happened well before the injury are more likely to be remembered the greater the amount of time that they preceded the injury (hence the designation, temporally graded). This kind of amnesia is known to involve the diencephalon and medial temporal regions of the cortex, so it may be that information in these parts of the brain is used to determine the ages of memories. Unfortunately, there is insufficient evidence at present to tell whether the temporal characteristics of consolidation make it a plausible candidate for explaining the time functions reported in the sections on developmental and adult studies of distance-based processes.

Finally, it is worth mentioning recent findings that throughout life new nerve cells are created in one of the regions believed to be involved in the storage of new memories. Studies of adult marmoset monkeys (Gould *et al.*, 1998) and adult humans (Eriksson *et al.*, 1998) have shown that new neurons are created and mature in the dentate gyrus of the hippocampus. There is some evidence in the latter study that the new cells may die in the succeeding weeks and months. Although it is highly speculative at present, this process of cell creation and death may be involved in the temporary storage of new information and perhaps our ability to judge the ages of memories.

CONCLUSION

In the previous sections, we have seen that two distinct processes, distance and location processes, play important roles in humans' memory for the times of past events. Table 5.3 summarizes the characteristics of the two processes. Neither reconstruction (column 1) nor assessing direct impressions of recency (column 2) requires special coding of events at the time when the events are experienced. Reconstruction does not depend on a special time code assigned at the time of an

TABLE 5.3 *A summary of the characteristics of two processes underlying memory for the times of past events*

	Location	*Distance*
Special processing at time of encoding?	No	No
Information in memory	Associations, context	Vividness (not a unitary strength quantity)
Process at time of recall	Link event to locations via inference	Judge vividness
Speed	Slow	Fast
Development	Late (limited by knowledge of time patterns)	Early
Brain structures	Prefrontal cortex + distributed traces in other regions	? (Consolidation in the hippocampus?)
Role in human thought	Predicting the future	Updating information,

event but rather on the storage of 'ordinary' information, such as what we saw, heard, did, or felt when the event happened. In distance-based processes it is assumed that temporal information is created by the passage of time, not by special processing at the time an event is encoded in memory.

Furthermore, neither process requires that memory be organized by time of occurrence. For location-based processes, the crucial information is the contents of memories, such as details about the context in which the event occurred, relations to other events, and even information added later, including at the time of recall. For distance-based processes, it is also intrinsic properties of memories that are used, such as the clarity, accessibility, or the elaborateness of the memories. These intrinsic properties do not appear to be the ones that cause differences in the memorability of events, rendering unitary strength theories unlikely.

Different processes are assumed to take place when an event is recalled and its age is judged in the location and distance explanations. Method reports indicate that reconstruction is a slow, strategic process in which we attempt to infer events' locations in time by relating what we remember about them to our general knowledge of time patterns. Information used to infer distances is presumed to be directly available. Participants in one of the studies reported in the section on distance-based processes were able to judge times of occurrence in just over one second, and they reported doing so by assessing the vividness of their memories or the amount remembered about the events.

Location- and distance-based processes develop in different ways during childhood. Location-based processes develop gradually, as children learn about different time patterns, and perhaps as they develop effective strategic processes that allow them to reconstruct past locations. With some help, even 4-year-olds can reconstruct past times on a time-scale they understand, parts of a day. But not until nearly 10 years of age can children consistently use their knowledge of the calendar to compare locations in the past. In contrast, children have access to distance-based processes at least by 4 to 5 years of age, and they can use this information to judge relative distances in the past with some accuracy. These abilities show that information about the ages of memories is present early in development.

Evidence from patients with brain damage suggests that location-based processes depend on strategic processes carried out in the prefrontal cortex. Memory representations themselves are not stored in this region; instead the prefrontal cortex must be drawing on various kinds of information about particular events stored in more posterior regions of the brain. We do not know what brain regions underlie humans' ability to directly judge the ages of memories. It is possible that some quality of memories is created by the mechanisms that cause some memories to become stable and others to be forgotten and that this quality underlies impressions of the distances of events in the past. If so, the hippocampus and related structures must play an important role in distance-based processes.

In modern conceptions time is viewed as a uniform continuum, encompassing all events, and psychologists who study memory for time are tempted to assume that this linear order is somehow represented in the brain. But for most of human history, linear chronology was largely irrelevant to the day-to-day problems that humans needed to solve in order to survive. More important would have been memory for when in a cyclic pattern an event occurred. Cyclic information can be used to predict future events, such as the time of year when a particular animal migrates. For this reason, locations in cycles have been far more important than linear chronology throughout most of human experience.

If the chronological order of memories is not represented in the brain, why are humans able to judge distances with such speed and from such an early age? The answer may be that distance-based processes provide an 'inexpensive' way to judge which information in memory is probably current and which out of date or, for example, to judge which of two areas have been hunted more recently. Adequate information to make these sorts of judgements may simply require assessing the vividness of memories. Such a process is inexpensive in the sense that no special memory processes are required. We do not need special encoding, storage, or retrieval mechanisms to compare distance-related qualities of memories; they are an automatic concomitant of retrieval itself. Another important function of distance-based processes is in temporal orientation, determining our current location in time. The ability to rapidly compare the ages of events, such as meals, lets us know where we are in the present, and thus what we need to be doing now.

Of course, the basic abilities to reconstruct past locations and compare distances in the past can be applied not only to the temporal environments in which our ancestors evolved but to the elaborate temporal patterns of the modern world. Locations in the artificial time structures of clocks and calendars have become at least as real for most of us as the cycles of the seasons or the sun, and when we try to remember the times of past events, it is usually so that we can place the events in these conventional patterns. In a similar way, our impressions of distances in the past are readily translated into conventional time units (e.g. about a month ago, within the past week). Biology has given us two ways to remember the times of past events. Culture provides the time systems to which these abilities will be applied.

REFERENCES

BADDELEY, A. D., LEWIS, V., and NIMMO-SMITH, I. (1978), 'When did you last . . .?', in M. M. Gruneberg and R. N. Sykes (eds.), *Practical Aspects of Memory*. San Diego: Academic Press, 77–83.

BARTLETT, J. C., and SNELUS, P. (1980), 'Lifespan memory for popular songs', *American Journal of Psychology*, 93: 551–60.

BLOCK, R. A. (1982), 'Temporal judgments and contextual change', *Journal of Experimental Psychology: Learning, Memory and Cognition*, 8: 530–44.

BREWER, W. F. (1996), 'What is recollective memory?', in D. C. Rubin (ed.), *Remembering our Past: Studies in Autobiographical Memory*. Cambridge: Cambridge University Press, 19–66.

BROWN, N. R., RIPS, L. J., and SHEVELL, S. K. (1985), 'The subjective dates of natural events in very-long-term memory', *Cognitive Psychology*, 17: 139–77.

—— SHEVELL, S. K., and RIPS, L. J. (1986), 'Public memories and their personal context', in D. C. Rubin (ed.), *Autobiographical Memory*. Cambridge, England: Cambridge University Press, 137–58.

BRUCE, D., and VAN PELT, M. (1989), 'Memories of a bicycle tour', *Applied Cognitive Psychology*, 3: 137–56.

BURT, C. D. B. (1992), 'Retrieval characteristics of autobiographical memories: event and date information', *Applied Cognitive Psychology*, 6: 389–404.

ERIKSSON, P. S., PERFILIEVA, E., BJÖRK-ERIKSSON, T., ALBORN, A.-M., NORDBERG, C., PETERSON, D. A., and GAGE, F. H. (1998), 'Neurogenesis in the adult hippocampus', *Nature Medicine*, 4: 1313–17.

FOZARD, J. L., and WEINERT, J. R. (1972), 'Absolute judgments of recency for pictures and nouns after various numbers of intervening items', *Journal of Experimental Psychology*, 95: 472–4.

FRIEDMAN, W. J. (1978), 'Development of time concepts in children', in H. W. Reese and L. P. Lipsitt (eds.), *Advances in Child Development and Behavior*, xii. New York: Academic Press, 267–98.

—— (1982), 'Conventional time concepts and children's structuring of time', in W. J. Friedman (ed.), *The Developmental Psychology of Time*. New York: Academic Press, 171–208.

—— (1987), 'A follow-up to "Scale effects in memory for the time of events": the earthquake study', *Memory & Cognition*, 15: 518–20.

—— (1990), 'Children's representations of the pattern of daily activities', *Child Development*, 61: 1399–412.

—— (1991), 'The development of children's memory for the time of past events', *Child Development*, 62: 139–55.

—— (1992), 'Children's time memory: the development of a differentiated past', *Cognitive Development*, 7: 171–87.

—— (1993), 'Memory for the time of past events', *Psychological Bulletin*, 113: 44–66.

—— (1996), 'Distance and location processes in memory for the times of past events', in D. L. Medin (ed.), *The psychology of learning and motivation*, xxxv. Orlando, Fla.: Academic Press, 1–41.

—— and DEWINSTANLEY, P. A. (1998), 'Changes in the subjective properties of autobiographical memories with the passage of time', *Memory*, 6: 367–81.

—— and HUTTENLOCHER, J. (1997), 'Memory for the times of "60 Minutes" stories and news events', *Journal of Experimental Psychology: Learning, Memory, and Cognition*, 23: 560–9.

—— and KEMP, S. (1998), 'The effects of elapsed time and retrieval on young children's judgments of the temporal distances of past events', *Cognitive Development*, 13: 335–67.

—— and WILKINS, A. J. (1985), 'Scale effects in memory for the time of past events', *Memory & Cognition*, 13: 168–75.

—— GARDNER, A. G., and ZUBIN, N. R. E. (1995), 'Children's comparisons of the recency of two events from the past year', *Child Development*, 66: 970–83.

GOULD, E., TANAPAT, P., McEWEN, B. S., FLÜGGE, G., and FUCHS, E. (1998), 'Proliferation of granule cell precursors in adult monkeys is diminished by stress', *Proceedings of the National Academy of Sciences*, 95: 3168–71.

GUENTHER, R. K., and LINTON, M. (1975), 'Mechanisms of temporal coding', *Journal of Experimental Psychology: Human Learning and Memory*, 97: 220–9.

HASHER, L., and ZACKS, R. T. (1979), 'Automatic and effortful processes in memory', *Journal of Experimental Psychology: General*, 108: 356–88.

HINRICHS, J. V. (1970), 'A two-process memory-strength theory for judgment of recency', *Psychological Review*, 77: 223–33.

HINTZMAN, D. L., and BLOCK, R. A. (1971), 'Repetition and memory: evidence for a multiple trace hypothesis', *Journal of Experimental Psychology*, 88: 297–306.

—— —— and SUMMERS, J. J. (1973), 'Contextual associations and memory for serial position', *Journal of Experimental Psychology*, 97: 220–9.

KEMP, S. (1988), 'Dating recent and historical events', *Applied Cognitive Psychology*, 2: 181–8.

—— and BURT, C. D. B. (1998), 'The force of events: cross-modality matching the recency of news events', *Memory*, 6: 297–306.

LIEURY, A., CAPLAIN, P., JACQUET, A., and JOLIVET, C. (1979), 'La contraction du temps dans la datation des souvenirs anciens [The contraction of time in the dating of old memories],' *Année Psychologique*, 79: 7–22.

LINTON, M. (1975), 'Memory for real world events', in D. A. Norman and R. E. Rumelhart (eds.), *Explorations in Cognition*. San Francisco: Freeman.

McANDREWS, M. P., and MILNER, B. (1991), 'The frontal cortex and memory for temporal order', *Neuropsychologia*, 29: 849–59.

McTAGGART, J. E. (1927), in C. D. Broad (ed.), *The Nature of Existence*, ii. Cambridge: Cambridge University Press.

MANGELS, J. A., GERSHBERG, F. B., SHIMAMURA, A. P., and KNIGHT, R. T. (1996), 'Impaired retrieval from remote memory in patients with frontal lobe damage', *Neuropsychology*, 10: 32–41.

MILNER, B., CORSI, P., and LEONARD, G. (1991), 'Frontal-lobe contribution to recency judgments', *Neuropsychologia*, 29: 601–18.

MORTON, J. (1968), 'Repeated items and decay in memory', *Psychonomic Science*, 10: 219–20.

MOSCOVITCH, M. (1995), 'Models of consciousness and memory', in M. S. Gazzaniga (ed.), *The Cognitive Neurosciences*. Cambridge, Mass.: MIT Press, 1341–56.

—— and MELO, B. (1997), 'Strategic retrieval and the frontal lobes: evidence from confabulation and amnesia', *Neuropsychologia*, 35: 1017–34.

MURDOCK, B. B., JR. (1974), *Human Memory: Theory and Data*. Potomac, MD: Erlbaum.

NADEL, L., and MOSCOVITCH, M. (1997), 'Memory consolidation, retrograde amnesia and the hippocampal complex', *Current Opinion in Neurobiology*, 7: 217–27.

NAVEH-BENJAMIN, M. (1990), 'Coding of temporal order information: an automatic process?, *Journal of Experimental Psychology: Learning, Memory, and Cognition*, 16: 117–26.

SCHACTER, D. L. (1987), 'Memory, amnesia, and frontal-lobe dysfunction', *Psychobiology*, 15: 21–36.

SHIMAMURA, A. P., JANOWSKY, J. S., and SQUIRE, L. R. (1990), 'Memory for the temporal order of events in patients with frontal lobe lesions and amnesic patients', *Neuropsychologia*, 28: 803–13.

SQUIRE, L. R. (1992), 'Memory and the hippocampus: a synthesis of findings from rats, monkeys, and humans', *Psychological Review*, 99: 195–231.

—— HAIST, F., and SHIMAMURA, A. P. (1989), 'The neurology of memory: quantitative assessment of retrograde amnesia in two groups of amnesic patients', *Journal of Neuroscience*, 9: 828–39.

THOMPSON, C. P. (1982), 'Memory for unique personal events: the roommate study', *Memory & Cognition*, 10: 324–32.

—— SKOWRONSKI, J. J., and LEE, D. J. (1988), 'Telescoping in dating naturally occurring events', *Memory & Cognition*, 16: 461–8.

TOGLIA, M. P., and KIMBLE, G. A. (1976), 'Recall and use of serial position information', *Journal of Experimental Psychology: Human Learning and Memory*, 2: 431–45.

TULVING, E., and MADIGAN, S. A. (1970), 'Memory and verbal learning', *Annual Review of Psychology*, 21: 437–84.

TZENG, O. J. L., and COTTON, B. (1980), 'A study-phase retrieval model of temporal coding', *Journal of Experimental Psychology: Human Learning and Memory*, 6: 705–16.

UNDERWOOD, B. J., and MALMI, R. A. (1978), 'An evaluation of measures used in studying temporal codes for words within a list', *Journal of Verbal Learning and Verbal Behavior*, 17: 279–93.

WELLS, J. E. (1974), 'Strength theory and judgments of recency and frequency', *Journal of Verbal Learning and Verbal Behavior*, 13: 378–92

WHEELER, M. A., STUSS, D. T., and TULVING, E. (1997), 'Toward a theory of episodic memory: the frontal lobes and autonoetic consciousness', *Psychological Bulletin*, 121: 331–54.

WHITE, R. T. (1982), 'Memory for personal events', *Human Learning*, 1, 171–83.

—— (1989), 'Recall of autobiographical events', *Applied Cognitive Psychology*, 3: 127–35.

WINOGRAD, E., and SOLOWAY, R. M. (1985), 'Reminding as a basis for temporal judgments', *Journal of Experimental Psychology: Learning, Memory, and Cognition*, 11: 262–71.

WRIGHT, D. B., GASKELL, G. D., and O'MUIRCHEARTAIGH, C. A. (1997), 'Temporal estimation of major news events: re-examining the accessibility principle', *Applied Cognitive Psychology*, 11: 35–46.

YNTEMA, D. B., and TRASK, F. P. (1963), 'Recall as a search process', *Journal of Verbal Learning and Verbal Behavior*, 2: 65–74.

ZIMMERMAN, J., and UNDERWOOD, B. J. (1968), 'Ordinal position knowledge within and across lists as a function of instructions in free-recall learning', *Journal of General Psychology*, 79: 301–7.

6

Memory Demonstratives

John Campbell

THE CLASSICAL MODEL

Perceptual demonstratives—terms such as 'this man' or 'that building', used to refer to currently perceived objects—seem to be fundamental to our understanding of concepts and language. There are two ways in which they display this fundamental character. First, they are used in the explanation of observational concepts like 'red' or 'square'. These terms are learnt in the context of propositions like, 'that chair is red', or 'that box is square', where the demonstrative refers to a currently perceived object. Secondly, other types of reference to concrete objects, such as our use of proper names, seem to depend, directly or indirectly, on our use of perceptual demonstratives. The use of a name like 'Sigmund Freud' is ultimately dependent on it having been possible to introduce and use the name in contexts such as 'this man is Sigmund Freud'. And even a singular term such as 'the Big Bang' which does not refer to a perceptible event at all, can refer only because we understand how its referent is causally connected to objects which we can perceptually demonstrate.

It seems to be a datum that there are memory demonstratives—terms which refer to currently remembered objects. Suppose you and I meet someone for the first time one evening. The next day you say, 'Was that man a doctor?' and I, knowing immediately who you mean, reply, 'Yes, he certainly was'. Suppose the man was simply one of a number of people present. How do I go about interpreting your use of the demonstrative 'that man'? Here it seems that one way I have of interpreting the demonstrative is by consciously recollecting him. It is not enough, for understanding, merely that your behaviour be affected in one way or another by your past encounter with the thing. The ordinary way of understanding the demonstrative is by consciously recollecting the object. The use of such a memory demonstrative need not be confined to past-tense judgements. You might ask, 'Will that doctor be there tomorrow?', and of course the use of the future tense makes perfect sense even though a memory demonstrative is being used. But it would be a reasonable initial supposition that someone who understands a memory demonstrative will be in a position to make knowledgeable past-tense judgements about the thing.

A great deal of work has been done on perceptual demonstratives. Memory demonstratives have attracted little attention since Russell.[1] In this chapter I want

---

[1] Russell, 1967: chs. 5 and 11; Russell, 1984; Russell, 1921: ch. 9. See also Pears, 1975.

to address the question how we understand memory demonstratives, and to set out a classical realist framework for describing our understanding of these terms. One way to approach setting out a model of our understanding of memory demonstratives is to look at what is perhaps the theoretically most tractable case of singular reference: descriptive names. These are terms introduced by us for theoretical purposes; it is not obvious that there are any examples in everyday language, though there may be. Suppose, then, that we construct an example. Suppose we consider the name 'Woody', introduced as an abbreviation for the description 'the palm tree in this garden'. In the case of a logical constant, we can give introduction and elimination rules for the use of the term. Just so, in the case of 'Woody', we can give introduction and elimination rules which state how to verify or find the implications of judgements involving the term. The introduction rule is:

there is just one palm tree in this garden	any palm tree in this garden is G

$$\text{Woody is G}$$

The elimination rules are:

Woody is G	Woody is G

there is just one palm tree in this garden	any palm tree in this garden is G

On a verificationist analysis of descriptive names, grasp of the introduction rule will be fundamental to your understanding of the term. All other aspects of the use of the term will have to be derived from your grasp of the introduction rule. In particular, the elimination rule will be justified by reference to the introduction rule: if that is the introduction rule for the term, if that is what it takes to verify a use of the term, then surely you are entitled to draw these conclusions from a correct use of the term. Moreover, all other methods of verifying a judgement involving the term will have to be validated by being shown to be methods whose successful application guarantees that the introduction rule could have been used.

On a pragmatist analysis of descriptive names, on the other hand, grasp of the elimination rule will be fundamental to your understanding of the term, and all other aspects of the use of the term will be derived from that. The introduction rule will be justified by appeal to the elimination rule: given that these are the conclusions you are going to draw from propositions involving the term, this had better be what you demand for verification of a use of the term. And any other conclusions you draw from a use of the term will have to be drawn by way of the use of the elimination rule.

On a classical realist analysis of descriptive names, however, neither the introduction nor the elimination rules will be basic to your understanding of the name. Your understanding of the name will be provided by your knowledge of what it refers to, and this knowledge of what it refers to will not be a matter of knowing how to use the term, either in verifying statements involving it or in finding the consequences of statements involving the name. Your knowledge of reference will be more fundamental than either your knowledge of how to verify, or your knowledge of how to find the implications of judgements involving the term. Your knowledge of reference will be what causes you to use these introduction and elimination rules for the term, and it will provide you with your justification for the use of those procedures. Your knowledge of the reference of the term will be provided by your knowledge of the definition:

'Woody' refers to the palm tree in this garden.

So on the classical realist analysis, knowledge of the reference of a singular term is what explains and justifies the use of particular procedures for verifying and finding the implications of judgements involving the term. I want now to ask what it is to know the reference of a memory demonstrative, and how this relates to the use we make of memory demonstratives.

Memory demonstratives are made available by memory of events. There are a number of distinctions we can draw among types of event memory. For example, we can distinguish between memory of repeated events: 'that walk we took so often last summer'; memory of extended events: 'that trip to the coast'; and episodic events: 'the time you cut your finger'. It is striking that each of these types of event memory may involve conscious imagery, appropriate to the type. I may have an experiential memory of the walk that does not relate to any one occasion, but draws on many; or a series of images which relate to different aspects of the trip, as well as memory of your cry of pain. Each of these types of experiential memory can sustain memory demonstratives referring to objects. I may refer to 'that tree', which was part of the walk, 'that cottage', which figured in the trip, or 'that knife', which divided the flesh. It seems likely that memory is hierarchically organized among the types of event memory. The nesting of an experiential memory in a hierarchy of event memories can provide the temporal and spatial context for the remembered object. If I try to locate 'that knife', with which you cut your finger, I can do it by saying I am remembering the knife as it was while we were out walking during that trip to the coast (Barsalou, 1988).

Psychologists working on memory distinguish between memory with aware-ness and memory without awareness, conscious and unconscious memory, or explicit and implicit memory. Straight off, it seems that memory demonstratives depend on conscious memory. In unconscious memory, the past affects the subject without there being any conscious recollection. There is a famous anec-dote from Claparède which illustrates the distinction. He shook hands with an amnesic woman, having hidden a pin in his hand. The next day she refused to shake hands with him, although she had no conscious recollection of the earlier encounter. She said, 'Sometimes pins are hidden in people's hands.' (Kelley and Jacoby, 1993). This woman is evidently not in a position to understand a memory demonstrative referring to 'that pin'. There is a parallel here between memory demonstratives and perceptual demonstratives. In a case of blindsight, the subject may be differentially affected by a light in the blind field without having conscious awareness of it. The subject might be able to use a term like 'that figure', in the sense that he has some ability to verify propositions like 'that figure is square', or to act with respect to the figure, say by reaching for it. But although he has some capacity to use the term appropriately, this subject still does not understand the demonstrative 'that figure'. Since he is not conscious of the figure, he does not know which thing is in question; he does not know the reference of the demonstrative (Campbell, 1998). The central problem we have to address, in explaining how memory demonstratives work, is to characterize the role that consciousness of the past object plays in knowledge of the reference of the demonstrative.

KNOWLEDGE OF THE REFERENCE OF A MEMORY DEMONSTRATIVE

If we mechanically apply the model of descriptive names to the case of memory demonstratives, we will suppose that knowledge of the reference of a memory demonstrative is a matter of knowing a descriptive condition which an object must meet in order to be the referent of the term. If we bear in mind the role of conscious imagery in understanding a memory demonstrative—that using a memory image of the object may be an essential part of your understanding of the term—then we will suppose that the role of the image is to provide descriptive conditions which must be met by an object for the term to refer to it. The image will provide what we might call pictorial conditions on what the object must be like for the term to refer to it—the sort of object, its colour, size, shape, and so on. The image will not of itself provide any information about the time and place at which the object has to have met these pictorial conditions. This marks a sharp contrast between perceptions and memory images. Perception of an object in general does provide information about when and where: the time is now and the place is in the immediate vicinity of the subject. A memory image, in contrast, could relate to any of endlessly many different times and places—at least as many as the subject has ever perceived. In general, if a memory image is to provide uniquely identifying descriptive conditions, time and place will have to be anchored, even if only approximately. For time and place to be anchored, the image needs a context, specifying the time and place. The time and place need not be specified using any particular canonical system for specifying times and places. They may be given in terms which relate to one or another memory narrative, locating the time and place with respect to other remembered events and places.

Something like this approach, treating the demonstrative as having its reference fixed by a descriptive condition, seems to be the only one possible for demonstratives referring to future objects. Suppose you are in your usual café. You have ordered a coffee. All that is sustaining you through the next few minutes is the thought of the arrival of the coffee. You know exactly what it will look like when it comes. You have a vivid image of it. 'That cup', you say, 'will taste good'. There seems to be no particular reason to deny that this image could sustain a demonstrative referring to the future cup. But it does seem that this could only be by fixing a descriptive condition which an object must meet in order to be that cup. I am not considering a case in which you know which particular cup will be brought to you, and have a memory of it. Rather, since this is your usual café, you know in general what the cups look like, so you know what your next one will look like, and you use that knowledge in forming your image. And you have knowledge enough to provide a context for the image—you know roughly when and where the cup will arrive. So you have enough to have a descriptive condition uniquely identifying that cup. And the only way the demonstrative 'that cup' can have a reference is by having as referent whatever cup best fits that descriptive condition.

There is an evident contrast here between memory images and images of future objects. Suppose that someone, your sister, say, is trying to remind you of the oddly shaped window in your childhood bedroom. 'It was circular, with spokes running out from the centre, like the wheel of a ship', she says. As she talks you form a vivid image of the window. The image may be correct, detailed, and reliable. Even at this stage, it seems that you could, on the strength of the image, form a demonstrative, 'that window'. Still, you cannot be said to remember the window. It may be, though, that as your sister continues talking, she finally succeeds in jogging your memory, so that eventually you say, 'Aha! Now I remember!' After the shift, your image of the window may be exactly the same as before. There need be no pictorial change in the image. And it may be no more reliable than it was before. But this non-pictorial shift, whatever it is, marks the transition from your merely having an accurate, reliable, conscious image of the past window, to your consciously recollecting it.

On one analysis, what this shows is that there are two elements in conscious recollection of the past window. One element is having an accurate, reliable, conscious image of the thing. The other element is whatever it is that is gained by the non-pictorial shift. In the above example, the first element is in place before the second, but in general their onset may be simultaneous. The point of the example is just to make vivid the distinctness of the two elements. What differentiates images of past objects from images of future objects is that in the case of future objects, such as my projected cup of coffee, only the first of these two elements is ever available. I can form an accurate, reliable image of my future cup of coffee. But I am irredeemably stuck at that stage, and there is no such thing as my moving to the second stage and saying 'Aha! Now I have it!' (except in the altogether irrelevant sense in which I might make that remark when the coffee finally arrives).

In these terms, the question is what difference the second element makes to demonstrative reference. One analysis of the situation is that the second element is an experienced shift in the causation of the image. Of course, even before the shift, there was a causal chain running from the past window, through my sister's memory of it to my current image. But the present suggestion is that what happens after the shift is that the image is causally sustained not by my sister's

description, but in some more direct way by my own past perception of the thing
and the impact it made on me. And I can experience this shift in causation. It
seems possible that I could think my memory had been jogged when it had not,
so that I had an illusion of a shift in causation. It also seems possible that there
might have been the shift in causation without my realizing it, so that I took the
image still to have been formed merely in response to my sister's description
when it was actually a memory of mine. But in the ordinary case, the 'Aha!' will
express both the experience and the underlying shift in causation. It expresses my
experience of an underlying shift in the causation of the image (cf. Johnson,
1988).

What difference, if any, does this make to the kind of demonstrative that the
image can sustain? On the face of it, you might think it does not make a lot of
difference. Of course, since there is now an experienced causal link between the
image and the past object, there can be a causal dimension to the way in which
reference is fixed. But a causal link was there anyhow in the case in which I form
the image in response to the description given by my sister. In that case, there is
still a causal link between my image and the past object, although it is one that
goes by way of my sister's memory rather than my own. And that causal link is
one which is again quite apparent to me. So when, in this case, I use the demonstrative 'that window', to refer to the window of which I have formed an image,
there may well be a causal dimension to the way in which the reference of the
term is fixed. So there does not yet seem to be a radical difference between the
demonstrative I use in this case and a memory demonstrative. The causal links to
the object which serve to fix the references of the two types of demonstrative will
be somewhat different in detail. In one case the causal link goes by way of
another person, in the memory case it does not. But that difference of detail is all
there is to it.

I think you might wonder if there is not a more radical difference between, on
the one hand, the case in which the reference of the demonstrative is fixed by a
purely descriptive condition, and the case in which the reference of the demonstrative is fixed by a causal chain which goes by way of another person, and, on
the other hand, a memory demonstrative. The first two, it is natural to feel, are
only dubiously cases of demonstrative reference at all. With the memory demonstrative we come to a quite different case: here we have a kind of direct connection between the present subject and the past object which means that we have
demonstrative reference proper. I think this is a natural reaction. The problem is
to explain what the radical difference is, in the case of memory demonstratives.
Do we not, in all these cases, just have conscious imagery, which may or may not
have one or another kind of causal link to an object?

To articulate the view on which there is a radical difference here, we can
appeal to the general notion of being 'conscious of an object'. The central case of
being 'conscious of an object' is that in which you can perceive the thing; it is
right in front of you, staring you in the face. But there is also the case in which
you consciously recollect an object, and in that way are conscious of it. What is

it to be conscious of an object in memory? On one analysis it is a matter of having a conscious image of the thing. But you can have a conscious image relating to a future object, or one about which you have been told by someone else. All that the 'Aha!' of memory proper adds, on this analysis, is the experience of a particular type of causation. You might respond to this, though, by saying that there is in the case of memory proper more to consciousness of the past object than that. What the 'Aha!' of memory proper signals is not an experience of causation, but a shift from merely having a conscious image to being directly conscious of the past thing itself. To use Russell's term, it signals a shift to being directly acquainted with the past object. It is this kind of direct awareness of an object that alone is capable of supporting demonstrative reference proper.

JUSTIFYING THE INTRODUCTION RULE FOR A MEMORY DEMONSTRATIVE: THE ROLE OF TEMPORAL DECENTRING

So much, for the moment, for consciousness and knowledge of the reference of a memory demonstrative. Let us consider what an introduction rule for a memory demonstrative might look like. In general, memory exploits broadly logical links between differently tensed statements made at different times. For example, the statement 'Yesterday it rained', made on Tuesday, is true if and only if the statement 'Today it is raining', made on Monday, is true. The two statements are truth-value linked. Our ordinary use of memory exploits the existence of these truth-value links. What happens, in our ordinary use of memory, is that you shift from the judgement 'Today it is raining', made on Monday, to the memory-judgement, made on Tuesday, 'Yesterday it rained'. This procedure depends on the existence of logical connections between differently tensed judgements made at different times. We find this exploitation of truth-value links also in our use of memory demonstratives. Suppose you see someone standing in a shop doorway during a downpour and you think, 'that man is drenched'. The following day, remembering the scene, you think, 'That man was drenched'. This is a memory-demonstrative judgement, and in making it you exploit its being truth-value linked to the earlier demonstrative judgement. The truth-value link here is between a present judgement such as 'That (remembered) man was drenched', and a past present-tensed judgement such as 'That (perceived) man is drenched'. In this case, even to articulate the truth-value link, we have to be considering the connection between two different types of demonstrative, memory demonstratives and perceptual demonstratives.

The point now is that an observational predicate like 'drenched' is first introduced and explained in the context of present-tense propositions involving perceptual demonstratives, such as 'that (perceived) man is drenched'. Even to understand the use of the term in a memory-based judgement, you have to grasp the link between the way in which the perceptual judgement is verified and the way in which the memory-based judgement is verified. It can happen that you are in a position to recall the perceived scene on an earlier occasion—for example, the shop doorway yesterday—and now to make a memory-demonstrative judgement about someone you saw then, even though at the time you did not formulate any perceptual-demonstrative judgements about them. Still, the epistemic soundness of this procedure—its capacity to provide you with knowledge—depends on you relying on memory of perceptions on the basis of which you could have formulated knowledgeable perceptual-demonstrative judgements at the time. Only in that way can your use of the observational predicate in memory-based judgements be linked up to its use in the perceptual contexts in which it was first introduced and explained. So the introduction rule for a memory demonstrative will be something like:

$$\frac{\text{that (perceived) man is drenched [judged on Monday]}}{\text{that (remembered) man was drenched [judged subsequently]}}$$

As I said, the complication is that it seems possible that a knowledgeable memory-judgement could derive from a past perception, even though you made no judgement at the time. You might not have thought anything about the bedraggled figure in the shop doorway at the time, though he was in your field of vision, but still formed the memory-judgement later. In that case, we can say that your memory is knowledgeable just because your past perceptions provided the basis for a past perceptual-demonstrative judgement, even though you did not in fact make the judgement. You had the basis for an application of the introduction rule.

This lets us deal with another complication. In the case of a perceptual demonstrative, there is something paradoxical about a judgement like 'that (perceived) man is not currently being thought about by anyone'; simply making the judgement seems to be enough to guarantee that it is false. But if you think, 'that (remembered) man was then not being thought about by anyone', this might well be true, and indeed an expression of knowledge, as in the case of the bedraggled figure in the doorway that no one thought about at the time. However, if a condition for the judgement to be knowledgeable were that it should be derived from an actual application of the introduction rule, this should be impossible, since the application of the introduction rule would require you to have actually made a perceptual judgement at the time. What lets us deal with this is the fact your current memory-experiences may provide you with knowledge that (*a*) your past perceptions may have provided the ground for a perceptual-demonstrative judgement that could have served as input to an application of the introduction rule, and (*b*) that (*a*) could be true even though you did not actually form the perceptual-demonstrative judgement. It is consistent with all this that the introduction rule for the memory demonstrative is as shown above.

The transitions we make over time, from one tensed judgement to another, are in effect temporally extended inferences. They play a similar role, in our understanding of tense, to the role that introduction and elimination rules play for a logical constant. On a classical realist account, however, we do not simply make these moves: our grasp of the truth-conditions of the propositions involved is what causes us to make these transitions, and it justifies us in making these transitions. I am talking here about grasp of the truth-conditions of judgements made at different times. So what is involved is what I will call 'temporal decentring'. By temporal decentring, I will mean the capacity to understand tensed judgements, or statements, made at times other than the present.

We have to separate different types of skill involved in a grasp of tense. We have to distinguish between diachronic aspects of one's grasp of tense, which have to do with how one thinks over time, and synchronic aspects of one's grasp of tense, which have to do with one's ability to think in tensed terms at a particular time. Memory, as I have described it so far, exploiting the truth-value links, has to do with diachronic aspects of grasp of tense. Decentring, on the other hand, is synchronic. It has to do with your capacity, at some one time, to understand tensed statements which may have been made at any of a variety of times.[2] If, at some moment, you are to understand the logical link between two differently tensed statements made at different times, then you will have to exploit the understanding you have, at that moment, of those two statements made at different times. It is almost a tautology that your understanding of the logical link between statements made at different times will have to exploit your capacity for temporal decentring.

There is a parallel here between the way in which decentring causes, and justifies, our use of the truth-value links, and the way in which grasp of the truth-table for a classical propositional connective can be seen as causing, and justifying, the use of the classical introduction and elimination rules for the sign. You can think of memory as a kind of temporally extended inference, taking you from a judgement made on one day to a judgement made some time later, whose truth is implied by the truth of the earlier judgement. Of course, you have to use your empirically grounded capacity to keep track of time to ensure that you have come to a judgement which is implied by the earlier judgement, and that is not itself a purely logical matter. But there is none the less a logical aspect to the transition, in that if the empirical condition is met then the truth-value link holds as a logical matter. With what right do we take the truth-value links to hold? The answer I propose is that just as our use of classical introduction and elimination rules for the propositional constants is justified by our grasp of the classical truth-tables, so our use of the inferential links between differently tensed judgements made at different times is justified by our capacity for temporal decentring.

How does this apply to the case of memory demonstratives? How does my knowledge of the reference of the memory demonstrative 'that (remembered) man' play its role in justifying me in making the transition over time, from yesterday's judgement, 'that man (perceived) is drenched', to today's judgement, 'that (remembered) man was drenched'? I think it helps to begin on this by thinking first about my own understanding of a perceptual remark I made yesterday.

---

[2] For a review of the notion of temporal decentring as it figures in the psychological literature, see McCormack and Hoerl, 1999.

Suppose, for example, that yesterday I was standing in the doorway writing in my journal as the stranger walked in. And I wrote, 'that man is drenched'. Today, looking at the remark in my journal, how am I to interpret it? How do I, from today's perspective, understand yesterday's perceptual demonstrative?

You might say that understanding yesterday's perceptual demonstrative is actually impossible. As I used it yesterday, my use of the term depended on my then current perceptions. But those perceptions are gone forever, and so I have no way now of understanding the demonstrative I used yesterday. If this is correct, then there is no way in which temporal decentring can justify my use of the transition from 'that (perceived) man is F' to 'that (remembered) man was F'. We would find ourselves compelled to make these transitions, but lack any comprehension of why they were correct. A parallel for the situation would be that I find there is a logical connective '*', which I simply do not understand, though I used to understand it and back then I accepted a proposition of the form 'A*B'. Now, I find myself compelled, for no reason I can give, to make the transition from this judgement 'A*B', to the conclusion A. In this case I think we would have no hesitation in saying that my making the transition from the judgement 'A*B', which I do not understand, to the conclusion A, which I do understand, is not rational, and that the conclusion A cannot be knowledge. But this is exactly parallel to the situation in which yesterday's perceptual demonstrative is no longer comprehensible to me, but I find myself compelled to move from yesterday's judgement to the conclusion 'that man was drenched'. If yesterday's perceptual demonstrative is no longer comprehensible to me, then the transition is not rational and the conclusion is not knowledge. So if we are to acknowledge the status of memory as a form of knowledge, we have to find some way in which I can now be said to understand yesterday's perceptual demonstrative.

The simplest approach is to try to recall my perceptions as I stood in the doorway. But this just is memory imagery. My current understanding of yesterday's perceptual judgement will have to rely on just the same memory imagery as is relied on by my understanding of today's memory-based judgement, 'that (remembered) man was F'. So my knowledge of which thing was in question in yesterday's perceptual judgement automatically grounds my use of the current memory demonstrative. It provides me with a guarantee that it is one and the same thing that is in question both times.

At this point, though, you might say the problem has simply been shifted back a stage. Through decentring we have found a connection between my present understanding of yesterday's perceptual judgement and my present understanding of today's memory-judgement. And the connection does seem to be enough to validate my making the transition from yesterday's judgement to today's judgement. The problem now, though, is that we seem not to have any connection between the way in which I now understand yesterday's perceptual judgement, on the basis of memory imagery, and the way in which I understood it yesterday, on the basis of perception.

You might ask whether there really has to be any such linkage. Could we not say that there is an incommensurability between the ways in which we understand the perceptual judgement at different times, but still insist that we do grasp the justification for our ordinary procedures; that decentring is enough to justify our exploitation of the truth-value links? If we have that, what more is needed? The trouble with this is that the way we actually use memory does seem to demand a commensurability between the way in which we understand a perceptual judgement at the time at which it is made, and the way in which we subsequently understand it. We think that whether the current memory-judgement is knowledge depends on whether the earlier perceptual judgement was epistemically sound. In making the earlier judgement and in making the current judgement, you were aiming at truth both times; and your success in the earlier enterprise affects your prospects of success in the later enterprise. But if your ways of understanding the proposition at different times were incommensurable, there would be no way in which the two enterprises could be connected. So, to respect the way in which we do use memory, we have to find a linkage between my current understanding of the earlier perceptual demonstrative and the way in which I understood it earlier.

SURFACE V. DEEP DECENTRING

If memory imagery were one style of representation, and perception another style of representation, with no commensurability between the two, then it would indeed be impossible to find any connection between my current understanding of a past perceptual demonstrative and my past understanding of it. For I would be using incommensurable styles of representation in the two interpretative exercises. Of course, conscious recollection causally depends on past perceptions. But the point we have reached is that there has to be a linkage between the content of my present conscious memory and the contents of my past perceptions. This linkage has to be what we exploit in the decentring that justifies the use we make of memory demonstratives.

We can ask to what extent this linkage between current memory and past perception can be acknowledged by the two views of conscious recollection that I distinguished earlier. One of these views was the two-component view. On this view, conscious recollection of an object is a matter of having a conscious image of the object, together with an experience of the image as having been suitably caused by the past object. On the alternative, direct-acquaintance view, conscious recollection is a relational act that straddles time; consciousness of the object is a primitive relation that connects the present rememberer to the remembered object.

Straight off, we might expect that the direct acquaintance view will have trouble in acknowledging the link between a present memory and past perceptions. On the face of it, if direct acquaintance with the past object is indeed a primitive relation that you stand in to it, then there is no very evident reason why that should involve perception of the past object at all. Russell, who first articulated this kind of view of memory, thought that memory acquaintance with a past sense-datum did not even depend on it having been previously sensed. On this view, then, memory acquaintance and perceptual acquaintance may simply be different types of acquaintance we can have with objects, and there may be nothing very informative or substantive to be said about connections between them. So there will be nothing to be said about how a capacity for temporal decentring could justify the use that we make of memory demonstratives. Russell's view seems extreme, because it hardly makes sense to suppose that we could have experiential memories of scenes we had not previously perceived. But if temporal decentring is to play the role I am envisaging for it, it is not just that there must be a causal dependence of recollection on prior perception. The content of the recollection has to be commensurable with the content of the prior perception, so that the move from the prior perception to the current recollection can be seen by the subject to be justified.

It is important to bear in mind that we are not looking for anything very heroic in the way of justification here. If the classical realist picture can be sustained at all, it has to be that the ordinary person does, in grasping a memory demonstrative, grasp the justification for shifting from the past perceptual judgement to the current memory-based judgement. So the kind of justification that is sought must be available to anyone who grasps a memory demonstrative. It is not to be given by some complicated argument known only to philosophers.

I think it helps here to draw a distinction between different ways in which temporal decentring might work. Suppose you consider a tensed statement made at a different time, such as 'that (perceived) man is drenched'. And suppose that you know that time at which the statement was made, using a time-specification from a suitable temporal framework. How are you to use the time-specification to interpret the statement? The simplest way is simply to delete the use of the present tense, and replace it with the time-specification. So you might have something like, 'that (perceived) man is drenched at noon on Monday'. Just to try to make it unmistakable what process I have in mind here, notice that this interpretation process loses information. By the time the process is complete, the fact that we were dealing with a tensed sentence at the outset has been lost. So you might try to meet this point by keeping a log of the process, so that you record that you began with a tensed sentence. Notice, though, that if you approach temporal decentring in this way, there seems to be no obvious route by which the link between the present memory demonstrative and the past perceptual judgement, as you understood it then, could be made apparent to you simply by your having an understanding of the memory demonstrative.

There is, though, another way in which you might go about the interpretation process in temporal decentring. I will call the process I just described 'surface decentring'. The process I am about to describe is 'deep decentring'. This is a more complex, two-stage construction. In the first level of the construction, you adopt the hypothesis, or the supposition, or the pretence, that it is now noon on Monday. Then, in the second level, you consider, within the scope of the hypothesis, the sentence, 'that (perceived) man is drenched' as a sentence which is currently being uttered. There is no need for any further interpretation of the sentence.

This procedure exploits the fact that in my current use of tense, I do not need knowledge of the time to interpret the tenses I use. I might have lost all track of what the time is, and I still understand perfectly well what my tensed utterances mean. That is why it makes sense to raise such questions as 'What time is it now?', 'Is it still January?', and so on. That such questions make sense exploits the fact that I do have a current temporal location, that these sentences are being uttered at determinate times, but I can understand them without knowing what those times are. In contrast, to understand a use of tense at another time than the present, I do need to know the time of utterance.

In this second way of understanding a use of tense at some time other than the present, tense is used, not mentioned, in the final understanding one reaches. One reaches imaginatively to the past time and, within the context of the imaginative project, thinks the tensed thoughts. This way of understanding a past use of tense is deep decentring. You might think of it on analogy with simulating the mental states of another person than yourself; this is simulating the properties of another time than the present.

The question I left hanging earlier was the relation between my current understanding of a past perceptual demonstrative and my past understanding of it. This seems to turn on the relation between my current memory imagery and my past perception of the object. But it seems possible to think of the relation like this: that grasp of the memory demonstrative just consists in deep decentring to the past time, the time at which the past perceptual demonstrative was used. We can think of knowledge of the reference of a memory demonstrative as actually provided by deep decentring to the past time. To understand the memory demonstrative is to simulate the time at which a past perceptual demonstrative could have been used. If you think of knowledge of the reference of the memory demonstrative in this way, then I think you can see how it could validate the use of the kind of introduction rule I mentioned for memory demonstratives.

The crucial point is that deep decentring is not simply a matter of knowing how to verify or to find the implications of the demonstrative proposition. It actually provides you with knowledge of which thing is being referred to. It is what causes, and justifies, your use of the particular methods that you use to verify or find the implications of judgements involving the demonstrative.

Does this approach favour the two-component view of conscious recollection over the direct-acquaintance view? At first it may not seem that a direct-acquaintance view could acknowledge any need for deep decentring in understanding a memory demonstrative, since acquaintance was thought of as a primitive relation between the present rememberer and the past object, which would not be mediated by any representation of past perceptions. On a two-component view, on the other hand, the current conscious image just serves as the basis for deep decentring. The current conscious image is a potential perceptual image, and knowing the temporal and spatial context for the image just provides for the second phase of deep decentring. So the two-component view of conscious recollection and the view of grasp of a memory-demonstrative as involving deep decentring seem to support one another.

Of course, memory images are not simple copies of past perceptions; they are reconstructed from compilations of past perceptions. This is immediately apparent when you reflect even on the contrast between the course of your perceptions as you enter a room—jerky, rapidly switching from shot to shot, disorganized—and your imagistic memory a few moments later of your entry to the room, which is a smooth, carefully edited, coherent sequence. The constructed character of memory imagery—the fact that we cannot view the memory image as a simple copy of an earlier perception—also shows up in the fact that many people, reporting the contents of their memories of scenes in which they played a part, report that they have a third-person image of themselves as one among the people in the scene, rather than remembering the scene from their own past point of view (Nigro and Neisser, 1983). Finally, there may be no one past perception from which your current memory image derives. Suppose you are asked, 'Do you remember that woman who sold flowers by the railway station?' You may well be in a position to understand the memory demonstrative here, but there may be no one past perception from which your current memory image of that woman derives—it may be that your memory imagery of that woman, which you use to interpret the demonstrative, is in effect a compilation from many past perceptions of her, which you could not now separate. None the less, memory images are still linked to past perceptions. It sometimes seems to be supposed that memory is somehow discredited by the fact that it has this reconstructive character, as if the point of the reconstruction were inevitably to distort your memories of how things happened. Of course there can be distortion. But the point of the reconstruction is more typically to keep your memory images on track; to ensure that they are credible images of what actually happened. In effect, what you are doing is constructing an image of the past scene which could have been the content of an accurate perception of it, whether or not there was just such a perception.

Still, this point does indicate one concession that has to be made to the direct-acquaintance view: namely, that grasp of the memory demonstrative requires the existence of the past object. Since the use that we make of memory demonstratives depends in general on compilation of images, the correctness of your current use of the memory demonstrative will depend on whether you have compiled together perceptions that are indeed all perceptions of one and the same object. So your grasp of the memory demonstrative will depend on it being true that there is just one object from which your current memory derives. And that in general will not be something that can be guaranteed by the contents of your memory images or perceptual images alone—they could be exactly the same whether they derived from one object, a number of objects, or no objects at all. Whether your grasp of the memory demonstrative can justify the use you make of it will depend on what objects there are around you. So since grasp of the memory demonstrative has to validate your using the demonstrative as if there is just one object in question, your having grasped the memory demonstrative at all will depend on the existence and uniqueness of the thing from which your memory images derive.

A view which would accommodate all these points would be one on which (*a*) your current experience, in memory, of the past object, reaches all the way to the past object itself. That is, just as on Russell's original theory, the memory experience includes the past object as a constituent, so that there is a sense in which the existence and uniqueness of the object referred to is apparent to the subject. None the less, (*b*) there is a further aspect to your current experience of the past object, the 'way' in which the past object is given to you, which does provide you with the capacity for deep decentring to a past perception of the thing.

Finally, suppose we consider how these points bear on scepticism about memory. Russell famously said that there is no inconsistency in the proposition that the whole world, with all its records and apparent memories, sprang into existence just five minutes ago. He also said that there is no interest in the hypothesis, since ordinary knowledge does not demand infallibility; the hypothesis marks only a bare possibility which need not disturb our ordinary knowledge claims; you do not have to refute the sceptical hypothesis to have knowledge (Russell, 1921: ch. 9). But there is more threat contained in the hypothesis than this reaction acknowledges. To take a parallel case, suppose that you and I enter a laboratory, with various pieces of equipment scattered around. I know nothing about these instruments, but, wishing to impress you, I seize on one meter at random and tell you, 'This is a voltmeter. See, it is measuring the current in that wire. Now it's 9 volts, now it's 4.5 volts . . .', and so on. Even if I have been lucky, and what I picked on is as it happens a reliable voltmeter, my remarks do not express knowledge. I have no reason to think the instrument is connected to voltage rather than to anything else. Just so in the case of memory. Even if everything is as we think, so long as we use memory blindly, with no particular reason to think it is a way of finding out about the past, rather than being as described by Russell's sceptic, it could not be said to provide us with knowledge of the past. We need some reason to think that the procedures we use—whether it is the meter or memory—are connected in any way to the phenomena we find out about by using them. Otherwise what we have is not knowledge. In the case of the voltmeter, what would be needed—if I am not simply to rely on the testimony of other people—is some understanding of how a voltmeter can work, how it can be that the swinging of the needle varies with the voltage in the wire. But this kind of theoretical understanding seems unlikely to be of any help to us in the memory case, since any such theoretical understanding we might bring to bear is likely itself to depend on the exercise of memory. What I am suggesting is that, instead, consciousness of past objects plays the role here of giving us the reason why our introduction rules for memory demonstratives are correct.

We have to acknowledge that a machine could mimic the use that we make of memory demonstratives. That is, we could construct a machine which could verify sentences involving memory demonstratives much as we do, and which could find the implications of sentences involving memory demonstratives much

as we do. That is, we could enable the machine to go into states which had imagistic content parallel to the imagistic contents of our memories. These imagistic
contents might indeed be reconstructed from earlier quasi-perceptual states of the
machine's sensors, in parallel to the way in which our memory images are reconstructed from past perceptions. So the machine would be able to use imagery to
verify demonstrative judgements much as we do, and it could use them in
constructing verbal narratives about past events much as we do. All this without
the machine being conscious. So what is missing in the machine's understanding
of memory demonstratives? What the machine does not have is the core of our
understanding of memory demonstratives: the knowledge of reference that
causes, and justifies, our use of particular procedures for verifying and finding the
implications of judgements about the past. It mimics our use of the procedures;
but it has no grasp of the justification for the use of those procedures. That is what
is provided by our consciousness of the past object.

TOP–DOWN V. BOTTOM–UP MEMORY DEMONSTRATIVES

I began by saying that there are two reasons why perceptual demonstratives seem
to be fundamental to our grasp of concepts and language. One was that they play
a basic role in our understanding of observational concepts, which are first introduced and explained in the context of propositions involving perceptual demonstratives. The second reason was that perceptual demonstration seems to be
fundamental among the types of singular reference. It does not itself depend on the
availability of other types of singular reference; but other types of singular reference, such as our use of proper names, seem to depend on their connections to
perceptual demonstratives. Do similar points apply to memory demonstratives?
Do they have any claim to be fundamental to our grasp of concepts and language?

Do memory demonstratives have any role in explaining observational
concepts? On the face of it, the answer seems to be that they can play a role in
explaining observational concepts but that they need not do so. For example, if
you are trying to explain to me what 'Wedgwood blue' is, you might say,
'Remember that room we were in yesterday? Those walls were Wedgwood blue.'
But this does not give memory any special place in the explanation of observational concepts. It can play its role here only because of its link to perception;
only because when I say 'those walls' I am deep decentring to perception of those
walls as they were yesterday.

Are memory demonstratives fundamental among the types of singular reference? I think that here we have to make a contrast between different ways in
which a memory image might be constructed. In one kind of case, you have a
clear objective in constructing a memory image, which is defined by some non-
demonstrative designator such as 'Jerry Lee Lewis'. Suppose I am trying to
remember what Jerry Lee Lewis looks like. I construct an image of him, using the
stored information I have. Once I have a vivid image, I might say, 'that man is

probably dead by now', using a memory demonstrative. But there does not seem to be any sense in which this memory demonstrative is any more fundamental than the name 'Jerry Lee Lewis'. The judgement, 'that (remembered) man is Jerry Lee Lewis', is a priori. In contrast, perceptual demonstratives seem always to achieve reference independently of our capacities to identify objects descriptively, or to recognize them. So a judgement like 'that (perceived) man is Jerry Lee Lewis' is always empirically grounded rather than being a priori.

In the case in which I form an image of Jerry Lee Lewis, the objective in constructing the memory image on which the memory demonstrative depends is specified using a non-demonstrative designator. We might call such memory demonstratives, 'top–down memory demonstratives', because there is a top–down specification of the intended referent governing the construction of the memory image. There are also, however, 'bottom–up memory demonstratives'. Suppose we return to the scenario on which you and I are standing talking in a shop doorway during a heavy rainstorm and, as we talk, a bedraggled figure stumbles into shelter. The next day you say to me: 'Do you remember that man in the shop doorway yesterday? He was really drenched.' In this case I understand your use of the demonstrative by consciously recollecting that bedraggled figure. My formation of the memory image here is not top–down, in the sense that I have an objective in forming the memory image which can be specified using a non-demonstrative designator; though you are certainly supplying me with retrieval cues. My aim is simply to form an image of the scene in the doorway, and consequent upon that, I can refer to that individual as 'that man'. There is in this case no designator D such that I express a priori knowledge when I say 'that (remembered) man is D'. So this is a bottom–up memory demonstrative.

The use of bottom–up memory demonstratives does not seem to depend on the use of any other types of singular reference. So in that sense they might be said to be basic. They do not yet, however, seem to have any claim to being fundamental, in the sense in which perceptual demonstratives are fundamental. That is, we do not yet have any reason to think that other types of singular reference depend on the use of memory demonstratives. The most intriguing and problematic line of thought here was once again set out by Russell. Explaining the need for experiential memory of past objects, Russell wrote:

But for the fact of memory in this sense, we should not know that there ever was a past at all, nor should we be able to understand the word 'past' any more than a man born blind can understand the word 'light'. Thus there must be intuitive judgements of memory, and it is upon them, ultimately, that all our knowledge of the past depends. (Russell, 1967: 115)

We can imagine someone who claims to have no experience of the past, in Russell's sense. This person might be able to construct memory narratives which reliably reflect the course of events. The question raised by Russell's remark is whether there is not here a sense in which this is just empty talk. (Similarly, someone born blind might, one way or another, manage to use a colour vocabulary reliably; but he or she would have no grasp of colour concepts and this would just be empty talk.) Certainly, it is hard to see how someone who had precognition, but no experiential memory, could have the concept of the past. But, although it has some immediate plausibility, it is not easy to see how you would make out a detailed case for Russell's view here. Moreover, this view immediately raises a problem. As I said, we do not have experience of the future in the sense in which we have experience of the past. But we certainly have the concept of the future. Why should there be this asymmetry between past and future? If you think that we do need experience of past objects in order to have the concept of the past, you owe an explanation of why we do not need experience of future objects in order to have the concept of the future.

Thanks to Naomi Eilan, Philippa Foot, Christoph Hoerl, Teresa McCormack, Christopher Peacocke, and John Sutton for discussion of these topics. Earlier versions were presented to a workshop at Macquarie University, and to the ANU, and I learnt a lot from these discussions. I began work on this paper during tenure of a British Academy Research Readership, and I am grateful to the Academy for its support.

J.C.

REFERENCES

BARSALOU, L. W. (1988), 'The content and organization of autobiographical memories', in U. Neisser and E. Winograd (eds.), *Remembering Reconsidered*. Cambridge: Cambridge University Press.

CAMPBELL, J. (1998), 'Sense and consciousness', in P. Sullivan and J. Brandl (eds.), *New Essays on the Philosophy of Michael Dummett* Grazer Philosophische Studien, 55: 195–211.

JOHNSON, M. K. (1988), 'Reality monitoring: an experimental phenomenological approach', *Journal of Experimental Psychology: General*, 117: 390–4.

KELLEY, C. M., and JACOBY, L. L. (1993), 'The construction of subjective experience: memory attributions', in M. Davies and G. Humphreys (eds.), *Consciousness*. Oxford: Blackwell.

McCORMACK, T., and HOERL, C. (1999), 'Memory and temporal perspective: the role of temporal frameworks in memory development', *Developmental Review*, 19: 154–82.

NIGRO, G., and NEISSER, U. (1983), 'Point of view in personal memories', *Cognitive Psychology*, 15: 467–82.

PEARS, D. (1975), 'Russell's theories of memory', in *Questions in the Philosophy of Mind*. London: Duckworth.

RUSSELL, BERTRAND (1921), *The Analysis of Mind*. London: George Allen and Unwin.

—— (1967), *The Problems of Philosophy*. Oxford: Oxford University Press.

—— (1984), *Theory of Knowledge: The 1913 Manuscript*. London: Allen and Unwin.

7

Aware and Unaware Memory
Does Unaware Memory Underlie Aware Memory?

Andrew R. Mayes

IS THERE A PROBLEM IN EXPLAINING HOW AWARE MEMORY ARISES?

Most people think that provided one can explain how information is stored in the human brain there is no extra problem that must be solved to explain why we usually know that we are remembering. In this section, it will be argued that even if the processes of storage were understood, there is an extra problem requiring solution.

The human brain not only processes information, it stores it as well. There is growing evidence that most, if not all, regions of the central nervous system are plastic and, therefore, capable of storing memories. Memories are not stored in special storage sites. In fact, most researchers believe that each memory representation is stored in the same network of neurons that was responsible for making the representation in the first place (Rose, 1992; Mayes, 1988). Some support for this assumption can be derived from neuroimaging studies (see Ungerleider, 1995 for a review). When facts or episodes are represented by their brains, humans are often conscious of the factual or episodic information being represented. Such awareness is necessary for the occurrence of aware memory, but it is not the same thing. One can be aware of facts or episodes without being aware that one is remembering them, that is, that one has encountered them before in some form. Broadly, one could believe that one is remembering such information for two reasons: one could see that the information of which one was conscious was consistent with other memories in which one believed and hence infer that one must be remembering or one could feel that one was remembering more directly. It is certainly the case that humans often feel that they are remembering and such aware remembering is often accurate.

It is this latter kind of aware remembering, where one is directly aware that the information of which one is conscious is a memory, that needs to be explained. Having such a memory experience either means that one is directly aware that one has encountered the information of which one is conscious as part of an experienced episode (episodic memory) or that one has previously encountered it as a true fact (semantic memory). Explaining how such aware memory is generated is the focus of the present chapter. The chapter does not address the more general problem of what processes are responsible for our being conscious of the information we feel ourselves to be remembering (or indeed not remembering). Without such consciousness, however, aware memory is not possible. It is very important to note that we are often conscious of information which we do not feel that we are remembering even though memory is occurring. Such instances of unaware memory depend on storage of the information and are indicated by changes in the way that the information is processed. There is no awareness that the remembered information has been encountered before in the ways indicated above. The occurrence of such unaware memory indicates that the occurrence of aware memory is not an automatic consequence of storage, but requires an explanation.

The problem of aware memory can be illustrated most easily by considering the case of recognition memory. If one perceives a face that has never been seen before, a specific pattern of activation in a network of neurons in the posterior cortex is probably critical for making one aware that a particular face is being perceived. Assuming that a representation of the face is stored in memory, then the next time it is perceived a similar set of neurons or a subset of them will be activated and the perceiver will be aware of the same facial information as before. But awareness of the facial information cannot by itself indicate whether the face has been seen before or not, as it is common to novel and familiar faces, and cannot possibly distinguish between the two accurately.

Two things might be argued to explain from where the memory awareness emerges. First, it might be suggested that seeing the face triggers other information which was present when the face was initially perceived so that perceivers know they are remembering. But how do they know that they are not imagining that the other information occurred with the face or that the face and the information are just 'good companions'? In other words, the same problem appears again if one argues that awareness that one is remembering X arises because being aware of X triggers awareness of Y. Also, the argument cannot explain all cases of accurate face recognition even if it is correct. This is because experience indicates that people often feel that faces are familiar even when they can recall nothing about them including the contexts in which they were previously seen.

Secondly, it might be suggested that aware memory occurs when the neural activity that produces consciousness of a particular face feeds into a 'memory awareness or familiarity mechanism'. The objection to this proposal is not so much that it is circular and deliberately vague, but that it completely fails to indicate why aware memory is not random, but a process that is generally accurate. It does not explain why the neuronal activity that produces consciousness of a face sometimes triggers the familiarity mechanism, and why, when it does so, true memory is usually present. Once again, it is difficult to accept that merely being aware of information that is in memory is sufficient to trigger the mechanism because this should be equally likely with conscious representations of novel information.

In this chapter, a redundancy model is proposed according to which aware memory is triggered not by merely being conscious of specific information, but by the way in which that information is brought back into consciousness following the encoding of more or less complete components of it. This process is very similar to what has been referred to as priming (see Wiggs and Martin, 1998) and which can also be referred to as information-specific implicit memory (ISIM) (see Mayes, Gooding, and Van Eijk, 1997). Four kinds of mechanism, familiar from the memory research literature, and the ways in which they interact, will provide the framework for this proposal. These mechanisms should be sufficient to explain recall, recognition, and ISIM for facts and episodes and, in modified form, may be able to explain all forms of procedural or non-declarative memory. The framework is consistent with a redundancy relationship existing between ISIM and aware memory in which aware memory for specific information of *any* kind does not occur without ISIM (indicated by an enhancement of fluency) occurring for the same information. The next section outlines what these four mechanisms are. The redundancy model is then explained in more detail in the following section, before possible problems are briefly considered in the final section. The argument is that there is reasonable support for the redundancy model that is derivable from the four-component framework, and although it is far from proved, there are currently no other explanations of what generates aware memory. The redundancy model is also testable and its adoption would be heuristically beneficial.

THE FRAMEWORK

The framework, explicit memory, and implicit memory

Performance on indirect memory tasks in which no reference is made to a study episode or to memory is often believed to depend mainly on priming, which will be referred to in this chapter as ISIM because it is the subtype of implicit memory (Schacter, 1987) that is information-specific. In contrast, performance on direct memory tasks in which reference is made to a study episode and to memory is usually believed to depend mainly or even solely on what will be referred to here as explicit memory (Schacter, 1987; Roediger, 1990). Examples of typical indirect memory tasks include preference judgements, word stem completion, lexical and object decision, and word and picture naming or categorization (see Graf and Masson, 1993 *passim*). Examples of direct memory tasks include yes/no and forced-choice recognition, and cued and free recall (see Richardson-Klavehn and Bjork, 1988, for a review). ISIM and explicit memory are the hypothetical memory processes that are postulated to underlie performance on these two kinds of memory task. Implicit process(es) are believed to lead to unaware memory whereas the explicit process(es) lead to aware memory. Most workers believe that these processes are distinct from each other (Schacter, 1992, 1994; Squire, 1992). If they are correct, then almost certainly the implicit and explicit processes should be mediated by separate brain regions.

The theoretical framework, outlined in this section, comprises four kinds of process or mechanism: memory representations (see Mayes, 1988, for a discussion); enhanced fluency (see Jacoby and Dallas, 1981); attributions (see Jacoby, Kelley, and Dywan, 1989); and active retrieval search (see Gillund and Shiffrin, 1984). These mechanisms, all of which have been discussed to some degree in the literature, can explain how performance is mediated not only on indirect memory tests (usually regarded as primarily sensitive to ISIM), but also on the direct memory tests of recall and recognition (usually regarded as quintessentially explicit memory tasks). Indirect memory test performance usually depends primarily on only ISIM which is typically dependent on one of the four mechanisms, namely enhanced fluency. When the indirect memory test involves a non-memory attribution (e.g. where repeated words are judged to have been shown for longer than baseline words shown for equivalent times), ISIM depends on an attribution mechanism as well as enhanced fluency. These mechanisms can operate on different kinds of memory representation depending on the kind of information tapped by the indirect memory task.

Memory representations, or storage

Memory representations store specific kinds of information and should presumably be defined in terms of what that information is and the way in which it is stored. As already indicated, memory representations are believed to be stored within the set of neurons that represented the information before it was stored in memory. This implies that memory for different kinds of information will be stored in different neurons because it is known that different kinds of sensory and other information are processed and represented by distinct brain regions. Storage is universally believed to involve structural changes at synapses that affect the ease with which neurons in a neural network can activate each other (see e.g. Rose, 1992). Explicit memory and ISIM tap semantic, perceptual, and episodic information which is likely to be represented primarily in the neocortex, so the synaptic changes should increase the degree to which the neurons representing the separate informational components of the memory are interconnected. Thus storage probably involves forming stronger links between the neocortical neurons that represent the basic components of the information stored. In this sense, all memory, whether of items or complex sets of items, is associative and new memories should depend on strengthening links that either did not previously exist or were weaker. They may also depend on weakening pre-existing links that represent information disruptive of that which needs to be stored.

It is possible that there are different kinds of memory representation corresponding to those kinds of association that are stored in distinct ways. For example, it could be that storage of single items (words or faces) in memory depends on associations that are formed between neurons in one neocortical region whereas associations between items and their study context (and perhaps associations between different kinds of item) depend on very different kinds of association formed across distinct neocortical regions (Cohen, Poldrack, and Eichenbaum, 1997; Curran and Schacter, 1997; Schacter, 1994). It needs to be shown that not only do single-item and item-context associations involve storage in different brain sites, but that the storage operations mediated by these brain sites depend on biochemically and structurally distinct processes that work according to different rules. Storage operations might differ not only within neurons, but also with respect to the kind of inter-neuronal reorganization they produce. Abel *et al.* (1995) have argued that explicit and implicit memory (and presumably their subtypes) 'seem to share a common molecular logic for initial consolidation' and, therefore, they probably share storage processes at the intra-neuronal level. If they are correct, then any differences in the storage of different representations must relate to organizational differences at the inter-neuronal level.

That something external, like a face or a film, can be encoded in different ways so that different information is represented in memory is obvious. It is nevertheless hard to show that the representations of the different information encoded are stored in distinct ways. Whether *exactly* the same information can be stored twice according to algorithmically distinct principles seems much less likely. Even so, it has been argued that ISIM for what might be regarded as inter-item associations is organized differently from explicit memory for the same associations. Whereas explicit memory representations of inter-item associations have been postulated by Cohen, Poldrack, and Eichenbaum (1997) to be componential, they have argued that ISIM representations of the same information are inflexibly merged into a new Gestalt. On this hypothesis, componential representations retain the identities of their components so that the whole representation can be flexibly retrieved from different componential features. In contrast, ISIM representations show the property of hyperspecificity, which means that they can only be accessed when the precise cues encoded during the study phase are presented during retrieval. Flexible memory representations are initially mediated by storage changes in the hippocampus which link to the neocortical regions that represent the component features of each representation. Inflexible memory representations, in contrast, depend on direct neocortical connections being strengthened as soon as the memory is created.

We should stress, however, that the evidence for the same kind of information being stored twice according to different principles currently does not exist. One reason for this, highlighted by the notion of memory representation, is that it is far from a trivial problem to determine exactly what information is being retrieved. Performance on different memory tests for the same *nominal stimulus* may tap retrieval of distinct encoded features of the stimulus or of semantic features that were encoded in association with the stimulus when it was perceived. For example, ISIM for a specific item may just involve retrieving some of the perceptual features of the item whereas, if the dual process theory of recognition is correct (e.g. Mandler, 1980; Jacoby and Dallas, 1981), then recognizing the item often involves retrieving the association between some of the item information and its study context. Thus, it is hard to know whether particular instances of ISIM and explicit memory for the same nominal stimulus involve retrieval of exactly the same information.

In summary, memory representations involve strengthening or weakening the connections between the components that make up the stored representations. This is achieved by intra-neuronal modifications in synaptic structure and functioning in the brain regions and neural networks in which the stored information was initially represented. The location of memory representations, therefore, differs depending on the information stored because of the way that different information is processed and represented by distinct brain regions. How the synaptic changes alter the organization of neural networks is poorly understood, but the result is a marked increase in the effectiveness with which remembered representations are reactivated when some of their components are re-encoded.

Enhanced fluency

In other words, studied information has its memory representation activated more rapidly, easily, and strongly when cues that are components of the representation have been encoded (see Jacoby and Dallas, 1981). This enhancement in fluency is relative to the fluency with which the same encoded cues would have activated the representation on a previous occasion before the memory had been stored or strengthened. Fluency enhancement is often caused by the strengthening of the information's memory representation and this mnemonic enhancement of fluency is postulated to be, in some sense, automatic (Jacoby, 1983; Jacoby and Dallas, 1981; Jacoby and Witherspoon, 1992; Jacoby and Kelley, 1992). However, fluency of reactivation can also be influenced by non-mnemonic factors such as arousal level. For example, if visual cues are presented with various degrees of masking, the masking will strongly influence the ease with which the related representation is reactivated. Reactivation of the representation is triggered by cues that constitute varying degrees of the original information. They may be very partial in the case of stem completion (where the cues correspond to those provided in cued recall) or perhaps total in the case of the cues in a perceptual identification task (where the cues correspond to those used in recognition). The ease with which a memory is reactivated depends not only on the strength of the memory, but also on the degree of match between the encoded cues and the memory representation in accordance with the encoding specificity principle (see Tulving, 1983). It is postulated that subjects have some awareness of the fluency with which representations are activated, but that the fluency feeling is similar regardless of whether it is caused by mnemonic or non-mnemonic factors.

More interestingly, fluency can be increased by subliminal priming with the same item that is then immediately afterwards presented in a normal manner. A plausible explanation of this phenomenon is that the representation is still partially active because in subliminal priming there is a delay of less than a second between prime and normal presentation of the item. Continued activation of the representation is unlikely to explain ISIM at longer delays. There is also evidence against this possibility. Thus Reinitz and Alexander (1996) have shown that perceptual identification priming of words and pictures depends on reactivating the memory representation at a faster rate from an initial level of activation equivalent to that of unstudied items. They found no evidence that memory representations were reactivated at a normal rate from an already partially activated state that had been maintained during the delay. Fluency, therefore, varies when (*a*) the rate at which a representation is reactivated is increased because its components are linked more strongly in long-term memory, (*b*) non-mnemonic factors, such as arousal, either increase the speed with which a representation is activated or reduce the processing needed to activate it, or (*c*) factors such as subliminal priming may activate short-term, but not long-term, memory, thus reducing the amount of processing needed to reactivate a representation because it is still partially active.

The proposal being made here is that when the enhancement of fluency is automatically triggered by the strengthening of long-term memory for the target information, priming or ISIM has occurred. Of course, not all priming involves reaction time measures or measures of increased accuracy of identification from brief presentations. In these cases, the evidence for enhanced fluency of activation of the memory representation from the encoding of some of its components is direct.

In other cases, priming provides less direct evidence of enhanced fluency. This is so when it involves tasks such as stem completion where the encoding of a part of the memory representation makes it more probable that the full representation will be automatically activated. Two comments on these kinds of priming task are warranted. First, it remains possible that the target memory is generated faster from the encoded cues than when a memory representation has not been strengthened or created. There is indeed some unpublished evidence that such target generation is performed more rapidly than baseline generations. For example, Rajaram (personal communication) found that word fragment completion was significantly faster for studied items and that there was a trend in the same direction for word stem completion. These effects might have been greater if only correct rather than all completions for studied items had been analysed. The second comment is that the generative phenomenon itself (as an indication of accuracy) suggests ready reconstruction of the whole of a studied item from a part. Whether increased accuracy of generation is driven by the same process as that driving increased speed of generation remains to be determined. The simplest assumption, however, is that there is one underlying process responsible for both, which may be operationally defined best in terms of reaction time measures, but this remains to be proved.

If priming or ISIM occurs when memory storage changes enable a representation to be automatically reactivated more rapidly, readily, or strongly from whatever proportion of its components has been encoded, then how are such priming or enhanced fluency effects manifested by the brain? There is growing evidence from neuroimaging studies with both positron emission tomography (PET) and functional magnetic resonance imaging (fMRI) that priming is most often associated with reductions either in blood flow or in blood oxygenation in those brain regions where the retrieved information is likely to be represented (see Wiggs and Martin, 1998). For example, Martin and his associates (see Martin *et al.*, 1995) found reduced activation in the ventral occipitotemporal, parietal, insular, and prefrontal cortices when visually presented objects were shown for the second time in an object-naming task. There is also considerable evidence from animal single unit recording studies that there are neurons within these brain regions which show reductions in firing rate when stimuli are re-presented (see e.g. Brown, Wilson, and Riches, 1987). As Wiggs and Martin point out, this repetition suppression effect mirrors many of the characteristics of behavioural priming. For example, it is long-lasting, increases with further repetition, and occurs despite manipulations of the characteristics of a stimulus. They suggest that the effect could reflect a tuning process in which some of the neurons which originally represented specific information gradually cease to respond so that the representing network becomes progressively sparser and more selective.

The suggestion by Wiggs and Martin raises several issues. First, they propose that the memory representational changes are specific to priming or ISIM. But this need not be the case and, indeed, Aggleton and Brown (1999) have discussed repetition suppression in the context of aware or explicit memory. It seems more likely that there is one memory representation for precisely the same information which subserves both unaware and aware memory. If so, aware and unaware memory for the information must depend on somewhat different expressions of the same memory representation. In contrast, the proposal of Wiggs and Martin seems to require that there are two memory representations for identical information, one of which subserves priming (unaware memory) and one of which subserves explicit or aware memory. Secondly, making the representing network sparser and more selective does not necessarily mean that fewer components of the original information are now being represented, as Wiggs and Martin suggest. Rather, it could simply be that tuning leads to the brain representing individual features in a more efficient manner so that a smaller network of the originally activated neurons does the same representational job more cleanly and efficiently as a result of synaptic changes that increase connectivity. Thirdly, it is plausible to argue, as Wiggs and Martin do, that the effect of such reorganization of the representation is that the memory representation can be reactivated from encoding some of its components in a more rapid and stronger fashion. Thus enhanced fluency which should correspond to a behavioural priming effect would be expected to result from the storage changes.

As Wiggs and Martin discuss, attempts to explore priming using evoked response potentials (ERPs) have generally, but not always, revealed increased positivity of the ERP fairly soon after stimulus presentation. Nearly all such studies of the ERP correlates of priming have confounded the priming with aware memory, so that it is hard to be sure that a correlate relates specifically to unaware memory. A conspicuous exception is a study by Rugg *et al.* (1998) which examined ERPs of words that were recognized or not recognized following a low-level orienting study task. Relative to correctly rejected new words, both recognized and unrecognized old words showed an enhanced positivity of the ERP between 300 and 500ms, which was of a very similar size in the two cases. This enhanced positivity was found at posterior electrode sites, so may correspond to unaware memory processes that relate to the perceptual appearances of the words. The similar size of the effect for recognized and unrecognized words strongly suggests this rather than that weak aware memory drove the effect. If weak aware memory had driven the effect with unrecognized words, then one would have expected enhancement to have been greater for recognized words for which memory was presumably stronger. As ERP effects presumably depend on synchronized neuronal activity, it is possible that the memory changes underlying priming (and also probably aware memory) lead the representing network of neurons to work in a more highly co-ordinated manner, one effect of which is that the representation is more rapidly and strongly reactivated (i.e. priming occurs).

In summary, it has been argued that storage of representations causes those representations to emerge more rapidly, easily, and/or strongly into consciousness when components of the representations have been encoded and act as cues. It is important to realize that it is being suggested that the same enhanced fluency process is involved whether all, many, or few of the components of a stored representation have been encoded. Also, such enhanced fluency is being proposed as equivalent to ISIM. If ISIM could occur without enhanced fluency, the proposal would be wrong.

Attributions

If (because of the development of a memory representation) repetition of some or all of what has been learnt, leads to the more rapid reactivation of conscious awareness of the remembered information, then it is likely that subjects will be aware of a change in the way in which the target information emerges into consciousness. This may lead to an automatic inference or attribution, which is the third kind of memory mechanism. The concept of attribution is regarded as involving a rapid, automatic, and unconscious inference based on some aspect of enhanced fluency. This aspect of enhanced fluency gives rise to a feeling that is different for the fluently processed memory representation than it is for otherwise equivalent representations for which there are no memories or weaker memories.

Most research work has been focused on attributions about perceptual or aesthetic qualities of studied items or things related to them. For example, it has been reported that subjects mistakenly judged studied stimuli to have been present on a screen for longer than non-studied stimuli shown for equivalent times (Witherspoon and Allan, 1985; Paller *et al.*, 1991) or that the studied stimuli were judged to be more aesthetically appealing than equivalent non-studied stimuli (Bonanno and Stillings, 1986; Zajonc, 1980). Some of these attributional effects are robust and still occur even when subjects are informed about what is going on. For example, when spoken sentences are presented against a background of white noise, the white noise is judged to be quieter when the same sentences are repeated than when similar new sentences are presented, presumably because repeated sentences are more fluently activated (Jacoby *et al.*, 1988). Even when subjects are told about this, Jacoby and his co-workers have claimed that the noise background of studied sentences still seems to be quieter than the equivalently noisy background of new sentences. This finding rather strongly suggests that the feeling produced is generated by an automatic process that is not readily affected by conscious intervention or effortful monitoring processes. Whether a perceptual/aesthetic attribution is likely to be made is determined to some degree by whether the context directs the subject's attention towards the perceptual or aesthetic qualities of interest. Thus, when subjects are thinking about making noise judgements, enhanced fluency of processing a spoken sentence in noise will be automatically interpreted as related to the noise level (Jacoby *et al.*, 1988). This issue does, however, require systematic exploration with perceptual and aesthetic attributions.

The attribution process produces not only particular perceptual or aesthetic feelings. It is centrally related to the redundancy model of the relationship between aware and unaware memory that is proposed in this chapter. This is because it has been argued by Jacoby and his colleagues that, in certain situations, the enhanced fluency with which a memory representation is brought back to consciousness leads to the automatic attribution that the reactivated representation is a memory (see e.g. Jacoby and Kelley, 1992). Fuller discussion of this proposal will be left to the next section. The one point that will be made here is that attribution is probably the memory mechanism about which least is known. It remains unclear whether the process is really inference-like and hence whether the notion of 'automatic inference' is an appropriate one. Whether the process is like automatic inference or not, it is supposed to be triggered by a fluency enhancement which probably corresponds to priming. As the brain activity which underlies different processes can now be explored indirectly by neuroimaging procedures, it is pertinent to ask whether when attributional effects occur additional brain activity can be detected. If so, it is important to know whether they occur in the same region in which priming deactivations occur or in a different brain region. Equally important, it needs to be known whether different regions are affected depending on (*a*) the kind of attribution being made (i.e. perceptual, aesthetic, or mnemonic), and (*b*) the nature of the remembered information. Relatedly, it needs to be determined to what extent the triggering conditions of perceptual/aesthetic and mnemonic attributions differ from each other.

Active retrieval search

The fourth mechanism of the theoretical framework is active search (see e.g. Gillund and Shiffrin, 1984, for a discussion of this mechanism). This is typically important in direct memory tests of recognition, cued recall, and, particularly, free recall. In these tasks, subjects are given different degrees and kinds of cueing and then search for further cues that are components of the target memory, with the aim of increasing the number of components that they can encode so that eventually they are able to reactivate the entire memory automatically through a fluency mechanism. In essence, subjects engage in a directed search that uses their existing semantic and episodic memory in a problem-solving fashion to generate cues that will reactivate the target memory automatically. Active search refers to the effortful processes that may lead to several automatic retrievals in the course of the search before the target memory is retrieved. The redundancy model proposes that, in the final stage of any memory retrieval, a memory is automatically reactivated through a fluency-based process. This means that active search will always be combined with a fluency mechanism when retrieval is successful. Indeed, both these processes may be repeatedly used as rememberers approach the state in which they have sufficient cues to reactivate the target memory (as opposed to incorrect memories) automatically. It needs to be indicated why the process or processes that make up active search are effortful. Very little is known about the true reasons, but one reason why effort is involved could be that the rememberer has to monitor the products of retrieval and then make a decision about what to search for next, and hence what to encode. Retrieved information is used to direct the selection of cues that are encoded and used for the next automatic retrieval. The central point is that a memory representation can be immediately retrieved and reactivated (brought to consciousness) using a fluency-based process alone or it can be retrieved through a multistage effortful process or set of processes which interact with an automatic fluency-based retrieval process. The final stage of active search is verifying that what has been retrieved is the desired target memory. This stage of intentional retrieval is probably effortful, as it may often involve the directed retrieval of confirmatory information and the use of inference.

As already indicated, active search probably comprises several distinct subprocesses, although these are not necessarily used in all instances where aware memory occurs. One often becomes aware of a memory without having deliberately retrieved any information. Such involuntary retrieval does not involve active search processes and probably need not involve any monitoring processes to check that the memory of which one becomes aware is appropriate for some purpose. These processes only operate when retrieval is intentional. The encoding specificity principle (Tulving, 1983) explains why active search is sometimes vital. If the initial cues encoded do not overlap sufficiently with what was encoded at study to create the target memory, then it becomes necessary to increase the set of encoded components that correspond to this target until it emerges automatically into awareness. The implication is that although active search may take some time (and hence may be the antithesis of fluent reactivation), the final stage of the search is associated with an automatic and fluent reactivation of the target memory. Whether monitoring processes are then engaged will depend on the nature of the information retrieved and the purposes of the rememberer.

There is extensive evidence from both lesion studies (see Mayes, 1988; Moscovitch, 1995a and b; Schacter et al., 1996) and from neuroimaging studies (see Nolde et al., 1998) that the prefrontal cortex plays an important role in mediating active search and monitoring processes. This region is believed to mediate the kind of planning activities which are related to problem-solving, and which are likely to underlie active search. Neuroimaging studies have found that episodic memory retrieval produces activations not only in posterior regions such as the parietal cortex and precuneus, but also in the frontal cortex (see Nolde et al., 1998). Squire et al. (1992) found a right frontal cortex activation with verbal cued recall, but not with stem completion. This is consistent with the notion that active search is often needed to retrieve an aware memory, but that primed information is retrieved automatically. Active search should be used more when aware memory retrieval is intentional rather than incidental. This notion was supported by an elegant study of Rugg and his colleagues (Rugg et al., 1997). They found that intentional, relative to incidental, recognition produced more activation in the right frontal cortex.

Confabulation is often associated with lesions to the prefrontal cortex (see Kapur and Coughlan, 1980), so it is tempting to argue that it results from an impairment of one or more of the active search processes. In this disorder, patients produce a very high level of false memories about which they are confident. Having poor memory is not sufficient to produce this state. Indeed, Moscovitch (1995b) has argued that it may even be necessary to have at least a moderate level of memory in order to produce confabulations. The condition can clearly be produced by lesions that are unrelated to amnesia. As implied above, explanations of confabulation have always focused on disordered active search processes. Thus patients are deemed to be poor at monitoring whether memories that may contain 'true' components, but which do not accurately correspond to a target episode or fact, fail to match the target appropriately. This is most likely when the frontal neocortex is damaged because of its hypothesized role in planning. The framework, however, allows that confabulation might also result from an abnormality of either the enhanced fluency or the memory attribution processes. If there are patients who show pathological confabulation for either or both of these reasons, they are likely to have damage to non-frontal cortex regions that mediate either fluency or memory attribution processes, and may frequently produce memories with no 'true' components.

A full explanation of both aware and unaware memory for facts and episodes, therefore, requires a good understanding of four mechanisms: (1) how such information is stored at the microscopic and macroscopic levels and how this varies with the information being stored; (2) how such changes alter fluency or the rapidity and strength with which remembered information emerges into consciousness; (3) how such fluency changes trigger automatic inference processes (attributions) and whether the mechanisms underlying these differ depending on whether they involve memory or perceptual/aesthetic inferences; and (4) how the intentional search and monitoring processes work so as to ensure that appropriate information is encoded (or strictly re-encoded) so that target memories can be automatically reactivated with enhanced fluency.

WHAT PROCESSES UNDERLIE ISIM AND EXPLICIT MEMORY?

The redundancy model proposes that aware or explicit memory for specific information always depends on enhanced fluency for the same information-triggering memory attribution processes (see Jacoby, Kelley, and Dywan, 1989). In other words, if enhanced fluency is equivalent to ISIM, then aware memory for specific information cannot occur without ISIM for this information also being present. Both aware and unaware memory for identical information depend on the same memory representation, and aware memory also involves an automatic memory attribution triggered by the ISIM-related enhanced fluency.

Aware memory also often requires an active retrieval search mechanism. The mechanisms underlying aware memory can operate on different kinds of memory representation depending on the kind of information tapped in the task. For example, if the dual processing account of item recognition is correct (see Mandler, 1980, 1991; Jacoby and Dallas, 1981), then this form of memory depends on enhanced fluency and memory attribution operating on memory representations of items (familiarity), item-context associations (recollection), or both. Active retrieval mechanisms will often be used to assist the search, but solely or at least primarily for memory representations of item–context associations. Like recognition, recall also always depends on enhanced fluency and attribution. It is likely to depend on active search mechanisms to a greater extent than recognition. This would be needed because recall requires the retrieval of inter-item associations as well as the associations of these to the study context whereas item recognition probably only requires the retrieval of item–context associations. In summary, ISIM is equivalent to enhanced fluency and sometimes involves perceptual or aesthetic attributions. In contrast, although aware memory always depends on enhanced fluency and a memory attribution, it sometimes also depends on active search to ensure that sufficient components of the target memory representation are re-encoded so as to ensure that it is brought back to consciousness with enhanced fluency.

Jacoby and his colleagues have been major proponents of this hypothesis although they have primarily focused on the non-specific form of recognition memory for items, known as familiarity. Nevertheless, Jacoby, Kelley, and Dywan (1989) proposed that even specific and more 'analytic' forms of aware memory, such as recollection, rely on attributions of pastness so that there can be illusions of recollection, generated by encouraging subjects to make misattributions. Few people realize that Jacoby and his colleagues ever believed that all aware memory relies on memory attributions based on enhanced fluency. For example, Squire (1995) seems to believe that Jacoby and his colleagues only believe this view as it applies to the narrow sense of familiarity (which excludes recollection), and Squire is critical even of this narrower view.

There are perhaps two reasons why so few realize that Jacoby ever espoused the full redundancy model. One reason is that the broader view was not developed and was only explicitly stated once over a decade ago (Jacoby, Kelley, and Dywan, 1989). When it was, the term 'familiarity' was treated as equivalent to all kinds of aware remembering rather than the non-specific and automatic kind of aware memory. This non-specific kind of aware memory corresponds both to current usage and the way that Jacoby and his colleagues now use the term (for example, Jacoby, Toth and Yonelinas, 1993).

The second reason is that intentional recollection is indeed more analytic than familiarity and usually involves an effortful and active search, so that sometimes aware memories are only found after a prolonged search. This seems to be the very opposite of a fluently reactivated memory as is required by the hypothesis. As this problem was not addressed and, subsequently, Jacoby and his co-workers (e.g. Jennings and Jacoby, 1993) have emphasized that recollection is an active, analytic process, his current views are not equated with the idea that recollection involves retrieving item–context associations with enhanced fluency so that memory is then attributed to the associations. Most importantly, Jacoby and his co-workers have not attempted to reconcile the apparent contradiction between the view that intentional recollection often requires a prolonged retrieval search and the view that it always depends on a memory attribution consequent on enhanced fluency of reactivation of item–context information.

The redundancy model advanced in this chapter specifically addresses this apparent contradiction. Critical to the model is the idea that active search involves progressively finding new cues to encode so that, if it is successful, the target item–context memory will 'pop out' with enhanced fluency when the final set of cues is encoded. Central to this idea is the view that whether free recall, cued recall, or recognition is involved, there is a common sense in which the target memory is reactivated with enhanced fluency in all three cases. Tests of the idea will require good methods of measuring this hypothesized enhanced fluency or its neural correlates. If the view is correct, then the fluent way the item–context association emerges into consciousness must lead automatically to a memory attribution whether there is an intention to remember or not. However, if recollection is intentional, then rememberers will monitor whether the memory retrieved is appropriate to their aims.

Unaware memory processes cannot be making an essential contribution to aware memory, if the processes underlying the two forms of memory are completely distinct from each other. However, it is widely believed that aware and unaware memory are completely distinct from each other because many researchers believe that ISIM and aware memory are different memory systems which depend on radically different processes and brain regions (see Schacter and Tulving, 1994, *passim*). Support for their belief is derived from either single or double dissociations of the kind that have been reported between performance on direct and indirect memory tests. If the processes underlying the two forms of memory are not only partially distinct from each other, but also functionally independent (i.e. they operate in parallel), then double dissociations should occur between direct and indirect memory tasks even when these involve retrieval of the *same* information. Evidence of such dissociations would be inconsistent with the redundancy model. This is so because the model states that enhanced fluency is vital for aware as well as unaware memory, whereas a double dissociation could occur only if there are unaware memory processes that do not contribute to aware memory.

If the processes underlying ISIM and aware memory are partially distinct, but there is a serial (or redundancy) relationship between them, then the appropriate kind of single dissociation must be found. The only acceptable kind of serial relationship is one in which the processes of ISIM contribute to those of aware memory, but aware memory requires the operation of some further and distinct process or processes. If this is the way that ISIM and aware memory are related to each other, then one should expect to find a single dissociation in which there are variables that only affect aware memory, but not variables that affect only ISIM for the same information.

Double dissociations between indirect and direct memory test performance have often been reported. For example, semantic orienting tasks typically improve direct memory test performance, but often have little or no effect on indirect memory test performance. In contrast, shifts of sensory modality between study and test typically affect performance on indirect memory tests, but not on direct memory tests (see Roediger and McDermott, 1993, for a review). There are, however, two possible kinds of interpretation for such dissociations. First, they could arise because different kinds of process underlie performance on direct and indirect memory tests. This would apply if performance on the two types of test depended on different kinds of encoding, storage, and/or retrieval processes. Secondly, they could arise because direct and indirect memory tests depend on the retrieval of different kinds of information. In such cases, double dissociations will not be found when the information retrieved is matched across the aware and unaware memory tasks.

There is good evidence that the examples of double dissociation given in the previous paragraph depend on the direct and indirect memory tasks compared requiring the retrieval of mainly semantic and mainly perceptual information respectively. Thus indirect memory test performance was unaffected by semantic encoding at study because it depended on retrieving perceptual information (with tasks such as stem completion) whereas direct memory test performance was very little affected by shifts in sensory modality between study and test because it depended primarily on retrieving semantic information (with tasks such as cued recall). However, performance on semantic indirect memory tasks, such as category generation, is affected by semantic orienting tasks, whereas performance on more perceptual direct memory tasks, such as memory tests for the fount in which different words have been presented, is affected by a shift in sensory modality of presentation from visual to auditory between study and test (Roediger, 1990). In other words, double dissociations of this kind do not occur when 'semantic' direct and indirect memory tasks are compared, or 'perceptual' direct and indirect memory tasks are compared.

Double dissociations between tasks that probably depend on aware memory and unaware memory or ISIM respectively are, therefore, only problematic for the redundancy model when they reflect the operation of non-overlapping memory processes. Some, if not all, double dissociations between ISIM and aware memory do not require one to assume that aware and unaware memory depend on partially distinct processes working in parallel. Are there any dissociations which can plausibly be ascribed to processing differences underlying performance on direct and indirect memory tasks? One can be confident that distinct processes underlie ISIM and explicit memory if there is one process variable that affects only ISIM and one process variable that affects only explicit memory. The problem is how to determine whether or not a variable is selectively affecting a process. One can only be sure that process variables are operating if one knows that ISIM and explicit memory are for the same information. The fact that lesions in different brain regions can selectively disrupt aware and unaware memory respectively does not of itself provide this knowledge because different kinds of information are represented in different brain regions and the aware and unaware memory tasks may involve retrieval of different information.

This problem is illustrated by a study in which Keane *et al.* (1995) reported a double dissociation between performance on a word recognition memory test and performance on two verbal indirect memory tasks. Recognition memory for visually presented words was disrupted in patients with amnesic impairments, which had no effect on two visual word-priming tasks whereas a patient, MS, who had a lesion that was mainly located in the right occipital lobe, showed the reverse pattern of deficit. If the dual process theory of item recognition is correct, then the word recognition measure should depend on both familiarity and recollection. It is, therefore, of interest that Gabrieli *et al.* (1995) have also reported that MS showed intact familiarity when this was measured either by the Process Dissociation procedure or the Remember/Know procedure. Although these procedures may not have given accurate estimates of familiarity, they do reliably show that it contributed to recognition, and, given that performance was estimated to be normal in MS, familiarity may well have been approximately normal. However, Wagner, Gabrieli, and Verfaellie (1997) have found that familiarity as measured by both Process Dissociation and Remember/Know procedures is influenced by semantic manipulations more than perceptual ones. This suggests that even the familiarity component of MS's recognition performance could have involved the reactivation of semantic more than perceptual information, whereas the priming tasks were basically dependent on retrieving perceptual information. As MS has been shown to be normal at semantic priming (Fleischman *et al.*, 1995), it is not, therefore, surprising that he may also show normal familiarity memory in a word recognition task.

It has now been demonstrated that MS is unimpaired at recognition even when this is of perceptual characteristics, such as fount and modality (Fleischman *et al.*, 1997). Does this prove that enhanced fluency cannot be triggering memory attribution to produce familiarity memory in MS? The answer has to be 'no' because

MS is not impaired at all kinds of visual perceptual priming, so stronger evidence is needed to show that the familiarity for which he shows preservation involves retrieving exactly the same perceptual information as that retrieved in the priming tasks for which he shows clear impairment. It should also be pointed out that impaired fluency processes for perceptual features of words should affect familiarity, but not recollection, and it is unknown to what degree familiarity contributes to recognition. If its contribution is very small, it would be very hard to demonstrate a significant familiarity deficit in MS.

Amnesia is often regarded as a deficit in aware memory for facts and episodes in which unaware memory for all kinds of information is preserved (see Mayes, 1988). This would be compatible with the redundancy model provided that amnesia is caused by a breakdown in memory attribution or active search. But no one has proposed that a breakdown in either of these processes underlies the syndrome, whereas it is most commonly argued that amnesia is caused by a failure to store certain kinds of association that are critical for fact and episodic memory (e.g. Cohen, Poldrack, and Eichenbaum, 1997). If this hypothesis is correct, then the redundancy model would be wrong unless amnesics also show impaired ISIM (unaware memory) for the kinds of association they fail to store properly.

So it is very important to determine whether priming for all kinds of fact and episode information is preserved in amnesia. Although amnesics show apparently normal priming for items that were already in memory prior to the study episode, they quite often show deficits in priming for information that was novel at study (see Mayes and Downes, 1997). These studies are hard to interpret because it is difficult to know whether amnesics are impaired at indirect memory tasks because of a deficit in ISIM for certain kinds of information or because, contrary to experimenters' wishes, normal subjects use intentional retrieval to boost their performance. The latter explanation is perhaps unlikely because a meta-analysis (Gooding, Mayes, and Van Eijk, 2000) has shown that, with tasks that only differ with respect to whether information was novel or familiar prior to study, amnesics were impaired only at the novel information indirect memory tasks. This conclusion is strongly supported by a study in which amnesics, unlike normal subjects, showed no speed-up in visual search when arrays were repeated (Chun and Phelps, 1999), even though the normal subjects' recognition for the repeated arrays was at chance (so that intentional retrieval was impossible). This study and the meta-analysis provide strong evidence that amnesics' ISIM is impaired for the kinds of complex association which many believe patients cannot store. More studies like that of Chun and Phelps are needed to resolve the issue fully.

Although the redundancy model is not refuted by the pattern of dissociations that memory researchers have so far found, there is little direct evidence for it. The available evidence relates primarily to item familiarity. Thus subliminal priming at test (Jacoby and Whitehouse, 1989) has been shown to selectively enhance familiarity memory in an item recognition task (Rajaram, 1993). In this procedure, preceding a test word with a subliminally presented version of itself increases the likelihood that a subject will report the test word to be familiar, whereas preceding the test word with a subliminally presented irrelevant word has no effect. Jacoby and Whitehouse showed that familiarity was enhanced when the priming presentations were brief, so that subjects were largely unaware of them, but with longer presentations, so that subjects were aware of the primes, familiarity was actually inhibited. Whether prime duration or awareness is actually critical has, however, been disputed (Joordens and Merickle, 1992). The critical point to note here, however, is that brief and primarily subliminal priming selectively affects familiarity. The most plausible explanation of this effect is that the priming boosts the enhanced fluency process that underlies the feeling of familiarity. In support of this interpretation, it has also been shown that a non-mnemonic manipulation of semantic fluency which does not involve subliminal priming also increased familiarity feelings (Whittlesea, 1993; Whittlesea, Jacoby, and Girard, 1990). Thus, when words were produced more fluently because they were presented at the ends of sentences with which they fitted well, greater familiarity was felt for the words in a recognition situation.

Other experiments which have also used non-mnemonic means to manipulate the fluency with which information is brought to consciousness have found similar results. For example, Lindsay and Kelley (1996) showed that when subjects were given a list of easy and difficult word fragments in a cued recall test, so that particular words were either fluently or non-fluently generated, the subjects reported remembering an increased number of fluently generated items whether or not these had been previously studied. The authors interpreted this as an illusion of item familiarity similar to the ones that Whittlesea (1993) found with recognition memory. If they are correct, fluency-related effects on aware memory must occur with cued recall as well as recognition. They also suggested that similar illusions may be found with recollection (retrieval of item–context associations) when manipulations (such as giving misinformation about a whole event or its details) cause a whole event to come more fluently into consciousness. The redundancy model must also predict that subliminally priming aspects of item–context associations immediately prior to test should enhance recollection in recognition tasks and also in free and cued recall tasks.

Showing that non-mnemonic manipulations of the fluency with which information reaches consciousness when some of it is encoded influence cued and free recall, and for recollection as it occurs in recognition is particularly important, remains to be done. All these ways of testing aware memory rely on some form of recollection and work in our laboratory and by others (for example, Jacoby, 1991) has shown that dividing attention at *test* disrupts recollection in recognition, but leaves item familiarity unaffected. Item familiarity may be automatic because all or nearly all of the target information may be encoded at test, whereas this is much less likely to be true of item–context associations. When it is true, then retrieval may be involuntary and automatic, but otherwise it will be necessary to engage the effortful processes of active search. Recollection, therefore, often seems to be the antithesis of the automatic enhanced fluency that I am postulating is equivalent to ISIM. Given this, it is particularly important to show that recollection can be increased by non-mnemonic manipulations that boost fluency.

It might be argued that the false memory effect (see Roediger and McDermott, 1995) provides support for the view that enhanced fluency of item–context associations leads to recollection. In this effect, normal subjects are shown several lists of words in each of which presented words are strong associates of a non-presented word. Later, the subjects not only falsely recall or recognize about as many of the strong associates as they truly remember target words, but they claim to be recollecting the same proportion of false memories as they do true memories. Item–context associations related to the non-presented words are likely to be retrieved with enhanced fluency because at encoding subjects repeatedly think about the non-presented strong associates when other list words are shown. Direct evidence is needed, however, that this occurs and leads to a feeling of recollection. The false memory effect is also interesting because recollection that the non-presented items were thought of in the study context may be correct, but this does not mean that they were presented in that context. The effect shows that intentional recollection depends on monitoring whether a memory truly identifies a context, and that such monitoring can be made very hard.

The memory tasks, discussed so far, would normally be regarded as relating to episodic memory because they depend on memory for information encountered in personally experienced contexts. Nothing has been said about semantic memory. But the redundancy model proposes that aware fact memory (semantic memory) also depends on memory attributions triggered by the more fluent emergence into consciousness of studied facts. If familiarity memory, construed as enhanced fluency plus memory attribution, applies not only to items, but also to more complex associations between items, then it should underlie all semantic memory. There is evidence that this is the case because manipulations which enhance fluency, or at least a correlate of fluency, lead to false judgements that certain statements are true, a form of semantic memory that clearly involves item–item associations (Begg, Anas, and Farinacci, 1992). This illusion of semantic memory provides direct support for the view that semantic memory typically involves enhanced fluency for factual information which leads to a memory attribution of familiarity for the fact (or item–item associate).

As with recollection, familiarity for factual associations may sometimes be achieved via enhanced fluency and a memory attribution alone, but it will often also require active retrieval search, as does recollection. Facts can be about item–situation associations and it is hard to see how the mechanisms of aware memory of these can differ much from the episodic recollection that is central to the aware memory of personally experienced item–context associations. In other words, episodic memory and semantic memory for item–situation associations should be based on memory representations for similar kinds of association and, in both cases, the redundancy model proposes that aware memory is the product of the same fluency and attribution processes and often of the same active search process.

SOME POSSIBLE PROBLEMS FOR THE REDUNDANCY MODEL

The model predicts only that enhanced fluency is a necessary condition for aware memory without specifying the precise nature of the relationship. One would expect, however, if other factors are constant, that memory attribution would be triggered more frequently when the fluency increase is more striking and hence ISIM is stronger. This remains to be tested. It is striking, however, that aesthetic attributions seem to be triggered sometimes when recognition is at chance. This is illustrated by a well-known experiment of Kunst-Wilson and Zajonc (1979) in which subliminal presentation of polygons led to an increase in the positivity of aesthetic attributions that subjects made about them, but did not produce above chance memory attributions. If they occur, why were accurate memory attributions not made when aesthetic ones clearly were?

There are two possible and related reasons. One is that subjects must recollect a critical amount about the study context if they are going to make item familiarity attributions. This would explain why familiarity as well as recollection seems to be impaired in amnesics (Knowlton and Squire, 1995; Yonelinas *et al.*, 1998) and that in severe amnesics recognition can be at chance when some forms of perceptual ISIM are preserved (Hamann and Squire, 1997). The other possibility is that subjects have to be aware that information was shown at study if they are later going to make memory attributions about it. Nevertheless, the redundancy model needs to specify the conditions necessary for the making of memory attributions more fully if it is to be heuristically valuable. For example, the intention to remember cannot be necessary for memory attributions to occur because, if it was, then unintentional aware memory would not exist.

Even if all the necessary conditions required for making a memory attribution apply, the model still requires that the brain can monitor small fluency changes with considerable precision. This requirement may be hard to meet because the fluency baseline is likely to fluctuate considerably over time, as it will be strongly influenced by non-mnemonic factors. The evidence from subliminal priming, nevertheless, strongly suggests that the brain can monitor fluency with precision relative to a baseline that probably fluctuates. Future work needs to determine just how much the fluency baseline does fluctuate and to identify precisely which features of fluency relate most closely to memory attribution.

It has been assumed that enhanced fluency is equivalent to the unaware form of memory known as priming or ISIM, and that all aspects of fluency are highly interconnected. These assumptions may be wrong if some forms of enhanced fluency are unrelated to ISIM. In unpublished work, we have examined the ERP correlates of recognized and unrecognized pictures that were studied a week earlier versus unstudied pictures. Although the paradigm was different, we obtained results very similar to those of Rugg *et al.* (1998). Unlike Rugg, however, we found enhanced positivity only at latencies between 500 and 1200 msec for old items at electrode sites where enhanced positivity had already been found between 300 and 500 msec after presentation. In the earlier time window, enhanced positivity was the *same* for recognized and unrecognized old pictures, but whereas the effect then rapidly disappeared for unrecognized pictures, it continued relatively unabated for over a second for recognized pictures. One interpretation of these results is that encoding old items produced enhanced and more synchronized activity in the posterior neocortical picture representing neural network. Between 300 and 500 msec this activity corresponded to the enhanced fluency that produces behavioural priming and was related to unaware memory. The longer the enhanced positivity continued after this the more likely there was to be a feeling of aware memory for the picture. The two effects may well have occurred in the same representational system of neurons, but it remains to be established whether or not the prolonged positivity enhancement was associated not only with recognition, but also with the enhanced fluency/strength processes that underlie ISIM.

The study clearly requires replication and an extension in order to see whether the prolongation of the enhanced positivity that occurs after 500 msec is unrelated to any form of behavioural priming that can be measured. If it is unrelated, then it could still be true that aware memory depends on the way that the representation of an episode emerges into consciousness, but that this kind of emergence into consciousness is somewhat different from the fluency that is equivalent to ISIM. It should be noted, however, that behavioural measures of fluency are only indirect measures of the fluency of reactivation of memory representations, and Ostergaard (1992) has argued that the contribution of memory to performance in such tasks may be small, with unrelated factors making a greater contribution.

If the redundancy model is correct, then the way that information emerges into consciousness from its encoded components must trigger a memory attribution that causes an aware memory feeling. There is currently no neurobiological evidence that this kind of attribution exists. In principle, however, neuroimaging studies have the potential to address this issue. In situations where memory attribution is supposed to have occurred, we need to know whether there are associated activation changes. If there are, then we need to determine whether these changes occur in specific structures (such as those implicated in amnesia) that are concerned with memory attributions for all kinds of fact and episode information, or whether the changes are co-localized with each representing system of neurons.

These issues need to be addressed in order to determine whether the redundancy model provides a useful account of aware memory or whether it needs radical modification. In concluding, I wish to re-emphasize two things. First, memory researchers should not assume that they know what information is retrieved in memory tasks. Rather, they should carefully identify this and distinguish between information-based and process-based effects. Secondly, even if the specific account of aware memory given here is wrong, it remains true that there are no other proper accounts of the mechanism of this phenomenon. Furthermore, this mechanism cannot relate directly to the content of the information itself, but must relate in some way to the manner in which the represented information emerges into consciousness as a result of storage changes.

I would like to thank Dr Daniela Montaldi for helpful feedback on the text. The work was supported by Grant G9300193 awarded by the Medical Research Council.

A.R.M.

REFERENCES

ABEL, T., ALBERINI, C., GHIRARDI, M., HUANG, Y.-Y., NGUYEN, P., and KANDEL, E. R. (1995), 'Steps toward a molecular definition of memory consolidation', in D. L. Schacter (ed.), *Memory Distortion*. Cambridge, Mass.: Harvard University Press, 298–325.

AGGLETON, J. P., and BROWN, M. W. (1999), 'Episodic memory, amnesia, and the hippocampal–anterior thalamic axis', *Behavioural and Brain Sciences*, 22: 425–89.

BEGG, I. M., ANAS, A., and FARINACCI, S. (1992), 'Dissociation of processes in belief: source recollection, statement familiarity and the illusion of truth', *Journal of Experimental Psychology: General,* 121: 446–58.

BONANNO, G. A., and STILLINGS, N. A. (1986), 'Preference, familiarity, and recognition after repeated brief exposures to random geometric shapes', *American Journal of Psychology,* 99: 403–15.

BROWN, M. W., WILSON, F. A.W., and RICHES, I. P. (1987), 'Neuronal evidence that infer-omedial temporal cortex is more important than hippocampus in certain processes underlying recognition', *Brain Research*, 409: 158–62.

CHUN, M., and PHELPS, E. (1999), 'Memory deficits for implicit contextual information in amnesic subjects with hippocampal damage', *Nature Neuroscience*, 2: 844–7.

COHEN, N. J., POLDRACK, R. A., and EICHENBAUM, H. (1997), 'Memory for items and memory for relations in the procedural/declarative memory framework', *Memory*, 5: 131–78.

CURRAN, T., and SCHACTER, D. L. (1997)', 'Implicit memory: what must theories of amnesia explain?', *Memory,* 5: 37–48.

FLEISCHMAN, D. A., GABRIELI, J. D. E., REMINGER, S. L., RINALDI, J. A., MORRELL, F., and WILSON, R. S. (1995), 'Conceptual priming in perceptual identification for patients with Alzheimer's disease and a patient with right occipital lobectomy', *Neuropsychology*, 9: 187–97.

—— VAIDYA, C. J., LANGE, K. L., and GABRIELI, J. D. E. (1997), 'A dissociation between perceptual explicit and implicit memory processes', *Brain and Cognition*, 35: 42–57.

GABRIELI, J. D. E., WAGNER, A. D., STEBBINS, G. T., BURTON, K. W., and FLEISCHMAN, D. A. (1995), 'Neuropsychological dissociation between perceptual fluency and recognition fluency in long-term memory', *Society for Neuroscience Abstracts*, 21: 753.

GILLUND, G., and SHIFFRIN, R. M. (1984), 'A retrieval model for both recognition and recall', *Psychological Review*, 19: 1–65.

GOODING, P. A., MAYES, A. R., and VAN EIJK, R. (2000), 'A meta-analysis of indirect memory tests for novel material in organic amnesics', *Neuropsychologia*, 38: 666–76.

GRAF, P., and MASSON, M. E. J. (1993), *Implicit Memory: New Directions in Cognition, Development and Neuropsychology*. Hillsdale, NJ: Erlbaum.

HAMANN, S. B., and SQUIRE, L. R. (1997), 'Intact perceptual memory in the absence of conscious memory', *Behavioral Neuroscience*, 111: 850–4.

JACOBY, L. L. (1983), 'Remembering the data: analyzing interactive processes in reading', *Journal of Verbal Learning and Verbal Behavior*, 22: 485–508.

—— (1991), 'A process dissociation framework: separating automatic from intentional uses of memory', *Journal of Memory and Language*, 30: 513–41.

—— and DALLAS, M. (1981), 'On the relationship between autobiographical memory and perceptual learning', *Journal of Experimental Psychology: General*, 110: 306–40.

—— and KELLEY, C. (1992), 'Unconscious influences of memory: dissociations and automaticity', in A. D. Milner and M. D. Rugg (eds.), *The Neuropsychology of Consciousness*. New York: Academic Press.

—— and WHITEHOUSE, K. (1989), 'An illusion of memory: false recognition influenced by unconscious perception', *Journal of Experimental Psychology: General*, 118: 126–35.

—— and WITHERSPOON, D. (1982), 'Remembering without awareness', *Canadian Journal of Psychology*, 36: 300–24.

—— KELLEY, C. M., and DYWAN, J. (1989), 'Memory attributions', in H. L. Roediger III and F. I. M. Craik (eds.), *Varieties of Memory and Consciousness: Essays in Honor of Endel Tulving*. Hillsdale, NJ: Erlbaum, 391–422.

—— TOTH, J. P., and YONELINAS, A. P. (1993), 'Separating conscious and unconscious influences of memory: measuring recollection', *Journal of Experimental Psychology: General*, 2: 1–16.

—— ALLAN, L. G., COLLINS, J. C., and LARWILL, L. K. (1988), 'Memory influences subjective experience: noise judgements', *Journal of Experimental Psychology: Learning, Memory and Cognition*, 14: 240–7.

JENNINGS, J. M., and JACOBY, L. L. (1993), 'Automatic versus intentional uses of memory: aging, attention and control', *Psycychology and Aging*, 12: 283–93.

JOHNSON, M. (1996), 'ERP studies of source monitoring'. Paper presented at the meeting of the Memory Disorders Research Society, Boston, 24–6 October.

JOORDENS, S., and MERICKLE, P. M. (1992), 'False recognition and perception without awareness', *Memory & Cognition*, 20: 151–9.

KAPUR, N., and COUGHLAN, A. K. (1980), 'Confabulation and frontal lobe dysfunction', *Journal of Neurology, Neurosurgery and Psychiatry*, 43: 461–3.

KEANE, M. M., GABRIELI, J. D. E., MAPSTONE, H. C., JOHNSON, K. A., and CORKIN, S. (1995), 'Double dissociation of memory capacities after bilateral occipital-lobe or medial temporal lobe lesions', *Brain*, 118: 1129–48.

KNOWLTON, B. J., and SQUIRE, L. R. (1995), 'Remembering and knowing: two different expressions of declarative memory', *Journal of Experimental Psychology: Learning, Memory and Cognition*, 21: 699–710.

KUNST-WILSON, W. R., and ZAJONC, R. B. (1979), 'Affective discrimination of stimuli that cannot be recognized', *Science*, 207: 557–8.

LINDSAY, D. S., and KELLEY, C. M. (1996), 'Creating illusions of familiarity in a cued-recall remember/know paradigm', *Journal of Memory and Language*, 35: 197–211.

MANDLER, G. (1980), 'Recognising: the judgement of prior occurrence', *Psychological Review*, 87: 252–71.

—— (1991), 'Your face looks familiar but I can't remember your name: a review of dual process theory', in W. E. Hockley and S. Lewandowsky (eds.), *Relating Theory and Data: Essays in honor of Bennet B. Murdock*. London: Erlbaum.

MARTIN, A., LALONDE, F. M., WIGGS, C. L., WEISBERG, J., UNGERLEIDER, L. G., and HAXBY, J. V. (1995), 'Repeated presentation of objects reduces activity in ventral occipitotemporal cortex: an MRI study of repetition priming', *Society for Neuroscience Abstracts*, 21: 1497.

MAYES, A. R. (1988), *Human Organic Memory Disorders*. Cambridge: Cambridge University Press.

—— and DOWNES, J. J. (1997), 'What do theories of the functional deficit(s) underlying amnesia have to explain?', *Memory*, 5: 3–36.

—— GOODING, P. A. and VAN EIJK, R. (1997), 'A new theoretical framework for explicit and implicit memory', *Psyche*, 3(2).

MOSCOVITCH, M. (1995*a*), 'Recovered consciousness: a hypothesis concerning modularity and episodic memory', *Journal of Clinical and Experimental Neuropsychology*, 17: 276–90.

—— (1995*b*), 'Confabulation', in D. L. Schacter (ed.), *Memory Distortion: How Minds, Brains, and Societies Reconstruct the Past*. Cambridge, Mass.: Harvard University Press.

NOLDE, S. F., JOHNSON, M. K., and RAYE, C. L. (1998), 'The role of prefrontal cortex during tests of episodic memory', *Trends in Cognitive Sciences*, 2: 399–406.

OSTERGAARD, A. L. (1992), 'A method for judging measures of stochastic dependence: further comments on the current controversy', *Journal of Experimental Psychology: Learning, Memory & Cognition*, 18: 413–20.

PALLER, K. A., MAYES, A. R., McDERMOTT, K. B., PICKERING, A. D., and MEUDELL, P. R. (1991), 'Indirect measures of memory in a duration-judgement task are normal in amnesic patients', *Neuropsychologia*, 29: 1007–18.

RAJARAM, S. (1993), 'Remembering and knowing: two means of access to the personal past', *Memory & Cognition*, 21: 89–112.

REINITZ, M. T., and ALEXANDER, R. (1996), 'Mechanisms of facilitation in primed perceptual identification', *Memory & Cognition*, 24: 129–35.

RICHARDSON-KLAVEHN, A., and BJORK, R. A. (1988), 'Measures of memory', *Annual Review of Psychology*, 39: 475–543.

ROEDIGER, H. (1990), 'Implicit memory: retention without remembering', *American Psychologist* , 45: 1043–56

—— and McDERMOTT, K. B. (1993), 'Implicit memory in normal human subjects', in F. Boller and J. Graffman, (eds.), *Handbook of Neuropsychology*, viii. Amsterdam: Elsevier, 63–131.

—— (1995), 'Creating false memories: remembering words not presented in lists', *Journal of Experimental Psychology: Learning, Memory and Cognition*, 21: 803–14.

ROSE, S. (1992), *The Making of Memory*. London: Bantam.

RUGG, M. (1996), 'Studies of episodic memory retrieval with brain potentials and functional neuroimaging'. Paper presented at the meeting of the Memory Disorders Research Society, Boston, 24–6 October.

—— FLETCHER, P. C., FRITH, C. D., FRACKOWIAK, R. S. J., and DOLAN, R. J. (1997), 'Brain regions supporting intentional and incidental memory: a PET study', *Neuroreport*, 8: 1283–7.

—— MARK, R. E., WALLA, P., SCHLOERSCHEIDT, A. M., BIRCH, C. S., and ALLAN, K. (1998), 'Dissociation of neural correlates of implicit and explicit memory', *Nature*, 392: 595–601.

SCHACTER, D. L. (1987), 'Implicit memory: history and current status', *Journal of Experimental Psychology: Learning, Memory and Cognition*, 13: 501–18.

—— (1992), 'Priming and multiple memory systems: perceptual mechanisms of implicit memory', *Journal of Cognitive Neuroscience*, 4: 244–56.

—— (1994), 'Priming and multiple memory systems: perceptual mechanisms of implicit memory', in Schacter and Tulving (1994), 233–68.

—— and TULVING, E. (1994), *Memory Systems 1994*. Cambridge, Mass.: MIT Press.

—— CURRAN, T., GALLUCCIO, L., MILBERG, W. P, and BATES, J. F. (1996), 'False recognition and the right frontal lobe: a case study', *Neuropsychologia,* 34: 793–808.

SQUIRE, L. R. (1992), 'Memory and the hippocampus: a synthesis from findings with rats, monkeys and humans', *Psychological Review*, 99: 195–231.

—— (1995), 'Biological foundations of accuracy and inaccuracy in memory', in D. L. Schacter (ed.), *Memory Distortion*. Cambridge, Mass: Harvard University Press.

—— OJEMANN, J. G., MIEZIN, F. M., PETERSEN, S. E., VIDEEN, T. O., and RAICHLE, M. E. (1992), 'Activation of the hippocampus in normal humans: a functional anatomical study of memory', *Proceedings of the National Academy of Science, USA*, 89: 1837–41.

TULVING, E. (1983), *Elements of Episodic Memory*. Oxford: Oxford University Press.

UNGERLEIDER, L. G. (1995), 'Functional brain imaging studies of cortical mechanisms for memory', *Science*, 270: 769–75.

WAGNER, A. D., GABRIELI, J. D. E., and VERFAELLIE, M. (1997), 'Dissociations between familiarity processes in explicit-recognition and implicit-perceptual memory', *Journal of Experimental Psychology: Learning, Memory and Cognition*, 23: 305–23.

WHITTLESEA, B. W. A. (1993), 'Illusions of familiarity', *Journal of Experimental Psychology: Learning, Memory and Cognition*, 19: 1235–53.

—— JACOBY, L. L., and GIRARD, K. A. (1990), 'Illusions of immediate memory: evidence for an attributional basis for feelings of familiarity and personal quality', *Journal of Memory and Language*, 29: 716–32.

WIGGS, C. L., and MARTIN, A. (1998), 'Properties and mechanisms of perceptual priming', *Current Opinion in Neurobiology*, 8: 227–33.

—— WEISBERG, J., GARBER, S., and MARTIN, A. (1996), 'Brain regions associated with semantic and episodic memory', *Neuroimaging*, 3: S568.

WITHERSPOON, D. A., and ALLAN, L. G. (1985), 'The effects of a prior presentation on temporal judgements in a perceptual identification task', *Memory & Cognition*, 13: 101–11.

YONELINAS, A. P., KROLL, N. E., DOBBINS, I., LAZZARA, M., and KNIGHT, R. T. (1998), 'Recollection and familiarity deficits in amnesia: convergence of remember–know, process dissociation, and receiver operator characteristic data', *Neuropsychology*, 12: 323–39.

ZAJONC, R. B. (1980), 'Feeling and thinking: preferences need no inferences', *American Psychologist*, 35: 151–75.

8

Is Memory Purely Preservative?

Jérôme Dokic

TWO FORMS OF MEMORY AND GOETHE'S PROBLEM

Let us start with a familiar distinction between two forms of memory: episodic memory (remembering a thing or an episode) v. factual memory (remembering that something is the case).[1]

Factual memory does not necessarily give rise to the corresponding episodic memories. For instance, we colloquially use formulations such as the following:

(1) I remember (I know) that I broke my leg when I was a child, yet I don't remember the incident itself.

I remember that the incident was painful, but I do not remember the pain. I know that I broke my leg, because I learnt it from my parents, but I have forgotten (in the relevant, episodic sense) the painful experience itself. In general, factual memory that p does not imply episodic memory of x, where x is an objective constituent of the proposition that p.

Many things which I know about myself and my own past life I learnt from others. This is especially true of events in my early childhood. A central question in the philosophy of memory is how we should explain the distinction between those of my autobiographical memories (i.e. the memories whose expression requires use of the first-person 'I') which are genuinely episodic and those which belong to personal folklore—to things that friends and family members told me at various times after the remembered events.

One suggestion is that the relevant difference between episodic and factual memory has to do with the memory's *causal history* (rather than with its content). Arguably, any memory—episodic or not—which refers to a particular past experience causally derives from that experience itself. (This is a consequence of the causal theory of singular thought.) But there are memories which come *directly* from the subject's past experience, in the sense that neither external testimony (verbal or not) nor internal reasoning are essential links in the causal chain connecting past and present. For instance, my memory that I broke my leg when

---

[1] Various versions of this distinction can be found, *inter alia*, in Russell, 1921; Bergson, 1939; Ayer, 1956; and Malcolm, 1963. In what follows, I freely oscillate between saying that a subject remembers an incident and saying that a subject remembers *experiencing* the incident. As we shall see, the latter description is more perspicuous than the former as far as episodic memory is concerned.

I was 3 does not come directly from the past incident, since it causally depends on my parents' testimony. My present memory (or knowledge) that the incident was painful does not come directly from the incident either, since I inferred this some time ago, from the parental narration.

I suppose that there is an intuitive notion of 'coming directly' from the remembered experience, even if a more precise definition is certainly needed. We can provisionally content ourselves with the following negative definition: a memory comes directly from the remembered experience only if the memory's causal history does not essentially involve testimony or inference.

The envisaged suggestion, then, is that a given memory is episodic if and only if it comes directly from the remembered event—otherwise it is factual. Is this suggestion plausible?

Unfortunately, it is not. To see why, it is worth considering a remark made by Goethe at the beginning of his autobiographical work *Poetry and Truth*:

> When we wish to remember what happened to us in the early times of childhood, it is often the case that we confuse what we heard from others with what we genuinely know from our own experience.[2]

On one way of reading this passage, episodic memory is not intrinsically associated with a specific *experience* or *feeling*. We have to reject the idea of a 'phenomenology of episodic memory', that is, the myth of a memory experience immediately recognizable by its phenomenal properties.[3] This reading is compatible with the envisaged suggestion. Episodic memories are those that come directly from the remembered event, but we often confuse episodic memories with factual ones, if only because (it is assumed) memory does not wear its causal history on its sleeves.

However, there is another interpretation of Goethe's remark, which I think brings it closer to the true nature of episodic memory. The memories alluded to by Goethe in this passage are precisely *not* episodic. An episodic memory normally appears to the subject *as* coming directly from his own past experience, in a way which excludes the alternative possibility that it is immediately grounded on testimony or reasoning. Episodic memory normally reveals its own immediate origin. In general, I do not *confuse* an episodic memory with a factual memory deriving from external testimony. Of course, a seemingly episodic memory might not trace directly back to the relevant past experience, and I might wonder, at a reflective level, whether this is so with a particular memory of mine.[4] However, if good reasons convince me that this is indeed so, I have to admit that I was somewhat *deluded*. Even if I can recover veridical pieces of factual information from my memory, there was something wrong about it, in so far as it *presented* itself as episodic.

On the proposed reading of Goethe's passage, a factual memory does not

---

[2] Goethe, *Dichtung und Wahrheit* (1811): translated from p. 15. My attention was drawn to this passage by Anscombe, 1974.   [3] This is Anscombe's reading.
[4] I do not want to exclude the possibility that Goethe was also thinking of such a case.

become episodic just because it happens to come directly from the remembered event. The following description is not self-contradictory:

> (2) I remember (I know) that I broke my leg. For all I know, my memory might come directly from the past incident, yet I don't remember the incident itself.

Goethe's point is that factual memory does not reveal its own immediate origin. So I may presently possess the information that I broke my leg when I was a child, while I have *forgotten* how I acquired this piece of information. I cannot just read off the causal history of my factual memory from that memory itself (or from its content). Therefore, although coming directly from the remembered event is a necessary condition of episodic memory, it is certainly not a sufficient condition, since it can also be satisfied by merely factual memories.

Further reflection on Goethe's remark shows that other claims about episodic memory cannot be sustained. For instance, one might suggest that a given memory is episodic if and only if (i) it comes directly from the relevant past incident, and (ii) the subject *remembers* that it comes directly from this incident. In other words, an episodic memory is defined as a factual memory which comes directly from the remembered experience, and which is the object of a further meta-memory about its immediate origin. (It is a meta-memory in the sense that it is a memory about another memory.) However, this account of episodic memory does not work. Suppose that I spontaneously tell my parents a story about a past incident, without knowing whether the story comes directly from my own experience, or from external testimony. My parents declare that the story must come from me, since (they say) there is no way I could have learnt this from someone else. I acquire thus the further, factual meta-memory that my memory (or the set of memories constituting my story) comes directly from my own experience. These memories do not necessarily amount to episodic memory of the relevant incident. The following description may be perfectly accurate:

> (3) I remember (I know) that I broke my leg, I also remember (I know) that the first memory comes directly from my past experience, yet I don't remember the incident itself.

This description will be appropriate in a context in which I have forgotten the immediate origin of my meta-memory (for instance, that it comes directly from my parents). Obviously, insisting that I remember that the second-order memory comes directly from my own experience leads us nowhere, because this would simply raise the corresponding question about the causal history of the third-order memory. Episodic memory does not seem to be (easily) definable in terms of a structured set of factual memories, even if some of them are metarepresentational.

In general, the possibility that a factual memory comes directly from the remembered experience and the possibility that it does not are *equally* compatible with the memory's being veridical or correct, even warranted. In contrast, the possibility that a seemingly episodic memory does not come directly from the past experience is *not* compatible with its correctness. It follows that the epistemic value of episodic memory is different from the epistemic value of factual memory. Factual memory gives the subject a reason to believe that the remembered event really happened, and is not the result of fiction or imagination. However, genuine episodic memory gives the subject something more: it provides him or her with a reason to believe that the information carried by it does not essentially derive from testimony or inference but comes directly from the subject's own past life.[5]

I shall call 'Goethe's Problem' the philosophical problem of accounting for this epistemic gulf between episodic and factual memory. An important task of a theory of episodic memory is to solve Goethe's Problem, in showing how that form of memory can have the substantial epistemic role it appears to have.

FACTUAL MEMORY IS PURELY PRESERVATIVE

What emerges from these preliminary considerations is that factual memory does not *have* to carry information about its own causal history. Arguably, this is a consequence of the fact that it is *purely preservative*: the piece of information the subject is said to remember must have been originally acquired by other cognitive means (e.g. perception or testimony), retained and faithfully preserved since then. Since most, if not all, pieces of information acquired by perception or testimony do not say anything about how they have been acquired, the same is true of information retained and preserved by factual memory.

In this section, I shall make a little more precise the claim that factual memory is purely preservative. Although I shall ultimately argue that there is a connection between memories being purely preservative and them *not* being episodic, I do not want to exclude at the outset the possibility that episodic memory is purely preservative (and even is a kind of factual memory).

Let us start with a reasonably straightforward case. I see that there is a book on the table in front of me, and I acquire the corresponding perceptual knowledge. Later, having left the room, I remember that there was a book on the table then in front of me. I have factual memory knowledge about the book. Obviously, in this case, memory is not a *source* of knowledge, since the remembered piece

---

[5] This way of formulating the epistemological difference between episodic and factual memory is all right as far as it goes, but in the light of the main conception presented in this chapter, it does not go far enough. For there is another crucial difference between the two forms of memory. Consider a particular factual memory which involves information originally acquired by perception. If the relevant piece of information has been properly retained and faithfully preserved, but is in fact wrong (and so is a piece of misinformation), all the blame goes to the perceptual experience which introduced the information into the cognitive scene. In contrast, episodic memory is a *sui generis* experience, and as such it is always, so to speak, epistemically responsible for the veridicality of the carried information. Thus, if a seemingly episodic memory carries what is in fact misinformation, there is something wrong with the memory itself (it is at least partly illusory), and not (or not only) with the relevant past experience.

of knowledge has been acquired by cognitive means other than memory, namely visual perception and judgement. As Dummett puts it: 'I cannot separate the knowledge I suppose myself to have now from the knowledge I surely had at the past time. For the former is derived from the latter; more exactly, it simply *is* the knowledge I had as an eyewitness, maintained in being' (1993: 414–15). If memory were a source of knowledge in this case, we would have to say that each time I remember that there was a book on the table, I *re-acquire* the same piece of knowledge over and again. This seems absurd.[6]

Sometimes, of course, what is preserved from the original acquisition of information to the present memory need not be knowledge, even if the present memory itself is knowledge. Suppose that I did not believe that there was a book on the table when I saw it, because I (wrongly) thought that I was faced with, say, a hologram. I saw that there is a book on the table, but I did not *know* it (because I did not even believe it). Later, becoming aware of my mistake, I believe that there *was* a book on the table after all. Intuitively, my present belief is a case of factual memory knowledge, in so far as it carries well-grounded or warranted information faithfully preserved over time.[7] My memory is still purely preservative, since its content is information originally acquired by perception. I remember, and know that there was a book on the table partly because such was the content of my original perception.

A first claim about factual memory, then, is that it involves a *continuous* information-link between the original cognitive state (e.g. visual perception) and the present memory. (I ignore the possibility of innate knowledge and information.) Part of the explanation of why my factual memory is knowledge is that I successfully preserved a single informational state originally capable of grounding knowledge. There should not be any (substantial) interruption in the informational chain. If I have lost track of the relevant information, I have lost track of the memory, and the matter is forgotten (although I might have later another factual memory with the same content). Of course, we might be temporarily unable to retrieve information we in fact possess, as when I have someone's name on the tip of my tongue. This is, so to speak, a performance and not a competence problem. There is a distinction to be drawn between possessing a piece of information we cannot access because of independent and momentary interference, and having completely forgotten the information. Interruption in the informational chain has the latter as a consequence.

A second claim I think we should make about factual memory is that the information-link underlying factual memory is *doxastic*: it is always by means of some

---

[6] Cf. Shoemaker, 1967: 272. Factual memory can be a source of knowledge in a different sense, since it is always possible to draw knowledge-preserving inferences from it.

[7] The fact that information acquired by perception has been retained and preserved over time is among the 'ground-floor' conditions on memory knowledge, in the sense defined by Campbell, 1994: 234. There are other, 'reflective' conditions on memory knowledge, though. The mere fact that warranted information has been retained and preserved is not sufficient for knowledge. What I have to say here about factual memory is compatible with what Peacocke, 1986: 161, calls 'The Model of Virtual Inference'.

belief that information carried by factual memory is preserved over time. One motivation for this claim is the following. A central and much-discussed feature of factual memory is that it allows us to retain a propositional content without keeping track of the specific *reasons* for which the content has been originally formed. How is it possible, then, that a *present* factual memory amounts to knowledge? It cannot be knowledge if it is carrying a piece of information which was *merely entertained* by the subject, outside any belief context. What epistemic value would we attach to a piece of information which is retained as a merely entertained piece of information (if indeed this makes sense at all), as opposed to something which is actually *believed* by the subject? For all the subject knows, this information might have been once entertained in the context of fancy or imagination. (Remember that one can have a factual memory while having forgotten the circumstances in which the remembered information has been acquired.)

A partial solution to this problem has already been suggested by Dummett: sometimes, the present memory is *identical* with a belief that was properly grounded on the relevant past experience. In the first case described above, there is a single belief, to the effect that there is (or was) a book on the table, which is preserved over time as a single piece of knowledge. The case in which I do not believe that there is a book on the table when I see one is more complicated. Here, the formation of the belief that there was a book on the table does not coincide with the acquisition of the corresponding information. This does not contradict the second claim. The information-link between past and present is still doxastic since it is crucially relayed by the metarepresentational belief that I have (or had) a visual experience with a definite character and content. When I realized that I was wrong, and that my past experience was veridical after all, I *detached* the belief that there was a book on the table from this metarepresentational belief.[8]

Combining the two claims together, we can say that factual memory involves a continuous information-link which is guaranteed, at any time between the past acquisition of the information and the present memory, by some belief carrying the relevant information. Either the present factual memory is the very belief that was grounded on the original cognitive state, or it is a belief which has been validly derived from a set of beliefs which contained the information, until a point has been reached at which a belief is immediately grounded on the original cognitive state. (This is only a rough formulation.) In either case, the memory's epistemic credentials depend on there being a continuous doxastic information-link between past and present.

One consequence is that, since beliefs have conceptual contents, the information retained in factual memory is always conceptual (even though it may be partly or fully indexical). Another consequence is that the content of factual memory need not concern the past. The remembered information might have

---

[8] It follows that some, but not necessarily all, factual memories depend on metarepresentational abilities.

been originally acquired not only through perception but also through testimony or reasoning. For instance, I have been told some days ago that I have an appointment tomorrow. I have kept track of the days, and today I remember that I have an appointment tomorrow, but I am unable to recall the past circumstance in which this information was acquired. Or what I have been told is that I will have an appointment on 9 November 1998, and inferred that it is in three days, then keeping track of the days as before. In one case, what I remember has been acquired directly through testimony; in the other case, it has been acquired through reasoning based on testimony and other knowledge.

REFLEXIVITY AND CHILDHOOD AMNESIA

Factual memory is purely preservative. Is this true of episodic memory as well? In this and the following sections, I shall discuss two conceptions which lead to an affirmative answer to this question. As we shall see, both conceptions raise serious problems.

On the first conception of episodic memory to be presented, episodic memory is purely preservative because it is assimilated to a kind of factual memory. At the end of the first section, I envisaged a possible account of episodic memory in terms of a structured set of factual memories. The proposal was that an episodic memory is just a factual memory associated with the further, metarepresentational memory that the former memory comes directly from the subject's past experience. Now this proposal has similarities with the theory of episodic memory put forward by Perner in his important book (1991). Suppose, for example, that the subject remembers, in the episodic sense, a particular word on a list he has seen before. According to Tulving (1985), the subject has access to 'episodic trace information' which Perner (1991: 163) claims is a 'metarepresentational comment' on how information was obtained:

> (4) I have information that 'pear' was on the list, and I have this information because I have seen 'pear' on the list.

On Perner's view, an advantage of the meta-comment theory is that it accounts for the phenomenon of 'childhood amnesia', namely the fact that adults generally (i.e. statistically) have no memories of the first three or four years of their childhood. The explanation is that before that age children do not have the necessary metarepresentational abilities, so they have difficulties in forming long-term memories of their experiences.

There is one interpretation of Perner's theory which invites the objection raised in Section 1. On this interpretation, we can take (4) as the description of two separate pieces of knowledge—'I have information that "pear" was on the list' and 'I have this information because I have seen "pear" on the list', the latter involving a representation of the former. The objection is that even if the phrase 'I have this information because I have seen "pear" on the list' is read as meaning that the relevant information (that 'pear' was on the list) comes directly from one's past experience (in the sense already introduced), someone could possess both pieces of information and fail to have an episodic memory of seeing the word on the list.

However, there is another interpretation of Perner's theory which escapes this objection. Instead of saying that (4) describes two pieces of information, we stipulate that it describes a *single* piece of information which refers to itself. The reflexivity of the memory information can be more explicitly indicated as follows:

> (5) I have information (that 'pear' was on the list and this information comes directly from my past experience of the list).[9]

Reflexivity comes from the deictic term 'this information', which refers to the very piece of information it contributes to express. If the information is conceived as a Russellian proposition, it contains as an objective constituent the memory state or event which carries it. The general idea is the following: when I remember *x* in the episodic sense, I have a collection of factual memories not only about *x*, but equally and simultaneously about the fact that this same collection comes directly from my past experience. Episodic memories are reflexive factual memories. Since (arguably) reflexivity entails metarepresentation (although the converse is not true),[10] the proposed account can still be invoked to explain childhood amnesia.

Let us grant that the reflexive account of episodic memory deals with Goethe's Problem: the piece of information described by (5) could have been acquired neither by reasoning nor by testimony, at least not while preserving the essential reflexivity. My memory provides me with a reason to believe that it *itself* comes directly from my own experience. The question is, is this a plausible account of episodic memory?

Note first that it is essential to Perner's explanation of childhood amnesia (as it is to account for the positive epistemic value of the relevant factual memories) that the retained piece of information was acquired *at the same time as* the remembered experience. If it were allowed that it can be acquired later, it would be unclear, in particular, why people are unable to recall events from a time of their lives (before the age of 3 or 4) when they lacked the capacity to metarepresent. The reflexive account of the distinction between episodic memory and (mere) factual memory points to different ways in which the remembered events were *encoded* when they were first experienced by the subject. Something like the view that memory is purely preservative is presupposed here. At least, it

---

[9] In a later work, Perner (2000) presents something like this refined formulation to avoid the style of objection raised here. Perner's actual formulation is: 'I have information (that "pear" was on the list and that I have this information because I have seen "pear" on the list)'. For similar proposals, cf. Searle, 1983, and Owens, 1996.

[10] For details on this point, cf. Dokic, 1997, in which I tried (I now think wrongly) to assimilate episodic memories to reflexive factual ones.

seems to be required that there be a continuous, reflexive information-link between the remembered experience and the present memory: episodic memory involves the preservation of a special kind of information over time.[11]

However, such a view is a source of difficulties for the reflexive account. In particular, there is the question of how the piece of reflexive information was *acquired* in the past. Consider the following unwelcome consequence of this account. I can remember a particular incident in the episodic sense only if (i) the incident was (consciously) experienced by me, and (ii) I had a roughly simultaneous second-order representation of my experience. This does not fare well with many relevant cases, in which I suddenly remember something to which I barely paid attention when I first perceived it. Suppose I was absent-minded, thinking about something else. Surely I *saw* the book (it was in my visual field), but it is implausible to suggest that my visual representation of it was *at that time* the object of a (reflexive) metarepresentation.

In a recent paper (2000), Perner expresses some sympathy for a version of the 'higher-order thought' (HOT) theory of consciousness, according to which consciousness of a fact requires awareness of the state with which one beholds the fact.[12] Perhaps, then, he would argue on the following lines. It seems implausible, on phenomenological grounds, that every conscious experience is accompanied by a higher-order representation that makes it conscious, but it is only because we implicitly assume that the latter is itself conscious. HOT theories of consciousness usually reject this assumption. My visual experience of the book was conscious because it was the object of a metarepresentation which does not itself have to be conscious. That is why it does not *seem* to me that I have a representation of my visual experience when I simply see the book.

However, it is not clear that this strategy is available in the present case. When I remember having seen the book, I have a fully conscious piece of information, but it is argued that it was unconscious at the time of its acquisition (at least as far as its reflexive component is concerned). In the HOT picture, what makes an occurrent mental state conscious is the fact that it is the *object* of a metarepresentation. By definition, an essentially reflexive thought is already its own object; it is at once presentational and metarepresentational, so to speak. How, then, could the HOT theory allow for it to be unconscious? The point here is not so much that reflexive information cannot be *retained* unconsciously, when the subject does not actually use the information but is merely disposed to retrieve it. It is rather that it cannot be *acquired* unconsciously, because of its essentially reflexive structure. The HOT theory of consciousness must see with suspicion the very notion of acquiring reflexive information unconsciously.

Moreover, one might wonder how my present memory can give me a reason

---

[11] In Perner (2000), it is said that one has to 'encode *(or later reconstruct)*' (my italics) the metarepresentational comment. Reconstructing cannot mean here acquiring the information expressed by such a comment *after* the remembered experience; otherwise, why should I be unable to reconstruct metarepresentational comments about experiences I had before the age of 3?

[12] Cf. Armstrong, 1980; Rosenthal, 1993.

to believe that I saw a book in the past if it emerged, at some point, from unconscious acquisition of the remembered information. For what is the difference,
from the subjects' point of view, between a memory which *becomes* conscious
and a piece of information, or belief, which merely comes to them as something
they did not have before? Of course, I might discover that I had an unconscious
belief, by realizing that I behaved in surprising ways in various past situations,
but such a discovery is possible only if I have the independent means of establishing that my unconscious belief was there for some time. Intuitively, this seems
to require genuine episodic memory (of my past behaviour), precisely of the kind
that, I shall argue, the reflexive account cannot invoke.[13]

Alternatively, one might claim that there *was* an appropriate metarepresentation at the time I saw the book, namely the indexical representation of one's
global perceptual experience as *that* experience, or as being *thus*. One might
conceptualize an experience as being *thus* but not as containing a representation
of the book, even if one's experience contained such a representation. The claim
is that I suddenly remember the book by discovering that *that* experience has
always contained (*inter alia*) a representation of it. Even if we accept the idea that
perceptual experience is always accompanied by a metarepresentation of this
kind (which I think we should not), it is doubtful that the indexical concept '*that*
experience' continuously carries a potentially conscious information about the
book if the latter was completely unattended to at the time of the experience.

To sum up, Perner's reflexive account faces a dilemma. Either episodic
memory is purely preservative, or it is not. In the first case, we are bound to
postulate metarepresentations formed at the same time as the remembered experiences, but this seems to misdescribe the phenomenology of many relevant
cases. In the second case, justice is done to the phenomenology, but we have lost
a possible explanation of childhood amnesia. The striking fact that episodic
memory emerges at about the same time as the ability to have metarepresentations is left unaccounted for.

EPISODIC MEMORY AND NON-CONCEPTUAL INFORMATION

As we have just seen, episodic memory cannot be assimilated to reflexive factual
memory. Factual memory is purely preservative, and it is implausible to suppose
that everything that we can remember in the episodic sense was initiated by a
reflexive experience or state. Our discussion so far strongly suggests that episodic
memory is not a kind of factual memory. We should not conclude too hastily,
though, that episodic memory is not purely preservative. What we have to examine is the conception according to which, just as factual memory was described

---

[13] This speaks equally to those versions of the HOT theory of consciousness which hold that an
unconscious metarepresentation about a first-order representation is not enough to make the latter
conscious; see Carruthers, 1996. As far I as I can see, Carruthers does not explicitly address here the
question of how an unconscious piece of information can become conscious.

as the preservation of doxastic information, episodic memory can be understood in terms of the preservation of a different kind of information—non-doxastic, indeed non-conceptual information.

Consider a proposal that Gareth Evans made *en passant*, in a footnote. He suggests that the distinction between remembering that there was such-and-such a thing and remembering that thing, or between remembering that there was such-and-such an episode and remembering the episode, 'turns on the kind of information retained' (Evans, 1982: 267 n. 1). If we read the distinction between factual and episodic memory into this passage, the proposal is that factual memory is the retention of conceptual content, whereas episodic memory carries non-conceptual information about the past. The distinction between factual and episodic memory corresponds to different kinds of content—conceptual in the former case and non-conceptual in the second. Both forms of memory are purely preservative, although different kinds of information are retained. Does this suggestion provide an adequate solution to Goethe's Problem?

To begin with, I think that we should exclude the following explanation as a satisfactory answer to our problem. Suppose that I have an apparent memory, and reason as follows. 'This memory has a non-conceptual content, so it *has* to come directly from my own past experience (if it is not illusory). After all, testimony always carries conceptual information, embodied in language, and inference always involves conceptual contents. So if my memory is veridical, it comes directly from the remembered event.' Such a reasoning cannot be what makes the difference, among my present memories, between those that are episodic and those that are not. Episodic memory is *non-inferential* in the intuitive sense that it immediately presents itself as episodic. I do not need to infer its episodic character from features of its content.

Still, one might insist that episodic memory yields a reason to believe that it comes directly from one's own experience precisely in virtue of the fact that it has a special kind of content. There are at least two worries with this proposal, though.

One worry, which I do not want to dwell on here, concerns the sense in which the non-conceptual information carried by episodic memory can immediately ground *past-tense* judgements. Evans (1982: 239) says that when the subject has (what we call) an episodic memory, he is in a 'non-conceptual informational state' which puts him in a position to judge, being immune to error through misidentification, 'I *was* facing a burning tree'.[14] This non-conceptual informational state differs from that which is involved in perception, and which allows us to judge, being equally immune to error through misidentification, 'I am facing a burning tree'. Both states carry non-conceptual information, but the difference

---

[14] The notion of immunity to error through misidentification comes from Shoemaker (1968). What it means in this context is that my memory cannot ground knowledge of the fact that someone was facing a burning tree without at the same time grounding knowledge that *I* was facing a burning tree. There is no possibility for me to make a mistake as to the identity of the person whose experience I am remembering. On this aspect of memory, cf. also Wiggins, 1993.

lies precisely in the reference to the past: 'If the subject is in the memory state, it seems to him that such-and-such *was* the case.' The difficulty, which Evans himself notes, is to understand how there can be such non-conceptual states which are in some sense about the past. The worry is especially pressing if we think that only *conceptual* states, whose contents are wholly expressible in language, can carry past-tense information, at least if that information is about a particular, non-repeatable past event, as opposed to being merely about temporal phases (cf. Campbell, 1994: ch. 2).

Another worry arises even if the notion of non-conceptual information about the past is shown to be intelligible. Evans's proposal raises Goethe's Problem again: how are we to exclude the possibility that such information, which I possess in the present, derives *indirectly* from my past experience? Suppose, for instance, that at some time in the past I was shown photographs and films of an incident in which I was involved before that time, but had completely forgotten. Testimony by films and photographs surely carries non-conceptual information in some sense. It is not impossible, then, that non-conceptual information about the incident has been retained in the present, which I can express with 'I remember that fight; it was pitiful'. The point is that my present memory may not be *episodic*: I may still wonder whether the information preserved in the present memory has been relayed by external testimony, especially if I do not remember that I was shown films and photographs. This hypothesis, as well as the hypothesis that the information-link is direct (in the sense that it does not involve testimony or reasoning), are equally compatible with the veridicality of my memory. Therefore, the mere fact that my memory involves the past-tense demonstrative concept 'that fight', based on non-conceptual information about the past, does not make it episodic—in the story just told, it is a factual memory.

I do not wish to dispute the fact that there are many contexts in which understanding past-tense demonstratives *requires* having relevant episodic memories. Evans gives the following example: S prompts A to remember a particular bird they saw together on a hunting trip. S asks: 'Do you remember that bird we saw years ago?' Eventually, A has the right memory: 'Oh yes! Now I remember. You mean *that* bird' (Evans, 1982: 308). Clearly, in that kind of context, the understanding of 'that bird', as used by S, requires an appropriate episodic memory from A. It does not follow that such uses of past-tense demonstratives must be invoked in an *explanation* of what is special about episodic memory as opposed to mere factual memory. On the contrary, we need an independent notion of episodic memory to understand the intelligibility of the dialogue.[15]

In order for Evans's proposal to work, it must be shown that the information carried by episodic memory is of a kind which *cannot* be transmitted by testimony, in particular testimony aided by pictures and (physical) images. It is plausible to suggest that, as far as memory is concerned, there is no such information *at the personal level*. At that level, any information carried by episodic memory

---

[15] For more on memory demonstratives, cf. Campbell, Ch. 6, this volume.

could in principle be carried by testimony or reasoning.[16] There is no need to invoke non-conceptual contents to account for episodic memory; even if there are such contents, in memory they are always backed up by suitably indexical conceptual contents. It is important to note that this is not an objection to Evans's notion of an information-link. His notion is different from the one used here, since it is specifically introduced to capture the (anti-intellectualist) insight that there is a non-conceptual informational system which constitutes 'the substratum of our cognitive lives' (Evans, 1982: 122). We might sympathize with the insight, but claim that Evans's notion of an information-link is not the key to understanding the distinction between episodic and factual memory. Indeed, a main claim of the present chapter will be that a theory of memory should recognize at most two central kinds of link between past and present: doxastic information-links at the personal level, and neuropsychological causal links at the subpersonal level, whose nature is to be investigated empirically. Non-conceptual information-links at the personal level need not enter the picture.

PRESERVATION, ACQUISITION, AND RE-ACQUISITION OF INFORMATION

As we have seen, Goethe's Problem creates difficulties for the view that episodic memory involves, at the personal level, the continuous retention of information acquired by other cognitive means. These difficulties encourage us to explore a different avenue, according to which episodic memory is not in general purely preservative; its epistemic credentials do not depend on there being a personal-level information-link between present and past.

The phenomenological facts are at least compatible with the claim that episodic memory is not purely preservative. Consider the phenomenon of *suddenly remembering* something that is re-considered for the first time since the original perception. When we have such an experience, we have the feeling that we acquire an *original* memory, which we did not have just before. This is very different from the experience of recalling something which we had momentarily forgotten. In the latter case, there is a sense in which the memory was *there*, only we could not access it. In contrast, when we suddenly *realize* that there was a book on the table, to which we barely paid attention, we do not actualize a memory which was already 'there' in the same dispositional sense (at the same level of potentiality).

From an epistemological point of view, the rejection of the view that episodic memory is purely preservative means that we have to take seriously the possibility that episodic memory is a 'stopping point' in the process of justification (cf. Dummett, 1973: 619). *Pace* Ryle (1949: ch. 8), it is often perfectly all right to

---

[16] This is true even for reflexive information, although in that case, the content of episodic memory could not have been *taken from* testimony or reasoning (cf. Section 3).

declare 'I remember it' as an answer to a challenge as to how I know something. Of course, when my answer is intended to express an episodic memory, it presupposes that I previously witnessed something (in the typical case). It does not follow, though, that the information I now possess is just old evidence. On the contrary, it is fresh evidence in the sense that I did not possess that information just before my sudden awareness. My memory has enabled me to *re*-acquire it.

I suggest that episodic memory is a stopping point in the process of justification because it is a genuine source of knowledge and information. We might say that it is analogous to a form of acquaintance like perception. However, surface grammar notwithstanding, episodic memory cannot be just acquaintance of things. It is true that we tend to report episodic memory using phrases of the form 'I remember *x*' rather than of the form 'I remember that *p*' (although there are exceptions).[17] Episodic memory, though, must be capable of grounding knowledge about what happened at a particular time, which requires that a concept of a particular time and a concept of what happens then be articulated together. When I have an episodic memory of Pierre, Pierre cannot be the sole object of my conscious awareness. Otherwise, 'I remember Pierre' would have the same force as 'I can recognize Pierre', which involves no reference to a particular past time. What I am conscious of is meeting Pierre two days ago. In general, the proper object of episodic memory seems to be an event rather than a thing.

There is a significant difference between perception and episodic memory which suggests that the matter is more complicated. This difference concerns the cognitive dynamics of the two faculties. Perception essentially involves the capacity to keep track of things and events in the various states, phases, and relations in which they present themselves to the perceiver at different times. For instance, I can compensate for the perceived thing's movement by adjusting my relative position to it. In contrast, memory need not be contemporaneous with a capacity to keep track of the remembered events in this sense. I can remember the flight of a particular bird long after I have perceptually lost track of it. What I keep track of in memory is at best *facts* and not events, but here the notion of 'keeping track' has a different sense. There is no need to compensate for spatiotemporal changes in the remembered facts, for a fact has neither a spatial nor a temporal location; it is immutable. This does not mean that the maintenance of a memory over time is automatic. When an occurrent episodic memory is formed for the first time, it can persist after that as a dispositional state. At this point, we might recognize active requirements on grasping the same content over time and maintaining a state of memory knowledge. The description of what it means to grasp the same content over time and to possess persisting knowledge is a task for the theory of concepts and epistemology.

Episodic memory, then, is present awareness of facts which is not grounded on

[17] For instance, I can say that I remember Pythagoras' theorem, but what I mean, of course, is that I have a set of factual memories corresponding to the various propositions which constitute the theorem.

present awareness of events, although it is typically grounded on *previous* aware-ness of the remembered events. In this sense, my episodic memory of meeting Pierre is a case of direct knowledge of a fact involving an event—meeting Pierre—while I am not at present acquainted with that event (I might have lost track of it). It is analogous, in this respect, to introspective self-knowledge according to Shoemaker, that is, a case of knowledge of a fact about oneself which does not simultaneously involve acquaintance with the self.[18]

It might seem that Goethe's Problem is immediately solved by the concession that episodic memory is not purely preservative, but is a form of acquaintance with remembered facts. My having a particular episodic memory is a *sui generis* experience, and if I have no reason to doubt that it is veridical, it is misleading to ask how I know that the remembered piece of information comes directly from my own past life. I am directly *en rapport* with a fact concerning my own past, apparently without the help of reasoning or external testimony. For instance, if I suddenly remember that there was a (previously unattended) book on the table, I know that I am in possession of a piece of information which I did not have just before. The logical form of my memory is the following:[19]

> (6) I have a memory experience which carries the information that there was a book on the table.

However, one grossly misrepresents the true nature of episodic memory if one takes (6) as a complete description of the content of my memory experience. At best, (6) would fully describe a very different cognitive faculty, perhaps *clair-voyance* (assuming that the notion of clairvoyance makes sense). Unlike clair-voyance, episodic memory carries, and presents itself as carrying, information which the subject already possessed once. As Campbell (1994: 233) puts it, episodic memory (like factual memory) is *stepwise*: it depends on there being other ways of finding out how things are. More precisely, when there is no contin-uous information-link at the personal level, it is the *re-acquisition* of a piece of information acquired in the past, that is, the faculty of *reproducing* in the present a past informational state. The following description is slightly better as far as this distinctive feature of episodic memory is concerned:

> (7) I have a memory experience which carries the information that there was a book on the table, and this piece of information presents itself as some-thing I acquired in a previous experience.

However, (7) is still incomplete, for it does not *entail* that I have an episodic memory of the book. Suppose that I was perceptually aware that there was a book on the table. Later, when I have *definitely* forgotten this fact, someone

---

[18] One crucial difference is, of course, that (in Shoemaker's theory) the self is *never* experienced as a thing. Cf. Shoemaker, 1996: essay 10, where the distinction between awareness of facts and awareness of objects (things or events) is discussed.

[19] In this and the next formulations, the phrases 'a book' and 'the table' should be read, more real-istically, as complex demonstratives: 'this book' and 'that table'.

tells me that I really did perceive the book. Description (7) might correctly refer to a still later experience in which I re-acquire the information that there was a book on the table and this information presents itself as something I have witnessed in the past. Still, I do not have a genuine episodic memory of the book, since past testimony is among the conditions that make my present memory experience possible (although I may not know it). In this particular example, I can have the experience described by (7) *only if* there is previous testimony—without it, I would be totally unable to *gain* the memory that there was a book on the table.[20]

Of course, this is just Goethe's Problem in a different guise. It shows that the content of an ordinary episodic memory must be more complex than (7) suggests. In particular, it should not be compatible with being completely unable to re-acquire the relevant information between the past experience and the actual, present memory. I would like to claim that when I remember something in the episodic sense, I have a piece of information which presents itself as being *directly* re-acquired from my past experience, in a way which excludes the essential intervention of reasoning or testimony. Thus, (8) might be the correct description of (a central case of) episodic memory:

(8) I have a memory experience which carries the information that there was a book on the table, and this piece of information presents itself as being directly re-acquired from my past experience.

If we adopt this description of episodic memory, Goethe's Problem is dealt with in a very special way. Episodic memory is the experience of re-acquiring a piece of information *as* something which is taken directly from the past experience itself, without the essential mediation of reasoning or testimony. More generally, episodic memory gives me a reason to believe that it comes directly from my own past experience because the fact that it does so is presented in the memory experience itself. However, the notion of 'coming directly from one's own past experience' is interpreted here in a crucially different way than in the accounts presented above in Sections 3 and 4. There is no suggestion that the metarepresentational information carried by memory is preserved at the personal level from the time of the past experience to the present; very often, my episodic memory won't involve a continuous information-link from past to present. Of course, there must be some subpersonal link between the past experience and the present memory, but this link is not supposed to ground, at the personal level, an episodic memory at each time between past and present. At best, the link must guarantee that the relevant memory can be *gained*.

---

[20] Similar points apply to Locke's and William James's theories of memory. For Locke, memory is the capacity of the mind 'to revive perceptions, which it has once had, with this additional perception annexed to them, that it has had them before' (Locke, 1997: 148). For James, 'memory proper . . . is the knowledge of an event, or fact . . . with the additional consciousness that we have . . . experienced it before' (1890: 648). If I am right, these are crucially incomplete descriptions of episodic memory.

It is worth comparing the present account with proposals made by two authors from quite different philosophical horizons. Merleau-Ponty, just after having stressed the non-inferential character of genuine memory ('memory that reaches to the past'), writes about his memory of when he ordered a particular English cloth:

When . . . I find again the concrete origin of the memory, it is because it is replaced in a particular stream of fear and hope which goes from Munich to the war; it is because I go back to the lost time; and it is because, from the considered moment to my present, the chain of retentions and the successive overlapping horizons ensure a continuous path. (1945: translated from p. 478).

What Merleau-Ponty seems to suggest is that a genuine memory must enable one to 'see through the past' to the remembered experience. He would probably agree that in cases in which the remembered information is essentially relayed by testimony or reasoning, there is no continuous path (once again, at the personal level) leading to the original experience. There is precisely no path of this kind in the example discussed above, when (7) was rejected as a non-perspicuous account of episodic memory.

Some years earlier (in 1927), G. F. Stout proposed a similar account. He draws a distinction between reminiscence, that is, what we call here 'episodic memory', and retentiveness, which concerns in general the persistence in the present of the results of past mental processes. He writes:

In remembering past experience as such we are cognisant of it as past relatively to our own actual present in the moment of remembering it. Our total object is a complex unity which includes present and past in relation to each other. We are aware of the actual present as continued back into a certain past specially connected with it; and of this past as prolonged forward to the present. (Stout, 1930: 175)

I have no objection to this account of episodic memory, except perhaps as far as the notion of retentiveness is concerned. Stout says that retentiveness is an indispensable condition of reminiscence. If 'retentiveness' means that there is a continuous causal link, possibly at the subpersonal level, between past experience and present memory, he is surely right. If, on the other hand, he means that there must be an information-link between past and present at the personal level, I disagree. As I said before, the phenomenon of suddenly remembering something seems to indicate that episodic memory involves the re-acquisition of a piece of information which has not been preserved by the *subject*, whether doxastically or otherwise.

Note that the claim that episodic memory presents a piece of information as something which is directly connected to one's past experience does not entail that the subject is always in a position to keep track of the time or date of the original experience. The subject might have the strong feeling that she recently saw the book she is now looking for, without being able to remember exactly when. Indeed, she might remember two past experiences as being connected to the present and be unable to recover from her memory the temporal relations between the experiences, or their relative order.[21] What is important is that at least some episodic memories provide more precise temporal information about the remembered events, and that in general the subject can legitimately impose on his memory a conception of time as linear (cf. Campbell, 1997).

Finally, the present analysis of episodic memory can account for the following situation. I have a visual experience of seeing a book which is a complete hallucination, although I do not know it. Later, I have a memory experience of seeing the book which is not veridical, and I may know it, if I realized in between that my past visual experience was a hallucination. How is it possible, then, to remember my past hallucination itself? I suggest that whereas my past experience was a hallucination, my present memory is only an illusion. Here I mean something like Austin's (1962) notion of an illusion, according to which an experience is illusory if something is perceived as having the wrong properties. Similarly, there is something veridical in my present memory experience: I am not presented with the fact that there was a book on the table (for there was no such fact), but I am presented with the fact that a piece of information (which is in fact misinformation) comes directly from my past experience. Thus I can remember the past experience itself even though it did not warrant the information that there was a book on the table.

CONCLUSION

In this essay, I have explored an intermediary position between two antagonist conceptions of memory: on the one hand, a conception of memory as a mere form of knowledge, involving possession of information preserved over time (the 'purely preservative' view of memory), and on the other hand, a conception of memory as a genuine source of knowledge and information, possibly acquired for the first time. There is an intimate connection, then, between memories being purely preservative and them being not episodic. The mental state which I am in when I have a factual memory is much like the one I was in before, whereas the fact that my episodic memory has been caused in a certain way has made a difference to what kind of mental state it is (and not only to what kind of content it has). I do not want to exclude a priori the possibility of reflexive factual memories, whose causal history is somehow written into their contents, but we have to realize that the range of episodic memory is in a sense much wider. In particular, I can have an episodic memory of a past scene even though there is no information-link at the personal level (let alone a reflexive information-link) connecting past and present.

Episodic memory requires metarepresentational abilities, since its content

---

[21] The matter is different if the content of memory includes specific indexical concepts like 'yesterday' or 'the day before yesterday'.

describes or refers to a previous experience, and is essentially reflexive. The *core* information carried by this form of memory need not be reflexive, though. It is the information originally acquired by the subject, typically through perception. So how should we explain the striking fact that we have episodic memories only of events experienced at times when the metarepresentational abilities are in place? As the Editors remind me, the theory that there is a necessary connection between childhood amnesia and the development of metarepresentational abilities is actually quite controversial, and the fact that our first memories come on the scene at roughly the same time as these abilities might be a mere coincidence. Still, I shall end this chapter with a brief and speculative remark about why I think the conception of episodic memory sketched here is not utterly incompatible with there being a connection between episodic memory and the emergence of metarepresentational abilities, wherever the truth lies with this particular issue.[22]

As we saw, there is a sense in which (episodic) memory is a kind of 'vision' through our past life to the remembered experience. Now perhaps such a 'vision' is possible only if the subject is at least *capable* of self consciousness at any time between the remembered experience and the present. How can we 'see' through our past life if it consists in a mere succession of first-order mental states and episodes, neither unified nor bound together by any reflection? In this perspective, episodic memory requires a present exercise of self consciousness, but it also requires that the capacity of self consciousness be in place from the remembered experience to the present. Since such a capacity appears to emerge at around the age of 3 or 4, the phenomenon of childhood amnesia would be explained by the presence of a 'block', at about that time, beyond which episodic memory is simply blind. Of course, this is merely a speculation, and further work on the role of self consciousness in episodic memory is called for.

I would like to thank the Editors, Christoph Hoerl and Teresa McCormack, for their very valuable comments on earlier drafts of this paper.

J.D.

REFERENCES

ANSCOMBE, G. E. M. (1974), 'Memory, "Experience" and Causation', in *The Collected Papers of G. E. M. Anscombe*, ii. Oxford: Basil Blackwell, 120–30.

ARMSTRONG, D. (1980), 'What is consciousness?', in *The Nature of Mind*. Ithaca, NY: Cornell University Press, 55–67.

AUSTIN, J. L. (1962), *Sense and Sensibilia*. Oxford: Oxford University Press.

AYER, A. J. (1956), *The Problem of Knowledge*. London: Macmillan.

---

[22] For further reflection on the relationship between self consciousness and episodic memory development, cf. McCormack and Hoerl (forthcoming).

BERGSON, H. (1939), *Matière et mémoire*. Paris: Presses Universitaires de France.

CAMPBELL, J. (1994), *Past, Space, and Self*. Cambridge, Mass.: MIT Press.

—— (1997), 'The structure of time in autobiographical memory', *European Journal of Philosophy*, 5(2): 105–18.

DOKIC, J. (1997), 'Une théorie réflexive du souvenir épisodique', *Dialogue*, 36: 527–54.

DUMMETT, M. (1973), *Frege and Other Philosophers*. London: Duckworth.

—— (1993), 'Testimony and memory', in *The Seas of Language*. Oxford: Clarendon Press.

EVANS, G. (1982), *The Varieties of Reference*. Oxford: Basil Blackwell.

JAMES, W. (1890), *The Principles of Psychology*. London: Macmillan.

LOCKE, J. (1997) [1690/1694], *An Essay Concerning Human Understanding*, ed. R. Woolhouse. Harmondsworth: Penguin.

MCCORMACK, T., and HOERL, C. (forthcoming), 'The child in time: temporal concepts, self-consciousness, and the development of episodic memory', in C. Moore and K. Skene (eds.), *The Self in Time: Developmental Issues*. Hillsdale, NJ: Erlbaum.

MALCOLM, N. (1963), 'Three lectures on memory', in *Knowledge and Certainty*. Englewood Cliffs, NJ: Prentice-Hall, 187–240.

MERLEAU-PONTY, M. (1945), *La phénoménologie de la perception*. Paris: Gallimard.

OWENS, D. (1996), 'A Lockean theory of memory experience', *Philosophy and Phenomenological Research*, 56(2): 319–32.

PEACOCKE, C. (1986), *Thoughts: An Essay on Content*. Oxford: Basil Blackwell.

PERNER, J. (1991), *Understanding the Representational Mind*. Cambridge, Mass.: MIT Press.

—— (2000), 'Memory and theory of mind', in E. Tulving and F. I. M. Craik (eds.), *The Oxford Handbook of Memory*. New York, NY: Oxford University Press.

ROSENTHAL, D. (1993), 'Thinking that one thinks', in M. Davies and G. W. Humphreys (eds.), *Consciousness*. Oxford: Basil Blackwell.

—— (1996), *Language, Thought, and Consciousness*. Cambridge: Cambridge University Press.

RUSSELL, B. (1921), *The Analysis of Mind*. London: Allen and Unwin.

RYLE, G. (1949), *The Concept of Mind*. London: Hutchinson.

SEARLE, J. (1983), *Intentionality*. Cambridge: Cambridge University Press.

SHOEMAKER, S. (1967), 'Memory', in P. Edwards, *The Encyclopedia of Philosophy*, 8 vols. New York: Macmillan/Free Press; London: Collier Macmillan, 265–74.

—— (1968), 'Self-reference and self-awareness', *Journal of Philosophy*, 65: 555–67.

—— (1996), *The First-Person Perspective and Other Essays*. Cambridge: Cambridge University Press.

STOUT, G. F. (1930), 'In what way is memory-knowledge immediate?', in *Studies in Philosophy and Psychology*. London: Macmillan, 166–81.

TULVING, E. (1985), 'Memory and Consciousness', *Canadian Psychology*, 26: 1–12.

WIGGINS, D. (1993), 'Remembering directly', in J. Hopkins and A. Savile (eds.), *Psychoanalysis, Mind and Art*. Oxford: Basil Blackwell.

III

Memory and Experience

9

Phenomenological Records and the Self-Memory System

Martin A. Conway

The problem of the intentionality of mental states (Brentano, 1874/1973)—their 'aboutness'—has often preoccupied students of consciousness and it seems that conscious states must always be about something: a thought, image, feeling, etc. In analogous ways I want to consider here what memory might be 'about', and I will focus particularly on *autobiographical memory* (AM) or memory for the experiences of our lives. I start from the view that specific AMs are mental states or processes more or less effortfully constructed from several different types of knowledge (Conway, 1996a). These states are transitory and difficult to maintain, at least in their initial full form—that is, in the form in which they first enter conscious awareness. Moreover, the knowledge which is brought together from several sources, including the present, critically includes some knowledge of near-sensory experience quality. This near-sensory experience knowledge may originate from processing in the present that corresponds or 'maps' onto near-sensory experience knowledge in long-term memory, or it may originate solely from long-term memory itself which contains this type of knowledge. I will refer to near-sensory experience long-term knowledge as the phenomenological record (Conway, 1992) and I shall propose that when phenomenological records enter into an act of autobiographical remembering they promote, or bring about, distinctive states of conscious experience. These states of consciousness, which are 'about' AMs, will be considered later but by way of a preview the following passage from Proust's profoundly perceptive essay on autobiographical remembering, in the chapter 'Impressions Regained' from his uncompleted autobiographical novel, *Jean Santeuil*, touches on several of the issues considered below:

When a sensation comes to me in the present though as a sensation belonging to the past, there springs from the impact of that clash something that seems as it were to be a sensation freed from the *trammels of the senses,* and within the field of the imagination which, having now offered to it an eternal object, can know it, and know it so well that in a flash I find myself confronted by a reality liberated from the temporal circumstances of my life, by something which I once saw only as a passing show preserved in memory: but preserved in such a way that instead of being conscious of the melancholy that hangs over a collection of pictures drawn from the past, instead of living though not living, I have the feeling not only that I *have* lived, but rather that I have lived something which is living still, which *I* may live again tomorrow. (Proust, 1955: 409)

When filtered through the skills of a great writer this metaphysical view of remembering (memories as 'eternal objects') appears to fit a type of discourse far removed from that of the memory researcher. However, Proust's idea that people might have a past of which they are aware (the 'collection of pictures') *without* recollectively experiencing that past and the same past now recollectively experienced, and as a consequence giving rise to a different type of conscious experience, corresponds closely with current thinking about states of awareness in remembering (Gardiner, 1988; Tulving, 1985; Wheeler, Stuss, and Tulving, 1997). People might at one time 'just know' (cf. Conway *et al.*, 1997) they went to a certain infant school whereas on another occasion the same individuals might recollectively experience a specific event from their school days or even, perhaps, recollectively experience the entire period. When the past is recollectively experienced, as Proust later comments, AMs 'have not the flatness of pictures but the rounded fullness of reality' (p. 409), a reality which is experienced by the 'I'. This too fits with current thinking about the construction of AMs in the present by a self that may have different goals and aims from the self that existed when an experience first entered long-term memory (Conway, 1996*a*; Conway and Pleydell-Pearce, 2000). Thus, when knowledge is accessed there may be a Proustian 'clash' between that knowledge (the product of a different self) and the current self and, possibly, it is this that leads to the distinctive experience of remembering—it is this that makes memories more than 'flat pictures', makes them 'living still'.

AUTOBIOGRAPHICAL MEMORY AND THE SELF

As we do not know what the self is, it may be thought disingenuous to make it a central component of a theory of human memory. Nevertheless virtually every writer on AM, from memory researcher to poet, has seen an intimate connection between the self and memory generally and AM in particular (cf. Conway, 1996*a*). What could this relation be? One recent theory postulates a reciprocal relation between self and memories (Conway and Pleydell-Pearce, 2000). In this account the self is conceived as a hierarchy of currently active goal structures—*the working self* (e.g. Markus and Ruvolo, 1989). Autobiographical memory is the database of the working self and constrains what goals can be adopted and stipulates what goals should be pursued. For example, a person who has become a father cannot maintain a goal 'to be a father for the first time' *if* some sort of record of becoming a father is represented in the autobiographical memory knowledge base. On the other hand, if no such record exists then the goal can be adopted (to become a father). Autobiographical memory then is in effect, although this is rarely explicit in individual memories, a record of successful, abandoned, and failed, attempts at goal attainment. The AM knowledge base *grounds* the working self, it constrains the universe of 'possible selves' (Markus and Nurius, 1986) available to the individual, and it requires that the goal structures of the working self be consistent with the contents of the knowledge base. When currently active goals are inconsistent with the AM knowledge base, then the individual may be in a pathological state. It does not follow from this that people cannot maintain contradictory beliefs but rather more simply that beliefs/goals should not contradict or be wholly incompatible with what can be remembered. Of course, if some memory cannot be accessed, then it may be that the failure of access will itself allow the holding of a belief which is in reality a contradiction (cf. Conway and Tacchi, 1996; Ramachandran, 1995). Such inaccessible knowledge, assuming it remains in long-term memory and has not been forgotten, may have indirect or implicit effects on cognition (Freud, 1915; Kihlstrom, 1997).

The reciprocity of the relationship between the working self and the AM knowledge base rests on the ability of the working self to control access to the knowledge base and to determine what will and what will not be encoded (this latter, only to a limited degree). The goal-structure of the working self 'gates' what knowledge will be attended to and, as a consequence, encoded in accessible ways. The working self also plays a critical role in access to the knowledge base and in memory construction and this is considered in detail later: first we need to have some conception of the nature of the knowledge base itself. Conway (1992, 1996*a*; Conway and Pleydell-Pearce, 2000; Conway and Rubin, 1993) reviews the evidence from several different and independent lines of research and notes that they converge on the view that AMs are constructions featuring knowledge at several different levels of abstraction. Autobiographical memories contain knowledge of *lifetime periods*, such as when I was at school X, worked for company Y, lived with Z, etc., *general event knowledge*, such as holiday in A, eating out at B, working project C, etc., and *event specific knowledge* or *phenomenological records* (PRs). It seems a strong possibility that these different types of AM knowledge might be stored separately, possibly in different locations in the brain (Conway and Pleydell-Pearce, 2000), but have indices that connect them into AM knowledge structures. For example, a lifetime period such as *when I worked for company X* will contain knowledge of activities, locations, others, feelings, goals, and beliefs characteristic of the period and which endured for some extended time, if not for the whole period. Note that lifetime period knowledge is considered to be schematic and may often take the form of generic images of locations, objects, others, etc., common to the period, such as images of a school attended (cf. Whitten and Leonard, 1981, and Haque and Conway, 2000). Lifetime periods may also contain broad temporal knowledge of the *order* of occurrence of general events which they can access, for example, work projects, phases in relationships, holidays, etc. (Conway and Bekerian, 1987). Lifetime period knowledge can be used to access or index more temporarily limited and more event-specific general events. So the general event 'My interview at company X' may be indexed by lifetime period knowledge of activities, etc., common to the period, that is, a generic image of building in which the interview took place.

General events, in contrast, are more specific and at the same time more heterogeneous and numerous than lifetime periods. Barsalou (1988) found that general events encompassed both repeated events, such as *evening hikes to meadows,* and single events, such as *My trip to Paris.* Robinson (1992) pointed out that general events may also represent sets of associated events and so encompass a series of memories linked together by a theme. For example, Robinson (1992) studied what he called 'mini-histories' for activities such as *learning to drive a car* and *first romantic relationship.* Initial findings suggested that these were organized around individual memories representing events featuring goal-attainment knowledge (both positive and negative) that appeared to convey significant information for the self, for example, about how easily a skill was acquired, and about success and failure in intimate interpersonal relations. Interestingly, both types of mini-history featured highly vivid memories for critical moments of goal attainment. Virtually all Robinson's (1992) subjects had vivid memories for the first time they drove a car alone and for a first kiss. Obviously, other types of event may also lead to local organization, for example, a holiday, a period performing some particular piece of work, a period of illness, and so on. N. Brown and Schopflocher (1998) have demonstrated how when one memory is used to cue recall of a second then striking event clusters emerge, and this suggests quite extensive local temporal organization of general events. General event knowledge, then, represents knowledge of others, activities, locations, goals, temporal order, etc., which can be used to access PRs and so form specific and, sometimes, vivid AMs. General event knowledge itself, however, appears to be in a more propositional, less imagistic form of representation and it is only when PRs are accessed that imagery enters the memory construction (see Martin, Ch. 10 this volume, for related comments). By this scheme, then, lifetime periods access general events and general events access PRs, and a stable pattern of activation over these structures linked to the goals of the working self is the representation of a specific AM. Critical to this process is the access of PRs and before turning to consider these in further detail it will be useful to review briefly some of the evidence for this type of knowledge in autobiographical memory.

SENSORY-PERCEPTUAL KNOWLEDGE IN AUTOBIOGRAPHICAL REMEMBERING

Specific autobiographical memories are often accompanied by visual imagery, a fact noted by many researchers from the original studies of Galton (1883; see Conway, 1990, for a review) to Brewer's (1986) theoretical analysis of the predominant role of imagery in autobiographical remembering (see also Brewer, 1996, for a historical review). Indeed, in the more specialized study of flashbulb memories (R. Brown and Kulik, 1977; see Conway, 1995, for a review of this area) recall of event specific details is a defining feature of memory vividness. In the most extreme form of flashbulb memories that occur following the experience of trauma, the intrusive recollection of highly specific single details is taken as a symptom of the clinical illness of Post Traumatic Stress Disorder (PTSD) (American Psychiatric Association, DSM-IIIr, 1986). In recent studies it has been suggested that intrusive memories in PTSD, especially following a single trau-matic experience, initially take the from of an unrelated set of sensory-perceptual details which only over time come to be associated with more abstract general event and lifetime period knowledge (Ehlers and Steil, 1995; van der Kolk and Fisler, 1995; but see Howe, 1997). This unorganized representation of PRs contrasts with the organization of event details typical of everyday, non-trau-matic, memories. S. J. Anderson and Conway (1993) found that the event details that make up a single specific memory could be accessed in either of two ways: in one form of access a distinctive or thematic detail was recalled first and other details were accessed subsequently; in another form of access, knowledge was accessed sequentially from details of first occurring activities to last (see also Burt *et al.*, 1996). In both cases, however, after initial access additional memory details were accessed in forward temporal order, suggesting that this was how these representations were organized in long-term memory. In other studies (S. J. Anderson, 1993) participants were asked to recall details from their memories exhaustively. For example, a participant who listed an activity such as *Talking to Z* as a detail of a memory would be asked to recall this conversation. Overall, participants were able to do this for one-third of the details listed to several memories but there was very marked variation and for some memories many additional details were retrieved whereas for others few or no additional details were available. This variability is what might be expected, as it has been shown that PR links to general event structures are fairly rapidly lost (within one week of encoding) unless these links are rehearsed (Burt *et al.*, 1998). As recall (rehearsal) rates will differ for different memories, it follows that some memories will preserve more links to PRs than others. Nevertheless, when additional knowledge was accessed in the S. J. Anderson (1993) study, it was virtually always in the form of visual images. These images did not appear to be recalled in any particular order but rather, according to the participants, they simply 'popped' into mind. This latter finding suggests that PRs are not subject to detailed pre-stored organization and instead come to mind in response to inter-nally elaborated cues that by the process of encoding specificity (Tulving and Thomson, 1973) make contact with specific PRs.

A number of other studies have also demonstrated the centrality of sensory-perceptual knowledge to autobiographical remembering more generally. For example, Johnson, Foley, Suengas, and Raye (1988) found that sensory-percep-tual knowledge was the key feature that distinguished memory for experienced events from memory for imagined events. Conway *et al.* (1996) found recall of sensory-perceptual information to be associated with both correct and incorrect recognition of previously experienced events, further suggesting that this type of knowledge and the imagery to which it gives rise is critical in leading remem-berers to believe the truth of their memories. As Conway *et al.* (1996) point out, however, this may not be as dysfunctional a strategy as it may first seem: Brewer

(1988) observed that the more sensory detail available at recall the more accurate an autobiographical memory was and, in general, Conway and colleagues found recall of sensory-perceptual knowledge to be very strongly associated with correct recognition. Thus, in most instances the more sensory-perceptual knowledge the more likely that a recalled event has actually been experienced, although in exceptional circumstances evidence of sensory-perceptual knowledge can mislead a rememberer into erroneous and even false memories (Conway, 1997a; Conway et al., 1996). That sensory-perceptual knowledge can take the form of the recall of 'minutiae' (R. Brown and Kulik, 1977; Heuer and Reisberg, 1990) in even low-emotion memories was further demonstrated by Ross (1984), who found that people learning to use a word processor over a number of training sessions were often reminded of the exact words they had edited in a previous session. Ross (Blessing and Ross, 1996; Ross, Perkins, and Tenpenny, 1990) has further proposed that such 'remindings' (Schank, 1982, 1986) provide critical support for category learning and the creation of generalizations. Finally, a recent study by S. J. Anderson (1998) demonstrated the role of sensory-perceptual knowledge in the construction of autobiographical memories. In a series of experiments in which participants retrieved memories to self-generated cues while performing a secondary task, Anderson (1998) found that, when a secondary task took up visual processing capacity, the knowledge initially accessed was abstract and verbal whereas, when a secondary task took up verbal processing capacity, the knowledge initially accessed was sensory-perceptual and represented in the form of visual images.

Given this critical role of sensory-perceptual knowledge in AM, and especially that of visual imagery, it is not too surprising that in some cases of retrograde amnesia following brain damage access to the PR may be abolished while access to some lifetime period knowledge and general events remains intact (reviews of this area can be found in Conway, 1993, 1996b, Conway and Fthenaki, 2000, and Rubin and Greenberg, 1998, see too Nadel and Moscovitch, 1997). For example, investigations of several patients (e.g. Cermak and O'Connor, 1983; Stuss and Benson, 1988; Tulving et al., 1988) with very dense focal retrograde amnesias (Kapur, 1993) and widespread brain damage encompassing frontal, temporal, and limbic regions, found an inability to retrieve specific memories while access to knowledge of lifetime periods and general events from the period covered by their amnesias remained intact. An unusual case of this was Cermak and O'Connor's (1983) patient, S.S., who spontaneously provided what initially appeared to be descriptions of memories but which upon further investigation turned out to be well-established stories or narratives that the patient was in the habit of relating. Thus, when his memory was tested more formally S.S. proved unable to recall virtually any specific memories but nevertheless he had good retention of his 'stories' and in addition retained knowledge of lifetime periods and general events. Other patients in this group retained only fragmentary access to lifetime period and general event knowledge with fairly complete focal retrograde amnesias for specific memories. As these patients also had very dense anterograde amnesias, it seems unlikely that they could have relearned this knowledge following their brain injury, although this possibility cannot be ruled out for patients with less extensive injuries (cf. Hunkin *et al.*, 1995). More recently a series of patients have been reported who have marked damage to regions of the occipital lobes (Hunkin *et al.*, 1995; O'Connor *et al.*, 1992; Ogden, 1993). These patients typically cannot retrieve memories from the pre-morbid period prior to their injury, but often have, in comparison, fairly intact memories for events in the post-morbid period, although these are less detailed and vivid than the memories of non-brain damaged controls (Hunkin *et al.*, 1995). One common feature of these patients is an inability, or strikingly reduced ability, to generate visual images of events experienced prior to their brain injury. For example, Ogden's (1993) patient could recall virtually no memories from his pre-morbid period and those few he could recall were typically dominated by non-visual sensory-perceptual details such as sounds (particularly music), smells, or movements. Nevertheless, this patient, like the patients of Hunkin, *et al.* (1995) and O'Connor *et al.* (1992) appeared to have good access to lifetime period and some general event knowledge. It appears that in order to have an intact and functioning AM those brain networks that mediate representation of the *type* of retained knowledge (visuo-spatial in the case of most PRs) must be unimpaired.

PHENOMENOLOGICAL RECORDS

Lifetime period and general event knowledge may be a (delimited) part of a much larger declarative long-term memory knowledge base which encompasses many different varieties of semantic knowledge. A defining feature of semantic knowledge, as originally proposed by Tulving (1972, 1983), is that it is knowledge which does not preserve information about the spatio-temporal context in which it was acquired and because of this lack of experiential know-ledge semantic memory cannot be *recollectively experienced* (cf. Conway *et al.*, 1997, for a demonstration of this). The concept of 'recollective experience' was introduced by Tulving (1985) to further characterize episodic remembering and separate it from other types of memory. The central feature of recollective experience is that it is a form of autonoetic consciousness in which the current self becomes aware of itself in the past and this may entail (vivid) imagery of various sorts, recall of thoughts, goals, personal strivings, and feelings, all highly specific to the event remembered (see Gardiner and Conway, 1999, Gardiner and Richardson-Klavehn, 2000, Gardiner, Ramponi, and Richardson-Klavehn, 1997). In a further revision of the concept of episodic memory Wheeler *et al.* (1997) proposed that recollective experience was exclusive to, and defining of, episodic memory. Indeed, these authors postulated that networks in the right prefrontal cortex mediated recollective experience and that damage to these brain regions could impair or even ablate the ability to recollectively experience the past (cf. Wheeler, Stuss, and Tulving, 1995). In contrast, semantic memory is not associated with recollec-

tive experience and instead is characterized by feelings of familiarity/knowing—
a type of noetic consciousness.

The strong claim that recollective experience is *the* defining feature of
episodic memory can, however, be questioned. For instance, one problem is that
some autobiographical knowledge which undeniably is *about* experience, even a
specific experience, may not be recollectively experienced when accessed:
people may simply 'know' that last year they took their annual holiday in Italy. It
also seems possible that the opposite could be true and they could remember,
recollectively experience, a general event, for example, that they had once been
on a school trip to Italy. Lifetime period knowledge and especially general event
knowledge pose difficulties for theories of episodic memory that postulate recollective experience as the major defining feature of this type of memory.
Additionally, it is difficult to see how such an approach could account for false
memories (Conway, 1997*b*) which must, almost by definition, be semantic but
which none the less can be recollectively experienced (Conway *et al.*, 1996;
Roediger and McDermott, 1995). Thus I suggest that it is not the state of
conscious awareness that defines episodic/autobiographical memory, although
recollective experience is characteristic of this type of memory, but rather that
which initiates or triggers recollective experience—phenomenological records
(PRs).

Another issue of some interest here is whether or not generic personal images
also invoke recollective experience. My view is that they do not. Unlike PRs,
generic images are not strongly associated summaries of specific conscious states
of the self from the past. Instead they are abstractions which derive from PRs.
Thus, the notion of a 'PR' attempts to capture the idea of an encounter (during
retrieval) of the current self with a fragment (or fragments) of a past self, and the
proposal is that it is this encounter which triggers recollective experience. Such
an encounter does not occur at the level of lifetime period knowledge and generic
imagery. Of course, the retrieval process might incorrectly identify an accessed
item of long-term knowledge as a PR when it is not. When this occurs recollective experience is still triggered but a false memory results. What, then, is a PR?
A PR is a summary record of a period during which the contents of consciousness
remained constant (Conway, 1992; see also Newtson, 1976). A PR is automatically encoded when the contents of consciousness change, and this is signalled by
a redirection of attention. So, for instance, when a person stops thinking about
one subject and turns to another, or switches attention to an external task, or
switches from one external task to another, in all cases PRs are formed. However,
it is assumed that PRs represent comparatively short periods, that is, of seconds
and minutes in duration, and fluctuations of attention while performing a task
trigger the automatic encoding of the preceding period. PRs, then, represent
moment-by-moment sustained periods of attention and in so doing implicitly
represent information about goals (it is after all these that direct attention). In
representing in summary form the contents of consciousness, PRs must also
contain some record of the non-conscious processing that led to the contents of

consciousness in the first place. Thus PRs represent near-sensory knowledge of moment-by-moment experience as this was guided and interpreted by the working self (see Barsalou, 1999, for a related account of representation in terms of 'perceptual symbols'). They are like snapshots of what the goal structure of the working self was attending to and, because of this, PRs can (potentially) be used to infer past goal states or even recreate them. When PRs are accessed they have a potential to reinstate a part of a previous version of the working self, and I suggest that it is this property that triggers recollective experience. By this view one of the functions of recollective experience would be to *signal* to the cognitive system as a whole that it is remembering an old goal state and not running a current one.

Conway (1992) proposed that PRs as a whole might be represented separately from other forms of AM knowledge, that is, lifetime periods and general events, in an independent memory store or system. One interesting possibility is that the PR system might have properties similar to those of the random storage model of memory originally proposed by Landauer (1975). In Landauer's model a large number of loci are homogeneously distributed throughout a memory store and a pointer directed at a specific point marks the place where a PR will be stored. After a record is registered (as the content of consciousness change) the pointer randomly jumps to a nearby location in preparation for the registration of another record. Thus organization is random with temporally contiguous memories being stored at physically close locations within the store. Note that, in a simulation of this model, Landauer demonstrated that many well-documented memory phenomena, such as retroactive and proactive inhibition, recency effects, etc., can be modelled assuming a simple cue-based search process. Within the store, records are accessed by cues by a process of encoding specificity (Tulving and Thomson, 1973) or by searches of adjacent spaces (temporally contiguous records tend to be stored in physically close locations: Landauer, 1975). Clearly, such a store would have to be very large indeed to contain a complete record of all the fluctuations in conscious experience in, for example, the life of a typical 70-year-old. However, it is not proposed that the phenomenological record contains a complete record of conscious experience. On the contrary the evidence from autobiographical memory research (cf. Conway, 1996a) is that records are incomplete and fragmentary. Therefore, although it is assumed that all fluctuations in the contents of consciousness are encoded, it is only those PRs which are indexed by some higher-order structure (i.e. a general event) that are protected from overwriting. Assuming that the phenomenological record, as a discrete store, is limited in the amount of records it can contain, then when this limit is reached records not indexed by more abstract knowledge will be overwritten. Moreover, everyday conscious experience is highly structured by goals, plans, and sequenced activities, and a further possibility is that rather than all fluctuations in phenomenal experience being encoded it may be that it is only those experiences directly associated with event-specific goals, plans, and activities that are retained. Thus an unrealistically large memory store is not required for the phenomenological record. But note also that one implication of these proposals is that once the PR store is filled with records indexed by higher order structures it will not be possible to encode further PRs unless some preserved PRs are over-written (forgotten). This view then proposes that long-term memory is not infinite but rather has a limited capacity, although that limit may be very large indeed.

NEUROANATOMY OF PHENOMENOLOGICAL RECORDS

It is suggested that PRs are represented in sensory processing networks in the posterior of the neocortex, where they were originally processed. Of especial importance here are networks in the occipital lobes which mediate visual imagery (Conway, Pleydell-Pearce, and Whitecross, 1999; Fletcher *et al.*, 1996; Rubin and Greenberg, 1998). In a neuroimaging study using slow cortical potentials Conway, Pleydell-Pearce, and Whitecross (1999) found that while an autobio-graphical memory was held in mind activation of right posterior temporal and anterior occipital lobes was strong and that this pattern was most marked for those memories later judged to be most vivid. Other neuroimaging studies have not, however, observed exactly this pattern of activation. For instance, Fink *et al.* (1996) in a positron emission tomography (PET) study found AM unique increases in relative cerebral blow flow (rCBF) largely in lateral and medial regions of the right temporal lobe (hippocampus, parahippocampal, amygdala), right temporoparietal junction, right prefrontal cortex, and other right hemisphere sites (see Fink *et al.*, 1996, table 1). Conway, Turk, Miller, Logan, Nebes, Meltzer, and Becker (1999), also in a PET study of AM retrieval, failed to find any striking right side rCBF increases while memories were recalled but did find very marked increases in the left frontal lobe, corresponding to the findings of Conway, Pleydell-Pearce, and Whitecross (1999), who also observed increased activation of the left frontal lobes in the early phase of AM retrieval just prior to formation of a memory (cf. Nolde, Johnson, and Raye, 1998). Conway *et al.* (1999) further found in their PET study rCBF increases in the hippocampus bilat-erally. Collectively these findings illustrate the complexity of AM construction and suggest a flow of activation, over time, commencing with activation of networks in the left frontal lobes during the memory construction phase with a conjoint but slower rise of activation of networks in the right frontal lobes, followed by a switch in activation to the right temporofrontal networks as a memory is formed, and right side temporo-occipital activation as a memory is held in mind. Crucial sites in all of this are the right temporofrontal junction (Kroll *et al.*, 1997), the right temporo-occipital connections (Conway, 1996*a*; Conway and Fthenaki, 2000; Rubin and Greenberg, 1998), and the (right) hippocampal formation (Fink *et al.*, 1996).

I suggest that it is hippocampal networks which create and reinstate PRs. Activation in other areas reflects the operation of other processes in AM construc-tion. Conway and Pleydell-Pearce (2000) argue that the activation of left frontal networks present early in effortful retrieval reflects the operation of working-self goal structures in defining a retrieval template against which accessed knowledge can be evaluated. Networks at the right temporofrontal junction may be involved in accessing AM knowledge structures, in particular lifetime periods and general events stored, perhaps, in temporal cortex (Moscovitch, 1995). It is through these routes that hippocampal networks are accessed, and the role of these networks is to reactivate the summary records of sensory perceptual processing—the PRs—associated with the cue information already accessed at the general event and lifetime period level. This view is consistent with McClelland, McNaughton, and O'Reilly's (1995) proposal that hippocampal networks generate a 'condensed' code that summarizes sensory-perceptual processing activities which occurred in posterior sensory processing networks. Hippocampal networks, then, might generate a representation of moment-by-moment experience with each representation being triggered by a change in the contents of consciousness. But note that hippocampal networks are not considered to generate code for event-specific conceptual knowledge, that is, the meaning of an event or its gist. Representations of this latter type of AM knowledge are most probably generated by networks in neocortical sites in temporal and frontal lobes. The condensed hippocampal code, or PR, represents previous states of sensory-perceptual networks and, given that most AMs are encoded in terms of visual features it might be that the hippocampally generated PRs activate occipital networks via routes through temporal cortex. If this were the case, then, possibly, PRs would activate networks in visual recognition rather than localization systems (see Conway, 1996b; Rubin and Greenberg, 1998).

DIRECT AND GENERATIVE RETRIEVAL

A central aim of retrieval, then, is to access and activate a PR or set of PRs in order to have recollective experience and remember. An individual or associated set of PRs can only be accessed by a cue that activates their content and this cue can be generated in two different ways: either through the process of generative retrieval or by direct retrieval. The type of cue elaborated in generative retrieval uses the structure of AM to build a stable pattern of activation that will become the memory once unique PRs are accessed. In this case the activation spreads through AM knowledge structures and is channelled by control processes which shape the pattern by continuously revising and elaborating the cue on the basis of an evaluation of each item of accessed knowledge. Essentially this is a 'many-to-few' search which starts with access of a lifetime period followed by general events and, eventually, PRs. In contrast, a cue which is able to bypass the cue elaboration phase gains direct access to PRs and sensory-perceptual information. Conway and Bekerian (1987) collected lifetime period and general event information from people and then used these to cue memory retrieval. They found that retrieval times were far faster to personal cues compared to non-personal cues. In response to personal cues participants retrieved memories in about 2.5sec, whereas typical retrieval times to non-personal cues were two to three times this. Similarly, Fink *et al.* (1996), in their PET study, in which participants recalled cues drawn directly from descriptions of their own emotional memories, found no activation of left frontal networks suggesting that these highly AM-specific cues also bypassed the generation phase. In contrast, Conway *et al.* (1999) in a similar PET study but using cue words found extensive left frontal activation, as did Conway, Pleydell-Pearce, and Whitecross (1999), also using cue word prompted recall. It appears, then, that a sufficiently specific cue can bypass generative retrieval and give rise to spontaneous construction of a memory. This may occur because of the structure of AM in which PRs access a single general event which in turn accesses a lifetime period. Activation spreading from the PR will be channelled by the organization of AM knowledge into a distinct and stable pattern that forms a memory. In this way AMs are constructed in direct retrieval without the elaborate and extended processing characteristic of generative retrieval.

In everyday cognition, as patterns of activation constantly arise and dissipate in response to externally presented and internally generated cues, at some point a pattern will arise that can trigger the hippocampal networks to access PRs, and when this occurs a memory will be spontaneously formed. The hippocampus, too, may be constantly active, at least during conscious periods, and part of this activity may be the continuous encoding of new PRs. This hippocampal activity may keep regions of the whole PR highly active and render individual PRs in these locations highly accessible. Recent studies suggest that direct retrieval may occur with some moderate frequency in everyday life (twice per day in Berntsen, 1996), although with respect to the number of patterns spontaneously formed in the database the frequency is low. Many writers have described how specific cues have suddenly and spontaneously 'brought back' memories previously thought to have been forgotten, perhaps the most famous of these being Proust's recall of his childhood which was cued by the taste of a piece of tea-soaked madeleine cake (see Conway, 1997*a*, for a review of this and other cases). More recently and more dramatically cases of recovery from retrograde amnesia have been documented which apparently occurred in response to highly specific cues, cues which would have been likely to have had their effect by giving rise to sensory perceptual processing that could have gained direct access to a PR or set of PRs and so to memory as a whole (Lucchelli, Muggia, and Spinnler, 1995).

A potential problem, however, in recalling specific AMs, whether by direct or generative route, is that other processing sequences have to be suspended or run in attenuated form as limited resources are diverted into sustaining retrieval mode and promoting recollective experience. By way of illustration consider the nature of remindings during problem-solving when a specific AM comes to mind in response to the conceptual structure of a current problem or cued by some more specific detail (Blessing and Ross, 1996; Schank, 1986). No matter how the reminding is cued, the effect is to *halt* problem-solving while the memory is recalled and reviewed. Thus it is of some importance that remembering should be controlled, as uncontrolled, cue-driven, spontaneous, or direct recall would disrupt cognition and, ultimately, severely impair behaviour (see Sacks, 1985: 127, for an informal account of two transient cases of incessant and involuntary recall following temporal lobe damage). Of course, when this occurs in generative retrieval it is not generally a problem, as the act of remembering is intentional and other processing sequences have been powered down to facilitate memory construction. The problem of direct retrieval and other problems common to both types of retrieval are considered further in the next section.

THE CONTROL OF MEMORY BY THE SELF-MEMORY SYSTEM

If memories were *literal* records of the past, then when they were recalled perception of the present could, during the period of recall, be disrupted or even obliterated altogether. Thus one of the major issues confronting human memory is how to represent the past without overwhelming the representation of the present (failure to solve this problem may lead to the type of destabilizing intrusive recollection present in disorders such as PTSD). One solution would be to retain, in long-term memory, summary or abstract knowledge of experience which did not encompass sensory-perceptual details and, indeed, much AM knowledge appears to be of this type. People can recall that they took a holiday at resort X, worked for company Y, lived in town Z, etc., without any apparent change in consciousness or behaviour. It is only when PRs are accessed that attention becomes strongly focused internally and awareness of the present weakens. A conjecture I want to consider in relation to this is: *the point at which a memory is formed is a point where there is no conscious awareness of the external world.* Thus I suggest that in every act of fully constructing a memory there is a *moment of disengagement* from the present, which perhaps may persist for only a few seconds, and this occurs as PRs when accessed. Such disengagement might endure for longer periods in a weaker form (as in Proust's case) and, whether weak or strong, it is this loss of conscious contact with reality that makes remembering such a potentially destabilizing process. Thus, when remembering occurs, it seems that the rememberer at least briefly, and possibly for longer periods, becomes more or less disconnected from the present. Resources are diverted from current processing sequences to the memory and this may give rise to behavioural changes too, such as cessation of a current activity. Spontaneous remindings (Berntsen, 1996), often induce this rapid switching of attention from the external to the internal or from one form of processing to remembering, and in some rare cases the negative effects of spontaneous remembering (traumatic) experiences may be even more far-reaching and give rise to permanent physiological changes (Markowitsch *et al.*, 1998). Clearly, if we were constantly or even frequently reminded, then we could not function effectively, causing behavioural disruption and impairment of goal-attainment.

Conway and Pleydell-Pearce (2000) propose that one of the main roles of the

Self-Memory System (SMS) is to control remembering in such a way as to ensure that it does not disrupt other types of cognition. We assume that the accessibility of knowledge in long-term memory is determined by the degree to which it is compatible with currently active goal hierarchies in the working self: the greater the compatibility the greater the accessibility. We also assume that knowledge which is incompatible, that is, which if retrieved might destabilize active goals, is inhibited. However, the extent to which the SMS can inhibit incompatible knowledge is limited, and such knowledge cannot be permanently removed from the knowledge base. Also, the SMS may non-consciously monitor patterns of activation continuously arising and dissipating in the knowledge base in response to internally generated cues while at the same time maintaining a general inhibition on those networks (possibly located in the region of the temporofrontal junction: Kroll *et al.*, 1997) that could bring this knowledge into consciousness. Despite this monitoring and inhibitory control, the SMS can be disrupted by the activation of PRs and the spontaneous construction of a memory. When this occurs in response to a specific cue that activates PRs directly, bypassing the process of generative retrieval, then the SMS may be forced into retrieval mode, causing the disruption of other cognitive processes, especially those focused on external events.

Apart from this, hypothesized, direct inhibitory control of AM, there are a range of other ways in which the working self can control access to the knowledge base and determine the way in which new knowledge is integrated with existing knowledge. In *retrieval inhibition* (Bjork, Bjork, and Anderson, 1998), for example, one of the effects of retrieving a specific item of knowledge is the inhibition of closely associated items. Recalling a word such as 'apple' from a list that included other fruits, for example, orange, banana, etc., inhibits the later recall and recognition of these strongly associated items (M. C. Anderson, Bjork, and Bjork, 1994; M. C. Anderson and Spellman, 1995). The SMS could, then, inhibit access to goal-negative knowledge by directing access to closely related goal-neutral or goal-positive knowledge. Persistent use of selective access in this way might lead to a more permanent inhibition or overshadowing of goal-negative knowledge. In this way retrieval inhibition could be used to produce specific incidents of what Freud (1899) called 'screen memories' or in a more general way it might be used to shape a 'personal myth' (Kris, 1956/1975). A critical point about the process of retrieval inhibition, however, is that it shapes the accessibility of long-term knowledge but does not, directly, influence its availability (Tulving and Pearlstone, 1966). Thus inhibited knowledge can be retrieved if the inhibition is removed, and presumably this knowledge continues to influence cognition and behaviour implicitly (cf. Kihlstrom, 1997).

Freud (1915, 1926) on the basis of his clinical experience argued that two commonly encountered forms of repression were repression of the emotion associated with an experience with preserved access to other knowledge of that experience and the reverse, repression of the content of an experience with preserved access to the emotion. Retrieval inhibition could be used to bring about such a selective pattern of access by constant rehearsal of either the emotional or non-emotional aspects of an event. Recent findings by Schooler, Bendiksen, and Ambadar (1997) with individuals who recovered memories of childhood sexual abuse—in which both the abuse and amnesia were independently corroborated—lend some support to Freud's suggestion. The Schooler, Bendiksen, and Ambadar patients often knew, or provided evidence to others that they knew, that they had been sexually abused. This knowledge, however, appeared to be unassociated with any emotion and was itself difficult to bring to mind. Interestingly, in some of these patients the sudden recall of more detailed and emotional memories occurred in response to a specific cue, that is, by the direct access of PRs.

Another form of retrieval inhibition, and hence control of remembering, is demonstrated in the directed forgetting (DF) procedure. In this procedure a set of items are studied one after the other for later recall and, at some point, usually half-way through the set, the learner is instructed to forget all items already studied and concentrate on learning the remaining to-be-remembered (TBR) items. Powerful inhibition of the to-be-forgotten (TBF) list is observed in this type of procedure and this has been observed across a wide range of experiments that converge on the view that the entire set of TBF items is inhibited in response to the forget instruction (Bjork, 1989; see MacLeod, 1998, for a review). There are several features of the DF procedure that must be held constant if the inhibition is to be effective; of these, however, one of the most important is that there must be a period of acquisition of a second list of TBR items closely following the forget instruction and it may be this that triggers the inhibition of the TBF items. The goal structure of the SMS may use a process like this to control the retention of new knowledge by selecting PRs that carry goal-consistent knowledge and in so doing inhibiting goal-inconsistent knowledge (Conway *et al.*, 2000). Inhibited PRs are less likely to be recalled and, therefore, receive less rehearsal, and because of this they are only poorly integrated with structures in the knowledge base and have low accessibility. An extreme example of these DF effects was reported by Christianson and Engelberg (1997), who observed that a serial killer when reminded of one of his crimes would engage in intense acts of distraction such as repetitively reading aloud the contents from the label on a can of food until the dysphoric memories passed. More prosaically indulging in new learning in order to control the accessibility of recently acquired knowledge may be a fairly general and basic form of control of memory.

Inhibitory processes, triggered by goal compatibility, can then be used to determine the accessibility of different types of AM knowledge and in this way 'shape' individual memories as well as AM as a whole. There may, however, be more powerful, if less subtle, processes which can also be employed to control remembering. Ramachandran (1995) describes a study of patients with damage to the right parietal lobe resulting in paralysis of a limb. These patients were unaware (anosognosic) that they had a paralysed limb and so dense was their anosognosia that they believed themselves to be uninjured. For instance, one patient when asked to clap hands claimed that a paralysed armed had moved and that the sound of the clap was audible. Another patient subjected to a procedure that stimulated the vestibular system became aware that her arm was paralysed and recovered memories that indicated the paralysis had lasted for several days. Eight hours later, when questioned again about her arm, she then denied that there was any problem and, although she could recall her responses from earlier in the day, these had now been 'edited' to exclude any mention of the impaired arm. The function of these striking forms of denial and repression was to allow the belief that no injury had been sustained. In a patient with bilateral temporofrontal injuries Conway and Tacchi (1996) observed a similar phenomenon when the patient 'recalled' a set of confabulated memories that depicted a close and supportive history with certain key family members. The function of these persistent confabulations was to maintain a personal history that had been desired but which had not in fact occurred, and the relations with family members had been more marked by indifference than intimacy. Thus memories can be fabricated, denied, and/or repressed if the working self is sufficiently motivated and if, perhaps, the effects of brain damage are such that networks that might otherwise prevent such distortions are themselves damaged or inoperative (Conway and Tacchi, 1996; Ramachandran, 1995).

CONCLUSIONS

Perhaps it was no accident that Proust spent much of the latter half of his life in a cork-lined room in a Parisian apartment which he very rarely left. It was in this room that he wrote his masterpiece *A la recherche du temps perdu* working alone at night and sleeping through the day. The intensity of his writing about the past suggests that he had become a supreme exponent of recollective experience and expert in accessing sensory-perceptual details of the past. The cost of this was, of course, an almost complete retreat from daily life. According to the theory developed above this was inevitable as it would not have been possible to perform even the most routine of actions while maintaining such sustained and intense recollective experience. Autobiographical remembering, as this occurs every day, can destabilize the active goal structure of the working self, lead to premature cessation of actions, sudden changes in cognition and action, and disconnect attention from the present. It is, therefore, a volatile form of cognition which requires control. My closing suggestion is that the hippocampal, temporo-occipital, route to access of PRs is a phylogenetically older form of memory: one present in animals whose behaviour was largely externally driven by stimuli in the environment. By this view the primary function of PRs is to stimulate action by reminding the organism of very specific past experiences that are activated by some aspect of the present experience. Phylogenetically more recent systems, which have perhaps evolved to control the cue-driven automatic sensory-perceptual memory system, reduce the effects of PR activation by ensuring that activation occurs in the context of abstract knowledge of one's life, by the use of inhibitory processes, and by having a special state in which remembering occurs, retrieval mode, and a special signal that a mental representation is a memory, recollective experience.

REFERENCES

American Psychiatric Association (1986), *Diagnostic and Statistical Manual of Mental Disorders*, 3rd edn. *(DSM-IIIr)*. Washington, DC: APA.

ANDERSON, M. C., and SPELLMAN, B. A. (1995), 'On the status of inhibitory mechanisms in cognition: memory retrieval as a model case', *Psychological Review*, 102: 68–100.

—— BJORK, R. A., and BJORK, E. L. (1994), 'Remembering can cause forgetting: retrieval dynamics in long-term memory', *Journal of Experimental Psychology: Learning, Memory, and Cognition,* 20: 1063–87.

ANDERSON, S. J. (1993), 'Investigating the Structure of Autobiographical Memories'. Ph.D. diss., Department of Psychology, University of Lancaster, England.

—— (forthcoming), 'The role of working memory in autobiographical memory retrieval'. Under review.

—— and CONWAY, M. A. (1993), 'Investigating the structure of autobiographical memory', *Journal of Experimental Psychology: Learning, Memory, and Cognition,* 19: 1178–96.

BARSALOU, L. W. (1988), 'The content and organization of autobiographical memories', in U. Neisser and E. Winograd (eds.), *Remembering Reconsidered: Ecological and Traditional Approaches to the Study of Memory*. New York: Cambridge University Press, 193–243.

—— (1999), 'Perceptual symbol systems', *Behavioural and Brain Sciences*, 22: 577–609.

BERNTSEN, D. (1996), 'Involuntary autobiographical memories', *Applied Cognitive Psychology*, 10(5): 435–54.

BJORK, R. A. (1989), 'Retrieval inhibition as an adaptive mechanism in human memory', in H. L. Roediger III and F. I. M. Craik (eds.), *Varieties of Memory and Consciousness: Essays in Honor of Endel Tulving*. Hillsdale, NJ: Erlbaum, 309–30.

—— BJORK, E. L., and ANDERSON, M. C. (1998), 'Varieties of goal-directed forgetting', in J. M. Golding and C. M. MacLeod (eds.), *Intentional Forgetting: Interdisciplinary Approaches*. Mahwah, NJ: Erlbaum, 103–37.

BLESSING, S. B., and ROSS, B. H. (1996), 'Content effects in problem categorization and problem solving', *Journal of Experimental Psychology: Learning, Memory, and Cognition*, 22: 792–810.

BRENTANO, F. (1973), *Psychology from an Empirical Standpoint*. London: Routledge and Kegan Paul. (Original work published in 1874.)

BREWER, W. F. (1986), 'What is autobiographical memory?', in D. C. Rubin, (ed.), *Autobiographical Memory*. Cambridge: Cambridge University Press, 25–49.

—— (1988), 'Memory for randomly sampled autobiographical events', in U. Neisser and E. Winograd (eds.), *Remembering Reconsidered: Ecological and Traditional Approaches to the Study of Memory*. New York: Cambridge University Press, 21–90.

—— (1996), 'What is recollective memory?', in D. C. Rubin (ed.), *Remembering Our Past: Studies in Autobiographical Memory*. Cambridge: Cambridge University Press, 19–66.

BROWN, N. R., and SCHOPFLOCHER, D. (1997), 'Event clusters: an organization of personal events in autobiographical memory', *Applied Cognitive Psychology*, 12(4): 305–20.

BROWN, R., and KULIK, J. (1977), 'Flashbulb memories', *Cognition,* 5: 73–99.

BURT, C. D. B., WATT, S. C., MITCHELL, D. A., and CONWAY, M. A. (1998), 'Retrieving a sequence of specific autobiographical event components', *Applied Cognitive Psychology,* 12: 321–38.

—— MITCHELL, D. A., RAGGAT, P. T. F., JONES, C. A., and COWAN, T. M. (1996), 'A snap-shot of autobiographical memory retrieval characteristics', *Applied Cognitive Psychology*, 9: 61–74.

CERMAK, L. S., and O'CONNOR, M. (1983), 'The anterograde and retrograde retrieval ability of a patient with amnesia due to encephalitis', *Neuropsychologia,* 21: 213–34.

CHRISTIANSON, S.-A., and ENGELBERG, E. (1997), 'Remembering and forgetting traumatic experiences: a matter of survival', in Conway (1997*b*), 230–50.

CONWAY, M. A. (1990), *Autobiographical Memory: An Introduction*. Buckingham: Open University Press.

—— (1992), 'A structural model of autobiographical memory', in M. A. Conway, D. C. Rubin, H. Spinnler, and W. A. Wagenaar, (eds.), *Theoretical Perspectives on Autobiographical Memory*. Dordrecht: Kluwer Academic, 167–94.

—— (1993), 'Impairments of autobiographical memory', in H. Spinnler and F. Boller (eds.), *Handbook of Neuropsychology*, 8th edn. Amsterdam: Elsevier, 175–92.

—— (1995), *Flashbulb Memories*. Brighton, Sussex: LEA.

—— (1996*a*), 'Autobiographical memories and autobiographical knowledge', in D. C. Rubin (ed.), *Remembering Our Past: Studies in Autobiographical Memory*. Cambridge: Cambridge University Press, 67–93.

—— (1996*b*), 'Failures of autobiographical remembering', in D. Herrmann, M. Johnson, C. McEvoy, C. Hertzog, and P. Hertel (eds.), *Basic and Applied Memory: Theory in Context*. Hillsdale, NJ: Erlbaum, 295–315.

—— (1997*a*), 'Past and present: recovered memories and false memories', in Conway (1997*b*), 150–91.

—— (1997*b*) (ed.), *Recovered Memories and False Memories*. Oxford: Oxford University Press.

—— and BEKERIAN, D. A. (1987), 'Organization in autobiographical memory', *Memory & Cognition*, 15(2): 119–32.

—— and FTHENAKI, A. (2000), 'Disruption and loss of autobiographical memory', in L. Cermak (ed.), *Handbook of Neuropsychology*, 2nd edn.: *Memory and its Disorders*. Amsterdam: Elsevier, 257–88.

—— and PLEYDELL-PEARCE, C. W. (2000), 'The construction of autobiographical memories in the self memory system', *Psychological Review*, 107: 261–88.

—— and RUBIN, D. C. (1993), 'The structure of autobiographical memory', in A. F. Collins, S. E. Gathercole, M. A. Conway, and P. E. M. Morris (eds.), *Theories of Memory*. Hove: Erlbaum, 103–37.

—— and TACCHI, P. C. (1996), 'Motivated confabulation', *Neurocase*, 2: 325–39.

—— PLEYDELL-PEARCE, C. W., and WHITECROSS, S. (1999), 'The neuroanatomy of autobiographical memory: a slow cortical potentials (SCPs) study of autobiographical memory retrieval', Under review.

—— COLLINS, A. F., GATHERCOLE, S. E., and ANDERSON, S. J. (1996), 'Recollections of true and false autobiographical memories', *Journal of Experimental Psychology: General,* 125(1): 69–95.

—— GARDINER, J. M., PERFECT, T. J., ANDERSON, S. J., and COHEN, G. M. (1997), 'Changes in memory awareness during learning: the acquisition of knowledge by psychology undergraduates', *Journal of Experimental Psychology: General*, 126(4): 1–21.

—— HARRIES, K., NOYES, J., RACSMA'NY, M., and FRANKISH, C. R. (2000), 'On the disruption and dissolution of directed forgetting'. Under review.

—— TURK, J. D., MILLER, S. L., LOGAN, J., NEBES, R. D., MELTZER, C. C., and BECKER, J. T. (1999), 'The neuroanatomical basis of autobiographical memory', *Memory*, 7(5): 1–25.

EHLERS, A., and STEIL, R. (1995), 'Maintenance of intrusive memories in posttraumatic stress disorder: a cognitive approach', *Behavioural and Cognitive Psychotherapy*, 23: 217–49.

FINK, G. R., MARKOWITSCH, H. J., REINKEMEIER, M., BRUCKBAUER, T., KESSLER, J., and HEISS, W. (1996), 'Cerebral representation of own's own past: neural networks involved in autobiographical memory', *Journal of Neuroscience*, 18(13): 4275–82.

FLETCHER, P. C., SHALLICE, T., FRITH, C. D., FRACKOWIAK, R. S. J., and DOLAN, R. J. (1996), 'Brain activity during memory retrieval: the influence of imagery and semantic cueing' *Brain*, 119: 1587–96.

FREUD, S. (1899), *Screen Memories*, trans. J. Strachey, in *The Standard Edition of the Complete Psychological Works of Sigmund Freud*, ed. J. Strachey, iii. London: Hogarth Press, 1955.

—— (1915), *Repression.*, trans. C. M. Baines and J. Strachey, in *The Standard Edition of the Complete Psychological Works of Sigmund Freud*, ed. J. Strachey, xiv. London: Hogarth Press, 1957.

—— (1926) *Inhibition, Symptoms, and Anxiety*, trans. Alix Strachey, in *The Standard Edition of the Complete Psychological Works of Sigmund Freud*, ed. J. Strachey, xx. London: Hogarth Press, 1959.

GALTON, F. (1883), *Inquiries into Human Faculty and its Development*. London: Macmillan.

GARDINER, J. M. (1988), 'Functional aspects of recollective experience', *Memory & Cognition*, 16: 309–13.

—— and CONWAY, M. A. (1999), 'Levels of awareness and varieties of experience', in B. H. Challis and B. M. Velichkovsky (eds.), *Stratification of Consciousness and Cognition*. Amsterdam/Philadelphia: John Benjamin Publishing Co.

—— and RICHARDSON-KLAVEHN, A. (2000), 'Remembering and knowing', in E. Tulving and F. I. M. Craik (eds.), *Handbook of Memory*. Oxford: Oxford University Press.

—— RAMPONI, C., and RICHARDSON-KLAVEHN, A. (1997), 'On reporting recollective experience and "direct acces to memory systems" ', *Psychological Science*, 8: 391–4.

HAQUE, S., and CONWAY, M. A. (2000), 'Probing the process of autobiographical memory retrieval', *European Journal of Cognitive Psychology*.

HEUER, F., and REISBERG, D. (1990), 'Vivid memories of emotional events: the accuracy of remembered minutiae', *Memory & Cognition*, 18: 496–506.

HOWE, M. L. (1997), 'Children's memory for traumatic experiences', *Learning and individual differences*, 9: 153–74.

HUNKIN, N. M., PARKIN, A. J., BRADELY, V. A., BURROWS, E. H., ALDRICH, F. K., JANSARI, A., and BURDON-COPPER, C. (1995), 'Focal retrograde amnesia following closed head injury: a case study and theoretical account', *Neuropsychologia*, 33(4): 509–23.

JOHNSON, M. K., FOLEY, M. A., SUENGAS, A. G., and RAYE, C. L. (1988), 'Phenomenal

characteristics of memories for perceived and imagined autobiographical events',
Journal of Experimental Psychology: General, 117: 371–6.

KAPUR, N. (1993), 'Focal retrograde amnesia in neurological disease: a critical review',
Cortex, 29: 217–34.

KIHLSTROM, J. F. (1997), 'Suffering from reminiscences: exhumed memory, implicit
memory, and the return of the repressed', in Conway (1997*b*), 100–17.

KRIS, E. (1956), 'The personal myth: a problem in psychoanalytic technique', in *The
Selected Papers of Ernst Kris*. New Haven: Yale University Press, 1975.

KROLL, N. E. A., MARKOWITSCH, H. J., KNIGHT, R. T., and VON CRAMON, D. Y. (1997),
'Retrieval of old memories: the temporofrontal hypothesis', *Brain*, 120: 1377–99.

LANDAUER, T. K. (1975), 'Memory without organization: properties of a model with
random storage and undirected retrieval', *Cognitive Psychology,* 7: 495–531.

LUCCHELLI, F., MUGGIA, S., and SPINNLER, H. (1995), 'The "Petites Madeleines" phenomenon in two amnesic patients: sudden recovery of forgotten memories', *Brain*, 118:
167–83.

MCCLELLAND, J. L., MCNAUGHTON, B. L., and O'REILLY, R. C. (1995), 'Why there are
complementary learning systems in the hippocampus and neocortex: insights from the
successes and failures of connectionist models of learning and memory', *Psychological
Review*, 102 (3): 419–57.

MACLEOD, C. M. (1998), 'Directed forgetting', in J. M. Golding and C. M. MacLeod
(eds.), *Intentional Forgetting: Interdisciplinary Approaches*. Mahwah, NJ: Erlbaum,
1–57.

MARKOWITSCH, H. J., KESSLER, J., VAN DER VEN, C., WEBER-LUXENBURGER, G., ALBERS,
M., and HEISS, W.-D. (1998), Psychic trauma causing grossly reduced brain metabolism and cognitive deterioration', *Neuropsychologia*, 36: 77–82.

MARKUS, H., and NURIUS, P. (1986), 'Possible selves', *American Psychologist*, 41: 954–69.

—— and RUVOLO, A. (1989), 'Possible selves: personalized representations of goals', in
L. A. Pervin (ed.), *Goal Concepts in Personality and Social Psychology*. Hillsdale, NJ:
Erlbaum, 211–42.

MOSCOVITCH, M. (1995), 'Recovered consciousness: a hypothesis concerning modularity and
episodic memory', *Journal of Clinical and Experimental Neuropsychology*, 17: 276–90.

NADEL, L., and MOSCOVITCH, M. (1997). 'Consolidation, amnesia, and the hippocampal
complex', *Current Opinion in Neurobiology*, 7: 217–27.

NEWTSON, D. (1976), 'Foundations of attribution: the perception of ongoing behaviour', in
J. H. Harvey, J. W. Ickes, and R. F. Kidd (eds.), *New Directions in Attribution Research*,
i. Hillsdale, NJ: Erlbaum, 41–67.

NOLDE, S. F., JOHNSON, M. K., and RAYE, C. L. (1998), 'The role of prefrontal cortex
during tests of episodic memory', *Trends in Cognitive Sciences*, 2: 399–406.

O'CONNOR, M., BUTTERS, N., MILIOTIS, P., ESLINGER, P., and CERMAK, L. S. (1992), 'The
dissociation of anterograde and retrograde amnesia in a patient with Herpes encephalitis', *Journal of Clinical Experimental Neuropsychology*, 14: 159–78.

OGDEN, J. A. (1993), 'Visual object agnosia, prosopagnosia, achromatopsia, loss of visual
imagery, and autobiographical amnesia following recovery from cortical blindness:
Case M.H.', *Neuropsychologia*, 31: 571–89.

PROUST, M. (1955/1985), *Jean Santeuil*, trans. Gerard Hopkins. Harmondsworth: Penguin.

RAMACHANDRAN, V. S. (1995), 'Anosognosia in parietal syndrome', *Consciousness and
Cognition*, 4: 22–51.

ROBINSON, J. A. (1992), 'First experience memories: contexts and function in personal histories', in M. A. Conway, D. C. Rubin, H. Spinnler, and W. Wagenaar (eds.), *Theoretical Perspectives on Autobiographical Memory*. Dordrecht: Kluwer Academic, 223–39.

ROEDIGER, H. L., III, and McDERMOTT, K. B. (1995), 'Creating false memories: remembering words not presented in lists', *Journal of Experimental Psychology: Learning, Memory, and Cognition*, 21: 803–14.

ROSS, B. H. (1984), 'Remindings and their effects in learning a cognitive skill', *Cognitive Psychology*, 16: 371–416.

—— PERKINS, S. J., and TENPENNY, P. L. (1990), 'Reminding-based category learning', *Cognitive Psychology*, 22: 460–92.

RUBIN, D. C., and GREENBERG, D. L. (1998), 'Visual-memory-deficit amnesia: a distinct presentation and etiology', *Proceedings of the National Academy of Science*, 95: 1–4.

SACKS, O. (1985), *The man who mistook his wife for a hat*. London: Duckworth.

SCHACTER, D. L., NORMAN, K. A., and KOUSTAAL, W. (1998), 'The cognitive neuroscience of constructive memory', *Annual Review of Psychology*, 49: 289–318.

SCHANK, R. C. (1982), *Dynamic Memory*. New York: Cambridge University Press.

—— (1986), *Explanation Patterns: Understanding Mechanically and Creatively*. Hillsdale, NJ: Erlbaum.

SCHOOLER, J. W., BENDIKSEN, M., and AMBADAR, Z. (1997), 'Taking the middle line: can we accommodate both fabricated and recovered memories of sexual abuse?', in Conway (1997*b*), 251–92.

STUSS, D. T., and BENSON, D. F. (1986), *The Frontal Lobes*. New York: Raven Press.

SQUIRE, L. R. (1992), 'Memory and the hippocampus: a synthesis from findings with rats, monkeys, and humans', *Psychological Review*, 99: 195–231.

TULVING, E. (1972), 'Episodic and semantic memory', in E. Tulving and W. Donaldson (eds.), *Organization of Memory*. New York: Academic Press.

—— (1983), *Elements of Episodic Memory*. Oxford: Clarendon Press.

—— (1985), 'Memory and consciousness', *Canadian Psychologist*, 26: 1–12.

—— and PEARLSTONE, Z. (1966), 'Availability versus accessibility of information in memory for words', *Journal of Verbal Learning and Verbal Behaviour*, 5: 381–91.

—— and THOMSON, D. M. (1973), 'Encoding specificity and retrieval processes in episodic memory', *Psychological Review*, 80: 353–73.

—— SCHACTER, D. L., McLACHLAN, D. R., and MOSCOVITCH, M. (1988), 'Priming of semantic autobiographical knowledge: a case study of retrograde amnesia', *Brain and Cognition*, 8: 3–20.

VAN DER KOLK, B. A., and FISLER, R. (1995), 'Dissociation and the fragmentary nature of traumatic memories: overview and exploratory study', *Journal of Traumatic Stress,* 8: 505–25.

WHEELER, M. A., STUSS, D. T., and TULVING, E. (1995), 'Frontal damage produces episodic memory impairment', *Journal of the International Neuropsychological Society*, 1: 525–36.

—— (1997), 'Towards a theory of episodic memory: the frontal lobes and autonoetic consciousness', *Psychological Bulletin*, 121: 331–54.

WHITTEN, W. B., and LEONARD, J. M. (1981), 'Directed search through autobiographical memory', *Memory & Cognition*, 9: 566–79.

10

Out of the Past: Episodic Recall as Retained Acquaintance

M. G. F. Martin

When John Dean, former counsel to President Nixon, gave testimony before the House on the Watergate affair, his recall of particular incidents and the contents of conversations that had taken place in the Oval Office was so detailed and so complete that one of the senators dubbed him in disbelief 'the human tape recorder'. Dean denied this, explaining that he claimed no accuracy for the words he used, but merely that he could recount what had gone on and the import of what had been said. Unbeknownst to Dean, the affairs that he testified on had been secretly recorded by Nixon, so the case offers an unusual real-world experiment for work in memory. The psychologist Ulric Neisser (1981) undertook such a comparison of Dean's testimony and the tapes in a published survey. Neisser makes the observation that we have a kind of objective test for Dean's veracity: he was never prosecuted for perjury, nor criticized in any official reports for inaccuracy or misleading testimony; in general the conclusion has been that Dean told the truth. On the other hand, the comparison of tape and testimony reveals that there are significant discrepancies between the two. For example, in some cases, Dean supposes that participants in meetings spoke when they did not; and elsewhere he transposes some familiar turns of phrase and details of plans made from one meeting, in September, to another, earlier in March. So it is not that Dean merely fails to get the words right while still giving the gist, he does not even get the gist of particular meetings right. What he does get right is the general import of the various meetings. For example, at one Nixon does not declare his knowledge of the break-in and the intended cover-up, as Dean has him do, but in the context of the meeting it is clear that Nixon must know these things, even if he does not explicitly say so. In general, the narrative drift of the course of events as told by Dean is accurate, albeit sometimes the tale involves a bias towards Dean himself as occupying centre stage. So there is a clear sense in which Dean is not misleading the House committee, as long as we stand back from assuming that accuracy requires that he should be able to give us the correct details of particular events.

Neisser himself is very cautious about morals to draw from Dean's admittedly extraordinary situation. But one might think that the story invites one to draw a bold conclusion: we are tempted, so the claim might go, to suppose that, when we recount events that we have witnessed, we have some kind of distinctive access to the past. Dean would appear to be someone with an exceptionally good such memory for his past life. Yet what Neisser's case study suggests is that there is no such fundamental divide between memories which relate one to past episodes that one has witnessed, and memory simply as a store of information about the world. Dean was in a position to know many facts about the general course of events during the Watergate cover-up. When he came to recount particular episodes, he could rely on his general knowledge about what happened and about Nixon's character to reconstruct the episodes as they must have occurred. Rather than supposing that there is a fundamental contrast between episodic memory (or personal memory) of past events in one's life and semantic memory (or factual memory) by which one retains factual knowledge of the world, we should instead simply contrast the different kinds of use that retained information can be put to in memory tasks. In autobiographical memory, one uses the information one has about the past to construct narratives about oneself. Where memory is non-auto-biographical, one simply uses that information to describe how the world has been. We have the impression that Dean has special access to past events through having witnessed matters only because, in addition to his having at that time greater factual knowledge about those things than the committee he was report-ing to, the story that he told using those facts was a story that featured him as the central agent of the narrative.

Let us call this view about the differences among different kinds of memory *Constructivism*, sceptical as it is about a distinctive divide between memory of facts in general and of one's own past in particular.[1] Such a view need not be sceptical about the veracity, or standards of correctness for memory information (so it is not to be read as claiming that the past is a construct). Rather, construc-tion enters when we try to explain the difference between memories as reports of our own past episodes, versus memory as reflecting our general knowledge of the nature of past happenings. What is constructed is a narrative about one's past deeds: the contrast between personal memory and general knowledge is not laid down in the information retained but rather in the way that reports exploiting that information are constructed.

One will be opposed to this view, if one is inclined to defend the idea that there is an important cognitive distinction to be drawn between episodic memory which relates one to past episodes of which one was a witness, and other kinds of memory where one retains facts or abilities. That there is such a distinction to be drawn is the main thrust of Endel Tulving's work over the last thirty years (Tulving, 1972, 1982; Wheeler, Stuss, and Tulving, 1997). This approach within cognitive psychology to the study of memory stresses the important role that episodic memory plays in an account of memory and consciousness. The stress here on episodic memory echoes the centrality that the parallel notion of personal or direct memory has had in philosophical debates about the nature of memory. It is an interesting question how someone who takes as central the notion of episodic memory should respond to the Constructivist challenge, and indeed a

---

[1] For an example of such an approach to memory cf. Barclay, 1994.

nice question what they ought to say about the example of Dean. We shall return to Dean at the end of this chapter; for most of what follows I shall be concerned with the question of what substance there is in opposition to Constructivism as I have construed it here. What content is there to this idea of episodic memory as a special kind of contact with the past? What is it about this idea that makes it inconsistent with the claim that we simply construct a self-narrative on the basis of general information about the world when we recount autobiographical memories?

Within the philosophical discussion of memory, there are certain strategies of transcendental argument aimed at showing the fundamental role of episodic memory in our conception of being related to an objective world.[2] But that is not the concern here. I want to start at a more elementary level and ask why we might initially be resistant to simply accepting Constructivism. What is important about our conception of episodic memory? Can such a conception be made coherent?

In a recent survey paper, Tulving's research group offers a suitably grand picture of what is so central about episodic memory:

One of the most fascinating achievements of the human mind is the ability to mentally travel through time. It is somehow possible for a person to relive experiences by thinking back to previous situations and happenings in the past and to mentally project oneself into the anticipated future through imagination, daydreams and fantasies. In the everyday world, the most common manifestations of this ability can be referred to as 'remembering past happenings'. Everyone knows what this phrase means and what it is like to reflect on personal experiences, past or future, that are not part of the present. (Wheeler, Stuss, and Tulving, 1997: 331)

This suggests that what is central about episodic memory is that it is one component of our experience of time. That suggestion seems to be an interesting echo of a thought that Bertrand Russell had in his first account of memory in 1912, which he soon came to abandon. For at that time Russell took as central to his account of the mind the role of acquaintance with things, and he included on his list of types of acquaintance, acquaintance with the past through memory:

It is obvious that we often remember what we have seen or heard or had otherwise present to our senses, and that in such cases we are still immediately aware of what we remember, in spite of the fact that it appears as past and not present. This immediate knowledge by memory is the source of all our knowledge concerning the past: without it, there could be no knowledge of the past by inference, since we should never know that there was anything past to be inferred. (Russell, 1912: 26)

So Tulving and Russell would seem to give us a direct answer to why we should be resistant to accepting the Constructivist picture straight off: in episodic memory we have experience or acquaintance with the past; we lack such acquaintance in mere semantic memory. If there is no essential difference between

---

[2] A starting point here is Strawson, 1966; for a recent application with the above concerns in mind see Campbell, 1997.

episodic and semantic memory, but only a difference in the way information retained is used, either as a story about one's past self, or as an account of how the world in general is, then no such memory has a special link to the past. There can be nothing which counts as experience of the past. If Constructivism is correct, Tulving and Russell are both wrong.

Yet before we can even address that conflict, we need to ask whether there could be anything that counted as a distinctive experience of the past or acquaintance with the past. For certainly Russell's 1912 picture of memory is commonly taken in the philosophical literature to have been incoherent. Russell himself had repudiated it along with the notion of acquaintance by the time he offered a new theory of memory in *The Analysis of Mind* in 1921. In this he has been followed by many other commentators on the problems of memory.[3] So, if Tulving's conception of 'mental time travel' is tarred with the same brush, then we have no significant alternative to Constructivism.

The aim of this chapter is to defend the idea that there is a distinctive phenomenology of encounter with past against a charge of incoherence. In the first section, I shall focus on a group of assumptions embedded in our ordinary talk of memory and its connections with knowledge and other cognitive achievements. Philosophers often assume that Russell's picture of memory as acquaintance with the past is driven solely by Russell's strange theoretical assumptions about knowledge. I shall argue that our common-sense conception of memory commits us to the idea of episodic memory as retention of past apprehension. In the second part of the chapter, I turn to the challenge that Russell and others have raised against the idea that we have any distinctive experience of the past in having episodic recall. I shall argue that the challenge rests on a false assumption about the nature of sensation and imagery, and in rejecting that assumption I shall sketch an alternative conception of memory imagery and experiential recall. This, in turn, will give us a way of fleshing out the idea that we have some kind of experience of past in episodic memory consonant both with common sense and Tulving's theoretical approach. In the concluding section I turn back to the challenge that Constructivism poses for this picture, and briefly sketch what I take the consequences of that dispute are for the conception of memory here defended.

I

Tulving is noteworthy among psychologists of memory, in that the divisions he draws among kinds of memory correspond to distinctions drawn by philosophers in their discussions of memory. And arguably the distinctions he makes echo

---

[3] Russell appears to have abandoned the view by 1917, see Pears, 1975 for discussion of this. For criticisms of ideas related to the 1912 view, see Ayer, 1956; Anscombe, 1974; Pears 1975, 1990. An exception to this attack is Evans, 1982: chs. 5 and 8, where Evans develops the idea of an information link with the past, analogous to Russell's idea of acquaintance; Judson, 1987–8, exploits Evans's ideas in a critique of Pears.

distinctions we are ordinarily inclined to note in our ordinary speech about remembering or recall. Where Tulving writes of episodic memory, semantic memory, and procedural memory, philosophers have talked of personal or direct memory, factual memory, and practical or habitual memory. Of these, philosophers have been most interested in personal/direct memory, what Tulving more aptly calls episodic memory. Typically, such memory is singled out through two marks. First, only such memories can be properly reported by using the form, '*S* remembers/recalls [*x*] *f*-ing', as in 'Mary remembers John falling asleep in the talk', 'Jo remembers being inoculated for smallpox'. Secondly, it is held that such statements about memory can be true only where the person remembering meets what we can call the Previous Awareness Condition: that one can remember an event only where one previously witnessed it or was the conscious agent of it (Shoemaker, 1984: 19; Wheeler, Stuss, and Tulving, 1997: 333).

The focus of discussion here has been on one aspect of the Previous Awareness Condition, that the original witness should be the very same the person as is now remembering. It has been asked whether this condition is merely a prejudice embedded in English and similar natural languages, or whether the way we talk about memory reveals something interesting about the nature of memory itself. Those who wish to appeal to the notion of psychological continuity, and in particular to the role of episodic memory in such continuity, as central to an account of personal identity have been keen to argue that the identity condition is mere convention; their opponents have questioned whether we can make sense of the Previous Awareness Condition without this identity condition attached.[4] But few have stopped to ask why the locution in question should be associated with the Previous Awareness Condition, or indeed why this condition should hold for any form of memory at all.

Just as some psychologists have questioned whether there is any unity to the notions of consciousness and attention (cf. Allport, 1992), we can ask what the varieties of memory that we mark out in natural language have in common that should make them all memories. I want to suggest that we can give at least a limited answer to this question which reveals why the Previous Awareness Condition should apply to memories which are properly reported with the locution indicated above. Such reflection on the concept of memory in general will lead us to the idea of episodic memory as relating us to past experience as past in a way which echoes Russell's conception of memory as acquaintance with the past.

Consider the following range of locutions:

(1) Mary remembers that Pompeii was destroyed by a pyroclastic flow
(2) Sam recalls what the number is to open the safe
(3) Ellen remembers where to put the key when going out
(4) Arnold recalls the view from the Giralda
(5) Sophie remembers Bernard

---

[4] Shoemaker, 1984, introduces the idea of quasi-memory as a notion of memory with the identity condition removed; Parfit, 1985, exploits the idea further in constructing an account of personal identity; Evans, 1982: ch. 7, and Wiggins, 1995, attack the very notion of quasi-memory as incoherent.

In each case we can replace the words 'remembers' or 'recalls' with 'knows' or 'knew' and preserve significance—that is, the resulting sentences make perfect sense—and in many of these cases, the resulting sentences are true if the original is. From this, one might first conjecture that the objects of memory (i.e. the 'grammatical' objects of memory ascriptions—what can be remembered) are simply the same objects as those of knowledge (what can be known). It is common for philosophers to distinguish various kinds of knowledge. There is propositional or factual knowledge, where one knows that or whether something is the case; practical knowledge, where one knows how to do something; and knowledge by acquaintance, where one knows some individual, place, or thing. Factual or semantic memory would just seem to be the correlate in memory of the former. Procedural memory or habitual memory seems to mirror practical knowledge. And as we have knowledge of things so we can remember them.

But one might also conjecture a tighter link than just this. For people can only remember that something is or was the case where we can also say of them that they know it. This suggests that in the case of factual memory, remembering is simply retained knowledge, or knowledge preserved.[5] However, this proposal needs some clarification if it is not to be trivially falsified: that a subject knows something at the time of recall, and must previously have known it in order to recall it, does not require that he or she know it throughout the intervening period. For example, a subject may forget something and then later recall it. In general, there seems to be an accessibility condition on knowledge, so that where a subject simply cannot answer a relevant question when needed (not necessarily verbally—the answer to the question may require appropriate action from them guided by the answer), then we are inclined to say that the subject does not know the fact in question, and must have forgotten it. Such forgetting is quite consistent with later recall, and hence with the knowledge having been retained, in the relevant sense of retention.[6]

However, a focus on factual knowledge and memory obscures the complexity of the link. For it need not be true in all cases of remembering that the occasion

[5] Cf. Squires, 1969 and Williamson, 1995, who suggests that 'remembering that p', like 'can see that p', is a determination of the determinable knowledge. The idea that memory is a form of preservation is also a central theme in Burge, 1993a and 1997. This conception of factual memory is attacked by Harman in (1973: ch. 12). See also the critical discussion of this idea in Peacocke, 1986: ch. 10.

[6] A related type of example can be constructed from so-called cases of lost knowledge—for this idea see Harman, 1973; Ginet, 1980; Dretske and Yourgrau, 1983. Arguably, one can come to fail to know something without having forgotten it, but simply through acquiring misleading evidence which one reasonably takes to refute what one knew. I may mislead you into thinking that you don't know that *The Family of Darius Presented to Alexander* is in the National Gallery, since you can give me allegedly conclusive evidence that it is merely a copy the museum possesses. If convinced by you, I may no longer be said to know that the painting is there. On the other hand, if later I discover your malicious falsehoods, I may then be said to remember that the painting is in the gallery, and so to have retained the knowledge after all that I had earlier acquired. The issue also has bearing on Peacocke's critique of a pure preservative conception of factual knowledge. An irresponsible or unreliable subject who is as liable to exploit mere false opinion as knowledge acquired may not be counted as having proper access to the knowledge that he or she would otherwise have retained through memory.

of recall counts as a case of current knowledge, and that it is bound to do so with factual memory reveals something distinctive of our grasp of facts as opposed to those cases where we know, or are acquainted with, things. (Note the point here concerns knowing an individual or place, not knowledge *of* or *about* an individual or place.) Spurred to think about my schooldays, I may recall several of my classmates. If I have lost touch with them, and not concerned myself in the interval with their progress in the world, then I might comment that I did know S or X but that I know them no longer. On the other hand, I can certainly correctly report myself as remembering them. The contrast is even clearer when we turn to our relation to the dead. I cannot now know my maternal grandmother, for she died twenty years ago, but I did know her, in contrast to my paternal grandmother who died when I was first born. On the other hand I can certainly remember my maternal grandmother, and cannot remember my paternal one.

At least part of the difference here comes from the difference in the *object* of knowledge—that one knows an individual or place rather than a fact. For objects and places exist within time and can come to be, alter, and cease to exist over time. In contrast we tend to think of facts as immutable and eternal; if they hold as things actually are, then there is no time at which it will no longer be the case that something was true of a particular time. Now in relation to factual knowledge, it has often been pointed out that we think that someone who has knowledge thereby has to be sensitive to the holding of a certain truth if they are to be credited with knowledge of it: they must track this truth in order to know it.[7] Since facts are immutable, the conditions for tracking a truth at one time need not be different at any later time, so there seems no particular extra condition which must be met in order for one to continue to count as knowing the fact. We require more when it comes to knowing individuals or places, rather than merely knowing of them, or facts concerning them. In general (but not invariably, for this is a context-sensitive matter) knowing an individual requires having met them, and knowing a place requires having visited. But since both individuals and places may change, continued knowledge of an object or place seems to require more: that one be sensitive to or track alterations in that object or place. Where one fails so to track, then one may once have known the person or place, but can no longer be said to do so. For example, I do not know now anyone that I first went to school with; I once knew the town of Camberley but no longer do. Furthermore, where an individual dies, or a place is destroyed, then while one may have known them, one can no longer do so: as noted above, while I once knew my maternal grandmother, I cannot know her now simply because she died twenty years ago.

If we apply the idea of memory as preservative to knowledge by acquaintance, this would suggest that occasions of recall are examples of knowing the

---

[7] The idea that there is a tracking condition on propositional knowledge is developed in detail by Robert Nozick (1981: ch. 3). One tracks the truth of a proposition p, where it is true of one that one wouldn't believe p were it not the case that p, while one would still believe p to be so, given relevantly similar circumstances to the actual one in which p does hold.

individual or place recalled. But our discussion gives us reason to deny this: I recall my grandmother but do not now know her. However, this does not over- throw the original suggestion, but reveals an extra aspect to it. What is preserved is one's original knowledge of them, one's knowing of them when they were alive and still in appropriate contact with them. In the case of factual memory, past knowledge is sufficient for current knowledge, so there can be no contrast here; but as we have seen, the same is not so for knowledge by acquaintance. In this case, preserving knowledge from the past does not amount to current knowledge, it is rather current recall of an object with which one had acquaintance.

Consider, in turn, the case of episodic memory. The first point to note in this case is that we cannot conceive of such remembering as the preservation of *knowledge*, for one cannot have known what one now recalls in episodic memory.[8] In cases such as:

(6) Mary remembers John falling asleep in the talk

where the derived nominal here picks out an event or episode which is being recalled, there is no well-formed substitution using a term for knowledge.

(7) *Mary knows/knew John falling asleep in the talk

is simply not English. Likewise while

(8) Jo recalls being inoculated for smallpox

makes perfect sense,

(9) *Jo knows/knew being inoculated for smallpox

is not something that can be used to say anything in English, although one might have some sense of what someone using it might be getting at. While this lack of parallel might incline someone sceptical of a general shape to the concept of memory to reject the idea that there is any role for the idea of preservation or retention of something in remembering, we should pursue the idea further, for in doing so we will highlight something of interest about the concept of knowledge itself.

Note, though that while we can find no knowledge ascriptions of an appropri- ate form that are true at an earlier time of the person remembering, there are other truths about them which seem relevant to the truth now of a memory ascription. For the Previous Awareness Condition itself would direct us towards an obvious class of statements: on the one hand, statements about what the person remem- bering has perceived:

(10) Mary heard John falling asleep in the talk;

---

[8] Roger Squires notes that episodic memory poses this problem for the general proposal that memory is retained knowledge, but heroically attempts to retain the thesis unmodified (1969: 188–90).

on the other, statements about the person remembering as conscious agent, or about events through which the subject lived:[9]

(11) Jo was/lived through being inoculated for smallpox.

Using a variant on Russell's talk of acquaintance, let us talk of these all together as cases of *apprehension*.[10] We apprehend events through either perceiving the events or through being their conscious agent. Episodic memory, then, traces back not to past knowledge, but past apprehension.

We might then restate the general condition on memory as that of preserving either past knowledge or past apprehension. Put so baldly, the proposal may seem objectionably *ad hoc*: why should knowledge and apprehension be grouped together in this way to be preserved for posterity in memory? That worry will be laid to rest, if we can show some appropriate unity between knowledge and apprehension.

On this matter, first note that we are reluctant, to say the least, to talk of knowing events or episodes. I can know Paris, and I can have known the exhibition *Picasso's Picassos* drawn from the contents of the Musée d'Orsay, but I cannot be said to have known the Vietnam War, I can only have lived through it, or witnessed it (see footnote for an important qualification, though).[11] Why shouldn't we be able to know events?[12] To answer this we need both to reflect on the link between apprehension and knowledge, and to think about the kind of cognitive contact we generally assume we can have with events. Apprehension is episodic: seeing, feeling, tasting something are all events or occurrences. Knowledge itself is a standing condition—although one can come to know something at a particular time, knowledge itself is not episodic. Nevertheless the state of knowledge is closely linked to episodes of apprehension: one must have apprehended individuals at some time to know them, and to continue knowing them one must have the possibility of further apprehension of them. Now, while we can apprehend events through perceiving them or living through them, in general we do not take

---

[9] Note that in order to count as remembering an event, one must have been conscious during it or witnessed it. Even if it had happened to one, one could not recall being abducted by extra-terrestrials, if the abduction involved being unconscious throughout. Cf. the discussion of the concept of experience in Hinton, 1973: ch 1.

[10] The early sense-datum theorists such as Price used the terms acquaintance and apprehension pretty much interchangeably: see Price, 1932: ch. 1. But in English the terms mark a difference significant for our discussion. Apprehension unlike acquaintance is episodic. Acquaintance like knowledge seems to be a standing state: one can be acquainted with someone over a long period, involving a number of different encounters with him or her; it sounds odd to claim that one was acquainted with someone for only five minutes. Russell slides over this distinction in his use of the term 'acquaintance' for something, which by his own lights seems to require something episodic.

[11] There is a sense in which a historian can know the Vietnam War but not the Korean War without having lived through either, simply from knowing enough about it. In this sense of knowing an event, one cannot properly be said to have known the event, the locution is much closer to our talk of knowledge of or knowledge about a subject matter.

[12] Note that we can hardly think of the question here as one about logical form: there seems nothing different in form between the noun phrase 'the war in the East' and 'the exhibition of Picasso's works', yet one can know the latter but not the former.

ourselves to be in a position to re-apprehend them. Hence, apprehension of an event is not a precursor to a standing condition of cognitive contact with what is apprehended, and so does not lead to knowing the event, although one will, of course, tend to acquire knowledge of the event.[13]

There is reason to think of apprehension and knowledge as closely connected—the former is the episodic counterpart of the latter standing condition. Taken together the two have in common that they are forms of cognitive contact with an object. It is not *ad hoc*, therefore, to suppose that the general preservative function of memory applies across the range of cognitive contact, to both standing conditions and episodes. Just as we can differentiate the kinds of cognitive contact and the objects that they have, so too we can differentiate the kinds of memories that result. We can then conceive of memory in general as the preservation of cognitive contact in general and not just the narrower condition of knowledge.

This proposal easily distinguishes the kinds of memory we started with and the conditions on them. With factual memory the antecedent cognition is that of factual knowledge, where knowing a fact does not seem to require apprehension of any of the objects or events that the fact concerns.[14] Hence, we would predict that it is not a condition on remembering a fact that one has had any particular prior episode of apprehending the fact in question. On the other hand, memory of individuals or places seems to require that there has been a particular form of past knowledge: knowledge by acquaintance with the individual or place. In most such cases knowledge by acquaintance derives from apprehension of the individual, or place, in question, but commonly one will have encountered them more than once. Having had the knowledge may require that there has been apprehension in the past, but the knowledge itself need not rest on any one particular such encounter. The corresponding memory, then, need not trace back to any particular episode recalled. When we come to episodic memory, on the other hand, precisely what is being remembered is a previous event. For reasons rehearsed above, the only antecedent cognitive contact one can have had with an event is apprehension and not knowledge, so it is only this which can be required in the antecedent conditions required for such memory. This is just what the Previous Awareness Condition expresses. We can, after all, see it merely as a special case of a more general feature of memory.

---

[13] At first sight, it may seem easy to think of cases of re-encounter with events: one might see the ball hit the stumps, and then seconds later hear it; one might have intermittently watched the funeral of Diana on the television; one might have gone for a number of tours of the Vietnam War, and in the interval isolated oneself entirely from any information about it. But, interestingly, these still seem to contrast with our talk of apprehensions of continuants. In the latter case the various viewings of an object are not intuitively aggregatable into a superordinate event, one's viewing of the object. In contrast, there is such an event for the viewing of any event. For example, there is an event of one's viewing of Diana's funeral, which seems to take all the viewings of parts of the funeral as something like proper parts. The relevant notion of re-apprehension here requires that the events in question be entirely distinct and not related as parts to any superordinate viewing.

[14] *Contra* Russell's notorious suggestion that one must be acquainted with all constituents of a proposition to understand it: Russell, 1912: ch. 5.

The picture of episodic memory we have ended up with from the discussion above has echoes both of Tulving's idea that we have mental time travel with episodic memory, and of Russell's talk of acquaintance with the past. In the case of factual memory, what is preserved is the past knowledge of the fact. Since no further condition for knowledge need be met, one's past knowledge of fact can also be one's current knowledge of the same fact. As we have seen, in the case of cognition of things within time, objects, and events, the assimilation of past cognition to current cognition does not necessarily hold. We may think of our memory of a place as retaining the knowledge we had of the place, but at best that is past knowledge, and by itself is not sufficient to show that we now still do know the place in question. So, when we turn to episodic memory, if we are to ask what it is that is retained in such memory, the answer would, by parity, seem to be the past apprehension of the event now recalled. One's memory of the episode is simply the retained apprehension or acquaintance with a past happening. It has an experiential component in the idea of retention of apprehension, and it has a temporal component in the suggestion that what is retained is past apprehension, not current perception.

We should not accuse either Tulving or Russell of simply coming up with some theoretical notion of experience of or acquaintance with the past which has no grounding in our ordinary thoughts about memory. If their conceptions of memory are problematic, then there may equally be something problematic about how we ordinarily think of memory. So, is there something suspicious about the idea of retention of past experience?

II

Remembering someone is not the same as now knowing him or her: one can remember those who one does not now know. Likewise, episodic memory is not now apprehension of a past episode, but rather the retention of a past apprehension of that episode. But what sense can we make of this distinction between retained past apprehension and current apprehension?

Here is an arch example illustrating the need to draw the distinction. Suppose Miriam the astronaut bids her lover a fond farewell. Since she is never to return, NASA have set up an intricate system of image intensifiers and reflectors along the path of her journey, so that at various stages she can catch a glimpse again of her lover's fond farewell, by looking in the right direction towards a mirror. We allow that we can see the sun and the stars, even though what we see on these occasions is very distant and in our past. So it is conceivable in this situation that we should count Miriam as continuing to see her lover's farewell when she looks in the right direction. NASA have offered Miriam a way of sustaining possible apprehension of that event receding into her past, but they do not thereby seem to give her a new form of recall of her lover's farewell. So, one can ask, what is the difference between sustained apprehension, courtesy of NASA, and retained apprehension courtesy of one's powers of recall?[15]

Of course, Miriam's sustained powers of apprehension of her lover's farewell differ markedly in their causal ancestry from how we normally conceive of recall. The causal mechanisms which make it possible for her to catch a glimpse of fond tears again and again lie outside of her own body, and rely on the planning and design of NASA physicists. By contrast, her own powers of recall of the same event rely on mechanisms internal to her body. Some philosophers have claimed that the idea of a memory trace is in play within our conception of memory, and in that case Miriam's sustained apprehension of her lover's farewell will fail to be memory for at least that reason (C. B. Martin and Deutscher, 1966: 186–91).

Nevertheless, this does not get quite to the key problem here. The above consideration does not bear directly on the character of Miriam's state of mind. Wheeler, Stuss, and Tulving, in talking of 'mental time travel', emphasize the idea that in episodic memory one has a different kind of experience in recall from that which one has in perception of the world around one. Inasmuch as we can describe both Miriam's recall of her lover's farewell and her glimpse in the image intensifier as cases of apprehension of the same event, we play down any experiential difference between them. In both cases we simply have the apprehension of a past event. But just as retained past knowledge of an individual is not current knowledge of them, retention of past apprehension is not current apprehension either. But what can the difference amount to? If episodic memory is to be the experience of the past, and play any role in explaining our grasp of the concept of the past, as Russell claims it must, then in memory we need to have experience of past events as being past.

It is in the light of this demand that the whole conception of episodic memory as giving one some distinctive experience of the past is liable to seem incoherent. In fact, in *The Problems of Philosophy*, Russell states the essence of the problem that has been repeated again and again in discussions of this idea. At one point, Russell insists that memory and memory imagery need to be sharply distinguished:

memory of an object is apt to be accompanied by an image of the object, and yet the image cannot be what constitutes the memory. This is easily seen by merely noticing that the image is in the present, whereas what is remembered is known to be in the past. (Russell, 1912: 66)

Russell's argument here turns on a particular assumption, one which he shares with many of the parties to this debate who otherwise disagree with him. This is an assumption about the nature of imagery, sensation, or occurrent experiential aspects and what role they can play in perception, imagery, or experiential recall. In this context, the assumption is just that anything that deserves to be called

---

[15] Given our discussion above, we have an answer concerning our talk of why we would not count this as *re*-apprehension. The glimpses in mirrors would all count as parts of the one superordinate event of seeing her lover's farewell. But that point alone would not address the challenge in the text.

imagistic in the episode of recall must simply be an aspect of the present event describable purely in terms of the present moment.

The key problem that this assumption generates here can be posed as a dilemma. If we hold on to the idea of memory as retention of what was experienced in the past, then we should be inclined to suppose that the recall is more faithful to the original event the more it matches in character the initial experience which is allegedly retained. In that case, one might suggest, the current episode of recall should be just like a case of current perception in experiential character if it is entirely faithful. This both goes against our knowledge of episodes of recall, which in general are very different in character from ordinary perception, and against the suggested role of such recall as experience of the past. This may incline one to insist that there must be some essential phenomenological distinction between episodes of recall and episodes of current apprehension. But this forces one onto the second horn of the dilemma. To the extent that one insists on there being a genuine sense of past associated with the episode of recall, then one will not locate that in what is retained from any antecedent experience, but rather in some characteristic of the current episode of recall. For when Miriam originally saw her lover's farewell, the experience then had no character of pastness associated with it: the events were all as if located in the present. Any sense of the past comes to be associated only with an episode of recall, not with the original experience recalled. Hence, on this conception, the idea of acquaintance with a past episode as being in any way explanatory of a sense of pastness drops out, and we may as well appeal to something which can perfectly well exist simply in the present. We seem to be faced with a choice: either we insist on the idea of episodic memory as retained apprehension or experience, in which case we can have no distinctive experience of the past as past; or we insist on the idea that the episodic memory has a distinctive phenomenology associated with the past, but thereby give up the idea that this has anything to do with retaining something from earlier experience.[16]

This, I suggest, is the central challenge to Russell's idea of memory as acquaintance with the past. Without an answer to it, we can have no way of literally spelling out the idea of episodic memory as the retention of past apprehension in the way that we might think of factual memory as the retention of past knowledge. Many philosophers have thought this simply to be a problem about Russell's own theory. But our observations in the last section suggest that this is not so. If there is a problem for Russell here, there is a problem for the common conception of episodic memory we have, at least as reflected in our ordinary talk about memory and recall. So the challenge would seem to suggest that there is something incoherent in the way we ordinarily think about episodic recall. Before we rush to such a pessimistic conclusion, we need to look more closely at the assumptions this argument turns on.

---

[16] Cf. also Ayer's attack on the role of imagery in memory (1956: 138–42).

III

The dilemma posed above will be unanswerable as long as we are held by one particular conception of the role that imagery, sensation, or, more generally, occurrent experiential elements can play in mental episodes such as those of perception, imagery, or experiential recall. The dilemma is imposed on us, once we assume that if memory is to be the retention of earlier apprehension, then the experiential element of the episode of recall and the original perceptual experience recalled would have to be the very same. Once we grant this assumption, our options for explaining the phenomenological differences between the two kinds of episode are heavily restricted. If we conceive of the experiential element as purely sensational or qualitative, then the differences could amount to no more than differences in degree of intensity or determinacy of the qualities. On the other hand, if we conceive of the experiential element in representational terms, then the differences can amount only to how vague or replete the information contained in the one or the other episode can be. Since these are at best differences in degree and not kind, one may then be inclined to insist that any distinction in kind between episodic recall and perceptual experience would have to be drawn in terms of something extrinsic to the experiential character of the episodes; namely in the kind of functional roles that they play within the mind, or in the associations they have with particular beliefs about the present or the past.

However, we can simply resist the dilemma if we adopt a different conception of the way in which the experiential or phenomenological can be common among perception, imagery, and remembering. We should think of experience, imagery, and memory as being phenomenologically the same not in terms of literally sharing experiential properties, but in virtue of a representational or intentional connection between them—imagery is experientially the same as perception through being the representation of such a perceptually experiential event; and memory can be experientially the same as perception through being the representational recall of such an experiential encounter.

In developing this alternative conception of the link between perception and imagery it is interesting to look at a very different tradition on these matters, to be found in Sartre's development of the phenomenological tradition. Towards the end of *The Psychology of Imagination*, Sartre asserts:

Now, the hypothesis of the imaginative consciousness is radically different from the hypothesis of the consciousness of the real. This means that the type of existence of the object of the image *as long as it is imagined*, differs in nature from the type of existence of the object grasped as real. And, surely, if I now form an image of Peter, my imaginative consciousness includes a certain position of the existence of Peter, insofar as he is now at this very moment in Berlin or London. But while he *appears to me as an image*, this Peter who is in London *appears to me absent*. This absence in actuality, this essential nothingness of the imagined object is enough to distinguish it from the object of perception. (Sartre, 1991: 261)

It is clear from this that Sartre is rejecting the background assumption that we isolated above: that imagistic experience or consciousness is a neutral core common to perception and imagery. According to him we must deny that there is a form of experiential consciousness common to both perception and imagination. On the other hand, it is not entirely clear what it is that he wishes to put in its place. Sartre's talk of Peter having different types of existence is hard to make much sense of. The idea that there are different types of existence is sometimes proposed in relation to discussion of the contrast between figments of fiction and concrete objects such as tables and chairs, or between the latter and such abstract things as numbers or sets. Yet in such contexts it is difficult to make any more sense of this idea than in terms of the claim that there are just different kinds of object, all of which exist in just the same, unequivocal way. Sartre's position cannot be reformulated in these terms, though. For it is not as if Peter can be a different object from Peter. Yet according to Sartre the very same individual has a different type of existence as imagined and as perceived.

I want to develop out of Sartre's suggestion a way of making sense of this without having recourse to different types of existence. (The terms in which it will be developed, however, may well be unacceptable to followers of the phenomenological tradition in philosophy.) In this I draw on a suggestion made some time ago by John Foster (1982: 101–3), that we should see the fundamental difference between sensory experience and imagery in terms of the way one's state of mind relates one to its objects. The idea here is that although perceptual experience and imagery may coincide with respect to the objects of experience, the events or qualities which are present to the mind, they will still differ in the manner by which these objects are given or presented to the mind. In general, perceptual experience allows for the presentation of objects and qualities, where imagery allows only for the re-presentation of such things.

The key difference here can perhaps best be expounded by example. Consider a feeling of itchiness in one's left knee. This is a case which philosophers have a tendency to think of as involving *subjective* qualities. It is common to assume both that there can only be an instance of itchiness in a knee if someone feels the itch—awareness here is necessary for its object. And it is also common to suppose that feeling an itch is sufficient for there to be an itch: nothing more is demanded of the world than that one feel the itch for there to be one. Now, one can imagine 'from the inside' such a feeling of itchiness in one's left knee (i.e. one can imagine feeling an itch rather than just seeing someone else who looks like they have an itch) just as one can imagine seeing an apple. Conscious imagery has some similarities with conscious experience of the same objects or qualities. We are inclined to group together both the imagining of an itch and the feeling of an itch in talking of what they are like. But we also have reason to think that they are distinct in kind. For, while we might think that the feeling of an itch is sufficient for an instance of itchiness, we do not suppose that merely imagining an itch thereby makes it the case that there actually is an itch, however faint. So, we cannot suppose that what explains the similarity between feeling an itch and imagining an itch involves them both having the same qualities, and at the same time suppose that those qualities are sufficient for there being an itch.

Imagining an itch consciously involves the imagined qualities of a feeling of an itch, yet does not amount to the existence of an itch. If having an experience of itchiness is sufficient for the existence of an itch, then imagining an itch does not consist in having such an experience. So we should conclude that imagining an experience is not the same as actually feeling one—there is not a common experiential core to both kinds of episode, even though there is a phenomenological similarity between them. How, then, are we to explain this similarity? Imaginings are related to experiencings through a kind of representational relation to them. We characterize imagining by the qualities of the experience imagined, but we do not suppose that those qualities, or what is dependent on them, is actually realized when we imagine. Instead we think of the imagining as a way of representing, or bringing before the mind in absence, the kind of situation that would be present in sensory experience of it. Imagining is the representing of what experience is the presenting. More exactly, it is the re-presenting of the experiential presentation of such an event. When one imagines the itch, one represents the itch as it would be felt.

The point here is not to reduce the notion of imagining a scene to a more generally understood notion of representation. Clearly there are plenty of ways in which one can represent the situation of itchiness in a knee without thereby having a state of mind with the relevant similarity to feeling the itch: in writing the last sentence, presumably I did just that. So if imagining is representing experience, it is a particular or peculiar kind of representing. Foster marks the difference by talk of 'transparent conceiving', but this is just a label for the position rather than an explanation of the difference. It is unclear how, starting from a purely general conception of representation which covers both linguistic representation and imagery, one can explain what is distinctive of imagistic representation rather than merely label the difference as Foster does.

This limitation does not undermine the central reasons for claiming that imagining is a form of representing, though. When one has a sensory experience of some state of affairs, it is for one just as if that state of affairs is present (spatially related to one's point of view). When one imagines an itch, one neither feels the itch, nor does it even seem to one as if there is an itch there. Where sensory experience is *presentational*, it is as if its object must exist and be present. Imagination is *representational* inasmuch as that it allows for objects, events or qualities to be before the mind and yet in a way which does not require them actually to be present, or to be instantiated.

In the case of subjective qualities of bodily sensation, it is easy to see that the object of imagining is something internally related, or even an aspect of, some sensory experience. But there is also good reason to extend the model to other cases of sensory imagining where the objects of experience are taken to be mind independent. Arguably, when we think of examples such as visualizing, we can only explain the similarity between visualizing and visual experience in the same kind of terms: visualizing takes visual experience as its object. Where seeing involves the apprehension of objects in a visual manner, visualizing involves imagining so apprehending objects.

For example, when one visualizes a red light as to the left, it need not be that one visualizes it as actually to the left of where one is (that requires the projection of one's images), rather one visualizes it as to the left of the point of view within the imagined situation. We can think of the perspectival elements of the visualizing as aspects of the imagined visual experience. Were one actually visually experiencing the lights, then one would experience them as if to one's actual left or right. When one visualizes them, one need only visualize them as to the left or right in the imagined situation. Perspective in vision determines the actual orientation of objects relative to the subject, but does not do so in visualizing. We can explain this on the hypothesis that visualizing relates to visual experience as on the model suggested above for imagining and feeling an itch: we imagine visual experience in visualizing a scene. In general, then, we should think of sensory imagining along the lines proposed by both John Foster and Christopher Peacocke. One sensorily imagines things to be a certain way through imagining a conscious experience of them as being so:

> (DT) When one sensorily imagines a f, one does so through imagining consciously experiencing a f.

This Berkeleian hypothesis of course prompts ready objections about imagining unseen trees, but I do not want to explore here the extent to which one must accept or deny restrictions on what one can imagine given (DT).[17]

We can re-construe Sartre's talk of two types of existence in terms of this contrast between different ways in which an object may be given to the mind. When Sartre can see Peter, Peter is before the mind as actually present. It seems as if one couldn't so be related to Peter and Peter not be there. When Sartre visualizes Peter, however, it does not seem to him as if Peter must actually be present. He is merely representing such a presentation of Peter's presence. There is a difference not in the way that the object of these states of minds exists, but in the way in which the agent's mind relates to the object of sensory experience or imagination. There can, then, be no such common core of imagery between experience and imagination.

The moral to emphasize at this point is just that the assumption at work in so much philosophical discussion of memory is that the phenomenological or the sensational must be a common element to experience and imagery can and should be denied. We should not accept that there is a common core of sensation which is neutral between perception and imagination or memory of such perceptual encounter. Imagination and memory relate to perception not through replicating

---

[17] Peacocke (1985) puts forward a similar principle concerning the link between sensory imagination and experience and also discusses in detail the consequence of this kind of connection; see also Martin mss for a more extensive discussion of these issues and their consequences for the theory of perception.

the sensational or imagistic component of perception, but through being a form of representing such experiential encounter with the world. We are now in a position to resolve the problems indicated above for the idea of memory as direct acquaintance with the past.

IV

As Russell noted, it is common to think of some episodes of recall as involving imagery. Russell offers an argument to think that any such imagery must accompany and not constitute remembering. Now, in rejecting the idea that there is a simple common core to imagery and perception we are already in a position to reject one aspect of the dilemma about memory as a copy of past perception. It is possible, on the view of imagery sketched above, for perception and imagery to relate one to the very same objects and qualities, and so to that extent share a content, but yet be phenomenologically distinct. So there is no immediate route to the conclusion that, where recall is a faithful copy or retention of what was experienced, it must also be a case of perceptual experience.

If we apply this to the example of Miriam the astronaut, we can explain the essential· phenomenological difference between her recall and re-encounters so. When she looks through the image intensifiers she is presented (again) with the same farewell: each glance at the screen is a re-encounter with the same event.[18] In contrast, when Miriam recalls the event as a fond farewell, her episode of recall is a representing of a past experience of the farewell, not an occurrent presenting of the episode. The two coincide in object, the event of departure, but they relate to it in different ways. It is this difference in the manner in which something is present to the mind that accounts for the intrinsic difference in consciousness.

But if the account so far enables us to explain how there can be a fundamental phenomenological difference between imagery and perception, and consequently episodic recall and perception, does it do so through assimilating episodic recall to imagery? Should we think of experiential episodes of recall as simply examples of imagery put to use in recalling the past, or should we think instead of there being some intrinsic phenomenological difference between mere imagery and genuine recall of the past?

In fact, we will not get a proper view of the way in which we can think of episodic recall as retaining something from earlier perception until we recognize the ways in which recall can be different from pure imagery, a way which exploits Russell's idea of acquaintance with the past. For there is something that both sensory perception and episodic recall share which is lacked by pure imagery. As a first stab at this, we might put the difference as follows. In both perception and

---

[18] More strictly, each glance at the mirror is a further part of her encounter with the event, given the points noted in n. 13 above, that we treat different encounters with the same event as parts of our overall apprehension of it and not just different encounters with the same entity.

in memory we are related to aspects of reality or actuality: matters as they are now present to the mind, or as they once were present to the mind. In pure imagination, on the other hand, we are related to things only as they are conceivably, or can possibly be, not as they really are. If there is an intrinsic difference between experiential recall and mere imagery, then it must lie in the way in which the former relates us to actuality and the latter to mere possibility.

Put in these terms it is difficult to see how any difference between the actual and the possible could be a phenomenological difference within conscious experience itself. Surely our experience of the world can only be of the actual not the possible. Experience can only tell us how things actually are, not how they must be. So, in what way can our experience reveal to us that something is merely possible? The answer to this problem is to consider the different ways in which experiential states of mind can be particular or specific in their content; that is to say, the ways in which they can present to us particular objects or specific events.

When I see or taste an apple, there is a particular object, and indeed a specific event involving that object, which I come to perceive. Two episodes of seeing might present objects indistinguishable in their qualities, in the same relative locations to the viewer, and yet be experiences of different objects and different events. When we turn to imagery, however, the particularity and specificity drops away. If asked to visualize a green apple, you may well succeed in bringing to mind an image of an apple. But, in many contexts, it is simply inappropriate to press the question which apple you have imagined. In visualizing an apple, there need be no particular apple which is imagined.

This is not to say that particularity cannot be injected into our imagery. One can, if one wants, imagine the very green apple now nestling in A. A. Gill's pocket. For we can use imagery for particular imaginative projects, for particular tasks; and in such cases it is entirely appropriate to take the imagery to be the imagining of the particular objects or events that one sets out to have in mind. The important point, however, is the account that we can give of the ways in which imagery can be particular. Whether I recognize it or not, my current visual perception of an apple is a perception of a particular apple; the perception is veridical or misleading to the extent that that apple is as it looks to me to be. As one might say, the actual context of perception is such that it is sufficient to fix the particular objects and specific events that the perception concerns. On the other hand, with imagery there is no sense to the answer of what an image is an image, independent of the purposes to which the image is put in imagining a scene. Here the subject's intentions in so imagining determine the particularity of the imagined scene, and the imagery carries no intrinsic particularity or specificity of its own.[19] There is no room, then, for the agent to be corrected with respect to which object is being imagined. All that can determine what is being

---

[19] cf. here Ishiguro, 1966, Wittgenstein 1980: §115, Peacocke, 1985: 26–7, and Budd, 1989: 114–15.

imagined is what he or she intends to imagine. If he or she knows what is intended, then he or she also knows what is imagined.

We might, with some caution, appeal to an analogy with painting: a naturalistic depiction of a scene need not be a picture of one scene rather than another. It could be the depiction of a purely imaginary scene, and what would make it the depiction of one landscape or another would rather be how, as we might say, the picture has been labelled, to be used as the portrait of one scene rather than an identical one. Likewise, I suggest, what is the essence here of the purely imagined scene is simply that there is no specific scene that has been imagined: different actual scenes could equally well play the role of the event perceived were this not an imagined perceptual encounter but an actual one (cf. Goodman, 1969; Wollheim, 1980: ss. 11–13).

So the conjecture for the case of episodic recall is simply that any experiential aspect to it, in contrast to pure imagery, is particular or specific in character. In this way episodic recall would be analogous to perceptual experience, and would contrast with imagery. When one in fact recalls someone's throwing a ball at one, then one is recalling some specific episode of having a ball thrown at one, given that one's recall is genuine, and the ball which is represented before the mind is whichever ball it was that was then thrown. Memory imagery has a specific or particular content intrinsic to it, regardless of any construal one is inclined to place on it: one correctly recognizes what one recalls where one realizes that it is indeed that particular event which is now again before the mind.

Indeed, we should draw out one further aspect of this. We started with the idea that episodic recall should be the retained apprehension of a past event. We raised the question how this could differ from current apprehension of that event, the answer was that in recall one represents the original encounter, rather than having the experience over again. Now we can ask: In what sense is this present imagistic representation the retention of what was there before? Here the answer comes from seeing the way in which such recall can be particular or specific in content: one's current episode of recall comes to be an awareness of the past event, which was once apprehended, through being the retention of that very apprehension. The particularity of memory experience is a derived particularity, arising from the retention of the cognitive aspects of the initial experience.[20]

This offers a further response to Russell's observation that any imagery involved in recall must be wholly in the present and hence distinct from any acquaintance with the past. In connection with the first point, one might reason that, since the episode of recall occurs at a later time than the original episode recalled, then that very episode of recalling could have occurred whether the antecedent experience occurred or not. So any experiential or imagistic aspect of that episode of recall would be entirely independent of whether there actually was

---

[20] That there is such a derivational link between memory and experience is suggested in Evans, 1982: chs. 5 and 7; and Campbell, 1994: ch. 7. Neither, however, indicates how such a connection may be reflected in the phenomenological differences between the two.

an earlier sensory experience being recalled. This supports the thought that there can be nothing about the imagistic element of an episode of recall which is essentially linked to the past. If this conclusion is right, then although the Previous Awareness Condition can be applied to determine whether an episode apparently of recall is indeed a genuine case of memory, the applicability of the condition does not indicate anything distinctive about the phenomenology or experiential aspect of recall, since anything phenomenological could be present whether one is recalling or not.

The picture of memory developed here gives a rather different perspective on matters. For we have claimed that what is distinctive of experiential memory, in contrast to imagery, is that it has an intrinsic particularity of content inherited from earlier sensory experience, and it is this which is lacking in pure imagery. This fits with a picture of experiential content where intrinsic particularity originates in an original experiential episode. And this means that in any case where one has an apparent memory with no antecedent experience, then it will lack any intrinsic particularity. If pure imagery lacks an appropriate context to provide it with an intrinsic content, then the same will be true of mere apparent memories. Unlike pure imagery, though, a properly misleading false memory might seem to link one back to some past event. It is this purported link to a particular episode which marks the phenomenological differences between mere imagery and apparent recall.

Given this, we should deny that our episodic recall is such that it could have occurred whether we are genuinely remembering or not. For if it is intrinsic to my current episode of recall that I apprehend some particular event, then I could not have been just like this in a case of mere apparent memory.[21] This gives a sense in which even though episodes of recall happen at one time, they can intrinsically link one to another: for on this view, one could not have been in the state that one now is in without the antecedent event which one now recalls.[22] At least one aspect of how the world is now depends non-causally on how it was before.

[21] P. F. Snowdon (1990), who endorses the increasingly popular disjunctive approach to perception, questions whether there can be such grounds in the case of memory. If we think that being intrinsically of a particular episode is essential to a mental event, then the discussion in the text gives us a reason to endorse disjunctivism about memory episodes. On the other hand, one might here wish to follow Burge's account (1996*b*) of singular reference for perceptual states, and thereby resist disjunctivism, while admitting that imagery *per se* is not the common element.

[22] Does this commit us to claiming that there is no distinction to be drawn between an apparent memory of past perception and a genuine memory which traces back to a mere hallucination? In neither case will there be an original perception which links to a specific event involving particular objects, so the episode of recall, apparent or actual, will lack genuine specificity. Despite this, we are still in a position to contrast the two situations: with a genuine memory of a mere hallucination there is no external event which one can recall; but one does recall a genuine event of merely hallucinating an external event, and that fixes the memory as linked to a genuine past episode in the way that no mere apparent memory could be.

A similar point holds for the recalling of past imagining. Clearly in this case there is a specific event to be recalled, one's imagining, but the image recalled will not itself have any intrinsic particularity. This indicates a further difference between imagery and experiential recall which flows from positing the intrinsic particularity of the latter. Arguably the imagery involved in imagining *j*-ing and imagining imagining *j*-ing is the same: after all one way of representing representing is just to instantiate it.

This discussion puts into place all the elements needed to rebut the charge of incoherence. When one recalls an episode, on the current account, one recalls the original episode of apprehension. That episode has as its object events which one perceived, or of which one was an agent. At the time that they are objects of apprehension, one is then in a position to attend to and respond to the various elements given to the mind. In recalling such an episode, the objects of that episode are recalled as the objects apprehended at that earlier time. Although an episode of recall has as its object the initial experience which was the apprehending of the event, it has thereby as a proper part of its content what was then apprehended. To that extent, one need not deny that in principle episodic recall and original sensory experience could coincide entirely in content. Of course, there are plenty of reasons to deny that such coincidence would in fact ever occur—recalling both tends to be more indeterminate than perception, and to involve elements through the process of retrieval that were no part of the original event. The point here is just to stress that we need not rely on an appeal to these differences in explaining how there can be a difference in kind between the phenomenology of episodic recall and sensory experience.

In the initial statement of the puzzle, the mere possibility that recall and experience might coincide in content raised the worry that the phenomenology of recall might then have to be identical with that of sensory experience. This would seem to rule out the claim that there could be any distinctive phenomenology of the past associated with episodic recall. The comparison with imagery shows that that is not so. In perceptual experience, one is presented with its object as present to one, in some relation to one's actual point of view. In episodic recall, although one is related to the same objects and qualities, one is not presented with them, rather one represents them, or rather recalls them as once presented to one's point of view. This phenomenological contrast, between objects as present in current sensory experience and as represented in recall, gives us a cognitive link to the past. In retaining the particularity of an earlier encounter, we retain a current cognitive link to a past encounter.

In the first section of this chapter I argued that we can find embedded in our ordinary talk of episodic memory something which echoes both Russell's idea that we have a distinctive experience of the past and Wheeler, Stuss, and Tulving's talk of mental time travel. Philosophers have been quick to dismiss such talk as fanciful and ultimately incoherent. I have suggested that we can trace this resistance to a very narrow conception of how distinct phenomenological

---

So the contrast between these two imaginative projects is one at the level of the use or context to which the imagery is put. The same cannot be true of recall experience, though, since it has a particular content. So there is a difference in content between recalling j-ing and recalling recalling j-ing, and so on.

On many theories of episodic memory, the retention of a memory requires that it be rehearsed and re-encoded. Someone who was utterly indifferent to what they recalled, such that there was no emotional difference for them from different rehearsals, could be in otherwise indistinguishable states which would be on the one hand recallings of recallings (of recallings) or simply some lower level of recalling.

states can be related and share a content. Once we embrace a conception of imagery as representational of sensory experience, then we can see distinctively memory imagery as that which represents particular encounters in sensory experience from the past. The distinctive phenomenology of our past experience is, then, the re-presentation of particular episodes in contrast, on the one hand, to the presentation of particular episodes in perception, and, on the other, to the non-particular representation of experienced episodes in sensory imagination.

V

Let us look back at the ideas from which we started and how the highly abstract philosophical account I have been spinning fits with a psychological theory of the structure of long-term memory. At various times in the development of his theory of episodic memory, Tulving has stressed different aspects of episodic memory, and one could think that the different theses could be developed by competing theories which took on board one rather than another of these claims. In the light of the above discussion, I suggest we can see how each of these different approaches illuminates a different aspect of the same phenomenon: all of them are needed in order to explain the sense in which we can have something like experiential memory.

In his earliest formulations (1972), Tulving stressed the idea of episodic memory as memory of events, of specific episodes in an individual's life. We can see the point of this within the terms of our account in two ways. First, if we think of instances of episodic recall as distinctively phenomenological occurrences, rather than simply whatever prompts a judgement in answer to a task, then specificity of what is recalled is essential in marking the contrast between memory and mere imagination. At the same time, I have claimed that we should think of experiential recall as the recalling, and hence representing, of a prior, specific experience. In later formulations, Tulving stresses the distinctive way in which episodic memory is connected to self consciousness. This, too, is reflected in the conception of memory offered here. To comprehend what one is doing when one recalls, one must recognize that one is not having the experience in question but merely recalling it. Hence the metarepresentational aspects of 'autonoetic consciousness', as Tulving calls it, will be essential to understanding what remembering is, and how one can be justified in making past-tensed judgements on the basis of such recall.[23] Finally, if we go back to the quotations with which we started, we can see the appeal of thinking of recall as a form of time travel: what one does in recalling some event is re-present the events that once one apprehended. One has here an immediate sense of the contrast between that which once was present and

---

[23] At the same time, however, the view leaves open the exact relation that must be claimed between self consciousness and the ability to recall episodically. On metarepresentational accounts of episodic recall it has been claimed that a necessary condition of such recall is that one be able to represent one's own states of mind, cf. e.g. Perner and Ruffman, 1995 and Owens, 1996.

is no more, and the present as actually experienced rather than represented as being experienced.

Discussion of the idea of a subjective feeling or quale of the past to be associated with memory has aroused much controversy recently. In part, theoretical opposition to it rests on the thought that our ability to make judgements about the past is a complex one, which could hardly be thought to be grounded in the presence or absence of a simple feeling of pastness. Our current picture indicates a way of respecting that thought while still holding on to the idea that there is an experiential element to our grasp of the concept of the past. For, on this account, consciousness of the past involves two things: (i) the representation in recall of apprehension rather than the occurrence of apprehension itself; (ii) representation which links one to an actual episode apprehended, rather than merely to a type of episode. We can then think of the plight of the infant in coming to have a full grasp of the notion of the past, one which is applicable directly to its experiential memories, as taking the following form. The infant needs to make sense of how there can be specific, and hence actual, events of which it has knowledge or conscious awareness, but which are nevertheless not part of the present scene. We can point to two things which might help it in this predicament: first a grasp of a concept of time as a causal structure in which earlier events cause later ones; secondly, an understanding of itself as located within that causal structure, such that recalled experiences have to possess a causal location prior to that of the present episode of recall. Past events are no less actual than current ones, but they are located in a different part of the structure that is time. The infant can have access to those different parts of time through the causal traces that the past events leave on it in memory.

The exact story here clearly needs more development and justification, but the idea that some such story needs to be told and can be told offers a response to the debate about qualia of pastness. We can deny that claiming that there is an experiential marker for the past or present means that one has to oppose the idea that coming to have a concept of the past is coming to have a theoretical understanding of time. We can see how the two claims are, instead, complementary. In this picture, there is a phenomenological difference between the experience of episodic recall and sensory experience, and a difference between both of these and mere sensory imagination. The difference is not one of the presence or absence of some simple quality, but rather a structural difference. And it is in this way that the need for sophistication in acquiring a concept of the past and of remembering it can mesh with the intuition that there is something phenomenologically distinctive in recalling past events. The phenomenological markers of past and present require that one come to have a theoretical grasp of time in order that such experience can appropriately ground tensed judgements.

Note that on this view the direction of time is not explicitly marked in consciousness: the past is given as not present but actual; on some views of the metaphysics of time, one might think of both the past and the future as equally actual. So, an objector might point out, there would be nothing to distinguish experiential representings of future apprehensions of particular events from my account of cases of recall. This is indeed a consequence of the view, but the objection raises no worry of substance. I take it that it is a deep fact about the world and us, that we can only be appropriately related to our past experiences and not to our future ones.[24] So we could not be creatures who had specific represented contact with future experiences. If indeed it is a metaphysical possibility that there could be creatures with such precognition of their own future perceptions, then on the account offered here, they could not have a conception of the past which is quite the same as ours. For we can immediately determine that anything we recall is in our past, and that where an event is recognized as past, that we must be recalling it; but such creatures would not be able to make such inferences. For remote contact with a specific event would for them, *ex hypothesi*, as easily relate them to the future as the past. I see no reason to think that our experience of the direction of time's arrow should require some feature which would be in common between us and these creatures. So the mere imaginability of their possibility does not give us reason to think that there is anything more to experience of the passage of time than I have indicated.

VI

How then, does this all relate to the challenge from Constructivism and the case of John Dean? Dean's example makes vivid something that we all already are well aware of: that in many of our memories, often our most treasured ones, there are fabrications. What seems to be recall of an episode may instead derive from earlier tales about it. To some extent, the idea that there are mechanisms involved in constructing narratives of our past exploits in the maintenance of long-term memory should not by itself threaten the idea that episodic recall which results is still retained acquaintance with the initial events. In the case of perception we are well aware that there are neurophysiological and psychological mechanisms which underpin our awareness of the world around us; we should not endorse any conception of acquaintance inconsistent with this. So, too, we can think of many of the mechanisms of memory as simply underpinning or supporting the preservative function of remembering.

But our recognition of what happens in Dean's case, and our sense of unreliability in many of our treasured memories, reflects something more than just that. It is difficult to read Neisser's description without feeling that Dean is in part responsible for the rewriting of his past encounters into memories congenial to

---

[24] One might suggest, though, that there is a sub-class of future events which we can be cognitively related to as particulars: namely those we intend. In making a decision, we might suggest I move from treating a future event as merely possible to definitely actual. To the extent that my will is indeed effective, my decision may give me knowledge of the future as memory can of the past. This does not affect the point in this chapter: it rather shows a way in which a different causal link might underpin awareness of specific episodes from that evident in perception and memory.

his self-conception. In a more pedestrian way, the same thought is reflected in the idea that in many episodic memories we 'see' ourselves in the scene, and often we cannot distinguish elements of the scene as then apprehended from the commentary or gloss on it we later are inclined to add. It is already part of our general conception of episodic memory that we ourselves have a hand in shaping it, and not merely that there may be unconscious psychological mechanisms involved in laying down memory traces and preserving them.[25]

Yet the thought that at the very least the ideal or central conception of what episodic memory is for us is a kind of direct contact with the past is still consistent with the idea that there is much fabrication in recall. This idea is what a purely Constructivist model of memory would enjoin us to give up. Of course, such a model may be concerned with keeping track of the sources of information—for it is important that one's information about events in the past should be reliable—but that concern will affect equally autobiographical and non-autobiographical memory. Such source monitoring notwithstanding, the main constraints on developing a self-narrative need have nothing to do with special access to past events in one's life. While examples such as Dean's memory provide support for the role of fabrication in memory of the past, they do not definitely show that a Constructivist view must be right. To settle the matter between a view which holds on to the idea of episodic memory as contact with the past and a view which just stresses the role of construction of self-narrative, we will need to look elsewhere.

For all that has been said here, a Constructivist model might turn out to be the best description of the mechanisms of episodic memory. The aim here has been just to spell out a coherent picture of what it is that matters for us in our recall of the past, and what would be lost if episodic memory had no special status in an account of our epistemic links with the past. If we can think of at least some of the mechanisms of memory not as purely fabricating stories drawn upon in recall, but rather as being means of retaining the kind of acquaintance we once had with events, then we can better understand the craving for such genuine episodes of contact with the past. The manifest fact that so much of our memories retain an emotional role for us while lacking that stamp of authenticity may reflect no more than that the picture of experiential memory sketched here is an ideal to which we can only sometimes conform, but which nevertheless informs centrally one aspect of why we value episodic memories in the way that we do.

This paper is based on talks to the HRB project on Consciousness and Self Consciousness; University of Hatfield; Scottish Graduate Conference at the University of Edinburgh; and a seminar in UCL. I am grateful to audiences there, and for discussion of these issues to John Campbell, Tim Crane, Jérôme Dokic, Naomi Eilan, Christoph Hoerl, Teresa McCormack, Tony Marcel, David

---

[25] For further discussion of the role of reconstruction in episodic recall among normals in comparison with confabulators see Burgess and Shallice, 1996.

Owens, Christopher Peacocke, Gabriel Segal, Paul Snowdon, and Timothy Williamson.

M.G.F.M.

REFERENCES

ALLPORT, A. (1992), 'Attention and control: have we been asking the wrong questions? A critical review of twenty-five years', in *Attention and Performance XV*. Cambridge, Mass.: MIT Press.

ANSCOMBE, G. E. M. (1976), 'Memory, "experience" and Causation', in H. Lewis (ed.), *Contemporary British Philosophy*. London: George Allen and Unwin.

AYER, A. J. (1956), *The Problem of Knowledge*. London: Macmillan.

BARCLAY, C. R. (1994), 'Composing protoselves through improvisation', in U. Neisser (ed.), *The Remembering Self*. Cambridge: Cambridge University Press.

BUDD, M. (1989), *Wittgenstein's Philosophy of Psychology*. London: Routledge.

BURGE, T. (1993*a*), 'Content preservation', *Philosophical Review*, 102: 457–88.

—— (1993*b*), 'Vision and intentional content', in R. v. Gulick and E. LePore (eds.), *John Searle and his Critics*. Oxford: Basil Blackwell.

—— (1997), 'Interlocution, perception, and memory', *Philosophical Studies*, 86: 21–47.

BURGESS, P. W., and SHALLICE, T. (1996), 'Confabulation and the control of recollection', *Memory*, 4(4): 359–411.

CAMPBELL, J. (1994), *Past, Space and Self*. Cambridge, Mass.: MIT Press.

—— (1997), 'The structure of time in autobiographical memory', *European Journal of Philosophy*, 5(2): 105–18.

DRETSKE, F., and YOURGRAU, (1983), 'Lost knowledge', *Journal of Philosophy,* 80.

EVANS, G. (1982), *The Varieties of Reference*, ed. J. McDowell. Oxford: Clarendon Press.

FOSTER, J. (1982), *The Case for Idealism*. London: Routledge and Kegan Paul.

GINET, C. (1980), 'Knowing less by knowing more', in *Midwest Studies in Philosophy, v. Studies in Epistemology*, ed. P. A. French, T. E. Uehling, Jr., and H. K. Wettstein. Minneapolis: Minnesota University Press.

GOODMAN, N. (1969), *Languages of Art*. London: Oxford University Press.

HARMAN, G. (1973), *Thought*. Princeton: Princeton University Press.

HINTON, J. M. (1973), *Experiences*. Oxford: Clarendon Press.

ISHIGURO, H. (1966), 'Imagination', in A. Montefiore and B. Williams (eds.), *British Analytic Philosophy*. London: Routledge and Kegan Paul.

JUDSON, L. (1987/8), 'Russell on memory', *Proceedings of the Aristotelian Society*, 88.

MARTIN, C. B., and Deutscher, M. (1966), 'Remembering', *Philosophical Review*, 75: 161–96.

MARTIN, M. G. F. Manuscript, 'The transparency of experience'.

NEISSER, U. (1981), John Dean's memory: a case study', *Cognition*, 9: 1–22.

NOZICK, R. (1981), *Philosophical Explanations*. Oxford: Clarendon Press.

OWENS, D. (1996), 'A Lockean theory of theory of memory experience', *Philosophy and Phenomenological Research*, 56(2): 319–32.

PARFIT, D. (1985), *Reasons and Persons*. Oxford: Clarendon Press.

PEACOCKE, C. A. B. (1985), 'Imagination, experience and possibility', in J. Foster and H. Robinson (eds.), *Essays on Berkeley*. Oxford: Clarendon Press.

PEACOCKE, C. A. B. (*cont.*) (1986), *Thoughts: An Essay on Content*. Oxford: Basil Blackwell.

PEARS, D. (1975), 'Russell's Theories of Memory', in *Questions in the Philosophy of Mind*. London: Duckworth.

—— (1990), *Hume's System*. Oxford: Clarendon Press.

PERNER, J., and RUFFMAN, T. (1995), 'Episodic memory and autonoetic consciousness: developmental evidence and a theory of childhood amnesia', *Journal of Experimental Child Psychology*, 59(3): 516–48.

PRICE, H. H. (1932), *Perception*. London: Methuen.

RUSSELL, B. (1912), *The Problems of Philosophy*, 9th edn. Oxford: Oxford University Press.

SARTRE, J.-P. (1991), *The Psychology of the Imagination*. New York: Citadel.

SHOEMAKER, S. (1984), 'Persons and their pasts', in *Identity, Cause and Mind*. Cambridge: Cambridge University Press.

SNOWDON, P. F. (1990). 'The objects of perceptual experience', *Proceedings of the Aristotelian Society,* suppl. vol.

SQUIRES, R. (1969), 'Memory unchained', *Philosophical Review*, 78(2): 178–96.

STRAWSON, P. F. (1966), *The Bounds of Sense*. London: Methuen.

TULVING, E. (1972), 'Episodic and semantic memory', in E. Tulving and W. Donaldson (eds.), *Organization of Memory*. New York: Academic Press.

—— (1982), *Elements of Episodic Memory*. Oxford: Clarendon Press.

WHEELER, M. A., Stuss, D. T., and Tulving, E. (1997), 'Toward a theory of episodic memory: the frontal lobes and autonoetic consciousness', *Psychological Bulletin*, 121(3): 331–54.

WIGGINS, D. (1995), 'Remembering directly', in J. Hopkins and A. Savile (eds.), *Psychoanalysis, Mind and Art*. Oxford: Basil Blackwell.

WILLIAMSON, T. (1995). 'Is knowing a state of mind?', *Mind*, 104: 560–2.

WITTGENSTEIN, L. (1980), *Remarks on the Philosophy of Psychology*, trans. C. G. Luckhardt and M. A. E. Aue, ed. G. H. v. Wright and H. Nyman. 2 vols. Oxford: Basil Blackwell, ii.

WOLLHEIM, R. (1980), *Art and its Objects*, 2nd edn. Cambridge: Cambridge University Press.

11

Attributing Episodic Memory to Animals and Children

Teresa McCormack

The term 'episodic memory' was first introduced in the psychological literature by Tulving (1972), and has persisted despite some subsequent difficulties in defining and measuring this type of memory. It is a term that many psychologists have been reluctant to abandon, perhaps because it captures an important aspect of our common-sense understanding of memory (see Martin, Ch. 10, this volume). In this chapter, episodic memory is considered in the light of different ways in which a connection can be made between the central themes of this book (time and memory). These considerations have implications for whether or not we wish to attribute episodic memory to animals and to children.

The attribution of episodic memory to animals or very young children is controversial. On the one hand, claims that some animals may have episodic memory, or at least 'episodic-like' memory, have received much attention recently. Most notably, Clayton and Dickinson have argued that their studies of memory in jays amounts to 'the first conclusive behavioral evidence of episodic-like memory in animals other than humans' (1998: 274). On the other hand, in the child development literature there have been recent attempts to link the emergence of episodic memory with 'theory of mind' understanding which is generally assumed to appear relatively late in development (Perner, 1991, 2000 and forthcoming; Perner and Ruffman, 1995; see also Dokic, Ch. 8, this volume).

Of course, how one interprets these claims hinges on the description one gives of what it is to remember episodically. A common description of episodic memory is that it involves recollecting a specific event from one's past. Episodic memory is contrasted with various other types of memory, and I mention just three of these contrasts here. First, episodic memory can be distinguished from factual or semantic memory. For example, although one may have acquired knowledge of a certain fact as a result of a specific learning event, remembering that fact need not involve recalling that event. Secondly, episodic memory can also be contrasted with generic memories about events. Episodic memories are always memories for specific events, whereas one may have more generalized memories about recurring events, such as remembering what one used to do at Sunday lunchtimes when one lived in London, or remembering the sequence of events that usually occur at staff meetings (of course, it is possible to view generic event memory as a type of factual memory). Thirdly, episodic memory is also sometimes contrasted with the familiarity-based responding involved in some recognition memory-judgements. The idea is that one could judge that, for example, one has met someone before simply because his or her face seems familiar, rather than because one can actually remember a previous episode of encountering that person.

The challenge to psychologists is to provide a definition of episodic memory that is sufficient to capture these types of contrast. What is special about episodic memory as a psychological category, and how should it be singled out? Faced with this question, one approach that has seemed appealing to at least some psychologists is to try to describe or define episodic memory in terms of the pieces of information about events that are stored in memory and subsequently retrieved. As I understand the literature, the issue can be put like this. All memories stem in some way or other from individual learning episodes, but not all memories are episodic. Episodic memories are memories of specific past events, but some of our memories that derive from specific learning experiences are factual memories, or generic event memories. Therefore, we can ask, what is special about the information that is encoded and maintained following a given learning episode that makes subsequent episodic remembering possible?

In fact, it is not obvious what such stored information could be. The main candidate that has been considered is whether that information is a specification of the time and place at which the remembered event occurred—what is sometimes called the spatiotemporal context of the event. In what follows I will refer to this idea as the *contextual* description of episodic memory. The motivation for such an account is considered in more detail in Section 2. Roughly speaking, the general idea is that whereas factual memory simply involves retrieval of the fact acquired during a given learning episode, the corresponding episodic memory would involve remembering something about the specific learning episode itself, namely the context in which the fact was acquired.

It is possible to interpret Tulving's (1972) original definition of episodic memory in precisely these terms. However, the idea that episodic memory can be defined in terms of the storage and retrieval of such information is one that Tulving himself has subsequently argued against. It may even be the case that, at present, no psychologist really subscribes to the contextual description of episodic memory. Nevertheless, I think it is fair to say that the contextual description of episodic memory still holds some lingering appeal for at least some psychologists. This is because it is traditional in experimental psychology to view memory primarily as a system for the storage and retrieval of types of information, and the contextual description fits with such a picture of memory.

Most notably in recent research, the contextual description of episodic memory is one that appears to have been at least part of what motivated Clayton and Dickinson's work on memory in jays. Clayton and Dickinson are in fact explicitly wary about claiming that they have demonstrated that jays have episodic memory, preferring to stick to the term 'episodic-like' memory (Griffiths, Dickinson, and Clayton, 1999). Nevertheless, their work seems to be guided by the general idea that demonstrations that animals can remember spatiotemporal contextual information about unique events connect closely with work on episodic memory in humans. In the first two sections of this chapter, I explore whether this is correct by considering in detail why the contextual description is appealing, and what problems it faces. Many of the points made in these first two sections are not new ones, but perhaps it is worth while, in the light of Clayton and Dickinson's work, to reconsider what motivates the contextual description of episodic memory and why this description is inadequate. In particular, it will be argued that the contextual account does not explain the fundamental feature of episodic memory: the fact that episodic memories are memories *about specific past events*.

It is suggested that to explain the specificity of episodic memory, it is necessary to consider not just the information about events that is stored in memory, but the way in which the rememberer represents such events during recollection. It is only by considering the distinctive way in which past events are represented at recall that we can reach a proper understanding of the processes involved in recollecting a specific past event. Further, a consideration of the representational demands of episodic memory raises fundamental issues concerning memory development. It is these issues which are considered in the third section.

EPISODIC MEMORY AND CONTEXT

The contextual description of episodic memory is one that Clayton and Dickinson (1998, 1999a) mention in connection with their work on memory in jays, and the first section of the chapter focuses on their study for this reason.

To explain many types of animal behaviour, we do not need to assume that animals have memories that stem from single learning episodes. Often, animal behaviour seems to be shaped over repeated learning episodes, resulting in the animal being able to return reliably to a certain location for food, or respond reliably after a given interval to receive a reward. Some studies of animal memory do demonstrate much more rapid acquisition of a response. For example, some studies suggest that animals can update their memories from trial to trial. However, Griffiths, Dickinson, and Clayton (1999) review these studies and argue that in all cases performance could be a result of familiarity-based memory, rather than episodic memory.

Clayton and Dickinson's own studies are based on the observation that, for some animals, the availability of a food source at a specific location interacts with time. For example, it is no longer worth while for an animal to return to a certain location if the food source that was previously there has moved or has decayed. It seems likely that animals are sensitive to such features of their environment, given that such sensitivity would be highly adaptive. Clayton and Dickinson's studies have examined this sensitivity in an experimental setting. They took as their aim to demonstrate that animals remember a combination of 'what', 'when', and 'where' information about specific events (see Griffiths, Dickinson, and

Clayton, 1999). The events that they used differed over trials, such that on any given test trial animals' performance needed to be based on what had happened during that trial.

In their study, a group of jays took part in a training phase in which they cached either worms (their preferred food) or peanuts in two separate sand-filled trays. During training, the birds were given the opportunity to 'learn' that the worms will have decayed, and thus be inedible, 124 hrs after they have been cached, whereas this is not true of peanuts. The sequence of events during test trials was as follows: (i) there was an initial session in which this group of birds cached either worms or peanuts in one side of a sand-filled tray; (ii) a second session took place 120 hrs later, during which they cached in the other side of the tray whichever one of the two foodstuffs they had not cached in the earlier session; (iii) a retrieval phase was held 4 hrs after the second session, during which the birds were allowed to search for the foodstuffs cached in both the previous sessions. The crucial finding is that if they had cached the worms in the first session, that is, 124 hrs before retrieval, the birds tended to search in the location in which they had hidden the peanuts (see Clayton and Dickinson, 1998, 1999b, for full details).

Clayton and Dickinson describe the birds as remembering 'what' (peanuts versus worms) they have hidden, 'where' they have hidden it (which of the two cache sites), and 'when' it was hidden (124 v. 4 hrs ago). They acknowledge that there is already abundant evidence which shows that various animals can remember some kinds of spatial information (Griffiths, Dickinson, and Clayton, 1999; for review and discussion, see O'Keefe, 1993b; Shettleworth, 1998) or keep track of time (see Wearden, Ch. 1, this volume; Gibbon and Allan, 1984; Bradshaw and Szabadi, 1997; Macar, Pouthas, and Friedman, 1992). What they take to be compelling about their study is that it demonstrates that 'what', 'when', and 'where' information can be remembered simultaneously about a specific unique caching event. Each event was unique because the caching locations varied across trials, so that animals could not learn rules about where to return to after a given delay. Thus, to perform well the animals were required to update their memory on every trial.

In assessing their claims, I consider two issues. The theoretical question I introduced above is whether the contextual description of episodic memory that seems to have been part of the motivation for their study is in any way useful. Before turning to that question, I consider another issue, an issue that may be possible to resolve empirically: is it correct to describe the birds in their study as remembering contextual information?

Remembering contextual information

It is by no means clear what contextual information is routinely stored about events, or how such information is supposed to become associated with event information in memory (an issue which psychologists are well aware of; see discussions in Davies and Thomson, 1988). The simple intuitive model seems to be that for each specific event there is a memory representation formed at encoding that either includes contextual features, or is in some way connected to or associated with the relevant features (e.g. Gallistel, 1990; Hasher and Zacks, 1979; see Block and Zakay and Brown and Chater, Chs. 2 and 3, this volume).

Thus the assumption is that, in at least some cases, contextual information is associated with event information at encoding, and thus that not all types of contextual judgements involve inferential processes at retrieval (Johnson, Hastroudi, and Lindsay, 1993). Should the behaviour of the birds in Clayton and Dickinson's task be described in terms of this simple contextual model? The temporal sensitivity that their task requires is sensitivity to how long ago the caching of the worms took place. Thus the issue is whether such sensitivity involves retrieval of stored temporal-contextual information.

It is possible to distinguish between at least two different types of explanations that could be given for the birds' sensitivity to how long ago an event occurred:

(1) Performance depends on the retrieval of previously stored temporal-contextual information. This is Clayton and Dickinson's claim. If they are correct, then the challenge is to describe the nature of this stored information, what encoding processes it depends upon, and how it is used to calculate elapsed time.

(2) Alternatively, the animals' performance exploits an interval timer (see Wearden, Ch. 1, this volume). Interval timers resemble stop-watches that can be set and reset. If caching worms in test trials triggers such a timer, then the output of this timer could be used to determine in the appropriate way whether or not to search for the worms.

Before discussing the plausibility of each of these possible explanations, it is important to consider the difference between them, and whether Clayton and Dickinson's claims about the birds' memory abilities hinge on one of them being correct. The contextual description of episodic memory suggests that episodic memory could be attributed if the birds have been shown to remember the temporal context of the past event. According to the simple version of the contextual model described above, episodic memory involves storage and retrieval of contextual information *associated with past events*. However, if (2) is correct, then it is possible that the temporal information used by the birds only concerns the *current state* of a timer (analogous to the current position of the hands on a stop-watch), rather than an encoded temporal location of a previous event. Of course, in principle, the temporal information provided by such a timer might be used to work out the temporal context of the previous caching event (analogous to using information about the time elapsed on a stop-watch to work out when it was switched on). However, there would be no need to assume that the birds actually derive that previous temporal context.

Why is the distinction between retrieving previously encoded temporal-contextual information and exploiting an interval timer important? If one were sympathetic to a strong interpretation of Clayton and Dickinson's findings in terms of episodic memory, one could respond that there is no need to insist that the temporal information exploited by the birds is something that is stored along with event information and subsequently retrieved. That is, one could argue that remembering 'when' something occurred just is a matter of showing sensitivity to how much time has elapsed since it occurred, regardless of the mechanisms underpinning such sensitivity.

The extent to which this is a good response depends upon what type of claim is being made about the nature of remembering in such a case. The claims made by Clayton and Dickinson, in their paper co-authored with Griffiths (Griffiths, Dickinson, and Clayton, 1999), seem interesting in so far as they take their study to be measuring a type of memory which involves actually recalling a previous past event, in contrast to, for example, familiarity-based responding. The title of the paper—'Episodic memory: what can animals remember about their past?'— makes this clear. Roughly speaking, they have in mind the idea of a type of remembering that involves thinking of or having before one's mind a previous event. The contextual features that they list—'when' and 'where' information— are described as features of the original caching event.

The contextual description of episodic memory would seem to require a demonstration that the animals are retrieving information about the context in which the past event occurred. Indeed, Griffiths, Dickinson, and Clayton make this clear in that they point out that 'the animal must be able to *encode* the information based on a single personal experience that occurred in the past, *and then accurately recall* the information about what happened, where and when, at a later date' (1999: 76–7, italics added). Thus a demonstration that the animals can respond appropriately given the current state of an interval timer would not seem to be sufficient. Animals, or indeed humans, could respond appropriately in this way without recollecting anything about previous events. Indeed, it is precisely those organisms that cannot recollect events that might be expected to make extensive use of such timers. The timers enable sensitivity to temporal features of the world without requiring thought about previous events.

Retrieving temporal context or exploiting an interval timer?

How should we explain the birds' sensitivity to elapsed time, given what is known about temporal processing in animals? Clayton and Dickinson's recent work rules out one particular explanation of the birds' sensitivity to duration. In their original study, birds could have used the rule that if more than 24 hrs had elapsed since caching the worms, then they should search for peanuts. In this way, their behaviour could perhaps have been the result of exploiting a circadian oscillator (the existence of such oscillators is well documented; see Gallistel, 1990). Clayton and Dickinson's more recent work rules out this particular possibility by demonstrating that the birds show a sensitivity to the fact that a degradable foodstuff will be edible one day after caching but not four days after caching (Clayton,

Yu, and Dickinson, forthcoming), or edible two or three days after caching but not five days (Clayton, personal communication).

Thus any attempt to explain the birds' behaviour in terms of the exploiting of an interval timer must account for their ability to keep track of very long periods of time (several days). On the basis of the existing literature, the main difficulty with such a proposal is that most models of such timers have been developed to account for the timing of much shorter intervals than those employed in their study (Clayton and Dickinson, 1999*b*). For example, pacemaker-accumulator models assume that intervals are measured in terms of the number of pulses produced by a pacemaker (e.g. Church, Meck, and Gibbon, 1994). However, the pacemaker is thought to generate pulses at a fairly high rate, appropriate for timing of seconds or perhaps minutes, rather than days (see Wearden, Ch. 1, this volume). Although it is possible that such a model could be altered for timing of much longer intervals, this has yet to be established in the literature. In particular, it is not obvious how a pacemaker that supported timing of very long intervals would be neurobiologically realized.

Church and Broadbent's (1990) oscillator-based model of timing is an alternative to the pacemaker-accumulator model that assumes that a timed interval is associated with a given state of a bank of oscillators (that is, a set of repeating signals of various periods). As with pacemaker-accumulator models of interval timing, such a model has (as far as I am aware) only been applied to shorter time intervals. However, it is possible that some animals possess oscillators with periods longer than 24 hrs that could be exploited in this way (see Gallistel, 1990, for discussion of intradian oscillators). Alternatively, it may be that animals can in some way keep track of the number of cycles that oscillators of shorter periods have completed (see Wearden's Ch. 1 above).

Thus, the plausibility of (2) depends on giving a satisfactory account of interval timing over very long ranges. Although there is already some evidence in the literature for the existence of interval timers which operate over periods of hours rather than minutes (see Gibbon, Fairhurst, and Goldberg, 1997), the functioning of timers over this range is not yet fully understood. It is also not clear whether such timers would also operate over the periods of several days used in the Clayton and Dickinson studies. However, the alternative explanation, that the animals in Clayton and Dickinson's study retrieve previously encoded temporal-contextual information, faces very similar difficulties. The temporal-contextual information that is assumed to be encoded must be the output of some type of temporal encoding process, and it must be able to be used to calculate elapsed time. It is not yet obvious what form that encoded information is supposed to take, based on what is currently known about animal timing and memory.

One possibility is that temporal context could be provided by a bank of oscillators, although in this case oscillators would be exploited in a manner somewhat different to that assumed in the Church and Broadbent (1990) oscillator-based interval timer. In their model, it is assumed that the output of the oscillators is initiated or triggered by the initial event (in this case the caching event). The alternative would be to assume that there are oscillators that are running continuously, independently of such salient events. Rather than initiating the output of such oscillators, salient events themselves could be associated with states of this continuous oscillator-based signal. In this way, a bank of oscillators might be able to be used as a temporal context to which memories can be associated (see Gallistel, 1990, 1994). The basic idea, then, is of a 'time-stamping process' for all memories, rather than an interval timer that functions like a stop-watch. At retrieval, time elapsed could be calculated by comparison of the previously encoded state with the current state of the oscillator-based signal. However, such a suggestion again depends on the plausibility of oscillators with long periods. It also remains to be established whether animals ever use oscillators in such a way to calculate elapsed time (Shettleworth, 1998).

In summary, it is not yet possible to decide what underpins the birds' sensitivity to elapsed duration, although it seems likely that this issue could be, and perhaps will be, resolved empirically. Since it is not yet clear whether the birds are remembering temporal context, it is not obvious what type of memory their procedure measures, even according to the contextual description of episodic memory. The issue I turn to in the next section is why, in their quest to find a parallel in animals to human episodic memory, Clayton and Dickinson might have thought it necessary to establish that animals remember temporal-contextual information.

BASIS OF THE CONTEXTUAL DESCRIPTION

I began this chapter with a puzzle that psychologists have faced, which I restate now. Even factual memory and familiarity-based memory can stem from specific, and sometimes unique, learning events. Episodic memories are different. They are memories that stem from specific learning episodes but, unlike factual memories, they are memories that are themselves about those specific events. What is special about the information that is encoded and maintained following a given learning episode that makes subsequent episodic remembering possible? What makes it the case that episodic memories are about specific events? In what follows, I consider why psychologists may have been drawn to a contextual description of episodic memory in trying to answer this question. In the first subsection, I explore whether the specificity of episodic memory is explicable in terms of stored temporal-contextual information. In the second subsection, I consider whether the difference between remembering a fact and remembering the episode in which the fact was acquired could ever be cashed out in terms of memory for contextual information.

The specificity of episodic memory

Historically, the underlying motivation for making a link between episodic memory and temporal-contextual information seems to have been the possibility that the specificity of episodic memory might be explicable in terms of the storage of such information. In explaining how the notion of episodic memory occurred to him, Tulving says:

One of the immediate consequences of thinking of word-events in memory experiments was my 'discovery' of what many wise philosophers from Heraclitus had known all the time: events do not repeat themselves, there is never another event exactly like a given one. Items may be repeated . . . producing events that have certain things (the nominal identity of the item) in common while differing in other respects (occurring at different times in different places). (Tulving, 1983: 19–20)

Thus, even if two events are similar, they will by necessity have occurred at different times. Roughly speaking, then, the idea seems to have been that, given this is true, what makes it the case that I am remembering a certain specific event is that I remember the event as having occurred in particular, unique, temporal context. And, the argument might be, remembering an event as having occurred in a certain temporal context is a matter of possessing stored temporal-contextual information about that event. Tulving argues that 'each event in the episodic system is referred to a particular instant, date, or period in time' (1983: 39). Similarly, Gallistel (1990) argues that what distinguishes one episodic memory from another is the availability of unique temporal addresses or indexes for each memory.

Whether or not it is correct that the specificity of episodic memory is due to stored temporal-contextual information (and I will argue that it is not correct), it is obvious on this sort of account that not all types of associated temporal information are going to be able to do this job. This is because not all types of temporal processes could provide unique temporal contexts. Internal oscillators would not appear to provide such contexts, as by definition they repeat at regular intervals. Thus animals, if reliant on timing mechanisms such as internal oscillators, have no way of representing the temporal location of events uniquely (see Campbell, 1994, for extensive discussion of this point). Although O'Keefe (1993a) has pointed out that by combining the output of oscillators of varying periods it may be possible to generate unique contexts, there is no evidence that oscillators are used in this way by animals. Indeed, it is not obvious how being able to assign unique temporal locations to events would be of any adaptive use to animals (Friedman, 1993).

However, perhaps in humans there is a type of temporal encoding process that does provide contexts that are unique. It has sometimes been claimed that unique temporal information is always encoded automatically with events in episodic memory (versions of such a claim are made by Hasher and Zacks, 1979; Gallistel, 1990; Schacter, 1987). However, there are a number of difficulties with such a possibility that are by now well recognized in the literature. First, when one is episodically remembering, one is often unable to make accurate temporal-contextual judgements. In particular, judgements about the temporal context of non-recent events are often inaccurate (see Friedman's, 1993, review for discussion of this and related issues; see also Brown and Chater's Ch. 3, this volume, for an alternative view). Secondly, not only is it not possible always to remember temporal-contextual information, but simply remembering such information does not seem to be associated in any straightforward way with episodic memory. For example, one can made judgements about the spatiotemporal context of events that one has not personally experienced, such as recalling the time and place that an event in the news occurred (Friedman, 1987; Friedman and Wilkins, 1985). Thirdly, even when one can make temporal-contextual judgements regarding personally experienced events, it is by no means clear that these are based on retrieval of a previously stored piece of temporal information. One may be making an inference on the basis of the content of one's memory, or its vividness, or by working out its relation to temporal 'landmarks' (e.g. Hintzman, Block, and Summers, 1973; Friedman, 1993 and Ch. 5, this volume; Robinson, 1986; Shum, 1998).

Someone who wishes to defend the role of temporal-contextual information in episodic memory is faced with the task of specifying exactly what the relevant information is and how it features in episodic remembering, while bearing in mind these points. If one did wish to defend the role of temporal-contextual information in episodic memory, one might argue that the stored contextual information is not always accessible for use in memory-judgements but nevertheless still plays a special role in episodic memory (such a position is related to that of Brown and Chater, Ch. 3, this volume). Further, perhaps the temporal-contextual information is of a form that is available only for personally experienced events. Thus the temporal information may be in the form of a code that is different from, for example, the date associated with a news event in semantic memory (see Tulving, 1983: 42). And, one might argue, the very fact that it is different in this way means that it may not be of a form that, even if it were retrievable, would easily support judgements required in some conventional temporal memory tasks. For example, there is no reason to assume that the temporal information may be of a kind that could be used to judge the temporal location of events according to conventional time-frames.

It is difficult to argue on empirical grounds against such a defence of the role of temporal-contextual information. Arguably, such a position means that claims regarding the role of context in episodic memory are not particularly useful empirically, since it means that measuring episodic memory can never be a matter of measuring the availability of contextual information. Further, the plausibility of such a position as an information-processing description of episodic memory must depend on the detailed description that is given of the contextual information that is thought to be stored along with events. Although there are several very successful accounts of the nature of temporal-contextual information in short-term memory (e.g. Burgess and Hitch, 1999; Brown, Preece, and Hulme, 2000; Henson and Burgess, 1998), attempts to specify the nature of stored temporal-contextual information in long-term memory have been much less fruitful (Friedman, 1993 and Ch. 5, this volume). In any case, the relevance here of a successful account of explicit judgements of temporal context is not clear. If the temporal-contextual information stored with episodic memories is argued to be of a type that is not necessarily available for retrieval, there is no reason to suppose that it is identical to any temporal information that supports explicit temporal-contextual judgements.

My own feeling is that, if it is argued that the temporal-contextual information is often not accessible for retrieval, it is not clear what is useful about introducing this type of information to do the job of ensuring the specificity of episodic memories.[1] One may as well simply assume that it is a fact about the episodic memory system that memories of specific events are retained, and that generalization over these memories need not always occur. Nevertheless, there does seem to be something correct about Tulving's original intuition that being able to think about a specific past event involves thinking about that event as having occurred in a unique temporal context. In the next section, I return to this issue by considering whether remembering an event as having occurred in a particular temporal context is a matter of having certain representational resources, rather than retrieving stored pieces of contextual information.

The focal element/setting distinction

One motivation for linking episodic memory to memory for contextual information was the idea that the specificity of episodic memory is due to stored temporal-contextual information. However, this suggestion is difficult to maintain. I now consider another way in which the case could be put for a contextual description of episodic memory.

The question that we are puzzling over is what is involved in having a memory that is about a specific past event as opposed to, for example, having a factual memory that stems from a specific event. In his 1983 book, Tulving discusses the difference between remembering a past learning event and remembering what is learnt. He makes the distinction between memory for the focal element of a learning event (e.g. a word in a list-learning task) and memories that include the 'setting' in which one encountered that element. It is the latter type of memories that are thought to be episodic.

It is not obvious how to interpret the focal element/setting distinction, but one possibility that may seem initially appealing is that remembering the setting involves remembering certain pieces of information. More specifically, perhaps remembering the setting is a matter of retrieving pieces of contextual information? Note that if one is going to make a case for defining 'setting' in terms of contextual information, it cannot be a type of contextual information that is stored with events but is unavailable or inaccessible at retrieval. Remembering the

---

[1] Brown and Chater (Ch. 3, this volume) have a different reason for assuming that temporal-contextual information is always stored along with memories for events. They argue that such information plays a fundamental role in memory retrieval.

setting is thought to be part of what it is to remember the episode itself. Therefore, if one is going to try to define setting in terms of contextual information, the information one describes must be something that the rememberer can report on at retrieval. It would seem, then, that someone arguing for a definition of setting in terms of pieces of stored contextual information could not include temporal-contextual information among these pieces of information. This is because, as we have seen, accurate judgements of temporal context are often not possible. Indeed, experimental research on memory for contextual information would suggest that it is not at all obvious what pieces of contextual information could be singled out as usually available in episodic memory.

According to Tulving's own analysis, remembering the setting of an event is not a matter of remembering pieces of contextual information. Rather, the distinction between focal element and setting is made clear if one bears in mind that, according to Tulving, episodic memory 'is capable of recording and retaining information about perceptible properties of stimuli that can be apprehended immediately by the senses' (1983: 41; see also Tulving and Markowitsch, 1998). For him, the focal element/setting distinction would seem to be a part of the difference between, for example, being able to remember a word from a list (the focal element), and remembering the *experience* of seeing/hearing the word previously. Remembering the previous experience puts before one's mind features of the setting or situation in which the word was encountered, whereas merely remembering the word itself does not.

The assumption that we should distinguish between remembering experiences and remembering facts is one that is made by several of the contributors in this volume (Campbell, Dokic, Hoerl, Martin). For example, Martin explicitly equates the notion of episodic memory with the notion in the philosophical literature of experiential memory. By this he means memory that has perceptual-like qualities (e.g. seeing past events in one's mind's eye or in some sense reliving previous experiences). Similarly, Conway argues that autobiographical memory often involves the retrieval of 'phenomenological records', which he assumes are like snapshots of our perceptual experience, laid down automatically as we engage in goal-driven activity in the world. These accounts have in common with that of Tulving the idea that in characterizing episodic memory we need to consider initially the distinctive way in which events are remembered—the fact that recollecting involves reliving past experiences in some way. I will call this type of account the *experiential description* of episodic memory.

Experientially remembering and memory for contextual information

The question I now turn to is the relationship between remembering one's previous experiences and memory for contextual information. There does seem to be a connection between being able to remember previous experiences and being able to make at least some types of contextual judgement. Remembering one's previous experience will often (but not always) allow one to make certain types of judgement about previous learning events. For example, in a word-learning task, remembering the experience of perceiving the word may allow one to judge the modality in which the word was presented, or make some types of judgement regarding the surroundings in which one encountered it. In other words, the very fact that one is remembering the experience itself will sometimes be sufficient to allow one to make some types of judgement which may be described as contextual.

Of course, it is quite compatible with this view that there may be many contextual judgements which are not based on experientially remembering. One may simply remember as a fact that one was presented with some words auditorily, rather than remembering one's previous auditory experience (Wheeler, Stuss, and Tulving, 1997). Further, the experiential view leaves open the possibility that there are some other memory processes which are dedicated to remembering particular types of contextual information, perhaps in the way described by the simple model in the previous section.

The point here is that in those cases in which one's ability to make contextual judgements is directly a result of the fact that one is experientially remembering, the contextual judgements are based on exactly the same memory as other judgements regarding the previous event. The implication of this is that which types of memory judgement are described as contextual and which are described as non-contextual may be a distinction made by the experimenter (on the basis of what is specified by the experimenter as the focal elements in the memory task), but may not always map onto any real psychological difference.

Thus there is a connection between the contextual description of episodic memory and the experiential description. When one is remembering a previous experience, one is likely (though not guaranteed) to be able to make particular kinds of memory-judgements, which, depending on the memory task, may be described as contextual. However, this does not mean that the contextual description of episodic memory is correct. Rather, the important implication of this is that while we may sometimes use the contextual description as a 'rule of thumb' in designing memory tasks, it cannot be what underpins our attribution of episodic memory. On the experiential view, the types of memory-judgement that one can make will depend to some extent on which aspects of one's experience one remembers, so it would not, for example, make sense to base attributions of episodic memory solely on the availability of particular types of contextual information.

It is true that the experiential description of episodic memory might seem unappealing to some psychologists. Suggesting that episodic memory involves remembering events in a distinctive way may be viewed by some as an unwelcome attempt to introduce tricky issues to do with types of memory experience. And it may be thought that raising issues to do with memory experiences does not sit well with the standard approach to memory as a system for storing and retrieving pieces of information.

It is beyond the scope of this chapter to address such a worry fully. However, there are two points to bear in mind. The first is that, at least as things stand, the contextual description seems to have been the only plausible attempt to describe episodic memory purely in terms of the storage and retrieval of pieces of information. But, as we have seen, it seems clear that in so far as the contextual description has any plausibility it is because it *derives from*, and thus is secondary to, a more basic notion of episodic memory as memory for specific past experiences. Without this more basic intuitive notion of experiential memory, it is difficult to see how or why one might go about trying to describe episodic memory in terms of contextual information.

The second point is that even if the experiential description of memory is correct, there must still be a story to be told about what types of information about events are stored in episodic memory, and the representational resources involved in episodic remembering. I cannot hope to provide all the details of such an account here, but in the next section I address one facet of this issue by considering the way in which episodic remembering seems to require a particular type of temporal representation.

EPISODIC MEMORY AS EXPERIENTIAL MEMORY

The experiential description of episodic memory presents various challenges to cognitive psychologists. For example, we need to give a good explanation of how the relevant experiential information is stored in memory (see Conway, Ch. 9, this volume) that is sensitive to the fact that episodic memories are not usually straight copies of perceptual experience. For example, Campbell discusses the work of Nigro and Neisser (1983), who found that images in memory sometimes correspond to what was perceptually available to someone other than the rememberer (so-called 'observer' memories in which the memory depicts rememberers themselves carrying out an action). The experiential description raises particularly difficult issues regarding memory attribution. The discussion of animal memory in the previous sections is compatible with Tulving and Markowitsch's (1998) analysis that there is no reason to ascribe episodic memory to animals. However, if we take experiential remembering to be the correct description of human episodic memory, there are pressing developmental questions regarding the correct description of children's memory.

Is experiential memory developmentally primitive?

On first consideration, it might appear that experiential memory is developmentally primitive. Given Conway's description of experiential memories as involving something like snapshots of past perceptual experience, it might seem that this type of awareness of past events is unmediated by reasoning or inferential processes. Further, according to Conway, there is a route to accessing such snapshots that is environmentally driven and available in the absence of search and retrieval processes governed by higher-order control processes. According to this description, it might appear that episodic memory is available to very young children. Consistent with this, reports in the literature suggest that very young children do sometimes verbally recall specific past events (Fivush and Hammond, 1989, 1990; Nelson, 1993; Pillemer, 1998). In addition, the fact that children of this age are already beginning to use tensed verb forms (especially the simple past; Harner, 1982; Weist, 1986) seems to indicate some kind of awareness of and orientation towards past events of the sort that is likely to be unavailable to animals.

Although this description of experiential memory as primitive may be appealing, the picture may be a bit more complex than this. Importantly, if young children did have experiential memories, for them to make use of such memories it would be necessary to have a way of handling the information derived from them. An important feature of such memories is that the information they yield is information about the past—facts about the world as it was, not as it is. Making use of such memories would seem to involve being sensitive to the fact that the retrieved experiences were ongoing in the past, rather than present experiences. Perner (1991) discussed this issue with respect to the distinctions that have to be maintained within the child's representational system. He argued that, like imaginings and pretence, memories have to be 'quarantined off' from representations of the world as it is, in order to prevent erroneous actions. In the case of memories, he described this as involving labelling or representing them in some way as 'past'.

There is a connection here with the issue of the specificity of episodic memories that was discussed in the previous section. There seems to be something correct about Tulving's (1983) original insight that being able to think about a specific past event involves thinking about that event as having a unique temporal location. That is, it does seem to be true that part of what makes it the case that my memory is about a certain specific event is that I think of the event as having occurred in a particular, unique, temporal context. However, as was shown in the last section, remembering an event as having occurred in a particular, unique, temporal location does not seem to be a matter of retrieving a stored piece of temporal-contextual information.

The link here with the quarantining of memories as 'past' is that part of what is involved in possessing a full-blown concept of the past is having the ability to think of previous events as having occurred in particular, unique, temporal locations (Campbell, 1994). The representational requirements of possessing memories about specific past events have been discussed in detail by Campbell (1994). He describes thought about the past, and thus episodic memory, as involving a *temporal framework* (a kind of cognitive map of time) which would, in principle, allow each event in our past to be assigned to a unique location. However, possession of such a framework does not guarantee that one actually possesses accurate information about the location of each specific past event. This is clear if one thinks about the spatial analogy. One could possess an accurate map of space, which could in principle be used to assign a unique location to any object.

However, there may be many objects that one knows exist but cannot place on the map, because one does not know where they are. Similarly, possessing a temporal framework that can be used to represent past events as having unique temporal locations does not have the implication that one can actually remember when each event occurred. Further discussion of temporal frameworks and their relation to the development of episodic memory can be found in McCormack and Hoerl (1999).

In what follows, I focus on two different views of children's early memory. According to the first, the *displacement view*, 2- to 3-year-old children do have memories which are like Conway's phenomenological records and which are quarantined off as in the past. In what follows, I will describe these as quarantined memory images (the term 'memory image' is used by Hoerl (Ch. 12, this volume) to capture the experiential aspect of episodic memory). On the displacement view, it would make sense to describe young children as having episodic memories. However, I argue that there are reasons to believe that children of this age do not have the conceptual resources to quarantine off such memories as in the past. I finish by considering an alternative view, the event-based view, which does not assume that such quarantining abilities are available or required to explain children's memory abilities.

The displacement view of early memory

According to the displacement view, children have an early capacity for displacement which amounts to (i) possessing memories of past experiences in the form of memory images of past experiences (or, in Conway's terms, phenomenological records), and (ii) the ability to quarantine off such memories as representations of events which were ongoing in the past.

Although there is disagreement in the literature over how children's early temporal concepts should be characterized, there is a general consensus that 2- to 3-year-olds do not have a mature concept of time equivalent to that of adults, even if they are able to use some tensed forms of verbs correctly (see Harner, 1982; Gerhardt, 1989; Nelson, 1996; Weist, 1986, 1989; Weist *et al.*, 1997). If we accept that 2- and 3-year-olds do not have a mature concept of time, but want nevertheless to maintain that they have experiential memories, it is necessary to describe what, in Perner's terms, quarantines off these memories so that they are treated as representations of the world as it was, not as it is.

On the basis of an extensive review of the literature on children's use of tensed forms and temporal language, Weist (1986, 1989) has argued that, while young children may have a concept of time that is a primitive one, nevertheless they can still think of some events as having happened in the past. Thinking of an event as having occurred in the past is a relational notion. It involves grasp of the relationship between the point in time at which the previous event occurred, and the current point in time. Specifically, use of the simple past tense involves marking an event as having occurred at a time *before* the present time. Weist argues that when children first use the simple past tense, they can think about events as having occurred previous to 'now'. Weist (1989) argues that such a grasp of the relation 'anterior to now' is limited because, for example, it does not yet involve actually being able to think of the event in question as occurring at a particular time in a time-line running from past to future. However, in so far as they have some capacity for mental displacement from the current time, Weist believes that 2- to 3-year-olds *do* have episodic memories and think of the remembered events as having occurred previously.

If Weist's description is correct, children of this age are not thought to be operating with the type of temporal framework mentioned above that allows them to think of events as having particular unique temporal locations. Further, because recalled events are not thought of as having occurred at particular points in time, there is no reason to suppose that children of this age can, for example, think about the temporal relation that any two remembered events have to each other. And at this early stage, Weist argues that children are not capable of flexibly adopting different temporal perspectives on events, unlike adults and older children, who can, for example, describe a past event from a previous point of view at which the event was still in the future (see also Cromer, 1971; Smith, 1980). In this sense, young children are not capable of the temporal decentring described by Campbell in the current volume (Ch. 6).

Nevertheless, if Weist's description of children's early temporal understanding is correct, it may appear that young children do have a primitive way of quarantining off memories of previous experiences as in the past, as the displacement view holds. Is the displacement view a correct description of young children's abilities? To answer this question, we need first to consider what is really involved in quarantining memories in this way.

Making use of episodic memories: the role of causal reasoning

Elsewhere, Campbell has described what is involved in thinking of events as having occurred in the past in terms of a requirement for reflective causal understanding (1994, 1997). In his chapter in the current volume (Ch. 10) Martin also argues that representing previous experiences as in the past in part amounts to having 'a grasp of a concept of time as a causal structure in which earlier events cause later ones'. One way of exploring this claim is to consider how such causal understanding would affect the way that memories of previous experiences could be put to use.

One can distinguish between (at least) two ways in which memory images might be put to use. First, these memories might be treated as potential descriptions of the way the world is now. One may remember the experience of seeing a cake in the kitchen, and thus adopt the hypothesis that the cake is in the kitchen. Exploiting one's memory in this way would not involve any type of reasoning about the causal relations that exist between events that occur at different times. It simply involves using a memory to revise or update one's model of the world.

I will call this ability using memory images for updating. The second way in which memory images could be put to use involves a more sophisticated type of reasoning. In this second way of using memory, one exploits the memory not as a potential description of the world, but as a basis for making informed inferences about how the world may or may not be now, given the way events were previously. For example, you could remember seeing it rain yesterday. Based on your memory, you might reason that there is no need to water the garden today. In this case, you are using the information that memory yields about past events in causal reasoning to work out the current state of the world, and to decide how to act accordingly.

Without the ability to reflect on the causal relationships between the remembered events and the current state of the world, it is clear that possessing memory images would be of limited value. The information yielded by such memories would function only as a possible description of how the world *might still be now*. That is, memory images could be used only for updating. Without the additional capacity to reflect on the causal relationships between events at different times, there would be real limitations on how one could exploit such memories.

Would the fact that a remembered event occurred *in the past* play any role in one's reasoning if memory images could be used only for updating? One way of trying to answer this question is to consider whether exploiting such memories for updating would be more sophisticated or useful than primitive reasoning that clearly does not involve reference to the past. There is, of course, a primitive way in which one's earlier experiences could affect one's subsequent behaviour without thought about the past. A child could see a cake in the kitchen, and construct a model of the world that includes the cake being in the kitchen. This enables her to return at a later point to the kitchen to look for the cake. However, episodic memory is not involved here. Rather, simply having the concept of object permanence would be sufficient to ground her behaviour. Note that in this case the quarantining problem mentioned by Perner does not arise, because her behaviour is always based on a model of the world as it is.

This more primitive case, in which the child has a model of the world that changes over time, is obviously not the same as using memory images to update one's model of the world. However, if use of such memories is limited to this updating function, it is not entirely clear what additional advantage they would provide over the more primitive case. If there is a difference between the two cases, it seems to be that using memory images, but not the primitive case, involves being *reminded anew* of the way the world is. Such reminders could be triggered by environmental cues (as Conway suggests) or even potentially be the outcome of some kind of memory search and retrieval processes. But in exploiting such reminders, there does not seem to be any role played in one's reasoning by thinking of the remembered past event specifically *as* being in the past. There would appear to be no use being made aware of the fact that the remembered events are something that occurred before now.

Causal reasoning and the displacement view

Such considerations provide some reasons to doubt whether, in the absence of reflective causal understanding, the fact that remembered experiences occurred in the past could really be exploited in one's remembering (see Campbell, 1994). Thus there are at least grounds for doubting whether, in the absence of reflective causal understanding, memory images would really be treated as quarantined-off representations of the past. It would appear that, at best, such memories could be used only as reminders of the world as it is. The implication of this is that in assessing the validity of the displacement view described above, we need to turn to considering whether 2- or 3-year-old children have such an ability to reason about the causal relations between events at different times.

A recent paper by Povinelli and colleagues (1999) has attempted to address precisely this issue, arguing that an inability to reason about causal relations in time is a central limitation of young children's temporal thought, and one which is not overcome until children are around four years of age. To demonstrate this, they showed 3- and 4-year-olds videotapes of a previous situation in which an experimenter was shown concealing a toy in a box, out of sight of the child who was at that time playing a game with another experimenter. They found that below 4 years children could not make use of the information about the previous hiding event subsequently provided by the videotape in order to search for the toy (see also Povinelli, Landau, and Perilloux, 1996; Povinelli and Simon, 1998; Suddendorf, 1999; Zelazo, Sommerville, and Nichols, 1999). They found that this was so even if the relevant information was provided verbally rather than in the form of a videotape. Povinelli *et al.* (1999) argued that, without the ability to reason about the causal relations that exist between the previous hiding event and the current state of the world, children cannot make use of the information provided to them about the previous event.

Although from an early age, children show considerable sensitivity in their behaviour to causal relationships in the world, it is possible to distinguish between this mere sensitivity to regularities in the world and the ability to reflect on and reason about causal relationships between events at different times (see Campbell, 1994: ch. 3, for this point in detail). If Povinelli is correct, then before 4 years, children do not have this latter ability. Clearly, further research is necessary to establish whether Povinelli's description of children's difficulties is correct.[2] However, the important point for present purposes is that in the absence of an ability to reason about the causal implications of past events, young children should have limitations in the way they could use memory images, just as they have difficulty using the videotapes of past events. It is likely that they would be limited to using such memories only to update

---

[2] Actually, it may be possible to argue that updating abilities alone would be sufficient to pass Povinelli's task, rather than an ability to reflect on causal relationships between past and present events.

their model of the world, rather than in causal reasoning about the way the world might be.

Where does this leave the displacement view? According to the displacement view, children have memory images of events ongoing in the past, and they have a way of quarantining off such memory images as representations of the past. However, if Povinelli is correct about children's limitations concerning causal reasoning, there are reasons to doubt that 2- or 3-year-olds have the concepts available to them that would perform this quarantining job.[3] If young children do have memory images, they would be exploiting them in a way that is quite different from adults.

Event representations and early temporal thought

I have queried whether a displacement view is correct by considering whether young children's conceptual limitations would mean that they could use memory images only for updating their current model of the world. What alternatives to the displacement view may there be?

There are a number of facts to bear in mind when attempting to characterize children's early abilities. It is quite clear from the literature that 2- and 3-year-olds are not limited to simply updating their model of the world as it changes. Their knowledge of the temporally extended world goes beyond the more primitive grasp of object permanence described above. As will be discussed, children of this age have some ability to keep track of what has happened and are often adept at predicting what is yet to come, given their current situation (overviews of the relevant literature are provided in Fivush and Hudson, 1990, and in Nelson, 1986, 1996). Two important issues are addressed in this final section. First, how do children do this if they are not capable of reflecting on causal relationships between events at different points in time? Secondly, do we need, in the end, to appeal to a notion of quarantined memory images to explain any of young children's abilities?

The first question can be addressed by considering children's knowledge of event sequences. Over the last two decades, a considerable body of research has examined children's memory for event sequences (e.g. Fivush, 1984; Nelson, 1986; Nelson and Hudson, 1988). Various studies have shown that even in the first year of life, children can learn structured sequences of events, with studies of deferred imitation showing that children can behaviourally reproduce event sequences that they have observed only on a single occasion (e.g. Meltzoff, 1990; Bauer and Dow, 1994; Bauer and Mandler, 1989, 1992). This early capacity to learn event sequences seems to provide the developmental basis for the subsequent emergence of richer representations of types of event sequences. Studies of

---

[3] Povinelli *et al.* themselves seem to assume that events could be represented as in the past before such causal reasoning emerges. The general issue being raised here is whether it is possible to have a concept of the past without an appreciation of causality in time.

2- and 3-year-olds' knowledge about event types have shown that children of this age have accurate memory representations of a wide variety of typical event sequences or routines (what happens when you go to nursery school, mealtime or bedtime routines, what happens on trips to the doctor, and so on). Experimental studies in which children are exposed to novel sequences of events, such as baking a cake, have shown that even after relatively little experience children can remember event sequences that they have encountered (Fivush, Hudson, and Nelson, 1984; Ratner, Smith, and Padgett, 1990). When such knowledge is verbal, it is usually described as being in the form of 'scripts' (Schank, 1982; Schank and Abelson, 1977). Children's scripts are often quite rich representations of event sequences, which are sufficiently abstract to allow some degree of flexibility. For example, a script might involve representing a number of options regarding what happens at a specific point in the unfolding event sequence—on visits to a restaurant the choice of foods may differ, or you may not stay for dessert.

Because scripts are primarily descriptions of regularities in the world, they allow children to form reliable expectations about what will happen in many situations. Note that, in using such memory representations, children need not explicitly reason about the causal relations between events. Rather, provided the child chooses the correct script, she or he will possess a description of how their current situation will unfold, and, at any given stage of the unfolding event sequence, will have expectations about what should happen next. In other words, scripts seem to provide a way of engaging in a reliable type of 'if–then' reasoning that does not involve explicit causal understanding. Katherine Nelson (1990, 1996) has argued that general event representations, often in the form of scripts, are fundamental in early reasoning. She has highlighted the essentially adaptive function that scripts have for the child in providing a means of behaving appropriately in common situations. And as general interpretative structures, scripts also provide a basis for category acquisition, language learning, and for making sense of discourse or stories and guiding play (see Nelson, 1996, for extensive discussion).

Scripts themselves are essentially tenseless, because they simply provide descriptions of what usually happens. When young children actually describe event sequences, such descriptions often use the present rather than past or future tense (see Gerhardt, 1989; Fivush and Hammond, 1990). In that sense, such descriptions are like 'timeless stories' (Bruner and Lucariello, 1989). However, there are reasons to believe that 2- and 3-year-olds are not limited to simply describing what usually happens in this way. As Weist's work, and that of others (for example, the detailed studies of the monologues of one child described in Nelson, 1989), make clear, children of this age do often use the past tense to talk about previous events. What does this suggest about children's abilities to keep track of what has happened?

We can distinguish between (at least) two ways of keeping track of what has happened. A primitive way simply involves being able to behave appropriately given what actually has happened. For example, there may be associative links in memory such that one action or event reliably cues the next action, and so on. This does not involve continuing to represent what has happened once it has finished. Of course, children's ability to talk about previous events using past tense morphology suggests that their ability to keep track of what has happened is more sophisticated than this. It suggests that they can actually represent previous events when they are no longer going on. The fact that the past tense is sometimes used to describe previous events suggests that these events are thought of as different in some way to what is currently ongoing. In the rest of this section I consider what might be underpinning children's use of the past tense, and whether we should describe children's ability to represent and recount past event in terms of quarantined memory images.

Event based view of early memory

On the displacement view described above, children's use of the past tense is a manifestation of their understanding of the relation of anteriority to current time. However, in the linguistic literature, there is an alternative account of children's first use of the past tense. According to the *aspect-before-tense hypothesis* (Antinucci and Miller, 1976; Bloom and Harner, 1989; Rispoli and Bloom, 1985; though see Shirai and Andersen, 1995; Smith, 1980; Smith and Weist, 1987), when children first use tensed forms, it is not to mark relations between points in time. Rather, tensed forms are used to mark actual *properties of events themselves* (usually called aspectual properties). According to the aspect-before-tense view, the past tense is used to mark the fact than an event has been completed, whereas the present progressive might be used to mark the fact that the event is ongoing. So, for example, the use of past tense in a statement like 'John made the boat' should be understood not as marking the fact that the boat-making occurred at a time previous to now, but as marking the fact that the act of making the boat is completed.

What are the implications of the aspect-before-tense view in terms of children's underlying concepts? If we take the aspect-before-tense hypothesis as one regarding limitations on children's concepts of time, the basic idea would seem to be that children of this age can think of previous events as being completed, but cannot yet think of them as being located at a point of time in the past. One way of making the contrast here with the displacement view is in terms of whether children can be said to think about points in time *independently* of the events that happen at those points. On the displacement view, young children use the past tense to mark a relation between two points in time. This, by definition, requires an ability to think about those locations in time separately from what happens or happened in such locations. According to the alternative aspect-before-tense hypothesis, children are sensitive to the status of events (e.g. whether they have finished), but they cannot think about the times at which events occur or have occurred *independently* of this. It is in this sense that children's understanding of the temporally extended world may be described as 'event-based'. Thus, in what follows, this view, which derives from the aspect-before-tense hypothesis, will be called the *event-based* view.

When children are in a situation for which they have a script, they have an ordered representation of the sequence of events that unfold in the situation. Children's earliest ability to represent events as completed may be grounded in this script-like knowledge of event sequences. Such an early ability may amount to an appreciation of the point they have reached in such a sequence. In other words, depending on the point that they are in the event sequence, they are able to think of the earlier events in the represented sequence as completed, while others are still ongoing or yet to come (see McCormack and Hoerl, 1999, for discussion). For example, while eating the main food course on a visit to the restaurant, they may represent the events of finding a table and ordering food as completed and the event of eating dessert as yet to come, and so on. Of course, as some of the examples described by Gerhardt (1989) and Nelson (1996) make clear, 2- and 3-year-olds do sometimes use the past tense to describe an entire event sequence that occurred at a previous point in time, rather than to describe the completed events in a currently active script. In this case, the child may be representing the *whole event sequence* as completed, rather than portions of a currently unfolding sequence.

The event-based view and experiential memory

Children's ability to talk about previous events using the past tense suggests they have a way of representing what has happened. The event-based view provides a particular interpretation of children's representations of previous events and use of the past tense that contrasts with the displacement view, in that it does not assume that young children have a concept of the past. The last issue I will consider is the implications of the event-based view for whether we describe young children's memory as episodic memory.

According to the experiential description of episodic memory, episodic memory involves the retrieval of particular types of memories—the quarantined memory images assumed in the displacement view. Does the event-based view assume that children's descriptions of past events are based on quarantined memory images? If we consider what is involved in having experiential memories, it becomes clear that the event-based view suggests that young children's memory descriptions are *not* generated in this way. Mature experiential memory seems to have two components. First, it involves orientation towards the past— thinking of the remembered event as something which occurred before now. The second component derives from its experiential nature. The notion of reliving past events in the form of memory images is one which brings in the idea of an event which is ongoing (in the way that current experiences are ongoing), but *ongoing in the past*. (See also Campbell's description of two components in recollection, in Ch. 6, this volume.)

The very fact that we use the terms 're-experiencing' or 'reliving' past events through memory images suggests that there is something similar about remembering in this way to current actual experiencing. And the term 'quarantining' itself implies that there is a possibility of confusing the representations of what was ongoing in the past and what is currently ongoing. In other words, it seems to imply a need for a distinction to be maintained between what is currently ongoing and what was ongoing at a previous point in time. It is precisely this distinction that the event-based view suggests is unavailable to young children. On the event-based view, young children do not have a notion of previous events that would allow them to think of such events as ongoing in the past. They are limited to thinking of previous events as completed. These considerations suggest that if the event-based view is correct, children's early memory descriptions are not based on quarantined memory images. Rather, they are likely to involve representations of facts about previous events, often based on their script knowledge (which is propositional). Of course, on the event-based view, children's sensitivity to the status of events as completed or ongoing means that they do not confuse previous events with what is currently happening. However, it is perhaps misleading to describe this as 'quarantining'. On the event-based view, it involves representing completed and ongoing events in different ways (as having different properties), rather than keeping apart representations which are themselves confusable. In so far as the event-based view does not seem to draw on the notion of quarantined memory images in explaining children's abilities, it is compatible with the claim that young children do not have episodic memory abilities (at least according to the experiential description of episodic memory).

SUMMARY AND CONCLUSIONS

The aim of this chapter has been to consider the ways in which time and memory are related. In the first two sections, I argued against a description of episodic memory that implies that ascription of episodic memory is in part a matter of establishing memory for temporal-contextual information. In the last section, I argued that the alternative experiential description of episodic memory has the consequence that we need to consider the role of temporal concepts in ascribing episodic memory to children.

Although remembering a past experience may appear to be a primitive ability, we need to consider what is involved in thinking of that experience as in the past. The concept of the past is not a primitive one, and may depend on having a reflective understanding of causality. There are reasons to believe that 2- and 3-year-olds' concepts of time are not as sophisticated as those of older children. Nevertheless, children of this age do use the simple past tense when describing previous events. Two possible descriptions of children's abilities were described. According to the first, the displacement view, children do have episodic memories, but their understanding of what it means for remembered events to be in the past is limited to grasping that they occurred before 'now'. According to the second, the event-based view, it is not assumed that children have episodic memories, and they are limited to thinking of events as having been completed, rather than having occurred in the past.

The appeal of the event-based description of children's understanding of time is that it provides a route into temporal concepts that is based on children's actual encounters with events. It is compatible with what we know about children's strengths in memory and temporal representation at this age, namely their knowledge of events and event sequences. However, if we accept the event-based view, is there any room left for Conway's original intuition that memory images (or in his terms 'phenomenological records') are available to primitive memory systems? It is quite possible that elements of both the event-based and the displacement views are correct. Children's early temporal thought and memory abilities could be similar to those described by the event-based view, but in addition they could have some access to memory images. These images may be used as a way of updating or reminding themselves of the way the world is, rather than featuring in mature causal reasoning about the past. The event-based view as it stands does not seem to rule out such a possibility.

It may only be with subsequent development of temporal concepts that children become capable of having episodic memory, in which in entertaining memory images they are thinking about and orientated towards the past. Current empirical research does not allow us to decide on the correct characterization of children's memory abilities, but the implication of the arguments put forward here is that future research needs to focus on the children's temporal concepts and whether there are limitations on the use that they make of their memories.

I am very grateful to Christoph Hoerl for many hours of discussion, and to all of the other contributors in the volume with whom I have discussed these and related issues. Many thanks also to Nicky Clayton, Jon Brock, Naomi Eilan, and Rik Henson, who read and commented on an earlier draft of this chapter. This chapter was prepared while the author was funded by a grant from the Medical Research Council (G9608199).

T.M.

REFERENCES

ANTINUCCI, F., and MILLER, R. (1976), 'How children talk about what happened', *Journal of Child Language*, 3: 167–89.

BAUER, P. J., and DOW, G. A. (1994), 'Episodic memory in 16- and 20-month-old children: specifics are generalized but not forgotten', *Developmental Psychology*, 30: 403–17.

—— and MANDLER, J. M. (1989), 'One thing follows another: effects of temporal structure on 1- to 2-year-olds' recall of events', *Developmental Psychology*, 25: 197–206.

—— —— (1992), 'Putting the horse before the cart: the use of temporal order in recall of events by one-year-old children', *Developmental Psychology*, 28: 441–52.

BLOOM, L., and HARNER, L. (1989), 'On the developmental contour of child language: a reply to Smith and Weist', *Journal of Child Language*, 16: 207–16.

BRADSHAW, C. M., and SZABADI, E., (1987), *Time and Behaviour: Psychological and Neurobehavioural Analyses*. Amsterdam: North-Holland/Elsevier.

BROWN, G. D. A., PREECE, T., and HULME, C. (2000), 'Oscillator-based memory for serial order', *Psychological Review*, 107: 127–81.

BRUNER, J. S., and LUCARIELLO, J. (1989), 'Monologue as a narrative recreation of the world', in Nelson (1989).

BURGESS, N., and HITCH, G. J. (1999), 'Memory for serial order: a network model of the phonological loop and its timing, *Psychological Review*, 106: 551–81.

CAMPBELL, J. (1994), *Past, Space, and Self*. Cambridge, Mass.: MIT Press.

—— (1997), 'The structure of time in autobiographical memory', *European Journal of Philosophy*, 5: 105–18.

CHURCH, R. M., and BROADBENT, H. A. (1990), 'Alternative representations of time, number, and rate', *Cognition*, 37: 55–81.

—— MECK, W. H., and GIBBON, J. (1994), 'Application of scalar timing theory to individual trials', *Journal of Experimental Psychology: Animal Behavior Processes*, 30: 135–55.

CLAYTON, N. S., and DICKINSON, A. (1998), 'Episodic-like memory during cache recovery by scrub jays', *Nature*, 395: 272–4.

—— (1999a), 'Memory for the content of caches by scrub jays (*Aphelocoma coerulescens*)', *Journal of Experimental Psychology: Animal Behavior Processes*, 25: 82–91.

—— (1999b). Scrub jays (*Aphelocoma coerulescens*) remember the relative time of caching as well as the location and content of their caches', *Journal of Comparative Psychology*, 113: 403–16.

—— YU, K. S., and DICKINSON, A. (forthcoming), 'Scrub jays (*Aphelocoma coerulescens*) can form integrated memory for multiple features of caching episodes', *Journal of Experimental Psychology: Animal Behavior Processes*.

CROMER, R. F. (1971), 'The development of the ability to decenter in time', *British Journal of Psychology*, 62: 353–65.

DAVIES, G. M., and THOMSON, D. M. (1988) (eds.), *Memory in Context: Context in Memory*. Chichester: Wiley.

FIVUSH, R. (1984), 'Learning about school: the development of kindergartener's school scripts', *Child Development*, 55: 1697–709.

—— and HAMMOND, N. R. (1989), 'Time and again: effects of repetition and retention interval on two-year-olds' event recall', *Journal of Experimental Child Psychology*, 47: 259–73.

—— (1990), 'Autobiographical memory across the preschool years: toward reconceptualizing childhood amnesia', in Fivush and Hudson (1990), 223–48.

—— and HUDSON, J. A. (1990), *Knowing and Remembering in Young Children*. Cambridge: Cambridge University Press.

——, —— and NELSON, K. (1984), 'Children's long-term memory for a novel event: an exploratory study', *Merrill-Palmer Quarterly*, 30: 303–16.

FRIEDMAN, W. J. (1987), 'A follow-up to "Scale effects in memory for time of events": the earthquake study', *Memory & Cognition*, 15: 518–20.

—— (1993), 'Memory for the time of past events', *Psychological Bulletin*, 113: 44–66.

—— and WILKINS, A. J. (1985), 'Scale effects in memory for the time of past events', *Memory & Cognition*, 13: 168–75.

GALLISTEL, C. R. (1990), *The Organization of Learning*. Cambridge, Mass.: MIT Press.

—— (1994), 'Space and time', in N. J. Mackintosh (ed.), *Animal Learning and Cognition*. San Diego: Academic Press, 221–53.

GERHARDT, J. (1989), 'Monologue as a speech genre', in K. Nelson (1989).

GIBBON, J., and ALLAN, L. (1984), *Timing and Time Perception*. New York: New York Academy of Sciences.

—— FAIRHURST, S., and GOLDBERG, B. (1997), 'Cooperation, conflict and compromise between circadian and interval clocks in pigeons', in C. M. Bradshaw and E. Szabadi (eds.), *Time and Behaviour: Psychological and Neurobehavioural Analyses*. Amsterdam: North-Holland/Elsevier.

GRIFFITHS, D., DICKINSON, A., and CLAYTON, N. (1999), 'Episodic memory: what can animals remember about their past?', *Trends in Cognitive Sciences*, 3: 74–80.

HARNER, L. (1982), 'Talking about the past and the future', in W. J. Friedman (ed.), *The Developmental Psychology of Time*. New York: Academic Press.

HASHER, L., and ZACKS, R.T. (1979), 'Automatic and effortful processes in memory', *Journal of Experimental Psychology: General*, 108: 356–88.

HENSON, R. N. A., and BURGESS, N. (1998), 'Representations of serial order', in J. A. Bullinaria, D. W. Glasspool, and G. Houghton (eds.), *4th Neural Computation and Psychology Workshop*. London: Springer, 283–300.

HINTZMAN, D. L., BLOCK, R. A., and SUMMERS, J. J. (1973), 'Contextual associations and memory for serial position', *Journal of Experimental Psychology*, 97: 220–9.

JOHNSON, M. K., HASTROUDI, S., and LINDSAY, D. S. (1993), 'Source monitoring', *Psychological Bulletin*, 114: 3–28.

MACAR, F., POUTHAS, V., and FRIEDMAN, W. F. (1992), *Time, Action, and Cognition: Towards Bridging the Gap*. Dordrecht: Kluwer.

McCORMACK, T., and HOERL, C. (1999), 'Memory and temporal perspective: the role of temporal frameworks in memory development', *Developmental Review*, 19: 154–82.

MELTZOFF, A. N. (1990), 'Towards a developmental cognitive science: the implications of cross-modal matching and imitation for the development of representation and memory in infancy', in A. Diamond (ed.), *Annals of the New York Academy of Science*, vol. 608: *The Development and Neural Bases of Higher Cognitive Functions*. New York: New York Academy of Science, 1–37.

NELSON, K. (1986), *Event Knowledge: Structure and Function in Development*. Hillsdale, NJ: Erlbaum.

—— (1989), *Narratives from the Crib*. Cambridge, Mass.: Harvard University Press.

—— (1990), 'Remembering, forgetting and childhood amnesia', in Fivush and Hudson (1990), 223–48.

—— (1993), 'The psychological and social origins of autobiographical memory', *Psychological Science*, 4: 7–13.

—— (1996), *Language in Cognitive Development: Emergence of the Mediated Mind*. Cambridge: Cambridge University Press.

—— and HUDSON, J. A. (1988), 'Scripts and memory: functional relationships in development', in F. E. Weinert and M. Perlmutter (eds.), *Memory Development: Universal Changes and Individual Differences*. Hillsdale, NJ: Erlbaum, 147–67.

NIGRO, G., and NEISSER, U. (1983), 'Point of view in personal memories', *Cognitive Psychology*, 15, 467–82.

O'KEEFE, J. (1993a), 'Cognitive maps, time and causality', *Proceedings of the British Academy*, 83: 35–45.

O'KEEFE, J. (*cont.*) (1993*b*), 'Kant and the sea-horse', in N. Eilan, B. Brewer, and R. McCarthy (eds.), *Spatial Representation: Problems in Philosophy and Psychology.* Oxford: Blackwell, 43–64.

PERNER, J. (1991), *Understanding the Representational Mind.* Cambridge, Mass.: MIT Press.

—— (2000), 'Memory and theory of mind', in E. Tulving and F. I. M. Craik (eds.), *The Oxford Handbook of Memory.* Oxford: Oxford University Press.

—— (forthcoming), 'Episodic memory: essential distinctions and developmental implications', in C. Moore and K. Skene (eds.), *The Self in Time: Developmental Issues.* Hillsdale, NJ: Erlbaum.

—— and RUFFMAN, T. (1995), 'Episodic memory and autonoetic consciousness: developmental evidence and a theory of childhood amnesia', *Journal of Experimental Child Psychology,* 59: 516–48.

PILLEMER, D. B. (1998), *Momentous Events, Vivid Memories.* Cambridge, Mass.: Harvard University Press.

POVINELLI, D. J., and SIMON, B. B. (1998), 'Young children's understanding of briefly versus extremely delayed images of the self: emergence of the autobiographical stance', *Developmental Psychology,* 34: 188–94.

—— LANDAU, K. R., and PERILLOUX, H. K. (1996), 'Self-recognition in young children using delayed versus live feedback: evidence of a developmental asynchrony', *Child Development,* 67: 1540–54.

—— LANDRY, A. M., THEALL, L. A., CLARK, B. R., and CASTILLE, C. M. (1999), 'Development of young children's understanding that the recent past is causally bound to the present', *Developmental Psychology,* 35: 1426–39.

RATNER, H. H., SMITH, B. S., and PADGETT, R. J. (1990), 'Children's organization of events and event memories', in Fivush and Hudson (1990), 65–93.

RISPOLI, M., and BLOOM, L. (1985), 'Incomplete and continuing: theoretical issues in the acquisition of tense and aspect', *Journal of Child Language,* 12: 471–4.

ROBINSON, J. A. (1986), 'Temporal reference systems and autobiographical memory', in D. C. Rubin (ed.), *Autobiographical Memory.* Cambridge: Cambridge University Press.

SCHACTER, D. L. (1987), 'Memory, amnesia, and frontal lobe dysfunction', *Psychobiology,* 15: 21–36.

SCHANK, R. C. (1982), *Dynamic Memory.* New York: Cambridge University Press.

—— and ABELSON, R. P. (1977), *Scripts, Plans, Goals, and Understanding.* Hillsdale, NJ: Erlbaum.

SHETTLEWORTH, S. J. (1998), *Cognition, Evolution, and Behavior.* New York: Oxford University Press.

SHIRAI, Y., and ANDERSEN, R. W. (1995), 'The acquisition of tense-aspect morphology: a prototype account', *Language,* 71: 743–62.

SHUM, M. S. (1998), 'The role of temporal landmarks in autobiographical memory processes', *Psychological Bulletin,* 124: 423–42.

SMITH, C. S. (1980), 'The acquisition of time talk: relations between child and adult grammars', *Journal of Child Language,* 7: 263–78.

—— and WEIST, R. M. (1987), 'On the temporal contour of child language: a reply to Rispoli and Bloom', *Journal of Child Language,* 14: 387–92.

SUDDENDORF, T. (1999), 'Children's understanding of the relation between delayed video representation and current reality: a test for self-awareness?', *Journal of Experimental Child Psychology,* 72: 157–76.

TULVING, E. (1972), 'Episodic and semantic memory', in E. Tulving and W. Donaldson (eds.), *Organization of Memory*. New York: Academic Press, 381–403.

—— (1983), *Elements of Episodic Memory*. Oxford: Oxford University Press.

—— and MARKOWITSCH, H. J. (1998), 'Episodic and declarative memory: role of the hippocampus', *Hippocampus*, 8: 198–204.

WEIST, R. M. (1986), 'Tense and aspect', in P. Fletcher and M. Garman (eds.), *Language Acquisition: Studies in First Language Development*, 2nd edn. Cambridge: Cambridge University Press, 356–74.

—— (1989), 'Time concepts in language and thought: filling the Piagetian void from two to five years', in I. Levin and D. Zakay (eds.), *Time and Human Cognition: A Life-Span Perspective*. Amsterdam: Elsevier, 63–118.

—— LYYTINEN, P., WYSOCKA, J., and ATANASSOVA, M. (1997), 'The interaction of language and thought in children's language acquisition: a crosslinguistic study', *Journal of Child Language*, 24: 81–121.

WHEELER, M. A., STUSS, D. T., and TULVING, E. (1997), 'Toward a theory of episodic memory: the frontal lobes and autonoetic consciousness', *Psychological Bulletin*, 121: 331–54.

ZELAZO, P. D., SOMMERVILLE, J. A., and NICHOLS, S. (1999), 'Age-related changes in children's use of external representations', *Developmental Psychology*, 35: 1059–71.

12

The Phenomenology of Episodic Recall

Christoph Hoerl

The concept of episodic memory has been highly influential in shaping psychological research over almost three decades now. It was first introduced into the psychological literature by Endel Tulving (1972). Yet Tulving was not the first to use the term 'episodic memory'. It had been used before in a book on the philosophy of memory by Stanley Munsat (1966). Given that Tulving acknowledges Munsat as his source of inspiration, one should expect that the two authors use the term in the same sense. Looking back over the two texts, however, it soon becomes clear that Munsat and Tulving are using the term 'episodic memory' to mark out two potentially quite different phenomena.

Tulving uses the term 'episodic memory' in order to characterize that faculty which allows us to receive and store 'information about temporally dated episodes or events, and temporal-spatial relations among these events' (Tulving, 1972: 385)—occurrences that have been experienced by the subject in the past. Roughly speaking, it is because the subject can report an episode that once happened to her that Tulving chooses the term 'episodic'. For Munsat, by contrast, memory is 'episodic' when the subject can report an episode that happens to her now. It is the kind of memory that our attention is drawn to, for instance, when something suddenly comes back to us. In Munsat's (1966: 47) words '[w]hen I say "I just remembered . . ." I am giving voice to something which just happened'—a conscious mental occurrence that takes place at the time of remembering.

My aim in this chapter is to explore in more detail whether there is a connection between a memory's being 'episodic' in Tulving's sense and a memory's being 'episodic' in Munsat's sense. More to the point, I wish to look at the question as to whether the particular kind of memory Tulving has in mind when he speaks of a faculty which allows us to remember specific past events can be defined in terms of the particular phenomenology involved in recalling those events.

I

At the heart of Tulving's work on memory is the attempt to make good some intuitive differences we see between different kinds of memory. In particular, we find it natural to distinguish cases which we would typically describe by saying that someone remembers a particular event from cases which we would typically describe by saying simply that someone remembers that something is the case. It is this intuition, that memory-ascriptions of the first kind answer to the presence of a distinctive kind of psychological state, which Tulving tries to sharpen up by introducing the term 'episodic memory'. Describing his own motives for introducing episodic memory as a separate psychological category, Tulving speaks of two 'discoveries' which he made thinking about standard procedures for assessing memory performance.[1]

His first discovery concerns something which 'many wise philosophers from Heraclitus on had known all the time: events do not repeat themselves, there is never another event exactly like a given one' (Tulving 1983: 19). The idea here is this. Over time, I may have learned, say, that the bus to the university stops a little bit further down the road from my house. I may have come by this knowledge in a variety of ways: walking past the bus stop and reading the sign, looking out the window and seeing people getting on and off the bus there, or asking one of the neighbours. But saying that I remember that the bus stops there is quite different from saying that I remember it stopping there. In the latter case there has to be a particular episode or episodes—individual, unique occasions when the bus stopped there—that I have in mind. By contrast, if all I remember is that it stops there, I know of something that happens there repeatedly, but my memory is not in any sense about any particular instances of it happening rather than others.

Tulving's second discovery concerns 'the relation between the learner's response and the internal cognitive state that it represented: identical responses could reflect different kinds of awareness' (1983: 20). What Tulving has in mind here is something like the following. Think of someone who asks me, 'Where does the bus to the university stop?' I may point in a certain direction simply because I remember that this is where the bus stops. No particular occasion when the bus has stopped there in the past may come to mind. Now think of someone who asks me, 'Where did the man in the blue coat get off the bus?' I may point to the same place, but this time because I remember the bus stopping there and a man in a blue coat getting off. The response to a question about a particular incident, the thought is, may be identical to the response to a question as to how things usually go. Yet, in so far as it reflects an episodic memory, it reflects a specific kind of awareness which goes beyond the awareness involved in remembering that something is the case.

---

[1] The points Tulving makes in the passages cited are somewhat obscured by the fact that he uses examples from word-list or word-association learning tasks to illustrate them. A central distinction he draws, for instance, is that between remembering the meaning of a word and remembering the token occurrence of that word on a list that one has studied before. However, it strikes me that 'word-events' (i.e. presentations of individual word-tokens) do not provide a good paradigm for remembered episodes. In particular, it is not clear whether one should say that a subject has an episodic memory of a word-event if she is able to say, for instance, which of the lists she has been asked to study before a word appeared on. To be sure, episodic memory does have a role to play in explaining the subject's performance. Without any memory of having studied word-lists before she will not be able to understand the instructions given to her. But it may well be that the information acquired while studying the word-lists was non-episodic, i.e. was simply how each list goes. Therefore, to say that the subject has episodic memories for each particular word seems implausible.

There is a problem, though, with Tulving's two 'discoveries', as they stand, if they are indeed supposed to explain the distinction we see between remembering particular events and remembering that something is the case.[2] The problem arises because, arguably, what is the case can include such things as that a particular event happened on a certain date. Thus, for example, it is true of a large number of people born after 20 July 1969 that they remember that Neil Armstrong first set foot on the moon on that day, but of none of them is it also true that they remember Neil Armstrong first setting foot on the moon on that day. Now take, for instance, the idea that episodic memory concerns particular, unique events. On the face of it, a grasp of the fact that events do not repeat themselves also seems to be presupposed when we say of a person that he remembers that something happened on a particular date, or that someone was the first to do something, even if the person does not remember the event itself. Similar problems arise with the idea that identical responses can reflect different kinds of awareness, depending on whether the subject merely remembers that something is the case or whether he remembers a particular past event. The problem here is that it rather trivializes matters to say that 'identical responses' can reflect different kinds of awareness if they are responses to different questions, as in the examples given in the previous paragraph. To be sure, a response to a question about a particular event may reflect a different cognitive state than that reflected in a response to a question which does not make reference to a particular event. But this may just be because the two questions deal with a different subject matter. Yet, even if we ask a person questions about a particular event, she need not always remember that event itself to answer them. And it is at least not obvious how the envisaged distinction between two different kinds of awareness can help us deal with such a case.

II

The problem I have just sketched is that there seems to be more to claiming that one remembers a particular event than saying that one could cash out that claim by, say, recounting what happened then. Consider the following example (adapted from Ayer, 1956, and Evans, 1982): asked whether one can remember a particular incident in one's childhood, one may find oneself in no doubt that it happened. One may even be able to visualize it. Yet one may still be quite unsure as to whether one can genuinely remember the event itself. However, as Ayer points out, 'it may also be that all of a sudden the event comes back quite clearly. One has no doubt that one remembers it' (Ayer, 1956: 146).

Now, there is one feature of episodic memory we have not considered so far, which Tulving sometimes puts by saying that episodic memory is essentially memory for 'personally experienced' events, or events that belong to our

---

[2] Tulving himself is, of course, aware of these problems; cf. Tulving, 1983: ch. 3.

'personal past' (see Tulving, 1983: 39). Take again the case of a person who remembers that Neil Armstrong first set foot on the moon on 20 July 1969, but does not remember Neil Armstrong first setting foot on the moon on that day, simply because she was not yet born then. Even though she may know a lot about the event, no episodic memories of the event could ever come back to her in a flash of recollection of the kind just described, as they might do for some-one who lived through the days of the first moon landing. Part of what under-lies the distinction we draw between saying that a person remembers that something is the case and saying that a person remembers a particular event is the thought that memory ascriptions of the second type carry with them a specific assumption about that person's history: namely that she has witnessed the event in question. By contrast, no such specific assumption is involved in saying that someone remembers that something is the case. Memories of this type can have been acquired in a variety of ways. Especially, it does not matter whether they have been acquired through one's own experience or through the testimony of others.

What I wish to suggest is that if episodic memory is to be a distinct psycho-logical category, and if part of what makes it the case that someone can episodi-cally remember an event is that she witnessed the event in question, the fact that she did witness that event must help us make sense of why episodic memory is a faculty for which Tulving's two 'discoveries' hold as a matter of necessity. To repeat, Tulving claims that episodic remembering is crucially a matter of having in mind a particular, unique occurrence. And, according to him, having in mind such a particular, unique occurrence involves a distinct kind of awareness, differ-ent from that involved in merely retrieving knowledge as to what is the case. My suggestion is that we must appeal to the fact that episodic memory is essentially memory for events which the subject witnessed herself to explain what these two claims come to.

With episodic remembering, what makes it the case that the subject has this particular event in mind rather than any other is not the fact that she can provide the date when it happened or give any other description which would single it out from others like it. Indeed, if someone episodically remembers an event, ques-tions such as 'When do you remember it happening?' or 'Which particular occa-sion do you have in mind?' still make sense for her even if she cannot provide an informative answer. It is transparent to her that there is an answer, that there is a particular event she remembers, and we need to turn to the fact that it is the event she witnessed to explain why this is so.

Clearly, however, saying that it is transparent to the remembering subject that she has a particular event in mind also means more than saying that her memory happens to stem from her having experienced one event rather than another. The real force behind saying that there is a different kind of awareness to consider here, as Tulving claims, must lie in the fact that the subject's having witnessed the event in question makes available to her a way of thinking about the event that would not be available to her had she not witnessed it. For this to be the case, however, her having witnessed the event in question must make a difference to what it is like for her now to remember it.

In what follows, I wish to flesh out these suggestions by looking more closely at the idea that episodic memory makes available a particular way of thinking about events. In particular, I wish to pursue the claim that this idea can illuminate both questions as to the content of episodic memories and questions as to the phenomenology of episodic recall. First, however, I wish to look in more detail at the kind of remembering that is at issue when we say that someone remembers that something is the case, and the way of thinking about the world it involves.

III

Developmental psychologists have pointed out that young children seem to be outstandingly effective at learning and remembering event sequences. For instance, there exists a large body of research (starting with Nelson and Gruendel, 1981) on children's competence in verbally recalling the course of events involved in certain commonplace activities, such as the sequence of events involved in having a meal at a restaurant, or in assembling a toy from various components. These cases are often referred to by saying that the child has acquired a *script* of a certain type of event sequence, and we find that children are capable of recounting such scripts after just one encounter with the kind of sequence in question (Ratner, Smith and Dion, 1986). Yet it is doubtful whether we can also say that these children have episodic memories. Even at a stage when children have become quite articulate in reporting sequences of events in the form of a script, it often seems exceedingly difficult to get them to generate reports of specific occasions when such a sequence took place.

It is arguable, however, that the emergence of scripts indicates the development of a particular form of declarative memory. It is the term 'declarative memory' which is typically used to capture that form of memory which we have so far described by saying that it involves remembering that something is the case. And, as I wish to argue, it is declarative memory which can, in a certain sense, count as the most basic form of retention of knowledge about the world.

The ability to learn from the word of others, or to put what one has learned into words oneself, is often seen as a hallmark for the possession of declarative memory. We can look at this ability to make clearer what is involved in declarative memory, and how it differs from more primitive learning capacities. Think, for instance, about knowing one's way about in a building. If we know the route from, say, the entrance to a particular office, we can usually also give someone else directions. And if we don't know the route, we can acquire that knowledge by asking someone else for directions and use it to get to where we want to go. But there is a more primitive way in which one may be said to have learned a route. An animal may have learned, through trial and error, how to negotiate a maze to get to a food source, without there being any sense in which it could manifest possession of that information other than through that practical ability, or any sense in which it could have acquired that information other than through repeated practice. The point here, of course, is not just that the animal has no capacity for verbal report or verbal comprehension. Rather, the point is that there are two quite different abilities for retaining information at issue.[3]

The claim, in short, is that the information retained in declarative memory is *accessible* to the subject in a way in which this is not the case for the information retained in what is usually called 'procedural memory', for the latter is contained in a specific practical ability. There are two important, interconnected, aspects to this notion of 'accessibility'. First, it involves the idea that information is available to the person in such a manner that it can be drawn upon by him in a variety of ways. What he has learned is not just how to do one thing or another, but how things stand, such that they call, say, for choosing certain words to give directions or certain movements to get to his destination. Secondly, it involves the idea that information is available to the person in such a way that it can be brought to mind. In talking about declarative memory, we can draw a distinction between a person's retrieving the information and his acting upon it, in a way we cannot do when we are talking about procedural memory. It is because the person's memory presents things as being thus and so to him that he knows, for instance, which words to choose to give directions or which movements to get to his destination.

Considerations such as these, I believe, are at the heart of the idea that declarative memory involves the retention of knowledge in a way in which procedural memory does not.[4] Ascriptions of declarative memory carry the implication that the subject is able to see what he is onto in doing certain things. In explaining a person's behaviour, to say that he knows that things are a certain way (or that they go a certain way, as in the case of children who have acquired a script) means more than that he can do certain things. It implies that there is a sense in which he knows why it is right for him to do those things, why doing them is the right thing to do. Talk about declarative remembering as a matter of retaining knowledge, thus, has its roots in a picture of declarative remembering as a way of making sense of why it is right for us to do certain things by bringing to mind how things stand.

---

[3] Indeed, it may be argued that the kind of memory we rely on when we make our way into our own office in the morning is of the same kind as the animal's, only that we also have the more sophisticated form of memory available. Conversely, I do not wish to imply that having a language is necessary for possession of declarative memories.

[4] Possession of practical skills is sometimes described as a matter of 'knowing how' instead of 'knowing that' (cf. Cohen, 1984; Squire, 1987). This distinction was originally introduced by Ryle (1949: ch. 2), who argued that the ascription of propositional knowledge had to go together with the ascription of a range of practical skills. It is less clear, however, whether Ryle himself would be prepared to describe the possession of practical skills alone as a kind of knowledge. Cf. Moore, 1997: ch. 8, on related issues.

IV

Human reminiscing about times gone by often seems an idle pursuit, and distracting from the task at hand. What, then, is the point of being able to remember particular past events? What I wish to argue, in short, is that our possession of episodic memories has a particular epistemic role to play in our knowledge about the empirical world. And it is in this light that questions about the content and phenomenology of episodic memories have to be addressed.

Let us again return to the example of children's use of scripts. I have said that the emergence of scripts can be seen as a manifestation of a particular form of declarative memory. This is not just plausible in view of the fact that the children can put what they have learned into words. Much research on scripts is also concerned with children's ability to replicate event sequences in action (see e.g. Bauer and Mandler, 1989). And what this research brings out is that they show a remarkable flexibility in recognizing different situations as falling under the same script, or in integrating new facts with what they have learned. Script formation appears to involve a certain ability to generalize from past experience. Yet, if it is true that children can acquire scripts without having the capacity to form episodic memories (see McCormack and Hoerl, 1999, for a more detailed defence of such a claim), we have to ask what kinds of limitation this nevertheless imposes on those children's reasoning capacities.

The issue we need to focus on, I believe, is to what extent scripts can count as generalizations from past experience. A child who has acquired a script can be said to know how certain things go, on the basis of certain past experiences she has had. Yet, what I wish to argue is that there are two quite different ways of spelling out what it might mean to say that a subject possesses such knowledge. And the difference lies with the question as to whether the subject herself can make reference to the particular past events she has experienced in justifying the beliefs she holds. Adopting a phrase coined by Bill Brewer (1996), I will argue that if children lack episodic memories, there is an important sense in which they miss out on 'how they are right' about how things go.

Robyn Fivush (1997) has usefully pointed out two core features of scripts. They are marked by the linguistic form script reports tend to take: scripts are often told in the timeless present tense and using the second person. What appears to be reported is not the occurrence of a particular event as distinguished from occurrences of events of the same type at other times, but rather 'what happens each and every time the event occurs' (1997: 142). And, in so far as script reports involve the appeal to an agent, they report not what the speaker did, but 'what you do' in the sense of 'what one does' (ibid.) in a certain type of situation. It is plausible to think that the co-occurrence of these two features is not just incidental. The idea here is this: the reason why scripts cannot be counted as records of token events as they happened to a particular person at a particular time is that events only figure in them in so far as there is an appropriate sequence for them to occur in. That is to say, scripts are concerned with constraints on what can count as the right kind of sequence in which events must be produced or be recounted. What they record, then, are the types which events must belong to in order to make up a sequence of that kind, rather than token occurrences of particular such events.

I think what these considerations show is that we have to be careful in describing what is entailed by declarative memory. I have argued that what is crucial about having declarative memories is that these memories enable the subject to see what she is onto in doing certain things, that is, why it is right to say one thing rather than another or do one thing rather than another. For instance, a child who can recount what is involved in having a meal at a restaurant can be said to have picked up on the conventional order in which things happen when one visits a restaurant. Or a child who can assemble a toy might be said to have picked up on the causal order in which one must put the pieces together to produce the toy. Yet at this point we must observe an important distinction. We must distinguish between seeing why it is right for me to do what I do, given the way I take things to be, and seeing why it is right for me to take things to be that way in the first place. In ascribing declarative memories to someone, we commit ourselves to saying that she has a grasp of certain constraints on what she says or does, but we do not as yet say what her grasp of these constraints comes to, what constitutes her grasp of the reality her beliefs are answerable to.

A comparison might perhaps clarify the point I am trying to get at. Consider, for instance, two different senses in which we can talk about someone knowing about the colour of things. In the case of a sighted person, an account of what it is for her to know about the colour of things will usually make reference to her ability to make out these colours by looking. Her grasp of the kind of circumstance that makes it rational to have certain beliefs about the colour of things is in part explained by her ability to enjoy certain experiences which present things as having these colours. The same cannot be said of a congenitally blind person. In as far as such a person can be said to know about the colours of things in the world, it is only because of what she has been told about the colours of certain objects and her ability to make certain inferences. Clearly, there is a difference between these two cases—a difference that needs to be spelled out in terms of what each of the two persons' knowledge about colours consists in. The blind person will have learned, for instance, that it is correct to say that grass is green or that the sky is blue when there are no clouds. Yet, her conception of the reality her beliefs about colour are answerable to differs from that possessed by a person whose knowledge can draw on her own visual experiences.

The point I wish to make can now be put as follows. When considering what it means to say of a child that she knows about, say, what happens at a restaurant, or what it takes to assemble a toy, we similarly have to ask what that knowledge consists in. To say that a child has a restaurant-script, for instance, might imply that she grasps that the dessert comes after the main course. Yet the child's knowledge about such event sequences may be more like a blind person's knowledge about colours, in so far as she cannot turn her mind to particular occurrences she has experienced. There is a sense in which the child's knowledge about event sequences cannot draw on particular experiences she has had, just like the blind person's knowledge about colours cannot draw upon visual experiences. To be sure, there is a difference here in so far as the child's problems lie with memory, rather than with experience itself. But this should not distract us from a very important respect in which the analogy still holds. If the child does indeed lack episodic memories, she cannot make use of the particular experiences she has had in grasping the kind of circumstances that make it rational to have the beliefs she holds, in the same way as adults can. While there is a sense in which she can generalize from past experience by forming a script, her memory abilities may still be limited in that they do not make available to her a way of thinking of specific occurrences she has witnessed which she could use in justifying the generalizations she comes up with.

The thought here is that episodic memory has a specific role to play in the kinds of knowledge about events and event sequences a person can be said to possess. In particular, a person's ability to remember particular past events can explain a sense in which she can grasp why it is right for her to hold certain generalized beliefs. A person who remembers how things went on previous occasions knows not just that there are instances of which certain generalizations are true. Her episodic memory will also provide her with a grasp of how she is right about those instances, that is, how she is in a position to know about them. There is a specific way of justifying the beliefs she holds which episodic memory makes available to her.

Clearly, this is not to say that we can only really be said to know what happens when one visits a restaurant, or what it takes to put together a certain toy, if we can cite or think of particular occasions when we experienced these things ourselves. Rather, the suggestion is that using a justification of this kind displays a particular grasp of the reality our beliefs are answerable to—a grasp, for instance, of a world in which very much the same thing can happen, or the same states of affairs can obtain, on different occasions. In other words, if a subject is able to turn her mind, in episodic memory, to particular past occurrences, her ability to do so will provide her with a particular grasp of the circumstances that make it rational to hold certain beliefs. In reminding herself of how things went on particular occasions in the past, the subject is aware of having a specific kind of information germane to the truth of or falsity of her beliefs as to how these kinds of things go. Thus, the appeal to episodic memory here serves to elucidate not just how the subject has come to know that certain things are the case, but also what that knowledge consists in, that is, what constitutes it as a piece of knowledge about the empirical world.

I think considerations such as the ones just put forward can help us explain what it means to say that episodic memory involves a different form of conscious awareness from that involved in mere declarative memory. If we see a difference between the two cases, it is because we think of episodic memory as a faculty which makes manifest to us instances of the kinds of event or state of affairs our beliefs are about. I believe that this is part of the force behind saying that, in order for someone to remember an event episodically, it must not just be the case that she experienced the event in question, but that her having done so must make a difference to the way she remembers it. There must be a connection between the specific epistemological status of episodic memory, as a particular way of retaining knowledge of events we have experienced in the past, and its phenomenology. However, this also means that any account of the phenomenology of episodic memory ought to make sense of the specific epistemological role I have sketched, and this is where I believe certain current conceptions of episodic memory fail.

V

One way of spelling out the phenomenology of episodic remembering is suggested by attributional theories of memory. The central contention of this group of theories is that 'people do not typically directly retrieve an abstract tag or label that specifies a memory's source, rather, activated memory records are evaluated and attributed to particular sources through decision processes performed during remembering' (Johnson, Hashtroudi, and Lindsay, 1993: 3). We can distinguish two kinds of such processes. There is, first, a rapid heuristic process of identifying the source of a memory on the basis of specific kinds of information which become available at the retrieval of records laid down in memory. Then there is a second, more systematic decision-making process by which we evaluate the outcome of the first. A memory attribution will only be upheld by the subject if it accords with what is otherwise known, that is, if it is supported by other memories, general knowledge, and our own assumptions about the functioning and strength of our memory.

According to one version of the attributional paradigm, episodic records inherit certain qualitative characteristics from the subject's initial encounter with the event he remembers. On this view, the sense in which episodic memory presents us with a piece of reality we experienced can be explained in terms of particular kinds of corollary information that were encoded when we experienced the event. Basically, the idea is that episodic remembering can be distinguished from other cognitive operations because it typically involves the retrieval of more sensory details, contextual information, or information about the modality through which the event was perceived. And it is these features that allow us to attribute our memory to a particular source.

Another variant of the attributional paradigm appeals not to qualitative characteristics of activated records themselves but to qualitative characteristics of their activation. Thus, according to this view, what guides the attribution is not something that has been encoded in the past, but the influence past experience has on present cognitive performance through transfer effects. For instance, it has been suggested that when we remember something we have previously experienced, it is the particular fluency with which details can be generated that leads us to make a memory attribution. The claim is that people learn to interpret such differences in fluency 'as a sign that they are using the past' (Jacoby, Kelley, and Dywan, 1989: 396).

What, though, does all of this mean when it comes to questions about the phenomenology of episodic remembering? The idea, in short, is that qualitative features of activated records or qualitative features of their activation can explain why it strikes us that we must have experienced the event in question, which in turn leads us to endorse such a source attribution unless there are other reasons counting against it. What I wish to show, however, is that there are at least two different ways of interpreting this idea. And, ultimately, neither of them provides us with a satisfactory account of the phenomenology of episodic remembering and its role in our knowledge of the world.

The attributional account derives part of its strength from the fact that there are various ways in which the effects of past experience on present performance can be measured. Indeed, they can be measured in tasks which do not involve the participant making judgements about the past at all, but rather judgements about perceptual or aesthetic features of currently presented stimuli, or judgements about one's own current mental state (cf. Mayes, Ch. 7, this volume). This may invite us to think that, when subjects are asked to make judgements about the past, they put themselves into the position of the experimenter attributing the measured effects to past experience (cf. Jacoby, Kelley, and Dywan, 1989: 397), only with the difference that the subject is immediately conscious of these effects in a way the experimenter is not. Yet there is an obvious problem with this suggestion. Suppose there were some way the subject could come by the knowledge, say, that particular mental occurrences are typically caused by past experience (which is not at all a trivial assumption). The subject could then infer that it is bound to be true that he has had certain experiences in the past. Yet, to come back to our discussion in the last section, this falls short of showing how the subject could know how it is right for him to draw such an inference, that is, what more there is to judgements about the past to answer to than the occurrence, now, of particular mental phenomena. Arguably, the experimenter can only arrive at that particular attribution because he already knows that the participant has had certain experiences before. Thus, knowing what is involved in making the right kind of attribution itself seems to depend on knowing what has gone on before (or at least knowing of other cases in which what went on before had such an effect), rather than vice versa.

However, attributional theorists need not think of the subject as making a conscious inference from phenomenal features of certain mental occurrences to the occurrence of certain experiences in the past. On an alternative reading, attributional theories detail the workings of inference-like, but essentially non-deliberative, processes. Thus, for instance, attributional theories also make much of the fact that people can be manipulated into making erroneous memory judgements. The idea, on this reading, would again be that such errors are to do with features such as the amount of perceptual details generated, or the fluency with which they are generated, in response to certain tasks. Yet these features are

exploited by information processes which operate outside the subject's awareness, which can make it seem to us as though certain events have happened even
though they never did. However, to think of such processes as essentially working outside conscious awareness also removes any justification for thinking of the
features they exploit as elements of the phenomenology of episodic remembering. All the attributional theory gives us, on this construal, is an account of the
mechanisms that give rise to situations in which it seems to us as though certain
events have happened. Arguably, though, there is a difference between explaining why things seem a certain way to us, in this sense, and explaining what it is
for them to seem that way to us. Attributional theories, on this reading, give a
causal account of what must be the case for us to have certain experiences when
we remember, but, if anything, they simply take for granted that we already know
what it is for us to have such experiences, that is, what the phenomenology of
episodic memory consists in.

VI

A very different approach to the phenomenology of episodic recall can be found
in metarepresentational theories of episodic memory. Those theories take as their
starting point William James's (1890: i. 648) description of 'memory proper' as
'the knowledge of an event, or fact, of which in the meantime we have not been
thinking, with the additional consciousness that we have thought or experienced
it before.' This 'additional consciousness', it is argued, requires the ability to
represent one's own mental states and thus the possession of mental concepts.
Furthermore, it is precisely the way one's own mental states are represented in
episodic memory which 'confers the special phenomenal flavor to the remembering of past events' (Perner and Ruffman, 1995: 517). The basic idea here can
be made clear by looking at an example Perner (2000) gives of the kind of representation involved in episodic memory (see also Dokic, Ch. 8, this volume):

> I have information (that 'pear' was on the list and that I have *this informa-
> tion* because I have seen 'pear' on the list).

The force of the argument that, in order to have episodic memories, one must have
mental concepts, is taken to arise from the claim that a remembered event 'must
be remembered *as* personally experienced' (Perner, 2000). Thus episodic memory
involves metarepresentational abilities, in the first place, because one must be able
to conceptualize the mental state one was in when the remembered event happened
(here, the seeing of the word 'pear'). Once this thought is in place, however, we
must acknowledge that episodic memory also involves metarepresentational abilities in a second sense. It is not enough that I have the information that I experienced the event. I must grasp that I have this information because I experienced
the event, rather than, for instance, because someone simply told me I was there.
Thus episodic memory must also be metarepresentational in the sense that I must

be able to conceptualize my present mental state (the bearer of the information in question, as highlighted in the quotation above), namely as a state which has been caused by my past experience.

If this is true, it gives us a way of understanding the phenomenology of episodic recall which is quite different from that provided by attributional theories. Here, the sense in which episodic memory involves conscious awareness must be spelled out in terms of the particular representational structure of my current mental state. Arguably, if it is part of my being in a certain mental state that I have the information that that very mental state has been caused by my past experience, I must be aware of being in that mental state. In other words, saying that my present mental state provides me with the information that its own presence and nature are due to my own past experience just is a way of spelling out a sense in which that state can be said to be conscious. We only need to spell out the particular self-reflexive structure of that mental state to see what puts me into a position to be aware of being in it. Episodic memory cannot fail to involve a conscious occurrence in the present, because it partly consists in the awareness I have of my present mental state as a particular sort of mental state.

On closer inspection, however, there is a problem with the metarepresentational theory when it comes to the question as to how the past experience is supposed to figure in the subject's reasoning. Clearly, there is a sense in which I know which event it is I episodically remember only because I have experienced it. But if I already have to remember a particular past experience before I make the judgement that it was the cause of my present mental state, there must be a more primitive form of remembering things that happened in the past than that suggested by the metarepresentational theory. We could then ask why this form of remembering should be thought of as falling short of episodic memory, and what is so special about past experiences, rather than past events, that we can remember them in this way.

The rejoinder on the part of the metarepresentational theorist, at this stage, would presumably be that there is no special faculty for remembering past experiences assumed in the theory. All the theory presupposes is the information that I have had a certain experience, and that this experience is the cause of my present mental state. That I have had a certain experience, however, is a piece of information that might simply be retained in declarative memory. It is the kind of information I could have come by in a variety of ways; for instance, someone else might have told me where I had been and what had happened to me on a certain occasion.

If this is true, however, it leaves us with the problem as to what it means to say that, in episodic memory, I also have the information that my current mental state was caused by my past experience of the remembered event. Arguably, all the metarepresentational theorist can point to at this stage is the particular propositional content of the subject's current mental state, and the fact that, if the subject is in such a state, her being in that state is usually caused by her having had certain experiences. Yet, this seems to leave out the crucial sense in which episodic memory provides the subject with a grasp of the reality her beliefs are answerable to. On the metarepresentational theorist's view, it would seem, the subject simply finds herself in a certain mental state. And the presence of that mental state, because of the particular kind of state it is, is supposed to alert the subject to the fact that this very mental state was caused by a certain past experience she has had. Yet, if all the subject can turn her mind to is that particular mental state, it is unclear how the world beyond the mental state she is in could enter into her reasoning in such a way that she might see how she is right about the fact that that mental state has a particular causal origin. If this is true, however, it is not clear what her grasp of that fact comes to in the first place.

Again, the problem here is not so much that there is no role to be played, within a theoretical account of episodic memory, by the kind of representational and conceptual abilities described by the metarepresentational account. It could well be that episodic memory requires some kind of ability for thinking about one's own past and present mental states to be in place, similar to that described by the metarepresentational account. But that does not mean that these representational and conceptual abilities can explain what it is to have an episodic memory, or can account for the role episodic memory plays in our knowledge about the world.

VII

In the remainder of this chapter, I shall outline an approach to the phenomenology of episodic recall which I hope can avoid some of the problems faced by the accounts discussed in the last two sections. At the heart of this approach is the notion of a memory image. My claim will be that there is a way of construing the notion of a memory image that can help elucidate what it means to say that a person has a particular past event before his mind. Yet I shall also argue that the notion of a memory image, thus construed, cannot be divorced from considerations about the particular nature of the project a subject is engaged in when she recalls particular past events.

At first, it may seem somewhat paradoxical to invoke the notion of a memory image at this stage. Traditional accounts of the role of images in memory have often incurred a similar sort of criticism to that which I have just applied to attributional and metarepresentational theories of episodic memory. The particular way the notion of an image figures in these accounts is illustrated in the following example by David Pears (1975). Perchance it might happen to me that I find myself with an image, say, of a certain person. This might then raise questions such as 'Who is this?' or 'Where did I meet this person?', and I may attempt to fit a name or an occasion to the image. As Pears points out, as long as we adhere to this kind of scenario, the image will at best be conceived as something that gets in the way between us and reality, something the occurrence of which calls for further inference or interpretation. It is that picture of an image James has in mind when he says that 'we paint the remote past, as it were, upon a canvas in our memory, and yet often imagine that we have direct vision of its depths' (James, 1890: i. 643). On this view, the phenomenology of memory is a matter of the subject having before the mind a particular mental state or occurrence in the present. But this was just the feature which turned out to be so problematic about the proposals discussed above, if they are read as proposals providing us with an account of the particular way of thinking about past events which episodic memory makes available to us.

Yet, as Pears points out, quite a different way of looking at the idea of a memory image emerges when we reverse the 'direction of fit' between the image and a question asked by the subject. Starting with a question like 'What does x look like?' or 'Who was at the party?' an image might come to me as the answer. On this view, talk about images assigns them a particular role in the project the subject is engaged in. Specifically, the fact that the image has the content it has is partly explained by the role it plays within that project. The image has the content it does only in virtue of being the outcome of the activity I am engaged in. Saying that the image arrives in answer to a question means saying that it is in virtue of having the image that I find the question settled.

In what follows, I wish to spell out a way in which this proposal may be applied in an account of the phenomenology of episodic recall.[5] What I wish to argue is that this proposal can provide us with a way of understanding episodic remembering, not as having before the mind some present mental feature, but as having before the mind a particular past event itself.

VIII

The basic thought I wish to draw on can be found in a late work by Ryle, where he says that the memory image 'is not something by means of which one gets oneself to remember. It is the goal, not a vehicle, of his struggle to remember' (1971: 398). The idea I will take from Ryle is that there is a particular connection between the nature of the memory image and the specific project a subject is engaged in when she remembers. The first thing I wish to do is to clarify precisely what this project might be. I will then try to clarify the role memory images play in that project.

I have suggested that episodic memory has a particular epistemic role to play in our knowledge about the world. Above, I have tried to elucidate this role by considering the situation children might be in before the capacity to form episodic memories develops. In particular, I have looked at the knowledge children can be said to possess in virtue of having acquired scripts of certain event sequences.

---

[5] My thoughts on this issue are heavily influenced by Roessler's (1999) account of perception on the one hand and Martin's account (Ch. 10, this volume) of the connections between memory, perception, and imagination.

Forming such scripts, I have argued, can be seen to involve a certain ability to generalize from past experience. Yet, in the absence of episodic memory, children's grasp of the kinds of circumstances that make it rational to hold the generalized beliefs they have acquired will still be quite limited. In particular, I have argued, using Bill Brewer's (1996) phrase, that there is a sense in which children miss out on 'how they are right' about the things they believe, in virtue of the fact that they cannot make reference to the particular past events they have experienced in justifying the beliefs they hold.

The arguments I have put forward in this context concern the consequences which a general lack of episodic memories might have on children's epistemic abilities. However, there are also occasions on which the consequences of a lack of episodic memories can become apparent to us as adults because we are unable to remember a specific past occurrence. On route to her holiday destination, a person may suddenly be struck by the thought that she might have left the gas cooker on at home. She may be quite sure that she switched it off, but what eludes her is why this is the right thing to believe. And the reason for her worry is that she cannot retrieve the right kinds of memory of the things she did before she left the house. I think cases such as this can help us understand more clearly the sense in which episodic remembering can be a struggle, as Ryle puts it. The point here is not so much that episodic remembering always involves a painful process of rooting around in memory (though it sometimes does). Rather, it is that episodic memory involves a project whose success is not guaranteed. It is, at least on occasion, something we set out to do, and which has a point for us in that it can provide us with knowledge as to how we are right in believing certain things.

I think that these remarks might help us understand better the idea of a memory image as a central ingredient in episodic remembering. In short, if we find it natural to think of episodic remembering as involving images, it is because we think of episodic remembering as an activity out of the same box as visual perception and imagination. In both perceiving and imagining, the subject is engaged in a particular sort of project. And talk about visual images or images created in imagination can be seen as an attempt at spelling out what is involved in the subject's succeeding in the particular project he is engaged in. In each case, the notion of an image, thus conceived, is part of an account of what it is for the subject to find a particular issue settled. The same, I wish to suggest, applies to episodic remembering and the idea of a memory image. What I wish to argue, in particular, is that episodic remembering involves bringing to bear a particular sort of causal understanding. In episodic remembering, the subject's activity is informed by a grip on a specific set of causal constraints going beyond the here and now. Looking at things this way, episodic remembering can be seen as sharing certain features with imagination, and others with visual perception.

What a subject can imagine is, in part, a matter of how things were with the subject in the past. For instance, it may be that a subject is only able to imagine Simon sitting on a chair because she has, as a matter of fact, met Simon (suppose she hasn't otherwise come across information about Simon). Had she not met

Simon, all that could be ascribed to her is the ability to imagine someone sitting on a chair who looks a certain way, where that, as it happens, is just how Simon looks. More precisely, reference to Simon can only enter into the subject's own imaginative project in so far as she has some grip on the fact that what she imagines is constrained by what Simon looks like. In other words, the subject must have a grip on certain causal constraints which govern the particular imaginative project he is engaged in, and her grip on these constraints must draw on information she acquired in the past—for instance in her past encounters with Simon. The appeal to the past must come in here to explain the subject's ability to recognize what it is to succeed in imagining Simon, rather than, say, some other person or no one in particular.

I think it is in this respect that episodic memory can be said to share a feature with imagination. The point is not just that, in order to be able to turn her mind to a particular past event in memory, the subject must draw on information she acquired when she experienced that event. More specifically, her having experienced the event in question must be part of an explanation as to how she can recognize what it is to succeed in turning her mind to that particular event rather than another, or rather than simply retrieving general knowledge. Just as in the case of imagination, the appeal to the past must come in here to explain the subject's grip on the causal constraints that govern the particular project she is engaged in.

Yet there is also a crucial difference between the two cases. In imagination, the subject's grip on the causal constraints governing the project she is engaged in may be quite minimal. Specifically, the particular circumstances in virtue of which her project meets those constraints may be quite opaque to her. Thus, while it may be true that her ability to imagine, say, a situation involving a particular person relies on knowledge acquired in certain encounters with that person, these encounters themselves need not enter into the subject's mind. This comes out, in particular, through the fact that the spatial circumstances represented in the subject's imagination need not be true to any particular past state of affairs she encountered. For instance, in imagining a situation involving a particular person, it is up to the subject where and in what posture she represents that person as being.

This is different for episodic memory. What I wish to argue is that episodic remembering involves an ability, on the part of the subject, to think of her memories of what happened as the result of particular encounters with the world. And the spatial content of episodic memory plays a crucial role in explaining that ability. Specifically, while there is a sense in which episodic remembering can involve a certain amount of reconstruction, I think it is nevertheless plausible to say that, in episodic memory, the subject is essentially passive with regard to the spatial content delivered. More to the point, I wish to suggest that the way in which episodic memory itself makes spatial information available plays a crucial part in explaining the subject's ability to recognize what it is to succeed in turning her mind to a particular past event.

To clarify this idea, we may look at a similar way in which causal under-standing and spatial content are connected in visual perception. A central claim in much recent work on visual perception is that making perceptual judgements involves having a grip on the spatial conditions underlying the perceptibility of objects. In Gareth Evans's words (1982: 222), it involves the ability 'to think of one's perception of the world as simultaneously due to [one's] position in the world, and to the condition of the world at that position.' Johannes Roessler (1999; see also Eilan, 1998) takes up Evans's idea in arguing that, in visual perception, the subject brings to bear a particular kind of causal understanding which can be spelled out in terms of a grasp, on the part of the subject, of these spatial enabling conditions of perception. That is to say, the subject is engaged in a project of informing herself about the world which is guided by her grip on the fact that what she can see depends on where she herself is located, for instance in the sense that there must be a clear line of sight between her and the object. The judgement the subject arrives at relies on the fact that, in visual perception, objects are presented in such a way that their spatial configuration and location is open to view.

What I wish to suggest is that making judgements about the past on the basis of episodic memory similarly involves having a grip on a particular set of causal conditions which must be fulfilled if the subject is to be able to remember them. And, again, the spatial content of memory plays a crucial role in explaining how the subject can bring this causal understanding to bear. As we might put it, the feature episodic memory shares with visual perception is that they both involve a grasp, on the part of the subject, of the fact that the information available to her is the result of an encounter with the world at a certain location. Only, when it comes to episodic memory, the information the subject relies on concerns spatial locations the subject has occupied in the past, that is, where she was when certain events happened. In other words, episodic remembering involves a project which is guided by the subject's grip on the fact that whether she can remember certain events depends on where she was at the time when they happened. It is in this sense that the subject's ability to recognize what it is to succeed in turning her mind to a particular past event relies on the spatial information delivered by memory. In episodic memory, the world as it was comes before the subject's mind in such a way that it solves at the same time for what happened and for what puts her into a position to know what happened, namely the fact that she was around to witness the event in question. By making apparent that things *were* open to view as they happened, episodic memory also makes apparent what allows us to remember them.

IX

If the proposal I have sketched is along the right lines, I think it might help us clarify the role memory images play in episodic remembering. I have said that episodic remembering should be seen as involving a specific kind of project the subject is engaged in. Success in that project is determined by a set of causal constraints, specifically by where the subject was at a particular time in the past. One way of making sense of the idea of the subject's having a memory image, on this view, is to think of it as the successful outcome of the project he is engaged in. Talk about memory images, in this sense, is meant to capture the way particular past events can come before our mind only if we have been around to witness them.

However, the idea of a memory image, thus construed, can also help us make sense of the particular role episodic memory plays in our knowledge of the world. Episodic memory, I have suggested, provides us with a grasp of the reality certain of our beliefs are answerable to, or, in other words, with a grip on how we are right about certain things. I have said that episodic remembering involves bringing to bear a specific kind of causal understanding. The project which the subject is engaged in, we might say, is informed by an understanding that there are further conditions to be met, apart from an event's actually having happened, before he can remember it. It is in this sense that episodic memory can be said to present the subject with a world that is mind-independent. It involves grasping that the events he remembers could have happened without his knowing about them. To say that the subject understands that there are further conditions to be met, apart from an event's having happened, before he can remember it, is precisely a way of spelling out how the subject can make sense of this independence. Yet, arguably, for the subject to be able to exercise this kind of understanding, the obtaining of those further conditions must be something which the subject is, in a certain sense, aware of when he remembers. And this is just the way in which the idea of a memory image, construed along the lines I have proposed, can come in: the image, in this sense, makes manifest to the subject the past accessibility of the remembered event in experience.

To clarify the picture of episodic memory I have in mind, let me draw out two important respects in which it differs from attributional and metarepresentational accounts of episodic memory. On my view, the causal understanding involved in episodic memory consists in a grasp of certain spatiotemporal constraints on remembering, that is, of the fact that we must have been around to witness an event before we can remember it. Note, however, that the form of reasoning this involves is quite different from similar forms of reasoning invoked by attributional or metarepresentational theories. First, in as far as mention of one's own past experience can be said to come into this form of reasoning, it is through the idea that one can only remember the past event because one was around to witness it. This kind of causal understanding may well be quite distinct from the ability to think of the causal relations in which one's mental states stand to each other or their representational nature, as attributional and metarepresentational theories seem to imply. Secondly, this kind of causal understanding is here invoked to explain what allows us to grasp the enabling conditions of memory. That is to say, it is supposed to capture the way in which we make sense of the fact that what we can remember is as much down to us (i.e. where we have been at certain times in the past) as to what has happened. This does not entail that we infer that we have had certain experiences in the past from the qualitative nature of certain mental occurrences in the present, as the attributional account suggests. It also does not entail that episodic remembering is a matter of being in a mental state which has as its content that it has been caused by a past experience.

To conclude, I wish to return to the suggestion made by Pears that episodic memory can be seen as an activity which is guided by a certain question the subject has, and that it is in virtue of having a memory image that the subject finds the question settled. What I have tried to do is draw a connection between the epistemology of episodic memory and its phenomenology. I have suggested that episodic memory can indeed be seen as providing us with answers to a particular kind of question. Turning our minds to certain events we have experienced allows us to see how we are right about certain things we believe. But I have also suggested that the idea of a memory image plays a crucial part in an account of what it is to turn our minds to the past in this way. The answer comes to us in virtue of our having a memory image that brings a particular past event before our mind.

I am very grateful to Naomi Eilan, Teresa McCormack, and Johannes Roessler for discussion on the issues raised in this chapter.

C.H.

REFERENCES

AYER, A. J. (1956), *The Problem of Knowledge*. Harmondsworth: Penguin.

BAUER, P. J., and MANDLER, J. M. (1989), 'One thing follows another: effects of temporal structure on 1- to 2-year olds' recall of events', *Developmental Psychology*, 25: 197–206.

BREWER, B. (1996), 'Internalism and perceptual knowledge', *European Journal of Philosophy*, 4: 259–75.

COHEN, N. J. (1984), 'Preserved learning capacity in amnesia: evidence for multiple memory systems', in L. R. Squire and N. Butters (eds.), *Neuropsychology of Memory*. New York: Guildford Press.

EILAN, N. (1998), 'Perceptual intentionality, attention and consciousness', in A. O'Hear (ed.), *Current Issues in the Philosophy of Mind*. Royal Institute of Philosophy Supplement, 43. Cambridge: Cambridge University Press.

EVANS, G. (1982), *The Varieties of Reference*. Oxford: Oxford University Press.

FIVUSH, R. (1997), 'Event memory in early childhood', in N. Cowan (ed.), *The Development of Memory in Childhood*. Hove: Psychology Press.

JACOBY, L. L., KELLEY, C. M., and DYWAN, J. (1989), 'Memory attributions', in H. L. Roediger and F. I. M. Craik (eds.), *Varieties of Memory and Consciousness: Essays in Honor of Endel Tulving*. Hillsdale, NJ: Erlbaum.

JAMES, W. (1890), *Principles of Psychology*. London: Macmillan.

JOHNSON, M. K., HASHTROUDI, S., and LINDSAY, D. S. (1993), 'Source monitoring', *Psychological Bulletin*, 114: 3–28.

MOORE, A. W. (1997), *Points of View.* Oxford: Oxford University Press

MUNSAT, S. (1966), *The Concept of Memory.* New York: Random House.

NELSON, K., and GRUENDEL, J. (1981), 'Generalized event representations: basic building blocks of cognitive development,' in M. Lamb and A. Brown (eds.), *Advances in Developmental Psychology,* i. Hillsdale, NJ: Erlbaum.

O'KEEFE, J., and NADEL, L. (1978), *The Hippocampus as a Cognitive Map.* Oxford: Oxford University Press.

PEARS, D. (1975), 'Russell's theories of memory', in *Questions in the Philosophy of Mind.* London: Duckworth.

PERNER, J. (2000), 'Memory and theory of mind', in E. Tulving and F. I. M. Craik (eds.), *The Oxford Handbook of Memory.* Oxford: Oxford University Press.

—— and RUFFMAN, T. (1995), 'Episodic memory and autonoetic consciousness: developmental evidence and a theory of childhood amnesia', *Journal of Experimental Child Psychology*, 59: 516–48.

RATNER, H., SMITH, B. S., and DION, S. A. (1986), 'Development of memory for events', *Journal of Experimental Child Psychology*, 41: 411–28.

ROESSLER, J. (1999), 'Perception, introspection and attention', *European Journal of Philosophy*, 7: 47–64.

RUSSELL, B. (1912), *The Problems of Philosophy.* Oxford: Oxford University Press.

RYLE, G. (1949), *The Concept of Mind.* London: Hutchinson.

—— (1971), 'A puzzling element in the notion of thinking', in *Collected Papers,* ii. *Collected Essays 1929–1968.* London: Hutchinson.

SQUIRE, L. (1987), *Memory and Brain.* Oxford: Oxford University Press.

TULVING, E. (1972), 'Episodic and semantic memory', in E. Tulving and W. Donaldson (eds.), *Organization of Memory.* New York: Academic Press.

—— (1983), *Elements of Episodic Memory.* Oxford: Oxford University Press.

IV

Knowledge and the Past:
The Epistemology and Metaphysics of Time

13

Understanding the Past Tense

Christopher Peacocke

What is it to understand a statement about the past? How are the truth-conditions of past-tense statements related to this understanding? And how are the conditions for knowledge of past-tense statements related to that same understanding?

Quite apart from the intrinsic interest of questions about time, the past is a subject matter where realist intuitions are at their strongest. The possibility of past-tense statements which are true, though unknowably so now and in the past, will be a by-product of the theory I will be developing in attempting to answer those opening questions. So one of the background motivations for pursuing the issues about understanding statements of the past is the hope that, in doing so, we may be able to construct a working account of at least one kind of realistic understanding. Examination of such an account ought to give us insight into some of the conditions which make possible a realistic attitude to thought about a particular domain, if indeed there are such conditions.

I will proceed by suggesting a theory of understanding of the past tense, a theory which has the required links both to the metaphysics and the epistemology of the past. The first step will be an identification of one element in our understanding of the past tense. This element is a principle which seems like, and perhaps is, a truism, but which also has significant metaphysical consequences. Then I will go on to identify a second, externalist element in temporal thought, and discuss its relations to the metaphysics and epistemology of this domain. Metaphysics and the theory of understanding will be intertwined throughout this discussion. The discussion also points to some more general conclusions about the relations, in this area at least, between metaphysics and the theory of meaning and content.[1]

THE PROPERTY–IDENTITY LINK AND ITS ROLE IN UNDERSTANDING

I begin by proposing a hypothesis about the role of a certain property–identity link in our thought about the past. It is the link which is the natural generalization of such instances as this:

[1] This chapter, a version of which was presented at Warwick University to members of the Joint Philosophy and Psychology Project on Consciousness and Self Consciousness in November 1997, expounds the core theory of understanding the past tense which later featured in chapter 3 of my book *Being Known* (Peacocke, 1999). I refer any interested reader to that chapter for further discussion of the relation of this theory to issues about explanation, and for its relations to other philosophical approaches to time and memory. The present essay offers (in Section 3) an elaboration and defence, not found in *Being Known*, of the much-disputed notion of the categorical. I thank Christoph Hoerl and Teresa McCormack for valuable advice and comments.

> A thought (utterance) 'Yesterday, it rained' is true if and only if ('iff') yesterday had the same property as today is required to have for a present-tense thought (utterance) 'It is now raining' to be true when evaluated with respect to today.[2]

The property–identity link generalizes what is here said about the thoughts (and utterances) 'Yesterday, it rained' and 'It is now raining' to all corresponding thoughts (and utterances) of the form 'Yesterday, it was the case that A' and 'It is now the case that A'. I call this generalization 'the property–identity link'.

The property–identity link is closely related to one of the principles which goes under the name of 'the truth-value link' in the literature. This is the principle which has such instances as

> A thought (utterance) 'Yesterday, it rained' is true iff the sentence-type (thought-type) 'It is now raining' is true when evaluated with respect to yesterday.

The property–identity link is equivalent to the truth-value link, under the supposition of Uniformity:

> For any temporally open sentence A (or corresponding thought-content), there is a property such that for any time t, 'Now A' is true when evaluated with respect to t iff t has that property.

The property–identity link also entails the truth-value link outright. (The converse, however, is less clear. It is not obvious that the truth-value link involves commitment to an ontology of properties.) I will be focusing on the property–identity link, since we have very clear and robust intuitions about what properties something must have for a present-tense predication of it to be true. If the property–identity principle is correct, those intuitions will also provide a constraint upon any account of what is involved in the truth of corresponding past-tense predications. Later on, I will be arguing that some extant accounts violate this constraint.

Almost everyone will agree that the biconditionals which are examples of the property–identity link are true biconditionals. But to agree that they are true leaves much else undecided. First, it leaves open the question of whether their truth is derivative from something else, or whether their truth has a primitive status. Secondly, it leaves open the question of whether the property–identity link itself explains anything, and if so, what. Thirdly, if the property–identity link does explain some aspects of linguistic understanding and of concept possession, the nature of the explanation also needs elucidation.

---

[2] Both this, and the truth-value link given further below, are to be distinguished from the biconditional with the same left-hand side, and which continues: 'if and only if an utterance yesterday of "It is now raining" would have been true.' That does not generalize correctly, as one discovers if one tries it for 'Yesterday, no one uttered anything', or (for the case of thought) 'Yesterday, no one thought anything about the rain'.

Theorists who hope to make explanatory use of the property–identity link might have one of several quite different goals. One goal might be that of trying to explain the capacity to think about past times at all. This we could call a 'domain-explaining' use of the property–identity link. Trying to pursue that goal solely by citing some kind of mastery of the property–identity links is a distinctly unpromising enterprise. The right-hand side of the biconditionals which are instances of the link simply use past-tense ways of thinking, in the way that the displayed biconditional simply uses 'yesterday' on its right-hand side. The link itself does not connect up mastery of 'yesterday' with anything else. If there is a question about what it is to be capable of such past-tense thoughts, citing some favoured kind of grasp of the property–identity link cannot be the whole of the answer.

A goal of domain-explaining is not, though, the only explanatory goal which reference to the property–identity links might serve. A second goal is simply that of saying something about what, constitutively, is involved in the understanding or grasp of past-tense predications. It can contribute to the attainment of this second goal to mention the property–identity link in stating part of what is involved in a thinker's understanding of what it is for it to have been raining (say) yesterday. This I call a *bridging* use of the property–identity link.

The particular bridging use I want to consider is the claim that a thinker's understanding of the sentence 'Yesterday it rained' consists in part in his having precisely the information given in the property–identity link. The claim is that his understanding involves his having the information that that past-tense thought is true just in case yesterday had the same property that today has to have for it to be true that it is raining today. In saying that the understanding involves the thinker's 'having' this information I mean that the thinker has implicit knowledge of this piece of information, and that this implicit knowledge contributes system-atically to the explanation of his past-tense judgements and his evaluation of certain past-tense claims. Henceforth I will understand the bridging claim to be this explanatory claim about understanding, taken as suitably generalized to other past-tense ways of thinking, and to other properties of times besides that of being rainy.[3]

It will be helpful to keep in mind the parallelism between this bridging claim about past-tense thought and a bridging claim about spatial thought. The bridging claim about spatial thought holds that implicit knowledge of (a suitable general-ization of) the following principle is, similarly, partially constitutive of grasp of thought about other places:

> A thought or utterance 'Ten miles to the east it is raining' is true if and only if the place ten miles to the east has the same property as here is required to have for the thought or utterance 'It is raining here' to be true.

---

[3] For more on implicit knowledge, and the way in which it can explain judgements, see Peacocke, 1998.

This spatial bridging claim seems to me as plausible as the temporal bridging claim.

The temporal bridging claim is not a claim about the nature of the evidence for past-tense statements, or about the manifestation of understanding, even though of course both topics have to be addressed by any theory which includes the bridging claim. The bridging claim itself aims to say something about the nature of a thinker's understanding of predications in the past tense. I want to start by discussing the attractions, obligations, and commitments of the bridging claim.

The bridging claim has two important initial attractions. The first attraction is that the bridging claim entails, and if true it gives an explanation of, the following datum: that if someone understands 'Yesterday', and also understands 'Today it's the case that A', then he is in a position to understand 'Yesterday, it was the case that A'. The datum holds for any past-tense operator, and also holds correlatively in the realm of thoughts and concepts. If someone has the concept *yesterday*, and knows what it is for a thought *Today it's the case that A* to be true, then he is in a position to know what it is for *Yesterday , it was the case that A* to be true. These data hold for arbitrary contents A, be they observational, theoretical, or of any other kind appropriate for embedding in temporal operators. According to the bridging claim, the explanation of the datum in the linguistic case is this. If someone understands 'Today it's the case that A', he must know what property today has to have for it to be the case that A on that day; the property–identity link entails that that property is the one required to have held of yesterday for 'Yesterday, it was the case that A' to be true; and knowing (via this means) what property yesterday had to have for that past-tense sentence to be true is precisely what is involved in understanding it.

A second attraction of the bridging claim is that, in itself, it leaves entirely open, as it should, what sort of evidence might establish the truth of a thought of the form *Yesterday it was the case that A*. It can often take hard thought to work out what, if anything, could establish the truth of a past-tense thought such as *Yesterday, there was a strong magnetic field in the garden*. In many cases it is a partially empirical matter what would establish such a past-tense claim. A good theory must explain how and why this is so. At the moment, the point to be emphasized is that the bridging claim does not at all proceed by trying to explain grasp of *Yesterday it was the case that A* by determining evidence-conditions for it from either evidence-conditions, or truth-conditions, for the present-tense content *Today, it is the case that A*.

A realist may be tempted to add that there is a third attraction of the bridging claim: that it allows a past-tense thought to be true even though there is not, nor will ever be, any evidence for it. Some anti-realists, however, have insisted that they are entitled to certain forms of truth-value links, Crispin Wright being prominent among them.[4] One would expect them, if clear-headed, to insist that they are

---

[4] See esp. his essay 'Anti-realism, Timeless Truth and *Nineteen Eighty-Four*', reprinted in *Realism, Meaning and Truth* (Wright, 1993).

entitled to the property–identity link too. I myself think that, on the contrary, the bridging claim does require a form of realism. At this stage, I just want to note that the question of whether a theorist who makes the bridging claim is also making the truth of past-tense contents always, or possibly, or sometimes, inaccessible to us is an issue which cannot be assessed without looking at the theorist's attendant account of the metaphysics, and his fuller account of the mastery, of temporal concepts.

The commitments of the bridging claim are substantial. The notion of a property as it is used in the property–identity link is to be taken seriously. If the present time and some past time can have the same property, that of being a time at which rain occurs, there must be some level of description of kinds at which they are things of the same kind. Similarly, its raining now and its having rained yesterday are, at some level of description, states of affairs of the same kind. Corresponding points apply if spatial and interpersonal property–identity links are used in the explanation of thought about other places or other persons. We will need certain intuitive judgements about the identity and distinctness of certain properties in order for the argument to proceed. Many of the further determinations which must be made by a philosophical theory of properties will not matter for my argument. I do note, though, that any notion of property which will serve the needs of the property–identity link must be quite general, since almost any content, with almost any subject matter, can be embedded in the past tense. In basic cases, some generalization of the notion of a property identified by Putnam and elaborated by Shoemaker, on which properties are individuated by their causal potentialities, will serve the purposes of the bridging theorist.[5] Certainly the causal potentialities of a time's having a certain property—for instance, the property of being a time at which it is raining—will play an important part in what follows. It is clear, though, that much substantive work remains to be done in metaphysics to develop a theory of properties which has the required generality.

The bridging claim need not and should not be accompanied by the thesis that someone could be capable of thinking about the present while not yet having the capacity to think about the past. A thinker who is capable of objective thought about the present must, it seems, also be capable of past-tense thought. Even the simplest present-tense observationally made judgement of an observational property must be subject to rejection if perception of the perceived object from a different position undermines the original observational judgement. Without such a sensitivity, this would not be a case of thought about mind-independent objects. This sensitivity involves mastery of the past tense. It requires the ability to think 'This object is the same as the one I saw from over there'; or at least to think 'This object is the same as the one to which I previously stood in such-and-such a relation'; and these both involve past-tense descriptions. The ability must be present,

---

[5] 'On properties' (Putnam, 1970); 'Causality and properties' (Shoemaker, 1984*a*); 'Identity, properties and causality' (Shoemaker 1984*b*: esp. 248 ff.).

even if on occasion circumstances are unfavourable for exercising it in a way which yields knowledge (if, say, everything is changing too fast, or if the subject is suffering from lapses of memory or attention). Even if the subject is thinking objectively only about events, rather than continuant objects, the objectivity of thought, and its connection with correction from other standpoints, seems at least to involve the identifiability of particular places over time. This again involves the use of past-tense ways of thinking. The same consideration can be applied to Strawsonian 'feature-placing' sentences, when understood—as they are in Strawson—as placing objective features in an objective world (1959: 202 ff.). The objectivity of the features requires the potential correction of such judgements from other points of view, which again involves the identification of a place at which the thinker currently perceives something with some place at which something was encountered earlier.

So on the view of the property–identity link I am pressing, there is no commitment to conceptual independence of thought about the present from thought about the past. The bridging conception is proposing a constitutive link between understanding of predications about the present and understanding of predications about the past. It is consistent with the existence of this link that present and past be co-ordinate notions, with no conceptual priority of either over the other. This is surely what we should say in the spatial case too. It is not tempting to hold that there is some conceptual independence of the idea of one's current location from the idea of other locations. In the nature of the case, the idea of one's current location and that of other locations are simultaneously grasped—or else none of these ideas is grasped. We have here another example of a local holism.

The bridging use of the property–identity links in both the temporal and the spatial cases does not involve some explanatory priority of the thinker's current location—that is, to the very particular place itself—or to the very time at which he is thinking or speaking. The most defensible use of the property–identity link is one in which understanding of predications of other places and times involves an explanatory link, not with a particular time or place, but rather with a type of way of thinking of a place or time, the present-tense way or the *here* way. To move from an agreed explanatory priority of such ways of thinking of places and times to some kind of alleged priority of the particular place or time, thought of in a way of these two types, would involve an illicit shift. It would involve an illicit shift from a thesis about the level of sense to a thesis about the level of reference. A formulation of the property–identity link which is explicitly about ways of thinking d other than the present-tense way is this:

> For any time t and utterance or thought u occurring at t of 'It rains at d', u is true iff the time referred to by d at t has the same property as any time has to have for an utterance of 'It is now raining' to be true with respect to that time t.[6]

---

[6] This a very relaxed use of inverted commas. Those whom it makes queasy will also know how to give a stricter version.

This is a constant principle which can be used without ambiguity at different times. Its spatial analogue can similarly be used at different places. The move to explaining the property–identity principle in terms of types which may in principle be employed anywhere in space and time serves further to emphasize the way in which the whole spatiotemporal framework is presupposed in the property–identity principle.

It would be fair at this point for someone to press the question of what it means to say that grasp of the property–identity links are partially constitutive of understanding. Perhaps, it may be said, it would not be hard to accept the claim that they are constitutive if present-tense thought were possible without past-tense thought, for then a philosophically prior understanding of the present tense would be drawn upon in the thinker's understanding of past-tense predications. But I have precisely denied such modal independence. And there is a further worry about the constitutive claim. I said it is an advantage of the bridging claim that it explains why, if someone understands 'It is now raining', and also understands 'yesterday', then he will be in a position to understand 'Yesterday it rained'. Yet it is equally a truth that if someone understands 'Yesterday it rained', and also understands 'today', then he will be in a position to understand 'Today it is raining'. So where, it may be asked, is the evidence for any asymmetry which must necessarily be present if the claim of constitutive status for grasp of the property–identity links is to be correct?

On any view, such as I would want to hold, that understanding consists in some specified kind of grasp of truth-conditions, the claim that implicit knowledge of the property–identity links are partially constitutive of understanding the past tense must unfold into the claim that there are features of the grasp of truth-conditions of which the links are explanatory. So any good case for the bridging claim must cite some data involving understanding, and develop the position that the bridging claim provides the best explanation of those data. The explanatory claim is crucial. It may be that some understanders, when presented with the bridging claim, are immediately struck by its plausibility as an explanation of their understanding of past-tense predications. But its so striking them cannot make it so (nor does any failure to strike them so make it false). It is the explanatory claim itself which it is important for the defender of the bridging claim to make good.

I will consider other major points in support of the bridging claim later. Here I will outline one broadly structural respect in which it seems superior to a competing hypothesis (or more strictly, a competing class of hypotheses), and which if correct are indeed data which support the asymmetry to which we noted the bridging claim is committed. On these competing hypotheses, someone who understands past-tense predications has some information about what it is for any given temporal predicate he understands to be true of an arbitrary time. On these competing hypotheses, this information, unlike the bridging claim, gives no special explanatory position to the present-tense way of thinking of a time. Rather, there is some informational state which can be applied indifferently to any time which is thought about, whether the time is given as present, as past, or in a way which leaves open its relation to the present. We can call this 'the indifference hypothesis'. The indifference hypothesis has no dispute with the correctness of what is strictly stated in the property–identity link itself. After all, the defender of the indifference hypothesis will say, the fact that this biconditional is true

> 'Yesterday it rained' is true iff yesterday had the same property today has to have for 'Today it is raining' to be true

is simply a consequence of the generalized condition of Uniformity we identified earlier, that is,

> There is a single property which is the property an arbitrary time t must have for the tenselessly constructed 'It is raining' to be true of t.

The problem for the indifference hypothesis lies in saying exactly what the content of its postulated informational state could possibly be. It has to be something which, together with the correct account of perceptual demonstratives and observational vocabulary, entails a certain truth-condition for an utterance of the present-tense sentence 'That piece of paper is roughly rectangular'. Let us take it (i) that the truth of this present-tense content requires the fulfilment of a range of commitments about how the paper looks from other angles (among other things); (ii) that checking that some of these commitments are fulfilled involves essentially practical capacities, including those involved in the ability to move to look at it from other positions, or at least the capacity when one is so moved to tell whether the commitment is fulfilled, in the context of suitable auxiliary information (and indeed to check, in so far as one can, that it is a piece of paper); and (iii) that understanding this content involves some sensitivity to the fact that its acceptance involves a commitment to the fulfilment of these commitments, a sensitivity possible only for someone able, in suitable circumstances, to check on the fulfilment of any one of the commitments.

The question then arises: what content of an informational state, within the terms required by the indifference hypothesis, could possibly entail this condition of understanding for the present-tense 'That piece of paper is roughly rectangular', and also entail a condition of understanding for its past-tense variants? What could the entailed truth-conditions for those variants be? It is not credible that understanding of a past-tense predication of shape, say, consists in possessing an unexercisable capacity, that of being able to check that the commitments were fulfilled yesterday if only one could travel back in time. And in any case, if one could travel back in time, what one would then be checking would be, at that past time, present-tense thoughts.

To these remarks, defenders of the indifference hypothesis may find themselves tempted to reply that even if that is not a credible account of understanding, then at least the past-tense predication involves the object of the predication in question having the same property whose presence is ensured by the fulfilment of the range of commitments in the present-tense case. The temptation to give that reply is, however, one to which the defender of the indifference hypothesis cannot consistently yield. Yielding to that temptation is just to adopt the bridging use of the property–identity link after all.

Perhaps instead it may be proposed that the informational content needed by the indifference hypothesis has the following character. It is one which—for our sample content—requires the truth of a range of counterfactuals at the time mentioned in the content. Perceptual checks can show that some of these are fulfilled when the time mentioned is the present. But when it is a past time that is in question, the present memories of a thinker who was suitably placed at the past time in question can also establish the fulfilment of some of the commitments. However, I am in the next section just about to make a case that

(1) the counterfactuals are neither necessary nor sufficient for the truth of the past-tense content; and

(2) when they do coincide with the truth-value of the content, they do so only because a condition best explained by the bridging claim is also met.

If this is correct, counterfactuals and memory will not provide resources which will allow the indifference hypothesis to meet the challenge. So once those arguments are developed, our provisional conclusion should be that the bridging claim has a structural advantage over the indifference hypothesis. The special status the bridging claim gives to *now*-thoughts in the elucidation of understanding allows us to reconcile the practical elements in the understanding of a present-tense thought 'It is now raining' with the existence of a uniform condition for 'It rains' to hold of an arbitrary time. The special practical elements in the understanding of the present tense, which do not exist for the other tenses, provide the asymmetrical data which justify the special place of *now*-thoughts in the bridging claim.

PAST-TENSE TRUTH: SOME METAPHYSICS

I now turn to develop some points about the nature of the truth-conditions—about the metaphysics, if you will—of past-tense statements and thoughts. Then, in a later section, I return to the question of accounts of understanding which integrate properly with the emerging metaphysics.

A past-tense statement 'Yesterday it was the case that *A*' resists reduction to counterfactuals in the same way, and for the same reasons, that its present-tense counterpart 'It is the case that *A*' also does. 'Yesterday at such-and-such place an event of kind *F* occurred' cannot ever be explained as meaning 'If someone had been at that place, he would have discovered (or would have been able to discover) an event of kind *F* occurring there'. There are two reasons they are not equivalent. First, if the presence of a person would affect whether an event of that kind occurs, the proposed equivalence fails. The counterfactual could be true and the past-tense statement false; and conversely. This problem is not circumvented by adding the qualification 'If someone had been there, and if his presence were not to have affected whether or not an event of kind *F* occurs there, then . . .'. The newly added clause 'and if his presence were not to have affected whether . . .' has not itself been explained in counterfactual terms. To attempt to explain it in terms of the counterfactual results of someone's investigating whether there is any mechanism linking the presence of a person at the place and the occurrence of *F*-events would be open to the same objection again. In general, when counterfactuals fail to ensure that some condition holds in the actual world, it is not a good idea to try to circumvent the problem by adding more counterfactuals. All these points apply equally to present and to past-tense statements.

The other reason why any such proposed equivalence fails is that even when there is no interaction between the presence of an investigator and the holding of some condition, the coincidence in truth-value between a past-tense statement and a proposed counterfactual elaboration of it still leaves a major difference between the two. The truth of the past-tense statement contributes to an explanation of why the counterfactual is true, when it is true. This by itself precludes analysing the past-tense statement as a counterfactual.

It would not be quite right to capture these points by saying outright that the past-tense statements are categorical. The present-tense counterpart of a past-tense statement may be highly dispositional, and if it is, its past-tense counterpart will also be highly dispositional. So one would better summarize the present set of points by saying that a past-tense statement or thought is *equi-categorical* with its present-tense counterpart. I am, then, endorsing the *equi-categorical thesis*, which states that past-tense statements are equi-categorical with their present-tense counterparts.

The equi-categorical thesis is not an isolated phenomenon, unconnected with our earlier reflections. On the contrary, it follows from them. The equi-categorical thesis follows from the property–identity link. If a present-tense statement is not to be given a counterfactual analysis, then it follows from the property–identity link that the past-tense counterpart is not to be given the corresponding counterfactual analysis either. If it were, then in making the past-tense statement we would not be attributing the very same property to the past time in question as we are to the present time in accepting the present-tense version.

Contrapositively, we can equally say that a theorist who insists upon the counterfactual analysis for the past-tense statement will be committed to denying the property–identity links if the present-tense version is not to be analysed in terms of counterfactuals. It is worth noting here that these points do not actually require the full strength of the bridging claim, which is an account of understanding. They require only the correctness of the principle—regardless of whether it is crucial to the elucidation of understanding—that the truth of a past-tense statement about a particular time requires that time to have the same property as its present-tense counterpart requires of the present time.

If our understanding of past-tense statements is elucidated along the lines of the bridging claim, then it is also explained why we find the possibility of an investigator's presence affecting whether an event occurs at a certain place and time quite coherent. Consider a case in which there would be such an effect, for instance, the statement that there was a squirrel on this wall yesterday at noon. The truth of this statement is still understood as requiring yesterday to have had the same property as today has to have for there to be a squirrel on the same wall today at noon. Yesterday still had that property even if it is true that no squirrel would have appeared had there been an observer around. Our intuitive judgements about the possibility of such examples is well explained by the hypothesis that we have implicit knowledge of the property–identity link.

Implicit knowledge of the property–identity link and its consequences unifies various characteristics of our understanding of the past. If we have implicit knowledge whose content entails that past-tense statements are equi-categorical with their present-tense counterparts, we are in a position to appreciate, as in fact we do, that the holding in the past of categorical conditions can explain the past perceptions of other persons too, and thereby determine the content of their present memories, and can also leave non-psychological traces. Correspondingly we are in a position to appreciate that effects of either of these two sorts can correct our own apparent memories. The possibility of these other effects of past states of affairs, and their potential role in the correction of our own memories, are not conventional elements in our conception of the past which could easily be deleted while leaving something coherent behind. Rather, these possibilities are already implicit in the conception of the past which conforms to the property–identity link.

The simple points illustrated in the example of the squirrel seem to me to undermine not just all forms of phenomenalism, but all species of verificationism, constructivism, idealism, and anti-realism about the meaning of statements about the past. Some such verificationist views can be traced back at least to Kant.[7] They also receive a detailed formulation in some of Crispin Wright's papers. He formulates a version of anti-realism according to which 'The facts . . . are always as they would have been determined to be if the opportunity to test them had been taken' (1993: 181). This is what Wright calls the 'In principle/Sometime' ('I/S') version. In cases in which the presence of investigators affects what they find, this anti-realist account of truth or 'the facts' gives the wrong extension to the truth-predicate. What would have been determined to be the case if the opportunity to investigate had been taken is not in such cases what would have been the case had the opportunity not been taken. For similar reasons, the irreducibility to counterfactuals of present-tense statements about other places correspondingly undermines the 'In principle/Now' and 'In principle/Now or Future' versions of the doctrine. Once again, the property–identity link would not be respected on these anti-realist accounts if the present-tense truth-conditions for statements about currently perceived objects are given correctly, in categorical terms, while the past- and present-tense predications of objects at other places are explained in terms of counterfactuals.

Wright's anti-realist ends up endorsing a version of the truth-value links, in an

---

[7] See *Critique of Pure Reason* at A493/B521, and at A495–6/B523–4, among several other passages. For further remarks on these passages, see Peacocke, 1999: ch. 3, section 2.

account with double-indexing.[8] My own variety of realism will not provoke any need for double-indexing. But the point I want to emphasize here is that even for someone who is happy to use double-indexing, those principles, however intuitively obvious, must both be justified, and be shown to be consistent with the rest of one's theory. That issue of consistency is pressing. Once you have fixed a plausible meaning for a present-tense utterance or thought, occurring at any given time, and you have also fixed some favoured account of the meaning of a past-tense utterance, you need then to show that these fixings of meanings entail whatever formulation of the truth-value links is favoured. If you have a certain kind of meaning for present-tense utterances, and go on to specify a kind of meaning for past-tense utterances, and then also want to hold on to a truth-value link relating the two, you need to show that doing all those three things in the particular way proposed is consistent. Otherwise, you will in effect have put forward three equations in two variables.

By contrast, the bridging account guarantees these links. The property–identity link, which entails the truth-value link, is the fundamental statement of what it is for a past-tense predication to be true. There is no other explication of the truth of past-tense predications, in terms of possible verification, with which the link must square, or from which it must be derived.

The equi-categorical character of past-tense statements with their present-tense counterparts entails that no qualitative present-tense conditions are ever constitutively and conclusively sufficient for the occurrence of an event of a certain kind at some particular place at some past time. (Here the caveat 'qualitative' is just to exclude present-tense conditions which write in requirements whose present satisfaction requires the world earlier to have been a certain way, such as 'fossil', 'footprint', and 'genuine, as opposed to merely apparent, memory'.) The equi-categorical principle ensures that present-tense qualitative conditions are never so sufficient because in the case of a present-tense statement that an event of the given kind occurs at a particular place, we can see only too clearly how it could, on this particular occasion, be false even though conditions obtain which are, in other cases, its effects. Conversely, there is no difficulty in seeing how the present-tense version could be true without having its normal effects, since any causal process can be blocked.

It should not be inferred from these points that the equi-categorical claim makes statements about the past epistemologically more problematic. The contrary is true. It is only if a past-tense statement expresses a categorical property of some event or object that it can feature in causal explanation, and hence in causal explanation of an experiential memory of that event or object. If the past-tense statements which are in fact known by experiential memory were not equi-categorical with their categorical present-tense counterparts, they would not after all be knowable by experiential memory.[9]

---

[8] His principles A*–D* (in Wright, 1993: 195).
[9] Wright holds that statements about the past are not capable of actual verification: see Wright, 1993: 120. For an argument against his position, see Peacocke, 1999, ch. 3, section 2.

The question then arises why thinkers have been attracted to verificationist and counterfactual accounts of the meaning of present- and past-tense statements about the natural world. There are at least three reasons, and they are interrelated. One reason stems from a particular reading of Dummett's manifestation challenge. Meaning must determine and be exhaustively determined by use, according to this view, and so for any particular meaning we attribute to an expression, we ought to be able to give a philosophical account of the use which legitimates that attribution of meaning. The manifestation challenge comes in several strengths and varieties. I am not going to question that there are forms of the manifestation challenge which need to be addressed, provided that the challenge is framed in a way which allows the use of intentional vocabulary in describing what is involved in someone's employing one concept rather than another. The particular form of the manifestation challenge most pertinent to the case of understanding the past tense is one which holds that meaning and content must be fundamentally determined by a thinker's intentional responses to observable, or decidable, conditions.[10] Once the manifestation challenge is thought to have that consequence, one can see how a theorist might be led towards a verificationist and counterfactual theory. Even if it is insisted that intentional responses to decidable circumstances must play a central (albeit not exclusive) part in the individuation of meaning and concepts, there would still be a non-sequitur in moving from that point to a counterfactual theory. We can agree that the statement that a certain material object is F can be verified by your being at its location and perceiving it to be F. It by no means follows that what it is for it to be true that the object is F when you are not there is for it to be the case that if you or anyone else were there, it would be perceived to be F. Your being there and perceiving it to be F may verify the original statement because it establishes that some categorical condition is met by the object. If that is why it is so verified, then nothing follows about what would be the case when neither you, nor anyone else, is there. What categorical conditions would hold if you were not there is not settled by that information.

A second explanation of the temptation to a counterfactual analysis may also have been the idea that a verificationist account of understanding is the right way of generalizing to the empirical world from the case of decidable arithmetical equations. For decidable arithmetical equations, understanding is inseparable from grasp of a decision procedure, whether the procedure is executed in a particular case or not. In the nature of the case, performing a computation cannot affect what the outcome of the computation is, in the way in which going there can

---

[10] Dummett does sometimes lean towards the particular construal of the challenge which I am questioning. In 'The philosophical basis of intuitionistic logic', he says this of the argument for intuitionism which starts from the premiss that use must fully determine meaning: 'The argument told in favour of replacing, as the central notion for the theory of meaning, the condition under which a statement is true, whether we know or can know when that condition obtains, by the condition under which we acknowledge the statement as conclusively established, a condition which we must, by the nature of the case, be capable of effectively recognizing whenever it obtains.' Dummett, 1978: 227.

affect what happens at a place. This fact encourages the verificationist account for the arithmetical case: but it also makes it the wrong model for the empirical case. The difference between the cases is a by-product of the underlying difference between a procedure which is a computation, and a procedure which consists in getting into the right position and state to be causally affected by a temporal state of affairs. One highly problematic variety of Platonism in the philosophy of mathematics seems to me to result in part from the attempt to assimilate arithmetical knowledge to the case of knowledge explained by contact with a categorical and temporally explanatory state of affairs.

A third source of the temptation to the counterfactual analyses of past-tense statements is scepticism about the whole idea of the categorical, to which I turn in the following section.

THE CATEGORICAL

I have insisted that some past-tense statements express categorical properties of events and objects, and have claimed that this fact is pivotal to the metaphysics and epistemology of the past. So the position I have been developing is tenable only if there is a class of categorical properties that are not dispositional. By 'not dispositional' I mean not explicable in terms of counterfactuals (or, more strictly, in terms of subjunctive conditionals). But is it the case that, when we carefully examine any given allegedly categorical property, it can be seen to be really dispositional after all? This is a fundamental issue not only about the past, but for metaphysics in general.

Many philosophers hold that apparently categorical properties can always be shown to be dispositional. Michael Dummett once asked 'Are not the notions of distance (length), mass and temporal duration intrinsically connected with the means for measuring them?'[11] Hugh Mellor writes:

Take the paradigm, molecular structure—a geometrical (for example, triangular) array of inertial masses. To be triangular is at least to be such that if the corners were (correctly) counted the result would be three. Inertial mass entails only subjunctive conditionals specifying acceleration under diverse forces. It is . . . nothing but a 'generic' disposition—that is, a conjunction of specific dispositions. (1991: 115)

Simon Blackburn holds that the categorical credentials of properties we are apt to think of as categorical grounds are poor. He says that 'science finds only dispositional properties, all the way down' (1993: 255). Karl Popper (1957: 70) and Peter Strawson (1980: 280) express similar views. Scepticism about the notion of the categorical seems to be a point of agreement among philosophers who would not agree on much else.

To address this scepticism, we first need a better understanding of the categorical. One approach attempts to explicate the notion of the categorical via the

---

[11] Personal communication, 1997.

idea of the actual world. Goodman, for example, writes that to apply a 'non-dispositional, or manifest' predicate 'is to say that something actually happens with respect to the thing in question; while to apply a dispositional predicate is to speak only of what can happen'(1965: 41). Goodman throws away some of the intuitions underlying the notion of the categorical when he additionally remarks that this characterization may be merely relative, and speaks of 'the general problem of construing dispositional predicates on the basis of whatever predicates may be chosen as manifest' (ibid., n. 7). He says that 'A predicate like "bends", for example, may be dispositional under a phenomenalistic system' (ibid.). But we can consider the characterization of the categorical in terms of the actual world independently of such relativism.

Let us say that an *actual-world property* is a property whose holding or not holding of a given object is settled only by the way the actual world is, and is not in general settled by the properties and relations of the object in counterfactual circumstances. So can we adequately explicate the idea of the categorical, or part thereof, by saying that categorical properties and relations are actual-world properties and relations?

I do not doubt that we have some notion of the actual world that is intimately tied to the notion of the categorical. I suspect, however, that the notion of the actual world which is so tied has itself to be explained in terms of the categorical, rather than conversely. The idea of the actual world which is so tied is just that of all true propositions which involve predications of categorical properties and relations, or of something which fixes or uniquely determines that set. Such a conception may very well be in good standing (I think it is): but it is hardly dialectically available against an opponent who doubts that there are any categorical properties or relations. It would be question-begging to appeal to it.

Suppose we try to use the notion of the actual world more neutrally, as the class of all true propositions (or Fregean Thoughts). How does the thesis that the extension of categorical properties and relations are those not settled by counterfactuals, or by what is the case at non-actual worlds, fare then? 'Settling' is obviously the crucial term in this thesis. Suppose we take it as meaning a kind of determination, so that the thesis in question becomes this: there can be two networks of worlds, each with its own accessibility relation and its own actual world, which are the same in respect of the worlds which it labels as non-actual, but which differ in respect of what is true at the worlds which they respectively label as actual. This is a species of modal non-determination thesis. The suggestion is that what is not so determined is the categorical. Does this suggestion work?

The suggestion seems to me to be incorrect. The friend of the categorical may well accept, and in my view should accept, that whenever there is a categorical difference between worlds, there will also be some difference in respect of which counterfactuals are true at those worlds. Could one not always set up some device which is sensitive to the instantiation of a categorical property, which reacts differently as the property is or is not instantiated? This possibility claim seems extremely plausible, and it does not commit one to accepting the reducibility of categoricals to counterfactuals. The claim that one could always set up some such device does not commit one to its being a priori what that device would be; nor does it involve a priori commitments about its background conditions of operation; nor does it commit one to anything about the reducibility of any alleged explanatory power of categoricals to counterfactuals. But if it is correct, the possibility claim does rule out the existence of two networks of worlds which differ only in respect of what holds categorically at their respective actual worlds, but which are nevertheless the same in respect of which counterfactuals are true at their actual worlds. The significance of the possibility claim is precisely that any difference in categoricals will mean some difference or other in counterfactuals.

It may be said that this objection means only that a criterion for the categorical must speak only of what is not a priori settled by counterfactuals. Once we move to the question of what is a priori settled, however, we are in the territory of irreducibility theses, rather than modal determination or non-determination theses. So let us move straight to considering irreducibility theses directly.

A predication of a categorial property never has a counterfactual equivalent—something to which it is equivalent as an a priori matter—unless the proposed equivalent contains, or presupposes something about, some categorical property or other. (It need not be the same categorical property, but some categorical property or other must be involved for equivalence to be attained.) We can label this thesis of the non-existence of any such a priori equivalence the *Ineliminability Claim,* and it can be illustrated as follows. Any definition of distance in terms of measurement by unit rods works only if we add or presume that the rods do not change their length when moved. This addition or presumption involves a spatial, categorical notion, that of length. An attempted definition of distance in terms of the time taken to traverse it works only if either we use the notion of 'uniform velocity', which is again explained in terms of categorical notions; or else we use some condition about clocks, and these in turn must be assumed to be operating uniformly with respect to time. A characterization of the mass of an object in terms of counterfactuals about the force required to change its acceleration works only if the application of force does not cause the object's mass to alter, one way or another. To use Davidson's phrase, there is pattern in these failures of proposed equivalence. In all these cases, the counterfactuals achieve sameness of truth-value with the predication of the categorical property only if we assume some categorical property is held constant between the actual and the relevant counterfactual situations.

The Ineliminability Claim, if true, explains why there is intuitively such a close link between the categorical and at least one conception of actual-world properties. If we accept both the existence of categorical properties and relations, and if we also accept the Ineliminability Claim, then which categorical properties something actually has will not be settled a priori by which counterfactuals, not involving categoricals, are true.

In some cases, connections arguably exist between the meaning of a term for a categorical magnitude and the measurement-procedures for assigning that magnitude a particular value. Investigations in the theory of measurement have enormously increased our understanding of some of these connections.[12] Sometimes we have relational structures identified in the theory of measurement of a magnitude which give sufficient conditions for the magnitude to take a certain value. These connections should not, however, be thought to support a case for explanation of the categorical in terms of the dispositional. There are two reasons why they offer no such support. First, in establishing representation theorems in the theory of measurement, it is important that there be relations such as *x matches y in length*, or *the Goodmanian sum of x and y balances z on a true balance*, which do not themselves involve the assignment of numbers. To say that a relation does not involve the assignment of numbers is not to say that it is not categorical. I think that all the qualitative, non-numerical relations used in these representation theorems are categorical. Counterfactual explications of them are sometimes offered by writers in the theory of measurement, but it is obvious that these are just rough equivalents which serve the purpose only if it is assumed that fulfilment of the antecedent of the counterfactual does not alter the underlying property—that bringing the object to a balance does not alter its mass, and so forth. That is the first reason why these points in the theory of measurement do not support a dispositional analysis of categoricals.

A second reason why they do not support a dispositional analysis is that the connections which are brought out by the theory of measurement should in any case be construed as reference-fixing rather than as metaphysically necessary. If we try to marshal these systems of relations used in the theory of measurement into an account of *what it is* to have given length, the result is not a metaphysical necessity, but a contingency. What we obtain by such marshalling is, for instance, that the mass of an object x in grams is 17.4 iff the unique function f meeting certain conditions formulated in terms of the relational structure, and also mapping the standard gram in Paris to the number 1, is such that $f(x)$ is 17.4. This biconditional is not a necessity. Its right-hand side could hold if the standard gram in Paris had a greater mass, but that would not mean that our object x would in those circumstances weigh 17.4 grams. It is no accident that Kripke originally introduced the distinction between reference-fixing and sustaining necessities in connection with standard measures (1980: 54 ff.). On the present view, he was right to do so.

Categorical properties are involved in the explanation of why counterfactuals are true. An adequate empirical explanation of why an object has a particular disposition must either cite or be committed to the existence of an underlying categorical state. The underlying categorical state explains the manifestation of the disposition when its antecedent triggering conditions are fulfilled. We can call

---

[12] See esp. Krantz, *et al.*, 1971. In their informal discussions, these authors do not, however, always sufficiently distinguish epistemic and metaphysical issues.

this the *Explanation Claim* about categoricals. The Explanation Claim is not to be understood as a principle about the explanation of the acquisition by an object of a certain disposition. It is concerned not with the history of, or the antecedents of, possession of the disposition, but with explanations which cite current properties of the object, which are capable of explaining why, as the object is now, it has that disposition now. Different histories of acquisition of a disposition are compatible with the same underlying categorical explanation of why, now, the object has a given disposition.

The Explanation Claim says what an explanation of a disposition must be like, if there is an explanation. It would be a further metaphysical claim that any disposition must be underlain by a categorical state. That further claim would be one form of the thesis that counterfactuals cannot be 'barely' true (Dummett, 1976: 89). I am sympathetic to that further claim as well, but must not meander too far from my main topic.

The Explanation Claim is not an isolated principle, but is part of a wider metaphysical conception. The Explanation Claim is a consequence of a particular view of the relation of causation. Explanation of the manifestation of a disposition by citing some ground of the disposition is a causal explanation. Causal explanations require a relation of causation between the events in question, and causation is itself an actual-world relation. This can be regarded as one of the lessons of the objections to counterfactual analyses of causation, such as the objection from interrupted blocking.[13] Now when one event causes another in virtue of the object's having a certain property—say, the striking causes the breaking of the vase in virtue of the nature of the chemical bonds in the vase's material—it would be highly puzzling if the property in virtue of which the event causes the manifestation were not an actual-world property.[14] If the causal relation held, between these events, in virtue of a property which is not an actual-world property, it seems that causation would not really be an actual-world relation after all. Here I assume that if P is an actual-world property or relation, and holds in some particular case in virtue of an object's having property Q, Q is also an actual-world property. So one seems to be committed to the Explanation Claim if one accepts that causation is an actual-world relation, and that causal relations hold in virtue of properties of the causing events. If the Explanation Claim is true, it gives some significance to the class of categorical properties and relations, as characterized in terms of irreducibility to counterfactuals. Only properties which are so irreducible can be causally explanatory. 'Only the actual can explain the actual', we might say.

The idea of the categorical as potentially explanatory of other events and states is a necessary condition of other features of the categorical. The categorical is equally the idea of what is there anyway, independently of probing and testing,

---

[13] My thanks to Ned Hall of MIT for a helpful discussion of interrupted blocking.

[14] For a healthy dose of empirical information about the actual categorical basis of the distinction between those things which bend when struck, and those things which break, see Eberhart, 1999.

and which explains the results of tests when tests for the presence of a categorical property do take place. This evidently requires the ability of categorical properties to enter causal explanations of actual phenomena. It also seems to me that the categorical is an essential element in a full philosophical account of empirical objectivity and the explanation of agreement on empirical matters. Take the fundamental case of perceptual knowledge of the instantiation of an observational property. The explanation of two perceivers' agreement that the object has the property will in that basic case include the fact that the object's having that property causally explains each of their perceptions that it does. Without that, we would have not objectivity, but (at best) a common subjectivity.

From these points it may seem plain that the categorical ought to occupy a central position in metaphysics. Why then have so many philosophers thought that a notion of the categorical which is irreducible to the dispositional cannot have any application at all?[15]

One major reason involves the idea that the close relation between properties and laws forces the rejection of the applicability of a notion of the categorical of the sort I have tried to characterize. There is a hint of the view in the quotation from Mellor above, but it is Blackburn who states the view with full generality:

Just as the molecular theory gives us only things with dispositions, so any conceivable improvement in science will give us only a better pattern of dispositions and powers. That's the way physics works.

Is it the way it has to work? I believe so. A quick route to this conclusion is to see the theoretical terms of a science as defined functionally in terms of their place in a network of laws.[16] A slower route is to reflect on what is needed from physical thinking. What is needed is the use of concepts—energy, temperature, entropy—that cover changes of state, permitting the formulation of conservation laws. Such concepts in effect tell us what is the same about a changing system, in terms precisely of its powers and dispositions. (Blackburn, 1993: 256)

I agree that many properties, both amongst those identified in folk physics, and among those identified in more advanced scientific theories, are individuated in part by their relations to other properties, and that the individuating relations are given by the laws which relate the former properties to the latter. We should, however, distinguish very sharply between *relational individuation* and *counterfactual explication*. The fact that many properties are relationally individuated, via laws involving them, in no way obviates the need, emphasized earlier, for assumptions about categorical properties in the actual world in drawing any counterfactual conclusions from a true predication of a categorical property. Perhaps the point is most sharply formulated in terms of possible worlds. The relational individuation of a property P implies that in any world in which P is possessed by

---

[15] This is not the place to attempt to address all the arguments which have been mounted by sceptics about the categorical. Blackburn, 1993, mounts several others which need to be addressed. I would aim to draw on the resources of the present section in any attempt to address those further arguments.   [16] Here Blackburn cites Lewis, 1983.

an object, that object will also have certain complexes of other properties, as determined by the laws. The property P and the complex of properties are instantiated together, if at all; and that holds both in the actual world and in relevant nearby worlds. It does not follow that for an object to have P in the actual world is simply for certain counterfactuals to hold. Someone who accepts the Ineliminability Claim, and for the reasons I gave, can consistently hold that a magnitude is mass, or distance, or electric charge, only if it stands in specified relations to other magnitudes. In a case in which, because of some special set-up, it is true that if an object were moved, its mass would alter (say, because of some resultant chemical or nuclear reaction), the lawlike relations between mass, force, and acceleration remain intact. So it seems to me that there is no good argument from relational individuation of a property, or even from merely a functional characterization of it, to a dispositional analysis of that property.

Some friends of categorical properties have also held that the fundamental explanatory categorical properties are intrinsic properties. The phrase 'categorical and intrinsic' is sometimes used in the literature as if the second conjunct is ensured by the first. 'Intrinsic' is a term of art, and we need to draw some distinctions. We have already agreed that many properties are individuated by their relations to other properties. This already means that their nature cannot be explained independently of everything else in the universe, if that is taken to include other properties and relations. By 'intrinsicness', however, what is often intended is a property of properties, where the second-order property is characterized in terms that relate to other individuals. The intuitive idea of an intrinsic property is then that of a property whose possession by an object does not depend, constitutively, on that object's particular relations to other individuals wholly distinct from itself. An intrinsic property is thus one with respect to which a pair of duplicates cannot differ.[17] Perhaps it is consistent to hold that mass is a categorical and relationally individuated magnitude, while also holding that the mass of an object is one of its intrinsic features in this sense.[18]

In general, however, it is not a condition of a property's being categorical that it be intrinsic in this sense. Many categorical properties are extrinsic. The property

[17] For some time, it was accepted, following Kim, 1982, that an intrinsic property is one which could belong to an object even if that object were the only thing in the universe. Rae Langton and David Lewis pointed out that this is not quite right, as it includes the property of being unaccompanied. They recommend that we say that 'P is *independent of accompaniment* iff four different cases are possible: something accompanied may have P or lack P, something unaccompanied may have P or lack P. P is *basic intrinsic* iff (1) P and not-P are non-disjunctive and contingent, and (2) P is independent of accompaniment' (Langton and Lewis 1998, from the abstract at p. 333). The intuitive formulation involving constitutive dependence in the text above could be accepted without commitment to these possibilities of lone existence.

[18] Those who do hold this combination, will, incidentally, also identify a third objection to taking the biconditionals delivered by the theory of measurement as constitutive accounts of physical magnitudes. If mass is, though relationally individuated, an intrinsic magnitude of an object, a constitutive account of its nature should not mention other objects, neither the standard gram in Paris, nor its comparative mass-relations to other objects. These are all merely contingently related to the magnitude itself. They have epistemic significance in an account of how we latch on to the magnitude, but are not essential to the magnitude itself.

of an object of resting on another physical object is evidently extrinsic. It can also enter explanations—it explains why an object falls when its supporting object is removed. There would, in my judgement, be no plausibility in the claim that only intrinsic properties can enter causal explanations. The psychological provides just one of many other kinds of counterexample to such a claim. If intentional content is externally individuated, and mental states with intentional content are causally explanatory, it again follows that some extrinsic states are causally explanatory.

Temporal location, temporal relations between events, and temporal magnitudes also all seem to me to be categorical in the sense outlined in this section. All these temporal characteristics have the power to explain other events and states of affairs, and are irreducible to counterfactuals that do not hold certain categorical conditions constant in the actual world. If the characterizations of the categorical of this section are along roughly the right lines, temporal properties and relations are in equally good standing in respect of their categorical status as other, more traditional paradigms of the categorical.

AN ARGUMENT FOR REALISM ABOUT THE PAST

I now turn to the question of the relation between realism, in Dummett's sense, about the past and the conception with which I have been elaborating the bridging claim. There is a highly intuitive argument, which I suspect articulates widespread realist intuitions, from that conception to such a realism about the past. The intuitive argument has three steps:

1. We can set up—or at least there could be—a present state of affairs of such a kind that all its effects, other than those involved in producing our perceptual states, do not distinguish between the state of affairs we have actually set up and some different kind. We shield off any such discriminating effects. So, for instance, a sealed, opaque incinerator may contain a wooden cube which, when burned, leaves a certain mass of ashes. We could set up things in such a way that a block of a different shape but the same mass would leave exactly the same mass and pattern of ashes of the same kind after incineration.

2. Such a state of affairs could exist even if we were not present and had no perceptual states to give us information that it obtains.

3. A state of affairs of exactly the same sort as is mentioned in Step 2 could have obtained in the past. In the nature of the case, this would be a state of affairs which could exist without our now being able to know that it did—since by hypothesis its effects to do not distinguish it from other states of affairs which could have obtained.

Now the transition here from Step 2 to Step 3 relies on the property–identity link being understood as it is formulated in the bridging claim. It is a legitimate transition if we are employing a notion of sameness of property, and endorsing the equi-categorical claim. It would *not* be a valid transition if truth were understood in either of the two anti-realist ways that Wright calls the I/N (In principle/Now) or I/NF (In principle/Now or Future). On the I/N conception, we may have evidence now that a certain state of affairs exists, and there is no evident reason not to allow that conception the modal claim that it would exist even if we were not aware of it. But the transition to Step 3 would be quite illegitimate on that conception. The transition involves the possibility of the existence of a state of affairs of which we have no present evidence, and need not have any in the future. A similar point applies to establish the illegitimacy of the transition for the I/NF (In principle/Now or Future) variant of anti-realism.[19]

It seems to me that the transition from Step 2 to Step 3 is not simply an instance of begging the question against the anti-realist.[20] It is an instance of a kind of non-philosophical reasoning found not only in ordinary thought, but in the work of any historian, or archaeologist, or other empirical scientist. It is simply the principle that a state of affairs of a given kind, which could exist at one place and time, could, prima facie, exist at any other. We use such a principle frequently when thinking through how some known end result might have come about, as when an archaeologist investigates, using current sequences of events, whether a find of objects close together indicates that they were used close together, or that they have just settled there together from different locations. The principle needs the prima-facie qualification. The apparent possibility it mentions may be successfully rebutted by all sorts of more specific considerations about the region of the spatiotemporal universe to which its application is in question. What does not seem to be the case is that there is any general pretheoretical restriction on its application having to do with verifiability or evidence. The defender of the bridging claim who reflects on this prima-facie general principle will be unsurprised that there is no restriction concerning evidential relations. The idea that it is the same properties whose instantiation is in question as in present-tense instances is enough, in the presence of the equi-categorical claim, to make such investigations as that of the archaeologist reasonable.

These points suggest some reflections on the very delicate question of the proper account of the relation between truth-value links and realism, in Dummett's sense, about the past. In his original discussion of these issues, Dummett represents the realist as claiming that 'by stipulating the validity of the truth-value link, we thereby provide that from which a realist conception of truth and falsity for these statements can be derived' (1978: 364). As we have in effect noted, some anti-realists have said they are entitled to certain formulations of the truth-value links, and their position may make one wonder whether there is any connection between those links and realism. But when one looks in detail at anti-realist

---

[19] I am not pressing the point for I/S anti-realism, for anti-realists like Wright are surely correct in doubting whether, by their own lights, that is a legitimate variant. In any case, even if it were, it would still be problematic to appeal to it to support the transition from Step 2 to Step 3. It would involve the counterfactual analysis that we have questioned. The I/N and I/NF versions do not have this problem, at least for actually encountered states of affairs, which is what the possibility in Step 1 involves.

[20] As Wright, 1993: 186–7, implies.

approaches to content, it seems very doubtful that they really are preserving truth-value links between, for instance, present-tense predications and those in other tenses, when they go on to explain the past tense in counterfactual terms. The explication of the links that we do have, in the bridging claim, seem to validate fundamentally realistic forms of reasoning. The argument formulated in Steps 1–3 does not rely on very special features of some particular example. On the contrary, it seems to go through whenever we have the possibility of later evidence not discriminating between two competing hypotheses about some temporal state of affairs. So there may yet be some internal connection between realism and the truth-value links in their most defensible form after all. The explanation of why there is some internal connection has to allude to the equi-categorical character of past-tense statements with their present-tense counter-parts, and to the ramifications of this fact. It is only when the truth-value link is placed in this context that one has the resources to explain why there is a connec-tion between the truth-value link, properly explicated, and realism in Dummett's sense.

EXTERNALIST ELEMENTS IN UNDERSTANDING THE PAST TENSE

Not only conditions which held in the past, but also the particular temporal rela-tions which hold between past events and past or present states of affairs can be causally explanatory. The fact that the wet summer immediately preceded the dry one can explain the current spatial relation between the wide and the narrow rings in the cross-section of the tree. Particular temporal relations can equally be explanatory of facts in the mental realm. Your impression that a certain person left the room a certain interval of time ago, an interval which is, in fact, about ten minutes, can be explained by that person's having left about ten minutes ago. That this temporal relation between an event and the present can be causally explanatory is not any more problematic as a matter of general metaphysics than is the fact that the spatial relation of some event to you now can explain your impression that it stands in that spatial relation to you now.

I have just been mentioning examples in which the content of the temporal or spatial impression is specific as to which (egocentrically identified) time or place it represents as being a particular way. But even when a genuine memory impres-sion, for instance, is not specific in its content as to the temporal relation between the events it represents and the present, it is still true to say that you have an expe-riential memory of (say) having swum from a yacht because at some past time you did so.

The claim that certain mental states are causally sensitive to temporal facts would not carry much weight if we had no idea how underlying subpersonal mechanisms could be sensitive to such facts. We do, though, have some idea. Computational mechanisms which are sensitive to the passage of time and which have been discussed empirically in some detail include mechanisms which are sensitive to the state attained by some regular oscillatory process, or to the state of something which acts as an accumulator.[21] The fact that an oscillator is at a given time in a certain state, or that an accumulator has reached a certain level, are each of them causally explained in part by the fact that the given time is a certain interval of time after some other event. The nature of the subpersonal mechanism is, evidently, an empirical matter. A good a priori case can be made that any being capable of temporal thought must possess some such mechanism or other. There is, however, no a priori argument, of any particular mechanism, that it must be possessed. There may also be more than one subsystem making possible the representation of temporal properties and relations. Different subsystems may also be relevant to the mental representation of temporal magnitudes when they fall in very different ranges.[22]

To possess a subpersonal mechanism which is, when functioning properly, thus temporally sensitive is, of course, not yet to have mastered temporal thought. Here again it can help to consider a spatial parallel. It is equally the case that to possess a subpersonal mechanism which is, when functioning properly, sensitive to spatial facts is not yet to have mastered spatial thought. I will return shortly to the question of what conditions are sufficient. At present, I want to emphasize that in both the temporal and the spatial cases, the presence of such subpersonal mechanisms is a necessary condition of mastery. Without such sensitive mechanisms, a person's thought would not be latching on to space or time at all. A philosophical account of temporal thought must have externalist elements just as our models of spatial and other kinds of thought do. Correlatively, an account of the manifestation of the meaning of temporal vocabulary must involve, among other elements, a sensitivity to temporal relations themselves.

Within impressions of the duration between two events, we should distinguish between those impressions that result when a subject is told in advance that he will be asked about the interval, and those which result when he is not so told in advance. The former kind of impression can be expected to reflect more directly the subject's ability to perceive temporal duration. The correctness of the latter impressions, when the subject's attention may be engaged by non-temporal matters, either in the external or the mental world, may be distorted by other matters. Again a spatial parallel may help. Your impression, on walking through a house, of the distance from its entrance to the rear of its kitchen is likely to be far more accurate when you are told in advance that you will be asked to indicate that distance, than when you take the same route, but your attention is focused on a philosophical discussion, or on looking after a child (or both). In the latter case, there are likely to be elements of reconstruction and of inference at the personal

---

[21] For an illuminating critical overview, see Gallistel, 1990, chs. 7–9.

[22] See e.g. Friedman, 2001 (Ch. 5, this volume). One can have the impression that one event (which in fact occurred six months ago) was earlier than another (which in fact occurred four months ago, say), without in either case having an impression of the duration from the event to the present. These cases are very different from the temporal perception of the interval between an event which occurred a few minutes ago and the present.

level in your answers to questions about that distance, elements which are not fundamental to a perceptual sensitivity to distance. The case in which temporal impressions result after the subject has been told in advance that the task is one of estimating duration has come to be called 'the prospective paradigm' in the psychological literature, while the case in which the subject is not so told has been labelled the 'the retrospective paradigm'.[23] What we have just given is a reason for thinking that, on an externalist account of temporal understanding, the prospective paradigm is more fundamental.

Impressions of duration have a representational content which does not involve units at all. In this, the perception of time is just like the perception of other magnitudes and qualities (Peacocke, 1986). One perceives the interval between the phone stopping ringing and the knock at the door as *that long*, where the italics pick out a demonstrative presentation of a temporal length. How long that is in minutes, or any other units, is always a further question. One can perceive an interval as having a certain temporal duration without having any conception of temporal units. The duration one has perceived the interval to have can be reflected in one's ability to indicate the same interval again. Such an indication of the perceived duration involves a manifestation in relation to the passage of time itself, rather than in relation to something qualitative or non-temporal correlated with it. The manifestation also does not involve any particular units. Both of these points are predicted by an externalist theory which attributes unit-free contents to temporal perceptions.

Since impressions of duration do not involve any units, thinking of an event as '*that* long ago' does not actually locate it in relation to any particular scale (second, minutes, hours . . .). In fact, the acceptability of any everyday means of measuring particular temporal units depends in part on its respecting genuine perceptions of intervals of equal duration. Units and scales are built upon a more fundamental capacity to perceive duration in a unit-free manner.

The examples I have given so far concern a thinker's impressions of the temporal relations of some remembered event to the present time. The cases in which temporal facts explain temporal impressions range much more widely than that. Consider an episodic memory of some particular event in which you participated. Even if you know when the event occurred, we can always make sense of the idea that we might be mislocating in time an event remembered in this way. Equally, you may be remembering the event in this way, and wondering just when it did occur. Was it this year, or last year; here or in another continent? Now, even if you do not currently have any beliefs about when it occurred, you can still raise

---

[23] See Block and Zakay, 2001 (Ch. 2, this volume), and the many references therein. William James is often cited as a forefather of this distinction: see *The Principles of Psychology* (James, 1983: 587). In fact, James's concern was slightly different. James was concerned with the difference between how long something seems to be taking at the time it occurs, and how long it seemed to take after it is over. (His view was that the interesting and the boring differ in these respects.) This overlaps with, but is not the same as, the distinction between those cases in which one's attention is engaged in estimating duration, and those in which it is not.

the questions: what happened next? And what led up to this event? Memory will
sometimes serve up further episodic memories which answer these questions. It
will sometimes serve up answers in which the events remembered in the new
episodic memories are remembered as occurring a certain length of time before,
or after, the initially remembered events. Again, these temporal impressions are
explained, when all is working properly, by those newly remembered events
standing in just those temporal relations to the initially remembered events.[24]

What is the difference between being merely responsive to the temporal interval which has elapsed since a particular event occurred, and taking it *as* a temporal interval? In the latter case, the event at the far end of the temporal interval is
assigned a position in one's own history, and, correlatively, in the history of the
world. The difference is analogous to that found in the spatial case. One similarly
goes beyond simply being causally sensitive to an instance of a spatial magnitude
in assigning some perceived event or object a location on one's spatial cognitive
map. To think of something as spatial, or as temporal, involves possession of
mental states with objective content, and correspondingly possession of at least
some rudimentary form of first-person contents. In both the temporal and the
spatial cases, what more specific consequences flow from the subject's appreciation of the event or object as having an objective character will depend on what
other objective beliefs, inclinations, and projects the individual may have. There
will be some general a priori connections between the capacity for objective
thought and first-person thought. For a creature with an objective conception of
the world, many of his actions will be explained under objective and first-
personal descriptions. Such explanations will sustain counterfactuals which
would not be supported for the actions of a creature whose psychology does not
involve any grasp of the objective. If you want to shake hands with that man you
perceive, you will move towards him. If he had been in a different location, you
would have moved to that location; and so forth.[25] It is important to note, though,
consistently with these points, that attribution of an objective conception may be
necessary to making sense of the subject's actions and mental life, without there
being any simple correlation of behavioural effects with particular objective
assignments. On this, I am entirely at one with Gallistel when he writes:
'Representational approaches make a much sharper or consequential distinction
between what has been learned . . . and the effects that the existence of this representation may have on diverse behaviors. Representational approaches assume
that these effects will be as diverse as are the computational mechanisms brought
to bear on the represented information by different behavioral readout systems'

---

[24] Note that the newly remembered events are temporally identified just by their remembered
temporal relations to the initially remembered events. So we have a phenomenon of event-relative
temporal identification. There are many ramifications of this point which would take us too far off
course here. One is that mode of access to a past event can determine the particular temporal identification one has of it. My own view is that reflection on the case suggests that not all episodic memories are accessed by their being mentally indexed by the time at which they are (represented as)
occurring. For a contrasting view, see Gallistel, 1990: ch.15.

[25] There is more on this and related themes in Peacocke, 1993.

(1990: 257). Indeed, two creatures with very different behavioural repertoires, at one level of description, may both be capable of states with objective representational contents.

There are several consequences of the presence of externalist elements in a philosophical account of temporal thought. One of them can be brought out by reflection on a passage from Russell. The first, but not the second, sentence of this passage is well known. Russell wrote

> There is no logically necessary connection between events at different times; therefore nothing that is happening now or will happen in the future can disprove the hypothesis that the world began five minutes ago. Hence the occurrences which are *called* knowledge of the past are logically independent of the past; they are wholly analysable into present contents which might, theoretically, be just what they are even if no past had existed.'
> (1968: 159–60)

What interests me for present purposes is not the sceptical hypothesis, but rather what immediately follows Russell's 'Hence' in the second sentence of this passage, and whether the 'Hence' is justified. If we accept the existence of externalist elements in an account of what makes something an impression that a certain event happened a certain length of time ago, we will want to distinguish between two notions of independence. They can be brought out by considering a spatial analogue of Russell's argument:

> There is no logically necessary connection between events at different places; therefore nothing that is happening here (at the location of a perceiver) can disprove the hypothesis that there is nothing anywhere else. Hence the occurrences which are *called* knowledge of what is happening elsewhere are logically independent of what is happening elsewhere; they are wholly analysable into contents about the location of the perceiver, which might, theoretically, be just what they are even if there were nothing anywhere else.[26]

Presented with this argument about space, I think we would be inclined to distinguish at least two kinds of independence. Even if what is happening at one place, or what objects are located there, has no necessary connection with what is happening at any other particular place, that specific independence does not entail that one could give an account of what it is to be capable of having thoughts and perceptions of other places which do not mention the complex relations of those thoughts and perceptions to other places themselves. What I am concerned with here is not the issue of whether the representational content of, say, an individual spatial experience is correct. I am concerned rather with the issue of what makes it an experience with a certain specific spatial content, as one which represents objects or events as being at such-and-such distances and directions from the subject. It seems to me that there is no hope of giving an account of what it is for

---

[26] Or should I conclude the spatial version 'even if no other place existed'? Russell's intentions are not wholly clear.

experiences and thoughts to represent certain things or events as being at certain distances and directions from the subject without at some point mentioning the role of those experiences and thoughts in explaining the various complex capacities the subject of the experiences has in relation to the places at those represented distances and directions. It would be an interesting and fruitful task to elaborate these complex capacities in more detail. The elaboration would certainly have to take into account the role of specific spatial contents concerning distance and direction in explaining, in the presence of a suitable background, the subject's actions in relation to places in those same directions and distances (whether he moves to them or is moved to them). But however the elaboration runs, if this point is sound, then there is at least one reading of the conclusion of this spatial analogue of Russell's reasoning on which it is an incorrect conclusion. An account of what it is for a perceiver at a given location to have experiences with a spatial representational content cannot be given without mentioning his complex relations to other locations, even if on this occasion, and perhaps on many others, his experiences misrepresent what is the case at those other locations. There would be no question of, in Russell's terms, 'wholly analysing the occurrences which are *called*' knowledge of other places without making at least some reference to other places.

The analogous point seems to me to hold in the temporal case. It is hard to see how one could give an account of what it is to have an impression that something happened a certain period of time ago—a period which is about five minutes, say— without mentioning that person's ability, in suitable circumstances, to track and mark out temporal intervals of roughly that length. The thinker must have an ability to be sensitive to the passages of certain-sized intervals of time themselves. Even if a thinker is wholly mistaken about what happened to him about five minutes ago, none the less an account of what makes it the case that it is about five minutes ago that it seems the events occurred is one which undermines one reading of Russell's conclusion. Thought about the past involves past-tense contents, and the fundamental abilities involved in having the capacity for past-tense thought cannot be explained in purely present-tense terms. In fact it is noteworthy that we understand the sceptical hypothesis of Russell's premiss as describing a case in which the initial illusory impressions of what was the case more than five minutes ago—say, about half an hour ago—are of the same subjective kind as those later impressions with similar temporal contents which *do* track the passage of time, and track the (apparent) state of the world at later times.

The presence of externalist elements in a philosophical account of temporal thought has not only constitutive, but also epistemological, aspects. It is only if a temporal impression has an externally individuated content—in this case, a content individuated by its relations to the passage of time itself—that it can yield, in appropriate circumstances, non-inferential knowledge with a temporal content. The way a mental state represents the world as being must be a way which is externally individuated, if taking it at face value is to be capable of yielding knowledge that the world is that way. Here, taking an experience at face value is simply judging that things are as—or are in one of the ways—the state represents them as being, and because it so represents them. More precisely, we can formulate the principle as stating that the representational content of a mental state must be individuated by its relations to objects, properties, or events of a given kind if a thinker's taking it at face value is to be capable of yielding non-inferential knowledge about objects, properties, or events of that kind. If it were not so individuated, any knowledge about objects, properties, or events of that kind obtained by being in the state would be at most inferential.

This principle seems to me also to be correct for ordinary perceptually based knowledge of current states of affairs. It also seems to explain why perceptual knowledge of the external world could never be accounted for were perceptual judgements regarded merely as responses to sensational, non-representational properties of experience, if such there be. Though the principle surely merits independent discussion in epistemology and the theory of content, I mention it here as a plausible additional element in the case for treating temporal impressions as externally individuated. If the principle is correct, it also poses a further problem for constructivist, anti-realistic accounts of temporal content. According to the principle, temporal content must be externally individuated if memory is to give a thinker non-inferential knowledge of the past. But the external individuation seems to proceed by reference to temporal relations between events and states of affairs of such a kind that these events and states of affairs could still exist in circumstances in which all causal paths which would lead to later evidence for them are blocked.

In epistemology, as elsewhere, we ought always to respect a threefold partition between (*a*) an entitlement; (*b*) a norm; and (*c*) a philosophical explanation of the existence of a norm. This is a natural series of distinctions to make once we acknowledge the importance of a Burge-like notion of entitlement, and follow Burge's important discussion of these topics (1993). A particular entitlement to judge a given content on a certain occasion will exist because such a judgement meets certain norms. The norms can be given a general formulation, which covers judgements made on other occasions. It is a philosophical task to formulate the general norms correctly, and it is another philosophical task to give a philosophical explanation of why they exist. This threefold partition applies equally to temporal contents. A temporal impression entitles the thinker to make a corresponding temporal judgement. The norm which underlies the entitlement is the more general one of the legitimacy of taking perceptual impressions at face value, in the absence of positive reasons for doubt. The philosophical explanation of the norm is evidently a vexed issue. It is certainly reasonable to expect that any account which explains the entitlement of a thinker to take spatial experience at face value will, other things being equal, apply also to temporal experience. I will not attempt to tackle that whole issue here. For the present, it suffices that, whatever the full philosophical explanation of the existence of the norm, the distinction between entitlement and the norm is already sufficient to explain how temporal impressions can lead to temporal knowledge without the subject's having the concept of temporal impressions or temporal experience. The temporal impressions themselves are entitling, regardless of whether the subject has the concept of temporal impressions.

In the previous section, I already argued that in general understanding of, for instance, 'Yesterday, it was the case that *A*' does not involve any kind of appreciation that any particular qualitative, purely present-tense conditions are evidence for its having been the case yesterday that *A*. What such evidence might be is always something which has to be worked out empirically in the general case. The most recent points about externalism underwrite the point that the possibility of experiential memory as itself evidence is no counterexample to this general principle about evidence. If what makes an experiential memory a memory state with a certain temporal content cannot in general itself be elucidated without alluding to the relations of states of that kind to what happened to their subjects in the past, then experiential memories are not purely qualitative traces concerning only the present. If it is insisted that 'purely qualitative' here should mean only that any particular apparent memory does not require any particular conditions to hold at earlier times in the history of the actual world, then the point must be agreed. But since apparent experiential memories are evidently not conclusive, they cannot give an account of a thinker's knowledge of *what it is* for a particular past-tense condition to hold. The content of that knowledge must rather be specified in part by citing the property–identity link.

MEMORY AND THE PROPERTY–IDENTITY LINK

A pivotal question about understanding now arises. On the account I have given, grasp of the property–identity link and some form of memory faculty are both involved in the capacity for thought about the past. What is the relation between them? We did note that any kind of grasp of the property–identity link presupposed some mastery of the past elucidated in some way additional to the property–identity link, and externally individuated memory is serving that additional function in the account I am outlining. There is, however, more that needs to be understood about this apparently simple division of labour. In particular, there are two pressing questions.

(1) If the property–identity link and an externally individuated memory capacity are both present in an account of thought about the past, must there not be some danger of overdetermination, perhaps even divergent determination, of the conditions for the correctness of a past-tense content? If there are not two independent sufficient conditions for the correctness of a past-tense content, what is the explanation of this fact?

The second question is prompted by the combination of the realistic position I have been endorsing with acknowledgement of a constitutive role for memory in understanding the past. In the nature of the case, apparently, truths delivered by means of memory are knowable truths about the past. So the other question is:

(2) How can an account of understanding the past tense which essentially involves a capacity for learning knowable truths about the past reach as far as legitimizing the intelligibility of unknowable truths about the past?

I will address this second question first, since it seems to me that a good answer to it contains the resources and approach for answering the first question. The issues involved in addressing the second question have been elaborated in some detail by Wright, who summarizes one of his own critical discussions of the issue thus: 'the evident problem is to make out how *experience* can teach us that the occurrence of certain factors within our experience reliably indicates the character of states of affairs beyond it' (1993: 394). It should be agreed that a model under which we have to investigate empirically, and then discover that in fact some favoured, 'decidable' class of statements is correlated with verification-transcendent ones is incoherent. The realist can, however, do much better than offering that unsatisfactory response. A much better response asserts that the alleged problem is only formulable on a highly questionable conception of what is involved in the capacity to have experiential memories in the first place.

Suppose we consider an analogous issue, this time not about experiential memory, but once again about perception. Imagine someone asking 'How can anything in our perception of the world teach us that the states of affairs we perceive are also capable of existing unperceived?' That is not, it seems to me, a good question, despite the fact that it was in effect the question also asked by Bishop Berkeley. Nothing can be a perception unless it is of objects, events, or states of affairs which could exist without being perceived. The possibility of unperceived existence is integral to the nature of perception itself. So it is not coherent to accept that one is perceiving, and then to wonder whether or not what one is perceiving is something that could exist unperceived. Similarly, if you are thinking of objects, events, or states of affairs in ways made available by perception of them—if, for example, you are thinking of them by using perceptual demonstratives—what is thus thought about must be capable of existing unperceived. A commitment to the existence of things which could exist unperceived is not, then, something to which one is entitled to make only because one's perceptions take a certain particular course. The commitment is already made in taking perceptions at their face value, whatever their detailed course.

The general point here is constitutive, not epistemological. Of course a person may on occasion be enjoying something which seems to be a perception, but is not in fact so. Yet even to enjoy something which seems to be a perception, a thinker must be capable of mental states which employ the ways the apparent perception represents the world as being. The correctness conditions of even the apparent perception must already concern perception-independent objects, events, or states of affairs.

This feature of perception, that it has objects which can exist independently of being perceived, is not a mere add-on, something which could be stripped away to leave a wider concept of equal philosophical significance. Stripping off this feature would not result in something of equal philosophical interest. The significance of the feature is multiple. I mention just two points, from epistemology and the philosophy of action respectively. It is only if perception is of perception-independent entities that it can yield non-inferential knowledge of a world whose existence is independent of being perceived. It is hard to see how any concept resulting from the stripping-away of the feature—if indeed any concept remains—could possibly sustain such non-inferential knowledge. The feature is also crucial to the role of perception in the explanation of action. Actions are explained under descriptions which relate them to the objects, properties, and relations of the objective world. An action may be explained as, say, a reaching-out to a particular object. As we noted earlier, the counterfactuals defeasibly supported by such an explanation correspondingly concern the objective world (Peacocke, 1993). If the object had been in a somewhat different location, then *ceteris paribus* the agent would have reached out to a different location, for the agent would have perceived that object at that different location; and so forth. Stripping away the objective aspect of perception would yield (if anything) a kind of mental event incapable of playing the role in the explanation of action under environmental descriptions which is actually played by perception.

The inextricability of the idea of experience-independent existence is further emphasized if the spatial property–identity link is endorsed as explanatory of our understanding of spatial contents (or indeed merely as correct for spatial contents). Suppose it is true that for some other place to be F is for it to have the same property as this place here has to have if it is to be F here. If this is correct, then the condition that one's current location has to satisfy for 'Here, it's F' to be true is one it could have met even if one had not been perceiving it. Indeed, if a corresponding bridging claim is correct in the spatial case, an understanding of what it is for an arbitrary place to be F is inextricably involved in possession of one's capacity to perceive one's current location to be F.

These points may elicit the following reply. Although these considerations show that the idea of the possibility of unperceived existence must be an inextricable part of the idea of genuine perception, that does not take us as far as the idea of unperceiv*able* states of affairs of the same kind as those which are actually perceived. It is hard to see, however, how we can avoid commitment to the intelligibility of that idea too, given the position we have built up so far. Once we have the conception of perceived states of affairs as categorical, whose existence is not to be explained in counterfactual terms, it seems that it must always be in principle possible for some such state of affairs somewhere to be surrounded by arrangements of such a kind that anyone investigating it would be unable to discriminate between the existence of one, rather than another, specific state of affairs there. The possibility of detectors which, when observations are attempted, destroy any traces of evidence that one rather than the other state of affairs existed is something which is conceptually unproblematic.

What has just been argued in outline for perception holds broadly analogously for memory (though with an extra layer of structure). Genuine experiential memory of an event or state of affairs must be memory of something which could have existed without having been remembered at all.

In the memory case, we can further distinguish two subspecies of possibility of unknowable truth which seem inseparable from the conception of memory as giving, via some form of storage, information about past states of affairs. (i) The first subspecies is already instanced by the examples of two paragraphs back. Suppose it is agreed that a currently perceived state of affairs is of a kind which could now obtain unknowably elsewhere. Suppose too that we accept the equi-categorical claim. It follows that in remembering, in experiential memory, perceiving some state of affairs, one is remembering a state of affairs of a kind which could have obtained unknowably somewhere else in the past. (ii) The second subspecies of cases are those specific to memory, and do not just ride on the back of present-tense possibilities. What is remembered is a state of affairs which could exist without being remembered, and which causally explains the remembering when it is experientially remembered. So, once again, it must in principle be possible for a state of the remembered kind to have occurred, while the subject is in some state which results in the failure of operation of the causal mechanisms needed for the formation of a memory trace. This sort of possibility, unlike subspecies (i), arises not only for memories of objective states of affairs, but also for memories of the subject's own pains and other subjective states.

After this discussion, the answer to our question (1) above should now be apparent. There is no possibility, even in principle, of the truth-conditions fixed by the property–identity link coming apart from those made available by an understanding which involves an externally individuated memory capacity. A properly functioning experiential memory capacity is sensitive to whether, at some earlier time, a truth-condition of the form 'It is *now* the case that *A*' obtained with respect to the earlier time. When functioning properly, it delivers later the information 'It was the case that *A*'. It follows from Uniformity and the property–identity link that, in these circumstances, later deliverance of memory has a correct content. The argument runs thus. In the given circumstances, 'Now it is raining' was true with respect to yesterday. By Uniformity, there is a uniform property any time must have for 'Now it is raining' to be true with respect to that time. So yesterday had the same property as today has to have for 'Now it is raining' to be true with respect to it. So, by the property–identity link, 'Yesterday, it rained' is true. Here I am in agreement with John Campbell's discussion (1994). It follows that, given Uniformity, there cannot be a case in which memory is functioning properly, and conveys the present information that it was the case that *A*, and yet the past-tense statement is not true by the criterion of the property–identity link. It is precisely the condition required by the property–identity link that memory confirms to be true. I conjecture that the use of experiential memory and grasp of the most primitive instances of the property–identity link for the past tense are necessarily coeval.

REALISM, METAPHYSICS, AND THE THEORY OF MEANING

What are the implications of this account for the correct way of conceiving of the relations between metaphysics and the theory of meaning and understanding? Dummett has written of this relation:

The task of constructing a meaning-theory can, in principle, be approached without meta-physical presuppositions or *arrières-pensées*: success is to be estimated according as the theory does or does not provide a workable account of a practice that agrees with that which we in fact observe. It thus provides us with a means of resolving the metaphysical disputes about realism: not an indirect means, but one which accords with their true nature, namely as disputes about the kind of meaning to be attached to various types of sentences. (1991: 13–14)

The account I have given does not accord with that description of the relation between the metaphysics and the theory of understanding. The bridging account has as an essential argumentative background the categorical character of many present-tense statements, the role of the categorical in explanation, and the claim that temporal properties and relations are capable of entering into causal expla-nations of mental and of non-mental phenomena. These are metaphysical theses, and they were presupposed and drawn upon in the above account of understand-ing past-tense predications. They did not fall out of the theory of understanding by itself.

Perhaps, though, it may be said that the opposition between the two accounts of the relation need not be so stark. Can we at least say that a metaphysics is to be tested by its capacity to dovetail with a good theory of understanding? Even if a theory of understanding has sometimes to draw on a metaphysics, still that is consistent with the position that the metaphysics is ratified by its ability to dovetail with the theory of understanding. However, the position I have been developing seems to me to be in tension also with this intermediate position. Presumably this intermediate position is saying more than just that a meta-physics must be consistent with a good theory of understanding. To say only that would be to give no special position to the theory of understanding. All the theories we accept had better be consistent with one another. The intermediate position is making the stronger claim that the fundamental source of ratification of metaphysical claims is their ability to dovetail with a theory of understand-ing. There is tension between the account developed here and this reading of the intermediate position, because the claim of the categorical character of many present-tense statements, the role of the categorical in explanation, and the claim that temporal properties and relations are capable of entering into causal explanations of mental and of non-mental phenomena were illustrated and argued for not in connection with any phenomena having to do with meaning, thought, or understanding, but in connection with ordinary explanatory claims about the world. Examination of our explanatory practices outside the realm of thought and meaning can sometimes give a rational basis for accepting or rejecting metaphysical claims. Our metaphysics, our theory of understanding, our epistemology, and our empirical psychology must all dovetail with one another; but no one of them determines in advance the pattern for all the rest.

REFERENCES

BLACKBURN, S. (1993), 'Filling in space', *Essays in Quasi-Realism*. New York: Oxford University Press.

BLOCK, R., and ZAKAY, D. (2001), 'Retrospective and prospective timing: memory, attention, and consciousness', in C. Hoerl and T. McCormack (eds.), *Time and Memory*. Oxford: Clarendon Press.

BURGE, T. (1993), 'Content preservation', *Philosophical Review*, 102: 457–88.

CAMPBELL, J. (1994), *Past, Space and Self*. Cambridge, Mass.: MIT Press.

DUMMETT, M. (1976), 'What is a theory of meaning? (II)', in G. Evans and J. McDowell (eds.), *Truth and Meaning: Essays in Semantics*. Oxford: Oxford University Press.

—— (1978), *Truth and Other Enigmas*. London: Duckworth.

—— (1991), *The Logical Basis of Metaphysics*. Cambridge, Mass.: Harvard University Press.

EBERHART, M. (1999), 'Why things break', *Scientific American*, 281: 44–51.

FRIEDMAN, W. (2001), 'Memory processes underlying humans' chronological sense of the past', in C. Hoerl and T. McCormack (eds.), *Time and Memory*. Oxford: Clarendon Press.

GALLISTEL, C. (1990), *The Organization of Learning*. Cambridge, Mass.: MIT Press.

GOODMAN, N. (1965), *Fact, Fiction and Forecast*, 2nd edn. Indianapolis: Bobbs-Merrill.

JAMES, W. (1983), *Principles of Psychology*. Cambridge, Mass.: Harvard University Press.

KIM, J. (1982), 'Psychophysical supervenience', *Philosophical Studies*, 41: 51–70.

KRANTZ, D., LUCE, R., SUPPES, P., and TVERSKY, A. (1971), *Foundations of Measurement*, i. New York, Academic Press.

KRIPKE, S. (1980), *Naming and Necessity*. Oxford: Basil Blackwell.

LANGTON, R., and LEWIS, D. (1998), 'Defining "intrinsic" ', *Philosophy and Phenomenological Research*, 58: 333–45.

LEWIS, D. (1983), 'How to define theoretical terms', in *Philosophical Papers*, i. New York: Oxford University Press.

MELLOR, D. H. (1991), 'In defence of dispositions', *Matters of Metaphysics*. Cambridge: Cambridge University Press.

PEACOCKE, C. (1986), 'Analogue content', *Proceedings of the Aristotelian Society*, Suppl. vol. 60: 1–17.

—— (1993), 'Externalist explanation', *Proceedings of the Aristotelian Society*, 93: 203–30.

—— (1998), 'Implicit conceptions, understanding and rationality', in E. Villaneuva (ed.), *Concepts: Philosophical Issues*, 8. Atascadero, Calif.: Ridgeview.

—— (1999), *Being Known*. Oxford: Oxford University Press.

POPPER, K. (1957), *Observation and Interpretation in the Philosophy of Physics*, ed. S. Körner. New York: Dover.

PUTNAM, H. (1970), 'On properties', in N. Rescher (ed.), *Essays in Honor of Carl Hempel*. Dordrecht: Reidel.

RUSSELL, B. (1968), *The Analysis of Mind*. London: George Allen and Unwin.

SHOEMAKER, S. (1984a), 'Causality and properties', in *Identity, Cause and Mind: Philosophical Essays*. Cambridge: Cambridge University Press.

—— (1984b), 'Identity, properties and causality', in *Identity, Cause and Mind: Philosophical Essays*. Cambridge: Cambridge University Press.

STRAWSON, P. (1959), *Individuals*. London: Methuen.

—— (1980), 'Reply to Evans', in Z. van Straaten (ed.), *Philosophical Subjects*. Oxford: Oxford University Press.

WRIGHT, C. (1993), *Realism, Meaning and Truth*, 2nd edn. Oxford: Basil Blackwell.

14

Apperception and the Unreality of Tense

A. W. Moore

My concern is with the issue whether tense is real. Broadly speaking, what this means is that I shall be investigating the *metaphysics* of tensed thought and talk. The sort of question on which I hope to cast light is this: can one and the same fact account both for the truth of a memory I have today, about how things were yesterday, and for the truth of a thought that I had yesterday, about how things were then?

Eventually I shall be concerned with how such questions relate to various aspects of what Kant calls 'the deduction of the categories' in his *Critique of Pure Reason*.[1] More specifically, I hope to see how the answers to such questions might depend on the answers to questions about (to use Kant's phrase) the unity of apperception.[2]

I begin with three disclaimers. First, although I talk about 'the' issue whether tense is real, and shall continue to do so throughout the essay, this is in full acknowledgement of the fact that I am discussing just one of many issues that could reasonably be referred to in this way. All sorts of debates have been conducted under this title. I make no pretence to be focusing on any one thing that has been in dispute in every case.[3]

Secondly, I am not so much interested in settling this issue as in characterizing it. This means that, granted the first disclaimer, I must beware that what I characterize is worthy of attention. In particular, I must try to respect what I shall call the Interest Constraint: to characterize the issue in such a way that neither the view that tense is real nor the view that tense is unreal is a straw man, in the sense of being easily refuted or completely without appeal.[4]

---

[1] Kant, 1933: A84-92/B116-24. The deduction is given in A95-130 and, differently, in B129-69.

[2] This phrase occurs e.g. in ibid., B135.

[3] For a very helpful survey see Le Poidevin, 1998. One of the issues that I shall not be discussing is whether a being that was completely outside time could have any conception of what the past, the present, or the future were: cf. Dummett, 1978a.

[4] There is another constraint that I might be expected to try to respect in this connection: namely, to characterize the issue in such a way that it is not terminological, i.e. in such a way that those who profess a belief in the reality of tense and those who profess a belief in the unreality of tense do not have at their disposal some (mutually acceptable) scheme of translation whereby they can recognize that they are not in dispute after all. But I am much less confident that the characterization I shall provide conforms with this second constraint than I am that it conforms with the Interest Constraint. For one thing, the two constraints are in some tension with each other: the clearer it is that neither of the opposing views in any given philosophical debate is a straw man, the less clear it is that what divides them *is* more than terminological. But I am also much less certain that respecting this second constraint is necessary for ensuring that the issue characterized is worthy of attention. The expression

The third disclaimer is that I shall not be doing any serious Kantian exegesis. Most of the claims that I shall make about Kant's deduction will, I regret, be unsubstantiated. But those who dispute my attributions might still find something of interest in the relationship between the issue on which I shall eventually fasten and the ideas that I shall claim to find in Kant.

Now I have said that there is more than one issue that could reasonably be called 'the' issue whether tense is real. Various points of controversy cluster together here, and they need to be distinguished. But they are not always distinguished. As a result, many of the debates that have been called debates about whether tense is real are little more than a tissue of confusion and failure of communication, so that some philosophers have reacted with scepticism— perfectly justified scepticism—about whether anything at all merits the label. To show that I take such scepticism seriously, I shall devote the first section of this essay to highlighting some of the issues that could *not* reasonably be what is meant by the issue whether tense is real, at least not granted the Interest Constraint, though they look at first blush as though they could.[5]

I

Tense is a feature of certain representations. That is, loosely, it is a feature of certain beliefs, judgements, thoughts, claims, and assertions.[6] It is that feature which indicates that they are from a temporal point of view. Thus if I say, 'It was

'terminological' has all sorts of pejorative overtones. But I see no reason why an issue cannot be terminological, in the sense defined, and also of considerable philosophical moment—if, for instance, it is an issue about which of two conceptual schemes is better equipped to meet certain theoretical and/or practical needs. (This is related to David Cockburn's project in his extremely interesting *Other Times* (1997).) Whether the issue on which I shall be focusing is an issue of this kind is a question that I find enormously difficult. Nothing I say in this essay will help to settle the question. But neither will anything I say depend on how it ought to be settled.

[5] I shall be relying heavily on Cockburn, 1997, which, in effect, gives voice to such scepticism. At the end of one particularly pertinent chapter (ch. 6), Cockburn says that he has been involved in 'an attempt to dissolve the dispute between tensed and tenseless theories [i.e. theories that do and theories that do not accept the reality of tense] as this is widely understood' (p. 127). 'As this is widely understood' indicates that he has in mind something metaphysical. (He allows room for a related ethical dispute.) Granted that my own concerns are broadly metaphysical, Cockburn's chapter challenges my aspiration to identify even one dispute in this territory while respecting the Interest Constraint.

[6] This is as much as I am going to say about how I shall be using the term 'representation', other than to add here that, on my conception, a representation is something that is true or false, without relativization. There is much more that could be said, obviously. In particular, there is much that could be said in response to the worry that, by assuming that there are things that are true or false without relativization, I may, in the context of this essay, be begging some crucial questions. Swinburne (1990: 120) says e.g. that the unreality of tense follows from the assumption that truth is timeless. However, I think I can allay this worry. For whatever relativization may be involved in ascriptions of truth and falsity—such as the obvious relativization of a sentence-type to a time of utterance, and perhaps also the relativization of an utterance to a time of evaluation (cf. Wright, 1987: §VII and Campbell, 1994: 228–30)—I hereby simply stipulate that all the relevant relata are to be thought of as already bound up in the notion of a representation, thus guaranteeing that any given representation can be regarded as true or false without further relativization. Cf. Percival, 1994: 205.

humid yesterday', both the grammatical form of the verb I use and my use of the word 'yesterday' are part of the tense of the representation I produce. Now very roughly, the issue whether tense is real—*any* issue that could reasonably be referred to in that way—turns on whether this feature of representations corresponds in some suitably direct way to a feature of what is represented. The task at hand is to make this less rough.

> *First suggestion*: The issue whether tense is real is the issue whether the truth-conditions of a tensed representation (a representation from a temporal point of view) can be given by means of a representation that is itself tensed.[7]

In due course I shall argue that the issue is a variation on this theme. But as it stands this suggestion is clearly wrong. It makes the view that tense is unreal a straw man, in violation of the Interest Constraint. For patently the truth-conditions of a tensed representation can be given by means of a representation that is itself tensed. If I say, today, 'It was humid yesterday', then what I say is true if and only if it was humid yesterday.

> *Second suggestion*: The issue whether tense is real is the issue whether it can be of material significance whether an event has occurred, is occurring, or is yet to occur.

That will not do either. That, too, makes the view that tense is unreal a straw man. Of course it can be of material significance whether an event has occurred, is occurring, or is yet to occur. My attitude to an excruciating pain that I recall feeling yesterday is very different from my attitude to that same pain two days ago, while I was still anticipating it. But it remains to be shown that *what* is of significance here is something that directly answers to the tense of my various representations of the pain, and not just the tense of the representations themselves.[8]

> *Third suggestion*: The issue whether tense is real is the issue whether properties such as lying in the past and lying in the future are properties

---

[7] By the truth-conditions of a representation I mean the conditions that must be satisfied—the way things must be—in order for the representation to be true. (This notion, it must be said straight away, needs all sorts of clarification. In fact, as we shall see, it needs clarification that is highly pertinent to the issue on which I shall eventually fasten. But because there is more than one acceptable way to clarify it, and because I think that the choice between these may itself be part of settling the issue— this relates to what I said in n. 4 about the possibility of the issue's being terminological—I am deliberately going to leave the notion in this unclarified form.) Note: the canonical way of giving the truth-conditions of a representation is to say that it is true if and only if things are a certain way. And sometimes it is possible to do this by simply reusing the sentence that was used in producing the representation in the first place. Thus I can give the truth-conditions of an utterance of the sentence 'Water contains oxygen', by saying, 'This utterance is true if and only if water contains oxygen.' But sometimes greater subtlety is called for. I cannot give the truth-conditions of an utterance *by you* of the sentence 'I am thirsty' by saying, 'This utterance is true if and only if I am thirsty.'

[8] The issues that arise here were classically brought into focus in Prior, 1959. They are pursued in MacBeath, 1983, and Mellor, 1983.

that events have 'intrinsically' (that is, not from any temporal point of view).

   The problem with this suggestion is that it is likely to make the opposite view, the view that tense is real, a straw man, again in violation of the Interest Constraint. I say 'it is likely to', rather than 'it will', because there is *a* way of construing the claim that events have these properties 'intrinsically' whereby (pending various metaphysical concerns about whether an event can still have a property even when evidence for its having that property is lost, or concerns about whether the future is open[9]) it is fair to say that they do.[10] For instance, I take it to be a simple fact that the Second World War has the property of being over. I do not say that the Second World War has the property of being over *from this temporal point of view*, as though it might not have the property of being over from some other temporal point of view, any more than I say that I am English *from my point of view*, as though I might not be English from yours (cf. Lowe, 1987, 1992). But still, when I say, 'The Second World War has the property of being over', I am producing a representation from a particular temporal point of view. This is illustrated by the fact that somebody could once have used the sentence 'The Second World War has the property of being over' to say something false (just as a German could use the sentence 'I am English' to say something false). The straw man is the view that the Second World War has the property of being over, construed in such a way that *any* utterance of the sentence 'The Second World War has the property of being over' would have succeeded, or would still succeed, in ascribing that property to it. Clearly, in so far as the Second World War has any such property, then it equally has the property of being yet to come; and in so far as there is any making sense of either of these properties, then no event can have them both.[11] A defender of this view might try to escape this contradiction by saying that the properties in question are implicitly relative, so that, to make explicit what is implicit, the Second World War has the property of being over *now* but (compatibly with that) of being yet to come *one hundred years ago*, say. But the response to this is familiar. If this is meant as a defence of the view on anything like the lines originally envisaged, then the original objections can themselves be reformulated: in so far as the Second World War has the property of being over now, then it equally has the property of being yet to come *now* (cf. McTaggart, 1993: 32–3).

   Fourth suggestion: The issue whether tense is real is the issue whether two tensed representations of the same type but from different temporal points of view (for instance, two utterances on successive days of the sentence 'It

---

   [9] See Wright, 1987, and Tooley, 1999 respectively. See further Section III below.

   [10] On this way of construing the claim, I think there *is* an issue here that could reasonably be what is meant by the issue whether tense is real—precisely because of these metaphysical concerns. However, it is not the issue on which I wish to focus.

   [11] This is reminiscent of one of the key steps in J. M. E. McTaggart's celebrated argument for the unreality of time: see McTaggart, 1993: 31–2.

was humid yesterday'[12]) have, modulo any other indexical features they share,[13] the same content.

The problem with this is that there is not really an *issue* here. In one sense the two representations have the same content. In another sense they do not. Nothing of substance hangs on which sense we choose to adopt.[14]

> *Fifth suggestion*: The issue whether tense is real is the issue whether physics needs to involve tensed representations.

I am probably more sympathetic than most to the idea that physics plays a unique and privileged role in informing our conception of reality. Indeed I am prepared to say that the only facts are physical facts, facts about how things are physically; see further Moore (1997: 75–6). But even if this much is granted, this fifth suggestion fails. For consider: physics does not need to involve representations about dogs. Yet not even the most strident physicalism can combine with that to yield the conclusion that dogs are unreal.

> *Sixth suggestion*: The issue whether tense is real is the issue whether, if there had never been any tensed representations (say, because there had never been any creatures capable of producing them), events would still have had such properties as lying in the past and lying in the future.

There is *an* issue here, certainly. But it does not seem to me to be a good candidate for the issue whether tense is real. Someone who denies the reality of tense can quite reasonably accept that, had things turned out in such a way that no creatures capable of producing tensed representations had ever existed, the Big Bang, say, would still have occurred some fifteen thousand million years ago. There is no reason why we should not use tensed representations to describe a world without tensed representations, even while denying that anything in that world corresponds in any suitably direct way to the tense of the representations we thereby use. It is rather as if someone who denied the reality of colour, because of its

---

[12] For more on this notion of a representation's type, see Moore, 1997: 9–11.

[13] The indexical features of a representation are those features of it which indicate that it is from a certain point of view, in the way that tense does. Thus, if I say, 'It is icy over there', my use of the phrase 'over there' is an indexical feature of the representation I produce: it indicates that the representation is from a certain spatial point of view.

[14] There are similar choices to be made with respect to 'proposition', 'belief', and other related terms; there is e.g. the choice about whether to say that the two representations express the same proposition. See Swinburne, 1990: §III and Mellor, 1998: §II for more on these choices. (I do not think that any of the choices generates a real issue. But it is a serious question why not—granted what I said above in n. 4 about the possibility of an issue's being both terminological, in the sense defined there, and 'of considerable philosophical moment'. I have nothing to offer in response to this question but an appeal to judgement. All the crucial distinctions that need to be drawn here, such as the distinction between a choice on which something of substance hangs and a choice on which nothing of substance hangs, are distinctions of degree, not of kind. My own judgement is that not enough hangs on these choices for there to be any serious philosophical point in debating them. This is what I mean by saying that none of the choices generates a real issue. I shall leave it to others to decide how far this distances me from either Swinburne or Mellor.)

secondary-quality status, nevertheless insisted that, even if there had never been any creatures with visual apparatus, grass, say, would still have been green.[15]

> *Seventh suggestion*: The issue whether tense is real is the issue whether a description of reality consisting only of tenseless representations (representations from no temporal point of view) would, no matter how exhaustive it was, be incomplete (cf. Dummett, 1978a: 356–7).

I take it that for a description of reality to be complete is for it to be such that, given any fact, it (the description of reality) entails that that fact obtains.[16] But then the very idea of a complete description of reality might be incoherent, for reasons having nothing to do with the reality of tense. (Perhaps some variation on Heisenberg's uncertainty principle, or on Gödel's theorem, might scupper the idea.[17]) If so, then the necessary incompleteness of a description of reality consisting only of tenseless representations would have no implications for the reality of tense. This suggestion also fails.[18]

> *Eighth suggestion*: The issue whether tense is real is the issue whether assimilation of a description of reality consisting only of tenseless representations would, no matter how exhaustive the description was, leave room for ignorance.

This suggestion is like the seventh, only worse. It is worse because, even if a complete description of reality were possible, and even if some being had assimilated such a description, there might still be things of which the being was ignorant. This is admittedly paradoxical; and the paradox deserves a fuller discussion than I can offer here. But the point is relatively simple. Granted that a complete description of reality is a description of reality such that, given any fact, it entails that that fact obtains, then there are all sorts of ways in which a being that had assimilated such a description might nevertheless lack knowledge. For one thing, the being's knowledge might not be closed under entailment (that is to say, the being's knowledge might not include everything it entails). But even if we put that consideration to one side, the being might lack non-propositional knowledge such as knowledge of how to write beautiful music. More pertinently, the being might lack tensed knowledge such as knowledge of what the date is. Or at least, some argument is required to show that this is not the case. Pending such an argument, the possibility remains open that the being's lacking this knowledge would be nothing but a failure on its part to know some of the facts from a temporal point of view—not a failure on its part to know these facts at all. And if that were

[15] Cf. the discussion of 'rigidification' in Wright (1992: 113–14).

[16] Dummett (1978a: 356) glosses 'complete' as 'observer-independent'. But he is presumably stating an entailment, not offering a definition.

[17] For discussion of each of these, see Penrose, 1989: 248–50 and 105–8 respectively.

[18] Can it not be turned into a good suggestion by a suitable insertion of the word 'thereby'? Perhaps. But something needs to be said about what work is being done by the word, and I suspect that, if the amended suggestion really is a good one, then it will turn out to be the same as the suggestion that I shall eventually endorse.

so, then nothing would follow about the reality of tense. Thus those who insist that tense is real because tenseless knowledge, no matter how exhaustive it was, would leave room for ignorance are guilty, it seems to me, of a straightforward *non sequitur*.[19]

II

I said in response to the first suggestion that it was a variation on the suggestion that I would eventually endorse. Indeed I think that if, in place of the word 'can', it had contained the word 'must', the suggestion would have been correct. I therefore propose the following:

> The issue whether tense is real is the issue whether the truth-conditions of a tensed representation must be given by means of a representation that is itself tensed.[20]

The point is this. Tense is first and foremost a feature of certain representations. The fact that something in reality admits of being represented in this way is not enough to license the claim that the feature is 'real'; that there is something in reality corresponding in some suitably direct way to the feature. But the fact that something in reality *demands* to be represented in this way, provided it were a fact, would be enough.

Objection: Would it not be more than enough? Suppose that the truth-conditions of a tensed representation do *not* have to be given by means of a representation that is tensed. Suppose, in other words, that they can be given by means of a representation that is tenseless. Does it follow that tense is unreal? After all, to echo a point that arose in connection with the fifth suggestion, it may be possible to give the truth-conditions of a representation about a dog without making any reference to the dog but rather by referring to its several parts and saying how they must stand in relation to one another in order for the representation to be true. If so, it certainly does not follow that nothing in reality directly corresponds to that feature of the representation which indicates that it is about a dog, nor that the dog is in any sense unreal.

Reply: There is a crucial difference between the reality of tense and the reality of a dog. The latter, unlike the former, does not have to be understood in terms of some antecedent grasp of a certain feature of representations. Or so I claim. If I am wrong about that—if there are decisive arguments for some sort of idealism whereby the reality of the dog does have to be understood in this way—then so be it: the dog is unreal.

---

[19] Examples are Swinburne, 1990: §§5 and 6; and Lucas (1998). For a fuller discussion of these issues see Moore, 1997: 53–8 and 171–2. Cf. Lewis, 1983, and Perry, 1993. Cf. also Butterfield, 1985, which connects with my essay at several points.

[20] Cf. Priest, 1986: 162–3. Cf. also Mellor, 1993: 59, with a slightly different but closely related gloss on the issue.

Second objection: According to the proposed characterization, if the truth-conditions of a tensed representation can be given by means of a representation that is tenseless, then tense is unreal. But might it not also be the case that the truth-conditions of a tenseless representation can be given by means of a representation that is tensed? And if it *is* the case, should not parity of reasoning force us to conclude that tenselessness is unreal too (cf. Priest, 1986)?

Reply: Yes, but there is no contradiction in this. Both tense and tenselessness are features of representations. It may be that *neither* corresponds in any suitably direct way to any feature of what is represented.

Third objection: Suppose that tenseless representations are not possible at all. Or, less dramatically, suppose that it is not possible to identify a temporal point of view tenselessly. Then must not the truth-conditions of a tensed representation be given by means of a representation that is itself tensed, but not for reasons that have anything to do with the reality of tense?

Reply: It is true that I am taking for granted the possibility both of tenseless representations and of tenseless identifications of temporal points of view.[21] The characterization above fails if either of these things is not possible. However, I have an alternative characterization of the issue for which I claim the following: if both of these things *are* possible, it is equivalent to the characterization above, and, if they are not, it succeeds anyway.

. According to the characterization above, if tense is real, then there is no giving the truth-conditions of a representation from a given temporal point of view except by producing a representation that is itself from some temporal point of view. But this can only be because there is no giving the truth-conditions of a representation from a given temporal point of view except by producing a representation that is from *that very same* temporal point of view. For suppose the latter is not the case. Suppose, for example, that I can give the truth-conditions of an utterance I made yesterday of the sentence 'It is humid today' by saying, 'My utterance yesterday was true if and only if it was humid yesterday.' Then there is nothing to prevent me from giving the truth-conditions of my utterance tenselessly, by tenselessly identifying the temporal point of view I had yesterday—say, by specifying yesterday's date. Or, at least, there is nothing to prevent me from doing this unless tenseless representations are not possible at all, or unless tenseless identifications of temporal points of view are not possible—say, because there is no tenselessly saying what is meant by '*anno domini*'. What this shows is that the heart of the view that tense is real is that something in reality corresponds in a specially direct way to the actual tense of any given tensed representation, not just to its being tensed. Thus, whether or not tenseless representations are possible, and whether or not tenseless identifications of temporal points of view are possible, the following will do as an alternative characterization of the issue:

---

[21] Arguments for and against the possibility of tenseless representations can be found in Le Poidevin, 1998–9, and Teichmann, 1998, respectively.

The issue whether tense is real is the issue whether the truth-conditions of a representation from a temporal point of view must be given by means of a representation that is from that very same temporal point of view.[22]

III

The question I must now address is whether this characterization of the issue violates the Interest Constraint. More specifically, does it make the view that tense is real a straw man?

Note first that the view does not impugn my right to say of yesterday's utterance of 'It is humid today' that it was true if and only if it was humid yesterday. For even if I am right to say this, it remains an open question whether I thereby give the truth-conditions of yesterday's utterance. On the view that tense is real, so characterized, I do not.[23] On that view, the truth-conditions of yesterday's utterance are not that it was humid yesterday. At most they correspond in some specially intimate way to the conditions that it was humid yesterday: the obtaining of either at most affords some sort of guarantee of the obtaining of the other. But they are not the same, because the truth-conditions of yesterday's utterance contain something that directly corresponds to the tense of the utterance, something that precludes my giving those truth-conditions except by re-producing that tense, which I can no longer do. This in turn means that, if yesterday's utterance was true, then the fact that made it true can no longer be so much as expressed.[24]

---

[22] *Counter-objection*: Is there not an intermediate position, based on a belief in the openness of the future, which undermines what I say in this paragraph: namely, the position whereby there are some tensed representations whose truth-conditions can be given by means of representations that are from the same temporal points of view *or later ones*, though they cannot be given by means of representations that are from earlier temporal points of view because the truth-conditions come into existence at a certain time and are simply not available to be given before then?—*Reply*: This position certainly muddies the waters. Unless it can be ruled out (which, ultimately, I think it can) then what I say in the main text needs modification—but not, I think, in a way that affects the main point that I am making. For even if the position is correct, there remains a sense in which it is not possible to give the truth-conditions of a representation from a temporal point of view except by producing a representation that is from that very same temporal point of view: the sense, namely, in which a temporal point of view is a (possibly infinite) period of time, not a point in time. For a very thorough discussion of the issues and complications that arise here, with its own distinctive angle on them, see Tooley, 1997: *passim*.

[23] I said in n. 7 that the canonical way of giving the truth-conditions of a representation is to say that it is true if and only if things are a certain way. It does not follow that saying that a representation is true if and only if things are a certain way always constitutes giving its truth-conditions. It may constitute giving other, correlated conditions. (See further below, in the main text.)

[24] Cf. Dummett, 1978*b*: 373, and Perry, 1993: 45–6. And cf. Frege, 1967: 24–6, for a similar view concerning personal points of view. Note, however, that Michael Dummett, in the first of these references, is talking about a particular philosophical thesis (a kind of anti-realism about the past, whereby the meanings of past-tense representations are given in terms of the conditions which we now recognize as establishing their truth or falsity) which is such that, if any statement of it is true, then what makes that statement true cannot be expressed at a later time—though the thesis in question *accepts* the unreality of tense, as characterized here (see e.g. Dummett, 1978*b*: 363–4). It follows that the issue whether tense is real, as characterized here, is not the same as the issue whether we should endorse the philosophical thesis in question, even though that thesis has importantly similar consequences. It may also follow, ultimately, that that thesis is internally incoherent.

Whatever there is to be said against this view, I do not believe that it is a straw man. For instance, on this view, representations from temporal points of view other than the present can still be acknowledged, now, as representations. They can still be acknowledged as either true or false. More particularly, they can still be acknowledged as having truth-conditions. And we can still talk about these truth-conditions, just as we can talk about the facts that make the representations true or false. In what terms? In precisely those terms—referring to them as we would to things of any other kind. (I can talk about 'the fact' that made something I said yesterday true, just as I can talk about 'the tree' that I was sitting under when I said it.) This much is necessary if the view is to have any intelligibility at all. What we cannot do, if the view is correct, is to *express* the fact that makes any one of these representations true or false. We cannot produce a representation, either tensed or tenseless, that is itself made true by the same fact.

The picture that supports this view—the only picture, so far as I can see, that *can* support it—is that reality fractures into different worlds, where a world is constituted by a set of facts. Each temporal point of view carries its own world with it. Some facts, say the fact that $e = mc^2$, may constitute more than one world.[25] But for each world, there are also facts that peculiarly constitute it, in the sense that they constitute no other world. These facts can be expressed only from the corresponding temporal point of view. For any one of these facts, there may be facts constituting other worlds that correspond in some specially intimate way to it (in the sense alluded to above). But such correspondence falls short of identity.

This picture does not seem to me to admit of any simple refutation.[26] To be sure, if there is a correspondence of the kind just referred to, then there are awkward questions that remain to be addressed about its nature, and about just what sort of guarantee there is that, if one of these facts obtains, then all the corresponding facts obtain too. But those who adopt this picture are not, *per se*, under

---

[25] To say that a fact constitutes a world is an elliptical way of saying that it belongs to the set of facts that constitute that world.

[26] Two comments are in order about how this squares with what I say in Moore, 1997. First, in ch. 3, I seem to regard the view that tense is real as incoherent. I do, but only because I am in effect taking for granted the unity of reality (see e.g. p. 49). Granted the unity of reality, the view that tense is real degenerates into an irremediable muddle about whether the facts that make tensed representations true or false obtain only relative to a temporal point of view or not. Secondly, the view that tense is real, as characterized here, seems to be nothing but the view that tensed representations enjoy what I call in the book 'inherent perspective' (p. 15). Yet I am perfectly happy, in the book, to acknowledge inherent perspective; I do not seem to think that it poses any threat to the unity of reality (see e.g. pp. 50–1). Have I changed my mind about this? No. The threat to the unity of reality comes not just from the inherent perspective in tensed representations, but from that together with the fact that, for most tensed representations, there are obvious candidates from other temporal points of view to answer to the same facts. What someone who believes in the reality of tense has to explain is not just why it is impossible to give the truth-conditions of a tensed representation from another temporal point of view, but why it is impossible to do so even by means of one of these candidates. I can see no other explanation but that there are different worlds associated with different temporal points of view. (This means, in the terms of the book, that if tense is real—on this conception—then not only is it impossible to endorse a tensed representation from another temporal point of view, it is impossible *indirectly* to endorse a tensed representation from another temporal point of view: see pp. 15–16.)

any obligation to answer these questions. For they are not, *per se*, committed to there being any such correspondence. Indeed they may expressly challenge my right to say of yesterday's utterance of 'It is humid today' that it was true if and only if it was humid yesterday,[27] in order to accommodate a certain kind of anti-realism about the past. (I have in mind a view which allows for the possibility that, although I am entitled to say of yesterday's utterance that it was true, I am not entitled to say that it was humid yesterday, because there is no longer any evidence available for yesterday's humidity—a possibility which rests on a distinction between evidence that is available today for yesterday's humidity and evidence that is available today for evidence that was available yesterday for it.[28]) Less radically, they may challenge my right to say the same sort of thing about an utterance I made yesterday in the future tense. 'Less radically' because the corresponding view about the future arguably constitutes a kind of common sense. Thus suppose I said yesterday, 'I shall be in London tomorrow.' And suppose I am now in London. Even so, according to the view I have in mind, the future is open in such a way that my utterance yesterday was not (yet) true: it was not (yet) the case that I would be in London today; there was no fact obtaining then that corresponds to the fact obtaining now that licenses my saying today, 'I am in London.'[29]

There are some large and fascinating philosophical questions, incidentally, about how these worlds compare with the possible worlds acknowledged by modal realists, or with the worlds acknowledged by those who accept the 'many worlds' interpretation of quantum mechanics.[30] Discussion of these questions would take us too far afield. I shall simply make the following three observations, which I think highlight important analogies and disanalogies between these worlds and other kinds of world. First, each of these worlds is part of reality. (The view is after all that tense is real.) Secondly, each of them is part of reality at the expense of something else. In other words, there are other worlds that reality might have contained: there are other ways that the facts might have been. Thirdly, an object that appears in one of these worlds, in the sense that it figures in a fact that constitutes one of these worlds, can also appear in another.[31] In

---

[27] Although the view that tense is real does not impugn my right to say this, neither does it secure my right to say it.

[28] This is a variant of the thesis mentioned in n. 24. Cf. Wright, 1987: §VI, and Campbell, 1994: ch. 7. (In §5 of the latter Campbell suggests that the view is unstable. But on p. 248 he admits that he is prescinding from the possibility that evidence that there was evidence for something is to be distinguished from evidence for that thing.)

[29] If this is right, or if there is a failure of correspondence of any other kind, then not only does each of the worlds fail to contain all the facts, it fails even to 'mirror' all the facts in Leibnizian fashion—unless, perhaps, there is a last moment of time. See Leibniz, 1973: §§56 and 61. Cf. Dummett, 1980: 391 ff.; and cf. n. 22 above.

[30] The *locus classicus* for the first of these is Lewis, 1986, and for the second, Everett, 1957.

[31] Indeed an object's thus appearing in more than one world is a necessary condition of its persisting through time. However, it is not a sufficient condition of the object's persisting through time. There can be facts about objects that no longer exist. Those who adopt this picture may even find it natural to deny, and are at liberty to deny, that objects ever do, strictly speaking, persist through time.

particular, a representation produced from one temporal point of view can be referred to from another temporal point of view. Nevertheless no tensed representation answers to any facts except those that constitute the world associated with the point of view from which it is produced.[32]

IV

The view that tense is real abnegates the unity of reality, then. The question now arises whether this can be turned into an objection to the view. Is the unity of reality something that can be argued for?

One might think that Kant's deduction of the categories provides such an argument. In particular, one might try to extract the following argument from the deduction.

Given any judgement I make, it must be possible for the 'I think' to accompany that judgement. It must be possible for me to think, not only that this is how things are, but that *I think* this is how things are. Otherwise the judgement would not be one of *mine*. Alternatively, if something is to count as a judgement, then its elements must be combined together in a certain way. They must be held together in a certain unity. And such unity must be capable of being acknowledged by the judge—by me, if the judgement is one of mine. But such unity is what I myself supply in making the judgement. So in acknowledging the unity I am in effect acknowledging the judgement as one that I have made. I am acknowledging that *I think* this is how things are. And the unity is the same for any judgement I make. It is what constitutes the judgement as one of mine. It is the unity of my own apperception. But now let f_1 and f_2 be any two facts. Assuming that it is in principle possible for me to judge that each obtains, then it must be in principle possible for me not only to make each of the two relevant judgements but to acknowledge the unity in which each of them is held together, the same in each case, the unity of my apperception. But then it must be in principle possible for me to acknowledge *both* judgements as ones that I have made. Hence it must be in principle possible for me to make a single judgement that embraces both. To telescope the argument: making separate judgements that each of f_1 and f_2 obtains enables me to make separate judgements that *I think* that each of f_1 and f_2 obtains, which enables me to make a single judgement that I think that both f_1 and f_2 obtain, which enables me to make a single judgement that both f_1 and f_2 obtain. This means that f_1 and f_2 are part of the same world. They are part of *my* world. The unity of my apperception signals the unity of reality. To quote Kant (1933: B141): 'A judgement is nothing but the manner in which given modes of knowledge are brought to the objective unity of apperception. This is what is intended by the copula "is".'

---

[32] The vast literature on these issues includes Evans, 1985*b*; Percival, 1992; Butterfield, 1995; and Fleming, 1995.

This argument fails, however. More particularly, there are Kantian reasons why it fails. Perhaps the most obvious objection to it is that it rests on the unargued assumption that, for any two facts, it is in principle possible for me to judge that each obtains. But this is not the objection I wish to focus on, for two reasons. First, this assumption is not one that an advocate of the reality of tense is liable to query, provided that I can make judgements from different temporal points of view, and pending worries about times at which I do not exist. (I shall say some more about this proviso below.) Secondly, the assumption is not one that prevents the argument from succeeding in Kantian terms. Suitably qualified and suitably understood, it is an assumption that Kant himself would have been prepared to grant.[33] The objection I wish to focus on is rather this. Even if it is possible for me to acknowledge each of two separate judgements I make as held together in the unity of my apperception, it does not follow that I can simultaneously acknowledge them both as held together in that unity, or at least not in such a way that I can endorse them both. If the two judgements are made from two different temporal points of view, then it is straightforwardly question-begging to suppose that I can do more, whether from one of those points of view or not, than see them as two judgements answering to how things are in two worlds. It is straightforwardly question-begging, in other words, to suppose that I can integrate them into a single judgement. Even though, in making the two judgements, I bring each of them into the unity of my apperception, there remains the possibility that I do so only as two essentially separate cognitive acts, each of which precludes any repetition of the other. To exclude this possibility, one would need to appeal to something about the character of the judgements themselves. One would need to show that it is in the nature of the judgements themselves to allow for such repetition (cf. Allison, 1983: 162).

But perhaps the very fact that each judgement is one of *mine* allows for this? Perhaps the two judgements cannot count as two judgements by the same person unless, in the passage from the point of view from which one judgement is made to the point of view from which the other is made, there is provision for a kind of 'constancy' of judgement, or a kind of 'retention' of judgement—the sort of thing that allows me at one time to see that things are precisely as I earlier predicted they would be, or to remember that things are precisely as I earlier saw they were. If I cannot now make any judgement that answers to the same fact as any of the tensed judgements I made yesterday, then we lose our grip on the idea that it really was *I*—not merely some counterpart of me—who made all those judgements.[34]

---

[33] This is for reasons that I hope will soon be clear. (Note: the assumption is interestingly related to, though importantly different from and independent of, Kant's famous claim in 1933: A493/B521, that '[to say] that there may be inhabitants in the moon, although no one has ever perceived them . . . only means that in the possible advance of experience we may encounter them.')

[34] Cf. Campbell, 1994: ch. 7. Cf. also what Gareth Evans calls 'keeping track of the passage of time' in Evans, 1985a: 309–10. But note that what Evans has in mind here does not just involve producing a representation at one time that answers to the same fact as a representation produced at an earlier time; it involves *in some sense* reproducing the very same representation. (This means that there is an issue about whether, and how, the representation counts as being from a temporal point of view at all.)

This suggestion, I think, cuts very deep. But it is ineffectual against an intransigent advocate of the reality of tense who is prepared to concede that it was indeed not strictly speaking I, but merely some counterpart of me, who made all those judgements. Such a person might argue that the unity of apperception, which enables any judgement to be made, cannot carry over from one world to another; that this would be contrary to its very unity; that the makers of judgements are essentially ephemeral (cf. n. 31 above).

V

I said that the argument given for the unity of reality fails even in Kantian terms. This is significant *vis-à-vis* Kant's project in the deduction.

Kant's project in the deduction is not to defend the unity of reality. It is to defend our right to apply the categories as we do.[35] And, as Dieter Henrich has famously argued, he undertakes to provide this defence, at least in the version of the deduction that appears in the second edition of *Critique of Pure Reason*, in two steps.[36] In the first step, he tries to show that we are justified in applying the categories to what is united in a certain way. In the second step, he tries to show that what we in fact apply the categories to—that which is in space and time—is indeed united in that way.[37] In the second step he appeals to the fact that 'space and time are represented a priori not merely as *forms* of sensible intuition, but as themselves *intuitions* which contain a manifold . . . and therefore are represented with the determination of the *unity* of this manifold' (Kant, 1933: B160; his emphasis). That is, he appeals to the fact, to which he has already appealed and attached much importance in 'The Transcendental Aesthetic' (A24-5/B39 and A31-2/B47), that space and time, and therewith that which is in space and time, are *given* to us as having the requisite unity. 'Fact' is the operative word here. Kant thinks it conceivable, in the abstract, that things should have been different. 'Appearances might very well be so constituted', he writes (A90/B123), 'that understanding should not find them to be in accordance with the conditions of its unity.' That is, they might be so constituted that they should lack the unity necessary for us to be justified in applying the categories to them. Had they been made up of different worlds associated with different temporal points of view, this would have been the case. We should have had no justification, for example, in applying the category of causation across such worlds. This is reflected in the fact that we could not have used the schema '*p* because *q*' to adjudge that one of the facts that (peculiarly) constituted one world was causally dependent on one of the facts that (peculiarly) constituted another. We could not have used this schema

---

[35] Kant, 1933: A84 ff./B116 ff. The 'categories' are twelve fundamental a priori concepts of ours that Kant claims to have identified. A prime example is the concept of causation.

[36] Henrich, 1982. For what follows, see esp. §II. Cf. also Turetzky, 1998: 92–3.

[37] The first step is completed by the end of §20. The second step is given, after some incidental observations, in §26.

because the two facts would have had to be represented from two incompatible points of view.[38]

We can now see better why the argument given in the previous section fails even in Kantian terms. It relies on certain highly abstract considerations about judgement and unity. But it is clear from the way in which Kant proceeds in the deduction that he does not think that the unity of *temporal* reality can be argued for in any such way, certainly not in any such abstract way. For Kant, this unity is something more like a brute fact, a fact about how time is given to us. If it is possible for someone to integrate two judgements from different temporal points of view into a single judgement, this is in part because of the quintessence of time (the quintessence of the 'space' in which each of the two different points of view is located).

As for the way in which time is given to us, on Kant's conception, this is through the 'transcendental synthesis of imagination', where 'transcendental' synthesis is defined as synthesis which 'not merely . . . [takes] place a priori, but also . . . [conditions] the possibility of other a priori knowledge', and 'imagination' is defined as 'the faculty of representing in intuition an object that is *not itself present*' (Kant 1933: B151; his emphasis. See also B151 ff.) It follows that time is given to us as having parts, as something that is partly past and partly future: imagination is the faculty that provides for the possibility of memory and expectation. Now this in turn may seem to conflict with the idea that time is given to us as having unity. But it does not. Past and future are indeed different parts of time, but they are parts that are (transcendentally) synthesized into a whole. They are features of a single temporal world. (This is why time is not only given to us as having unity, it is given to us as having the kind of unity that justifies our applying the categories to it and to its contents.[39]) Through memory we are able to recall, and thereby to represent, the very facts that we once witnessed as present. Through expectation we are able to anticipate, and again thereby to represent, the very facts that we shall later witness as present.

If this is on even broadly the right lines—and I am sure it is—then tense is unreal. The unreality of tense, or equivalently the unity of temporal reality, is of a piece with the unity of apperception. We can achieve insight into it through a kind of self-conscious reflection. But we cannot argue for it. Thus if we consider our own tensed representations and reflect on how we conceive them and what they answer to, then we can come to see them as representations, from different positions within a single world, of that single world—just as, if I consider my own representations (tensed or tenseless) and reflect on how I conceive them and my capacity to produce them, I can come to see them as representations produced

---

[38] To say that two points of view are incompatible is to say that no representation could be from both.

[39] See esp. §26 of the 2nd edn. version of the deduction in Kant, 1933. Cf. Allison, 1983: 160–4, and Turetzky, 1998: 93. Cf. also what Kant himself says later, at 1933: A581–2/B609–10, which, together with the footnote at A572/B600, in turn merits a striking comparison with Wittgenstein, 1961: 2.0124 and 5.524.

by a single self-conscious subject occupying different positions within a single world. Even so, if someone resolutely refuses to acknowledge the unity of temporal reality—if someone conceives of tense as a feature of reality—then there is no more basic principle we can adduce to force a change of mind. The unity of temporal reality is indeed, to that extent, akin to a brute fact. There is a great deal to be said about it. But there is nothing, or at least nothing with any suasive power, to be said in favour of it.[40]

I am extremely grateful to John Bigelow, Jeremy Butterfield, John Campbell, David Cockburn, Michael Dummett, Naomi Eilan, Christoph Hoerl, Teresa McCormack, Helen Steward, and especially Philip Percival for comments on earlier drafts of this essay.

A.W.M.

REFERENCES

ALLISON, H. E. (1983), *Kant's Transcendental Idealism: An Interpretation and Defense*. New Haven: Yale University Press.

BUTTERFIELD, J. (1985), 'Indexicals and tense', in I. Hacking (ed.), *Exercises in Analysis: Essays by Students of Casimir Lewy*. Cambridge: Cambridge University Press, 69–87.

—— (1995), 'Quantum theory and the mind: worlds, minds and quanta', in *Proceedings of the Aristotelian Society*, supp. vol. 69: 113–58.

CAMPBELL, J. (1994), *Past, Space, and Self*. Cambridge, Mass.: MIT Press.

COCKBURN, D. (1997), *Other Times: Philosophical Perspectives on Past, Present and Future*. Cambridge: Cambridge University Press.

DUMMETT, M. (1978a), 'A defence of McTaggart's proof of the unreality of time', repr. in his *Truth and Other Enigmas*. London: Duckworth, 351–7

—— (1978b), 'The reality of the past', repr. in his *Truth and Other Enigmas*. London: Duckworth, 358–74.

—— (1980), *Frege: Philosophy of Language*, 2nd edn. London: Duckworth.

EVANS, G. (1985a), 'Understanding demonstratives', repr. in his *Collected Papers*. Oxford: Oxford University Press, 291–321.

—— (1985b), 'Does tense logic rest upon a mistake?', in his *Collected Papers*. Oxford: Oxford University Press, 343–63.

EVERETT, H. (1956), ' "Relative state" formulation of quantum mechanics', *Reviews of Modern Physics*, 29: 454–62.

FLEMING, G. N. (1995), 'Quantum theory and the mind', in *Proceedings of the Aristotelian Society*, supp. vol. 69: 159–73.

---

[40] This echoes a recurring theme of Moore, 1997. I there make frequent use of two principles which are different expressions of the unity of reality: what I call the Fundamental Principle (pp. 21–2) and what I call the Basic Assumption (p. 74). I claim that such principles cannot be established by any arguments: see e.g. pp. 188–9. Cf. in this connection Michael Dummett's remarks about what he calls 'our prejudice' that there must be a complete description of reality (1978a: 356–7), and John Campbell's comments about the ineluctability of a realist view of the past (1994: 4). And see again the remarks in n. 4 above.

FREGE, G. (1967), 'The thought: a logical inquiry', trans. A. M. and M. Quinton and repr. in P. F. Strawson (ed.), *Philosophical Logic*. Oxford: Oxford University Press, 17–38.

HENRICH, D. (1982), 'The proof-structure of Kant's transcendental deduction', repr. in R. C. S. Walker (ed.), *Kant on Pure Reason*. Oxford: Oxford University Press, 66–81.

KANT, I. (1933), *Critique of Pure Reason*, trans. N. Kemp Smith. London: Macmillan.

LEIBNIZ, G. W. (1973), 'Monadology', trans. M. Morris and G. H. R. Parkinson, in his *Philosophical Writings*. London: Dent, 179–94.

LE POIDEVIN, R. (1998), 'The past, present, and future of the debate about tense', in R. Le Poidevin (ed.), *Questions of Time and Tense*. Oxford: Oxford University Press, 13–42.

—— (1998–9), 'Egocentric and objective time', *Proceedings of the Aristotelian Society*, 99: 19–36.

LEWIS, D. (1983), 'Attitudes *de dicto* and *de se*', repr. in his *Philosophical Papers*, i. New York: Oxford University Press, 133–59.

—— (1986), *On the Plurality of Worlds*. Oxford: Basil Blackwell.

LOWE, E. J. (1987), 'The indexical fallacy in McTaggart's proof of the unreality of time', *Mind*, 96: 62–70.

—— (1992), 'McTaggart's paradox revisited', *Mind*, 101: 323–6.

LUCAS, J. R. (1998), 'Transcendental tense', *Proceedings of the Aristotelian Society*, supp. vol. 72: 45–56.

MACBEATH, M. (1983), 'Mellor's emeritus headache', *Ratio*, 25: 81–8.

MCTAGGART, J. M. E. (1993), 'The unreality of time', repr. in R. Le Poidevin and M. MacBeath (eds.), *The Philosophy of Time*. Oxford: Oxford University Press, 23–34.

MELLOR, D. H. (1983), 'MacBeath's soluble aspirin', *Ratio*, 25: 89–92.

—— (1993), 'The unreality of tense', repr. in R. Le Poidevin and M. MacBeath (eds.), *The Philosophy of Time*. Oxford: Oxford University Press, 47–59.

—— (1998), 'Transcendental tense', in *Proceedings of the Aristotelian Society*, supp. vol. 72: 29–43.

MOORE, A. W. (1997), *Points of View*. Oxford: Oxford University Press.

PENROSE, R. (1989), *The Emperor's New Mind: Concerning Computers, Minds, and the Laws of Physics*. Oxford: Oxford University Press.

PERCIVAL, P. (1992), 'Thank goodness that's non-actual', *Philosophical Papers*, 21: 191–213.

—— (1994), 'Absolute truth', *Proceedings of the Aristotelian Society*, 94: 189–213.

PERRY, J. (1993), 'The problem of the essential indexical', repr. in *The Problem of the Essential Indexical and Other Essays*. New York: Oxford University Press, 33–52.

PRIEST, G. (1986), 'Tense and truth conditions', *Analysis*, 46: 162–6.

PRIOR, A. N. (1959), 'Thank goodness that's over', *Philosophy*, 34: 12–17.

SWINBURNE, R. (1990), 'Tensed facts', *American Philosophical Quarterly*, 22: 117–30.

TEICHMANN, R. (1998), 'Is a tenseless language possible?', *Philosophical Quarterly*, 48: 176–88.

TOOLEY, M. (1997), *Time, Tense, and Causation*. Oxford: Oxford University Press.

TURETZKY, P. (1998), *Time*. London: Routledge.

WITTGENSTEIN, L. (1961), *Tractatus Logico-Philosophicus*, trans. D. F. Pears and B. F. McGuiness. London: Routledge and Kegan Paul.

WRIGHT, C. (1987), 'Anti-realism, timeless truth and *Nineteen Eighty-Four*', in his *Realism, Meaning and Truth*. Oxford: Basil Blackwell, 176–203.

—— (1992), *Truth and Objectivity*. Cambridge, Mass.: Harvard University Press.

15

Memories, Traces and the Significance of the Past

David Cockburn

I

A certain, fairly widespread, pair of assumptions are, perhaps, implicit in the project which the present volume represents. It is assumed, first, that the notion of 'consciousness' should have a fundamental place in our attempts to understand the phenomenon of human memory; and, secondly, that that understanding will be enhanced by an attempt at dialogue between philosophy and psychology. Now it is perhaps worth saying at the start that this chapter is, in part, an attempt to raise certain worries about these assumptions. I say this at the start partly in order to stress that, perhaps contrary to appearances, my scepticism is far from total. I take it to be obvious that there is an important place for inter-disciplinary dialogue here; and that no discussion of the memory of experienced events can be complete without a consideration of, for example, the idea of a conscious reliving of past events. Still, I believe that there are dangers here: that we may end up setting an agenda for the discussion that skews it in quite the wrong direction, leading to a seriously distorted account of this phenomenon of human life.

II

One question that has had a prominent place in much of the philosophical and psychological discussion of memory might be formulated in this way: what happens in a person when she remembers some past event? The question assumes that remembering an event involves something *happening* within one. We might protest that remembering is a *state*, not a happening. Thus, we can say of Mary that she remembers what happened on that night even though she is thinking about something quite different at the moment; or, for that matter, is lying unconscious on the floor. Now it might be replied that such uses of the term 'remember' are secondary: that primary ascriptions of episodic memory to an individual involve datable happenings in the individual's life.[1] And whatever one may think

---

[1] I use the phrase 'episodic memory' to mean, not 'particular episodes of remembering', but 'memory of particular episodes'. There may, in some discussions, be a tendency towards equivocation here: a tendency behind which lies the idea that what makes something a memory of a particular episode—as opposed to an instance of 'habit memory'—can only be the way in which it involves a 'mental re-experiencing of events'. One of the aims of this chapter is to question that connection of

of the claim to primacy, we can, for the moment, simply acknowledge that there *are* such things as datable occurrences of 'remembering'. There is the phenomenon of suddenly recovering a memory that one (thought one?) had lost. And there is the phenomenon of dwelling on some event through mental imagery, discussion with another, or some other medium. There are, then, memory occurrences for the philosopher or psychologist to study.

But, I want to suggest, there are dangers here. First, we may find ourselves drawn into the idea that examining what happens at these times is what is *fundamental* to an understanding of memory and its place in human life. Secondly, it may lead to a focusing of attention on what can be studied in abstraction from any connection that it may have with the past. Thirdly, a study of 'what happens in a person when she remembers some past event' may lead us to think of remembering as something essentially 'inner': to think that we can get clear about the character of remembering while paying no attention to the ways in which a person's memories may find expression in her speech and behaviour.[2]

Central to my essay will be an attempt to substantiate the claim that these are correctly described as 'dangers'. In doing that, I will suggest—primarily by example—that greater philosophical illumination is to be found by focusing, not on the question 'What happens in a person when she remembers some past event?', but rather on the question 'What are we doing when we ascribe to another a memory of some event?' or 'What place do such ascriptions have in our lives?' This shift in focus brings with it a shift from a traditional philosophical emphasis on questions of the form 'How can we have knowledge of the past through memory?' to questions of the form 'How do the events that we remember provide us with reasons for doing and feeling certain things now?' And that, in turn, introduces questions about the *ethical* commitment involved in the ascription of 'memory', or of particular memories, to an individual.

III

In approaching these matters it will be helpful, first, to pick up a central strand in the interest in memory embodied in one philosophical tradition. Speaking of remembering what I had for breakfast, Russell writes: 'The process of remembering will consist of calling up images of my breakfast, which will come to me with a feeling of belief such as distinguishes memory images from mere imagination images' (1921: 175). Others speak, instead of 'images', of 'presentations',

---

ideas. (See, in this connection, the chapters by Christoph Hoerl, John Campbell, and Michael Martin (Chs. 12, 6, and 10) in the present volume. Incidentally, the contrast between 'conscious' and 'unconscious' memories often harbours a similar confusion—which is not, of course, to deny that there are perfectly legitimate uses of that contrast.)

[2] On these last two points, compare the question 'What happens when one person checkmates another?' Checkmating is a significant event for the chess player; so we might expect a close examination of what happens when a checkmating happens to reveal some pretty profound things.

'impressions', 'ideas', 'the immediate object in memory', and so on. And to the objection that we can say of someone that he remembers what he had for breakfast even though his mind is on quite other things at the moment it will be replied that such ascriptions of memory are secondary. The central cases of memory—those on which we must focus if we are to attain philosophical clarity—are those in which a representation of a past event is present to consciousness.

Views of this general form are almost inevitable products of the idea that memory is a source of knowledge of the past. While such views can survive its rejection, a brief consideration of that idea will, I think, be a helpful first step in the attempt to dislodge their hold. On the most familiar version of this idea, then, in remembering some event I find out what happened through examining an effect of that event in the present: the trace that it has left in my mind. Thus, as Russell says:

Our confidence or lack of confidence in the accuracy of a memory-image must, in fundamental cases, be based upon a characteristic of the image itself, since we cannot evoke the past bodily and compare it with the present image . . . I think the characteristic by which we distinguish the images we trust is the feeling of *familiarity* that accompanies them.[3]

I infer from this trace—this image, together with its distinctive feeling—that things probably happened as they are represented in the image.

There are familiar, and serious, problems about how memory *could* be a source of knowledge of the past. In presenting that view I said: 'I infer from this trace—this image, together with its distinctive feeling—that things probably happened as they are represented in the image.' But that raises the question: what grounds can I have for thinking that images that are accompanied by *this* feeling are representations of things that happened in the past? The story seems to require that there is some way, independent of memory, by which I can, on occasion, compare my mental imagery with the past, and so notice that images accompanied by this feeling are generally representations of things that have happened. But what could this way be? Of course, we do normally suppose that we have other forms of access to the past: for example, through written reports, physical traces, what others tell us, and so on. Now it is often suggested that our employment of any of these is *dependent on* memory—in which case they cannot provide independent support for it. Be that as it may, if these, too, are to be understood as '*sources*' of knowledge of the past, then the same question of grounding as arose about memory will arise about them: what grounds can I have for thinking that present states of these particular kinds are any guide to what happened in the past?

There are possible answers to these questions. Rather than address those, however, I want to suggest that we should take seriously a picture on which these questions will not arise. We should, that is, take seriously the (by no means new[4])

---

[3] Russell, 1921: 161. Comparing this passage with that quoted above, Russell appears to appeal to 'feeling' both in his account of the *basis* of belief and in his account of the *nature* of belief. Both stories appear, perhaps sometimes not clearly distinguished, in writers in this tradition.

[4] See e.g. Holland, 1954: 464–86; Malcolm, 1963, 1977.

suggestion that memory is *not*—at least not in a quite general way—a source of
knowledge of the past. To remember some event is not to have a present mental
trace from which one infers what happened. One who remembers an event is one
who already knows what happened because he observed it. One who remembers
an event does not, then, need present evidence—either internal or external—on
the basis of which he can infer what happened. The assumption that there *must* be
a memory trace—an internal state from which I can infer what happened—is the
assumption that at each instant of my life I must start again in a state of complete
ignorance: building up my picture of the past (and, presumably, of everything
else) on the basis of the evidence that is now available to me.

It is worth mentioning here a range of cases that might seem to corroborate the
Russell-type view. For example, when trying to recount who was at the party I
conjure up a mental image of the room full of people and 'read' the names off
from that. In such cases there is, I think, a fairly straightforward sense in which
memory may be a source of knowledge. The Russell view, of course, trades on
such cases: suggesting that even when there appears to be no mental image it is
there, at work, at some level. Perhaps the pull of this suggestion will be weakened
by the observation that this method of recounting who was at the party is dependent on my knowing, or at least believing, that this, that I now have, is an image
of the party. Do I, then, need another image from which I 'read' *that* off?[5]

The fundamental idea, then, behind the alternative view of memory is that
knowledge can be retained. One who remembers an event does not need a source
of knowledge about it, for he already knows what happened. Now that view, if
there is anything to be said for it, has implications for questions of the form: what
happens in a person when he remembers some past event? I suggested earlier that
there appears to be a confusion in the question in so far as, contrary to what it
presupposes, memory is a *state*, not a happening. That doubt should now be reinforced. So long as one thinks of memory as a source of knowledge one will think
that those moments of 'recall' when the knowledge is acquired are fundamental to
the phenomenon of memory. But if, as I have suggested, one who remembers is
one who knows, then there are no such privileged instants at which the knowledge
is, from time to time, acquired. Further, one will no longer suppose that there *must*
be some particular phenomenology that marks out 'remembering', for one will no
longer insist that there must be an answer to the question: what grounds does he
have for supposing that this image before his mind is of some past event?[6] What
is more, one will, or should, no longer suppose that there *could* be some particular phenomenology that marks out 'remembering' any more than—and because—
there is no particular phenomenology that marks out 'knowing'. Nothing
happening now—today—determines this as a case of 'remembering yesterday's

---

[5] See Ch. 8 by Dokic in this volume for a much more detailed, and highly illuminating, discussion of cases of this kind.

[6] A similar point may apply to any *completely general* form of the question: what grounds does
an individual have for his judgement about the relative recency of remembered events? In this connection, see William Friedman's Ch. 5 in this volume.

fight' since yesterday's fight itself is a crucial determinant: it is not remembering if there was no such fight.

I can imagine someone feeling that I have, in these remarks, offered a wholly inadequate response to the sceptical worry that I suggested is generated by the idea of memory as a source of knowledge. For to insist that one who remembers what happened is one who knows what happened clearly leaves us with the question: how does the individual know that what he now has is a case of 'knowledge of the past'? Must there not be something in his current experience that tells him that this *is* a case of remembering? So are we not back where we started? Well, not exactly where we started. One bit of progress is seen in the fact that we are now confronted with an *obvious* regress. If there *must* be a way in which he knows that he knows, then presumably there must also be a way in which he knows that he knows that he knows. It is, then, fairly clear that we had better grasp the bull by the horns and allow that we can sometimes remember what happened—know what happened through having been there—without *knowing* that we remember. This is progress. At the same time, it is a piece of progress that should make it clear that scepticism has not been *answered*. I have not shown, but simply taken it as given, that we do, in memory, have knowledge of the past. I will return to this: suggesting a sense in which this 'taking it as given' involves an *ethical* commitment. First, I want to take up, in the next two sections, the second and third 'dangers' that I spoke of at the end of Section II.

IV

I said that it is a danger in the question 'What happens in a person when she remembers some past event?' that it may lead to a focusing of attention on what can be studied in abstraction from any connection that it may have with the past. What is 'dangerous' in that? While it will not be the whole of what we can expect from a philosophical treatment, is it not a quite legitimate—indeed essential—starting point? Surely we can—perhaps must—get clear about the phenomenon of remembering, understood exclusively as an occurrence or state *in the present*, before we move on to the character of the relation between that and the event in the past that is (purportedly) remembered. In support of this, appeal might be made to the Humean idea articulated by Russell in the words: 'There is no logically necessary connection between events at different times' (1921: 156).

Russell's claim has the ring of a transparent truth. How, we might ask, could something that happens on Monday necessitate something that happens on Tuesday in anything stronger than a causal sense? Yet, for all its apparent transparency, there is an unclarity about just what the claim means. The unclarity is, in the first instance, a 'grammatical' one. Events do not belong to the category of things between which it can be said that a logically necessary relation holds. It makes no sense to say of a tree's falling down or my being rude to Fred that it logically entails anything else. The terms of the relationship of 'logically necessary connection' come from a quite different group of categories—a group that includes, perhaps: propositions, assertions, thoughts, and facts.

No doubt our tendency to see a transparent truth in Russell's claim—and, what is more, a transparent truth of deep metaphysical import—is in part explained by the particular character of the grammatical confusion that it contains. Be that as it may, consider a case in which, on Monday, Jones treats Mary in a way that is extraordinarily rude—indeed cruel. On Tuesday, remembering his disgraceful behaviour, he feels deeply ashamed and apologizes to Mary. Does it not logically follow from the claim that Jones remembers being rude to Mary on Monday that Jones was rude to Mary on Monday? In describing his condition on Tuesday as one of 'remembering' we commit ourselves to the claim that what he 'remembers' happened.

Now it is tempting to suppose that this kind of point raises no difficulty for an important truth that is embodied in Russell's claim. For, it will be said, this logical connection arises solely from the terms in which we have chosen to describe the situation. That our language contains terms, such as 'remember', whose correct application to what happens at one time depends on what happened at another, can show us nothing of *metaphysical* significance. It is simply a reflection of the way in which, for certain practical reasons, we find it convenient to describe experience. That this is so is clear from the fact that we can equally describe what happens on Tuesday in terms that carry no implications concerning what happened on Monday: 'Jones has a mental image of him being rude to Mary. He looks grim, shakes his head, and feels ashamed', and so on.

Well, perhaps this description carries no implications concerning what happened on *Monday*. But its sense is still deeply bound up with what happens at times other than, say, 4.17 p.m. on Tuesday. Think, for example, of the logical implications carried by the use of a particular proper name, such as 'Jones' or 'Mary': to identify this individual as Jones is to identify him as one with a particular place in an historical narrative. Again, think of the various kinds of logical implication of our description of his state as one of 'feeling ashamed': our characterization of what is happening now—say, in this three seconds—as 'shame' is not independent of our understanding of the development of this feeling over a longer stretch of his life.[7] I strongly suspect, but cannot argue here, that we will only achieve anything approaching the kind of 'purified' description that we are after if we describe the situation in something approximating to the traditional philosophical terminology of sense data. But setting that to one side we can ask: why should it be assumed that a description that has the narrowest possible 'temporal scope' is metaphysically purer than one that carries implications for what happens at other times? Why, that is, should it be assumed that our 'primary' relation to reality is through a, narrowly conceived, present: that descriptions of

---

[7] ' "For a second he felt violent pain."—Why does it sound queer to say: "For a second he felt deep grief"? Only because it so seldom happens? But don't you feel grief *now*? ("But aren't you playing chess *now*?") The answer may be affirmative, but that does not make the concept of grief any more like the concept of a sensation' (Wittgenstein, 1958: 174.)

the world that involve a temporal span must be conceived as a logical combination of more basic elements that describe time slices experienced in a series of such 'presents'?

The assumption runs deep in a great deal of philosophy, and I can do little, directly, to undermine it here. We can, however, approach it indirectly by way of a consideration of another kind of relation between events at different times. What Jones did on Monday provides him with a reason for doing and feeling certain things on Tuesday. Might *that* be a logically necessary connection? Suppose, for example, it was said: it logically follows from the fact that Jones was extraordinarily rude to Mary on Monday that he has, on Tuesday, reason to feel ashamed and to apologize to her.

As with the earlier kind of connection of which I spoke, there are several powerful strands within contemporary philosophical thinking that might underpin a denial of such a suggestion. One is the widely held, completely general, doctrine that it is only in conjunction with a relevant *desire* (or 'pro-attitude') that belief can lead to action. The belief that I acted badly, or that it is about to rain, cannot lead me to *do* anything unless I also have a desire to make amends, to keep dry, or whatever. Combined with the widely held view that the limits on what it is possible to desire are only psychological in character, this will entail that there are *no* logical limits on the ways in which a particular fact can be offered as a reason for action.

The denial that there can be a logical connection between what Jones did on Monday and what he has reason to do, or feel, on Tuesday might be defended by appeal to the more modest doctrine that all 'intrinsic' reasons for action and feeling lie in the present or future. There is a forward-looking strand in much philosophical ethics according to which past events can only provide me with reason to do or feel something now by way of contingent connections in which they stand to present or future events. That the possibility of intense pain in the near future is a reason for fear and for taking evasive action is not dependent on any contingent truth such as: pain is a sign of physical injury. By contrast, that Jones's rudeness yesterday gives him reason to apologize to Mary today is dependent on the contingent fact that past rudeness tends to lead to present hurt feelings, and apologies tend to lead to the relief of those feelings. Thus, if Jones fails to see that he has reason to apologize to Mary, that need not reveal any failure in understanding of what he has done. It may reveal, rather, his failure to recognize the contingent connections between rudeness and hurt feelings, or between apologies and the relief of such feelings. Alternatively, it may reveal his conviction that in *this* case those contingent connections do not hold.

There is room for the view that, by contrast with both of these suggestions, the connection between past events and what someone now has reason to do or feel is sometimes logical in character. For example, a full grasp of the meaning of the word 'rude' involves a recognition that if one has been rude to someone one has, other things being equal, reason to feel ashamed and to apologize to him or her. Or at the very least: it involves a recognition that past rudeness can intelligibly be offered as a reason for feeling ashamed and apologizing—as, in the absence of any special explanation, the fact that one has been kind to someone cannot.

V

To see the significance of this suggestion we need to turn to what I spoke of as a third 'danger' in the question: what happens in a person when she remembers some past event? I suggested that it may lead us to think that we can get clear about the character of remembering while paying no attention to the ways in which a person's memories may find expression in her speech and behaviour. We come to suppose that such outward expressions of remembering are merely a consequence of 'the remembering itself'; for we are looking for something that is common to all cases of remembering, and it is clear that there is nothing common at the level of public expression.

It is, in this connection, worth asking: in what circumstances do we say of someone that she remembers some event? But it might be more useful to focus, for the moment, on the more general question: what are the conditions that ground our judgement that someone shares with us the use of past-tense language as an articulation of personal memories? One relevant condition is, I take it, the fact that she offers (what we judge to be) true descriptions in the past tense of events that she observed. Another is that her 'memory reports' are integrated with the rest of her life in certain ways. For example, she offers the fact that she left the spade in the shed (or: that she remembers leaving the spade in the shed) as a reason for someone to look in the shed if he needs a spade; she offers the fact that she was very rude to Smith as a reason for feeling ashamed and apologizing to him; she offers the fact that Sam had the largest piece of cake last time as a reason for thinking that *she* should have it this time; and so on. And the integration that we look for here does not lie only at the level of verbal behaviour of this form. We see that she remembers in the fact that she looks in the shed when she needs a spade; that she feels ashamed, and apologizes to Smith, etc. In the absence of links of these latter kinds there would be serious doubt about whether we could take her verbal insistence that there is *reason* to do and feel these things at face value: that is, as an expression of understanding of what the past provides her with reason to do and feel. With that, we can, in the absence of any relevant verbal behaviour, see, in aspects of her feelings and behaviour that are appropriate to events she has observed, that she has some form of memory of past events.

We say of someone who speaks, feels, and acts in these ways that she 'remembers' things she has done or observed. We do not, in the normal course of things, take seriously the quite general suggestion that perhaps she does not *really* remember: on the grounds that perhaps the relevant 'inner states' are not taking place in her; on the grounds that perhaps we and she are collectively and systematically deluded about the past, so that none of our purported memories are really memories at all; or, most relevantly to our immediate purposes, on the grounds that perhaps, while her actual memories are wholly delusive, they combine with a systematically abnormal set of desires to produce actions and feelings that are indistinguishable from the norm. Perhaps the philosopher can offer reasons for thinking that we ought at least to consider these possibilities. And perhaps, once we have done so, we can present considerations that will lay the doubts to rest. But I want to ask how matters will look if we simply take our normal practice at face value.

The suggestion, then, is that the *primary* expression of the employment of past-tense language as an articulation of personal memories—as we might equally say, the *primary* expression of episodic memory—is not some 'inner' event or state from which action and feeling may flow; but rather, action and feeling themselves. The primary *locus* of what is commonly referred to as 'mental content' is not an 'inner representation of a past event'—however that is conceived—to which (on Russell's account) a feeling of belief is attached. It is, rather, particular configurations of action and feeling.

This proposal will, to some, have an uncomfortable 'behaviourist' ring to it: the charge of 'behaviourism' being, perhaps, the charge that such an emphasis on 'action and feeling' fails to acknowledge the fact that action and feeling only have for us the *significance* that they do in a particular case because of our understanding that they are an expression of *something else*—a memory—that lies behind them. A notion of 'mental content', understood as something logically distinct from, and prior to, action and feeling is essential if we are to do justice to the 'richness', or the 'depth', of what is involved in human memory.

Discussing a different issue Wittgenstein writes:

I tell someone I am in pain. His attitude to me will then be that of belief; disbelief; suspicion; and so on.

Let us assume he says: 'It's not so bad.'—Doesn't that prove that he believes in something behind the outward expression of pain?—His attitude is a proof of his attitude. (1958: §310)

I quote this passage primarily for the sake of this comment on it by Peter Winch:

We might say that what Wittgenstein is really protesting against in section 310 is a sort of *impatience*. . . . 'His attitude is a proof of his attitude' means 'Just stop and look at what his attitude does actually consist in, perhaps you will be surprised at the subtleties and complexities involved; and when you have noticed them perhaps you will be less inclined to suppose that their significance must depend on something below the surface of which they are merely symptoms' (1987: 142).

I am not able here (or perhaps at all) to bring out the relevant subtleties and complexities of action and feeling involved in familiar cases of remembering: bring them out, that is, in a way that is likely much to reduce the inclination to suppose that their significance must depend on something below the surface—an 'inner representation'—of which they are merely symptoms. The inclination to think in that way may be partially eased by the observation that among the actions of which I am speaking, and central to the place that memory has in human life, is '*linguistic* behaviour': this including, for example, the ways in which memories may be verbally articulated or challenged, the ways in which what has happened may be offered as reason for doing and feeling certain things now, and so on. It is possible that reflection on what this can involve may restore some sense of the 'richness' and 'depth' that we felt in danger of losing. It is, in this connection, perhaps important to stress that in speaking of what a person *says* as an aspect of her 'behaviour' I do not mean to suggest that the familiar contrast between, for example, 'words' and 'deeds' lacks significant content. My point is simply that its content has little (perhaps nothing) to do with the 'inner'/'outer' contrast as it figures in much philosophical thinking about people. We will only be tempted to think that it does if we think a person's words acquire their character as *words* from some 'inner' accompaniment; and that, of course, is an assumption that I am suggesting we should resist.

It may be worth adding that part of the problem here lies, not so much in assumptions about what is 'inner', but in the 'inner'/'outer' contrast as it appears in our philosophical thought. Feelings and actions—which I will regularly speak of in the same breath—are often thought of as lying on opposite sides of this divide. And *that* goes with, on the one hand, our thinking of 'actions' in terms of relatively crude bodily movements, and, on the other, our forgetting the fineness of grain of bodily expressiveness—and, in particular, of facial expressiveness— that is central to our normal understanding of 'feelings'. There is, of course, much in an individual human life that is, in one way or another, not open to the inspection of others; and this fact is of enormous importance in a variety of ways. We must not, however, allow that to blind us to the richness and depth that may be found in the configurations of action and feeling—configurations that should be understood to include what a person *says*—of which I have spoken: configurations that may be completely accessible to others.

In any case, I suspect that (for reasons that I will not explore) the grip of the idea of an 'inner representation' may be weakened if, in the discussion of memory, we give a more central place to examples in which verbal articulation of our memories fails us. Think, for example, of a case in which a friend and I observe a startling, and highly nuanced, play of expression on Mary's face. We can suppose that neither of us could begin to do justice in words to what we saw. Yet my friend's whole demeanour, along, we can suppose, with a more extended change in his relationship with Mary, shows me unambiguously that he saw what I saw: and that (as I will say) he has an accurate memory of the incident.[8]

My hope is that a consideration of the possible detail of my friend's responses (a detail that I must leave it to the reader to provide) will reduce the inclination 'to suppose that their significance *must* depend on something below the surface of

---

[8] I am speaking here of the man who 'remembers' the shade of desolation on her face; not of the man who is now 'remembering'—actively recalling—the shade of desolation. Some of what I say in this paragraph applies equally to the latter case. However, the notion of an 'inner representation' does, on the face of it, have a significant role to play in the latter case: a role that I cannot, at the moment, quite see how to characterize.

which they are merely symptoms'. The example might help, too, to dislodge the idea that an 'inner representation'—where this notion is modelled on that of visual representations such as photographs—*could* achieve what is needed here: could be what is fundamental to the idea that someone remembers what she saw on the face. For we can ask: how will the 'inner representation' of those who saw and remember what they saw differ from that of someone who, while she could identify a pictorial representation of the face as it was at the time, completely missed what was there to be seen: the quite particular shade of utter desolation for example?

When my friend's behaviour—understood in the rich sense that includes *expressiveness*—modifies in relevant ways we say that he saw the desolation in Mary's face and that he remembers what he saw. In a case of this kind there is, I would suggest, little, if any, room for a separation of an 'endorsement of his memory-judgement' and an 'endorsement of his response to what we both saw'. Yet there is a temptation to say that he only really *knows*, through memory, what was there in Mary's face if behind the action and feeling there lies something else: a belief, that is, an appropriate 'inner representation'; and, further, if that belief is grounded in a present 'mental trace' that is evidence for, because an effect of, the past event in question. The idea, we might say, is that adequate grounds for *present* action and feeling must be *present* states; and adequate grounds for *present* belief—grounds, that is, that are required for it to be knowledge—must be *present* grounds.

From this perspective our ascriptions of memory in *practice* will appear to involve some rather sloppy, if understandable, short-circuiting. We say 'He knows' straight off; and, provided his response is sufficiently rich in the relevant ways, we regard any expression of doubt about whether he really remembers what he saw as absurd. Now it could be that we do that because we have substantial grounds in past experience for supposing that where we see *this* behaviour the two relevant links are in place. But if we abandon the dogma that 'There is no logically necessary connection between events at different times', and the dogma that all the magic in human life is to be found beneath the skin, another possibility opens up. Perhaps the key to a proper philosophical understanding of memory is to be found in a direct connection between past event and present feelings and actions; and perhaps feelings and actions can be a direct manifestation of a person's memories. The connection between these ideas, which I have developed in the previous and present sections, can be brought out in this way. If what I witnessed can, by itself—without, that is, the intermediary of *either* a present 'representation' *or* a trace that grounds it—be a reason for certain action and feeling now, then nothing—such as a 'desire', for example—is needed to convert a memory into action and feeling: and so action and feeling themselves can be an unmediated manifestation of memory.

VI

I have not presented an argument in defence of the claim that that is how things are. For my aim in this chapter is not to defend our present ways of thinking of 'memory', but to try to get a clear picture of the phenomena of human life that should be the object of our study in so far as we are concerned with memory. I have suggested that it is a confusion to suppose that we can deal with the question of how past events can provide us with reasons for action and feeling *after* we have got straight about the character of our knowledge of the past in memory. For one of the central relevant 'phenomena of human life' is our readiness, in certain cases, to ascribe to someone 'knowledge of what she saw' on the basis of her present feelings and actions. That readiness, I am suggesting, should be seen, *not* as involving various hypotheses about 'underlying mechanisms', but, rather, as a rejection of certain demands that are characteristic of the dominant philosophical tradition. In many, central, cases the endorsement that is involved in our readiness to speak of someone as 'remembering'—the endorsement that is involved in our readiness to speak of his state as one of 'knowledge'—is an endorsement, at one and the same time, of his memory-judgement and of his response to what he saw: it is an endorsement of the former *through* being an endorsement of the latter.

Of course, this is only so in, as I expressed it, 'central cases'. I may, in many cases, question the appropriateness of her current feelings and behaviour while accepting that she has an accurate memory of what happened: while it is true that John treated her just as she remembers it her response to that is quite out of proportion to the offence. But there are limits to what is intelligible in this direction, just as there are limits on the possibilities of saying that someone has mastered the use of the past tense as an expression of memories and yet fails to judge in conformity with the rest of us. For in acknowledging her as one who uses the past tense as we do—and, in particular, uses the past tense as we do as an expression of personal memories—we are accepting her as one who shares much with us. Among what she shares with us is her seeing in past happenings a *significance* of the same kind as we do. One who shares with us the language of 'memory' is one who accepts that, other things being equal, *these* actions and feelings are in place when one has witnessed an event of *this* kind.[9]

I am, then, linking 'understanding what she saw' with 'responding with'—or, at least, 'accepting as in place'—certain forms of feeling and action now.[10] At a

---

[9] The picture that I am offering has in common with the view known as 'simulation theory' the idea that ascriptions of—in this case—memories to others are closely bound up with features the ascriber shares with the other. A fundamental difference, however, is seen in the fact that on the view presented here what is crucially shared is not helpfully characterized as an 'experiential element'. What is shared is, rather, a certain way of living; or, perhaps, a certain conception of the importance of various responses.

[10] John Campbell has, in discussion, objected that to follow any suggestion of this form would be to lose a crucial distinction: that between, for example, the person who does not realize that what he did hurt another, and the person who realizes this but simply does not care. The objection deserves more detailed treatment than I can give it here. Part of a response to it might involve appeal to the distinctions between 'recognizing that something can intelligibly be offered as a reason', 'accepting it as a reason', and 'being moved by that reason'. Perhaps it would also be helpful to make explicit my appeal to the Wittgensteinian notion of 'meaning as use'. The ways in which the term 'hurt', or 'rude', can feature in a presentation of reasons e.g. for feeling ashamed and apologizing are only two

more general level, I am linking 'mastery of the use of past-tense language as an expression of memories of events of this kind' with 'accepting that the past occurrence of such an event provides reason for these forms of feeling and acting now'. Only someone who accepts this general framework of reasons for action and feeling—that embodied in our use of the past tense as an articulation of personal memories—understands assertions in the past tense as we do.

We could express the matter in terms of a mutual logical relationship between past and present. Our understanding of what is going on now—our characterization of what he is doing as 'apologizing', and, with that, our acceptance that that is something that he has reason to do—embodies the idea of the connection of what is happening now with what *has* happened. And our understanding of what *has* happened—our understanding of that past deed as an act of 'rudeness'—is embodied in our acceptance that it provides reason for certain forms of feeling (such as shame) and action (such as apologizing) now. More briefly: we say that someone has memory in the rich, 'self-conscious', sense when she offers claims about what she has observed as reasons for present action and feeling; and it is, in part, in this way such claims are offered as reasons that we see the sense of our talk about the past.

Relating these remarks very briefly to the dispute between realist and anti-realist treatments of the past might help some (though not others!) to locate philosophically the position I am trying to occupy.[11] The idea of a 'truth-value' (or 'property–identity') link is given the central place in realist thinking: to get clear about the sense of the past tense we need to give central place to the fact that it is a matter of logic that if yesterday it could be truly asserted that 'It is raining', today it can be truly asserted that 'It rained yesterday'. While the anti-realist is not likely to *deny* this logical link he will (at least in his more reductive moods) try to interpret it through another claimed logical link: a logical link between the present grounds on which an individual bases a past-tense judgement and the content of that judgement. Now the forms of logical link on which I have focused are different from both of these. In particular, they differ from the reductive version of anti-realism in that I have insisted that many of our central past-tense judgements do not have, or need, present grounds. The logical link that I have stressed relates, not grounds for judging and what is judged, but *judging* and what is judged: it is in our readiness to ascribe memory of some event to one who behaves in certain ways and manifests certain feelings that the sense of our talk of the past, and of our talk of particular kinds of past event, is seen. To question in a particular area whether such behaviour and feeling can be a direct manifestation of such a memory is one and the same thing as to question whether the remembered event itself provides reason for such behaviour and feeling: for it is

of many relevant aspects of our use of these words. A breaking of this pair of connections in a particular individual's use of the words may leave sufficient standing for us to be able to ascribe to him, fairly unambiguously, an understanding of the terms—and, with that, a realization that what he did hurt another.

[11] See Christopher Peacocke's contribution to this volume, Ch. 13.

to suggest that *something else* is needed—a particular desire perhaps—to convert the memory into such action and feeling. And one who, in a particular area, questions this link in a sufficiently radical way is one who does not mean by past tensed talk in this area what we do.[12]

VII

I have stressed that nothing that I have said amounts to an answer to scepticism about the past. I have not shown that we do, in memory, have knowledge of the past. One might say that part of what I have tried to do is to offer an understanding of what is involved in memory that does not have the implication that we *must* take scepticism seriously. The picture that I have opposed is one that gives a central place to the idea of a memory trace from which I infer what happened in the past. On the view of the matter that I have offered one might say: an inference is needed only if I *don't* remember.

Now those under the sway of a certain picture of the task of philosophy will hear such remarks in a way that links them closely with talk of memory as 'direct awareness of the past'; and, with that, will hear them as an attempt to answer scepticism about the past. But to hear them in this way would, in my view, be to misunderstand the proper work of philosophy here; and would involve a failure to appreciate the character of the logical link that I have attempted to outline.

One way to see this is to note the way in which I can, for particular purposes, think of myself and of my relation to some past event in terms of the model that I have rejected as a general account of memory. For example: the way I remember it, whenever I made a contribution to the discussion Jones completely ignored what I said and turned to address someone else. But there are things that make the suggestion that that is how it was rather implausible (one of them perhaps being that his behaviour did not particularly strike me that way at the time); and I can distance myself sufficiently from my current—independent—fury at Jones for a question to arise in my mind as to how I am to think of this 'memory'. Now we can imagine a spectrum of postures that I might adopt in relation to my memory impression. At the far end of this spectrum—perhaps as a limiting case—I might think of my impression that that is how it was as simply an *effect* of the earlier events. The fact that I remember it this way is simply one piece of evidence to be weighed in the balance along with other forms of evidence for and against the claim that Jones behaved in that way.

A rather different kind of case would be this. Suppose that I remember some incident in my life with deep shame. I may, in a familiar, everyday, way, think of my shame as itself an expression of my grasp of what I have done—as we might

---

[12] It is perhaps worth adding that (so far as I can see) the character of the logical link that I have proposed leaves intact the thought that things having happened exactly as they did in a particular case is quite independent of whether or not anyone remembers them—or, for that matter, whether or not they have left any trace.

take an individual's lack of shame when he has behaved disgracefully as a mark of (*not* 'evidence' of) his failure properly to understand what he has done. If I think of my shame in this way—in the way that has been central to my treatment of memory in this chapter—then I must acknowledge (or rather: then I *do* acknowledge) that any attempt to smother the shame is an attempt to close my eyes to the character of what I have done. Suppose, however, that I think of my shame as simply one of the effects of my past action: people tend to suffer from this kind of after-effect when they behave like that, just as they tend to have a hangover when they drink too much. To think of the shame with which I remember in *this* way is to think of it—not as an aspect of my understanding of what I have done—but as an unpleasant condition which, other things being equal, it is only reasonable that I should try to remove.

There are a number of circumstances, and spirits, in which I might treat shame about some past event in this way. For example, I might employ it, or encourage another to employ it, as a defence mechanism in a case in which a particular memory is simply too painful to bear. But, rather differently, such a stance might, for a particular individual, reflect a more systematic policy in relation to incidents of a certain kind. Perhaps, as a result of my upbringing, there is a whole class of my behaviour that I cannot help but remember with shame. Yet I have now come to think that this response is irrational: there is nothing to be ashamed about here. And so I now regard my shamed response as simply a characteristic *effect* of certain forms of action. That is to say, I no longer think of the shame as an aspect of my recognition of what I have done. With that, I no longer regard the category of the 'shameful' as one that is appropriate in connection with behaviour of this kind. As we might express this: that response no longer enters into my conception of the kind of behaviour in question.

In such a case, the change in one's thinking about this aspect of one's memories and the change in one's conception of the remembered event are two sides of the same coin: two faces of the move from thinking of one's response in terms of its 'appropriateness' to what happened, to thinking of it as simply an effect—a trace—of some past event. That is the logical link that I attempted to capture in my previous section.

Now a first point that I want to make about such examples is that nothing that I have said shows that this kind of move would be a mistake. And closely linked with that, talk of memory as 'direct awareness of the past' simply obscures what is at issue in a move like this. Reflection on 'the character of my awareness' is *not* what is needed to resolve any doubts I may have about the appropriateness of the move. For example, in my second case what is needed is, rather, of the form of *ethical* reflection on how past behaviour of that kind should enter into one's subsequent thinking.

Something else is closely linked with that. In each of these examples I come to think of my current state as, not one of knowledge of some past event, but, rather, one in which there is in me a present trace of that event. What lies behind the shift in each case is not, however, of a form that creates any pressure towards

generalization: towards thinking of all 'remembering' as involving a mental trace
on the basis of which one may draw conclusions about what probably happened.
Such a generalization would involve the claim that action and feeling can never
themselves be a form of knowledge of the past; and that is to say: nothing that
lies in the past can ever itself provide reason for certain action and feeling now.
That, as I remarked earlier, is a characteristic claim of a powerful tradition in
philosophical ethics: a claim which, if the general direction of my argument has
been sound, is closely linked with the idea that all memory-judgements are
grounded in the individual's awareness of a present mental trace of the past event.

VIII

I have tried to bring out what I believe is a crucial link between the idea of
memory as being a *form* of knowledge of the past (as opposed to 'a *source* of
knowledge of the past') and the idea that remembered events—what *has*
happened—can in themselves provide us with reasons to do and feel certain
things now. The link between the ideas runs through the fact that action and feeling are the primary expression of personal memories: primary manifestations of
one's understanding of what has happened. This stands in contrast with certain—
one might say 'dominant'—styles of philosophical thinking which encourage us
to think of all the emotional and motivational charge that may be carried by
memories as simply *effects*, by way of an intermediary mental trace, of the
remembered event. I have tried, however sketchily, to suggest that these styles of
philosophical thinking involve a range of confusions. Most significantly, they
involve a denial, or, perhaps, a failure to remember, that the past may be of irreducible significance: can provide us with irreducible reasons for action and feeling. I am not sure that there is much that philosophy can do to show that that *is* a
confusion. But my hope is that in bringing out the connections between this idea
and the philosophical idea of a 'memory trace' both ideas may lose something of
their, sometimes mesmerizing, power.

Finally, I should stress that nothing that I have said rules out questions about
the inner physical mechanisms that, in some sense, 'underpin' memory in human
beings. While I am unclear how those questions should be formulated, the main
message of my essay here is this: if we do our philosophy with too firm an eye
on questions about 'inner mechanisms' we will be in danger of producing a seriously distorted account of this phenomenon of human life.

REFERENCES

HOLLAND, R. F. (1954), 'The empiricist theory of memory', *Mind*, 63: 464–86.
MALCOLM, N. (1963), 'Three lectures on memory' in his *Knowledge and Certainty*. Ithaca,
    NY: Cornell University Press.

—— (1977), *Memory and Mind*. Ithaca, NY: Cornell University Press.

RUSSELL, B. (1921), *The Analysis of Mind*. New York: Macmillan.

WINCH, P. (1987), '*Eine Einstellung zur Seele*', in his *Trying to Make Sense*. Oxford: Basil Blackwell.

WITTGENSTEIN, L. (1958), *Philosophical Investigations*, ed. G. E. M. Anscombe and G. H. von Wright, trans. G. E. M. Anscombe. Oxford: Basil Blackwell.

Author Index

Subject Index